THE CAUSE

THE CAUSE

The Fight for American Liberalism from
Franklin Roosevelt to Barack Obama

Eric Alterman

and Kevin Mattson

VIKING

VIKING

Published by the Penguin Group

Penguin Group (USA) Inc., 375 Hudson Street, New York, New York 10014, U.S.A. • Penguin Group (Canada), 90 Eglinton Avenue East, Suite 700, Toronto, Ontario, Canada M4P 2Y3 (a division of Pearson Penguin Canada Inc.) • Penguin Books Ltd, 80 Strand, London WC2R 0RL, England • Penguin Ireland, 25 St. Stephen's Green, Dublin 2, Ireland (a division of Penguin Books Ltd) • Penguin Books Australia Ltd, 250 Camberwell Road, Camberwell, Victoria 3124, Australia (a division of Pearson Australia Group Pty Ltd) • Penguin Books India Pvt Ltd, 11 Community Centre, Panchsheel Park, New Delhi – 110 017, India • Penguin Group (NZ), 67 Apollo Drive, Rosedale, Auckland 0632, New Zealand (a division of Pearson New Zealand Ltd) • Penguin Books (South Africa) (Pty) Ltd, 24 Sturdee Avenue, Rosebank, Johannesburg 2196, South Africa

Penguin Books Ltd, Registered Offices: 80 Strand, London WC2R 0RL, England

First published in 2012 by Viking Penguin, a member of Penguin Group (USA) Inc.

10 9 8 7 6 5 4 3 2 1

Grateful acknowledgment is made for permission to reprint excerpts from the following copyrighted works:

"Brilliant Disguise" by Bruce Springsteen. Copyright © 1987 Bruce Springsteen (ASCAP). Reprinted by permission. International copyright secured. All rights reserved.
    "How Can a Poor Man Stand Such Times and Live" (Bruce Springsteen version). Words and music by Alfred Reed. Additional lyrics by Bruce Springsteen. Copyright 1930, 2006 Peer International Corporation and Songs of Peer, Ltd. All rights reserved. Used by permission.
    "Worlds Apart" by Bruce Springsteen. Copyright © 2002 Bruce Springsteen (ASCAP). Reprinted by permission. International copyright secured. All rights reserved.

LIBRARY OF CONGRESS CATALOGING IN PUBLICATION DATA

Alterman, Eric.
    The cause : the fight for American liberalism from Franklin Roosevelt to Barack Obama / Eric Alterman and Kevin Mattson.
        p. cm.
    Includes bibliographical references and index.
    ISBN 978-0-670-02343-1
    1. Liberalism—United States—History—20th century.   2. Liberalism—United States—History—21st century. 3. United States—Politics and government—20th century.   4. United States—Politics and government— 21st century.   I. Mattson, Kevin, 1966–   II. Title.
    JC574.2.U6A43 2012
    320.51'30973—dc23   2011045497

Printed in the United States of America
Designed by Carla Bolte • Set in Palatino

Acknowledgments and Dedication

I began the research for this book in 2004 upon signing a contract with Viking to write two books on American liberalism, allegedly over a period of four years. The contract, which was negotiated by my friend, adviser, and agent for the past fourteen years, Tina Bennett, together with my friend, adviser, and editor for the past twenty years, Rick Kot, resulted in *Why We're Liberals* (Viking, 2008; Penguin 2009)—a present-oriented work still happily available for purchase and perusal—and now *The Cause*. At the time, I thought it was a pretty clever idea to create one body of research to be spread over two books, but instead I found myself burned out on the topic after spending four years on the first book. I needed a break, but I also had a contract to fulfill.

After fighting a losing war with the mountains of material I had amassed, I eventually admitted to myself that I needed help to sharpen both my focus and narrative strategies. Following a lengthy search, I found Kevin Mattson, an American historian and public intellectual whose earlier books I had admired and, though we had never met, whose views both on historical and contemporary matters appeared to closely mirror my own. Kevin accepted my offer and together we came up with an outline for this book and I then turned over all of my research to him and invited him to contribute his own. After sending me early rough drafts of all but the final sections of the book, Kevin was forced to drop out of the project owing to long-held travel plans and other writing commitments (and so should not be held responsible for the final results). The drafts, thankfully, gave me the raw material I needed to relocate my original inspiration and get back to work. I rewrote each chapter, adding additional research as necessary, and finally—four years (and one short book, *Kabuki Democracy*) later than initially intended—I was able to submit my much too long manuscript. Just as he has done for me since my first book, 1992's *Sound and Fury*, Rick Kot then flew into action to perform the painful surgical operations necessary to give the book coherent shape and (one hopes) manageable size. Following considerable back-and-forth, to say nothing of the yeoman efforts in the areas of copyediting, fact-checking, design, and everything else that goes into the publication of a big book like this one, here we are.

Kevin would like to offer his thanks "first to my coauthor; my family, Vicky and Jay; my colleagues at Ohio University; the support of Pat Connor Study; George Cotkin for cheering me up at times; and my closest friend Jeff (b.s.-free) Boxer." I would like to thank Kevin; Rick, who remains, as far as I am aware, the most conscientious line editor in all of New York publishing; and Tina, upon whose perspicacious advice I depend, together with her assistant, Svetlana Katz. At Viking I would also like to offer my deepest gratitude to Laura Tisdel, now of Little, Brown, whose friendship and guidance have been and remain invaluable to me in more ways than I can explain or even enumerate. Also to Rick's new assistant, Kyle Davis; my crack copy editor, Susan Johnson; and Louise Braverman and Rebecca Lang, in Viking's publicity department. Massive thanks also to the book's prepublication readers, the estimable trio of Mike Kazin, Tom Edsall, and Kai Bird, and to its team of fact-checkers Allie Tempus, Erica Hellerstein, Silvia Liu, and especially Jed Bickman. My appreciation as always to my friends, editors, and indulgent colleagues at *The Nation* and The Nation Institute, the Center for American Progress, *The Forward, The Daily Beast,* the English and journalism departments of Brooklyn College, and the CUNY Graduate School of Journalism. Finally, I remain indebted to my girls, Diana Silver and Eve Rose Alterman, and to my parents, Carl and Ruth Alterman, for their continued indulgence in good and bad, sickness and health, and everything in between. Per usual, whatever mistakes remain in the text are entirely their fault.

One of the oddities of this political moment is that contemporary conservatives have somehow settled on teachers as alleged enemies of the public good. I think I understand why they are doing this, but even after writing this book, it remains a kind of mystery how the rest of us have allowed it to happen. Personally, I would never have become the writer I am were it not for the commitments made to me over the course of my life by dedicated teachers who believed in what they did and repeatedly demonstrated why teaching and scholarship were the basis of not only a profoundly honorable life, but too often a significantly underappreciated one at that. In this spirit, I would like to recognize a group of people—many no longer living and most no longer teaching—whose wisdom and dedication to their craft I continue to carry in my head and in my heart. In rough chronological order, they are: Ed Grossman, Lawrence Kaye, Judith Kessler, Neil Maloney, Werner Feig, Judy Oksner, Richard Liebowitz, Walter LaFeber, Richard Polenberg, Isaac Kramnick, Benedict Anderson, George Quester, John Najemy, Robert Dahl,

Paul Kennedy, Donald Kagan, Max Ticktin, Arnold Eisen, George Fredrickson, David Kennedy, and Barton J. Bernstein. For the past five years, I have been fortunate to be able to continue my classroom learning every Saturday morning with the remarkably erudite Rabbi David Gelfand at Temple Israel, Park Avenue. Finally, Ellen Tremper, chair of the English department at Brooklyn College, deserves a special mention for all her hard work in making it possible for me to enjoy the honor of the title as well. It is to these teachers of mine, and to those whom they represent, that I should like to dedicate this book.

ERA
November 8, 2011

Contents

Introduction: Nothing to Fear

The existence of Franklin Roosevelt relieved American liberals for a
dozen years of the responsibility of thinking for themselves.
                                     —Arthur M. Schlesinger, Jr., 1947[1]

Felled by a sudden cerebral hemorrhage, Franklin Delano Roosevelt died
on April 12, 1945, in one of his favorite places: his "Little White House,"
in Warm Springs, Georgia. His demanding excursion to Yalta two months
earlier had appeared to add years to his sickly complexion, provoking a constant state of anxiety in those around him and forcing the president to acknowledge publicly for the first time his own mortality. On March 1, 1945, in
what would be his final address to Congress, in which he described—actually,
vastly exaggerated—the achievements of his negotiations with Winston
Churchill and Joseph Stalin, FDR finally put an end to his "splendid deception" and allowed himself to be taken in a wheelchair down the aisle to reach
the lectern rather than lean on a friend or use crutches. "I hope that you will
pardon me for the unusual posture of sitting down during the presentation
of what I want to say," he entreated, "but I know that you will realize that it
makes it a lot easier for me in not having . . . legs; and also because . . . I have
just completed a fourteen-thousand-mile trip."

Sitting for an artist's portrait barely six weeks later in Warm Springs, the
president complained of a "terrific pain in the back of my head" and slumped
down in his chair.[2] He had to be carried out of the room and died later that
afternoon. While it was a brain hemorrhage that killed him, a plethora of other
ailments might have done so otherwise. His inability to focus on matters of
state for more than two to four hours a day had come to limit his effectiveness,
but the president had proved so adept at masking his infirmities during the
1944 election campaign that his personal physician, Dr. Ross McIntire, had
confided in his diary, "It made me doubt my accuracy as a diagnostician." In

1

December of that year another doctor, Robert Duncan, had conducted a thorough examination and had given the president only a few months to live.[3]

Almost immediately after the reports of the president's passing, large crowds began to descend on the White House. All across America entire communities mourned in churches, in synagogues, in union halls and bars, and in their homes. That night the Hotel Association of New York City forbade all music and dancing, and the Yankees and Dodgers games were called off out of a combination of grief, respect, and, undoubtedly, fear for the future.[4] A day later half a million people crowded onto the streets of Washington, D.C., to view the coffin. They stood twenty or more deep along Pennsylvania Avenue, silently watching as first lady Eleanor Roosevelt rode in a black car behind the carriage carrying her husband's coffin. A *New York Times* editorial spoke for many when it declared, "Men will thank God on their knees a hundred years from now that Franklin D. Roosevelt was in the White House."[5]

What President Roosevelt left as his enduring legacy was the modern American welfare state, and with it the foundation of modern American liberalism. Americans looked to Roosevelt as a leader who had remembered the "forgotten man," almost regardless of why, exactly, they happened to feel forgotten. While Franklin Roosevelt had enjoyed many enviable political talents, perhaps the most valuable of these was his uncanny ability to leave virtually everyone to whom he spoke—whether individually in the Oval Office or by the millions on radio—with the distinct impression that he had heard their concerns, valued their contributions, and had everything under control. Nearly sixty years after his death the journalist Bill Moyers recalled his father, Henry Moyers, an ordinary man who had dropped out of the fourth grade to pick cotton, voting for Franklin Roosevelt in four straight elections, and telling his son, "The President's my friend."[6]

Roosevelt appeared to many to be almost above politics, dismissing both supporters and opponents with an optimistic "Fine! Fine! Fine!" at every turn[7] as he refused to define himself ideologically or show his hand in advance. The intellectuals who constituted the early New Deal brain trust and the advisers with whom he surrounded himself during his later years often worried that FDR's presidency lacked any form of consistency, whether with regard to policy or principles. To a considerable extent the New Deal was less a series of coherent policies than an expression of the philosophy of "bold, persistent experimentation" that FDR had celebrated early on in his presidency. But it was also a set of often ideologically incompatible proposals that competing advisers sent his way. Some argued for fiscal conservatism; others for antimonopoly efforts; still others for stronger public works and redistributing income and land more directly. A month after Roosevelt's death, the liberal author Sidney Hertzberg lamented the manner in which the late president had become "for so many a household God" whose policy proposals they rarely scrutinized, criticized, categorized, or even considered with much thought.[8]

This president of the forgotten man had been born into America's aristocracy, passing his youth with Swiss tutors; an overprotective, often coddling mother; and a father who, as the historian Alan Brinkley puts it, "sought to train his son in the life of a landowner and gentleman." Raised as an Episcopalian, he attended Groton, Harvard, and Columbia Law School and followed a none-too-strenuous path to political success based on the connections of his family and friends, moving smoothly from the New York State Assembly to the Wilson administration during World War I to the governorship of New York before reaching the presidency.[9]

Once elected, Roosevelt betrayed his class with a zeal that surprised virtually everyone. While celebrating capitalism in principle, Roosevelt despised its American practitioners, whom he viewed as too shortsighted and parochial to recognize their own self-interest. He built the welfare state—but a peculiar version that attempted to balance the need for social solidarity and citizen sacrifice with the (often enforced) largesse of the ruling classes. He imposed, in the words of the historian William Leuchtenberg, "a welfare state on a capitalist foundation."[10]

FDR was not entirely comfortable with the role of father of the modern labor movement, assigned to him by many, but with his support for the Wagner Act of 1935, which, though it excluded both domestic and agricultural workers to gain the support of southerners, unleashed grassroots organizing campaigns and fostered the growth of labor's political muscle. With the Fair Labor Standards Act of 1938, he empowered American workers by offering them a labor-based democracy. Unions such as the United Auto Workers (UAW) gained power not just from their own organizing initiatives but also from a growing assurance that they finally had their government on their side.

In the blighted areas of southern Appalachia, he created the Tennessee Valley Authority (TVA), unleashing a massive public investment program that brought hydroelectric power to people who had never had electricity before. Even more significant was the TVA's role in creating what its director, David Lilienthal, termed a new "grassroots democracy." Lilienthal struggled to ensure that local citizens and governments participated in making decisions about the extension of dams and the distribution of electricity. Roosevelt described the TVA as the illustration of his belief that "big government need not be absentee government . . . that great national powers can be exercised as government at hand, at home, working with the people and their local governments where the people are."[11] In this respect FDR sought to unite distinct American values—for instance, an instinctive distaste for the dole (which he viewed as distinctly un-American and inimical to individual initiative)—with a belief in the power of community, collective care for others, and the importance of individual dignity in labor.[12]

When it came to ideology, the president spoke the language of Christian civics—basic teachings from the Bible—which could be used to justify America's embarking on the largest expansion of federal power ever seen. FDR would personally chase the plutocrats from the temple of democracy. "Let us be frank in acknowledgment of the truth that many amongst us have made obeisance to Mammon, that the profits of speculation, the easy road without toil, have lured us from the old barricades. To return to higher standards we must abandon the false prophets and seek new leaders of our own choosing."[13] For Franklin Roosevelt, as for Lincoln before him, the nation was a spiritual entity. Asked by a reporter about his political philosophy, FDR replied, "Philosophy? I am a Christian and a Democrat—that's all."[14]

Here FDR was not only giving voice to the "simple" religious views of most Americans but was also paying tribute to the Social Gospel movement, embodied by those like the settlement house worker and suffragette Jane Addams (who was also an enormous influence on the thinking of Eleanor Roosevelt, who had spent a period of her youth working in the movement). It was characterized by the belief that Christianity's teachings had to move outside of the churches and take a role in the implementation of social and welfare legislation. Christianity, Addams insisted, "cannot be proclaimed and instituted apart from the social life of the community . . . it must seek a simple and natural expression in the social organism itself."[15]

Throughout his political career Roosevelt also drew upon a long tradition of political and social reform dating back to the late nineteenth century. His rhetoric—especially the dramatic tones of his 1936 campaign—reflected the spirit of the Populist revolt of the 1880s and 1890s, when America's farmers rose up to resist the predatory practices of the banking classes and their punitive credit policies. Reaching further back, Arthur Schlesinger, Jr., suggested that the origins of FDR's liberalism could be found in Andrew Jackson's desire to check the power of "privilege," build up the influence of "the laboring classes," and use the state "to restrain the power of the business community."[16]

But FDR could never comfortably embrace Jacksonianism, with its nostalgia for a rural democracy of rustic producers, nor, as Schlesinger admitted, could he view with even remote consistency that tradition's faith in states' rights and its angry distrust of the federal government.[17] To be a successful politician in tune with his times, Roosevelt needed a liberalism capable of both embracing and helping to shape the realities of industrial, urbanized capitalism and the modern state.[18] When he did try to chart his political trajectory, he would draw from the Progressive activists of a generation before him who had struggled to rid American politics of special interests and the power of money (by creating direct primaries and the secret ballot), to nurture the cause of social justice for the poor, and to elect two of the most robust presidents in history, Theodore Roosevelt (1901–1909) and Woodrow Wilson (1913–1921), while at the same time holding out hope for a prosperous, peaceful future.[19]

Initially liberalism had been synonymous with a faith in reason, which had arisen out of the Enlightenment as a reaction to claims of divine rule by the clergy and royalty of the late Middle Ages. It found expression in the thoughts of many writers across Europe and the British Isles, including John Stuart Mill, John Locke, Baron de Montesquieu, Voltaire, David Hume, and Immanuel Kant, as well as in the political arguments of America's founders, particularly Thomas Jefferson, Thomas Paine, and James Madison.[20] Liberal freedoms were primarily freedoms of the mind: freedom of thought, of expression, of religion, and of self-invention without regard to the customs of caste, creed, or crown. Above all, liberalism implied both an ability and a responsibility of people to think for themselves, to create their own destinies, and to follow their own consciences. Examining the evolution of liberal belief since its founding, the liberal theologian Reinhold Niebuhr observed in an article published on July 4, 1955, in *The New Republic*, that liberalism in the broadest sense was characterized by a commitment "to free the individual from the traditional restraints of a society, to endow the 'governed' with the power of the franchise, to establish the principle of the 'consent of the governed' as the basis of political society; to challenge all hereditary privileges and traditional restraints upon human initiative."[21]

Over the course of the nineteenth century, however, the traditional or "classical" understanding of liberalism came to represent a kind of conservatism, as powerful institutions (including, primarily, corporations and trusts) found ways to constrict the freedom of individuals through the onerous working conditions of early industrial factories while at the same time paying tribute to the liberal virtues of self-reliance and freedom to choose one's own path to prosperity. To address these developments the great liberal philosopher John Dewey called upon liberals to rethink some of their most fundamental assumptions. Dewey defended the same Enlightenment-based liberalism of old but redefined it so as to allow its believers to adapt to contemporary conditions. Liberalism, he wrote:

> came into use to denote a new spirit that grew and spread with the rise of democracy. It implied a new interest in the common man and a new sense that the common man, the representative of the great masses of human beings, had possibilities that had been kept under, that had not been allowed to develop, because of institutional and political conditions. . . . It was marked by a generous attitude, by sympathy for the underdog, for those who were not given a chance. . . . [And] it aimed at enlarging the scope of free action on the part of those who for ages had had no part in public affairs and no lot in the benefits secured by this participation.[22]

In his famous 1932 speech at the Commonwealth Club in San Francisco, Roosevelt expressed his admiration for Woodrow Wilson as a politician who "saw the situation" of industrial power "more clearly."[23] Even though, for political reasons, he needed to demonstrate his respect for his former boss and predecessor in office as America's most recent Democratic president, FDR likely felt a greater affinity, as an example of the presidency, between his older cousin Teddy rather than Wilson. TR had been a rarity: a successful politician who was a genuine man of ideas (and a historian himself). He gravitated toward other such men, and in Herbert Croly, the founding editor of *The New Republic*, he found one able to articulate the kind of grand sweeping notion upon which he could not only base an entire political lifetime of proposed reform but even found a movement that almost succeeded in displacing the two established political parties.

The "promise" in Croly's *The Promise of American Life* (1909) professed his belief that the United States would avoid the grotesque social and economic inequality found in Europe and could chart an independent course premised on its democratic faith. This faith was grounded in the Jeffersonian worldview, which was now being challenged by the closing of the frontier and the "concentration of economic power" in corporate trusts.[24] Suddenly Alexander Hamilton's vision of America as a future industrial powerhouse with a strong central government was looking a great deal more prophetic than the agrarian republic envisioned by his famous philosophical adversary. By the turn of the century, Croly reasoned, the only power capable of counteracting the transformation of the American economy would have to be national in scope, for the nation itself remained "the best machinery as yet developed for raising the level of human association."[25] But because he viewed the Hamiltonian tradition in American history as corrupted by its attachment to wealthy interests, particularly banking, he sought to employ Hamiltonian mechanisms in order to achieve a Jeffersonian vision of political equality: "The whole tendency of his programme," he explained, "is to give a democratic meaning and purpose to the Hamiltonian tradition and method."[26] The result would be a new definition of the hallowed tradition of American individualism.

Teddy Roosevelt laid the building blocks of the modern activist presidency through his belief that the office represented the will of the nation.[27] He made this point explicitly upon the passage of some of the most sweeping legislation in American history—the monitoring and regulation of the meat industry and drug trade—in 1906: "It is an absurdity to expect to eliminate the abuses in great corporations by State action. The National Government alone can deal adequately with these great corporations."[28] He did so in part by channeling populist rhetoric to mobilize the American people, deriding the "malefactors of great wealth" in ways that foreshadowed FDR's chiding "economic royalists."[29] TR's conception of "new nationalism"—the slogan for his run in 1912 as the candidate for the Progressive Party—also reflected a radical rethinking of liberalism, from which his younger cousin would later draw. In 1918, a year before he died, TR outlined a program of public works, hydroelectric power development, agricultural aid, pensions, and social insurance.[30] From these, it was a short step to the New Deal.

Franklin Roosevelt drew on all these traditions when he gave his famous speech on the "Four Freedoms" in his 1941 State of the Union address. There he enumerated what he defined as the rights everyone "everywhere in the world" ought to enjoy. These were "freedom of speech and expression," "freedom of every person to worship God in his own way," "freedom from want," and "freedom from fear."[31] Though it was hardly evident at the time, these foundational four freedoms proved the culmination of a far broader and significant intellectual project. As early as 1932 FDR had proclaimed, "Every man has a right to life, and this means that he has also a right to make a comfortable living."[32] No longer would freedom be defined simply as protection *from* or *against* the abusive powers of government—the central idea of classical liberalism. (The philosopher Isaiah Berlin famously defined this as "negative" freedom.) While FDR accepted the importance of protection from an overreaching government, he sought to create one that could provide "positive" freedoms as well. This radical reworking of the American creed could be seen in Roosevelt's near-revolutionary State of the Union address—the last he delivered directly to Congress—on January 11, 1944, in which he called for a

"Second Bill of Rights."[33] The key concept in this speech was "security," which FDR now expanded to include almost all areas of life. "Essential to peace," the president insisted, was "a decent standard of living for all individual men and women and children in all nations. Freedom from fear is eternally linked with freedom from want." He demanded a "realistic tax law—which will tax all unreasonable profits, both individual and corporate, and reduce the ultimate cost of the war to our sons and daughters." We "cannot be content," he went on, "no matter how high that general standard of living may be, if some fraction of our people—whether it be one-third or one-fifth or one-tenth—is ill-fed, ill-clothed, ill-housed, and insecure." Then he listed the new rights he now considered to be fundamental to the American way of life:

- The right to a useful and remunerative job in the industries or shops or farms or mines of the Nation.
- The right to earn enough to provide adequate food and clothing and recreation.
- The right of every farmer to raise and sell his products at a return which will give him and his family a decent living.
- The right of every businessman, large and small, to trade in an atmosphere of freedom from unfair competition and domination by monopolies at home or abroad.
- The right of every family to a decent home.
- The right to adequate medical care and the opportunity to achieve and enjoy good health.
- The right to adequate protection from the economic fears of old age, sickness, accident, and unemployment.
- The right to a good education.

FDR tied these rights to the struggle then underway to win the war. "America's own rightful place in the world depends in large part upon how fully these and similar rights have been carried into practice for our citizens. For unless there is security here at home there cannot be lasting peace in the world."[34]

Abroad, FDR hoped to replace traditional American unilateralism with what he called Americanism, a term he never really defined but that appeared to envision the slow, peaceful spread of the values of American-style democracy generally and the principles of the New Deal especially throughout the world.[35] Knowing what he did about the internal politics of Congress and the fears and aspirations of the nation's citizens, Roosevelt had always been careful to link his discussions of foreign policy issues to what he understood to be Americans' understanding of their role in the world. Despite the nation's long history of involvement in the global marketplace, the American people were new to the concept of diplomatic realpolitik. The country's history until then had involved a counterproductive swing between viewing foreign policy as akin to commercially profitable missionary work and the equally implausible desire simply to withdraw from world affairs whenever foreigners failed to appreciate America's plans to improve them. Their nation's unique characteristics—buffer of two oceans, territory that encompassed a vast expanse of land, a dearth of powerful or hostile neighbors, and the idealism of a successful revolution against the British empire—had combined to create habits of mind that led Americans to believe that they could construct a world system based on what they considered their own universally applicable principles rather than on more traditional considerations of balances of power. Many Americans understood their role in history as a "chosen" people akin to the ancient Israelites, a tradition that harkened all the way back to the Puritans. Americans were confident that their revolution was a new "chapter in the history of man," in Thomas Jefferson' words.[36] As the political philosopher Leo Strauss once noted: "The United States of America may be said to be the only country in the world which was founded in explicit opposition to Machiavellian principles."[37]

Roosevelt evinced little sympathy for such sentiments. The president had already begun the process of postwar planning in a series of meetings with Churchill and Stalin in Tehran and Yalta and had dispatched his financial advisers to Bretton Woods to deal with the creation of new international economic institutions. Though he often paid rhetorical tribute to the realization of Woodrow Wilson's dream to create a league of nations—now called the United Nations Organization (UNO)—Roosevelt was really interested in re-creating a modern-day Concert of Europe for the entire world, with each of the remaining four great powers responsible for maintaining order within its sphere of influence. Roosevelt remained at heart a realist who knew full well that the United States could not police the world, and that its people had no interest in trying to do so. For that reason—together with the fact that the Red Army was already occupying most of Central Europe, where the fiercest fighting of the war had taken place—the president felt he needed to secure whatever cooperation was possible from Stalin and the Soviet Union and do so in the language of universal peace and brotherhood.

Roosevelt viewed the creation of the UN Security Council as a potentially valuable institution for great power bargaining, accompanied by a "talking shop"—not unlike Wilson's ill-fated League of Nations—to be called the General Assembly and open to all nations. He recognized the power and position of the Russians as well as the need to try to dampen the likelihood that they would exploit postwar instability and unrest. America's only hope would be to try to ameliorate the problem as best it could through a mixture of economic carrots, military sticks, and traditional diplomacy.[38] As the Roosevelt scholar Warren F. Kimball smartly observes, "Roosevelt believed that the USSR could become a reasonable member of international society, but only if it felt secure. That meant that the United States should not and would not threaten the Soviet system."[39] But such complex and sophisticated trade-offs would remain the secret provenance of Roosevelt and his closest advisers throughout the war.

The prewar world offered precious few clues about how to construct a suitable structure for postwar peace and prosperity. Nor did it prepare the nation to deal with the problem that was poised to become America's most significant political fault line: the fact of legal apartheid in the South and de facto apartheid in the North. Despite the shimmering rhetoric of FDR's "Four Freedoms" and "Second Bill of Rights" speeches, he did nothing to address the question of racial equality in the South. In fact, he was so fearful of losing the southern states that he declined to listen to those, including his wife, who insisted that he try to put an end to lynching. Numerous New Deal agricultural programs, including those overseen by his otherwise progressive secretary of agriculture, Henry Wallace, discriminated against blacks, were administered locally by racists, and did nothing to overturn or upset "local elites."[40] FDR knew full well that while southern "liberals" might look favorably on moves toward socioeconomic equality, they remained extremely reticent—at best—regarding race.

Black leaders, pledging themselves to the now famous "Double V" strategy of victory abroad and at home, were eager to leverage the idea that the war being fought abroad was bringing racial discrimination at home into a different light. Their patience, however, grew thin, and A. Philip Randolph, leader of the almost entirely black Brotherhood of Sleeping Car Porters, called for an immediate end to discrimination in the armed forces and among defense contractors. Eleanor Roosevelt heard of his efforts and set up a meeting between him and her husband. When FDR failed to meet his demands, Randolph began organizing for a mass march on Washington, D.C., to embarrass the government into action. At their second meeting, the president asked, "Well, Phil, what do you want me to do?" Randolph told him to outlaw discrimination in war plants. "You know I can't do that," FDR protested, but he did precisely that: Executive Order 8802 addressed that issue and also created a Committee on Fair Employment Practice (COFEP) to monitor the situation and enforce the rules. It was a temporary and in many ways unsatisfactory compromise but one that set the stage for the expansion of freedoms and democracy in the future.[41]

Many drew confidence on this front from *An American Dilemma,* a much-celebrated multivolume 1944 study of the race problem by the Swedish scholar/politician Gunnar Myrdal. As Myrdal explained, the "American Creed" of democracy and equality was in conflict with the reality of black American lives. Negroes, he argued, were certain to become "more and more vociferous" in their demands that the nation live up to the promise of its rhetoric. Not only were whites behaving contrary to the spirit of their own Constitution and Bill of Rights in this regard, but also to "the American Creed, which is firmly rooted in the Americans' hearts." Not since Reconstruction, Myrdal wrote, "has there been more reason to anticipate fundamental changes in American race relations, changes which will involve a development toward American ideals."[42]

Southern apartheid was anathema to northern liberals, but given the dependence of the New Deal political coalition on the cooperation of die-hard segregationist southern conservatives, no one could imagine just how, short of revolution, the status quo could be changed. The only potential salvation on the horizon seemed to be that graceful push coming from A. Philip Randolph—the nudge of conscience, the threat of embarrassment, the use of mass mobilization—coupled with the reaction of a leader who knew when a breaking point had been passed.

The president's sudden death took those around him by surprise. It was Mrs. Roosevelt, wearing her pain valiantly, who broke the news to Harry Truman, who had been vice president for only eighty-two days. When he asked how he could help the first lady during her mourning, she reportedly said: "You're the one who needs help."[43]

At the time of the president's passing, Truman had met with his predecessor only twice as vice president and never on substantial matters. And yet now he himself was president, and leader of the greatest wartime alliance in history; the de facto mayor, police chief, and first citizen of what *The New Republic* was calling the newly created "World-Capital-on-the-Potomac," the most powerful nation the world had ever seen, boasting what Secretary of War Henry Stimson—the man who advised Truman to use it—would call "the most terrible weapon ever known in human history."[44] Truman addressed the

American people in eloquent tones that balanced wariness and confidence: "Tragic fate has thrust upon us grave responsibilities. We must carry on. Our departed leader never looked backward. He looked forward and moved forward." He knew that Americans would eventually look ahead, and he might have known that Roosevelt's doctrine—the "Second Bill of Rights," a New Deal for the world and for America's own citizens—would have to be developed apart from the power of FDR's personality. Liberalism was now, more than ever, on its own.

FDR had bequeathed a context in which postwar liberals would operate for years to come: an entire New Deal order made up of values and institutions that long outlived the president and his policies.

First and most obviously, he inspired the notion that American government might play a positive role in improving the lives of its citizens. Certainly postwar liberals held memories of a time before FDR when their eighteenth- and nineteenth-century predecessors defended the "rights" of an individual from egregious governmental intrusion. Indeed, the English philosopher Isaiah Berlin's notions of negative freedoms remained central to the story of postwar liberalism.

While FDR had permanently changed Americans' conception of rights, he never defined the boundaries of benevolent government intervention in the economy or individuals' lives. Despite Americans' historical aversion toward the trappings of a powerful central government, Roosevelt managed, in the crisis of the Depression, to provide an example for future generations to create collective initiatives aimed at social amelioration.[45]

Consider the New Deal infrastructure. Programs such as the Works Progress Administration (WPA), the Civilian Conservation Corps (CCC), and National Youth Administration (NYA) all provided models of how the government could do good, and personal experiences with them inspired the next generation of postwar liberals.[46] For instance, Lyndon Johnson's work in the NYA as a young man during the thirties influenced his building of the Great Society in the sixties, while the "public work" FDR initiated with the WPA and CCC reappeared in John Kennedy's Peace Corps, the Great Society's community action programs, and Bill Clinton's AmeriCorps. Or consider wartime regulatory agencies such as the Office of Price Administration (OPA). Short-lived though it was, the OPA not only oversaw price ceilings and rationing but also provided a forum in which liberal economists like John Kenneth Galbraith could apply Keynesian ideals and test the government's ability to nurture a sense of fair play under trying circumstances. Ideas about "full employment" and redistributive social policies—central to the story of postwar liberalism—would have been more difficult to craft if the OPA had never existed.

If FDR had not succeeded in generating a national consensus around his programs, liberalism, which had previously been relegated to the margins of American policies, would not have occupied the "center," between the extremes of communism on the left and laissez-faire capitalism on the right. Liberal historian Arthur Schlesinger, Jr., recognized this as one of FDR's key accomplishments: "The whole point of the New Deal lay in its faith in 'the exercise of democracy,' its belief in gradualness, its rejection of catastrophism, its denial of either-or, its indifference to ideology, its conviction that a managed and modified capitalist order achieved by piecemeal experiment could best combine personal freedom and economic growth."[47] Long before Bill Clinton's presidency, FDR happily employed "triangulation" as a tool to achieve liberal legitimacy, playing himself off against Supreme Court conservatives on the one hand and socialist visionaries on the left. FDR inherited a party of the American southland and northern urban machines but helped to enlarge it, adding labor, the newer immigrants, Negroes, women, and intellectuals, among many others.[48] Postwar liberals inherited this polyglot coalition just as the means by which it was held together—an unspoken agreement to ignore the conditions of apartheid in the American South—was coming undone. Liberals who sought to make progress on race were often forced to move their advocacy outside of the party itself into independent organizations, such as Americans for Democratic Action (ADA) or the National Association for the Advancement of Colored People (NAACP).

Postwar liberals also remained loyal to FDR's belief in the importance of a strong labor movement as a key foundation for almost all forms of social progress. "Labor unions," historian Mary McAuliffe explains, "had provided the mass constituency for the American left during the 1930s and early 1940s, for the Communist Party as well as for the liberal-labor New Deal coalition."[49] While the question of Communist sympathies loomed large in the labor movement, providing an opportunity for anti-Communist union leaders to define the left-wing borders of "responsible" liberalism in the postwar era, unions, and particularly the mighty United Auto Workers, led by Walter Reuther, fought not only for higher wages for their workers but also for social justice for blacks and other minorities.[50]

FDR also opened the gates for intellectuals to enter politics. He was no ideologue, but he assembled his brain trust and enjoyed listening to new ideas.[51] During the war, for instance, he relied heavily on the Office of Strategic

Services (OSS), the Central Intelligence Agency's (CIA) precursor, and on the intellectuals it employed to perform intelligence work necessary for military combat.[52] More broadly, intellectuals started to mature—what historians have labeled a process of "deradicalization"—as they drifted away from the romanticism of the "Red Decade" of the 1930s. In a biographical sketch of Reinhold Niebuhr's early years as a revolutionary socialist during the 1930s, Arthur Schlesinger, Jr., describes how the man who would become liberalism's most influential theologian had been unable to bring himself to vote for Franklin Roosevelt until 1944. Niebuhr found this history embarrassing. "My negative attitude towards Roosevelt is really a scandal considering that he elaborated a pragmatic approach which I should have appreciated long before I did," he admitted.[53] What matters here less is the tardiness of Niebuhr's conversion, but rather the manner in which Roosevelt and the New Deal paved his path, just as it would for so many influential Jewish intellectuals, black intellectuals, playwrights, novelists, and other radicals who had previously viewed themselves to be living and working at the margins of mainstream society, in critical opposition to its central values.

FDR provided another keynote for the postwar period: liberals had international responsibilities. The war against fascism had excited liberals far more than conservatives or radicals of any persuasion, and they had come out of it with a hope and a belief in the importance of international cooperation, even transnational governance. But Roosevelt also bequeathed a legacy of realism: he inspired the creation of the United Nations but refused to cede to it the power and political independence that would have been necessary to allow it to act independently to preserve peace and punish transgressors. This strategy was a product of FDR's own diplomatic approach, for while he engaged in typical give and take, often in secret, he lied about it to the country and pretended to transcend it in his speeches. He even misled his closest advisers—and, indeed, his own successor—so committed was he both to secrecy and freedom of action. At the time of his death, what shone most brightly about Franklin Roosevelt was his "first-rate character." He naturally projected hope and self-confidence, a sense that one could, like the crippled president, overcome any obstacle if one demonstrated the right spirit. Americans had "nothing to fear but fear itself," he told them, and to an amazing degree, they believed it. That was his gift to liberals, as well as his curse.

1

Henry, Harry, and Eleanor:
Three Faces of Liberalism

A liberal is a man who is constantly and simultaneously being kicked
in the teeth by the Commies and in the pants by the National Association of Manufacturers.

—Frank Sullivan, 1949

By August 10, 1945, Harry S. Truman had decided the war was over. Many
of his advisers, including his secretary of state, James "Jimmy" Byrnes,
wanted unconditional surrender from the Japanese, but the president had
grown weary of the conflict, and by now the Japanese themselves knew they
had been beaten and asked only to retain their emperor. On the advice of the
secretary of war, Colonel Henry Stimson, the president told himself the world
could live with a politically enfeebled Japanese emperor if it meant saving
countless lives.

Just as he had done a week earlier when deciding to drop two atomic bombs
on Japan, the president came to his momentous decision without, apparently,
ever second-guessing himself. As he explained afterward to Anthony Eden:
"I'm here to make decisions, and whether they prove right or wrong, I am
going to make them."[1] Like Walt Whitman, Truman "contained multitudes."
He manifested a deep sense of political responsibility but also an enormous
chip on his shoulder, and both his gruffness and his boldness would be defining elements of his presidency, for better or for worse. The journalist I. F. Stone
admiringly described the new president as "devoted" and "decisive," but also
"humble about his own knowledge and capacities."[2] At 4:05 p.m. on Tuesday,
August 14, the Japanese offered surrender, and the Swiss chargé d'affaires
delivered the official text to the State Department two hours and five miutes
later, owing to a mishap with its bicycle messenger. Within the hour, reporters
were crowded into Truman's office as the president, standing beside his desk

and flanked by Byrnes, Chief of Staff Admiral William Leahy, and Bess, together with much of the cabinet, gave everyone the scoop. Truman, however, fudged the truth, promising the crowd the "full acceptance of the Potsdam Declaration, which specifies the unconditional surrender of Japan."

The president later addressed the crowds gathering in Lafayette Square just outside the White House gates: "This is a great day, the day we've been waiting for. This is the day for free governments in the world. This is the day that fascism and police government ceases in the world. . . . We will need the help of all of you and I know we will get it."[3]

This was a moment with few precedents: the deadliest conflict in human history had just ended, and to consider the career of the man responsible for this momentous achievement was to meditate on the mystery of history. At times Harry Truman appeared to have stepped out of Sinclair Lewis's novel *Babbitt*. He was a Mason and a Shriner, a member in good standing of the American Legion and Veterans of Foreign Wars, and a farmer and small businessman.[4] It was easy to paint him as a hayseed, especially in contrast to the easy aristocratic charmer FDR. But Truman's career was marked by a meticulous consideration for politics and power.

A failed haberdasher rescued by a patronage job in a corrupt Kansas City political machine at the onset of the first Roosevelt administration, Truman owed pretty much his entire career to the fact that as a forty-year-old Army captain in World War I, he had impressed his fellow soldiers, including the son of the local political boss, Tom Pendergast. His rise from county judge to senator, once it began, had been a rapid one as Pendergast picked him each time as the least objectionable option—just as FDR would do in 1944. In his first senate election, in 1934, Truman rode "the Roosevelt wave," and became Missouri's junior senator, though one who was by and large ignored by the White House.[5] "After six years in the Senate, he had no significant legislative initiative to his credit," historian Robert Dallek recounts. And at the same time that Truman seemed to be pursuing a nonillustrious career, his patron, Pendergast, found himself facing a prison term on charges of tax evasion.[6] Truman, now his own man, sought a second Senate term by positioning himself as a responsible reformer.

While FDR might not have been an intellectual in the manner of so many of his brain trusters, to a remarkable degree, the man chosen by him as his likely successor was his opposite. Truman actually took pride in his anti-intellectualism and treated those who did traffic in ideas as effete and untrustworthy. Not only did he speak a plain cornpone English, lacking in both gravitas and good grammar, he communicated a kind of nervous anger that led him to snap judgments and stubbornness about refusing to rethink them once he had made them.

Wholly unschooled in the ways of international diplomacy, the Missourian viewed global politics through the prism of his experience with the Kansas City machine that had launched his career. "If you understand Jackson County," he once remarked, "you understand the world."[7] Joseph Stalin, he would likewise observe, was "as near like Tom Pendergast as any man" he knew;[8] the Soviets were "like people from across the tracks whose manners were very bad."[9] Before becoming president, Truman's best-known statement on foreign affairs had been "If we see Germany is winning we ought to help Russia, and if Russia is winning we ought to help Germany, and that way let them kill as many as possible."[10] As late as June 1948, long after Truman had directed the entire national security apparatus of the U.S. government toward a Cold War policy of opposing the Soviets at every turn, he told an assembled crowd, "I like Old Joe! He is a decent fellow. But Joe is a prisoner of the politburo. He can't do what he wants to. He makes agreements, and if he could he would keep them; but the people who run the government are very specific in saying that he can't keep them."[11]

When the Democratic Party's more conservative leaders, especially those from the South, objected to Roosevelt's renaming the fiery liberal Wallace as vice president, the still unknown Truman was chosen at the 1944 convention as an unobjectionable compromise: a candidate who offended no one and inspired an equal number.

Though he had done so reluctantly, Roosevelt's rejection of Wallace in favor of the largely unknown Truman remained an open wound for liberals. Most of them had nothing against Truman per se, but he was no Henry Wallace, and his ascension to the presidency was widely considered to be a lost opportunity of tragic proportions.[12]

The young Minnesota politician Hubert Humphrey spoke for many when, upon hearing of FDR's death, he wrote Wallace, "How I wish you were at the helm." Arthur Schlesinger, Jr., later recalled that "like many liberals," he considered Wallace to be FDR's ideological heir, a judgment he would soon regret. If Wallace had become president, Schlesinger would soon speculate in a special FDR issue of *The New Republic*, "The collapse of the New Deal might not have been so complete or so pathetic as it has been under Truman."[13]

Henry Wallace was in most respects the polar opposite of both Roosevelt and Truman. While the two presidents were, each in his own way, men who enjoyed the company of other men, Wallace was shy. He was, as former underscretary of agriculture Gardner Jackson observed in *The Atlantic Monthly*, "ill at ease in public places, sloppy in his dress, tousled of hair, and completely incapable of small talk." He seemed humorless, unable to "know how to have a belly-laugh—least of all at himself."[14] "I like Henry," admitted his close friend and biographer Russell Lord, "but he certainly makes it hard to do so."[15]

He ran for public office only once in his life before World War II, and that was as FDR's vice president. "It's hard to be a politician and be honest with yourself," he said after he had retired. The fear of sacrificing his integrity often left him without options in the horse-trading world of American politics, and he regarded those who actually did the dirty work of actually getting things done as fallen: "Fascists" became his frequent term of derision, together with "Hitlerite," a term he applied even to President Truman at one point.[16]

Before becoming a politician, Henry Wallace had been a scientist, a horticulturist, and most oddly, a dedicated disciple of a mystical White Russian guru. But he also remained a practicing Christian, deeply devoted to the Bible and, particularly, its prophets. He believed in prophecy and the search for ways, in his own words, "of bringing about the kingdom of heaven on earth."[17]

As a combination Christian socialist and farmer-capitalist, Wallace rarely fit neatly into any ideological category. FDR admired him, explaining in 1940, "He's not a mystic. He's a philosopher. He's got ideas. . . . He'll help the people think."[18] A less charitable if more common viewpoint in Washington was given voice by the pundit Walter Lippmann, who criticized Wallace as a "prophet" who couldn't relate to the "real world," because he possessed none of the "intellectual resources to decide the issues and the emotional steadfastness and stability to endure responsibility."[19]

Wallace was, in fact, as much a man of ideas as he was a man of action. As a young man, Wallace steeped himself in theory and theology. He began with William James's writings on pragmatism and religion but then quickly shifted his attention toward one of the most revolutionary thinkers in America's past, the economist and sociologist Thorstein Veblen. Veblen is perhaps best known for his theories of "conspicuous consumption," a critique of how the ornate display of wealth projected the power of elites in industrializing America. But Wallace was equally inspired by Veblen's writings on society's increasing reliance upon technical experts—"engineers," as he labeled them—and the control they were coming to exert over the scientific processes of advanced capitalist production. Veblen believed such expertise foretold a battle between production for public use versus that for private gain, waged by the "engineers" and the "capitalists."[20]

Wallace applied Veblen's teachings to the world of agriculture in his first book, *Agricultural Prices* (1920). He foresaw a transition toward a new form of economic production that involved more government regulation and, by result, further empowerment to "production engineers" and "statistical economists."[21] This was to be a peaceable revolution where regulation and planning would start to displace the capitalist hunt for short-term profit.

In *New Frontiers* (1934), which appeared a year after he became secretary of agriculture, Wallace wrote about the need to not "compete with each other for enough of this world's goods" but to build what he called a "cooperative good life."[22] As the historian Richard Pells points out, Wallace appeared "hostile to individualism and competition" and in favor of "community, social responsibility, balance, centralization, cooperation, and control." The historian Robert Westbrook describes the vision as one of a "rationalized society . . . managed in the public interest by expert planners."[23]

For American intellectuals of the 1930s, capitalism seemed on the brink of self-destruction, and its demise represented a moment of revolutionary potential, not merely politically but socially, culturally, and intellectually. Many—even many non-Marxists—saw the Soviet Union not as an adversary but as a road to the future. Henry Wallace swam in these intellectual currents and carried them with him into Franklin Roosevelt's White House.[24]

Wallace came to his cabinet job almost by inheritance, as his father had served as secretary of agriculture under Warren Harding. In that position under FDR, Henry Wallace oversaw programs aimed at improving agricultural prices by limiting supplies of goods in the market, a goal that dated back to the Populist Party of the 1890s. A Teddy Roosevelt Republican like his father, Wallace did not decide to become a Democrat until 1936, when FDR was preparing to run for his second term. When the president picked him as a running mate in 1940, he had begun his journey on a peaceful path away from laissez-faire capitalism toward a far more highly regulated social order.

Like Wallace, countless liberals, progressives, and socialists—including luminary independent thinkers and activists such as John Dewey, Walter Lippmann, and Upton Sinclair—threw their full weight behind U.S. entry into the war, which they regarded not only as a necessary battle against German autocracy but as an opportunity for America to move in a more progressive direction, one in which government would play a larger role in regulating the economy for the common good. John Dewey, who had no particular faith in militarism or war itself, argued—in his inimitably unwieldy prose—that the war could throw "into relief the public aspect of every social enterprise" and produce "instrumentalities for enforcing the public interest in all the agencies of modern production and exchange." Dewey believed the war could do away with the "individualistic tradition," as it demonstrated "the supremacy of public need over private possession."[25]

As vice president, Wallace had offered liberals as grand a vision as any they had been offered in decades in his response to Henry Luce's pronouncement of a new "American Century."[26] The founder of a growing magazine empire that already included *Time*, *Life*, and *Fortune*, Luce had answered FDR's famous 1941 "Four Freedoms" speech with his declaration of the dawning of an "American Century" characterized by "a sharing with all people of our Bill of Rights, our Declaration of Independence, our Constitution, our magnificent industrial products, our technical skills." Luce sketched out a vision of a future driven by "a passionate devotion to great American ideals . . . a love of freedom, a feeling for the equality of opportunity, a tradition of self-reliance and independence, and also of cooperation." For, he continued, "we are the inheritors of all the great principles of Western civilization—above all Justice, the love of Truth, the ideal of Charity. . . . It now becomes our time to be the powerhouse from which the ideals spread throughout the world and do their mysterious work of lifting the life of mankind from the level of the beasts to what the Psalmist called a little lower than the angels." It was America's "manifest destiny," he announced, to be "the Good Samaritan of the entire world."[27]

Wallace's May 1942 response became known as "The Century of the Common Man" speech, although its actual title was "The Price of Free World Victory." Here he set aside the language of technocracy and turned instead to Christian civics and his love of prophecy. Like Luce—who had been raised in China, the son of Christian missionaries—Wallace, as Alan Brinkley notes, also steeped his response in scripture and defined America's victory over evil as the center of a vision of a new, peaceful world. The basis of that victory was the principles embodied in Franklin Roosevelt's "Four Freedoms" speech, which, as the president had proclaimed, were "at the very core of the revolution for which the United Nations have taken their stand." And just as Luce's vision of an American Century included American industrial abundance spreading throughout the world, Wallace likewise promised that "the peace must mean a better standard of living for the common man, not merely in the United States and England, but also in India, Russia, China, and Latin America—not merely in the United Nations, but also in Germany and Italy and Japan."[28] That speech established Wallace, in the admiring words of the editors of *The New Republic*, as "a statesman capable of the grand conceptions for which the world has never had a greater need." His "lonely, eloquent words," wrote the liberal pundit Marquis Childs, had expressed "the vague aspirations and desires that are in men's hearts everywhere."[29]

Henry Wallace had more than fresh ideas and committed institutions behind him as the war wound to its close; he also had the support of Eleanor Roosevelt. Not long after his famous speech calling for the elimination of "economic cartels, colonialism, social injustice, and poverty," the first lady herself gave a speech in which she proposed "a partnership between those who work with their hands and those who work with their heads. They must all insist on their common interest because they are workers of the world." Eleanor envisioned a postwar world with international aid programs, full employment, global free trade, and eventually, an end to proverty and war.[30]

Ironically, Eleanor had not approved of Wallace as her husband's agriculture secretary, as she disliked Wallace's farm programs and thought he could do more for rural blacks. (At one point he was heard to tell an aide that the New Deal might be "undertaking to do too much for the Negroes."[31]) Once Wallace became vice president, though, he and Eleanor became close allies, if not close friends. She championed her husband's decision to make Wallace his running mate in the 1940 election, and both Roosevelts viewed Wallace as a worthy successor to Franklin, given his strength with liberals, organized labor, and farmers. Upon choosing Wallace, the president said he sought to demonstrate that the Democratic Party had made "overwhelmingly clear its stand in favor of social progress and liberalism" and had not shaken off "all the shackles of control fastened upon it by the forces of conservatism, reaction, and appeasement."[32]

Eleanor soon came to view Wallace as a kindred political soul, and she frequently asked the vice president to join her at speeches and other political functions. Like Wallace, Eleanor felt that Franklin had allowed Dr. Win the War to supplant Dr. New Deal. Her husband, she believed, was "no longer guided by warm human emotion."[33] FDR's willingness to abandon Wallace for the compromise choice of Truman left Eleanor feeling even more depressed and dejected, but their mutual admiration had continued through the final year of her husband's life. The day she moved out of the White House she wrote to him, "You are peculiarly fitted to carry on the ideals which were close to my husband's heart."[34] Wallace, said Eleanor, had become "the outstanding symbol of liberalism in the United States."[35]

And yet despite the privileged place he occupied in so many liberal hearts, Wallace's influence on Truman from his perch as secretary of commerce—his consolation prize after losing the vice presidency in 1944—was negligible. The president thought Wallace a showboat, a dreamer, and far too eccentric to be trusted. And while it was not Truman's fault that FDR and the party elders had picked him to replace Wallace as vice president, it surely did not endear him to Wallace, who thought Truman too easily swayed by conservative members in his administration.[36]

While Truman did consider himself a "liberal" when the occasion called for it, he had little affinity for those who worked and lived in that world. "There should be a real liberal party in this country, and I don't mean a crackpot professional one," he wrote in his diary in September 1945. "The opponents to liberalism and progress should join together in the party of the opposition."[37] And yet among Truman's first acts as president was to replace almost all of Roosevelt's veteran New Dealers—"the lowest form of politician," he called them—with his own political cronies and allies.[38] Within a year of FDR's death, in fact, the only one left was Henry Wallace.

Truman's and Wallace's temperamental and policy differences should not be allowed to obscure their similarities. By the standards of the day, they were both undeniably liberals, and shared similar beliefs with regard to many of the most important problems facing the nation in the coming aftermath of the war: Could the regulation of the economy during wartime serve as a bridge to postwar economic justice? Could the entry of the government into the economic sphere continue apace amid demilitarization?

Following the 1942 election, conservatives in the Republican Party had begun to grow in number and in boldness, and by 1943 they had succeeded in eliminating a number of key New Deal programs, including the Civilian Conservation Corps (CCC), the Works Progress Administration (WPA), the Farm Security Administration (FSA), and the National Youth Administration (NYA). Truman fought back. On September 6, 1945, just days after the Japanese surrender, he went to Congress and delivered one of the most ambitious speeches ever given by an American president. Though most historians believe the Fair Deal was formally formulated much later, Truman insisted that "it was on that day and with this message that I first spelled out the details of the program of liberalism and progressivism which was to be the foundation of my administration."

Truman's outline that day included extending unemployment benefits and raising the minimum wage. From there he warned against lifting price controls instituted during the war and reluctantly explained that some rationing would remain as well, especially when necessary to provide goods to prevent starvation in war-ravaged Europe. He then spoke highly of the possibility of "a full production peacetime economy" and, citing FDR's Second Bill of Rights, promised "a national reassertion of the right to work for every American citizen able and willing to work." He also outlined a "universal training program" for the military, believing that conscription was fair in that it distributed sacrifice evenly across the American population. He ended with this vow: "I shall shortly communicate with the Congress recommending a national health program to provide adequate medical care for all Americans and to protect them from financial loss and hardships resulting from illness and accident." And while civil rights was not an explicit part of this proposal, it was embedded in Truman's belief that the best way to uplift the Negro position in society was to do so for all poor people.

As secretary of commerce, Henry Wallace likewise fought the conservative rollback effort with every weapon at his disposal. In 1945 he published another book of extraordinary vision, *Sixty Million Jobs*, in which he called for full employment and a balance between the free market and government activism. Tipping his hat to the new president, he argued that Harry Truman would make good on FDR's Second Bill of Rights by fighting for such policies.[39] Wallace did his best to turn the Commerce Department, usually a sleepy backwater whose secretaries were often patronage appointments, into what one historian called "a clearinghouse for economic planning and for the creation of a balanced full-employment economy and expanded world trade."[40]

The first battle between the two men occurred over the innocuous-sounding but hotly contested bureaucratic base called the Office of Price Administration (OPA). Created in August 1941, it was charged with the responsibility of overseeing the wartime economy, setting price limits for consumers at home, and rationing to ensure that enough goods could be shipped to the men overseas. In 1942 the OPA announced the General Maximum Price Regulation—known as General Max—which set ceilings on prices based upon levels in March that year.

The OPA was headed originally by Leon Henderson, whom FDR once called "the toughest bastard in town," but who left the job early in the war to be replaced, following a short interregnum, by Chester Bowles in 1943.[41]

Bowles was no radical, but he did have a vision of what the OPA could accomplish in the postwar world. In 1946 he authored a short pamphlet titled "Tomorrow Without Fear," in which he argued for a strong role for government in the postwar American economy; though, paradoxically, he reasoned that "the firmer the commitment of the government, the less the government will be called upon actually to do." As businessmen came to recognize that government infrastructure was bolstering the economy, their fear of investment—a fear that had paralyzed the country during the Depression—would dissipate. Bowles was crafty here, arguing for both more and less government intervention in the economy, depending on the economic and political circumstance. His view of the future of the economy was rosy—he foresaw a thirty-hour workweek by the 1960s, increased wages, and higher levels of consumption, which would require firm and patient oversight by the federal government, including such measures as increasing the minimum wage, creating more foreign trade, building affordable housing, and most important, a continuation of price controls that could prevent inflation.[42]

Conservatives fixed their sites on the OPA as public enemy number one in the postwar world. Wisconsin's junior senator, Joseph McCarthy, earned his nickname as the "Pepsi Cola Kid," fighting OPA price controls on sugar.[43] When the young California congressman Richard M. Nixon was discovered to have (briefly) done some OPA work, he quickly announced his innocence from infection by the "slide-rule boys" and "snoopsters" of the agency.[44] Conservatives consistently attacked the OPA for "communist infiltration" and succeeded in forcing the young Canadian economist John Kenneth Galbraith from his job (and, not incidentally, contributing to his nervous breakdown in the process).[45] They resented not only regulation but also what they termed the "imperial presidency," which war and depression had helped birth. More significant, they were inspired by their vision of an almost pristinely "free" market untouched by government regulation, and this was a vision that millions of Americans shared with them.

Although conservatives had watched with frustration as the OPA had been renewed in 1944, they knew that 1946 would be their year to take it on, as the agency's charter was due to expire that June, just as they were on their way to vastly increasing their power and influence in Congress. As the debate began, Bowles warned that the Republicans wished to "throw away all the fruits of our four-year battle against higher rents and prices" and create an "inflationary joyride."[46] Citizens organized "Save the O.P. A." rallies, and labor threw its weight behind the agency, believing it to be a bulwark against the nasty "wage-price spiral" that had stymied its political and economic ambitions. But in June 1946, Congress produced a "severely weakened price control bill that turned OPA into a paper tiger."[47] Truman refused to sign it, and prices of goods, particularly beef, shot upward as the industry intentionally withdrew product from the marketplace to increase consumer pressure on Congress. By July, Truman received yet another weak version of the OPA bill from Capitol Hill, but this time it came with increasing pressure to sign. Instead, he decided to lift price controls on beef, which contributed to his image as a spineless vacillator who could be rolled by his right-wing opponents.[48]

Republicans also took aim at Truman's second big-ticket item: an economy based on "full production and full employment."[49] In January 1945, Senator James Murray (D-Montana) had sponsored the Full Employment Bill that presaged, in many respects, Truman's plan by requiring that the federal government find employment for those "able to work and seeking work."[50] Republicans were decidedly unimpressed, deriding the concept of full employment as both inflationary and none of the government's business.[51] Instead of supporting attempts to measure just how many people were employed at any given moment—and thus how close to full employment the country might be—they created a strictly advisory Council of Economic Advisers (CEA), which liberals naively believed might become influential by virtue of the example of FDR's brain trust. The final version of the legislation—the Employment Act of 1946—did next to nothing to bring the country closer to full employment, but neither did it deny all governmental responsibility for the public good. Liberals learned, however, that if they were to achieve any progress at all on their lofty postwar economic goals, they would have to work with big business to enlarge the overall economic pie, with the hope that more of it would fall into the hands of the unemployed, underemployed, and working poor.

Truman's feeble response to the opposition he faced regarding both the OPA and the Full Employment Bill worried liberals, who complained, notes the author Richard Parker, that among his senior appointees, "49 were bankers, financiers, and industrialists, including his secretaries of Commerce, War, and Defense, and his undersecretary of State. . . . [Another] seventeen were corporate lawyers."[52] Arthur Schlesinger, Jr., spoke for many at a dinner in October 1946 when, plagiarizing a line from British politics, he credited the Truman administration with "all the attributes of a jelly-fish except the sting." Not only was the president a man of decidedly limited ability, he wrote in *The Atlantic Monthly* in November of that year, "but, after considerable hiring and firing, he has managed to surround himself with his intellectual equals."[53]

Eleanor Roosevelt worried as well about Truman's weakness, but while her anger and frustration were no doubt politically motivated, this was also very much a personal issue for her. Eleanor's passion for working people—and those without work—had always been far stronger than her husband's, a fact that was evident to the millions of Americans who wrote to her and reached out to her for help during the Depression and the war.

Like FDR, Eleanor had been born into the American aristocracy, but she had had a far lonelier childhood. She lost her mother when she was only eight, and her father's uncontrollable alcoholism led relatives to place him in an insane asylum, where he died when Eleanor was just nine. That she was labeled an ugly duckling—not least of all by her own mother—only heightened her natural shyness. As a young girl, she was prepared for the future expected of her, a school for young ladies, Allenswood Academy outside London, run by feminist pioneer Marie Souvestre. She returned to the United States in 1902, at seventeen, and was presented as a debutante at the Waldorf Astoria. Through the New York Junior League, she volunteered to work with the poor and indigent, soon joining the Rivington Street settlement house, and her work in the slums on the East Side of New York City transformed her life, as it did those of so many privileged young girls who came of age during the Progressive Era. The movement helped well-to-do young women find purpose in "giving back" through social work and civic education, a principle that helped sustain Eleanor throughout her life. She came to believe that liberalism was grounded in personal "generosity," and by embodying this belief, she would soon stand accused as symbolizing its infamous "bleeding heart."[54] With Franklin dead and the war over, Eleanor became a fully independent actor and thinker on the political scene, and an informal kingmaker within the party. She continued her regular newspaper column, "My Day," and grew more outspoken in her calls for a national commitment to full employment, wage and price controls, and fair employment for all races and creeds. In doing so, she became a role model for liberals who could not fully trust either President Truman or the increasingly apostate Wallace.

While liberals grew more frustrated with both the style and substance of Truman's politics, the exasperation became more than mutual, particularly as it related to the most muscular manifestation of liberalism in America: the labor movement. The war had bottled up the labor movement's energies; a "no-strike pledge" policy prevented its members from exercising much pressure on their employers, many of whom were enjoying huge profits supplying the government with war-related products. When the war ended, union after union decided to walk out at once. Historian James Patterson calls 1946 "the most contentious in the history of labor-management relations in the United States, with 4,985 stoppages by 4.6 million workers, or about one of every fourteen Americans in the labor force."[55]

Truman was undoubtedly a friend to organized labor. Though he had, in the past, warned of "labor leaders" who "shirk their responsibility and permit widespread industrial strife," it was widely understood that he was referring almost exclusively to the United Mine Workers' John L. Lewis, a Republican who consistently had been a thorn in FDR's side during the war. But in the same September 1945 speech, Truman promised to "look to collective bargaining, aided and supplemented by a truly effective system of conciliation and voluntary arbitration, as the best and most democratic method of maintaining sound industrial relations."[56]

But America's labor leaders were in the mood for confrontation, not compromise. The ailing but angry Congress of Industrial Organizations (CIO) leader Sidney Hillman argued that big business wished to "break down everything that has been done in the last decade and get a situation that will give them Fascist powers under some other name."[57] John L. Lewis had no fears about alienating Democrats or the president. He was a near anarchist when it came to the relationship between government and labor—he wanted none— and usually endorsed Republicans rather than Democrats for the presidency. He represented, as the liberal journalist Jimmy Wechsler put it, a combination of "three deep strains in our history—the 'public be damned' adventurism of our earlier industrial barons, the cynicism of our political bosses, and the anti-intellectualism that has flared up intermittently in sectional and racial movements."[58]

From mid-1945 to early 1946, steelworkers, railroad workers, autoworkers, meat-packers, and coal workers went out on strike. Worried about the stability of the postwar economy as well as strikes in the coal and railroad industries threatening the fragile economies of war-torn Europe with additional starvation and death, Truman tried desperately to persuade industry leaders to negotiate with their employees. "I am a friend of labor," he declared when the railroad workers walked out, but "it is inconceivable that in our democracy" random individuals could "stifle our economy and ultimately destroy our country."[59] He wrote a speech in which he threatened to draft the strikers into the Army as punishment for their disobedience—"Let's give the country back to the people. Let's put transportation and production back to work, hang a few traitors, and make our country safe for democracy."[60] Fortunately, the president was dissuaded from delivering it

Within a mere year of FDR's passing, liberalism looked to be on the ropes almost everywhere in America: the OPA was dead, full employment was a pipe dream, and the passage of a program for national health insurance was even less likely. With those defeats came a flagging of the liberal spirit and, as so many historians have argued, the evolution of the fighting faith of the New Deal into a far more conciliatory and less ambitious agenda. The tribulations of the new world order, the uncertainties of the postwar economy, and the dawning of the Cold War demanded leadership on a scale at least equal to that of FDR, and yet no one—likely not even Truman—believed the new president to be up to the task. Suddenly the deeply rooted differences in personalities and approaches toward politics became public in explosive disagreement—disagreement that would define much of the future course of American liberalism.

2

"Scare Hell"

> I should observe of the liberal mind in actuality that it was inclined to give Communism an unreasoned and un-intelligent sympathy, sentimental in its first impulse, though often very hard and bitter in its tenacity.
>
> —Lionel Trilling[1]

In the spring of 1944, Henry Luce's popular *Life* magazine rejected an excerpt from Walter Lippmann's forthcoming book, *U.S. War Aims,* because Luce found its overall orientation to be "too anti-Russian." Had Lippmann offered the piece to Luce four years earlier, when *Time* termed Soviet dictator Joseph Stalin to be "the world's most hated man," he might have made a sale. Had he waited three more years, by which time Luce was calling Lippmann "naive" and *Life* was now proclaiming that the Soviets were intent upon causing "chaos, the collapse of civilization and the Communization of the Eurasian continent," his article might also have met with a favorable response. But Lippmann had submitted an essay critical of the Soviet Union's totalitarian character at a time when Luce publications were pronouncing Stalin "a great wartime leader" and the Russians, "one hell of a people," who "look like Americans, dress like Americans and think like Americans."[2] Two months into his presidency, in June 1945, Harry Truman promised that Americans had no reason to be afraid of Russia. "They've always been our friends," he insisted, "and I can't see any reason why they shouldn't always be."[3] By March 1948, however, the influential insider columnists Joseph and Stewart Alsop had reported, "The atmosphere in Washington today is no longer postwar, it is prewar."[4]

Franklin Roosevelt had believed that he could handle the Soviets, and the Soviets themselves, Molotov once explained, had "full confidence" in his sincerity and commitment to cooperation in working out differences.[5] Roosevelt was hardly naive about Stalin's intentions for Poland and Eastern Europe, but he believed that peace depended on the ability of the four great powers—the United States, the USSR, Great Britain, and China—to work together under the umbrella of the United Nations to keep order within their respective spheres of influence. As the historian Warren F. Kimball has observed, "His concept was vague, ill defined, and full of distinctions so subtle (or ignored) that even his closest advisers were uncertain about how it would work." Eleanor Roosevelt, for her part, thought her husband's concept to be "fraught with danger."[6] Truman later speculated, "If Roosevelt had been in a position of good health, he probably could have gone further than anyone else. . . . He had this appeal to world opinion that no one else had."[7] Whatever his plans may have been, Roosevelt kept them largely to himself, which left Truman at a complete loss to understand Roosevelt's machinations at home or abroad. No one had even bothered to inform him about the Yalta conference.[8]

The accidental president admitted that he "was very hazy about the Yalta matters," especially Poland.[9] As president, he naturally found himself highly dependent on his predecessor's staff to bring him up to date on past policies and decision making. But owing to Roosevelt's obsessive secrecy, no one could definitively clear up his confusion. Lacking a firm grasp on the issues, Truman had no choice but to trust his gut instincts.

His new nostrums about the world were evident as early as April 1945. A key meeting on the twenty-third of that month with Soviet foreign minister Vyacheslav Molotov would set the tone for many thereafter, when Truman, according to his own account, took a tough-guy attitude toward Molotov, as if he thought he could dictate the terms of agreement with the Soviets rather than negotiate them.[10] (His actual behavior that day is described differently in the several versions of the story told later.[11]) Truman probably warned Molotov that the United States would demand that "the Soviet government carry out the Crimea decision on Poland." He also handed him a memorandum that equated fulfillment of the Yalta decisions with establishment of a "new" government in Poland.[12] In Truman's ghostwritten memoirs, a shocked Molotov responded, "I have never been talked to like that in my life." Truman recalls replying, "Carry out your agreements, and you won't get talked to like that."[13] No one else in the room remembered it that way, but in any case, Truman told his advisers, "Our agreements with the Soviet Union so far had been a one-way street. . . . If the Russians did not wish to join us they could go to hell."

From the Commerce Department, Henry Wallace exercised little influence, much less authority, over U.S. foreign policy, but he grew increasingly alarmed by what he deemed to be a dangerous drift toward war with Russia. Wallace's "go-easy-on-the-Soviets" attitude put the former vice president at odds with many of the city's most influential citizens. Writing in *Life,* Joseph Alsop called him a "symbol of the terrible confusion which now afflicts American liberalism."[14]

Wallace began the autumn of 1946 as a loyal Democrat, but given his increasing anxiety about Truman's direction, the break was inevitable. Events came to a head one evening in mid-September after Wallace had been invited to give an address about the future of global relations at New York's Madison Square Garden by the CIO's political action committee, National Citizens Political Action Committee (NCPAC), and the celebrity-oriented cultural organization, the Independent Citizens Committee of the Arts, Sciences and Professions (ICCASP), two Popular Front groups friendly to the Soviets. The text of the address began circulating through Washington the afternoon of its presentation, and when Undersecretary of State Will Clayton got a copy, he tried frantically to get it rewritten. He called the White House at 6:00 p.m. and reached Press Secretary Charles Ross, but unfortunately for everyone concerned, Ross decided that the better part of prudence would be to allow the president to play poker over at Clark Clifford's house undisturbed.

Wallace showed up in New York to find the rally's organizers in a panic for exactly the opposite reason that had Washington insiders buzzing: they hated what they deemed to be the anti-Soviet tone of his proposed address and thought it altogether too evenhanded when it came to parceling out blame for the increasingly testy state of U.S.-Soviet affairs. Wallace agreed to edit this and other critical comments out of the talk, though he later claimed to reporters that he did so only for reasons of brevity.

As delivered, Wallace's remarks could only be interpreted as a repudiation of, if not an attack on, Truman's policy toward Russia and an attempt to blame Britain, and to a lesser degree, the United States for the world's difficulties in creating a lasting peace. Republican senator Arthur Vandenberg immediately joined with Democratic senator Tom Connally to attack Wallace for damaging "American unity." Senate minority leader Robert Taft took to the floor of the Senate to accuse the president of caving in to his party's "radical" wing. Byrnes was in a rage and angrily cabled Truman, "If it is not possible for you, for any reason, to keep Mr. Wallace, as a member of your cabinet, from speaking on foreign affairs, it would be a grave mistake from every point of view for me to continue in office, even temporarily." A day later, he thought it over and added: "I do not think that any man who professes any loyalty to you would so seriously impair your prestige and the prestige of the Government. . . . You and I spent 15 months building a bipartisan policy . . . a permanent policy upon which the world could rely. Wallace destroyed it in a day."[15]

Walter Lippmann "revived his portrait of Wallace as a man out of touch with reality, 'a man trying earnestly to deal with a world which is too much for him, and like many another he is cracking under the strain.'" Truman was loath to mention what he termed "Henry's wild statements" lest he help publicize them , but he went on the attack by proxy. He unleashed his conservative attorney general, Tom Clark, to chastise Wallace at a political banquet. A man who "tells the people of Europe that the United States is committed to a ruthless imperialism and war with the Soviet Union tells a lie," Clark declared. Truman also sought to distance himself from previous statements in which he had not only supported Wallace but had also endorsed the very speech that was now making his life miserable.[16] He did not, however, give up on Wallace immediately, knowing how important a symbol Wallace was for the administration's liberal political base, but tried to work out some accommodation "without cutting the ground out from under Byrnes." But Wallace did not help matters by issuing a statement that read: "I stand upon my New York speech," and "I intend to continue my efforts for a just and lasting peace."[17]

Later Truman complained to his diary:

Mr. Wallace spent two and one half hours talking to me yesterday. I am not sure he is as fundamentally sound intellectually as I had thought. He advised me that I should be far to the "left" when Congress is not in session and should move more to the "right" when Congress is on hand and in session. . . . He is a pacifist one hundred percent. He wants to disband our armed forces, give Russia our atomic secrets and trust a bunch of adventurers in the Kremlin Politboro. I do not understand a "dreamer" like that. The German-American Bund under Fritz Kuhn was not half so dangerous. The Reds, phonies and the "parlor pinks" seem to be banded together and are becoming a national danger.[18]

Wallace had to go, and once the deed was done, the president explained that the secretary had "resigned" because his views were in "fundamental conflict" not only with those of the administration but also, Truman said, with those "shared, I am confident, by the great body of our citizens."[19]

Wallace's departure provided a major turning point in the history of American liberalism. However accidentally it may have occurred, history had now provided liberals with a definitional moment, one in which they were forced to choose sides on the issue of communism and the Cold War. Wallace's break with the Democratic Party established an impermeable barrier between those liberals who embraced the assumptions that underlay U.S. Cold War strategy and those who rejected them. The refusal to embrace these assumptions—particularly those that held the Soviets to be solely responsible for the breakdown of global cooperation and the creation of a world of hostile "blocs," each seeking to undermine the other—was henceforth deemed out of order among politically respectable liberals. The notion that it was Truman and the United States rather than Stalin and the Soviets who were the aggressors in this conflict—a belief held, if not by Wallace, then by many if not most of his supporters—would remain cordoned off from respectable discourse among American liberals until the Vietnam conflict eventually revived it. Similarly, Wallace's hopes for a more humane, "managed" version of capitalism also fell out of fashion with most liberals as they made peace with a less ambitious, albeit uniquely American brand of laissez-faire tempered with Keynesian adjustments in tough times.

"The crackpots are having conniption fits," a delighted Truman mused about the reaction to Wallace's departure, while issuing an executive order that forbade any member of the executive branch from offering any public criticisms of U.S. foreign policy.[20] Given his opinion that almost all of the people who opposed his policies from the left were "crackpots," he worried little about the possibility that Wallace could cause any significant political problems.

Wallace misjudged the Soviets in fundamental ways and later admitted that he had been deceived when he visited Soviet Asia as vice president in 1944 and judged them to be building an economically democratic society in Siberia. He could not bring himself to condemn the Communist coup in Czechoslovakia in February 1948 and blamed Truman, pretty much exclusively, for the outbreak of the Berlin crisis of the same year, in which the Soviets sought to starve the citizens of that free city into submission.[21]

Whoever was more right than wrong on matters of judgment, clearly Truman had the better of the political argument. For not only had Harry Truman decided that the Soviets were not to be trusted, so, too, had his advisers, his cabinet, and the increasingly influential political establishment that had arisen around the Roosevelt administration, together with just about every newpaper editorial writer in America.

By the late 1940s, Americans had come to regard their security and their way of life to be remarkably fragile and beleaguered in the face of the Communist challenge, despite a significant degree of superiority in virtually every significant measure of power and influence. The Soviets had no long-range air force, no atomic bomb, and no surface fleet—and thus no capacity to attack America or to inflict significant damage on its economy. The opening of the Communist Party archives following the collapse of the Soviet Union revealed that the Soviets probably did not have the aggressive intentions toward Western Europe that at the time so concerned U.S. policy makers and politicians. Soviet leaders had more than enough trouble merely managing those nations they had already conquered, while deepening and extending their rule in Eastern Europe and trying to recover from the unprecedented devastation they had experienced during the war. While they most definitely saw themselves as competing for influence with the United States everywhere, and did whatever they could to support indigenous Communist movements wherever they arose, they lacked the resources, if not the ambition, to rule nations beyond their own extensive periphery. As Dean Acheson told a friend, the Soviets would not instigate war with the United States "unless they are absolutely out of their minds."[22] Even so, Truman and Acheson took no chances. The historian Melvyn Leffler argues that the priority of U.S. grand strategy was "to prevent a totalitarian adversary from conquering or assimilating resources of Europe and Asia and using them to wage war against the United States."[23]

Meanwhile, February 1946 provided a cavalcade of conundrums that together demonstrated just how fast and far U.S.-Soviet relations had fallen from their apex a year earlier at Yalta. Stalin's deeply ideological "election" speech—termed by Justice William O. Douglas to be a "declaration of World War III"—came on the ninth. The following day Winston Churchill visited the White House, where he previewed the "Iron Curtain" address he was to deliver shortly in Fulton, Missouri. A week later Canadian authorities announced the arrest of twenty-two alleged atomic spies. George Kennan's famous "Long Telegram" from Moscow appeared six days after that, both crowning and summing up a series of extremely pessimistic reports he had been sending steadily since the end of the war. ("I think there can be no more dangerous tendency in American public opinion than one which places on our government an obligation to accomplish the impossible by gestures of good will and conciliation toward a political entity constitutionally incapable of being conciliated," Kennan explained.[24]) *The New York Times* editors wondered if "the West did not fight one totalitarianism . . . to yield to another."[25]

By summer, Truman had declared—falsely, as it turned out—that the Soviets were "chiseling" on their agreements[26] and ordered a formal indictment outlining all the violations of the accords that Roosevelt and Truman had signed with Stalin.[27] Unfortunately for the president, the "Clifford-Elsey Report" of September 1946 had a hard time coming up with any clear examples, but what they lacked in specifics, they made for up with rhetoric. The Russians, they argued, believed that "the conflict between Capitalism and Communism [was] irreconcilable and must eventually be resolved by the triumph of the latter." Their ultimate aim was "to weaken the position and to destroy the prestige of the United States in Europe, Asia and South America." Virtually any action the United States took to frustrate their efforts would be justified, according to the authors, until the Soviets "realize that we are too strong to be beaten and too determined to be frightened."[28] Truman considered the report's language to be so potentially incendiary that he ordered all twenty copies of it locked in his safe, and it remained under wraps for the next twenty-two years. But he endorsed both its logic and conclusions and conducted his policies accordingly.

Following his contretemps with Truman, Wallace decamped to become editor of liberalism's flagship weekly magazine, *The New Republic*. Since its founding in 1914 by Herbert Croly, backed by the fortune of Willard Straight and boasting such luminaries as the wunderkind Walter Lippmann, *The New Republic* had offered liberals a combination of advice, vision, criticism, and education. Together with the much older *Nation*—founded by ex-abolitionists in 1865— *The New Republic* helped define the debate among liberals, policy makers, journalists, and others. Both publications were a great deal more sympathetic to Popular Front pieties than were the members of the Truman administration, though this was slightly truer of *The Nation* than *The New Republic*, and considerably more patient with regard to Soviet demands for indulgences, whether it be to crush non-Communist opposition in Eastern Europe or receive extra votes in the UN General Assembly. Many liberals associated with both *The New Republic* and *The Nation*, unaware of the degree of Stalin's brutality, viewed their philosophies as broadly consistent with that of the Soviets. Despite communism's exclusive emphasis on the working classes, its call for a (temporary) "dictatorship of the proletariat," and its contempt for slow systemic reform, they viewed their comrades as little more than "liberals in a hurry."

Wallace did not prove an especially good editor. He tended to fall asleep during editorial meetings, and little of what had made *The New Republic* so vibrant a read, whether in politics or the arts, survived during his tenure.[29] He viewed the magazine less as a place to engage in political and literary discussion and instead turned its focus more toward his own rather hazy thinking about politics. Upon assuming the editor's job, he announced that "jobs, peace, and freedom can be attained together" and "can make possible One

World, prosperous and free, within our lifetime."[30] Michael Straight (who had inherited the magazine from his father, Willard) came to regret the idea almost immediately. "I had bound *The New Republic* to Henry Wallace," Straight wrote in his memoirs. He, in turn, had allowed himself to be bound to the P.C.A. [Progressive Citizens of America]. Wallace, he recalled, was "heading for the land of illusions from which I had come. I knew from experience that collaboration with the Communist party would destroy Wallace, but I could not share my experience with him."[31]

Pro-Soviet liberals and leftists had formed the PCA in December 1946 by merging the CIO's NCPAC with the more culturally oriented ICCASP. From its inception the PCA's vision of politics included floating the idea of a third party to be led by Wallace and open to both Communists and non-Communists. At its founding convention Wallace promised, in his inimitable purism, "We must make it clear to the administration that we, as progressives, would prefer the election of an out-and-out reactionary like Taft in 1948, to a lukewarm liberal. We want this to be a genuine two-party country and not a country operated by a fake one-party system under the guise of a bi-partisan bloc."[32]

It was a stunning line of reasoning. In October 1947, nearly two of every three Americans surveyed said they believed that Communists should not be allowed to hold public office or important positions in any labor union. A similar percentage approved of the provisions of the Taft-Hartley Act demanding that the leadership of all unions swear they were not Communists.[33] Wallace and the PCA, meanwhile, had concluded that the problem with the Democrats was that they were insufficiently radical and overly anti-Communist, a misjudgment in which they were hardly alone. Writing in *The Nation*, its editor, Freda Kirchwey, advised, "Henry Wallace has issued a summons to action and a platform to which all progressives can rally. Only if we take up that challenge, and take it up with courage and determination, can we check the steady drift in American reaction and prevent a new war."[34]

What infuriated many liberals during this period was that Truman appeared to consistently betray the core principles of liberalism while never taking himself entirely out of their fold. He pressed for legislation more in response to political pressure than as a reflection of his own beliefs; liberals watched and wondered what was truly at the core.

For his part, Truman felt himself to be under attack from all sides: by liberals in his party and in the media, by conservative southern Democrats, and by the Republicans in Congress, who grew more confident with each passing day. During March 1947, for instance, faced with the withdrawal of the British from an area of the world they had traditionally policed, Truman put the United States squarely on the side of authoritarian anti-Marxist forces in Greece and Turkey with an astonishing $400 million in military aid. To secure this enormous sum, the formerly isolationist senator Arthur Vandenberg advised the president that he had to "scare hell" out of the American people, which is precisely what Truman and Acheson did. These countries were like "apples in a barrel," Acheson warned congressional leaders: let one become "corrupted" by communism, and it would "infect Iran and to all the East."[35]

In adopting these policies, Harry Truman proclaimed a new foreign policy doctrine: "I believe that it must be the policy of the United States to support free peoples who are resisting attempted subjugation by armed minorities or by outside pressures," he told Congress. "I believe that we must assist free peoples to work out their own destinies in their own way."[36] Fully twenty-five years later, Senator J. William Fulbright would observe, "More by far than any other factor, the anti-communism of the Truman Doctrine has been the guiding spirit of American foreign policy since World War II."[37]

Shortly thereafter, in June, Truman's much-admired secretary of state, General George Marshall, traveled to Harvard University to proclaim what would become known as the Marshall Plan. Far more expansive than the Truman Doctrine, it represented a complete reversal of America's age-old policy of aspiring, as President Washington put it in his iconic Farewell Address, "to steer clear" of foreign entanglements. The Marshall Plan sought to rescue virtually the entire Continent from the potential of postwar economic collapse, a collapse that would, according to the Truman Doctrine, invite Soviet subversion on a massive scale. The goal, Marshall announced, would be to "provide a cure rather than a mere palliative."[38] While Winston Churchill would call the speech "a turning point in the history of the world,"[39] Truman well understood the political risks he was assuming. The proposal flew in the face of both traditional Republican isolationism—and stinginess—and the Wallace-ites' increasing hostility toward the British Empire. The president looked to General Marshall to lead the charge and isolate his opponents on both flanks.[40] "Anything going up there bearing my name," he told Clark Clifford, "will quiver a couple of times, turn belly-up, and die."[41]

At first it appeared that even the Soviets might be eligible for Marshall aid, which would have made it all but impossible to sell to Congress. Until they learned that the conditions of participation would prove unacceptable to the Soviets, pro-Communist liberals were not quite sure how to react. Wallace, for his part, initially embraced the plan. "The Marshall Doctrine looks toward an overall program which is what I have been advocating all along," he wrote in *The New Republic*. But once it became clear that the plan was aimed at containing the Soviets rather than helping them to rebuild, he began attacking it. As it happened, William Z. Foster, who headed the U.S. Communist Party, followed a similar trajectory in his own criticism, and began calling on fellow Communists to support Wallace in a run for the presidency in the coming election, which suited Harry Truman just fine.[42]

To shore up his support with an increasingly insecure American public, Truman coupled this aggressive response to Soviet expansionism with a domestic loyalty program designed to root out Communists and their sympathizers from the federal government. Here he tried to find a middle ground between those who demanded the dismissal of all Communists, ex-Communists, and likely Communist sympathizers and those who viewed the threat of a new postwar Red Scare with greater alarm. Truman did not think that the federal government should be employing card-carrying Communists, but he did share the concern about potential abuse of civil liberties that a crackdown would inevitably invite. He was especially apprehensive about giving unlimited power to Congress and the FBI to harass those with un-popular views.[43] But under pressure from not only Republican right-wingers in Congress but also the powerful and obsessive FBI director, J. Edgar Hoover, he felt pressured to act politically in order to stave off something far worse.

The loyalty program quickly ballooned out of control, as it "required full-scale loyalty investigations of every new federal employee, whether an atomic scientist at Los Alamos or a janitor in a Department of Agriculture office in Peoria."[44] Too often the program became a pretext to rid the government of those with unpopular beliefs, for instance, employees who refused to condemn interracial marriages and alleged "sexual perverts" (that is, homosexuals).[45] The NAACP complained that many loyalty investigators were questioning government employees on their attitudes toward racial integration. The American Civil Liberties Union condemned the Truman program, and *Nation* editor Kirchwey spoke for many when she termed the program "an organized system of thought control."[46]

As the loyalty boards were investigating a wide range of employees, the House Committee on Un-American Activities (often called the House Un-American Activities Committee and thus abbreviated as HUAC), already active when FDR was president, began its notorious hunt for actors, writers, and directors accused of surreptitiously slipping Communist messages into America's movie theaters, Broadway shows, and soon enough, television programming. It discovered not a single instance of such espionage in its relentless search but did ruin many a career and did deep and lasting damage to the quality of America's cultural, political, and social discourse.[47]

Truman's troubles on the domestic front were hardly limited to the loyalty issue. It had long been the goal of conservatives in Congress to halt the growing power of labor under the New Deal, and in June 1947 they introduced the Taft-Hartley bill, which stripped labor of many of its most important victories of the Roosevelt era. Taft-Hartley sought to undermine the "closed shop," a practice that required a newly hired employee to join a union if one was in place. It bolstered state right-to-work laws and made it much more difficult for workers to organize their plants by such measures as banning secondary boycott, which made it impossible for unionized workers in one firm to boycott the products of another in support of their strike or organized drive. As historian Nelson Lichtenstein explains, "The strong could not come to the aid of the weak, which in practice proscribed the organizing techniques so effectively deployed by the transport and longshoring unions to extend unionism into retail trade, food processing, and warehouse work."[48]

Perhaps most significant for the long-term political balance of the nation, as well as that between capital and labor, the bill defined shop supervisors as "management" rather than labor, and thereby detached them from the union. Lichtenstein argues that this "deunionization of the foremen and their forced-draft conscription back into the managerial realm was therefore essential to the reghettoization of the union movement and the victory of management all along the white-collar frontier."[49] Coupled with the myriad unhappy implications of the increasingly widespread red-hunting machine arising in the Republican Party, the effect was to divide and weaken liberal forces for the coming political battles at home and abroad.

Shrewdly, Truman used the threat of Taft-Hartley to try to undo some of the damage done to his relations with labor by presenting a new ideological rationale for his presidency and his party. He took to the airwaves to call Taft-Hartley "a shocking piece of legislation" that would "take fundamental rights away from our working people."[50] He promised to veto it when it reached his desk, well aware that the Republican Congress would override him but knowing the gesture would please his party nevertheless. The *New Republic*'s Richard Strout wrote, "Let's come right out and say it, we thought Truman's labor veto thrilling." Columnist James Wechsler added, "Mr. Truman has reached the crucial fork in the road and turned unmistakably to the left."[51]

Truman took another, braver, step to shore up his left flank that same month by agreeing to become the first American president to deliver an address before the National Association for the Advancement of Colored People

(NAACP), on June 29, 1947. During the 1920s and 1930s the organization had lobbied hard against the poll tax and for an antilynching law without ever receiving the explicit support of President Roosevelt. (Naturally, Eleanor was much more eager to lend her assistance.) But in general the NAACP resisted direct action or mounting a campaign of conscience. It had already shifted its strategy from trying to persuade Congress to pass legislation—an approach that had proved impossible, given the hostility of powerful southern Democrats—toward winning their battles in the courts.

The organization's leadership understood that as the Cold War expanded into Asia and Africa, the question of race at home would become an increasingly significant embarrassment to the Truman administration abroad. When, for instance, a mob of five hundred whites attacked a small party of blacks seeking to make use of public swimming facilities in Cicero, Illinois, Soviet foreign minister Andrei Vishinsky seized the opportunity to mock the United States at the United Nations, noting sarcastically, "This is human rights in the U.S.A.," and the event was covered widely in Third World nations based primarily on U.S. press reports.[52] Eleanor, who had joined the NAACP Executive Board in 1945, was already making the connection between civil rights and Communist propaganda. "We have to make sure that we have civil rights in this country," she argued, because it is no longer "a domestic question—it's an international question. It is perhaps the question which may decide whether democracy or communism wins out in the world."[53] Truman's decision to speak to the NAACP thrilled Eleanor. She saw herself and Truman standing in the shadow of Lincoln, doing what that president never did do: bequeath full civil rights to the freed slaves. It was here that Eleanor started to see Truman as an ally, and found occasion to praise what she termed his "courage."[54]

Truman looked out over the black and white crowd and gave eloquent testament to his unpretentious midwestern faith in equal opportunity for everyone, now to be guaranteed by the federal government. "The extension of civil rights today means not protection of the people *against* the government, but protection of the people by the government." This was an attempt to expand FDR's Second Bill of Rights beyond where the former president had thought of extending it: race relations.

"To Secure These Rights," issued in October 1947 by the committee Truman appointed to report on civil rights in America, called for the immediate institution of antilynching laws—a demand that would eventually split off the Dixiecrats from the rest of the party for the upcoming election—the abolition of poll taxes, and an end to segregation on interstate transportation networks, where federal law held sway. Truman might have been thinking about the increasing voting power of blacks who were settling in northern urban areas in larger numbers at the time—and reducing Wallace's appeal, should he mount a challenge—but there can be no doubt that Eleanor's heartfelt moral support for the cause did a great deal to persuade the president as well. Whatever the reason, it was the beginning of the Democratic Party's commitment to civil rights legislation that would dominate its identity—and that of modern liberalism—for much of the coming half century.

Clark Clifford, Truman's trusted political adviser, recalled 1948 as "an incredible year": "The Communists took over Czechoslovakia, Israel was born, Stalin lay siege to Berlin, and the Airlift saved it, Whittaker Chambers confronted Alger Hiss and Harry Truman defied the predictions of every political pundit and expert in the nation—except himself."[55] For all of the historical world drama these events represented, it was the coming election that proved the focus of liberals' obsessions.

Having returned from a lecture tour of Europe—where he was met in every city by dueling telegrams from both pro- and anti-Communist liberals either disputing or proclaiming his credentials as America's liberal leader—Wallace began barnstorming America. Drawing enormous paying crowds, he condemned Truman in increasingly bitter terms for his Hitlerite methods. "If the Democratic Party" is the "war party, if my party continues to attack civil liberties, if both parties stand for high prices and depression," he told a PCA rally in September, "then the people must have a new party of liberty and peace."[56] He then called on his followers to become "a Gideon's army" of equally uncompromising soldiers of virtue.[57] By the end of 1947, Wallace had decided he was ready to run for president, his moralistic enthusiasm easily triumphing over his pragmatic political instincts.

The election of 1948 proved to be among the most bizarre in American history. It was really three elections held simultaneously, each with a surprise outcome. In most of the country, the crime-fighting Republican candidate, New York governor Thomas E. Dewey, faced the Democrat, Harry Truman. But in the South the choice boiled down to Truman versus a segregationist Dixiecrat, South Carolina governor Strom Thurmond. On the left, and among many liberals, the choice was a newly invigorated Truman and an increasingly Communist-influenced Wallace, while a few ended up supporting Dewey.

The Democrats were the first to convene as a party, and they met in early July in hot and humid Philadelphia. With Wallace still riding relatively high on the left and Dewey soaring in the polls, "arriving delegates found an atmosphere of gloom and despondency and encountered a spirit of defeatism among the party leaders," *The New York Times* reported. "Not since the South rebelled against Stephen Douglas in 1860," *Time* oberved, "has the party seemed so hopelessly torn and divided."[58] The mayor of New York told a reporter, "We are here to honor the honored dead. Won't you please act accordingly?"[59]

When the party liberals succeeded, finally, in passing a strong civil rights plank, Handy Ellis, Alabama's chairman, said, "We cannot participate further in this convention" and then led a walkout to a chorus of boos from the floor, all the while displaying the Stars and Bars of the Confederate flag.[60] Soon Strom Thurmond took over, giving speeches and then forming a new party that broke to Truman's right. The States Rights Democratic Party, or Dixiecrats, met in Birmingham in mid-July. Their platform attacked Truman's "infamous and iniquitous" civil rights planks, terming them a "totalitarian" plan to enforce a "police state" on the United States. The Dixiecrat slogan was "Segregation Forever." And while Thurmond had originally planned to make what he said would be a principled campaign in support of states' rights, he could soon be heard crying: "There's not enough troops in the Army to break down segregation and admit the Negro into our homes, our eating places, our swimming pools and our theaters."[61]

During the final week of July, the Progressive Party held its convention in Philadelphia as well. Paying crowds proved so large and enthusiastic that the final night of the gathering had to be moved to the local baseball stadium, where a capacity crowd of thirty-two thousand bought tickets to hear their hero speak. "It will remain a thing of awe to professional politicians that people paid hard cash to see a man baptize his own party," wrote the Associated Press's man there, Hal Boyle. "This was something new."[62] But the size and enthusiasm of the crowds did not change the fact that the Communists had seized control of the campaign. "If it had not been for the Communists, there would have been no Progressive Party," mused the decidedly ambivalent Wallace supporter, I. F. Stone.[63]

Following the convention, Wallace made a point of showing up the Democrats by bravely traveling through the South and refusing to accept the strictures of segregation, even as events grew increasingly unruly. Wallace's speeches, whose audiences he always insisted be strictly integrated, were often marred by violent attacks by local whites on black participants, resulting in at least one fatal stabbing. At virtually every speech he gave, Wallace faced a deluge of hurled food, some landing squarely on his face. "I don't mind a little good-natured throwing of eggs and tomatoes," he would say, demonstrating considerable grace along with extraordinary personal courage, "but I'd much rather see that food being fed to children."[64] Facing a mob twenty-five hundred strong on a hot, hazy day in Burlington, North Carolina, Wallace went so far as to pick a protester up by his lapels and challenge him: "Are you an American? Don't you believe in free speech? Why won't you let me speak?"[65]

He was a "genuinely distinguished figure," admitted anti-Wallaceite James Wechsler. "His journey," said *The Nation*, "may well turn out to have been the redeeming feature of an otherwise ill-advised candidacy."[66] But Wallace all but did in his own cause, whatever that may have been, by refusing to support his country during the Berlin crisis, and by such statements as calling Communists "the closest things to the early Christian martyrs." It would have been amazingly bad judgment—to stay nothing of bad timing—for any politician to take an adversary's side in any international conflict, but to do so during a presidential campaign was surely an act of political suicide on Wallace's part, even exclusively within the confines of his left-liberal cocoon.[67]

Wallace's message was woefully out of tune with a country whose economy was in the midst of an almost unprecedented economic boom. In 1947, for instance, Americans were producing roughly one-half of the world's manufactures, including 57 percent of its steel, 43 percent of its electricity, and 62 percent of its oil. Americans drove three of every four cars in the world and its companies built four out of every five.[68]

Liberals everywhere shared a palpable sense of imminent catastrophe, as virtually every opinion poll showed Truman getting trounced in the November 1948 election. But the young political genius Clark Clifford saw opportunity amid the crisis. He concluded that if the president moved leftward on domestic issues as a kind of bookend to the harsh Cold War rhetoric he was now employing vis-à-vis the Soviets, he might capture parts of both flanks simultaneously as he also staked a claim to traditional Democratic working-class constituencies across the agricultural Midwest and urban Northeast.

In January, Truman presented Congress with a decidedly leftward-leaning program of increased taxes, a higher minimum wage, civil rights, price controls, and national health insurance—a set of programs he would later term "the Fair Deal"—the successor to FDR's New Deal. When combined with his fierce opposition to the Taft-Hartley legislation and his soaring speech to the NAACP, Truman successfully presented himself as a candidate who would fight hard for liberal causes, even hopeless ones, so long as they remained untainted by a Communist or quasi-Communist association.[69] He toured the country on a specially equipped sixteen-car train and promised to "give 'em hell" at every stop. And he embraced the liberal label to a degree that must have surprised even himself, telling a rally in Los Angeles, "The Democratic Party is the party which truly expresses the hopes of American liberals, and which has power to fulfill those hopes."[70] *The New Republic*'s "TRB" column (authored by Richard Strout) cheerfully observed that Truman's speeches put him "as far to the left as Roosevelt ever was in his most leftish days."[71]

Eleanor Roosevelt viewed the election from afar, working away at the United Nations in San Francisco. Surprised by Wallace's initial popularity, she worried that he was striking a nerve with liberals who felt betrayed by Truman. Having worked with Communist front organizations during the 1930s, she was loath to trust them.[72] Meanwhile, Eleanor was preoccupied with the drafting of what was to become the Universal Declaration of Human Rights. "I knew that as the only woman, I'd better be better than anybody else. So I read every paper," she later explained. "And they were very dull sometimes, because State Department papers can be very dull."[73] Even so, her greatest frustration at the UN was the Soviet delegation and its quisling allies, as Soviets increasingly saw human rights as subterfuge for class domination.[74] She understood that the Soviets were eager to manipulate the language of rights to justify their abnegation of exactly these rights with the kind of Orwellian doublespeak in which their diplomats had by this time come to excel.

Eleanor gave voice to her frustration when she used her syndicated column to criticize the Soviet tactic of delay and then takeover by late-night vote—one at which American Communist labor leaders and others were also adept. Eleanor complained: "One must be alert since if they cannot win success for their point of view in one way, they are still going to try to win in any other way that seems to them possible."[75] She had watched as delegation member W.E.B. Du Bois, onetime head of the NAACP and intellectual avatar of much of black America, threatened to bring the vexing question of America's treatment of its black citizens to the UN debate. Eleanor blocked this, knowing the ruckus it would cause at home. And when, in 1948, the NAACP booted the increasingly radicalized Du Bois out of its ranks, he immediately rushed into the welcoming arms of the Wallace camp, and then from there to an embrace of the Soviet Union.[76]

Roosevelt was quick to recognize the self-defeating nature of Wallace's chimerical quest. "As a leader of a third party," she wrote, Wallace would likely "accomplish nothing. He will merely destroy the very things he wishes to achieve." In January 1948 she predicted that "the American Communists will be the nucleus of Mr. Wallace's third party." She told the Oregon ADA, "Any use of my husband's name in connection with that party is from my point of view entirely dishonest."[77]

Just before the election took place, Eleanor finally made it official and gave Truman her endorsement. As such testimonials go, it was not much, but Truman used it, especially in New York, where the former first lady's backing might mean the difference between winning and losing. Far more surprising, undoubtedly to Wallace as well as Truman, was *The New Republic*'s endorsement of the president as the candidate of "militant liberalism" who deserved the "full support" of its readers as well.[78]

Truman famously surprised virtually the entire country by eking out a razor-thin victory. Just about every newspaper had predicted that he would lose, and the president was shown gleefully holding up a copy of *The Chicago Tribune* with its famously wrong headline, "Dewey Defeats Truman." No less amazing to observers was Wallace's anemic performance. He finished *fourth*, behind even Strom Thurmond, who carried four states and 39 electoral votes, based on 1,169,021 total votes cast for him. Wallace wound up with just 1,157,172 votes, or 2.38 percent total, and zero electoral votes.[79]

By 1952, Wallace would renounce his candidacy and the role he played in challenging the American Cold War consensus, admitting that he had "failed utterly to take into account the ruthless nature of Russian-trained communists" in the Czechoslovak coup. "What I did not see," he explained, "was the Soviet determination to enslave the common man morally, mentally, and physically for its own imperial purposes."[80]

With the Wallaceites having amputated the Democrats' most leftward extremities and the Dixiecrats, those on the right, the election of 1948 offered a rare opportunity for postwar American liberalism to define itself without the compromise and co-optation that usually characterized such efforts. Many on the liberal left believed their moment had finally arrived. *Commentary*'s estimable founding editor, Elliot E. Cohen, sensed a hunger among Americans for a "middle-of-the-road social democracy."[81] *The New Republic*'s Strout argued that Americans had now embraced the most "radical" reformist platform in the nation's history.[82] Truman won himself considerably more respect among liberals than he had previously enjoyed going into the campaign. Freda Kirchwey admired his "pugnacious and stout-hearted campaign," and I. F. Stone called his victory "a magnificent display of moral courage."[83] When he delivered his 1949 State of the Union address, he was ready to offer the country a bold program and a set of principles around which almost all liberals could comfortably unify, and one that intentionally echoed both the rhetoric and programmatic purpose of the New Deal. "Every segment of our population and every individual has a right to expect from our Government a fair deal," he declared and then provided a wish list that one historian summarized as "widespread economic controls; new taxes to balance the budget and lower the national debt; repeal of Taft-Hartley; a higher minimum wage; an agricultural program providing 'abundant farm production and parity income'; major resource-development projects and the creation of new valley authorities based on the TVA; large-scale extensions of the Social Security program; 'a system of prepaid medical insurance' and other health initiatives; federal aid to education; creation of a cabinet-level department to manage health, education, and Social Security; an extensive housing bill emphasizing slum clearance and public housing for the poor; a fairer and more generous immigration bill aimed at the admission of greater numbers of displaced persons; comprehensive civil rights legislation."[84]

On Election Day, it was Truman's tough-minded liberalism that had won the day, even if he had been pushed toward that stance by the visionary romanticism of Henry Wallace and by the power of Eleanor Roosevelt's own savvy combination of realism, idealism, and emotional intensity. Each would live within American liberalism to fight another day.

3

"The Self-Righteous Delusions of Innocence"

American liberalism, partly because it is impotent and frustrated and partly because it has learned scarcely anything since the eighteenth century, has little understanding of the fact that politics are morally ambiguous even on the highest level.

—Reinhold Niebuhr, 1946[1]

Harry Truman's tough-guy self-image matched many of the themes of America's pop culture of the period, with its hard-boiled depictions of unshaven, dark antiheroes facing a world out of control in the film noir of the era personified by Humphrey Bogart's wise-cracking Sam Spade in Hollywood's rendering of Dashiell Hammett's *The Maltese Falcon,* along with its many imitators. ("I'll have some rotten nights after I've sent you over," said Spade to Mary Astor's Brigid O'Shaughnessy as he handed her over to the authorities, "but that'll pass."[2]) Postwar America called for no-nonsense, tough-talking leaders willing to do whatever was necessary to protect the country from those prepared to do it harm.

But there was also a more deeply considered version of anti-Communist liberalism than Truman's, one that had been worked out by liberal intellectuals well versed in the foundational theories of the liberal Enlightenment as well as in those of the more intellectually fashionable Marxist tradition. These thinkers, who also helped define liberalism in the late 1940s, believed that an American president could educate the public in the principles of liberalism to the point where it could become the dominant creed not just of the United States but of democrats the world over.

The American thinker who best embodied this ambition was, ironically, a man of the cloth. The Reverend Reinhold Niebuhr spent his life pondering the paradox of how to square the existence of evil with the existence of God. He inherited this charge from his father, who had ministered to the plains dwellers of Illinois and who was proud to see his son pursue this path as well. Upon completing his graduate studies at Yale, the younger Niebuhr accepted a ministry in Detroit, where he witnessed exploitation in the preunion auto industry in its most brutal phase. His appreciation for the human consequences of such exploitation turned him into an early champion of the revolt against the market-dominated society of the 1920s, and he enrolled in the Socialist Party in 1929 after embarking to teach theology at Union Theological Seminary in Manhattan the previous year.

Upon his arrival, Niebuhr immediately established a reputation as a popular and intense lecturer. He would stand at the lectern, tall, lean, and prematurely balding, his words tumbling out in a losing race with his thoughts.[3] In 1932, Niebuhr published his masterwork, *Moral Man and Immoral Society*, which focused on the question that so many had asked during the past two decades and that had vexed both the Roosevelt and Truman administrations: How could modern industrial society be made more just? Niebuhr knew that in most progressive circles, this question was often answered with reference to the teachings of the Social Gospel movement, one that had originated among mainline Protestant churches and employed explicitly religious arguments to justify liberal activism in support of ending the exploitation of child labor, promoting workmen's compensation, and the like. The "arc of justice" pointed toward mutual improvement in society, they argued. Man's sinfulness was not a permanent condition but rather a reflection of the selfishness to which a pecuniary society drove him. Conditions could change, and so, therefore, could consciousness.[4]

Niebuhr set out to upend these principles, and in so doing hoped to drive away all sentimentalists from the liberal Christians he considered his primary audience. "Force" and "coercion"—ideas considered anathema to those who believed in a process of gradual and enlightened progress—were actually central to the project of improving society. Human nature tended toward self-interest, and power did not give up without a fight. Classes of people deprived of justice were entitled to "coercion" as "ethically justified" in certain cases, even if it was "morally dangerous." "It is sentimental and romantic," he warned, "to assume that any education or any example will ever completely destroy the inclination of human nature to seek special advantages at the expense of, or in indifference to, the needs and interests of others." Niebuhr sought to define nothing less than the limits and possibilities of a transformation of American public life. His teachings would also inspire the leadership of the coming civil rights revolution, as its tough-minded strategist and public face, Martin Luther King, Jr., came to consider himself a Niebuhr disciple.[5] (So, too, would Niebuhr's—and King's—close friend of later years, Rabbi Abraham Joshua Heschel, who would become the most influential American Jewish theologian and civil rights champion of the twentieth century.)

The outbreak of war in Europe engaged Niebuhr in the most critical concerns he had faced to date. Did Christian activists, he asked, really believe that the proper response to Nazism was pacifism? To address such questions, Niebuhr founded in 1941 a short biweekly, *Christianity and Crisis*. He aimed his arguments at the "irresponsibles," as Archibald MacLeish called them: intellectuals so fixated on the "lessons" of World War I that they blinded themselves to the threat that fascism posed.[6] Niebuhr's life became a torrent of argument, essays, and reviews written on train rides between lectures, in the midst of which he still managed to write books that set out further his views on Augustinian Christianity, human nature, and the myriad paradoxes of evil in God's kingdom.[7]

No less important than his published words and speeches were his organizing efforts. He threw himself into giving speeches, editing newsletters, and seat-of-the-pants fund-raising. In 1941 he created the Union for Democratic Action (UDA) to do battle on behalf of liberals and socialists opposed to pacifism and isolationism. It remained very much an elite-driven organization with few local chapters. Niebuhr explained that he didn't want to "build a political party" but rather a "general alliance to support the New Deal against efforts of reactionary democrats to destroy it."[8] UDA would remain a shoestring organization, but a significant one, as it came to provide, in the words of Niebuhr's biographer, Richard Wightman Fox, "a haven for former radicals in transit toward the liberalism of the Democratic Party."[9]

The war inspired Niebuhr to cast aside the socialism and pacifism of his youth and accept his fate as a liberal, but he was a liberal unlike any before him. The focus of Niebuhr's writing and speaking was what he called the "tragic necessities of history."[10] "The excessively optimistic estimates of human nature and of human history with which the democratic credo has been historically associated are a source of peril to democratic society," he explained, warning liberals in particular against allowing their hopes for a peaceful world to triumph over their need to prepare for one likely to be characterized by ceaseless conflict.[11] It was a jarringly self-critical and reflective perspective to ask a nation still drunk with wartime victory to adopt. Even so, in 1948, Henry Luce's *Time* would anoint Niebuhr "America's Theologian" and place him, alone, on the cover of the magazine's twenty-fifth anniversary issue.

Possessing a sprightly step and boasting a famously vivacious disposition, twenty-five years younger and almost a foot shorter, Arthur M. Schlesinger, Jr., stood in near-perfect physical contrast to Reinhold Niebuhr. Schlesinger's parents originally sent him to public schools in Cambridge, but his father, who was a Harvard history professor, upon hearing that Arthur's history teacher had taught him that Albanians were albinos, shipped Arthur off to Phillips Exeter Academy, before he returned home to attend Harvard College.[12] One night not long after Schlesinger finished his undergraduate studies in American literature and history, his wife, Marian, took him to hear Niebuhr speak at the university's Memorial Church. Schlesinger had been raised a Unitarian, a religion of optimism and hope about humankind and the prospects of justice in the world and with little use for what its proponents believed to be outdated notions of original sin. Niebuhr's lecture would change Schlesinger's thinking, as well as his life.

By the time Schlesinger attended Niebuhr's lecture, he had, like Niebuhr, chosen his father's career path and become an American historian—indeed, at the very same institution, Harvard. The son borrowed much from his famous father, most particularly his embrace of the theory of the power of "cycles" governing the swings of American political history. The nation's mood, both men believed, alternated between liberal hopes for reform and conservative fears based on the rising and waning of Americans' desire for reform and the inevitable disappointment that followed in its wake.

In 1939, Arthur junior published a study of the 1840s radical Orestes Brownson, whom he described as an "American Marxist before Marx." Brownson had developed from his own version of transcendentalism a "new church" that "found its God in man and looked for its heaven on earth."[13] Listening to Niebuhr speak, however, Schlesinger became a convert to darker teachings about sin and coercion, and soon became a leader of a group of intellectuals who were jocularly referred to on occasion as "Atheists for Niebuhr."[14]

Schlesinger's friendship with Niebuhr would define much of his work, both political and intellectual, for the coming sixty years, and would help guide him through the conflict that divided many if not most liberal intellectuals: that of a life of political involvement versus one of ideas and scholarship (and in Niebuhr's case, theology). The war made that question moot, at least temporarily. Schlesinger's eyesight kept him out of the Army, so he joined the Office of War Information (OWI) and then moved to the Office of Strategic Services (OSS), the precursor to the CIA, where he traveled to London and Paris.[15]

Schlesinger somehow found time during this period to research and write his second book, *The Age of Jackson,* which won the Pulitzer Prize in history in 1946. He cast Andrew Jackson as a hero for his times, who stood up for the "common man" against "privilege." Schlesinger found in America's seventh president an expression of homegrown radicalism that gave voice to an American creed. The inherent conflict in American society, Schlesinger argued, was "between the 'producing' and 'non-producing classes'"—not capitalist versus bourgeois, as Marx had theorized—and it was that split that characterized much of the struggle between Jeffersonians and Hamiltonians at the moment of the nation's founding. Jackson brought urban industrial workers into this fold and deployed the power of the state to protect the interests of the common man and woman, according to this interpretation, and Schlesinger deployed it as a model for contemporary liberalism. "American democracy has come to accept the struggle among competing groups for the control of the state as a positive virtue," he concluded.[16] Reviewing the book in *Time,* Whittaker Chambers judged it "a brilliant justification of the New Deal disguised as a history of the age of Jackson."[17] Niebuhr, in turn, praised the book for its value in helping to shape debate about American values and contemporary politics.[18]

Schlesinger emulated the examples of the progressive historians Charles Beard, James Harvey Robinson, and Vernon Parrington, among others, whose interpretations of American history self-consciously sought to create a "useable past" for contemporary American Progressives. But Schlesinger resisted any belief in an ineffable march of "progress," knowing that Niebuhr had destroyed such foolhardy optimism in a society wracked by conflict. Still, he looked to the past to at least offer some concrete lessons.

The book earned Schlesinger an enviable reputation among historians, policy makers, and liberal activists, and opened up myriad opportunities for future endeavors. He first considered journalism and briefly wrote for *Fortune* magazine but found that he had to scramble to publish freelance articles to support his growing family. This led him to propose a story for *Life* magazine for a scathing attack on the U.S. Communist Party, which granted communism's achievements "against local injustice and exploitation," and tried to avoid the excesses of hysterical anticommunism, but complained that Marxism remained subservient to Soviet foreign policy.[19]

Despite his misgivings about the parochialism and complacency of academia, he took a position in the Harvard history department, where he would remain for the next fifteen years. Harvard and the city of Cambridge provided a valuable circle of like-minded liberals, most notably his soon-to-be lifelong friend and political ally, John Kenneth Galbraith, and Bernard DeVoto, a conservationist and civil libertarian whom Schlesinger had long admired.

Like Niebuhr, Schlesinger remained committed to putting liberalism on a more pragmatic footing for the postwar world. "Whether you invoke Augustine or Freud or Pareto," he wrote, "there are moody and destructive impulses in man of which official liberalism has taken no serious account."[20] As he would explain just a year after joining the Harvard faculty, "The first major job for liberals today is surely to establish their belief in a democratic society on a solider and profounder conception of man—on a conception which takes into account the actualities of human nature, whether as disclosed in the ancient insights of Christianity or in the modern discoveries of psychiatry."[21] "Nations, as individuals, who are completely innocent in their own esteem," Niebuhr had written, "are insufferable in their human contacts," to which Schlesinger added, "The self-righteous delusion of innocence [has] encouraged a kind of Manichaeism dividing the world between good (us) and evil (our critics)." It was his ambition, as well as that of his new mentor, to help guide the new superpower on its journey between the twin dangers of hubris and wounded pride.[22]

If Schlesinger and Niebuhr had been philosophical anti-Communists from the beginning of their careers—Niebuhr due to his socialism, Schlesinger due to his liberalism—the liberal journalist James "Jimmy" Wechsler came about his ideology through personal experience. He had joined the Communist Party as a young man during the Great Depression, a time when communism was perceived by many in intellectual circles as the only manly response to the ongoing crisis. The literary critic Alfred Kazin later explained his flirtation with campus Communists at Columbia University as driven by a desire for "action" over mere personal virtue. He defined the differences between liberal notions of social democracy and communism as those between "ethical general ideas that are essentially drawn from the tradition of nineteenth-century liberal humanitarianism" and an ideology that "deals with the particulars, with the living seething contemporaneity of contemporary capitalism, rather than a vague general reformism. . . . Communism thrives on the offensive."[23]

Following his graduation from Columbia, Wechsler joined the American Student Union, a precursor to the Communist National Student League, writing and editing a great deal of its propaganda and in the process impressing even Schlesinger, a dedicated opponent. When asked to write something that supported Stalin's notorious purge trials, however, Wechsler's faith began to waiver, and when he asked too many questions, he was taken off the project.

On a trip to Moscow he listened to a drunken literature professor mock the party line on literature to Wechsler, raising further doubts in the previously loyal party member. He soon found himself falling asleep at Communist Party meetings[24] and noted that the circles in which he traveled felt increasingly claustrophobic. In 1937 he quit the party in search of a more pragmatic road to social justice.

Initially Wechsler joined the staff of *The Nation* but found there a similar insularity. "I was troubled," he later explained, "by that ancient disease of liberal journalism—the feeling that we were talking to ourselves, and to those who agreed with us, rather than to the great multitudes who daily received their guidance from Hearst, McCormick, and the other conservative press lords."[25] He then joined the leftist New York City daily newspaper *PM*, a bold but ultimately unsuccessful experiment in news unsupported by advertising. Though the newspaper didn't succeed financially, it offered Wechsler a glimpse of his future, in which he would write strongly opinionated liberal journalism for the city's working class.[26]

Following a short stint in the Army, he joined *The New York Post*, where he would remain for most of the rest of his life, moving from reporter to leading editor, columnist, and close adviser to its owner, Dorothy "Dolly" Schiff. The *Post* excelled in typical tabloid fare, especially sports, entertainment, and show business gossip, but once Wechsler arrived, it grew as interested, as one reader observed, in "racial integration" as in "Hollywood bust measurements."[27] Wechsler was hungry for something he saw evidenced abroad but not in America: "In Europe, there was a growing 'Third Force,'" he wrote, but in America "there was a rising Republican reaction, a pro-Communist left and nothing in between except the still inept, bumbling presidency of a man who wished he wasn't there."[28]

Liberal leaders were not much interested in attempting to create a mass movement in support of their program during the postwar years. This was an age of distrust in "the masses," which were now associated with both Stalinism and fascism among both intellectuals and much of the general population. Still, liberals needed to find a way to push Democrats—including Harry Truman—to turn their ideas into policy. The one institution capable of doing this at the time was organized labor. Unions had been the linchpin of New Deal activism, and FDR had helped galvanize the movement through his creation of the National Recovery Administration (NRA) and then his successful push to pass the Wagner Act in 1935. But the issue was complicated by the large-scale Communist infiltration of some of America's most influential unions, including the United Electrical Workers, the International Longshoremen's Association, the National Maritime Union, and the International Union of Mine, Mill and Smelter Workers.

The liberals turned to their favorite among the nascent national labor leaders, the firebrand Walter Reuther of the United Auto Workers (UAW).[29] As a young socialist, Reuther had begun organizing in Detroit during the Depression. He had had a brief moment of hope in Soviet Russia as a model for the future and his trip there did nothing to disabuse him.

Although his original support within the UAW began with a tenuous alliance of socialists, Communists, and other militants, Reuther turned on the Communists when they adopted a noninterventionist policy toward Hitler following the German-Soviet Nonagression Pact. He began his battle to transform the union in August 1940 at a UAW convention in St. Louis and continued it through his run for the top job in the union. Following a narrow victory for the UAW presidency in 1946, Reuther consolidated his power by purging more than a hundred Communist staffers from every level of the organization. "The Communists are to be pitied more than despised, because they are not free men," he continued. "Their very souls do not belong to them."[30] This was, in many respects, a turning point for the American labor movement. As the historian Steven Gillon points out, of the three largest CIO unions, only the 650,000-member United Electrical Workers maintained close ties with Communists; they were significantly outnumbered by the anti-Communist UAW and the United Steelworkers (USW), each one boasting more than one million members.[31]

Reuther was more than ready to seek out more civilized ways to do business with business, hoping that union-company relations might eventually mature. Unlike some more militant labor leaders—or Republican-friendly ones, especially the United Mine Workers' John L. Lewis—he was also eager to cooperate with the government during the war. He insisted that Ford and other automakers could retool and produce planes and the like and still treat their workers with fairness, dignity, and respect. He also supported, albeit quite reluctantly, the no-strike pledge demanded by the government. "The smart, dancing-eyed Reuther," explained a *Harper's* editorial during the war, "is something special among labor leaders, a person who moves in a world of ideas that includes a concept of the general welfare as distinct from short-term labor welfare."[32]

Following the war, Reuther felt he needed to switch gears and adopt a militant position for his workers. The UAW launched a strike against General Motors that demanded not only a 30 percent wage increase but also insisted that the company absorb the costs in the form of reduced profits rather than pass them along to consumers in the form of higher prices, as was customary. In doing so, Reuther sought to break the famous wage-price spiral that connected pay increases to inflation in the public mind. Even more significant, however, he was making an implicit argument about capitalism, one that drew upon the battles for the OPA and the Full Employment Bill and that would underlie the liberal vision of the economy for much of the postwar era. "The war," he said in a speech, "has proven that production is not our problem; our problem is consumption." In Reuther's view—resting, naturally, on that of John Maynard Keynes—everyone would enjoy greater prosperity from a demand-driven full-employment economy. Corporate profits would be ensured by high-volume production, which would enable prices to remain low and the fruits of capitalism to spread outward in a virtuous circle of increased distribution, technological innovation, and greater leisure time for all. Growth would float almost all boats, and the welfare state and the Social Security net could assist those in danger of sinking without them.

"We are not going to operate," Reuther explained, "as a narrow economic pressure group which says 'we are going to get ours and the public be damned' or 'the consumer be damned.'. . . We want to make progress with the community and not at the expense of the community." *The Nation* praised Reuther for "fighting the government's battle and the consumer's battle," while *The New Republic* saw the "most advanced unions" following Reuther's lead, acting "not only in the interest of their members but in the interest of sound national policy as well."[33]

Reuther demanded that the company open its books so he could demonstrate to all concerned that there would be plenty of profit to pass along to shareholders even after granting the UAW's proposed wage increase. The company responded with a condemnation of the union's demands as an attack on the fundamentals of free enterprise. As one GM official helpfully explained, "We don't even open our books to our stockholders."[34]

Truman responded to the UAW's demands by creating a fact-finding panel to explore the situation in Detroit, which found for Reuther and the UAW and also demanded that GM open its books. The board proposed a lower pay increase below what the union had demanded, but one that could be carried out easily without raising prices of cars. GM refused, alas, and the strike continued, further aggravating Truman. With the strike fund exhausted, the union finally settled for a far smaller raise than the administration recommended, much less what it had initially demanded.

Two years later, in 1948—and following a failed assassination attempt—Reuther did win his workers a major victory: a cost-of-living adjustment that tied pay to prices and overtime and produced almost all of the autoworkers' wage increases for a generation.[35] The agreement also included more generous pensions and benefits and obviated the need for future strikes. While Reuther praised the agreement from his bed, where he was recovering from his near-fatal wounds, it effectively cemented the company's ideological victory over the labor movement, and with it, postwar liberalism.[36] Rather than the UAW, it would be General Motors—the company that refused to share power or responsibility with its workers or take responsibility for its community beyond its shareholders—whose identity became inseparable in the public mind with the overall health and wealth of the nation itself.

What made Reuther unique was that he cared about more than just his own rank and file. In a time when so many labor leaders appeared to the public as fat-cat bureaucrats Reuther projected a different image entirely.[37] His own brand of democratic socialism, much like Niebuhr's, was converted to liberal anticommunism, but he never gave up on his belief that a labor movement ought to fight for more than just its members' material interests.

Walter Reuther, James Wechsler, Arthur Schlesinger, and Reinhold Niebuhr could all agree on one point: the need for an anti-Communist liberal organization that could press the Democratic Party to take liberal ideas seriously as policy prescriptions and political platforms. They found a friend in Eleanor Roosevelt. On January 4, 1947, Americans for Democratic Action (ADA) announced itself to the world at a conference presided over by Niebuhr.[38] Eleanor Roosevelt gave the keynote address, and Wechsler wrote the organization's opening statement:

> Liberalism is a demanding faith. It rests neither on a set of dogmas nor on a blueprint, but is rather a spirit which each generation of liberals must learn to apply to the needs of its own time. The spirit itself is unchanging—a deep belief in the dignity of man and an awareness of human frailty, a faith in human reason and the power of free inquiry, a high sense of individual responsibility for oneself and one's neighbor, a conviction that the best society is a brotherhood that enables the great numbers of its members to develop their potentialities to the utmost.[39]

While its founders promised to fight "to insure decent levels of health, nutrition, shelter and education," as well as protection of civil liberties from the power of concentrated wealth, they were clearly focused on their fundamental differences with Popular Front liberals in the PCA and elsewhere: "We reject any association with Communism or sympathizers with Communism in the United States as completely as we reject any association with Fascists or their sympathizers."[40]

ADA liberals tried to attract those whose hearts drifted toward Popular Front propaganda about "peace" and "progress" with rational arguments about how their hearts should not lead them to split progressive forces or ally with authoritarian leftists. They criticized Wallace supporters not merely for their errant views on the Soviets, but also for their soft-headed sentimentality when it came to American politics. The Wallaceites underestimated, as Niebuhr wrote Wechsler, the "continuing threat of reaction"; that is, the reality of an American right that was active and ready to leap into the opportunities offered by a divided left.[41]

Schlesinger and Niebuhr also attempted to map out the rudimentary principles of a liberal postwar foreign policy: "We must purposefully use our strength and prosperity to restore social and economic health to a broken world; and we must recognize that our power must be used wisely and discreetly, else we activate profound misgivings about American imperialism. And we must fully realize that this is not a great-hearted favor to the world, like tossing a quarter to a cripple selling shoe-laces; it is an absolute necessity from the viewpoint of the peace and prosperity of America as well as the world."[42] They cautioned against military excess in American foreign policy and sought to chart a middle ground between extremes posed by the "roll-back" ideas of James Burnham, then a rabid Communist turned anti-Communist conservative, and the appeasement and pacifist policies offered by Popular Front sympathizers and Communist Party fellow travelers.[43] "The realm of international politics is particularly filled with complexities which do not yield to the approach of a too simple idealism," Niebuhr had written during the war. "On the other hand the moral cynicism and defeatism which easily results from a clear-eyed view of the realities of international politics is even more harmful."[44]

The most vexing problems facing these liberals in this period were those raised by Truman's loyalty program. Schlesinger worried, as had Eleanor Roosevelt, that the government would embark on a policy of conformity, not just loyalty.[45] The key distinction to be drawn was that between ideas and actions: the former posed no danger and could be countered via argument; the latter could bleed into subversion and espionage, and must be crushed.

The liberal project now was to work within the system: to state one's principles clearly and declaratively and then ally with the Democratic Party and accept losses when they came. Liberalism was not, after all, a protest movement. It embraced dissent, but never disengagement, much less more radical forms of disagreement.

The most promising and ultimately influential politician to throw in with ADA in its infancy was undoubtedly Hubert Horatio Humphrey. Schlesinger described him as "a cocky, brass-lunged young man of courage, indefatigable energy, and inexhaustible political sex appeal."[46] Ironically, Humphrey never felt comfortable with eastern intellectuals like Schlesinger.[47] He had grown up on the plains of South Dakota, his father a supporter of William Jennings Bryan and a fervent believer in social justice. He attended the University of Minnesota, working at a drugstore to sustain himself and eating food scrounged from behind the lunch counter. His graduation was delayed by his need to return home to mind the family drugstore while his father pursued an unsuccessful political career. Before doing so, however, he attended pharmacy school in Denver and completed the two-year course in just six months.[48]

It was not until he finally landed in graduate school during the 1930s, attending Louisiana State University, that Humphrey discovered the political ideas that would guide him through his life. Unlike other student leftists during the time, Humphrey never drifted toward radicalism but embraced the New Deal faith that "government should do for the individual what he could not do for himself," that political experimentation and pragmatism were better than ideological starting points, and that communitarian values should trump "pecuniary" ones.[49] Humphrey also learned firsthand about the human cost of the South's apartheid culture. "The shock and outrage at what I saw there gave flesh and blood to my abstract commitment to civil rights," he later explained.[50]

Following his first failed run for mayor of Minneapolis, he won the office in 1945 as a progressive Democrat in the mold of Henry Wallace. As mayor he proved strongly prolabor, refusing requests from local industry to deploy the local police as strikebreakers and fighting racial discrimination in the workplace. Humphrey brought a fair employment practices ordinance and human rights commission to Minneapolis, and committed himself to erasing the city's earlier reputation as what Robert Caro called "the anti-Semitism capital of America."[51] Despite these then-controversial stances, he proved extraordinarily popular, both personally and politically, and easily won reelection.

Nineteen forty-eight turned out to be a wild political year for Democrats, and nothing demonstrated its raucousness so much as that year's convention. For liberals this was a genuine opportunity to both define their postwar principles and do so in a fashion that might define the Democratic Party for the coming generation.

Most delegates believed that Truman would be nominated, but there was still a scurrying of discussion about other possibilities. Many liberals, including some in ADA, had actually set their sights on General Dwight Eisenhower before learning that not only was he not a liberal, but not even a Democrat. The cabal of seventy-five or eighty ADA members gathered in a rented fraternity house on the University of Pennsylvania campus and argued among themselves over how to proceed. Still disgusted with Truman, but even more disillusioned with Wallace, they reluctantly accepted Hubert Humphrey's argument that it was "ridiculous" for the organization "to delay making a commitment, that Truman was the incumbent President, and that no convention was going to reject him." At that point, reality set in, and, according to Humphrey, "the issue of the civil rights plank took over our thoughts."[52]

Initially the liberals mistakenly expected the president to join their crusade. Truman had spoken out before the NAACP, at the Lincoln Memorial with Eleanor Roosevelt, and his Civil Rights Commission had come out in favor of creating a new and powerful civil rights division within the Justice Department. It had also strongly supported new federal antilynching laws, an end to segregation in the armed forces, and the termination of all poll taxes that prevented blacks from voting in the South. Clark Clifford viewed these changes in the party's traditional noninterference position vis-à-vis southern apartheid as crucial to winning the urban support necessary to keep the most populous states in the Democratic column, particularly because they were running against the popular governor of New York, Thomas Dewey.

But Truman was not on board at all. Under Clifford's tutelage he had rushed in a rather headstrong fashion into the winds of southern resistance, and soon found himself paying the very price that the prudent Roosevelt had always studiously avoided. As southerners threatened to bolt, Clifford told Truman to keep quiet about civil rights until after the election. Truman tried this approach, supporting a one-paragraph civil rights plank stating: "We favor legislation, recommended by President Truman, by which the Federal Government will exercise its full constitutional power to ensure that due process, the right to vote, the right to live and the right to work shall not turn on any consideration of race, religion, color or national origin."[53] But this ostensibly innocuous language satisfied neither side. The southerners demanded a pledge that the federal government would "not encroach upon the reserved powers of the states by the centralization of the government or otherwise." The liberals resubmitted their own proposal, and the result was a stalemate.

When the ADA delegation returned to its fraternity house to try to plan the next day's battle, Humphrey grew anxious. He was a candidate for the U.S. Senate in Minnesota that year and needed the support, both political and financial, of a party establishment whose ire he was about to earn. But the party was not the only source of Democratic money and support, and the liberals sought to stiffen Humphrey's backbone. At one point, Leon Henderson apparently warned him, "Hubert, I'll tell you this. If you don't speak for the minority plank, I promise you that you won't get a dime of Jew money out of New York."[54]

There was a furious fight on the convention floor the following day. A Trumanite complained, "You ADA bastards aren't going to tell us what to do,"[55] while Truman confided in his diary his fury upon hearing that these "crackpots" were going to cost him his presidency by forcing the South "to bolt."[56] David K. Niles, Truman's assistant for minority affairs, pulled aside Joe Rauh in a hotel hallway and explained furiously, "Joe, you won't get fifty votes here and Hubert will lose Minnesota, too."[57]

Humphrey stepped up to the precipice a nervous but confident young man. The journalist Irwin Ross—using Truman's own language—reported that "he was sacrificing a brilliant future for a crackpot crusade," and would "kill any chances we have of winning in November." Although the extremely ambitious thirty-seven-year-old knew that "the traditional thing to do was to make a gesture toward what was right . . . but not so tough a gesture that the South would leave the Democratic coalition," Humphrey decided to throw caution to the wind. "I'll do it," he told his friend Orville Freeman. "If there's one thing I believe in this crazy business it's civil rights."[58] Hubert Humphrey finally rose to the occasion as he did perhaps no other in his long and distinguished career, giving what many remember as the finest speech of his life: "To those who say that we are rushing this issue of civil rights," he cried, his voice pitched, his fist raised, "I say to them, we are 172 years too late. To those who say that this civil rights program is an infringement of states' rights [deafening applause], the time has arrived in America for the Democratic party to get out of the shadow of states' rights and walk forthrightly into the sunshine of human rights."[59]

He was a rhetorical equivalent of his old hero Henry Wallace but working *inside* the system, or at least inside the convention gathering. Though no Democrat had ever been popularly elected to the Senate from Minnesota, Humphrey became an overnight hero to his constituents and was literally carried through the streets of Minneapolis when he arrived home.[60] Barely six months later he appeared on the cover of *Time*, where he was described as "the No. 1 prospect for liberalism in this country."[61]

At barely more than eight minutes, it was among the shortest speeches of Humphrey's famously long-winded career—one that would eventually include twenty-six years in the Senate and four unsuccessful runs at the presidency—but it would transform the politics of civil rights in the Democratic Party forever. One would have to go as far back as William Jennings Bryan's famous 1896 "Cross of Gold" oration to find a single speech in the party's history that had galvanized so many people so powerfully on so central a political principle. And Humphrey's principle, unlike Bryan's, was a winner.

The plank passed by a thin 651½ to 582½ votes, and in later years Humphrey would credit the victory in part "to conscience" and in part "to political realities." The bosses of the large urban states of the Northeast needed to pick up the votes of liberals, blacks, and other minorities and labor. And the threat of Henry Wallace on the left made the traditional solution of ignoring the problem of civil rights out of deference to southern Democrats potentially far more costly than in the past. ADA had "licked the South" as Minnesota National Committeewoman Eugenie Anderson heard a reporter say. "Can you beat that?"[62]

All three southern resolutions were easily defeated. And when Truman rose to ascend to the podium a few hours later, he sounded like the liberal of the ADA's dreams. He attacked the reactionaries in Congress and promised to call it back into session on Missouri's Turnip Day, July 26, to enact his agenda. Jack Kroll, who headed up the left wing CIO-PAC, would report upon leaving that he witnessed "great enthusiasm over Truman's acceptance speech and great enthusiasm among liberals over the Convention proceedings as a whole."[63]

The victory was obviously not without costs. The South did bolt the convention with Thurmond, and most southerners would eventually leave the party entirely. But as Niebuhr argued, "Every advance that we make in better racial relations (and we have made some genuine advances) represents not only an intrinsic gain for the moral quality of our own civilization but an extrinsic gain for our relations to the world."[64]

In the meantime, ADA did not feel its work was done. While it had succeeded in moving the Democratic Party leftward, it also had to destroy its competition on the same field: namely, Henry Wallace. It circulated a thirty-four-page pamphlet, largely authored by Niebuhr, filled with innuendo and decontextualized quotations and Red Scare–style guilt by association designed to discredit Wallace as "inept, indecisive, and insincere."[65] But such tactics probably did not make any significant difference in the election, as Wallace had all but ended his own chances—first, by refusing to support Truman during the Berlin crisis and, second, by comparing Communists to Christian martyrs.[66]

Though the internecine warfare would continue on the left, ADA had clearly won the battle for relevance to and influence over actual existing American politics. After all, Truman went on to win the election and soon thereafter enunciated his Fair Deal. ADA had not only made a virtue of compromise but had even upheld compromise as a more astute strategy than Wallace's purist calls for a third party.

Nineteen forty-eight also marked the beginning of the end of the dominance of Democrats in the South. The "Solid South" had always been an anachronism, a vestige of the Civil War, rather than a reflection of present-day reality. The liberals and labor leaders who directed the national party were about as welcome in the South as weevils on a cotton crop. And whenever the hegemony of the local ruling elite—almost feudal in its attachment to tradition—was challenged, it tended to send back home the upstart in question who had thought to stir up trouble. A prime example of this can be found in what is perhaps the last attempt by the labor movement to plant its flag south of the Mason-Dixon. "Operation Dixie" was the CIO's attempt to complete the organization of the American mass-production industry that it had begun in the 1930s.[67] But the CIO's organizing model, which had been so successful in northern factories during the Great Depression, proved disastrously misapplied to the South, where industry was spread across many smaller towns and cities and where the largest enterprises often controlled their hometown or even owned it outright. And the threat of the mixing of the races almost always trumped the hope of working-class solidarity as the companies' "divide and rule" tactics proved effective in quashing organizers' hopes time and again.[68]

Outside the forbidden zone of the apartheid-ridden American South, however, the postwar years were also abundant with intellectual energy, infused in part by the diaspora of European intellectuals escaping Nazism and its aftermath. *Partisan Review*, a "little magazine" with an outsized influence, would publish letters from thinkers such as George Orwell, Ignazio Silone, and Arthur Koestler challenging America to rise to the moment and rejuvenate liberalism's challenge to totalitarianism, now spreading westward from Stalin's Soviet Union. Dwight Macdonald's *Politics*, published from 1944 to 1948, also served as a forum for writers to ponder the new world of dehumanization symbolized by the concentration camp and atomic war. Jean-Paul Sartre and his longtime comrade Simone de Beauvoir would visit the United States during this time, hosted by the Cultural Relations Section of the French Ministry of Foreign Affairs. They introduced readers to a philosophy of gloom, absurdity, and despair that focused on the tragic nature of making freewill choices in a time when there was so much "blasting of plans and the meaningless of effort" around people.[69] Those who fought in the French resistance, including particularly Camus, struck the proper chord for a world still reeling from the shock of discovering the horrific human consequences of both Nazi and Soviet mass murder.[70]

Following the bruising but exhilarating election of 1948, Arthur Schlesinger sat down to try to define what he, Niebuhr, and their fellow liberal anti-Communists believed in a positive rather than a merely negative sense. The result was *The Vital Center* (1949), a book Schlesinger hoped would reach a "new and distinct political generation" unscarred by the ideological bloodletting of the 1930s.[71] *The Vital Center* drew upon many of the intellectual trends of the moment. "Western man in the middle of the twentieth century is tense, uncertain, adrift. We look upon our epoch as a time of troubles, an age of anxiety," Schlesinger explained. As Western life grew increasingly impersonal and bureaucratic, its institutions growing larger and larger, it lost sight of any sense of personal responsibility. Dwight Macdonald had done a great deal to elucidate these themes in various essays he published in *Politics*, and he had explored any number of philosophies of abnegation and secession from capitalism and consumerism that would eventually have an impact on numerous New Left thinkers of the 1960s. But Schlesinger saw such intellectual tendencies as spinning a "quietist dreamworld." He was especially hostile to those "intellectual escapists" who upheld "conscientious objection" during World War II, which a surprising number of *Partisan Review* contributors had done. (It was surprising because so many were Jewish, though Macdonald was not.) It was precisely in the act of political engagement in a world of "imperfect alternatives" that Americans could appreciate the nature and scope of their responsibilities in the postwar world.[72]

Historically, liberalism had always been divided between two different intellectual tendencies: the pessimism evidenced in the Federalist Papers (where Madison noted that "if men were angels," government would not be necessary), and the optimism of Thomas Jefferson, who believed in democracy virtually without limits. Schlesinger, drawing heavily on Niebuhr, clearly sided with Madison, and he sought to bury definitively the likes of Henry Wallace, who drew heavily on the more hopeful John Dewey and his supporters. Progressives, Schlesinger argued, had allowed themselves to be corrupted by a "sentimental belief in progress" and naïveté, that is, they went along believing that things would improve for the better even while allying with forces that were corrupt. They abdicated the responsibility of making choices in life. The dough-faced progressive "never dreams of facing a question in terms of responsibility for the decision." Just as dough-faced politicians of yore had believed that slavery would disappear without a struggle, now Progressives imagined Soviet communism could evolve into an improved version of American liberalism, with greater emphasis on equity and fairness for the downtrodden.[73]

Progressives, like both Communists and Facists, had placed their faith in utopian politics that held out the hope of a world somehow freed of all human contradictions and conflict. For Schlesinger, reasserting classic liberal ideals, the challenge was to find a way to balance "individual liberties" against the "democratic control of economic life." Pessimism needed to guide political action in order to check liberal hubris. "It is a moderate pessimism about man which fortifies society against authoritarianism," which Schlesinger believed sprang from those who believed themselves to be pure at heart and incorruptible once in power. Schlesinger thus offered not only a pragmatic argument for tempered reform, such as Keynesianism and a mix of markets and government regulation, but also a philosophical one as well.[74]

The reform democratic tradition in the American past—one that Schlesinger believed extended from Andrew Jackson to Harry Truman—was the tradition that accepted "responsibility" and "choice." It was the only political approach that allowed for the imperfect nature of man. "A liberalism which purports to shape a real world must first accept the limitations and possibilities of that world," Schlesinger wrote. To be honest as well as politically successful required a "searching doubt about human perfectibility" of its proponents, an argument, Schlesinger believed, that could be located throughout the pessimistic philosophies of America's greatest political thinkers, from Madison to Niebuhr.[75]

But together with almost all critics of liberalism throughout the centuries, Schlesinger recognized that a philosophy based so heavily on process lacked the ability to inspire, to stand up for itself. "Why does not democracy believe in itself with passion?" he asked, a question he really directed toward liberalism. "In part because democracy, by its nature, dissipates rather than concentrates its internal moral force. The thrust of the democratic faith is away from fanaticism; it is toward compromise, persuasion, and consent in politics, toward tolerance and diversity. . . ." And yet, Schlesinger pointed out, America was a country that fell victim to frequent patterns of "hysteria" in its national life—and, indeed, was preparing to embark on yet another one, perhaps its most destructive. How to inspire passion for a philosophy that itself distrusted passion? With that question Schlesinger identified the challenge with which liberals would forever struggle without ever really finding a satisfactory solution.[76]

The significance of *The Vital Center* in its time and place can hardly be overstated. Schlesinger published it at a moment when most Western intellectuals had lost faith in Marxism and other totalizing ideologies.[77] Schlesinger offered up a liberalism without intellectual apology, one that could hold its own with what had been considered more ambitious—and indeed, exciting—European-style ideological systems. And while they might lack inspiration for passionate engagement, the arguments of democratic liberalism were tried and true, and worthy of respect and devotion by men and women of good faith and political commitment. They provided the backbone of liberalism and with a little luck, would serve as the foundation for the *vital center* of American politics.

4

Patient, Firm, and Vigilant

Great as it is, American power is limited. Within its limits, it will be greater or less depending on the ends for which it is used.
—Walter Lippmann, 1945[1]

Harry Truman said nothing particularly controversial, or even unusual, when, during the election campaign of 1948, he proclaimed the United States of America to be "the greatest [country] in history, the greatest that the sun has ever shone upon."[2] Philip Roth's fictional alter ego, Nathan Zuckerman, described the period as "the greatest moment of collective inebriation in American history."[3] Even the unrepentant British Communist historian Eric Hobsbawm could not help but admit in his 2002 memoir that the United States was "by any standards the success story among twentieth-century states. Its economy became the world's largest, both pace- and pattern-setting; its capacity for technological achievement was unique; its research in both natural and social sciences, even its philosophers, became increasingly dominant; and its hegemony in global consumer civilization seemed beyond challenge."[4]

These sentiments certainly held sway among liberals, who believed their ideals to be at the foundation of America's great good fortune. And yet the moment was also one fraught with great peril. The threat of the destructive power of the atom—knowledge that could never be unlearned and hence never fully controlled—left humankind dependent on the wisdom and prudence of its leadership to a degree that many people, understandably, found frightening, particularly now that the decidedly human Truman had replaced the sainted Roosevelt. "History," wrote the economist Lewis Corey at the time "is at another great divide in an age that may move toward unlimited good or unlimited evil."[5]

Liberal intellectuals understood the challenges America faced in shaping the new world, but they could not and did not allow themselves to be paralyzed by the enormity of the task. They sought to embrace both realism and idealism in their quest to increase the degree of freedom and security enjoyed by the populations of all nations, including especially those whom they had recently defeated in war, as they believed lack of freedom and a resulting insecurity to be at the root of the aggressive behavior that had resulted in such unprecedented death and destruction.

Liberals believed in the power of exporting American ideals abroad, particularly with regard to authoritarian governments. But they also knew the world was not theirs to mold, that different nations enjoyed unique traditions and histories and were not eager to trade their own for those of an alien culture, however touched by God it might be. They also understood that Americans had historically proved themselves to be deeply averse to what George Washington had so memorably termed "foreign entanglements," especially very expensive and time-consuming ones. Liberals understood the necessity of establishing multilateral institutions, but given Woodrow Wilson's failure to persuade his countrymen to embrace the League of Nations at the end of the previous world war, they had to tread extremely carefully. The problem of U.S.-Soviet relations, moreover, if mishandled, could frustrate hopes not only for the creation of functional, cooperative bodies to secure the peace and rebuild Europe and Asia, but also for the realization of any of the larger goals liberals might have for the creation of a more peaceful and prosperous world.

At the end of the war liberals turned quite naturally to Roosevelt's most important institutional innovation, the United Nations, as their first stop on the road to what they hoped would be a lasting peace. At the moment of its founding in San Francisco, in June of 1945, President Truman called on his fellow world leaders to consider the consequences of the League of Nations' failure, arguing that "experience has shown how deeply the seeds of war are planted by economic rivalry and by social injustice."[6] Perhaps most remarkable of all, given Americans' historic penchant for unilateralism in the conduct of world affairs, the UN had broad support domestically as well. Following the Yalta conference, American popular support for the UN rose from 60 to 80 percent.[7] The Senate approved its charter by a vote of 89–2.

Truman quickly appointed Eleanor Roosevelt as a delegate to the General

Assembly of the new organization, at least partially as a means of keeping her as far away as possible while at the same time retaining her loyalty for his team. He knew that the appointment might improve his shaky relationship with Eleanor, but he also had to be aware of her deep yearnings for the UN to become a beacon of liberal internationalism.

The collective shock and horror that accompanied the discovery of the Nazi death camps, together with the destruction wrought not only by atomic bombs but also by the Allied firebombing of Dresden and Tokyo, charged the talks in San Francisco with significant moral and political urgency. How the world might avoid such catastrophes in the future through enforced international rules of governance was a task that naturally inspired people of all political beliefs. Given the fact that whatever arrangements would likely emerge, it would be up to the United States of America to ensure their adoption and enforcement, so Eleanor's views assumed critical importance.

Inside the UN, Eleanor focused first on the postwar repatriation and refugee crisis, as approximately thirty million people had been uprooted by the conflict.[8] She then moved immediately to the UN's Commission on Human Rights, whose preliminary work began in early 1947. She appreciated the scope of the challenge ahead and worked hard, pushing her delegates "like a slave driver," in the estimation of one of her biographers, Lois Scharf.[9] She took advantage of the popularity of the UN to bring focus to the body's attention to civil rights, and liberties came to full fruition.

It was surprisingly philosophical work, and Eleanor quickly found herself in the thicket of debates about the nature of liberalism, individualism, and the foundational basis of human rights. The basic principles of modern liberalism, which were difficult to define under the best of circumstances, could not easily be translated into universal terms; they were not even "universally" accepted at home. Charles Malik, a world-renowned philosopher with day jobs as Lebanon's ambassador to the United States and president of the UN Economic and Social Council (and who would succeed Eleanor as the Human Rights Commission's chairman), served as the commission's rapporteur. He posed a series of questions to Eleanor and the rest of the representatives to provide a starting point for a discussion of the relationship between individualism and the conception of universal rights: "Is man merely a social being? Is he merely an animal? Is he merely an economic being?" A Soviet representative responded: "The psychology of individualism has been used by the ruling class in lost countries to preserve its own privileges."[10]

In the end, the Soviet Union, together with its quislings, withdrew from the process entirely, and thereby enabled those who remained to reach a consensus.

On December 10, 1948, after much haggling, the General Assembly voted unanimously to adopt what has become known as the Universal Declaration of Human Rights. It declared: "All men are born free and equal in dignity and rights. They are endowed by nature with reason and conscience, and should act towards one another like brothers." This was the language of liberalism at its most far-reaching. Embodying, simultaneously, the respective discourses of civil rights, protofeminism, and the New Deal, it continued, "Everyone is entitled to all rights and freedoms set forth in this Declaration, without distinction of any kind, such as colour, sex, language, religion, political or other opinion, property status, or national or social origin." "Everyone has the right to rest and leisure" as well as protection from "unemployment, sickness, disability, old age or all other lack of livelihood for reasons beyond [a person's] control."

However inspiring the declaration may have been to liberals, its utility was strictly rhetorical, as it lacked any enforcement provisions. As Eleanor put it, the Declaration was something "to which all men may aspire & which we should try to achieve. It has no legal value but should carry moral weight."[11] Eleanor was convinced that people could now employ its rhetorical power and international prestige to acquire rights in their own countries. But she was also a realist on such matters, and understood that this would not happen by itself. She also had to deal with the complication—no doubt an extremely painful one—of the challenge to the Declaration from her sometime ally, W.E.B. Du Bois, who had grown increasingly more radical over the years, and who served as an associate consultant to the American delegation. Du Bois had been lobbying her to bring the case for equal rights for African Americans directly to the United Nations. Forced to put pragmatism ahead of principle, Roosevelt not only silenced Du Bois's voice within the delegation but also successfully pressured the NAACP to marginalize him. Though she was personally deeply committed to the cause, she knew that it would destroy the support she was building for the UN at home—and not only among southerners and conservatives.

Truman, meanwhile, was having trouble making up his mind whether to cast his lot with those who advised him to seek some sort of modus vivendi with Stalin and the Soviets or with those who had already decided that a break was unavoidable and therefore might as well come sooner rather than later. W. Averell Harriman, ambassador to the USSR, was clearly in the latter category. After flying home immediately after Roosevelt's death to try to talk Truman into a more confrontational stance vis-à-vis the Russians, he continued to San Francisco. There he informed the U.S. UN delegation that the Russians were working by "chisel, by bluff, pressure and other unscrupulous methods" to subvert the Yalta accords, and pronounced the two sides' differences as irreconcilable.[12] I. F. Stone, writing in *The Nation,* wondered "if the main business of the United Nations conference on International Organization is not to condition the American people psychologically for war with the Soviet Union."[13]

While a variety of figures filled roles as advisers to the president, the person who emerged as undoubtedly the most influential figure over the formulation of U.S. foreign policy under Truman was Dean Gooderham Acheson, who served in a variety of high-level State Department posts before assuming the top job upon the retirement of General Marshall. Though reviled by conservatives, Acheson was hardly a typical liberal in the sense embodied by, say, Mrs. Roosevelt. He had no sympathy for the poor or dispossessed in Third World nations and he lost not a moment's sleep over racial discrimination, whether at home or abroad. Believing in "liberty everywhere," said Acheson, bespoke "a very emotional and shallow" view of how the world worked, and he wanted no part of it.[14] However, the system of international institutions he helped to create and support, and strengthen, served as the foundation of liberal internationalism in the postwar world, protected and supported by American hegemony. As G. John Ikenberry rightly notes, "Between 1944 and 1951, American leaders engaged in the most intensive institution-building the world had ever seen. They helped launch the United Nations, Bretton Woods, GATT, NATO and the US-Japanese alliance. They assumed costly obligations to aid Greece and Turkey and reconstruct Western Europe. They helped rebuild the economies of Germany and Japan and integrate them into the emerging Western system. And with the Atlantic Charter, the U.N. charter and the Universal Declaration of Human Rights, they articulated a new vision of progressive international community."[15] This commitment to Cold War internationalist institutions had a domestic corollary that included not only new regulations impinging on free speech and freedom of information but also vast spending increases in education, transportation and scientific research, all justified in the name of "national security."[16] Racial progress at home was also, on occasion, the beneficiary of Cold War thinking. As the fair employment advocate John A. Davis argued to American businessmen in *Fortune* in 1952, "In a world that is about 65 percent nonwhite the Communist charge of racial exploitation in America reverberates with a crashing emphasis."[17]

Born the son of the Episcopal bishop of Connecticut—the unofficial faith of the American establishment—Acheson attended the Groton School, Yale University, and Harvard Law School before earning a clerkship with legendary liberal Supreme Court Associate Justice Louis Brandeis. Stoical in persona while dapper in dress, he boasted a famously severe guardsman's mustache that conveyed gravitas with nearly comic pomposity. Possessed of a rapier wit and unabashed Anglophile sympathies, Acheson viewed life as "a pilgrimage from birth to death through a battleground between good and evil." His impressive self-regard is evidenced by his decision to title his memoir *Present at the Creation*, with no irony intended. Its introduction described the Truman administration's postwar task to be "just a bit less formidable than that described in the first chapter of Genesis."[18]

Many observers thought the plainspoken "no airs" Harry Truman would be oddly matched with the patrician Acheson, yet Acheson displayed a profound loyalty to the president over the years, and remained deferential to his boss, at least in public. ("Truman is like a boy you tell not to stick peanuts up his nose," he told one friend. "The minute you turn around, there he is sticking peanuts up his nose."[19]) Truman, for his part, stuck by Acheson during the frequent conservative attacks he endured even when the political costs made this loyalty difficult to justify.

For all of his personal flaws, Acheson was undoubtedly one of the most able American public servants of the twentieth century, and certainly one of the few who thought like a traditional European diplomatic statesman in the mode of a Talleyrand or a Metternich. Unimpressed with ideals of any kind when it came to politics between nations, he thought in purely power-political terms, with particular emphasis on the importance of alliances, both formal and informal. His efforts did not involve "a lot of abstract notions," such as those that had occupied Wilson, but "what you do—the business transactions, credit through central banks, food," and the like. When it came to foreign policy, Acheson believed, "there are moral problems and real problems."[20]

To a considerable extent, Acheson's outlook on the Soviet Union mirrored both that of the nascent American establishment and much of public opinion. As undersecretary of state (1945–47), he thought the two remaining great powers could work out some mutual understanding based on each other's vital interests, their opposing ideologies notwithstanding. "As late as spring 1946," John Lewis Gaddis writes, Acheson "still favored negotiations with the Soviet Union, so much so that J. Edgar Hoover thought him a security risk."[21] This was, in fact, the final window of opportunity for more cordial relations with the USSR, and Acheson saw a chance to settle perhaps the most daunting question facing the Truman administration: how to deal with the bomb.

Colonel Henry L. Stimson was a conservative Republican Wall Street attorney who had served as secretary of war under both presidents William Howard Taft and Franklin Roosevelt, as well as secretary of state under President Herbert Hoover and governor-general of the Philippines under President Calvin Coolidge. He also headed the Manhattan Project, with final authority over its director of operations, General Leslie Groves. It was Stimson's recommendation that the bomb be used on the cities of Hiroshima and Nagasaki, but that the cultural treasures of Kyoto be spared, and it probably guided Truman's decision to follow that path. It was unlikely that the president respected or admired anyone among Roosevelt's top advisers more than "the Colonel," an esteem that was all but universally held at the highest reaches of the government. Stimson is often referred to by historians as the first, and perhaps, wisest of the "the wise men."[22]

Stimson believed it folly for the United States to retain the atomic bomb for military advantage and strongly advised Truman to try to find a means to turn it over to international control. He felt certain that its use—and the apparent threat (though it was a bluff) that many more might be used—had succeeded in persuading the Japanese to surrender. But he couldn't imagine a situation in the future where it would serve any valuable military purpose. He believed that the bomb unleashed "forces of nature too revolutionary and dangerous to fit into the old concepts."[23] He also felt strongly that relations between the United States and the USSR need not fall into a pattern of ceaseless hostility, and he worried that the political fallout from America's sole possession of the bomb might drive them in that direction. Stimson called on Truman to try to create a sense of trust with the Soviet Union by sharing the "basic scientific data" of the bomb with them, confident that it would serve both "commercial and humanitarian purposes."[24] Truman, who understood that the bomb was, from a practical standpoint, useless, could not help but take Stimson's advice seriously, however counterintuitive.[25] Naturally, Eleanor Roosevelt was arguing for much the same thing and was never shy about making her feelings known to her husband's successor.[26]

Dean Acheson, then the assistant secretary to Byrnes, was charged with convening a State Department task force to examine the question of turning the bomb over to international control. Still in his friendly-to-Russia phase, Acheson had decided that "what we know about the bomb is not a secret which we can keep to ourselves." With considerable foresight, moreover, he considered international governance of atomic weapons to be the world's best hope for preventing a dangerous and expensive atomic arms race. "The advantage of being ahead in such a race is nothing compared with not having the race," he explained.[27] He sent a strongly worded memo to the president supporting Stimson's arguments, calling continued secrecy "futile and dangerous."[28]

Acheson invited FDR's hard-charging Tennessee Valley Authority chairman, David Lilienthal, to develop the plan that Stimson had imagined. They were both convinced that the bomb had unleashed such a terrible force that it had to be brought under rational control—a significant and necessary challenge for liberal principles to find expression in the new realities of the postwar world. Many writers and thinkers envisioned an imminent man-made apocalypse because humankind's technological know-how had outpaced its wisdom about how to live on a deeply but unevenly divided planet. Physicist J. Robert Oppenheimer, the scientific director who oversaw the Manhattan Project at Los Alamos, New Mexico, where the bomb had been built, would later say that he and his fellow scientists had been compelled by their work to "have known sin."[29]

To Dwight Macdonald, the dropping of the bomb signaled a fundamental moral cleavage in world history in which science shifted from being a boon to humankind to a curse on it. The atomic bomb signified to Macdonald the creation of a new society of remote technological and governmental processes far removed from the control, or even understanding, of its citizens, a society where "things happen *to* people."[30] The "white coat of the scientist" had turned "blood-chilling as Dracula's black cape." The bomb was a warning, therefore, to reject "traditional liberal" ideas, which were "scientific, materialist" and based upon ideas of progress.[31]

Considerably more liberal, idealistic, and democratic than Acheson, Lilienthal was born in Illinois but raised in a series of small towns in Indiana, the eldest son of Eastern European immigrant Jewish parents. He attended DePauw University and Harvard Law School, where he was fortunate to study with Felix Frankfurter. A labor lawyer during the conservative 1920s, he went to work for the Wisconsin Public Service Commission, imbibing the legacy of that state's strong history of Progressive reform. He entered the New Deal in 1932 as head of the Tennessee Valley Authority (TVA), which he believed built upon the promise of "grassroots democracy," a way that top-down action on the part of the federal government could work in synergy with local governments and citizen initiatives. The spread of electricity and technology to the masses didn't necessarily *ensure* progress, but it certainly placed in the hands of citizens the ability to "use the machine to augment the dignity of human existence," as he explained in his 1944 book, *TVA: Democracy on the March.*[32]

But as he witnessed the destruction of World War II, Lilienthal reconsidered this faith. Addressing his daughter's commencement class, he wondered, "Are machines to control men, or are men to control machines?"[33] This was the key question that faced the Acheson-Lilienthal committee on the bomb. Together they assembled a set of advisers that included as a first among equals, Oppenheimer. As the only physicist in the group, "Oppie," as everyone who knew the man called him, could and did dominate discussion.[34] Lilienthal remembered his conversations with the brilliant Oppenheimer to be "one of the most memorable intellectual and emotional experiences" he had ever had.[35]

The committee's report proposed the creation of an international "Atomic Development Authority," accountable to the UN Security Council, which would have "control over raw materials and ownership of all processing and production facilities."[36] The proposal called on the United States to relinquish its atomic monopoly voluntarily and place the weapon under the authority of this new international body in exchange for a promise from everyone never to develop such weapons. The plan would have outlawed the production of new atomic bombs while allowing the United States to keep its small stockpile—at least during its early stages—a condition that would likely have caught the attention of the Soviets.[37] Like so many liberal schemes, however, it lacked a clear enforcement mechanism, as both men knew that the Soviets would balk at so detailed a policy that lacked space for negotiation. Soviet fears of intrusive inspections were certain to be yet another sticking point, and so the plan skirted this issue as well.

Acheson thought the Acheson-Lilienthal draft "brilliant and profound," but when Byrnes read the document, he immediately objected. Like the right-wing editorials attacking the plan as a giveaway to the Soviets, he thought it dangerous from a policy standpoint and suicidal from a political one. He decided to strangle it in its cradle before it could live long enough to cause any genuine political trouble. With this task in mind, he called on the seventy-five-year-old financier, Wall Street speculator, and sometime economic adviser to presidents Wilson and (Franklin) Roosevelt, Bernard Baruch, to solve his problem. Acheson believed Baruch's sage reputation to be "without foundation in fact and entirely self-propagated," but Acheson was only an assistant secretary to Byrnes at the time with no direct line to Truman.[38] When Byrnes appointed Baruch to represent the United States at the UN Atomic Energy Commission as a way to sabotage the plan, he knew that given Baruch's reputation among policy makers and journalists, coupled with the financier's power as perhaps the Democrats' most important campaign funder, he needn't worry about being overruled by Truman, regardless of the president's feelings about the issue.[39]

Baruch, for his part, did not disappoint. He insisted on inserting a voting procedure into the plan that accorded the United States a veto over literally every aspect of the peaceful use of atomic power anywhere, including plants located inside the Soviet Union, and added some stern enforcement mechanisms as well. The Baruch Plan died in the Security Council, where the Soviets enjoyed a veto. When Baruch resigned at the end of the year, Congress had already passed the Atomic Energy Act, which made the sharing of any information related to the atomic processes not merely criminal but actually treasonous.[40] Though Lilienthal soon afterward would go on to become the chief in charge of the Atomic Energy Commission in the United States, the goal of controlling the nuclear genie—and avoiding a nuclear arms race—died with the plan.

Dean Acheson's views, meanwhile, were changing with the times. For the first part of the year, he resisted the drift toward outright hostility that appeared to be capturing so many, including most particularly Harry Truman. This may have been the result of his hopes for the Acheson-Lilienthal Plan, but it was almost certainly a reflection of his honest appraisal as well. At the beginning of 1946 he had called war with the USSR "unthinkable," but as the months wore on, he came to embrace the logic of the plan's opponents.[41] By spring 1947, Acheson the conciliator had been fully displaced by Acheson the Cold Warrior.[42] From 1947 onward, his vision was tripartite: free and open trade for America's and the world's goods; anti-Communist resistance everywhere it was practical, but particularly in Western Europe and those parts of Asia and the Middle East containing strategic resources; and a slow, perfectly orderly process of decolonization in the Third World that would help ensure the triumph of the first two. By now the UN played next to no role in his thinking; peace depended on America's "continued moral, military and economic power."[43] In November 1947, Acheson noted that while the United States might try "to draw the Soviet Union towards an accommodation," "practical men" needed to understand that it had better be prepared to "lick the hell out of them."[44] As a result, no doubt, U.S.-Soviet crises over Turkey and Yugoslavia the previous summer had met with far stronger responses than had earlier disputes, and by the end of the year, Acheson was not so subtly threatening war with the Russians over Iran. As the Cold War progressed, he more or less accepted U.S.-Soviet enmity as a permanent and reasonably "manageable" state of affairs.[45] "From this time forward—to the end of his life," the historian Robert Beisner observes, "Acheson barely budged from this altered outlook on the Soviet Union. He had become the very model of an American cold warrior."[46]

Dean Acheson's thinking about the Cold War had been deeply influenced by his conversations with a man who never enjoyed any position of signifi-cant authority in America's foreign policy apparatus, but whose difficult and demanding genius was recognized by Acheson and virtually everyone else responsible for shaping the contours of U.S. foreign policy: George Frost Kennan.

Born in Milwaukee to a tax lawyer and a mother who died two months after giving birth to him, the grandson and namesake of a famed Russian his-torian and explorer, Kennan lived briefly as a child in Germany with his father and stepmother before being sent to St. John's Military Academy in Delafield, Wisconsin, and then on to Princeton, where he developed a reputation as an unusually serious-minded loner, often moody, depressed, and considered by his fellow students to be rather prickly. The young graduate joined the newly formed Foreign Service because he could not afford law school, though he chafed at the class distinctions it demanded. His deep knowledge of Russian history and culture as well as his mastery of eight foreign languages served him well in a variety of diplomatic posts before he landed in Moscow in 1933, when the United States finally opened up diplomatic ties with the Soviet Union following FDR's election.

Like Acheson, Kennan was no liberal—at least not in the domestic sense of the term. But he frequently found himself arguing alongside American liber-als when opposing the increasing militarization of U.S. foreign policy. Kennan was an "organicist conservative," as his biographer Anders Stephanson puts it, who evinced "a strong belief in a natural, hierarchical and 'organic' order, where the inherent limits of things are recognized and strictly observed, where the best and the brightest rule for the benefit of the many and the innate ten-dency of humankind to transgress against nature and the natural is kept tightly under wraps."[47] His focus on foreign policy strategies—with their long-term planning and need to avoid the whims of public opinion—led to an ill-disguised contempt not merely for public opinion but also for democracy itself. "I hate democracy. I hate the press. . . . I hate the 'peepul,'" he once wrote his sister, later likening its practice to "one of those prehistoric monsters with a body as long as this room and a brain the size of a pin: he lies there in his primeval mud and pays little attention to his environment: he is slow to wrath—in fact, you practically have to whack his tail to make him aware that his interests are being disturbed; but once he grasps this, he lays about him with such blind determination that he not only destroys his adversary but largely wrecks his native habitat."[48]

Acheson and Kennan enjoyed a relationship of mutual respect and ex-tremely wary affection. Acheson sought to put Kennan's remarkable intellect and deep historical knowledge to work, but found himself frustrated by the man's unwillingness to temper his analyses—or sensibility—to what Acheson considered to be political reality.

Laboring away in Moscow, Kennan grew frustrated by the inability of American leaders to devise a grand strategy and stick to it. Replying to a February 3, 1946, Treasury Department request for information about the Soviets' unwillingness to adhere to rules established by the World Bank and the International Monetary Fund, Kennan decided to undertake the task of defining the "sources of Soviet conduct" himself. The result was his five-thousand-word treatise known as the Long Telegram—sent in five numbered parts. (As head of the newly created State Department Policy Planning office, Kennan later repeated its arguments in *Foreign Affairs* magazine under the title "The Sources of Soviet Conduct" under the pseudonym "X.") What Kennan wryly disparaged as an outrageous "burdening of telegraphic channel" was in reality a summation of the extremely pessimistic reports he had been steadily sending, but expressed with remarkable poetic flair. The argument succeeded in codifying the establishment's critique of communism and the Cold War and was enthusiastically embraced by liberals. In addition to the unchanging tradition of Russian expansion—and an incurable paranoia induced by its natural geographic vulnerability—Kennan argued, the scientific pretense of Marxism helped provide a sense of "infallibility" and "iron discipline" to the Russian mystical belief in the rectitude of its own actions and interests. The only sensible American policy would be the "long-term patient but firm and vigilant containment of Russian expansive tendencies." This would entail "vigilant application of counter-force at a series of constantly shifting geographical and political points." If this long-term strategy of containment was carried out, then the United States could rely upon the inevitable economic decline to work its way throughout the Soviet system and thereby plant the "seeds of its own decay."[49]

Kennan drew inspiration from Niebuhr, whom he has been quoted calling the "father of us all."[50] "Man," Kennan would explain, "would have to recognize, in short, that the device of military coercion could have, in the future, only a relative—never an absolute—value in the pursuit of political objectives."[51] He warned "about excessive reliance on the military" extension of power abroad.[52] Above all, he argued for realism rather than ideological fanaticism in a struggle that would likely last beyond the lives of most of the people engaged in it.

In many respects the policy prescriptions implicit in Kennan's containment framework were relatively modest ones. He believed that there were only four regions of the world that really mattered, and as long as three of them—the United Kingdom, Continental Europe, and Japan—remained allied with the West, the rest of the world might just as well be ignored. Given America's obvious advantages in wealth, know-how, geography, and natural resources, there was really no need for alarm. "Kennan came as close to authoring the diplomatic doctrine of his era as any diplomat in our history," in the undoubt-edly envious estimation of Henry Kissinger. But in part because of his own careless draftsmanship and his weakness for historical-world posturing, Ken-nan would later compare it with "one of those primers put out by alarmed congressional committees or by the Daughters of the American Revolution, designed to arouse the citizenry to the dangers of the Communist conspiracy." His argument wound up having the opposite of its intended effect on the American establishment and helped lay the ideological groundwork for ex-actly the kind of militarization of the conflict he professed to abhor.[53]

In an ironic twist, Kennan would spend the next half century acting as a kind of "one-man Greek chorus," in Andrew J. Bacevich's phrase, seeking to undo the damage he believed was caused by the misreading and subsequent misuse of his argument.[54]

Conservative intellectuals were quick to criticize containment's lack of am-bition. James Burnham, an ex-Trotskyist whose anti-Stalinism quickly swerved to the right after World War II, argued that containment was an overly reactive policy and essentially "defensive."[55] By 1947 he was arguing that America was already engaged in a "third world war" that would determine the future "conquest of the world."[56] "We are, historically," he wrote "in an extreme situation. It requires a novel and extreme solution." A war could only be ended when the other side was defeated, and this was not, to Burnham, such a bad thing: "Wars are not accidents in history, but integral and even normal parts of the process of history."[57]

But the policies implemented on the basis of Kennan's arguments turned out to be far more expansive than anyone—particularly the liberals who em-braced them—understood at the time. When in March 1947 Truman spoke of the "broad implications" from his call to provide military support to the gov-ernments of Greece and Turkey, he set out a program that enunciated few if any discernible limitations: "I believe that it must be the policy of the United States to support free peoples who are resisting attempted subjugation by armed minorities or by outside pressures."[58] Many critics thought they heard the word "everywhere" after "free peoples," and many ignored the fact that Truman had qualified that "our help should be primarily through economic and financial aid" soon afterward. Although Kennan himself criticized what he considered the Truman Doctrine's "sweeping nature"—arguing that a policy that had been designed to meet a "specific set of circumstances," in the manner of prudent diplomatic practice, had now been proclaimed to be "universal"—many attributed the doctrine to Kennan's ideas. Kennan would later complain that he felt "like one who has inadvertently loosened a large boulder from the top of a cliff and now helplessly witnesses its path of destruction in the valley below."[59]

Kennan's most perspicacious—and, sadly, prophetic—critic would turn out to be yet another conservative commentator who, like Kennan, was often mistaken for a liberal, even by most liberals. By 1945, Walter Lippmann was already decades into what would be regarded as one of the most important and influential careers of any American intellectual of any era. As a young man in his early twenties, he had already assisted in the authorship of Woodrow Wilson's "Fourteen Points" and helped found the flagship liberal publication *The New Republic*. Between 1920 and 1924 he authored three separate studies of American democracy that rank just a few notches below the Federalist Papers as perhaps the country's most significant contributions to the history of political philosophy; his masterpiece, *Public Opinion*, inspired a debate with the liberal American philosopher John Dewey that continues to resonate among scholars nearly a century later.

Like Kennan, Lippmann was deeply pessimistic about the possibilities of democracy and had precious little faith or patience with the vagaries of the American system as it applied to diplomacy. Lippmann compared the average citizen to a blind spectator sitting in the back row of a sporting event. "He does not know what is happening, why it is happening, what ought to happen . . . he lives in a world which he cannot see, does not understand and is unable to direct."[60] But like Kennan, Lippmann felt a sense of responsibility to his fellow citizens, and to history. He wrote a regular newspaper column, one that educated millions about the complexity of the various diplomatic quandaries faced by the United States and instructed policy makers as well.

Lippmann differed with the president and Kennan on the nature of the Soviet threat and how to handle it. He believed that Soviet foreign policy was driven by realist rather than ideological considerations. The USSR was not, as Kennan proclaimed it to be, remorselessly expansive, but understandably defensive and concerned about a renewed German threat to its security. Lippmann feared that the U.S. government was moving not only toward unnecessary conflict with the USSR but also putting itself at the mercy of corrupt dictators like those at the helm of the Greek and Turkish governments. Phrases like coming to the aid of all "free peoples who are resisting" might sound inspirational, but in practice they were bets that were simply too rich to cover.[61] He predicted that even if successful, the policy's costs would outweigh its benefits, for to implement it would entail "recruiting, subsidizing, and supporting a heterogeneous array of satellites, clients, dependents and puppets" as well as a massive military apparatus.

Lippmann argued that America should instead focus its energy on solving the problems of postwar Europe, "notably in reconstructing their economic life and in promoting a German settlement on which they can agree."[62] He continued: "The Truman Doctrine treats those who are supposed to benefit by it as dependencies of the United States, as instruments of the American policy for 'containing' Russia."[63] The great irony in this debate lies in the fact that not only would Kennan ultimately decide that Lippmann's analysis had been more accurate than his own, but that these two old-fashioned conservatives had actually constituted the liberal pole in a debate where conservatives were pressuring Congress and the president for a far more aggressive and ideologically charged policy that would have risked a much higher threat of all-out war, first with the Soviets and later with the Communist Chinese.

General George C. Marshall was a man whose heroism during World War II, coupled with his well-deserved reputation for the highest possible personal and political principles, positioned him to become a key statesman after the war.[64] His first postwar mission for Harry Truman was a great act of failed diplomacy, traveling to China to find a solution to the country's ongoing civil war. Though Marshall successfully negotiated a cease-fire, it didn't last long. When he left China in January 1947, his conclusions were prescient. The Nationalists were a "group of reactionaries who have been opposed" to forming a "coalition government." The Communists "do not hesitate at the most dramatic measures to gain their end."[65]

When Marshall agreed to put his considerable prestige at the service of the Truman administration by accepting the president's offer to replace the hapless Byrnes, who had replaced the even more inept Edward Stettinius, Jr., as secretary of state in early 1947, he immediately set to work on a plan to complement the Truman Doctrine that would emphasize economic aid to Europe as a means to prevent the spread of communism. Marshall knew he would need help and quickly employed as much talent as he could at the State Department. The general chose Acheson as his undersecretary, and their admiration was mutual. (The latter would observe that "in the field of ideas, there hardly was less a military mind than his."[66]) Marshall recalled Kennan to Washington, together with Charles "Chip" Bohlen, who was both a friend and a Lippmannesque critic of containment.[67]

Marshall wanted a plan that would confront the "very serious world situation" and guide the "rehabilitation of Europe," and he believed that for the next three or four years America would need to ship "food and other essential products" there. When Marshall summoned Kennan to his office to discuss his plans, the general seemed agitated and nervous, and bore down on Kennan to get to work, lest Congress interfere to tie their hands.[68] Kennan set to work, beginning with a program for the immediate improvement of European coal production. His long-term hope was to expand this notion into a much more ambitious sharing of agricultural and industrial resources to strengthen Western Europe economies and allow them to build resistance to Soviet pressures, all the while insisting that "the Europeans should themselves take the initiative in drawing up a program and should assume central responsibility for its terms."[69]

The plan he eventually helped construct was hugely expensive—$13 billion, or more than 5 percent of U.S. GDP at the time—and included technical assistance (goods as well as training), grants for key projects (rather than the loans the United States extended after World War I), basic agricultural goods, and monetary stabilization plans for local economies. Marshall announced his proposal in a famous June 5, 1947, address at Harvard, explaining, "It is logical that the United States should do whatever it is able to do to assist in the return of normal economic health in the world, without which there can be no political stability and no assured peace. Our policy is directed not against any country or doctrine but against hunger, poverty, desperation, and chaos." Knowing that his call for humanitarianism would likely face partisan opposition, he argued that "political passion and prejudice should have no part" in assisting European recovery.[70]

Congress debated the Marshall Plan for six months.[71] Republican isolationists unsurprisingly detested it, Senator Robert Taft (Ohio) dismissing it as a "European TVA" and a "giveaway program" and Senator Homer Capehart (Indiana) terming it "state socialism."[72] Some on the left believed that the Marshall Plan suffered, like the Truman Doctrine, from being a unilateral approach: aid should be deployed through the UN (just as Henry Wallace had proposed). The Soviets, meanwhile, gave little indication that they would abide by any set of rules that placed them in a supplicant position, no matter how desperate their economic condition. They also correctly viewed the plan as an attempt to seduce their East European "allies."[73]

The Truman administration understood the seriousness of the task before it: it needed to sell not only an extremely costly plan to an impecunious and unsophisticated public but with it the notion that the United States would now be involved in the global give-and-take it had hitherto shunned. Educational efforts had, in fact, been under way even before the Marshall Plan was formally announced. For example, in May 1947 Dean Acheson had been sent to Cleveland, Mississippi, to the Delta State Teachers College, where ten thousand people showed up to hear him speak. He began by explaining that Europe was on "the borderline of starvation," but added, "there is no charity involved in this. . . . We are obliged from considerations of self-interest and humanitarianism to finance a huge deficit in the world's budget."[74]

Business leaders, academics, religious and labor leaders barnstormed the country promoting the Marshall Plan. Marshall himself went to speak to agricultural organizations, meeting with one group in Ohio who had just left a meeting with Robert Taft, while Acheson did radio debates and talks with business associations. Truman called for ordinary citizens to take part in "national food-savings programs." Kiwanis clubs and other civic organizations sponsored local food drives for goods to be sent abroad, while 4-H clubs shipped farm implements to their counterparts in Europe. When ships filled with American grain started to leave for Europe, organizers made sure that their departures were well publicized, with marching bands and plenty of newspaper reporters and photographers, should anyone fail to get the message about the country's unparalleled generosity.[75] With its mixture of idealism and pragmatism, the Marshall Plan was nearly perfect from a liberal Cold Warrior's point of view. Not surprisingly, ADA endorsed it wholeheartedly and cheered its success when Congress passed it in the spring of 1948.[76]

In the end, the Marshall Plan proved a magnificent success, helping to stabilize European economies and provide sufficient food and coal to prevent famine and worse in the heart of Western Europe. As the historian Michael J. Hogan observes, it facilitated the creation of a market sufficient, finally, not only to absorb Germany's economic power but also to "boost productivity, raise living standards, lower prices and thus set the stage for security and recovery on the Continent and for a fully multilateral system of world trade."[77] The plan did not dispel resentment of the United States that was budding in many nations at the time, particularly among the pro-Soviet left. It was no surprise that the same year saw the formation of the Cominform (Communist Information Bureau), the international arm of Soviet propaganda, which denounced the Marshall Plan as an extension of American imperialism.[78] But if this was imperialism, it was imperialism of a uniquely benign sort. In order to win this argument, however, America would have to offer not only food and energy as a Cold War weapon, but attractive ideas and culture as well. And this was a fight that liberals were more than eager to embrace.

On June 26, 1950, delegates from around the world gathered in Berlin to launch yet another salvo on the rapidly expanding cultural front of the Cold War: the creation of the Congress for Cultural Freedom (CCF). Its participants signed a declaration that read: "We do not pretend that our democracies are anywhere near approaching an ideal state. *We are defending our relative freedoms against the total unfreedom of dictatorial regimes.*" The founders acknowledged that vis-à-vis communism: "Fanatical mass movements are always at a temporary advantage against the defenders of civilization. . . . Ours is a defensive battle."[79] Still, the CCF's defense of intellectual freedom served as an important rallying point for European and Third World democratic intellectuals of the center. Of course it was no accident that the event took place in Berlin (and no surprise when it was later discovered that U.S. intelligence agencies had played a significant role in CCF's funding).[80]

The CCF was ideologically internally divided between hard-line conservative anti-Communists—most famously Arthur Koestler, but also James Burnham—and anti-Communist liberal intellectuals, including Arthur Schlesinger, Jr., and Italian novelist and partisan Ignazio Silone.[81] It nevertheless provided a valuable forum for liberals to enunciate their principles to the world. The seeds for CCF were originally sown by Melvin Lasky, an American-born Jew who grew up in the Bronx and graduated from New York's City College. He joined the Foreign Service and became something of a roving intellectual, traveling throughout Europe and sending dispatches back to little magazines such as *The New Leader* and *Partisan Review*. In 1947 he showed up at a gathering of the East Berlin Writers' Congress, where instead of the usual extolling of the brilliance and beauty of the Communist future, those assembled heard a stocky man with a fierce goatee compare Stalin to Hitler and the Soviet Union to a prison camp. The audience erupted in cheers.[82] Excited by his moment of triumph, Lasky pitched what he thought of as an intellectual counterpart to the Marshall Plan to General Lucius Clay, whom General Eisenhower had appointed as military governor of Germany. His first step was to create a monthly magazine called *Der Monat*, copies of which General Clay agreed to help distribute by dropping them from the air.

The congress's origins can be traced back to 1939, when the intellectual firebrand Sidney Hook formed the Committee for Cultural Freedom to represent anti-Stalinist leftist intellectuals in their battles with those allied with the Communist Party of the USA.[83] Following a combative career as a student at City College, where he fought with Stalinists under the tutelage of the famously influential Minsk-born teacher and professor of philosophy, Morris Raphael Cohen, Hook spent the early portion of his brilliant career as a philosopher seeking to unite the writings of Karl Marx with those of John Dewey. He continued to do battle on behalf of what he considered to be democratic socialism while at the same time moving toward an almost obsessive anti-Communism.[84]

Hook organized Americans for Intellectual Freedom (AIF) as a counterpart to the Communist front organizations with which he sought to do battle, and it was this group that ultimately metamorphosed into the Congress for Cultural Freedom. Hook traveled to Berlin for the founding conference of CCF. Arthur Schlesinger, Jr., who joined him at both the Waldorf protests and in Berlin, and was attracted to Hook's City College–bred street fighter persona, later expressed some doubts about the romanticism of his cause. "He was quite excited by it all," Schlesinger recalled. "Many of them were. They thought they were going to be where the action was—especially those who hadn't been in the war."[85]

Within the State Department, a growing awareness arose of the unpopularity of the United States among many on both the left and right in Europe who shared the view that this new capitalistic colossus was both lacking in and hostile to the higher spiritual and cultural values that had given civilization its meaning across generations. The office that became known in 1947 as the Office of International Information and Educational Exchange was charged with finding ways to expose the rest of the world to America's cultural riches. It set up venues in West Germany, each called America House, to display the work of such American artists as Georgia O'Keeffe and Jacob Lawrence, and organized concert tours by jazz musicians such as Louis Armstrong and Duke Ellington.[86] By 1950, America Houses were attracting a million West Germans per month to conferences, lectures by visiting American writers and academics, exhibitions, movies, and the like. The Salzburg Seminar, begun in 1947 through the initiative of two graduate students and one instructor at Harvard University, also proved quite popular; it was staffed by professors from the United States and attended by students from all over Europe. The idea was to explain the American way of life to Europeans by emphasizing the country's literary traditions, music, and art and by hosting lectures by the likes of Alfred Kazin, Saul Bellow, and Margaret Mead.[87] (Despite its success, congressmen condemned the program as a boondoggle for good-for-nothings who didn't know the value of a hard-earned dollar, and even Harry Truman dismissed it as "the vaporings of half-baked lazy people."[88])

The 1949 publication of *The God That Failed,* a collection of essays by six enormously influential ex-Communist and fellow traveling intellectuals—Arthur Koestler, Richard Wright, Ignazio Silone, Stephen Spender, André Gide, and Louis Fischer—provided a much-needed manifesto of sorts for liberal anti-Communists on both sides of the Atlantic. These liberals understood that the Continental political spectrum—then as now—could be found well to the left of that in the United States. Its pro-Soviet left could be defeated only by a non-Commuist but pro-socialist liberal left, and these intellectuals, unlike most American politicians, were entirely comfortable swimming in these waters.

The CCF eventually lost its own left and right wings, owing to fights over McCarthyism. After Schlesinger quit the organization, he wrote in *Partisan Review* in 1952 that he could not work with those who "profess a belief in cultural freedom on the one hand, and refuse to condemn McCarthyism on the other," as America could not "hope to preserve cultural freedom and cultural pluralism in a society where political freedom and political pluralism become impossible."[89] The organization's membership had always been an unstable mix. As the historian Hugh Wilford points out: "One wing of the organization were upper-class bohemian dissenters like [Dwight] Macdonald, individuals who were highly sensitive about their intellectual independence and just as likely to sound off about American 'mass culture' as the threat of Communism. On the other were . . . intellectuals reared in the American Communist movement but now so bitterly anti-Communist that they even flirted with support for Joseph McCarthy."[90] Even before Nikita Khrushchev's explosive 1956 "secret speech" denouncing Stalin's gulag, though, the CCF had lost its raison d'être, as whatever attraction the Soviet Union had held for independent European intellectuals had all but evaporated of its own weighty contradictions. The University of Chicago scholar Edward Shils, attending a 1955 meeting in Milan, together with Daniel Bell, Raymond Aron, and Seymour Martin Lipset, among others, wondered aloud, "Have the Communists come to appear so preposterous to our Western intellectuals that it is no longer conceivable that they could be effectively subversive? Is it now thought that there is no longer any danger of the working classes in the advanced Western countries falling for their propaganda?"[91]

The source of the CCF's funding was much discussed in intellectual circles, but while many suspected, only a few were in on the secret source.[92] When the CIA funding of the CCF's efforts was revealed by radical American journalists in 1966, many who participated in its activities felt betrayed. Dwight Macdonald insisted that the "secret funding was immoral and unethical in itself," even if the CCF maintained autonomy from the policies of the CIA.[93] But Irving Kristol, who edited the CCF magazine *Encounter*, from London, insisted in 1967 that while he heard "rumors of government funding," he "never knew about the CIA financing of *Encounter*—and, by God, I will sue for libel anyone who says I did, if it takes the last cent I have."[94]

As the Marshall Plan and cultural diplomacy continued to work their way through Europe, the focus of the Cold War started to shift toward other parts of the world. Evident already in the battles over Greece and Turkey, the Cold War itself could not be comfortably contained—just as Lippmann had warned in his debate with Kennan. While the two sides would never go to war directly, they fought proxy wars with frequently devastating consequences for the local populace in countries as varied as Guatemala, El Salvador, Iran, Iraq, Indonesia, Laos, Nicaragua, Honduras, Bolivia, Congo, Angola, South Africa, South Korea, Czechoslovakia, Hungary, Mozambique, Afghanistan, the Dominican Republic, Chile, Cuba, Cambodia, Grenada, Panama, and Vietnam, to name just a few. From a political standpoint, perhaps none would prove as devastating to the fortunes of American liberalism as one from which the United States managed to refrain: China.

The shock to Americans of the "loss of China"—the term itself illustrated the sense of powerlessness that engulfed the nation—to the Communists in 1949 unleashed a particularly virulent form of conservatism in the United States, one with which liberals could not comfortably contend, at least in the high-minded fashion they had conceived for themselves. Even the heroic general George Marshall and the increasingly hard-line Cold Warrior Dean Acheson became prime political targets for the newly emboldened anti-Communist right.

Acheson offered an argument for U.S. nonintervention in what would become an infamous State Department white paper: "The unfortunate but inescapable fact is that the ominous result of the civil war in China was beyond the control of the government of the United States. . . . It was the product of internal Chinese forces, forces which this government tried to influence but could not."[95]

In 1949, Reinhold Niebuhr asserted that the appropriate American response to the fall of China was a policy of "folded hands." Yes, it was aggravating to watch communism expand abroad, Niebuhr conceded, but overextending

American power was hardly an appropriate reaction.[96] This philosophy of limits, as expressed by both Acheson and Niebuhr, was an essential aspect of the liberal interpretation of Kennan's policy of containment. But it was not a popular one in 1949, and not one that many liberals really knew how to defend in a nation accustomed only to military victory.

In June of 1950, as the participants in the Congress for Cultural Freedom's conference were gathered in Berlin, they heard the news that the North Koreans had invaded South Korea, crossing the now infamous 38th parallel. Soon Truman would make a fateful decision to commit the nation to war there, though he insisted on calling it a police action to avoid ratcheting up the conflict with the USSR, which was supplying the North Koreans. Coming so soon after the debacle in China, a military response by the United States was almost a given. The outbreak of the war inevitably served to dampen the dreams of liberal internationalism. Truman and Acheson committed themselves to the militaristic side of the doctrine articulated in 1947 regarding Greece and Turkey. The consequence was obvious, as the historian Nicolaus Mills points out: "Three days after fighting began in Korea, Congress slashed $208 million from the Marshall Plan and the ECA's budget and increased military spending by $4 billion."[97] In truth, Acheson and Truman had been looking for just such an opportunity to vastly increase the U.S. defense budget. The era's Magna Carta would prove to be an April 1950 internal report to President Truman titled "NSC-68." Though the document remained classified until 1975, it functioned within the government as the operational blueprint for the thoroughly militarized version of Kennan's containment policy. It argued that the Kremlin leaders were possessed of a "new fanatic faith," seeking "absolute authority over the rest of the world"; the authors argued that "the integrity of our system will not be jeopardized by any measures, covert or overt, violent or nonviolent, which serve the purposes of frustrating the Kremlin design."[98] With the dispatching of U.S. troops to the Korean peninsula, the Marshall Plan was effectively over. Asia became the new battleground.

5

The Best Years of Our Lives

> To the carrying out of the job of criticizing the liberal imagination,
> literature has a unique relevance . . . because literature is the human
> activity that takes the fullest and most precise account of variousness,
> possibility, complexity, and difficulty.
>
> —Lionel Trilling, 1949[1]

The social critic and literary scholar Irving Howe once called liberalism "a cast of mind, a structure of norms by means of which to humanize public life."[2] Here again we can see this definition embodied in the life and political principles of Eleanor Roosevelt. Her commitment to political activism was rooted in her witness to the suffering of others, originally at the Rivington Street settlement house in her youth. Eleanor lived her liberalism as a kind of personal democracy, a sentiment one felt as much as believed.

At the other end of the spectrum was the persona of Humphrey Bogart, the tough-guy actor who personified the popular-culture version of Truman's gruffness. Whether in the role of private detective Sam Spade or Philip Marlowe, or portraying the quiet heroism of Rick Blaine in the classic *Casablanca*, underneath the hard veneer beat a heart that was sensitive not only to his own self-interest (Blaine falsely proclaimed, "I stick my neck out for no man") but to that of the poor, the downtrodden, the fellow who needed a hand to fight the evil in life, evil in *Casablanca* represented by Adolf Hitler. The conservative cry of "bleeding heart" can be heard throughout the course of postwar liberalism's development, and for good reason: Liberalism bespoke powerful emotions, and these emotions can be seen most prominently in the cultural works it produced.

With the photographic images of concentration camps and the victims of the atomic bombs in Hiroshima and Nagasaki seared into their memories, most liberals left behind optimism during the 1940s, but they did retain the essential Enlightenment belief in the betterment of humankind. To open one's eyes and heart to the plight of the less fortunate remained an important foundation of liberalism, even as it tried to toughened itself to face the harsh realities of the postwar world. But these twin demands were never fully reconciled. As the liberal literary critic Lionel Trilling pointed out in 1950, "Liberalism stood in a paradoxical relation to the emotions." For though the doctrine was "concerned with the emotions above all else, liberalism somehow tends to deny them in their full possibility."[3] Much of Trilling's life was spent attempting to resolve this tension, particularly in his frequent warning to liberals against "wish-thinking and rationalization" as a substitute for the search for truth.[4] In his 1939 study of Matthew Arnold, written during the height of the Popular Front, Trilling, in Irving Kristol's words, held "up to scorn the modern radical-liberal-progressive, with his casual optimism, his blind adulation of the 'common people,' his condescending good will, his failure to face up to the less tractable aspects of human nature."[5]

The war's end ushered in what the literary critic Leslie Fiedler called "an end to innocence" in America[6] as the country's writers, artists, and critics grew more worldly and self-conscious. European intellectuals had long sneered at the country that was so adept at exporting its pop culture but precious little in terms of lasting value to the literary and cultural canon. The creative explosions of the postwar years challenged these perceptions. Before the war, jazz was perhaps America's singular contribution to Western music; it was democratic and innovative, with an apparently effortless amalgamation of high and low, urban and rural, black and white. After the war, such musicians as Charlie Parker, Dizzy Gillespie, and Miles Davis built on the earlier achievements of pioneers such as Duke Ellington and Louis Armstrong to add further depth and sophistication to this American art form. Unlike the big bands of the pre-war era, bebop artists played in smaller, more individualized and more improvisational combos, creating a sophisticated music that was for the purpose of listening, not dancing. The music fit the growing sense of freedom in the postwar years, especially for newly assertive blacks demanding their place at table after table.[7]

Much the same spirit struck the art world with the rise of abstract expressionism in the paintings of artists such as Willem de Kooning and Jackson Pollock. "Drip" and "action" painting, in which Pollock would stand above his canvas and allow his unconscious to spill over it, displaced the 1930s' Popular Front murals depicting American workers gleaming with muscles and pride, building the industrial infrastructure of the republic. Abstract expressionism drew upon two currents coursing through American culture simultaneously: it was difficult and brooding, reflecting the "anxiety" that

Schlesinger had identified as part of the postwar years, and profoundly original and expressive.[8] Robert Motherwell, another artist of the time, called abstract expressionism "rebellious, individualistic, unconventional."[9] The potency of this work made America and, more specifically, New York City the reigning cultural capital of the world, a magnet for Europeans rather than the other way around.[10]

Broadway found itself transformed as well. Eugene O'Neill's *The Iceman Cometh* and *Long Day's Journey into Night* challenged America's cherished sentimental notions of itself. O'Neill sought to awaken the nation from its "pipe dreams," providing troubling portraits of families struggling over addiction, sexual frustration, lies, and abuse. "I am going on the theory that the United States, instead of being the most successful country in the world, is the greatest failure," O'Neill explained.[11] Tennessee Williams's *The Glass Menagerie*, produced in 1944, offered up a similarly searing portrait of self-deception. The following year, Arthur Miller's *All My Sons* told the story of a young man's discovery of his father's corrupt business practices during the war and his complicity in making faulty airplane equipment that had caused the death of his brother. Two years later Miller would produce another classic, *Death of a Salesman*, which submitted the American dream to a merciless vivisection. Anyone looking for evidence of an end to an era of American cultural innocence could hardly do better than consider the success of these three postwar playwrights.[12]

The novel still stood as the high-water mark of cultural expression, and here, too, a cultural renaissance was clearly under way, as new novelists sprang from the ranks of "thousands of mud-flat Jewish-Polish-Russian generations," as the literary critic Alfred Kazin called them, challenging what had typically been an extremely genteel, even Waspish literary culture.[13] Brash young Norman Mailer offered up *The Naked and the Dead* (1948), a brutal depiction of soldiers' lives during the war, replete with anti-Semitism, racism, sadism, and stupidity as the defining characteristics of the men who had been romanticized in Hollywood newsreels and local newspaper reports. Saul Bellow struggled in these years with his early novels *Dangling Man* (1944) and *The Victim* (1947), works he would later describe as immature and rushed; he did not truly find his voice until *The Adventures of Augie March* (1953).[14]

Among the new voices that fell outside the WASP center of American culture were the first glimmerings of a mature black literature, a second act of the Harlem Renaissance. Richard Wright had published his naturalist novel *Native Son* in 1940, when he was still a Communist but was harboring doubts about the party. The story of a young black man coming into his "freedom" through murdering and then dismembering a white woman and facing jail and death, the novel inspired James Baldwin and Ralph Ellison to move beyond Wright's simplistic portrait of the sociopath as victim.[15]

Writers in general were discovering, as Kazin explained, that the central challenge of literature—as he believed it to be throughout the years of the twentieth century—was to balance "estrangement" with engagement in America's social life, embracing "alienation on native grounds—the interwoven story of our need to take up our life on our own grounds, and the irony of our possession." And it was in this tradition that the first battle of an undeclared culture war found its expression.[16]

In 1944, just as the war was winding down, a woman named Lillian Smith published a novel called *Strange Fruit*, which dealt frankly with racism, miscegenation, and lynching in the American South. The book was an immediate sensation, selling 140,000 copies in the first two months of its release.[17] A year later it became a play, opening first in Chicago before moving to Broadway for a successful two-year run. *Strange Fruit* was not a great novel by any measure. Smith's characters were flat, and she had too many of them. But unusually for the time—and particularly for a white author—it did not portray its black characters merely as victims.

The novel's title came to Smith one night when she happened into the club Café Society and heard the great Billie Holiday singing the song that would give it its name. "Strange Fruit" was written by Abel Meeropol, who sometime in the early 1930s came across a photograph of a lynching that he found shocking but also inspiring. Meeropol was a Communist inspired by the Popular Front ideal of an international, interracial movement for social justice. (He would become famous, together with his wife, Anne, for adopting the children of Ethel and Julius Rosenberg after their parents' execution.) Meeropol had written and submitted the lyrics as a poem to be published in the Communist magazine *New Masses*. After setting it to music, he persuaded Holiday to add it to her repertoire. With its spooky invocation of southern lynchings through the metaphor of "strange fruit" smelling of "burning flesh" and seen hanging off poplar trees, Holiday's reading of the lyrics would prove a bone-chilling mixture of art and artistry. The song stands today, in the opinion of many songwriters and musicians, as perhaps the most effective protest song ever recorded and one of twentieth-century America's singular cultural achievements.[18]

Lillian Smith, however, had her own ideas about the world, and particularly about the manner in which culture could advance social justice. Unlike most people associated with Popular Front politics, she actually deplored communism and had no use for the pieties that deliberately blurred its brutal practice with idealistic preaching. An unapologetic Cold War liberal, she sought to poach on the terrain of the Popular Front, particularly its antiracist and anti-Fascist strains, and use what she found there to liberal ends.

Throughout the 1930s, American writing had been marked by politicization. Popular American fiction felt frivolous in the face of the Depression, the war, and the threat of fascism. Writers associated with the Communist Party promoted "proletarian literature" designed to teach the working class what was good for it, emphasizing what the former fellow traveler Lionel Trilling would derisively term "the social responsibility of the writer."[19] This led to a "curiously moralistic stance" toward fiction, as the novelist Malcolm Cowley characterized it, and some truly awful novels. In its non-Communist version, however, it led to an interest in documenting America's social life and in explaining the country to itself.[20]

Lillian Smith chafed at the label of "race book" and argued instead that her novel was "a story about human beings and their relationships with each other."[21] *Strange Fruit* focused on the story of Nonnie Anderson, a young black woman, and Tracy Deen, a young white man, in the town of Maxwell, Georgia. Deen's sexual longing for Nonnie, which has resulted in her carrying his child, is described frankly and compellingly. He struggles with his desire, the prejudices of southern racist culture, and his religious upbringing. A local preacher tells him to marry off Nonnie to a black man, and then join the church and settle down with a white woman from a respectable family. Though rebellious up to a point, Tracy eventually gives in to the expectations of his class and caste. He tries to arrange to have Henry, a black man who works for his family, marry Nonnie. When Nonnie's brother Eddie discovers this, he murders Tracy, which leads the townspeople to lynch Henry in an act of blind vengeance.[22]

Smith drew from the documentary style prevalent in 1930s classics such as John Steinbeck's *Grapes of Wrath* (1939) but also offers an ongoing commentary on the psychological sources of her characters' feelings and actions, a technique pioneered in Sherwood Anderson's *Winesburg, Ohio* (1919). *Strange Fruit*, she later explained, was "a book about human beings journeying across deep chasms, and down into forbidding areas, but journeying also back to childhood, always back to the room where they were born, seeking to find wherever they travel, that which they left there, so long ago."[23] By focusing on the psychology of racism—Smith would call segregation an "ancient psychological mechanism"—she warned of the damage that segregation did to whites as well as blacks (much as Martin Luther King, Jr., would argue later).[24] Segregation, she insisted, not only created a lack of "self-esteem" in its victims, but also a "hardness of heart" in its perpetrators.[25]

Smith deployed her newfound celebrity to further the work that meant so much to her. In 1956 she joined the advisory committee of the Congress of Racial Equality (CORE), endorsing nonviolent direct action as a legitimate way to combat racism.[26] She also joined ADA and helped raise money among southern liberals. Arthur Schlesinger confided in his fellow ADA members that while Smith had good "moral character" and judgment, "her thinking and influence are somewhat irrelevant in the South" and she would therefore reinforce the perception that ADA was simply "another Yankee liberal outfit."[27] This would turn out to be an unfortunately accurate assessment.

Not long after Lillian Smith adapted her novel for the stage, the Post Office Department banned it from the mails due to its sexual explicitness. When the Board of Trade of Boston Book Merchants demanded that it be removed from bookstore shelves for its alleged obscenity, Smith knew that the controversy would improve sales and draw attention to the work. But she had also grown weary of the focus on the book's sexual passages and wrote her publisher to complain that everyone had reduced the novel to a "passionate love story." She went on: "There is a lot more about the book than a love affair and it continues to fix the image of 'dirt' in people's minds."[28]

The incident ended up having important implications not only for the debate over its racial and sexual content, but also because it caught the attention of a local liberal intellectual named Bernard "Benny" DeVoto, to whom fighting censorship in his adopted hometown of Boston came naturally. A stocky man with a barrel chest, DeVoto was raised in a combination Mormon/Catholic family in Ogden, Utah. His western roots helped provide a hint of libertarianism to his politics, the frontier ethic of freedom remaining a powerful part of his political and psychological makeup as he moved eastward. Famous for his honest and often blunt character, he served in the Army in World War I before becoming an unsuccessful novelist, and eventually an equally unsuccessful professor of literature. (DeVoto was denied tenure by Harvard in 1936.[29]) He eventually settled into a career as a journalist and popular historian of the West. After a stint at the *Saturday Review of Literature* in New York, he returned to Cambridge, where he continued his "Easy Chair" column for *Harper's*.

In Cambridge, DeVoto became fast friends with the Arthur Schlesingers, senior and junior. What Arthur junior admired about DeVoto was precisely what he admired about Niebuhr: his ability to move gracefully between "the poles of activism and skepticism." DeVoto, he recalled, displayed "a noncon- formist's love of freedom, a Populist's rage at injustice, and, though he would have indignantly denied it, a crusader's desire to knock sense into people's heads and build a better world."[30]

Once World War II began, DeVoto sought local outlets for activism and became "an air raid warden, a certificated first aider, and a lecturer to army camps."[31] When Schlesinger left the OWI in protest against its use of advertis- ing techniques to sell the war, DeVoto joined in his dissent, believing that a war for democracy need not devolve into dishonesty.[32]

DeVoto became chairman of the Massachusetts Civil Liberties Union Com- mittee on Censorship when *Strange Fruit* first appeared. The Massachusetts chapter was one of the ACLU's oldest, and it frequently focused on issues of literary censorship.[33] DeVoto believed that *Strange Fruit* warranted special protection because it was "conceived in the spirit of truth, charged with pity and the hope of a better social justice in America, and written with high artis- tic integrity and great literary power."[34]

When DeVoto learned that the Boston booksellers had prevented sales of *Strange Fruit*, he arranged to purchase a copy from a brave bookstore owner in Cambridge. The police immediately confiscated it and charged him "with buying an obscene book with intent to lend or circulate it, and charged the bookseller with possession of same, with intent to sell it as well."[35] The case moved quickly through the legal system. Joseph Welch, the young lawyer who would later famously challenge Joseph McCarthy, helped argue the ACLU's case. It moved to the Massachusetts Supreme Court, and on September 17, 1945, the court ruled that a novel could be deemed legally obscene "if it has a substantial tendency to deprave or corrupt its readers by inciting lascivious thoughts or arousing lustful desire."[36] In the vaguest and most inclusive terms imaginable, a literary work of significant merit was nevertheless ruled to be "obscene" because it "adversely affect[ed] a substantial proportion of its read- ers" and was "found to lower appreciably the average moral tone of the mass."[37]

DeVoto soon launched a personal campaign in opposition to the court's decision and reminded readers of the famous dictum of Justice Oliver Wendell Holmes, Jr., that it was "the hateful, the abhorrent idea whose freedom must be most vigorously defended, since there will be serious pressure against no other ideas."[38] DeVoto also particularly enjoyed pointing out that the high- minded citizens of Boston—home to Harvard University, *The Atlantic Monthly*, and, once upon a time, the abolitionist movement—believed themselves to be somehow threatened by a southern woman's book about lynching that was openly available in Atlanta and Birmingham.[39] The *Strange Fruit* case inspired a loosening of the Massachusetts obscenity law and helped to boost the cause of civil liberties in the United States in matters large and small.[40]

DeVoto was not only a civil libertarian but also an accomplished literary critic. His book *The Literary Fallacy* (1944) condemned what he considered the skewed view of America that was a legacy of the literature of the 1920s, especially the novels of Sinclair Lewis (author of *Main Street* and *Babbitt*). DeVoto believed that the 1920s generation had "scorned, condemned, and despaired of the American people and American democracy."[41] Attacks on what H. L. Mencken had once labeled the "booboisie" and Sinclair Lewis had derided as "Babbitry" rankled DeVoto, who believed such elitism isolated writers from society at large. Alfred Kazin came closer to the truth when he pointed out that Lewis "depended on the common life he satirized" and that his writing showed an "unflagging absorption of detail" and "grasp of life" that, in fact, connected it in many ways more deeply to the society he mocked than DeVoto allowed.[42]

Excluding perhaps only Edmuud Wilson, the most influential critic of the period was Lionel Trilling, who happened to be the first Jew to be tenured in Columbia University's English department, and who would emerge as one of liberalism's most subtle and sensitive thinkers. Trilling personified the cultivated literary gentleman, despite his background as the son of East European immigrants, and took on the reserved mores of the Protestant elite.

Trilling stood at the center of the group of writers who would become known as the New York Intellectuals, who came to prominence in the 1930s and 1940s. The group organized itself around the magazine *Partisan Review*, which nurtured the careers of Sidney Hook, Alfred Kazin, Dwight Macdonald, Mary McCarthy, Leslie Fiedler, Richard Hofstadter, Irving Howe, F. W. Dupree, Hannah Arendt, Clement Greenberg, Harold Rosenberg, Saul Bellow, and Delmore Schwartz, among others. Originally founded in 1934 as the "revolutionary" organ of the Communist Party's John Reed Club for writers, an early editorial statement promised dedication to "the defense of the Soviet Union" and a willingness to "combat not only the decadent culture of the exploiting classes but also the debilitating liberalism which at time seeps into our writers through the pressure of class-alien forces."[43] By 1937, its coeditors, Philip Rahv and William Phillips, were able to break it off from the party and relaunch it as a journal seeking to combine a commitment to (anti-Stalinist) Marxism in politics with modernist aesthetic culture. Originally supportive of Leon Trotsky, then living in exile in Mexico City, it would grow increasingly impossible to pin down ideologically as its members traveled through various permutations of liberalism, democratic socialism, and eventually for some, neoconservatism. The one constant for all of them would remain unremitting hostility to Stalinism and the Soviet Union.

During its heyday, the magazine functioned as a kind of base camp for an "American Bloomsbury," as the journalist Nicholas Lemann described it.[44] Its constributors liked to view themselves, in Trilling's formulation, as "an adversary culture," one whose purpose was "to liberate the individual from the tyranny of his culture in the environmental sense and to permit him to stand beyond it in an autonomy of perception and judgment."[45] In the beginning most of the group defined their politics as socialist, though this was not a terribly meaningful sobriquet. "Although I was a 'socialist,' like everyone else I knew," Alfred Kazin would later recall, "I thought of socialism as orthodox Christians might think of the Second Coming—a wholly supernatural event which one might await with perfect faith, but which had no immediate relevance to my life."[46]

The New York Intellectuals brought to their criticism a deep reading of European culture and history, together with a generalist's approach that was then alien to the American academy, where as Jews (mostly) they were almost uniformly unwelcome. (In 1939, Columbia University president Nicholas Murray Butler invoked his "summer powers" to appoint Trilling an assistant professor of English over the objection of its members, who had wanted no part of a professor who could be accurately described as "a Jew, a Marxist and a Freudian."[47])

Irving Howe would describe the typical *PR* essay as "wide-ranging in reference, melding notions about literature and politics, sometimes announcing itself as a study of a writer or literary group but usually taut with a pressure to 'go beyond' its subject, toward some encompassing moral or social observation." Stylistically, he noted, they adopted a manner "highly self-conscious in mode, with an unashamed vibration of bravura." It was "nervous, strewn with knotty or flashy phrases, impatient with transitions and other concessions to dullness, calling attention to itself as a form or at least an outcry, fond of rapid twists, taking pleasure in dispute, dialectic [and] dazzle."[48]

Although most members of what Norman Podhoretz would call "the family" were the children of Jewish immigrants—Edmund Wilson would constantly refer to the magazine as "Partisansky Review"—they rejected religious belief as a relic of a bygone era and self-consciously sought to shed this aspect of their cultural identities. Lost to the traditional Jewish community, they embraced the broad Western tradition in the humanities and the secular ideal of the intellectual life. As Kazin explained in 1944, it was the newness of America itself that defined his role as a critic. "Like any other American," he wrote, "I have had to make my own culture."[49] And make it, almost all of them did. The "beggarly Jewish radicals of the 30s" became the "the ruling cultural pundits of American society," as he later put it, marveling at his own journey.[50] It began, as the historian Edward S. Shapiro observed, with the representation of World War II in fiction, which proved to be almost a monopoly of young Jewish writers. Each service was portrayed in novels by veterans: The Army had both Mailer's *The Naked and the Dead* (1948) and Irwin Shaw's *The Young Lions* (1948); the Navy had Herman Wouk's *The Caine Mutiny* (1951); the Marine Corps had Leon Uris's *Battle Cry* (1953); and the Army Air Force, a bit later, had Joseph Heller's *Catch-22*.[51] Mailer's and Heller's work would remain classics of the American canon, more than half a century after their publication.[52]

Trilling had particular motivation to identify himself as an American writer, because his father, David Trilling, had been hastily shipped to the United States under deeply humiliating circumstances. The promising son of a distinguished Bialystok rabbi, thirteen-year-old David broke down and failed to present his haftarah at his Bar Mitzvah ceremony. Lionel was born in Queens and entered Columbia at age sixteen. He graduated in 1925 and married his wife and lifelong companion in the world of literature and leftist politics, the no less strong-willed Diana Rubin, four years later. The newlyweds moved to bohemian Greenwich Village, and Lionel helped edit *The Menorah Journal*, the small but influential publication of the Menorah Society, for young Jews, where he honed his writing skills. He taught English literature part time at Hunter College, struggling not only to support his family but his parents as well.[53] While Trilling did publish frequently in *Menorah*, he remained nervous about being perceived as a writer concerned exclusively with Jewish topics.[54] This act of self-abnegation was not uncommon in the *PR* circle, which, as the author Terry Cooney explains, "demanded a resistance to particularisms of nationality, race, religion or philosophy," and "celebrated richness, complexity, and diversity."[55] As the literary scholar Emily Budick would observe, "Jewishness, for many Jewish intellectuals from the 1930s and 1940s on, was, as it had been among European Jewish intellectuals before them, a card they played to lose, in order to win the hand and perhaps the game itself."[56]

In its earliest phase the refusal to engage with the world as Jews was simply a Marxist conceit. Sidney Hook disdainfully recalled his youthful belief that "the Jewish problem—and we all knew what that was—would be solved when the economically classless society of the future was established."[57] Alfred Kazin, who while still in his midtwenties would author a breakthrough study of nineteenth-century American literature, significantly titled *On Native Grounds* (1942), warned against "confusing the experience of being an immigrant, or an immigrant's son, with the experience of being Jewish." But Trilling went the furthest in capturing the prevailing mood of the young Jewish writer:

> I do not think of myself as a "Jewish writer." I do not have it in mind to serve by my writing any Jewish purpose. I should resent it if a critic of my work were to discover in it either faults or virtues which he called Jewish. . . . As the Jewish community now exists, it can give no sustenance to the American artist or intellectual who is born a Jew. . . . I know of no writer in English who has added a micromillimetre to his stature by "realizing his Jewishness."[58]

To a remarkable degree this generation of young Jewish intellectuals tried to live their lives according to the demanding precepts laid out by Marxist historian and philosopher Isaac Deutscher in his essay "The Non-Jewish Jew." To Deutscher the heroes of Jewish history were those thinkers who lived "on the borderlines of various civilizations, religion and national cultures" and were shaped by the "cross-fertilization of such diverse influences." They strove, "together with their non-Jewish comrades, for the universal, as against the particular, and for the internationalist as against the nationalist, solutions to the problems of their time."[59] Their cause, in Leslie Fiedler's words, was that of "universal reason" and "the dream of 'human' culture" that grew out of the Enlightenment; or in other words, liberalism at its most fully realized.[60]

In 1945 the American Jewish Committee founded *Commentary*, under the auspices of the fiercely anti-Communist Elliot Cohen, to help these young Jewish intellectuals navigate their way out of their Marxist-dominated intellectual ghettos and into the American mainstream. This "modern-day Moses," as Norman Podhoretz would call him, "wanted to lead the Jewish intelligentsia out of 'the desert of alienation'. . . and into the promised land of democratic, pluralistic, prosperous America where it would live as blessedly in its Jewishness as in its Americanness, safe and sound and forevermore, amen."[61] Just as their parents' generation on the Lower East Side shed their socialist aspirations during the war in appreciation of Franklin D. Roosevelt and the New Deal, the young intellectuals came to embrace the values and culture of America by first embracing those of a new liberalism they helped to create and define.

It is important to note that neither Trilling nor any important Jewish writer ever denied his or her Jewishness; this would have been a *shande* (cause for shame). But they consistently denied its *significance*. The Jewish historian Susanne Klingenstein views the story of Lionel Trilling's pathbreaking success in the gentile world of American letters as that of a man who "introduced the viewpoint of the Jewish rationalist into American literary criticism," and thus "managed to remain a Jew and to become one of the most celebrated figures in the American academy of his day."[62] He adopted an ironic and distanced stance toward life. "Irony," he wrote in his journal, "is the awareness with acceptance of the breach between spirit and the world of necessity—institutions, etc."[63] He found more inspiration in the teachings of Sigmund Freud than those of Karl Marx. Like Niebuhr, he was especially concerned with liberalism's weaknesses when faced with the irrationality that so frequently ruled human action.[64]

Trilling's interests lay in what he called "the dark and bloody crossroads where literature and politics meet." Like Lillian Smith, he struggled between wanting to write powerful stories and to teach important lessons but never fully realized either goal. One of Trilling's most successful stories, "The Other Margaret," published in 1945, focused on a precocious but naive young girl with a progressive worldview learned from her left-wing teachers in New York City schools. When her parents want to dismiss their black maid, the "other Margaret," who has destroyed a treasured possession in a quiet rage, the young Margaret intervenes on her behalf, blaming the woman's petty vindictiveness on social injustice: "She has to struggle so hard—against prejudice." Though her father also abhors racism, he believes that individuals can escape their social trappings and manifest what Reinhold Niebuhr termed "spiritual discipline against resentment." But at the end of the story, the heroine witnesses "the other Margaret" destroying a present she had made for her mother and concedes her father's argument. Her naïveté is no match for the power of painful reality.[65]

Trilling's only completed novel, *The Middle of the Journey*, appeared two years later. It focused on the journeys of John Laskell, an urban planner who, at thirty-three, is recovering from a life-threatening illness and decides to visit his friends Nancy and Arthur Croom, who are both fellow-traveling Popular Front leftists. Nancy is forced to confront the particularly ugly character of Duck, a man who does odd jobs for the Crooms, whose carelessness leads to his child's death. But the Popular Front fetish for a virtuous working class—captured in the "proletarian literature" of the 1930s—blinded both Crooms to his responsibility for the consequences of his drunken boorishness. "It's not his fault," Nancy Croom volunteers, though she adds, "but I couldn't stand having him around me. I'd think of it all the time. I couldn't stand seeing him. And yet it's not his fault, it's not." The author's judgment comes in his explanation that "the desire to refuse knowledge of the evil and hardness of the world can often shine in a face like a glow of youth."

Enter Gifford Maxim. Modeled after Whittaker Chambers—not yet the infamous protagonist of the Hiss-Chambers trial, whom Trilling knew through New York circles when Chambers was an editor at *Time*—Maxim approaches the Crooms to ask them to receive his mail for him, to free him to spy for the Communist Party. Like Chambers himself, Maxim is a character out of Dostoevsky, a classic absolutist who has transformed himself from a Communist apparatchik to a conservative reactionary without any stops in between. Maxim is a fanatic, but Nancy is convinced he is simply mad. John, however, comes to a different conclusion. Perhaps "we prefer not to think about the realities" of a Communist party, a common failing of liberalism at the time he was describing. Nancy cannot accept this and denounces her own "liberal shilly-shallying talk. I want to do something real. I'm so damned tired [of liberals with] their civil liberties and their Jeffersonian democracies." Maxim, meanwhile, turns to religion. Faith and fanaticism are as one in this world, and neither is available to Trilling's hero, the skeptical liberal. Trilling adds a dash of European existentialism—much in vogue with the *PR* crowd after the war—to Laskell's psychic makeup. He battles both extremes, injecting his ethics and political beliefs, as one critic observed, "with a sobered sense of possibility," and thereby becomes "a Camusian rebel of moderation."[66]

The novel was not well received. Criticized for being overly didactic and concerned more with making its points than with telling its story, Arthur Schlesinger, Jr., nevertheless found it a novelistic treatment of the argument he was trying to make in *The Vital Center*. He wrote Trilling: "Curiously enough, Maxim is so much more vital and vigorous a creation than Laskell that his questions, rather than Laskell's answers, remain in the reader's—or at least in my—mind." He recommended that "all liberals should read" what he termed "a searching and compassionate account of the liberal's dilemma of conscience in a world of absolutes."[67]

The real problem with the novel, however, was the fact that it was a Jewish story without Jews. Trilling, so fearful of failure from the start, had undermined his own talent by pretending to be something he could not be: an author in the tradition of Henry James or Henry Adams rather than the son of a long line of Bialystok rabbinical prodigies. As close as Trilling comes even to intimating a hidden Jewish background to any of the characters comes when Miss Paine, Laskell's British nurse, muses of his name, "It sounds quite English. . . ."

Laskell's mother, like Trilling's, observes the critic Adam Kirsch, "had been born in the first year of his grandparents' long English visit. But that did not make her or him English."[68]

Trilling's purpose, as he saw it, had to expose "the mentality of the Communist-oriented intelligentsia of the thirties and forties . . . presided over by an impassioned longing to believe."[69] But the "attack on the novel" deeply wounded its author, as he would later admit. "That it is gray, bloodless, intellectual, without passion, is always made with great personal feeling, with anger.—How dared I presume?"[70]

The Liberal Imagination (1950), Trilling's collection of essays written between 1940 and 1949, succeeded where his fiction had failed, and would prove itself to be one of the most influential arguments of the postwar era. Its chapters were loosely connected by the theme of "moral realism." Liberals, Trilling suggested, should hold firm to their ideals but with a sense of "dangers . . . which lie in our most generous wishes," especially the tendency to turn people into victims, to "objects of our pity, then of our wisdom, ultimately of our coercion." Liberalism, for Trilling, had a responsibility to set out "the quality of life it envisages, . . . by the sentiments it desires to affirm."[71] The role of the novel is to elevate the "moral imagination" of the reader-citizen. "Its greatness and its practical usefulness lay in its unremitting work of involving the reader himself in the moral life, inviting him to put his own motives under examination, suggesting that reality is not as his conventional education has led him to see it."[72]

Trilling believed a liberal citizen experienced a constant internal struggle of the sort Deutscher had described. "Life presses us so hard," he wrote, "time is so short, the suffering of the world is so huge, simple, unendurable—anything that complicates our moral fervor in dealing with reality as we immediately see it and wish to drive headlong upon it must be regarded with some impatience."[73] Trilling saw all humanity in a struggle between civilization's demands and its own irrational, emotional selves, and he warned against the sins of "intuition, inspiration, revelation; the annihilation of selfhood—perhaps through contemplation, but also through ecstasy and the various forms of intoxication; violence; madness."[74]

Trilling defined this new liberalism in extremely modest terms—as "a large tendency rather than a concise body of doctrine."[75] In this respect it was the opposite of Marxism, which, he wrote, combined "a kind of disgust with humanity as it is and a perfect faith in humanity as it is to be."[76] Liberalism without the corrective critique of conservatism grew "stale, habitual, and inert"; perhaps the most effective expression of liberalism was literature, because it was "the human activity that takes the fullest and most precise account of variousness, possibility, complexity, and difficulty."[77]

His eloquence notwithstanding, Trilling's liberalism suffered from a profound political flaw: it failed to inspire passion. Later in life, according to a story told by his friend Richard Sennett, when he was arguing with Trilling about the latter's maddening (to Sennett) inability to put himself clearly on one side or another of any argument, Sennett complained, "You have no position, you are always in between." "Between," Trilling replied, "is the only honest place to be."[78] Trilling's trademark phrases, his friend and colleague Jacques Barzun recalled, were "It's complicated," "It's much more complicated," and "It's very complicated."[79] One of liberalism's signature political problems is the demand—no better exemplified anywhere than in the world of Lionel Trilling—that political movements must accept such anodyne diagnoses and proceed not with excitement or enthusiasm, but with caution and modesty.

Populated almost exclusively by Jewish liberals, Hollywood at the time had its own ideas about liberalism, which had precious little in common with "complicated" notions of "irony," "moderation," and Matthew Arnold.

Hollywood's prospects looked bright as the war ended. The film historian Richard Sklar points out that "in 1946, the first full peacetime year, American movies attained the highest level of popular appeal in their half-century of existence."[80] The forties were a kind of golden age for Hollywood, as television had not yet replaced the motion picture as America's favorite form of mass entertainment. Because artists of every kind have always been interested in moving people's hearts toward visions of a better world, Hollywood has typically been populated by liberals, who have often sought to communicate their politics through their art.

Serious fare was on occasion produced by the same system that made the musicals, the love stories, and the spectacles, and the sheer numbers of well-educated people seeking entertainment at their local cinemas gave these artists considerable leeway in just how far they could take the concept of "entertainment." One such example was William Wyler's *The Best Years of Our Lives* (1946), the story of three returning veterans facing the challenges of peacetime. Its screenwriter, Robert Sherwood, had been a speechwriter for FDR.[81] Samuel Goldwyn contacted him after reading a story in *Time* about the alienation experienced by GIs coming home and wondered if there might not be a film in it.[82] Its central character, played by Dana Andrews, discovers a wife who has been unfaithful and who insists that he dress up in his uniform to impress her friends. Unable to find any other job, he suffers insults at the drugstore where he is forced to work. Another of the men finds himself pushed to deny GI loans to deserving clients and proceeds to consume massive amounts of alcohol as a result. In an especially daring move, Wyler cast nonactor Harold Russell, an actual soldier who had lost his hands in the war, as a vet struggling to find a way to reconnect with his girlfriend and family. A particularly pointed scene showed a wealthy man carrying golf clubs taking the place of a return-ing vet waiting for a flight home, a scene that led some in Congress to suggest that Sherwood be investigated for Communist sympathies.[83]

This being Hollywood, *The Best Years of Our Lives* needed a love story and a happy ending, and it got both. Somber endings were acceptable only in cer-tain circumstances, often for lone cowboys or for private detectives—the iconic archetypes that peopled the many excellent productions of film noir during the period. Other examples included Billy Wilder's *The Lost Weekend*, which depicted an alcoholic who dreams of becoming a writer and which swept the 1946 Oscars. Edward Dmytryk's *Crossfire* (1947) told the story of a deranged soldier who kills a member of his company in a fit of anti-Semitic hatred.[84] Stanley Kramer's *Home of the Brave* (1949) focused on an African American soldier discharged for a mysterious case of physical paralysis, the psychoso-matic cause of which was the brutal racism and discrimination the young man faced in the armed forces (as well as the war's horrors).[85]

Perhaps the most interesting case in liberal Hollywood of the period was that of the director Elia Kazan. Born to Anatolian Greek parents in Constan-tinople (now Istanbul), Turkey, in 1909, Kazan emigrated to New York at age four. After graduating from Williams College, he attended drama school at Yale before joining Stella Adler, Cheryl Crawford, and Harold Clurman's fa-mous Group Theatre. The Group was an extraordinarily influential troupe of actors, directors, and stagehands who pooled their money and committed themselves to creating a "social" theater that practiced the principles of "com-panionship," "security," and "a common faith."[86] Such grandiose visions were not always successful, but the Group Theatre struck gold when they decided to produce Odets's one-act play *Waiting for Lefty*. Like Kazan, Odets had se-cretly joined the Communist Party and committed himself to "put on the stage the lives of recognizable people struggling for life amidst 'petty conditions'" of Depression-era capitalism.[87] *Waiting for Lefty*, a piece of agitprop written in support of the New York taxi strike of 1934, tells the story of numerous char-acters coming to challenge the teachings of American capitalism. These in-clude a middle-class doctor who explains to the audience, "You don't believe theories until they happen to you."[88]

Kazan, meanwhile, began to chafe at the heavy-handed Communist inter-ference with the Group's productions, and was particularly miffed when a Communist Party functionary showed up and insisted that the Group "needed a little straightening out."[89] He quit the party, and while he remained active in the Group, he soon looked for opportunities outside its narrow ideological confines.[90]

After directing three of the most successful dramatic productions the the-ater world had witnessed in decades—Thornton Wilder's *The Skin of Our Teeth*, Arthur Miller's *Death of a Salesman*, and Tennessee Williams's *A Streetcar Named Desire*—Kazan became known as the "boy genius of Broadway."[91] He followed Odets to Hollywood, where his first film, *A Tree Grows in Brooklyn*, proved a touching tearjerker about a struggling family whose brilliant daugh-ter must cope with the disappointments of her alcoholic father.[92] More serious projects soon came his way, and Fox's Darryl Zanuck asked him to direct *Gentleman's Agreement*, based on Laura Hobson's 1947 novel about the scourge of polite anti-Semitism in American society. Zanuck was convinced that he could get away with the controversial subject matter if he wrapped the larger theme in a love story, but according to Kazan, "lots of rich Jews in Holly-wood" would have preferred to see the filming canceled.[93] Samuel Goldwyn, among others, asked Zanuck to drop the project, fearing that it would "stir up trouble."[94]

In the film, the gentile journalist Philip Schuyler Green, played by Gregory Peck, decides to write a magazine article about anti-Semitism by pretending to be a Jew. He experiences all manner of social slights and subtle forms of discrimination, including being turned away from a fancy hotel when he gives his Jewish-sounding name. His own girlfriend, the daughter of the owner of the magazine for which he works, starts to worry about the changes coming over him. It takes the intercession of Dave Goldman (played by the Jewish John Garfield, né Julius Garfinkle), Green's Jewish childhood friend, to show her the error of her ways.

The film was a box office hit, and in 1948, Academy voters awarded it the Best Picture Oscar and named Kazan the Best Director. Even so, he retained a low opinion of the film because he believed it merely skated over the surface of anti-Semitism and invited audiences to believe they were on the side of the angels without any commitment to changing their ways—something he found to be typical of the "liberal films" of the day.[95] It is rather significant that it made no mention of the Holocaust.[96] Ring Lardner, Jr., is one of many people credited with the quip that the movie's ultimate theme was: "Never be rude to a Jew again, because he might turn out to be a Gentile."[97]

Kazan's next film for Zanuck, 1949's *Pinky*, was about a woman who passes as white but is found out by her boyfriend. (The studio had considered the black actresses Lena Horne and Dorothy Dandridge for the lead role, which ended up going to Jeanne Crain, who was white.) When the heroine is left a fortune—despite the best efforts of a racist lawyer—the boyfriend suggests that the couple move out west, where she can continue to pass. After listening to advice from her grandmother, she decides to be what she was born, and opens up a clinic and nursery in the small southern town from which she had previously sought escape.

Kazan was no happier with *Pinky* than *Agreement* but thought the film did communicate a useful portrait of "human dignity," especially among its minor black characters.[98]

As the winds of McCarthyite fear and paranoia blew into town, films that looked patriotic during World War II suddenly stood accused of inspiring treason. Almost anything proved fodder for ideological investigation by self-appointed censors on HUAC, the House Committee on Un-American Activities. The committee was dominated by right-wing ideologues and xenophobes. One of its leading members, Mississippi's John Rankin, mused that every single member of the Soviet politburo was "either Yiddish or married to one, and that includes Stalin himself." In Rankin's view, Hollywood, dominated as it was by "long-nosed reprobates"—that is, Jews—seeking "to undermine and destroy America," was naturally at the center of the American Communist conspiracy and was as well "the greatest hotbed of subversive activities in the United States." The commie hunters were egged on by those working in the Motion Picture Alliance for the Preservation of American Ideals (MPAPAI). Founded in February 1944 in response to the "growing impression that this industry is made up of, and dominated by, Communists, radicals, and crackpots," the group capitalized on its support from the likes of John Wayne, Walt Disney, and Barbara Stanwyck.[99] Its executive director, Dr. John Lechner, insisted that he had identified "sizeable doses of Communist propaganda" in films such as *The Best Years of Our Lives*.[100] Perhaps not coincidentally, its attack mimicked that of crusading Christian evangelist Billy Graham, who termed Hollywood a "city of wickedness" and argued, "Communists are more rampant in Los Angeles than any other city in America." Its members, which grew to 7500, sometimes worked in tandem with J. Edgar Hoover's FBI agents, following the director's August 1942 order that the agency join in the Hollywood Red hunt.[101] (Screen Actors Guild president Ronald Reagan was one such informant.[102])

HUAC effectively began its Hollywood foray when, in the autumn of 1947, its members called in "friendly" witnesses such as Reagan, Robert Montgomery, and George Murphy along with members of the Motion Picture Alliance, including Ayn Rand and Adolphe Menjou and the much-beloved Gary Cooper, who complained that communism simply "wasn't on the level."[103] The still quite liberal Ronald Reagan, meanwhile, acquitted himself well with a strong condemnation of communism but a ringing defense of democracy and free speech. He closed with a warning to HUAC: "I hope we never are prompted by either fear or resentment of Communism into compromising any of our democratic principles in order to fight it."[104]

HUAC's chairman, J. Parnell Thomas, decided to go after those people whose names had come up as known Communists and demand that they, too, name the names of their associates and enablers. To this end, he subpoenaed forty-three known individuals. Of these, nineteen refused to answer questions about their associations. From this list, following a series of private negotiations—the émigré playwright Bertolt Brecht changed his mind and agreed to cooperate—the final list emerged at an even ten "unfriendly" witnesses.

In the closing days of the war, many Hollywood liberals had flocked to the newly formed Hollywood chapter of the Independent Citizens Committee of the Arts, Sciences and Professions (ICCASP), which featured Edward G. Robinson, Humphrey Bogart, and John Garfield on its executive committee. It began to disintegrate, however, in mid-1946 when the Soviets ordered all Communist Party organizations to end their Popular Front–era cooperation with liberals and began to move the organization toward an embrace of Soviet views. When Arthur Schlesinger, Jr., attacked the group in *Life* magazine as a Soviet front group, the organization fell apart in an acrimonious fight over whether or not it could issue a compelling denial that would simultaneously satisfy its liberals and radicals. It could not, and many of its liberal members drifted into the unashamedly anti-Communist ADA, which was more than happy to have them.[105]

In September 1947, in the face of the looming threat from HUAC, screenwriter Philip Dunne came up with the idea of forming a kind of successor, albeit more narrowly focused, organization to be called the Committee for the First Amendment (CFA), which would stand for the right to free cultural expression. He was joined by a who's who of Hollywood liberalism, most crucially, Humphrey Bogart. The actor who personified so many of liberalism's values during the 1940s recorded an announcement for the committee that included the words "This is Humphrey Bogart. Is democracy so feeble that it can be subverted merely by a look or a line, an inflection, a gesture?" He concluded by asserting that Congress had no right "to dictate what Americans shall think."[106] Fredric March, who had recently won an Oscar for his role in *The Best Years of Our Lives*, asked radio listeners, "Who's next? Is it your minister who will be told what he can say in the pulpit? . . . This reaches into every American city and town."[107]

To show its support for the free speech rights of the accused "unfriendlies," now termed the "Hollywood Ten," the CFA organized a group to travel to Washington to protest HUAC's investigations. But the members of the Hollywood Ten proved less interested in what they considered to be liberal platitudes on behalf of the Constitution and free speech than with exposing what they believed to be the "Fascist" threat to America represented by HUAC and the rest of the Red hunters. Rather than go to the CFA for support, they looked to the Progressive Citizens of America, the pro-Soviet organization that eventually morphed into Henry Wallace's presidential campaign. Their primary spokesperson, John Howard Lawson, was a barrel-chested Communist writer who never deviated from the party line and ran the Hollywood operation under direction from the party's national headquarters in New York, which was itself subservient to Moscow. The showdown between Thomas and Lawson, with its fist and gavel pounding, began on October 27, 1947, and generated just the controversy that Thomas sought, with Lawson playing the heavy and Parnell remaining the picture of good manners. (Ironically, Thomas would later claim the protection of the Fifth Amendment for himself during a trial in which he was convicted of fraud and sentenced to imprisonment with members of the Hollywood Ten.[108]) In November, the ten were accused of contempt of Congress and instructed that they would face formal proceedings before the entire House of Representatives.

When, at a CFA press conference that followed the hearing, a journalist shouted out, "Either you're for the commies or you're against them," Dunne retorted, "It's being for the Constitution or against it."[109] Numerous newspapers featured commentaries condemning the CFA as naive and politically ignorant outsiders at best, or as Communist stooges at worst. Bogart, under pressure from Jack Warner but also shocked at the anger and militance that characterized Lawson's performance, flipped overnight. Privately furious, he was heard screaming, "You fuckers sold me out!"[110] Publicly contrite, he explained to the press, "I went to Washington because I thought fellow Americans were being deprived of their Constitutional rights, and for that reason alone. That the trip was ill-advised, even foolish, I am very ready to admit. I am not a Communist."[111] When John Huston abandoned the CFA as well, director William Wyler told fellow members, "I guess it's no use. We oughta fold."[112]

The Motion Picture Association of America (MPAA) head, Eric Johnston, worried that public opinion was turning against not just CFA but Hollywood itself. The American Legion threatened a boycott. An audience in Chapel Hill, North Carolina, stoned the screen of a movie theater showing a Katharine Hepburn film. (She had been prominently featured as a supporter of the Committee for the First Amendment.[113]) This combination of vigilante action and public opinion frightened Hollywood's executives right into the arms of HUAC. Shortly after the disastrous hearing, a group of studio heads gathered at the Waldorf Astoria in New York to discuss the issue. While Johnston had earlier rejected the idea of a blacklist, he was now faced with a serious problem: recalcitrant ex-Communist screenwriters were unwilling to cooperate with the authorities, but the studios needed to find a way to pick and choose those writers and actors whose work they needed, and thus find a way to clear some radicals while effectively throwing the rest to the Red-hunting wolves.[114] The notion of *self*-policing—and what author Michael Wilson would term "the intimidation of a company town"—began to look more appealing.[115] Those assembled at the Waldorf concurred and endorsed a swift rebuke of the unfriendlies. The producers issued a statement in which they "deplore the action of the ten Hollywood men who have been cited for contempt" and announced they would not "knowingly employ a Communist or a member of any party or group which advocates the overthrow of the Government of the United States by force or by illegal or unconstitutional methods." Though they paid lip service to the ideals of "free speech and a free screen," they were, in reality, embracing the ethos of the blacklist.[116]

Within days, the socially conscious Hollywood film became an endangered species, and the sorts of projects that had inspired so much pride just a few years earlier were quickly abandoned.[117] Those who suffered most were actors with left-wing backgrounds, who found it difficult to find jobs once accused. *Counterattack,* a blacklist publication, accused Fredric March of propagating the Communist line "on eight separate occasions, starting October 17, 1947, and continuing to pound" that message "until March 5, 1948."[118] Elia Kazan later recalled March's wife explaining that after being "under assault by . . . *Counterattack* . . . the calls for Freddie's services could be 'counted on the fingers of one hand, with a finger or two left over.'"[119] Myrna Loy, who played March's spouse in *The Best Years of Our Lives,* saw her career suffer as well. Named as a Communist by the *Hollywood Reporter,* Loy found herself working primarily for UNESCO in the early fifties.[120]

A similar fate awaited many of those with roles in *Gentleman's Agreement*. Anne Revere, who played Gregory Peck's mother, refused to testify and didn't appear in another film for twenty years. John Garfield found himself hounded by HUAC as well. Though married to a party member, Garfield himself claimed that the Communist Party wouldn't take him, and he remained merely a fellow traveler. When Garfield appeared before HUAC later in 1951, he was so desperate to avoid the blacklist that he swore his support to outlawing the party and authored an unpublished article titled, "I Was a Sucker for a Left Hook." Refusing to testify against his wife, however, Garfield left Hollywood and returned to Broadway, where he died of heart failure at thirty-nine.[121]

In their defense, most Hollywood liberals might have believed themselves justified in concluding that they had been correct to refuse to risk their own careers in solidarity with the Communists in their midst, as the historian Jennifer Delton argues, "not because they feared them, not because they were hysterical, but because liberal principles were more effectively promoted by purging Communists than by defending their rights."[122] Sadly, the victim was the right of free speech itself. Admitting defeat, Philip Dunne explained that the blacklist "could not have been imposed if a few misguided souls had not provided the witch-hunters with" a "fatal linkage" between naive liberals and the dishonest Communists who manipulated them.[123] Liberal anticommunism, which respected the civil liberties of its opponents and did not fall prey to hysterical scare tactics, repeatedly found itself steamrollered by the more potent conservative forces. The liberal was now the man (or woman) in the middle who was standing precariously between fanatic extremes. Motivated by passion for social justice and appreciation of the complexity of defending unpopular views in the face of not only an outbreak of hysteria in the general public but also large-scale duplicity on the part of the accused, the liberal's stance was on shaky ground indeed. The liberal values of Smith, Trilling, Kazan, and company, based on a commitment to tolerance, fairness, moderation, and empathy, were never more necessary in America, but rarely more difficult to practice.

6

The Two Joes

I am beginning to think that if you have been a liberal, if you believe that those who are strong must sometimes consider the weak, and that with strength and power goes responsibility, automatically some people consider you a Communist.

—Eleanor Roosevelt[1]

Following the resignation of the onetime Red hunter Richard Nixon at the end of the Watergate affair, anticommunism itself fell into a brief but profound disrepute in much of America. Cold War liberals took it on the chin, as revisionist historians viewed their actions through the prism of Watergate and Vietnam. The British left-wing author David Caute, documenting the extensive damage McCarthyism had done to American politics, wrote, "Although the Cold War liberals were by no means in the vanguard of the forces pressing for the domestic purge, without doubt their obsessive anti-Sovietism blinded them."[2] The distinguished intellectual historian Richard Pells concurred, writing, "In one form or another, and with varying degrees of sophistication [liberal intellectuals] counseled or practiced collaboration—not as a matter of expediency, not so as to save their own or anyone else's career, but on principle." Pells added: "Unlike the terrified and now apolitical inhabitants of Hollywood, the intellectuals who adopted this stance were politically knowledgeable and philosophically resourceful. They should have known better."[3]

In the face of the threats emanating from "the two Joes"—Stalin and McCarthy—liberals found themselves caught in a decidedly difficult cunundrum. Stalin, it would turn out, would prove perhaps the single most heinous mass murderer in human history. But he lacked the capability to threaten the United States in any significant fashion, save symbolically. Senator McCarthy, on the other hand, did cause tremendous damage to the nation's politics, culture, and constitutional liberties, but he possessed no armies, no secret prisons, and no means of visiting physical violence on anyone. The damage was genuine, to be certain, but it was hardly comparable to the horrors Stalin wrought upon his millions of victims.

Moreover, the presence of Communists in the State Department and other branches of the U.S. government, to say nothing of their dominant role in the 1948 Wallace campaign, created significant discomfort for liberals, and many felt it necessary to demonstrate, repeatedly, that they were the "right" sort of liberal, the kind who could be trusted not to worry too much about the rights or welfare of accused Communists. Because the Communist Party refused to defend itself openly but instead resorted to evasion, obfuscation, and outright dishonesty when called to account for itself by Congress and other authorities, liberals found it almost impossible to come up with a position that gave simultaneous credence both to the precariousness of their political position as well as to their stated political principles.

In 1954, for instance, just as McCarthy was beginning his decline, Hubert Humphrey introduced the Communist Control Act in the Senate, which would declare the Communist Party "the agency of a hostile foreign power . . . an instrumentality of a conspiracy to overthrow the Government of the U.S." The bill would have made membership in the party punishable by a five-year prison sentence. Arthur Schlesinger, Jr., condemned Humphrey's act as "hasty and reckless."[4] (As early as 1948, Humphrey admitted that if he had had "to choose between being called a Red-baiter and traitor, I'll be a Red-baiter."[5]) ADA would eventually call for a presidential veto. Liberal pandering ultimately had its limits, though just what and where these were was often difficult to determine.

Right-wing anti-Communists had long argued that liberalism nurtured communism, that one was merely a gateway drug to the other. HUAC initiated its investigation of "un-American Activities" in the 1930s in order to discredit the New Deal. Joseph McCarthy began his career battling price controls and public housing, both continuations of policies originating with the New Deal. McCarthyites sought to sow fear of a liberal fifth column working hand in glove with the Communists to undermine America's defenses, morally and culturally as well as politically and militarily. At the very least, McCarthy and his followers insisted, liberals provided political cover—sometimes purposely, sometimes naively—for those "Communists within our borders [who] have been more responsible for the success of Communism abroad than Soviet Russia."[6]

McCarthy's triumph had many roots. The ex-Communist intellectual James Rorty called him "a kind of monstrous political robot unequipped with steering mechanism or reverse gear."[7] Much of his authority, however, derived from its appeal to Americans' deeply felt religious worldview. Catholicism, in particular, became imbued with right-wing anti-Communism during this period under the leadership of such church figures as New York's Francis Cardinal Spellman.[8] ("Only the batblind can fail to be aware of the Communist invasion of our country," he pronounced. [9]) McCarthyism enjoyed evangelical support as well: Billy Graham concluded that communism was a "tool of Satan" and also supported McCarthy.[10]

Paranoia was a key ingredient. In the McCarthyite mind-set, Communists were everywhere, pulling invisible strings and controlling institutions to a degree beyond anyone's comprehension.

McCarthy also lashed out at "the traitorous actions of those who have been treated so well by this Nation. It has not been the less fortunate or members of minority groups who have been selling this Nation out, but rather those who have had all the benefits that the wealthiest nation on earth has had to offer—the finest homes, the finest college education, and the finest jobs in Government we can give."[11] The enemy in this perspective was "elitists," meaning liberal establishmentarians and those perceived to be. As one scholar of McCarthyism has suggested, "the image of the enemy was *not* the Russian spy, but . . . the American intellectual with an Ivy League accent."[12] This right-wing populist resentment gave rise to America's postwar culture war—elites versus ordinary citizens—that would frame American politics from then on and would prove to be conservatives' fail-safe option and single most politically effective weapon whenever their political fortunes faded. When, during the 2004 presidential primary season, the conservative Club for Growth ran advertisements attacking ex-Vermont governor Howard Dean as the candidate of a "tax-hiking, government-expanding, latte-drinking, sushi-eating, Volvo-driving, *New York Times*-reading, body-piercing, Hollywood-loving, left-wing freak show," it was deploying virtually the very same stereotype, half a century later.[13]

The year 1949 was the beginning of the domination of the extremist version of American anticommunism in the nation's popular imagination. It began with the shock of Mao's victory over the U.S.-backed Nationalists and the ensuing "loss" of China. Dean Rusk compared the country's reaction to "that of a jilted lover."[14] That same year the Soviet Union exploded its first atomic bomb, followed shortly by the trials of accused spies Alger Hiss and Klaus Fuchs. Soon enough the country descended into what Supreme Court justice William O. Douglas would call a "black silence of fear" coupled with an obsessive search for secret culprits and hidden causes.[15] Conservative columnist

David Lawrence, the founder of *U.S. News & World Report*, compared McCarthyite "tactics used in ferreting out the subversives" to "bombing military targets—it is too bad if some of the civilians near the military installations get hurt, but they have no business being there . . . no business getting mixed up with subversive groups at all."[16]

One can find no better illustration of the dilemma facing liberals in this period than the infamous Hiss/Chambers Affair and its ensuing two trials, which resulted in the conviction of the liberal establishment darling Alger Hiss for perjury, and by implication, for being a Soviet spy. The shy, socially inept Whittaker Chambers had been a member of a Communist espionage cell during the 1930s before converting to a deeply religious and somewhat fanatical anticommunism and going to work for Henry Luce at *Time*. While Whittaker Chambers was described by Richard Nixon as "one of the most disheveled persons I have ever seen"[17] and by Alistair Cooke as "a fat, sad-looking man in a baggy blue suit," Alger Hiss would, in Cooke's estimation, prove an apt subject for "Henry James: a product of New World courtesy, with a gentle certitude of behavior, a ready warmth."[18] Raised fatherless in genteel poverty, Hiss made his way to Johns Hopkins followed by Harvard Law School. After serving in various New Deal posts, he had been recommended for the presidency of the Carnegie Endowment for International Peace by John Foster Dulles in 1946, and served as its president from 1946 to 1949, having been named by Secretary of State George Marshall as vice chair of a "citizen's committee" to celebrate the United Nations.[19]

Following his conversion experience, Chambers came to believe "that between the years 1930 and 1948, a group of almost unknown men and women, Communists or close fellow travelers, or their dupes, working in the United States government . . . affected the future of every American now alive. . . . If mankind is about to suffer one of its decisive transformations, if it is about to close its 2000-year-old experience of Christian civilization, and enter upon another wholly new and diametrically different, then that group may claim a part in history."[20] While Chambers's confession of his past, he acknowledged, would "no doubt continue to darken" his efforts to integrate himself "into the community of free men," it would be a small price to pay if he helped free America "from the grips of a secret, sinister, and enormously powerful force whose tireless purpose is their enslavement."[21]

As the young Richard Nixon explained to his HUAC colleagues, Hiss, who had been to Yalta as a midlevel State Department functionary, had conspired with the Soviets to sell out Poland and Eastern Europe by passing U.S. military secrets to the Russians. He then prevailed on his president, considerably weakened by illness, stress, and exhaustion and unable to resist the ministrations of a wily secret Communist, to set up a Communist takeover in China. The committee's acting chairman, Karl Mundt of South Dakota, accordingly announced, "There is reason to believe that he [Hiss] organized within the [State] department one of the Communist cells which endeavored to influence our Chinese policy and bring about the condemnation of Chiang Kai-shek."[22]

Meanwhile, Harry Truman decided to step into the proceedings by publicly mocking HUAC, accusing it of "slandering a lot of people who don't deserve it," and of creating a "red herring." Following Hiss's own rebuttal, the president took his attacks a step further: By giving voice to "wild and false accusation" against Hiss, HUAC, along with the Republican Party, Truman said, had become the "unwitting ally of the Communists in this country."[23] When Hiss demanded the right to confront his accuser outside the confines of a congressional committee—where libel and slander were protected by the constitution—the battle lines were drawn.

Alger Hiss's 1949 trial for perjury, which rested on his accusation that Chambers had invented the entire story of the two men's past espionage exploits, proved to be the first great political media trial of the postwar era. Alistair Cooke titled his account of the proceedings *Generation on Trial*.[24] "So we find this traitor hobnobbing through the years with the mightiest of the New Deal mighty," bellowed editors of *The Chicago Tribune*: "He advises the president. He is the favored protégé of two men who are kingmakers within the bureaucracy. One of them, Felix Frankfurter, is a man who moves the members of his personal entourage into ever greater posts of power and influence. He is the patron saint of Hiss." It concluded, "The guilt is collective" and "spreads over the New Deal, which sponsored and protected this monstrous conspiracy against America."[25]

In one of the great moments of historical anticlimax, the first jury returned deadlocked. Congressman Nixon immediately took to the airwaves and demanded an inquiry into Judge Samuel H. Kaufman's "fitness" for his position. The junior Republican representative and member of the bar admitted that while Judge Kaufman may have been on strong legal ground for his various rulings, "the average American wanted all the technicalities waived in this case."[26] On January 21, 1950, following a retrial under Judge Henry Goddard, the jurors found Hiss guilty of perjury, and by implication, of espionage as well. Secretary of State Acheson cited the Sermon on the Mount on behalf of Hiss, inspiring a tidal wave of right-wing anger and demands for his resignation (which he offered to Truman, who refused it). On the floor of the Senate, South Dakota Republican Karl Mundt blamed the fall of China on the "considerable coterie of Communist sympathizers in the Far Eastern Division of the State Department," who owed their allegiance not to America but to Alger Hiss.[27] Another senator, the junior member of the body from Wisconsin, Joseph McCarthy, wondered if Acheson's "most fantastic statement" meant he would also not "turn his back on other Communists who were associated with Hiss?"[28] Meanwhile, Representative Richard Nixon topped them all with a virtuoso four-hour performance, in which he explained that "five years ago, when Alger Hiss was arranging postwar conferences," the Soviet orbit drew in only 180 million people and "the odds were nine to one in our favor." Now 800 million souls lived "under the domination of Soviet totalitarianism" and "the odds are five to three against us." Closing with a dramatic flourish, he urged, "We owe a solemn duty to expose this sinister conspiracy for what it is."[29]

With an initial printing of a hundred thousand, serialization and promotion in a special edition of *The Saturday Evening Post*, and four full pages in *Time*, Chambers's subsequent memoir and morality tale of betrayal and redemption, *Witness*, was published in 1952. It dominated the top spot of *The New York Times* bestseller lists for nearly four months and would serve as an inspirational text for conservatives throughout the twentieth century.[30] Despite its equation of liberals with Communists, and Communists with spies, leftist luminaries, including Sidney Hook in *The New York Times Book Review* and Philip Rahv in *Partisan Review*, celebrated the book's publication.[31]

Meanwhile, just weeks after Hiss's conviction, Klaus Fuchs, a German refugee scientist who had worked on the Manhattan Project, was arrested for spying for the Soviets, a case that eventually led to the arrest of Julius and Ethel Rosenberg.[32] In June of 1950, North Korea invaded the South, and as Arthur Schlesinger, Jr., would later observe, "As long as our boys were getting killed by the Communists over there, people felt in a lynch-mob mood about Communists at home."[33] The Hollywood Ten were sent to jail, their judicial appeals having failed, and shortly thereafter, Julius and Ethel Rosenberg were arrested for helping the Soviets steal secret information relating to the manufacture of atomic weaponry. The result was an even more spectacular trial, though one in which liberals were loath to defend the accused.[34]

Shortly after the Hiss/Chambers trial ended, Joe McCarthy was scheduled to speak to the Ohio County Republican Women's Club of Wheeling, West Virginia. He had planned to address questions related to aid to the elderly or housing issues, but at the last minute he decided to borrow material from Nixon's impressive post-Hiss trial summation. "Alger Hiss," he told the women, "is important not as an individual anymore, but rather because he is so representative of a group in the State Department." He complained of "the traitorous actions of those who have been treated so well by this Nation"and then revealed his infamous list of 205 Communists "still working and shaping policy in the State Department."[35] The following day the figure had dropped to only 57 and fluctuated wildly thereafter.[36] Upon launching a national speaking tour immediately afterward, he boasted that he had "a sockful of shit—and knew how to use it."[37]

McCarthy soon became the second most influential Republican in America after President Eisenhower, who, significantly, declined to criticize him. As chairman of the influential Government Operations Committee and, soon, the Permanent Subcommittee on Investigations, he could demand fealty from virtually any government agency, and his energetic and equally obsessive staff, headed by the young lawyer Roy Cohn, used this power to ferret out liberals and other alleged "subversives" anywhere they imagined they could find one.

McCarthy's fall came swiftly. His judgment frequently impaired by alcohol, the senator opened a door that led to his own demise when, in 1953, he decided to go after not Hollywood starlets or State Department librarians, but four-star generals. McCarthy began leveling wild accusations against Irving Peress, a dentist with a Communist background who had been discharged from Camp Kilmer in New Jersey and implicated his commanding officer, General Ralph Zwicker. McCarthy lectured Zwicker: "You are a disgrace to the uniform. You're shielding Communist conspirators. You're not fit to be an officer. You're ignorant."[38] This time, unfortunately, he was up against a debonair, dignified lawyer hired by the Army, Joseph Welch, who consistently demanded that McCarthy support his allegations.[39] When McCarthy attacked a young lawyer on his staff, Welch cornered the squirming accuser, and in one of the most emotionally satisfying moments in the history of political schadenfreude, especially for liberals, he said, more in sorrow than in anger: "Until this moment, Senator, I think I never really gauged your cruelty or your recklessness. . . . Let us not assassinate this lad further, Senator. Have you left no sense of decency?"[40] When the gallery erupted in applause, it was clear that the monster had been slain. It took another seven months, but McCarthy was finally censured by his colleagues in the Senate in December of that year.

Liberals fought against, or capitulated to, McCarthyism in varying degrees. The toughest response naturally came from those who felt most secure in their status. Eleanor Roosevelt opposed him without hesitation or equivocation. In her editorials she condemned the idea of "thought crime" and the use of smear tactics.[41] Harry Truman, Murray Kempton observed at the time, was "gam-

bling that McCarthy [was] an overrated punk." The president had called Mc-
Carthy a "political gangster" who came from the "political underworld" and
who put forth a "big lie"[42] and even commissioned a staffer to do a study of
"hysteria and witch-hunting" in the American past.[43] William O. Douglas
derided the manner in which McCarthyism had been allowed to "narrow the
range of permissible discussion and permissible thought."[44]

Such unambiguous condemnations were rare, however. Literary critic Leslie Fiedler saw McCarthyism as an extension of much of the nation's historic
"distrust of authority, institutions, and expert knowledge," which fed off a
"populist conviction" with deep strains in the American grain. As such, it was
not easily counterattacked.[45] This concern also underlay the influential response of historian Richard Hofstadter, who, as much as anyone, helped liberals to sort out their feelings about the simultaneously frightening and perplexing
phenomenon.

Hofstadter, the son of a Polish Jewish father and a German Lutheran
mother, was raised in Buffalo, New York. He studied philosophy at the State
University at Buffalo, where he joined up with the Young Communist League
before attending Columbia University and spending some time with worker
cooperatives in the South. He joined the party in 1938, but shortly thereafter
found himself unable to accept the Nazi-Soviet nonagression pact and resigned right after its 1939 announcment (though he continued, he said, to
"hate capitalism and everything that goes with it").[46] Hofstadter moved from
the University of Maryland to Columbia, where he became a celebrated professor of history and author of a number of seminal bestselling tracts of liberal,
political, and philosophical inquiry.[47] Like his close friend Arthur Schlesinger,
Jr., Hofstadter shared a commitment to New Deal/Fair Deal-style liberalism
and its internationalist commitment via the American Committee for Cultural
Freedom. But in decided contrast to his friend, he remained purposely detached from political engagement.[48]

When the Red Scare erupted, Hofstadter was naturally concerned about
his own vulnerability as a former party member. He tried to explain rather
than challenge McCarthyism, and his arguments offer considerable insight
into the fears among once-radical, now liberal intellectuals of the time. For
Hofstadter, McCarthyism represented an almost predictable expression of
America's native "anti-intellectualism," a term his work popularized during the 1950s. Right-wing populist attacks on academe demonstrated "popular power's habitual suspicion of gifted minds."[49] He worried, in 1953, that
"everywhere in America, intellectuals are on the defensive" against the
forces of "populistic democracy."[50] He called McCarthy and his followers

pseudoconservatives who merely pandered to "the less educated members of the middle class" who were motivated by what he so memorably named "status anxiety," a persistent theme he professed to detect throughout American history."[51] (Ten years later, Hofstadter would extend these ideas to define what he called the "Paranoid Style in American Politics," a concept whose political relevance has only increased with time.[52]) "In a populistic culture like ours, which seems to lack a responsible elite with political and moral autonomy, and in which it is possible to exploit the wildest currents of public sentiment for private purposes," he warned, a year after McCarthy's Senate censure, "it is at least conceivable that a highly organized, vocal, active, and well-financed minority could create a political climate in which the rational pursuit of our well-being and safety would become impossible."[53]

In 1954 a symposium on anticommunism held at Columbia University resulted in a collection of essays, titled *The New American Right* (1955), that would constitute a crucial text in the history of liberalism. The contributors, especially Hofstadter, Daniel Bell, and David Riesman, were largely liberals who shared a belief that the psychological dimension of political belief mattered as much as its rational aspects—and indeed, far more so when it came to a matter like McCarthyism. Drawing upon the work of the neo-Marxist Frankfurt school scholar Theodor Adorno, Hofstadter argued that the "authoritarian personality" type who followed McCarthy believed "himself to be living in a world in which he is spied upon, plotted against, betrayed, and very likely destined for total ruin." Hofstadter reasoned that there was not much that could be done to stymie such a force in American politics.[54] In his essay, "Interpretations of American Politics," Bell argued that McCarthy had crossed a line when he started to smear the anti-Communist liberals in ADA, thereby transforming "issues into ideologies" and investing them "with moral color and high emotional charge" that made the "pragmatic give-and-take" of successful democratic politics all but impossible.[55] But liberals were hard pressed to find a politically effective response. As David Riesman and Nathan Glazer pointed out in their essay, "The Intellectuals and the Discontented Classes," liberal intellectuals had been "silenced more by their own feelings of inadequacy and failure than by direct intimidation." They held out little hope for any immediate relief from the irrational turn American politics had taken, as "intelligence without force or enthusiasm facing force" was no match for "enthusiasm without intelligence."[56]

These arguments reflected liberals' increasing distrust of mass democracy. "Mass politics" and "mass man" needed to be contained, as Daniel Bell suggested, by a democratic system that allowed "educated elites" to "mediate between the passions of the people and the realistic needs of a modern democracy." Reinhold Niebuhr, criticizing the views of his younger socialist self, added, "The rise of totalitarianism has prompted the democratic world to view all collectivist answers to our social problems with increased apprehension."[57]

The problem these liberals highlighted left them baffled not only about how to respond but also about what to propose as an alternative. Their political paralysis revealed itself further when the HUAC investigators turned their attention back to Hollywood in 1951. In came a new set of witnesses, including the ailing John Garfield and Fredric March. But most famous of all was Elia Kazan, who was, at the time, riding high on a wave of almost unmatched commercial and artistic success.

Kazan was well aware that his past associations with the Group Theatre and the Communist Party might result in an invitation from HUAC. When the summons came, he traveled to Washington, D.C., in mid-January 1952, in considerable anguish about what he would say to the committee. His first appearance was fairly perfunctory, and while he confessed to belonging to numerous front organizations, he informed the committee that he would not identify any of his fellow party members in the Group if asked.

It was at his second appearance, the following April, that Kazan decided to name names: "I believed it was the duty of the government to investigate the Communist movement in our country." As he later explained, "I believed that this committee, which everyone scorned—I had plenty against them, too—had a proper duty. I wanted to help break open the secrecy."[58] Kazan disagreed with the refusal of the Hollywood Ten—the "unfriendlies"—to come clean about their own Communist connections, whether past or present, and disapproved of their "contemptuous attitude" toward America's elected public officials.[59] Kazan had also come to believe that he had a responsibility to inform on people who colluded with the Soviet Union, whose repressive regime he had come to abhor.

Not surprisingly, perhaps, it was Kazan's frequent collaborator in art and politics, Budd Schulberg, who would make this case for cooperating most eloquently. Schulberg, whose screenplay for *On the Waterfront* (1954) came to be viewed as an extended metaphorical argument in favor of collaboration with the committee as well as the singular masterpiece of Kazan's career, admitted just before his own testimony that he had "felt guilty for having contributed unwittingly to intellectual and artistic as well as racial oppression" with his youthful support for Stalin and the USSR.[60]

Kazan gave HUAC a list of Group Theatre Communist Party members but "carefully avoiding naming anyone he might have suspected or known to be

Communists at a later period."[61] That decision changed the director's life forever, as with time HUAC grew increasingly shamed and discredited. Kazan, many liberals felt, had had the power to challenge not just HUAC but the blacklist itself. Instead, he protected his celebrity and his ability to work while those who stood up to the committee were jailed, ruined, or both. A few committed suicide and more than a few destroyed themselves with drink or drugs.[62] Kazan exacerbated the situation by purchasing and publishing an alternately self-pitying and self-justifing full-page advertisement in *The New York Times* to try to make his case for cooperation with the committee, arguing that "liberals must speak out."[63] In doing so, he effectively embraced a consistent conservative trope in American history: an insistence that liberals needed to prove their loyalty to America and the ideals for which it stood in a way conservatives never did and would never have to.

As with everything related to McCarthyism, liberals were bitterly divided by the course Kazan took. His friend Arthur Miller, who had never been a party member himself but was a particularly energetic fellow traveler, followed an alterative path. Also abjuring the Fifth Amendment defense as unmanly, Miller made the argument that the First Amendment gave him the right to speak via his own silence. (Miller was fined, a ruling that was later overturned.)[64] This stance was a riskier one at the time and so garnered him considerably more respect in artistic circles. In his masterful study of the period, *Naming Names* (1980), Victor Navasky tells the story (possibly apocryphal) of Miller's sending his 1955 play, *A View from the Bridge*—a harsh telling of the story of a Sicilian police informant who dishonors himelf within the tight-knit world of New York's waterfront—to the director. "I have read your play and would be honored to direct," Kazan may or may not have wired back. "You don't understand," went Miller's possible reply. "I didn't send it to you because I wanted you to direct it. I sent it to you because I wanted you to know what I think of stool pigeons."[65]

In a defense of Kazan, Arthur Schlesinger, Jr., asked *Nation* magazine readers: If the director "had been an ex-Nazi or even an ex-Klansman, telling the same story, would not *The Nation*'s reaction have been completely different?"[66] Schlesinger added, however, that the entire project of hunting for Communists in Hollywood was absurd and distracting. "The Communists themselves never looked sillier than when they were exposing Russian clowns or were detecting 'bourgeois tendencies' in Soviet circuses; and I should hate to see Americans imitating the Soviet Union in this respect."[67]

Quick to denounce anticommunism's abuses, without challenging the principle itself, Schlesinger differentiated, in classic liberal fashion, between ideas and actions. He reminded Americans of the famous "clear and present danger rule" in dealing with incendiary ideas: spies working in the U.S. government presented a "clear and present danger," but caution had to be exercised when dealing with such matters, as the demand for loyalty could turn too quickly to a demand for conformity. Liberals, Schlesinger insisted, had to respect traditional democratic methods of debate," even in the face of dangerous ideas. "In our detestation of Communism, we must not . . . do irreparable harm to our American heritage of freedom. . . . The important thing is to preserve the right to free discussion. This right includes the right to hold loathsome ideas."[68]

But neither was Schlesinger a paragon of principle during this period. He fought within ADA to soften the organization's condemnations of the Smith Act (1940), which was supposed to prevent speech that advocated the violent overthrow of the U.S. government but was widely used to silence suspected Communists, ex-Communists, and sometimes merely garden-variety liberals, because he feared that the organization would look soft on spying.[69] As Daniel Bell pointed out decades later, "What the Communists could have done was say, 'Yes, I'm a communist, and I will go to jail for my opinions.' In effect, justify themselves as people having beliefs. But they didn't. And they were trying to manipulate the situation by scaring the liberals, by saying, 'You see? We're under attack, and then you'll be under attack!'"[70] Issue after issue arose during this period for which liberals had no ready response, given their confusion about principle versus political palatability, coupled with their understandable refusal to appear to be on the side of people who were arguing deceptively on behalf of a cause they found abhorrent. Schlesinger wound up quarreling with Sidney Hook over the firing of Communist schoolteachers, which was hardly a merely theoretical question, given the left-wing orientation of so many urban teachers' unions. In New York City alone 321 schoolteachers and 58 college instructors lost their jobs either because of past Communist affiliations or because of their refusal to comply with investigators.[71]

Taking a position he termed "Heresy, Yes, Conspiracy, No," Hook argued that a "member of the Communist Party has transgressed the canons of academic responsibility, has engaged his intellect to servility, and is therefore professionally disqualified from performing his functions as scholar and teacher." Schlesinger accepted the idea that if teachers used their position to indoctrinate students, they were professionally incompetent and did not deserve to teach. He was especially concerned when it came to K-12 education, believing that college students had the wherewithal to see through propaganda. Nonetheless, Schlesinger parsed the issue and concluded that "membership in a subversive group" did not "ipso facto make the individual an obedient agent of that group."[72]

Though it hedged on the Smith Act, Americans for Democratic Action fought McCarthy on many fronts, albeit not always head-on. They demanded investigations of his shadowy finances and fund-raising practices.[73] ADA threw its support to Democratic senator William Benton of Connecticut, who was one of the very few to oppose McCarthy in the Senate (and who subsequently went down to electoral defeat).[74] Though McCarthy made no serious effort to expose any actual Communist spies, a successful demonstration of his demagogic intent was not an easy task. The fact that McCarthy was a duly elected U.S. senator made his pronouncements legitimate news, regardless of how little he cared about getting his facts correct. He would typically schedule his announcements for the late afternoon, leaving journalists with little time to search out the truth, or even obtain a response from anyone being accused. Because he was such a rich source of news, McCarthy enjoyed the favor of many reporters and editors, despite their tacit acknowledgment of his nefarious tactics. After all, the man sold newspapers.[75]

The hero of the story, as journalists tend to tell it, was CBS's Edward R. Murrow.[76] The case for Murrow's heroism rests exclusively on the *See It Now* show he hosted on March 9, 1954, one month before the Army hearings began. At considerable risk to the network, Murrow exposed the senator's methods and closed with the remarks: "This is no time for men who oppose Senator McCarthy's methods to keep silent. . . . We proclaim ourselves, as indeed we are, the defenders of freedom—wherever it exists in the world—but we cannot defend freedom by deserting it at home. The actions of the junior Senator from Wisconsin have caused alarm and dismay among our allies abroad and given considerable comfort to our enemies. And whose fault is that? He didn't create this situation of fear. He merely exploited it, and rather successfully."[77]

CBS owner William Paley was so nervous about allowing his reporter to criticize McCarthy—even though similar stories had already appeared in *The New York Times* and elsewhere—that he turned over an hour of network prime time for the senator's rebuttal. Looking sweaty and nervous, McCarthy denounced Murrow as "the leader and the cleverest of the jackal pack which is always found at the throat of anyone who dares to expose individual Communists and traitors." With that he managed to hold the allegiance of over a third of those polled, who had concluded that "Edward R. Murrow was either a Communist or a Communist sympathizer."[78]

Less well remembered is a much earlier stand taken by Jimmy Wechsler. Just one month after McCarthy's Wheeling speech, the ex-Communist *New*

York Post editor and ADA founder, wrote: "Day by day the undivided attention of a Senate committee is being held by the reckless, irresponsible outcries of a dreary character whose disrespect for human beings is equaled only by his disregard for facts."[79] Wechsler, in truth, didn't have much to risk: the *Post* enjoyed a largely liberal (and heavily Jewish) readership, and its owner, Dorothy "Dolly" Schiff, a onetime intimate of Franklin D. Roosevelt, didn't worry about advertiser reaction, because anyone who bought space in the paper was already well aware of its pugnacious reputation.[80]

In September 1951, the paper ran a series of articles titled "Smear Inc.," raising questions about any number of incidents in McCarthy's past, including potential income tax evasion, his personal and political dishonesty, and his former alliances with Fascists and known anti-Semites—not to mention his complete ineffectiveness in locating any actual spies.[81] Two years after the series ran, and with the witch hunts still in full force, Wechsler was called before the committee. On April 24, 1953, he went to Washington, D.C., and participated in what his colleague Max Lerner would call "one of the most dramatic clashes of personality and views in the history of Congressional hearings."[82]

Wechsler began by asking McCarthy why, in a closed hearing, he had a journalist, Howard Rushmore, sitting next to him. He received no response. When Wechsler sought to demonstrate his bona fides as an anti-Communist, pointing to his exposé of the 1948 Wallace campaign, McCarthy was unmoved.[83] When McCarthy raised the topic of Roy Cohn and David Schine's investigation of United States Information Service libraries abroad, Wechsler called it "one of the most absurd and fantastic wastes of taxpayers' money in history."

Wechsler knew the hearing's record would reflect badly on McCarthy and he wished to see it made public. The senator's condition was that Wechsler name names. Wechsler fretted: "It was wrong to expose others to McCarthy's wickedness, but it was equally wrong, in my judgment, to embrace the principle that a former Communist should tell nothing to anyone." It was the same cunundrum Kazan had faced, and Wechsler came to a similar conclusion: "By and large liberals have believed in giving wide scope to congressional committees. Moreover, there is in the American tradition a very real belief that the man who has nothing to conceal will speak up when spoken to: muteness has not often been equated with valor," he explained. "An American ought to be prepared to state his case in any public place at any time."[84]

As Leslie Fiedler, one of the few public sympathizers with this decision, argued, "Between the evasion of the non-cooperators and the over-cooperation of the confessors lies a troubled and difficult course: What seems to me the truly liberal one."[85] The only way to challenge McCarthy was through democratic means, and democracies require accurate information to operate. Wechsler ended his testimony with a judgment seconded by history: "You have done in my judgment serious damage to the battle against Communism by confusing liberals with Communists."[86] As his friend Arthur Schlesinger, Jr., wrote to Adlai Stevenson a month later, in May 1953, in one of history's great understatements, "Under better conditions, an event like this might be a turning point in the fight against McCarthy; but I fear that we have a little way to go."[87]

When North Korean troops crossed the 38th parallel in June 1950, Harry Truman decided instinctively that the encroachment must be resisted with force. Whether the decision was driven primarily by the Soviets, the Chinese, or the Koreans themselves, the United States needed to demonstrate to the world that such aggression would not be tolerated. Secretary Acheson called for an emergency meeting of the Security Council, which gave its blessing to the U.S. intervention. The rather brash move by the two men inspired little opposition outside of pacifist circles. Eleanor Roosevelt argued, "Had the United Nations permitted this to go on, their weakness would have been comparable only to the weakness of the League of Nations in its last days."[88] *The Nation* editors compared the invasion to Hitler's aggression, while those at *The New Republic* argued that Truman's response "undoubtedly gained new prestige among the Western powers." PCA leader Frank Kingdon praised the president for avoiding "the road to Munich."[89]

Truman initially believed the war to be in good hands under General Douglas MacArthur, the seventy-one-year-old hero of the war in the Pacific. But a rift soon opened between the two—one that revealed a great deal about differences between liberals and conservatives during the Cold War. MacArthur, like many conservatives, saw the war as an opportunity to take on Communist China, and thereby undo the humiliation of Mao's victory there. In September 1950, after a successful pushback of North Korean troops, Truman caved in to MacArthur's demand that he be allowed to take the war beyond the 38th parallel, despite clear warnings from the Chinese that this would force them to retaliate. When they did, what had been a successful and limited police action became one of the costliest and least conclusive conflicts in U.S. military history.[90]

As the war bogged down with little progress, but much carnage, on both sides, MacArthur began to flirt with open insubordination, telling reporters that the United States ought to prepare to invade the Chinese mainland. He sent a letter to Joseph Martin, the leader of the House and a Republican critic of Truman, in which he famously declared, "There is no substitute for victory," and thereby implied that perhaps the president was not man enough to see the struggle through.[91] By now Truman decided he had had enough and told Harley Kilgore, a Democratic senator from West Virginia, "I'll show that son of a bitch who's boss. Who does he think he is—God?"[92] On April 11, 1951, he relieved the general of his command.

MacArthur returned home to a hero's welcome. The general paraded down Pennsylvania Avenue to a boisterous crowd of three hundred thousand and at ticker-tape parades in New York City he was cheered by millions.[93] Truman's advisers were nervous about what MacArthur had in mind for the future, but MacArthur mania faded as quickly as it began, and the old man really did eventually fade away.

The president had taught the country a lesson in the importance of civilian control of the military, but his victory came at a significant price. As the war dragged on, both it and the president became increasingly unpopular.[94] As with Roosevelt before him (and LBJ afterward), his domestic agenda also fell victim to the bullets and bombing runs.[95]

Perhaps one of the bitterest ironies of all was that despite the willingness of so many liberals to pander to political paranoia at the expense of their principles, their accommodations did them little good. Even Arthur Schlesinger, Jr., who preferred not to challenge the Smith Act and who did everything he could to disassociate himself from communism and condemned those liberals who did not, became a McCarthy target. When the senator learned in 1952 that Schlesinger was drafting speeches for Adlai Stevenson, he accused him of writing admiringly of Russia, of disparaging religion, and of favoring Communist teachers in American universities. As a founding member of ADA, Schlesinger also naturally, according to McCarthy, supported Communist causes.[96] As the Jewish intellectual (and future godfather of neoconservatism) Irving Kristol wrote in *Commentary* in 1952, "There is one thing that the American people know about Senator McCarthy; he, like them, is unequivocally anti-Communist. About the spokesman for American liberalism, they feel they know no such thing. And with some justification."[97] That Kristol was, at the time he was offering legitimacy to McCarthy's witch hunt, viewed as a liberal writing in a liberal publication spoke volumes about the moral, intellectual, and political confusion with which liberals tried, and by and large failed, to meet the challenge of McCarthyism.

Richard Hofstadter had provided a fair warning: McCarthy's appeal drew on deep-seated elements of resentment and paranoia in the American character. The American public sphere was not governed by rules of fair and open deliberation. Frightening furies lurked in its shadows ready to reveal themselves in times of trouble. Liberals could not rely on the "good sense" of the American people to see the country through these moments—at least not in the short term.

Could liberals have stopped McCarthy if they had tried harder, if they had turned their attention away from Stalin and focused full time on the "other Joe"? As the anti-Communist liberal intellectual Nathan Glazer would muse, almost half a century after the fact:

> It is much easier to write a book describing what happened to these people and how excessive was their punishment in the light of their misdeeds or errors—all of which is true—than it is to explain just what role we should have played in that connection. There was no way of responding to the matter satisfactorily, to reconcile honesty as to our views, as to the affiliations and roles of certain people on the one hand, with consequences that were not up to use on the other. . . . In retrospect, we never managed to figure out a good position. By good I mean not one that was politically defensible but that was respectable and moral and responsive to all the complicated issues raised. And I still don't think we have one.[98]

7

Eggheads in the Wilderness

Eggheads of the world arise, you have nothing to lose but your yolks.
—Adlai Stevenson, 1954[1]

Adlai Stevenson was not blessed with a particularly strong or forceful appearance. His large oval head would arch up and give him a look that struck more than a few people as smug and self-satisfied.[2] No doubt his baldness helped inspire the term "egghead," a characterization that became a keyword of American politics during the 1950s. Though often rumpled in appearance, with holes in his shoes, his gleaming blue eyes contrasted with his shiny dome, and communicated an intensity that contradicted the coolness and distance his manner suggested. The overall effect was one that women frequently found attractive.[3] A divorced father, estranged from his mentally unstable socialite ex-wife, Stevenson surrounded himself with wealthy women who apparently enjoyed pampering him. He was also quite a snob. During his 1956 presidential campaign, a woman called out to him, "Senator, you have the vote of every thinking person!" Stevenson reportedly called back, "That's not enough, madam, we need a majority!" When he lost, and another woman tried to soothe his feelings by telling him that he had "educated the country," Stevenson replied, "Yes, but a lot of people flunked the exam."[4] It was Stevenson's high opinion of his own intellect, repeatedly demonstrated during his two presidential runs, that helped cement the notion of the effete, ineffectual liberal stereotype that has proved to be such rich territory for conservatives to mine since the mid-twentieth century.

Stevenson had been born to politics. His maternal grandfather had been campaign manager for Abe Lincoln, and his grandfather, Grover Cleveland's vice president; his mother had helped to found the Daughters of the American Revolution.[5] Born in Los Angeles and raised Unitarian in Bloomington, Illinois, Stevenson was a privileged but indifferent student who attended Choate and Princeton before flunking out of Harvard Law School. He eventually received a degree from Northwestern.

Stevenson had been laboring at a crusty old Chicago firm, Cutting, Moore & Sidley, after passing the bar exam when, in the summer of 1933, he was offered a New Deal position in the Agricultural Adjustment Administration (AAA), which at the time was run by Henry Wallace. He moved around a bit between regulatory bodies before briefly returning to law practice and then ended up in a top position in the office of the secretary of the navy in 1940, where he remained during the war, leaving for the State Department in 1945, before being appointed later that year to work on the creation of the United Nations. Returning home in 1947 to a Galena, Illinois, farm he had purchased but rarely used, he won the Illinois governorship in an upset when Truman's surprisingly strong 1948 campaign swept him into office as well.

Stevenson threw himself into the arena while rarely committing himself to anyone or any political issue in earnest. His moodiness and indecision during key campaign moments would drive even his strongest supporters to distraction and lead more than a few die-hard liberals to cast their votes for Eisenhower. (Armchair psychologists have speculated that a tragic accident that took place when Stevenson was twelve, when the boy accidentally killed sixteen-year-old Ruth Merwin with a loaded rifle at a family party, may have left him emotionally paralyzed when faced with difficult decisions.[6])

Ironically, the celebrated intellectual politician's impatience with the nuts and bolts of politics was exactly the quality that many liberals found most attractive about him. His high-minded disdain for the baby-kissing, glad-handing aspects of the profession warmed liberal hearts as it simultaneously infuriated those whose jobs (and hopes) rested on actually winning elections. Jimmy Wechsler remembers Stevenson campaigning at a factory early in the morning when a worker asked: "Governor, what the hell are you doing up at this hour?" Stevenson's response: "I'm damned if I know."[7] Another adviser once had occasion to instruct his candidate: "When you are shaking hands in a supermarket and a little girl in a starched dress steps out of the crowd and hands you a stuffed alligator, what you say is, 'Thanks very much, I've always wanted one of these for the mantelpiece at Libertyville.' What you *don't* say is what you *did* say: 'For Christ's sake, what's this?' "[8]

To many of those close to him it was Stevenson's bluntness that was his strongest selling point. As Schlesinger explained, "Stevenson knew what he was like and recoiled from giving the public any false impressions. He refused to make promises when he did not really believe there was a good chance of delivery."[9]

Perhaps the oddest aspect of Stevenson's career was the manner in which liberals anointed him as their standard-bearer in the 1950s. In 1952, ADA's James Loeb met with the presidential candidate, who had never joined their organization and whose overall views on a number of crucial issues remained murky to all concerned.[10] Pressed by Loeb, Stevenson complained, "What do you want from me? I don't agree with your programs."[11] In fact, Stevenson had next to no sympathy for much of the New Deal, despite his having made his career in it. He hated public housing, opposed "socialized medicine," and could hardly make up his mind on whether he supported the repeal of the antilabor Taft-Hartley Bill. On the central emerging moral and political issue of the moment—civil rights—he barely registered an opinion. (He considered himself a southerner at heart.) While he certainly opposed McCarthy, often with great eloquence, and bravely (or foolhardily) testified before HUAC on behalf of Alger Hiss, he had no problem with dismissing teachers for being Communist Party members or with using the Smith Act to prosecute others. Irving Howe would later term "Adlaism" to be "Ikeism . . . with a touch of literacy and intelligence."[12]

Stevenson himself explained to a friend in 1956 his view of political campaigning: "My experience is that the issues tend to take care of themselves satisfactorily if a man has proven qualities of mind, character, and temperament."[13] John Kenneth Galbraith remarked that "few men in American politics have ever aroused such a devoted and even passionate loyalty. . . . Increasingly . . . liberalism came to mean support of Stevenson."[14]

It was the pressures of the Cold War that compelled liberals to turn Stevenson into a liberal, a choice that made sense in context but one that ignored much about both the man and about liberalism. Arthur Schlesinger, Jr., who devoted much of his time and energies to writing speeches and politicking on behalf of Stevenson, noted in his journals on August 8, 1952, "that Adlai was probably even more conservative than I had thought." Months later, however, he added that Stevenson "seems to me more than ever the voice of the liberal future."[15]

Stevenson's tenure as governor was not much of a selling point, either. A good-government progressive, Stevenson focused on rationalizing the Illinois welfare system, cutting the state's bureaucratic costs, and cleaning up its government.[16] But he did little for civil rights, and much of his reputation in this area rested on his willingness to veto a single 1951 bill that was designed to outlaw the Illinois Communist Party. He laid out his argument in soaring language, acknowledging that the Communist Party was, indeed, a threat to America due to its faith in revolutionary activity, but at the same time, he warned Americans to consider the "methods" and "means" employed to meet this threat: "If this bill became law, it would be only human for employees to play safe and shirk duties which might bring upon them resentment or criticism. Public service requires independent and courageous action on matters which affect countless private interests. We cannot afford to make public employees vulnerable to malicious charges of disloyalty." He ended: "I must, in good conscience, protest against any unnecessary suppression of our ancient rights as free men."[17]

The 1952 presidential election began where the buck stopped—with Harry Truman, who had handpicked Stevenson as his successor. But Stevenson demurred repeatedly. Tennessee's crime-fighting, coonskin-cap-wearing Estes Kefauver was leading in the primaries, besting Hubert Humphrey, only four years in the Senate; the plutocrat Averell Harriman, who was now governor of New York; and Richard Russell, the regional candidate of the southern segregationists, as the Dixiecrats had now returned to the Democratic fold. Stevenson watched and waited, hoping, as Schlesinger recorded, that others "would come to him and ask him to run."[18] As the primary season continued, Stevenson grew increasingly popular with educated professionals, northern urbanites, and moderate southerners. A "Draft Stevenson" movement formed, but Stevenson continued to play the ingenue. He had secretly hoped that Robert Taft would win the nomination for the Republicans, which would have provided a political opening for an unapologetic Democratic internationalist, but the Republicans smartly liked Ike, whom ADA had sought out so desperately four years earlier on the vain (and rather pathetic) hope that he was a secret liberal.

The draft succeeded, in part because Stevenson's welcoming address to the delegates—Chicago was host to the 1952 convention—proved so winning that his supporters were able to sway the requisite number of Kefauver and Harriman voters in his direction. The words he chose framed his candidacy for the coming months, especially when he quoted scripture: "If this cup may not pass from me, except I drink it, thy will be done," he told cheering (if perhaps confused) crowds. Whether he was comparing himself to Christ or merely signaling his passive acceptance of the burdens that fate had placed on his shoulders, it was characteristic Stevensonianism.[19]

Stevenson did nothing to address concerns that many religious Americans had about his divorce. (An adviser, Lou Cowan, suggested the governor have his sons on stage during a televised debate, during which a camera could pan to them saying, "Good luck, Dad." Stevenson replied, "Lou, old boy, we don't do things like that in our family."[20])At a meeting with Truman, where the president threw himself into the campaign with gusto, Stevenson could not help but observe, "I think the President wants to win this campaign more than I do."[21]

The candidate characteristically resisted making the manipulative emotional appeals typical of American political campaigns. Indeed, as Arthur Schlesinger, Jr., complained to his diary, he recoiled "from this with a political puritanism which regards any popular political position (at least on the liberal side) as somehow immoral."[22] "Let's talk sense to the American people. Let's tell them the truth, that there are no gains without pains, that we are now on the eve of great decisions, not easy decisions, like resistance when you're attacked, but a long, patient, costly struggle which alone can assure triumph over the great enemies of man—war, poverty, and tyranny—and the assaults upon human dignity which are the most grievous consequences of each," he promised in his much-quoted acceptance speech.[23]

The high point of Stevenson's first presidential campaign came at the national convention of the American Legion, where he followed General Eisenhower on the podium. Stevenson, aware that he faced a much tougher challenge before an unsympathetic audience, rather characteristically told an adviser, "I would rather lecture them than try to win their votes by promising them material benefits."[24] "We talk a great deal about patriotism," he announced. "And I should tell you—my fellow Legionnaires—as I would tell all other organized groups that I intend to resist pressures from veterans, too." Then, drawing heavily on Reinhold Niebuhr, Stevenson gave the veterans a lecture on the meaning of "true patriotism." It was "based on tolerance and a large measure of humility," he explained. It celebrated the "freedom of the mind." "There are men among us who use 'patriotism' as a club for attacking other Americans," he warned. "The tragedy of our day is the climate of fear in which we live, and fear breeds repression. Too often sinister threats to the Bill of Rights, to freedom of the mind, are concealed under the patriotic cloak of anti-communism." It was a brave and eloquent speech, given the likely hostility of its audience, many of whom were sympathetic not merely to Eisenhower, but to McCarthy as well.[25]

Marquis Childs called him "Lincolnian." Max Lerner thought he was the first figure of major stature to have emerged since Roosevelt. Richard Rovere stated, rapturously, that "his gifts are more imposing than those of any President or any major-party aspirant for the office in this century." Liberal newspapers and magazines all jumped on the Stevenson bandwagon in a way they had not for Truman four years earlier.[26] *The New Republic* editors proclaimed that not only did he enjoy the integrity of Wilson and the compassion of FDR, but he brought to politics "moral honesty to challenge cynicism and corruption; intellectual ability to end mediocrity in government; open-mindedness to counter conformism and doctrinal rigidity; a belief in conciliation to overcome deep and disturbing divisions within this nation."[27]

Stevenson's remarks to the American Legion were directed less at Eisenhower than at McCarthy's surrogate on the ticket, Dick Nixon. Nixon hardly needed any prodding to tear into a politician who not only ran down Joe McCarthy but also took the stand for Hiss. He nicknamed their opponent "Adlai the Appeaser" and accused him of enjoying a PhD from "Dean Acheson's College of Cowardly Communist Containment."[28]

Stevenson's campaign was further frustrated by the McCarthyite tone of much of his press coverage. Right-wing newspapers went further than merely to endorse Eisenhower; they vigorously participated in the culture war against liberalism that McCarthy had launched as well. *The New York Daily News* called Stevenson "Adelaide" and condemned his "fruity" voice and "teacup words," making him sound like "a genteel spinster who can never forget that she got an A in elocution at Miss Smith's finishing school."[29] Ironically, it was the fear of McCarthyism, and the irresponsibility of so much of the Republican Party's base in the manner in which it pursued its prey, that led many moderates to vote for Eisenhower as a means of quashing it. The influential insider pundit Joe Alsop wrote Isaiah Berlin in London, "I find myself blackmailed by the virtual certainty that we shall have a first-class fascist party in the United States if the Republicans don't win. The real need for a change in this country arises, not from the decay of the Democrats, but from the need to give the Republicans the sobering experience of responsibility."[30] The same concerns motivated James "Scotty" Reston of *The New York Times*. As Schlesinger recorded in his diary, Reston's decision to "vote for Ike in order to spare the country four more years of Yalta, Hiss, McCarthy etc., . . . distresses me far less than it would have a few weeks ago. If we are going to have a Republican President it might as well be on the Republican ticket."[31]

The 1952 presidential election is best understood as a lost cause for liberalism, though this may have had less to do with the tough tactics of McCarthy and Nixon than with the fact of the Korean War. Stevenson did the best he could at defending the war and arguing against extension of the war into China, but in doing so, he was parroting the unpopular Truman, and appearing to support what looked to be a hopeless morass.[32] The sight of the ex-World War II hero, Ike, promising to "go to Korea" to, implicitly, at least, end the conflict put Stevenson in an all but impossible position. Nixon said nothing controversial when he mused that Americans would likely feel better protected by a "khaki-clad" president rather than one "clothed in State Department pinks."[33] Residents of America's booming suburbs voted overwhelmingly for Eisenhower;[34] they didn't want to hear about "greatness" so much as normalcy.

That year, 1952, was also the year *Partisan Review* ran its famous symposium, "Our Country and Our Culture." "Intellectuals for the first time in a hundred years discovered something to celebrate in America," observed Nathan Glazer, who was then an assistant editor at *Commentary*. "It has come to seem more reasonable," wrote Harold Rosenberg in the the same magazine's May 1951 issue, "to get to the top floor by taking an elevator than by blowing up the building."[35] As if to codify the intellectuals' new stance, *PR*'s editors announced that they believed that "more and more writers have ceased to think of themselves as rebels and exiles. They now realize that their values, if they are to be realized at all, are to be realized in America and in relation to the actuality of American life."[36] Such a pronouncement signaled an almost totemic transformation in the country's intellectual landscape. As the late intellectual historian John Patrick Diggins explained, during the twenties the questions and answers posed by the editors would have "disparaged their country" for its shallowness; in the thirties they would have "foretold of America's capitalist economy succumbing to Marx's prophecies"; but in the fifties they "felt . . . it was no disgrace, no shallow provincialism, to accept America and admire it."[37] (*Time*, characteristically, would celebrate the turn a mere four years later, in a June 1956 cover story titled "America and the Intellectual: The Reconciliation." It quoted Lionel Trilling observing that "for the first time in the history of the modern American intellectual, America is not to be conceived of as *a priori* the vulgarest and stupidest nation of the world."[38])

Yet to read the symposium as an expression of intellectual conformity would be unwarranted. Its editors explained, "The affirmative attitude toward America which has emerged since the Second World War may be a necessary corrective of the earlier extreme negation, but the affirmation cannot be unequivocal. For American economic and political institutions have not suddenly become ideally beneficent, and many intellectuals are not prepared to give up all criticism of them."[39] Sidney Hook argued that intellectuals had to be not too shy to "criticize what needs to be criticized in America."[40] C. Wright Mills and Irving Howe rejected the entire premise of the symposium. Mills, always the antiestablishmentarian, held fast to his "utopian" visions and his social and political criticism,[41] while Howe, not yet the full-fledged liberal he would later become, clung to his Marxism, which he believed to be "the best available method for understanding and making history."[42] The issue's two unapologetic liberals were hardly more celebratory. Reinhold Niebuhr complained, "We are engaged in such a perpetual liturgy of self-congratulations about the vaunted virtues and achievements of the 'American way of life' that we not only make ourselves odious to the world, but also rob ourselves of the political wisdom required to wield power in a world which refuses to be made over into the image of America." There was "no excuse for complacency" in America, Niebuhr argued, where there were "massive spiritual, moral, and cultural crudities."[43] Arthur Schlesinger, Jr., meanwhile, echoed his mentor, arguing that America's "cultural pluralism" and its principle of "free inquiry" were under siege by the combination of McCarthyism and mass culture. "The real *trahison des clercs* lies," he explained, "with those who collaborate with the foes of the mind—whether they are the demonic foes of the mind, like Hitler and Stalin, or the gangster foes, like McCarthy and McCarran."[44]

The primary difference between these liberal social critics and their Marxist counterparts was the former's willingness to pursue change from within society's institutions. The turn toward liberal reformism appears both entirely comprehensible and historically inevitable, rather than the simple "sellout" its critics would charge.

After all, the European ideologies of Marxism and other forms of socialism had arisen from a continent in crisis, but prosperity and abundance were everywhere in 1950s America. The nation's gross national product rose nearly 30 percent between 1950 and 1957.[45] At the center of this culture of consumption was the phenomenal success of television. No previous technological innovation in American history rivaled the rapidity with which the country took to TV. From a mere 172,000 households with television sets in 1948, the number grew to more than 15 million by 1952 and more than twice as many again, to 32 million, in 1955, accounting for roughly three-quarters of all American households. By 1960 the figure had risen to 90 percent, and that included homes without telephones or even central heating.[46]

David Riesman, a liberal sociologist at Harvard, argued in his bestselling book *The Lonely Crowd* (1950) that the American character was fast shifting from "inner directed" to "other directed."[47] The "inner-directed" personality of the past developed a moral "gyroscope" from within, internalizing strong parental morality—in Freudian terms via the self-punitive superego. The "other-directed" personality type took moral cues from colleagues and peers, creating someone who is "psychologically dependent on others for clues to the meaning of life."[48] In the postwar world, peer group and advertising were determining social behavior more decisively than the family. Riesman quipped, "The mass media are the wholesalers; the peer groups, the retailers of the communications industry."[49] Success at work now required gaining favor with one's coworkers as well as the boss, because of "what others think of one—and how competent one is in manipulating others and being oneself manipulated."[50] Though Riesman was not wholly critical of this change in character type—other-directed people could be, after all, sensitive and considerate to their peers—he did worry about the weakening of the "autonomous" person, "capable of conscious self-direction."[51]

The problem was especially prominent among middle-class urban residents—those whom C. Wright Mills characterized as "white collar." Mills, a motorcycle-driving Texan ensconced in the Columbia University Sociology Department with a penchant for tough talk and piercing prose, defined these individuals as "the small creature who is acted upon but who does not act, who works along unnoticed in somebody's office or store, never talking loud, never talking back, never taking a stand."[52] "Conformity" was now becoming a signal bone of contention among liberals, inspired in part by their unhappy experience with McCarthyism. As Daniel Bell and Irving Howe argued, "The criticism of mass culture" had come to "conveniently replace the criticism of bourgeois society" of the 1930s for America's liberal intellectuals.[53] Writing in *PR*, in 1954, Howe complained that these same intellectuals had "become . . . apologist[s] for middle-class values, middle-class culture, and the status quo" and "partisans of bourgeois society." He would accuse *Commentary*, in particular, of advancing a liberalism that is "most skillfully and systematically advanced as a strategy for adapting to the American status quo."[54]

America of the 1950s also belonged to "the man in the gray flannel suit," which was the title of a 1955 novel by Sloan Wilson that became a film starring Gregory Peck. The novel tells the story of Tom Rath, an alienated public relations executive with a bored wife, haunted by his war experiences, and numbed by the hollow domesticity of his suburban existence.[55] It was a theme that would soon be given the appellation Cheeveresque in honor of the masterful *New Yorker* short story writer, John Cheever. Like Wilson before him (and John Updike, who would follow the trail he blazed), Cheever portrayed suburbia as a pleasantly soul-destroying purgatory.

For some liberals, including many who worked with Stevenson, politics grew out of this abundance and the inner malaise it appeared to inspire. Conservatives could base their appeals upon Christianity, but to what could liberals, who embraced freethinking in matters cultural and religious, turn? Lionel Trilling had addressed exactly this question in his study of Matthew Arnold, undertaken originally as his doctoral dissertation at Columbia and written during a period when he was still a fellow-traveling Communist.[56] Trilling called Arnold, Oxford's famous professor of poetry who published his masterpiece, *Culture and Anarchy,* in 1869, a "liberal of the future." Arnold believed that the forces of culture—what he termed "sweetness of light"— could be harnessed by the Enlightenment to correct the excesses of the French Revolution and simultaneously counter the oppressive tendencies of the Church and the *ancien régime*.[57] Arnold held that the "future lay not with the working class but with the middle class."[58] And the culture offered to them must be, unlike politics, "affirmative, interesting, complete, human," so that each citizen might experience reason "as a kind of grace," and thereby be helped to create "a civilization into which workers can grow."[59] This was exactly the task that liberals felt it was their duty to assume nearly a century after Arnold's challenge, and more than a decade after Trilling's.

The Canadian-born economist John Kenneth Galbraith frequently found himself vexed as well by questions defined to be outside the confines of his discipline but central to those that postwar American liberals asked of themselves and their country. Reared by liberal parents in rural Ontario, Galbraith was deeply committed as a young man to the agrarian populism of his parents' faith.[60] After studying agricultural economics at the University of California, Berkeley, he became a kind of whirling dervish, spinning through the institutions of the New Deal. He began at the AAA, where he befriended Adlai Stevenson and developed an interest in the Swedish cooperative movement.[61] During the war Galbraith moved to the Office of Price Administration before settling on the General Maximum Price Regulation program. At OPA Galbraith learned how to "disperse sacrifice on an equal basis," his biographer Richard Parker observes, a crucial theme of the rest of his long and productive life.[62] Right-wing pundits, including especially the editors of *The Chicago Tribune* and the radio commentator Fulton Lewis, Jr., discovered his reports and painted him as a crypto-Communist, which led not only to the loss of his position but also, apparently, a nervous breakdown.[63] When he recovered, Galbraith took a job as a writer at *Fortune* magazine and then at the U.S. Strategic Bombing Survey in postwar Europe. From there Galbraith briefly stopped off at the State Department before finally winning an appointment to the Harvard Economics Department in 1949.

Like Stevenson, Galbraith had an almost uncontrollable penchant for mordant wit and irony. Parker speculates that the 1950 death of Galbraith's son from leukemia transformed him into the ironic and diffident character that became so well known the world over.[64] (In his *Ambassador's Journal*, published after he served in that position in India during the Kennedy administration, Galbraith actually takes credit for having coined "The shit hit the fan," a description he used regarding his confirmaion hearings, as when he "accidentally" answered a question honestly about Communist China.[65]) Unlike Stevenson, however, Galbraith was a genuine liberal's liberal, and one who consistently demonstrated the ability to join progressive policies to sophisticated political calculation.

When he began advising Stevenson in 1952, Galbraith was putting the finishing touches on his first major work, *American Capitalism*. In retrospect the book drew many lessons from another influential work in the canon of liberal economics, Adolf Berle and Gardiner Means's *The Modern Corporation and Private Property* (1932). *The Modern Corporation* maintained that the growth of big business had transformed corporations into de facto public institutions, and they therefore needed to be regulated as such. (Berle went on to become a key figure in FDR's brain trust, and his long life and deep desire to remain engaged in politics found him advising Stevenson in 1956.[66]) Galbraith expanded on Berle's redefinition of the role of the corporation, and predicted that during the postwar years its monopolistic economic and political power could only be expected to increase. Society therefore needed to encourage the creation of "countervailing power," such as labor unions as well as "food chains, variety chains, mail order houses," and "retail buyers."[67] The era's laissez-faire economics had come to an end, and Americans needed to prepare themselves for a future of regulation and government-mandated competition.[68] At the same time, however, liberals needed to come to terms with contemporary capitalism, as all forms of socialism had lost what luster they had once possessed in the United States as politically practical alternatives. The (then) liberal critic Max Lerner considered Galbraith's argument to be tantamount to surrender, terming it "Newtonianism": the faith in a "built-in self-regulating mechanism" of modern capitalism that encouraged liberals to grow fat, lazy, and complacent.[69]

Galbraith had little in common with his fellow academic economists in almost all aspects of his life and work, but none more so than in his concern with the quality of individual lives, rather than with the quantities of goods they produced and consumed, as was typical of his profession. Much as Riesman had been apprehensive about other-directedness, Galbraith worried that America was becoming a society dominated by the manufactured desires of advertisers. He warned of an American landscape characterized by "highway billboards, redundant service stations, glossy packages, bread that is first denatured and then fortified, high-pressure salesmanship, singing commercials, and the concept of the captive audience."[70]

Depressed at Stevenson's 1952 defeat, Galbraith began a book he planned to call *Why People Are Poor,* in which he hoped to examine what he told a friend were "hard-luck communities."[71] But over time issues of abundance took precedence in his mind over questions of poverty. He temporarily dropped the project, wrote a short, brilliant narrative, *The Great Crash, 1929* (1954) and then returned to work on what would be his masterpiece, *The Affluent Society* (1958).[72]

Galbraith focused America's attention on the juxtaposition of "private opulence" alongside "public squalor."[73] In what would become one of the most famous passages in all postwar social science, he wrote: "The family which takes its mauve and cerise, air-conditioned, power-steered, and power-braked automobile out for a tour passes through cities that are badly paved, made hideous by litter, blighted buildings, billboards, and posts for wires." They travel a "countryside . . . rendered largely invisible by commercial art" and "picnic on exquisitely packaged food from a portable icebox by a polluted stream and go on to spend the night at a park which is a menace to public health and morals."[74]

Deeply influenced by Riesman, Trilling (and therefore Arnold), and Galbraith, Arthur Schlesinger, Jr., tried to codify these vague notions under the rubric of what he called "qualitative liberalism." Schlesinger had become increasingly interested in the cultural criticism of the 1950s and tried to form a new magazine, to be called *The Critic,* though funds turned out to be unavailable.[75] He wrote Stevenson in 1955, encouraging the governor to develop an overarching message in 1956: "We feel that a key issue to be developed in the next twelve months is the anomaly of America's becoming simultaneously richer in wealth and poorer in public services and decencies under the Eisenhower administration."[76]

Schlesinger spoke of the "anxiety and discontent" besetting the middle class in the midst of a prosperous economy—a sense of unease quite different from that with which he described in the opening pages of *The Vital Center.* Its cause was not totalitarianism, but consumerism. "Qualitative liberalism" would be "dedicated to bettering the quality of people's lives and opportunities" and required that attention be paid to education, medical care, equal rights for minorities, and civic planning, as well as to attacking slums, improving national parks, and helping the aged. All of this would be wrapped in the mantle of what the historian James Kloppenberg has termed "aspirational nationalism," that is, patriotism.[77] Schlesinger wrote, "What the new liberalism must do is again something that is more subtle and perhaps more edifying:

It must make the point that our country can grow only if we develop a positive philosophy of the public interest to be asserted against the parochial interests of any special group."

Galbraith and Schlesinger were joined in this quest by their Cambridge neighbor Bernard DeVoto. The curmudgeonly critic had grown into an extremely energetic albeit gadfly environmentalist.[78] In 1955, much to Schlesinger's delight, DeVoto told the young historian what he had planned to tell Stevenson when they next met: "The Democratic Party needs a highly positive and highly specific resources program, and in order to get one, it will have to do some new and fundamental thinking." Liberals would have to question the idea of perpetual growth and progress stemming from America's postwar economy.[79]

But the failure of two Stevenson presidential campaigns should have warned liberals about the potential pitfalls of a pivot away from the New Deal/Fair Deal economic populism that had helped knit together the victorious constituencies of the 1930s and 1940s to a more culturally based liberalism that could easily upend these same political coalitions. A campaign for "quality" provided an irresistible target for identity-driven (and frequently class-based) attacks on perceived liberal arrogance and elitism. The tin ear that so many liberals displayed in the face of this inexorable fact of American political life would prove, in the coming decades, to be among the most costly of their political mistakes.

Democrats did well in 1954, as opposition parties tend to do in off-year elections. When Eisenhower suffered heart failure the following year, their prospects appeared to improve, however briefly, as Richard Nixon's forays into McCarthyism continued to define his political character for many for his first vice presidential term. Yet Eisenhower recovered and international crises in Suez and Hungary helped to remind Americans of what they liked and admired in the ex-general.

In the 1956 election Adlai Stevenson found himself facing another primary battle against the popular crime fighter Estes Kefauver, who would eventually make his way onto the ticket as its vice presidential candidate. Stevenson, moreover, did himself and the party no favors with a disorganized campaign, characterized by high-minded, philosophically inclined orations when the political occasion clearly called for meat and potatoes.[80] One former supporter wrote him, "I was a little disappointed in Senator Kefauver's corny poetry [in his peroration] but I was aghast at your quoting Arnold Toynbee."[81] Robert F. Kennedy, who worked on the campaign, ended up developing an almost irrational hatred and contempt for Stevenson, complaining: "It was ghastly. My feeling was that he had no rapport with his audience—no feeling for them—no comprehension of what campaigning required—no ability to make decisions. . . . In 1952, I had been crazy about him. I was excited in 1956, at the start. I came out of our first conversation with a very high opinion of him. . . . Then I spent six weeks with him on the campaign, and he destroyed it all."[82]

With Ike all but politically untouchable, Stevenson returned again and again in his speeches to the frightening possibility of a Nixon presidency. He warned one audience that the nation was at a forked road: "In one direction lies a land of slander and scare; the land of sly innuendo, the poison pen, the anonymous phone call and hustling, pushing, shoving; the land of smash and grab and anything to win. This is Nixonland. But I say to you that it is not America."[83]

In one respect, at least, those liberals who did count on Stevenson had reason to be proud: their candidate was now willing to embrace his liberalism. Urged on by Schlesinger and Galbraith, who volunteered as speechwriters, he spoke eloquently and openly of the need for "an emotional sympathy for the exploited."[84] He proposed a new program for the elderly and needy that would one day become Medicare. He also urged an end to nuclear weapons testing and presented a conservationist vision for the country's national forests and parks.

In the end, though, he lost by an even larger margin than he had four years earlier, carrying not a single state north of the Mason-Dixon line. And his success in the South was due exclusively to his complete moral abdication with regard to civil rights, which he entirely ignored during the campaign. Stevenson could not even bring himself to support the cause of black schoolchildren in the seminal 1954 Supreme Court decision *Brown v. Board of Education*—or at least not in language anyone could understand. He said it would "make no difference" what he thought of the decision as it was now the law of the land, which was quite similar to President Eisenhower's reluctant admission that he was sworn, as president, to uphold the law, but that was it.[85] Stevenson sometimes sounded not at all accidentially like an apologist for American apartheid: "We will have to proceed gradually. You do not upset the habits and traditions that are older than the Republic overnight."[86] Comments like this led the comedian Mort Sahl to quip: "Eisenhower is for integration, but gradually; Adlai Stevenson, on the other hand, is for integration but moderately."[87] When Schlesinger charged Stevenson with expecting "the Negroes to be more reasonable than he expected the southerners to be," and that this struck him as unfair, Stevenson replied, "Of course it was unfair; it was like expecting business to behave badly and labor to behave intelligently; but life was unfair."[88]

Following his second dispiriting defeat, *The New York Post* published a series asking liberal luminaries "Where Do Liberals Go from Here?" Reporter Irwin Ross solicited answers from Adlai Stevenson; Averell Harriman; Hubert Humphrey; Eleanor Roosevelt; the liberal lawyer and diplomat Thomas Finletter; Estes Kefauver; NAACP chief, Roy Wilkins; president of the International Ladies' Garment Workers Union, David Dubinsky; and Reinhold Niebuhr. Most of the answers were programmatic rather than visionary in character, insisting on a need to reform New Deal programs and improve political organization. Regarding civil rights, the focus was on ending the filibuster, so that southern senators could no longer prevent progressive measures from coming to a vote.[89] "Liberalism in America has not for thirty years been so homeless, baffled, irrelevant, and impotent as it is today," Schlesinger bemoaned in 1957.[90] Fortunately, however, liberalism's darkest hour had arrived, as the old cliché promised, just before its dawn.

8

We Shall Overcome

Are American Negroes simply the creation of white men, or have they at least helped to create themselves out of what they found around them?

—Ralph Ellison[1]

Today Communism and racism are the twin scourges of the world. Both of them take naked hatred and give it a mystical intensity and a feeling of absolute rightness.

—Max Lerner[2]

The boy appeared unremarkable. His father had died when he was three, and his mother, who married twice afterward, had tried her best to raise him with a sense of manners and religious faith, typical of middle-class African Americans born in Oklahoma around 1914. A combination of rage and alienation led him to seclude himself with what literature he found available. Though he had been named after Ralph Waldo Emerson, young Ralph Ellison developed an early devotion to the adventure stories of Mark Twain, particularly *The Adventures of Huckleberry Finn*, which, not coincidentally, contained what was then the richest and most fully developed black character in American literature, "Nigger Jim," Huck's devoted friend and protector.[3]

With no father and largely impermanent connections to other blacks in the community, he came to view identity as a fluid, contingent phenomenon. He briefly rode the rails as a teenager during the Depression before entering in 1933 the Tuskegee Normal and Industrial Institute. Though he passed away in 1915, the "bootstraps" educational philosophy of its first leader, Booker T. Washington, still dominated the institute's pedagogical approach. Washington had famously embraced segregation of the races as an unalterable condition in 1895, a year before *Plessy v. Ferguson* codified it legally. A former slave himself, Washington believed that African Americans should focus on internal economic and vocational development rather than work for the chimerical goal of equality, which the white power structure was unlikely ever to grant. "In all things that are purely social we can be as separate as the fingers, yet one as the hand in all things essential to mutual progress," he would explain to the large (segregated) crowds that attended his speeches in the mid-1890s.[4] Funded by the Carnegie and Rockefeller foundations, Tuskegee had by the time of Ellison's arrival added a few classes in the humanities to create at least the pretense of a well-rounded education for its students.

Ellison crashed headfirst into the limits of Tuskegee's vocational culture as he sought to investigate and inhabit the worlds of music and literature. By 1934 he had complained to his mother that he had made a "big mistake," as he did not think he should "have to listen to the ravings of a bunch of small minded niggers who won't be satisfied unless they show how important they are."[5] It was a place, he complained, where the students and faculty were "dumb and shallow and think that money is all there is in the world, never realizing that the finer things can't be bought, and that a few people in the world, yes even negroes, love books, music, art, beauty, nature and the other things that are good and great."[6]

W.E.B. Du Bois had written in a similar vein when he penned his classic critique of Washington, *The Souls of Black Folk* (1903). He derided Washington's "gospel of Work and Money" for its ability "almost completely to overshadow the higher aims of life."[7] He called instead for blacks to consider studying the liberal arts and to demand full political equality in immediate terms, rather than postpone such goals while hoping to improve their economic lot first. Du Bois articulated the need for a "Talented Tenth" among African Americans to lead the struggle for equality, a strategy that would influence the founding of the National Association for the Advancement of Colored People (NAACP) just six years after the publication of *The Souls of Black Folk*. The NAACP, formed by a coalition of socialists, liberals, and educated blacks like Du Bois himself, ultimately became the most important civil rights organization in postwar America. It sought to sue various public and private entities to force them to desegregate, and thereby challenge the courts to overturn Jim Crow laws in the South.[8]

Du Bois has framed his book with the question "How does it feel to be a problem?"[9] His suggestion that racism was as much a psychological problem as a political one for its victims both inspired and deeply vexed the young Ralph Ellison. Leaving Tuskegee without graduating, Ellison moved to Manhattan in 1936 and began to write fiction and essays while working for the Federal Writers' Project. Like Du Bois, who had moved there a quarter century earlier to edit the NAACP's magazine, *The Crisis*, he came to see the Communist Party as the black man's only true friend and joined its extremely active Harlem branch.[10] Ellison was inspired less by the writings of Karl Marx or even the desperate poverty he witnessed than by the famous and charismatic black Communists with whom he came into contact, including Langston Hughes and Louise Thompson, who worked with the poet in a Harlem theater.[11]

Richard Wright moved to Harlem a year after Ellison did, also to work for the party. He helped to organize a variety of cultural projects and wrote for *The Daily Worker*, *New Masses*, and smaller publications. Born in abject poverty, Wright spent time in an orphanage when his mother, a scoolteacher who became paralytic, proved temporarily unable to cope on her own following the abandonment of his father, an illiterate sharecropper. Having heard stories of his uncle's murder by a gang of white racists, Wright seethed with fury at his oppressors and looked to the Communists for a path to resistance. In 1933, at age twenty-five, he joined the Communist Party in Chicago—where he had lived since age three—in part inspired by the highly regarded proletarian novelist and CP member Nelson Algren. Seven years later, Wright's angry masterpiece, *Native Son*, would catapult him into fame.[12]

In yet another common rite of passage, both Wright and Ellison would resign from the party during World War II. Wright would write openly about his break, while Ellison made his break privately, as his stature did not approach that of Wright's at the time. Wright insisted that the party was patronizing toward its black membership and reduced them to mere tools in a larger struggle that barely took account of their needs.[13] But Wright remained a radical until his death, and like Du Bois, spent much of it abroad to escape the alienation he experienced as a result of both his color and radical politics. Ellison's rejection of communism, meanwhile, sent him into the arms of mainstream liberalism, where he found himself forced to fend off attacks from all sides. He would work with the Congress for Cultural Freedom and the Salzburg Seminar, and a variety of often unfashionable liberal causes and politicians, while many if not most high-profile black artists and intellectuals were growing increasingly radicalized throughout the 1960s.[14]

Ellison wrote slowly when he wrote at all. He began *Invisible Man* in 1945 and did not finish it until seven years later; it was the only novel he ever completed. During this period he grew more and more optimistic about the increasing militancy of blacks' demands for civil rights and increasingly angry about what he viewed as the patronizing response of whites, particularly white liberals. He authored one of the few critical reviews (outside of the South) of

Gunnar Myrdal's magisterial *American Dilemma.* "Can a people . . . live and develop for over three hundred years simply by reacting?" to racism, Ellison asked. "Are American Negroes simply the creation of white men, or have they at least helped to create themselves out of what they found around them?"[15]

Ellison was no less disturbed by the outpouring of uplifting "race" movies of the period and proved particularly hostile toward Kazan's *Pinky,* whose primary black character, he complained, "floats about like a sleepwalker, which seems to me to be exactly the way a girl so full of unreality would act."[16]

Invisible Man would prove a literary, political, cultural, and psychological breakthrough. Rejecting what he called "the tight, well-made Jamesian novel," the "hard-boiled novel," and the naturalism of Wright and Dreiser, Ellison sought to capture the "extreme fluidity and openness" of American life. Drawing on Joyce, Eliot, and the surrealists, he created his own variant of modernism, and in doing so, succeeded in replicating the magnificent achievements of nineteenth-century writers who also created new forms to speak to and for a new civilization. His primary role model was that most American of literary pioneers, Mark Twain, whose works he found to be "imaginative projections of the conflicts within the human heart which arose when the sacred principles of the Constitution and the Bill of Rights clashed with the practical exigencies of human greed and fear, hate and love."[17] Ellison intended the novel to capture these complexities on one hand and function simultaneously as the kind of "protest novel" that the younger black novelist James Baldwin had already dismissed in a much-discussed 1949 essay in *Partisan Review* on the other.[18]

The literary critic Morris Dickstein has linked the book "not only to the postwar discourse of anticommunism but to the closely related defense of liberal individualism and cultural pluralism in the work of such social critics" as Trilling, Niebuhr, and Schlesinger. Ellison's "arguments for the diversity of both black and American life, for a cultural rather than a strictly political approach, for discipline and self-mastery, and for an acceptance of complexity and contradiction" posed an "alternative to both black nationalism and Marxism."[19] To this the cultural historian John S. Wright adds that Ellison had moved the black novel away from the "strident protest fiction" of the naturalist, Richard Wright, toward a form of protest that held ambiguity at its heart.[20]

Invisible Man won the National Book Award in 1953 and was widely recognized, together with the Jewish renaissance in fiction then under way, as part of an explosion of ethnic diversity in American literature at the time. "Must I strive toward colorness?" the invisible hero asks in the book's final pages. "America is woven of many strands."[21] The promise of a renewed liberal America would be diversity plus unity; pluralism plus equality.

The year of *Invisible Man*'s publication would also prove to be that in which initial arguments were heard by the United States Supreme Court in *Brown v. Board of Education of Topeka*. The case had been a long time in the making. Like *Invisible Man*, it possessed a liberal anti-Communist "author," NAACP Legal Defense and Educational Fund (LDEF) chief legal counsel Thurgood Marshall.

Marshall had grown up in segregated Baltimore, a city with a proud "free black" population before the Civil War. Like Ellison, Marshall had a name with particularly resonant overtones; his birth certificate read "Thoroughgood."[22] Though blessed with a loving mother, Marshall's father was a famously ornery, hard-drinking fellow who loved to argue, sometimes abusively. It was here that Marshall learned how to spar verbally, a rather useful skill for a future trial lawyer. His father instructed him, "Anyone calls you nigger, you not only got my permission to fight him—you got orders to fight him."[23] The son would earn the high school nickname "Turkey," due to his "proud, head-high, defiant strut."[24]

Known as a cutup in high school (where he befriended future band leader Cab Calloway), Marshall displayed a lack of seriousness that continued into his days at the all-black Lincoln University in Chester, Pennsylvania, where he arrived in 1925. A heavy smoker, a gambler, and a man with a reputation among the ladies, he would brag to his friends, "I expect to die at 110, shot by a jealous husband."[25] What he really planned on was to become a dentist, but when the sciences stumped him, he looked around for something else. Reading Du Bois and experiencing discrimination at a local theater got Marshall thinking about politics.[26]

Discouraged from applying to the University of Maryland Law School because of its unreceptiveness to black applicants, Marshall chose to attend Washington's all-black Howard University, which had not yet been accredited by the American Bar Association. Fortunately, however, Marshall met Charles "Charlie" Houston there. A stern and rather cold man who intimidated many pupils but influenced them no less powerfully, Houston saw the role of his students to be "social engineers" in American society.[27] He was, at the time, legal counsel to the NAACP Legal Defense and Educational Fund and encouraged Marshall to join him. Upon graduation Marshall returned to Baltimore to try to begin a law practice, but when he didn't find enough work, he left for New York in 1936 to take a full-time position with the NAACP.

Marshall won a string of victories challenging segregation, including an especially satisfying one against the law school that had excluded him, and soon realized that the stakes of his work, together with his personal political profile, were rapidly increasing. In 1949 he quit the pro-Communist National Lawyers Guild and, together with Roy Wilkins, launched an anti-Communist purge of the NAACP as well, going so far as to cooperate with J. Edgar Hoover's G-men in doing so.[28] The organization's lawsuits, from this time on, focused largely on obtaining formal political rights for blacks, rather than taking part in the larger, more expansive social and economic struggles led by labor and other left-wing organizations.[29] "If children could sit in classes together," Marshall's biographer points out, "not only would all children get to know people of other races at an early age but they would have the benefit of a first-rate education."[30]

Marshall busied himself bundling together cases that would eventually serve as the basis of *Brown v. Board of Education*. He had to search for black families willing to fight in the courts to send their children to schools where they were unwanted and would be subject to harassment and perhaps far worse. The case therefore rested, in the legal scholar Randall Kennedy's words, on "the efforts of regular folk, many of whom were poor, vulnerable, and unlettered."[31] Marshall simultaneously combed his law books to find an argument likely to persuade a majority of the members of the United States Supreme Court to rethink the meaning of the Fourteenth Amendment almost a century after its 1868 passage. Marshall worried initially that "no one in the NAACP camp had come up with a persuasive rebuttal to the fact that Congress had permitted segregated schools in the District of Columbia from 1864 onward—and that, though the matter was debated thoroughly between 1871 and 1875, Congress had [also] declined to include a prohibition against segregated schools in the Civil Rights Act of 1875."[32] He asked for help from the historians John Hope Franklin and C. Vann Woodward, and sought the counsel of the social psychologist Kenneth Clark, whose famous doll test—in which black children were found to associate negative qualities with their own skin color—Marshall believed, demonstrated the psychological burden segregation imposed on them.[33]

The justices were themselves unsure of how best to proceed, as eager as most of them were to do so. Felix Frankfurter, a former adviser to the NAACP, worried about the difficulties of the implementation of any desegregation regimen, including the likelihood of a vicious backlash. Justice Robert H. Jackson received cold-blooded counsel from his then-young aide named William Rehnquist: "To the argument made by Thurgood, not John, Marshall that a majority may not deprive a minority of its constitutional right, the answer must be that while this is sound in theory, in the long run it is the majority who will determine what the constitutional rights of the minority are. . . . If the Fourteenth Amendment did not enact Spencer's *Social Statics*, it just as surely did not enact Myrdal's *American Dilemma*."[34] Then, finally, came what Felix Frankfurter called an act of God when Chief Justice Fred Vinson suffered a heart attack. To his lifelong regret, President Eisenhower appointed California's liberal Republican governor, Earl Warren, to the job.[35]

As governor, Warren had been an enthusiastic defender of FDR's highly controversial wartime decision to intern Japanese Americans in makeshift camps.[36] But he came to regret this decision, and later proved a civil rights champion.[37] While he was by no means a legal scholar or thinker in the mold of a Frankfurter or a Brandeis, this, ironically, left him more open to the sociological arguments that underlay Marshall's case. (As a later colleague on the court, Justice Potter Stewart, once told the-then-seventeen-year-old author of this book during a 1977 interview, "Justice Warren would first ask himself what was right? Then he would figure out the legal argument for it."[38])

In May 1954 the Warren Court finally issued its decision in *Brown v. Board of Education* and unanimously swept away the "separate but equal" racial doctrine that had governed American institutions, both public and private, since *Plessy v. Ferguson*. Warren explained that the discussion and debate on the Fourteenth Amendment's intentions were "inconclusive," but argued, also, that education's role had become more important to all citizens and therefore made a ruling on school segregation that much more pressing. Warren insisted that public education was now central to the formation of democratic citizenship, concluding, "Separate educational facilities are inherently unequal," due to the message of inferiority they inherently carried.[39]

Naturally, so profound and far-reaching a reversal of previous law was bound to meet with powerful resistance. When a year later the Court called upon schools to implement *Brown* with "all deliberate speed"—a phrase devoid of much in the way of either clarity or legal meaning—James J. Kilpatrick, editor of *The Richmond News Leader*, who had been relatively progressive on racial matters up to that point, announced, "When the court proposes that its social revolution be imposed upon the South 'as soon as practicable,' there are those of us who would respond that 'as soon as practicable' means never at all."[40] Southern segregationists rallied, and ranged from the terroristic violence of the Ku Klux Klan (KKK) to the putatively more respectable White Citizens' Councils. ("The KKK in gray flannel suits," was Bayard Rustin's characterization of the latter.[41]) In Congress, nineteen senators and eighty-two representatives signed the Southern Manifesto, proclaiming, "We regard the decision of the Supreme Court in the school cases as clear abuse of judicial power." The federal judiciary had decided to "legislate" and had thus encroached "upon the reserved rights of the States and the people."[42]

Warren and his fellow justices issued their decision but could not enforce it; the federal government, first under President Eisenhower and later under President Kennedy, was not eager to undertake measures that could lead to widespread violence and civil unrest. In the meantime, following decades of painfully slow progress, the liberals on the Warren Court decided that what race relations in America required was a revolution. Prodded, particularly by Justice William Brennan, the Warren Court ruled in *Cooper v. Aaron* (1958) to enforce desegregation in Little Rock; in *Baker v. Carr* (1962), it ruled that the unequal size of legislative districts—one legislator for a tiny rural district, and one for a huge urban district—violated the Equal Protection clause; and in *New York Times v. Sullivan* (1964), it ruled that the First Amendment barred southern authorities from suing newspapers or civil rights activists for libel.[43]

Even so, the revolution the justices said they wanted would prove quite different from the revolution they actually achieved, and liberals' failure to understand this distinction would go a long way toward undoing the gains they thought they had made in transforming America and overcoming the nation's "original sin." The past, as it quickly became clear, was not dead. Regarding race, it wasn't even the past.

The year 1954 was also the year that twenty-five-year-old Martin Luther King, Jr., took over the pulpit at the Dexter Avenue Baptist Church in Montgomery, Alabama.[44] Unbeknownst to him, he had entered a community in which powerful sentiments about resistance to racial oppression were already percolating. Jo Ann Robinson, head of the Women's Political Council and a community activist in Montgomery, heard the news about *Brown* and proposed a bus boycott to fight segregation on public transport. After all, blacks were "three-fourths of the riders of these public conveyances," she reasoned to her friends, and this meant that they'd have an easy time pushing through changes they desired by simply refusing to ride.[45]

The youthful minister was well educated and already famously wise beyond his years. He brought with him an intensity and self-discipline schooled by a stern father who had pushed his son from the start of his short life. The son of a sharecropper turned preacher, the Reverend Martin Luther King, Sr., led Atlanta's Ebenezer Baptist Church with a combination of fervid evangelicalism and conservative faith designed to "help its people prosper financially as well as spiritually."[46] To his children, "Daddy King" was a harsh taskmaster, one who might whip out his belt to administer punishment when his expectations of good behavior were not met.[47] His son grew anxious of failure, even contemplating suicide at low points in his life, but learned to calm himself by developing a dandyish side to his personality. Attending the all-black Morehouse College in Atlanta, which, together with Howard University, was then the primary training ground of the black elite, he embraced the school's ideal of the "successful, fun-loving gentleman."[48] In much the same manner, King departed from his father's stern fundamentalism and gravitated toward a less restrictive, more forgiving Christian liberalism. When he announced to his father that he planned to attend Crozer Theological Seminary in Pennsylvania, King senior worried that his namesake would be educated on what amounted to foreign soil: a white seminary noted for its liberal theological teachings.[49]

At Crozer, King began to study Niebuhr, whose work would help transform both his beliefs and character. "My reading of the works of Reinhold Niebuhr," King would later write, "made me aware of the complexity of human motives and the reality of sin on every level of man's existence. Moreover, I came to recognize the complexity of man's social involvement and the glaring reality of collective evil. I came to feel that liberalism had been all too sentimental concerning human nature and that it leaned toward a false idealism."[50] King pondered the relationship between "coercion" and "justice," and concluded: "Justice is a check (by force if necessary) upon ambitions of individuals seeking to overcome their own insecurity at the expense of others."[51] It was an insight he would retain for the balance of his brief life as he juggled the demands of redemptive love and the (unavoidable) coercion of evil.

(While Niebuhr would remain a powerful theological and intellectual influence on King's thinking, he would prove rather reluctant to commit his personal prestige to King's cause or to the cause of civil rights generally during the 1950s and early 1960s. He advised in 1957 that pressuring the South to enforce Supreme Court integration decisions would "do more harm than good" as it would appear to be "Yankee interference." Like so many other of the leading lights of liberalism of the day, Niebuhr looked to "the slow erosion of racial prejudice" to work its way through the South and end the evil of segregation.[52])

Upon finishing Crozer, King was accepted to a doctoral program in philosophy at Boston University, where he focused on theology. He "tamped, smoked, and fiddled with a pipe almost constantly, spoke with an air of detached reserve, and developed the far-off look of a philosopher," observes Taylor Branch, the most ambitious of King's many biographers.[53] King also met and married Coretta Scott while working on a dissertation on the theology of Paul Tillich and Henry Nelson Wieman. (Much of this work was discovered, long after his death, to have been plagiarized.[54]) He meanwhile inquired about teaching jobs at numerous black colleges in the South, including Morehouse, though his father still expected him to return to his own church and become copastor. When Dexter Avenue Baptist Church sent out feelers to King about ministering there, King senior balked at the idea and warned his son that Dexter was a "big-shots church" that chewed and spit out its pastors.[55] But King wanted to be free from his father and had decided to work among people rather than live the life of the isolated scholar. So on September 5, 1954, he gave his first sermon as resident pastor at Dexter.[56]

King became active in the executive committee of the local NAACP in Montgomery soon after he arrived, and in late 1955, after being approached by his parishioners, he agreed to head up the Montgomery Improvement Association, the organizational heart of what would become the bus boycott.[57] As Taylor Branch notes, one of King's aims was "to answer one peevish charge that" had been printed in early stories about the bus boycott: namely, "that the Negroes had borrowed the boycott tactic from the White Citizens' Councils, which had openly adopted a policy of harsh economic reprisal against Negroes who fought segregation."[58]

Preaching at the Holt Street Baptist Church, King challenged and inspired his audience of maids, janitors, and day laborers. "There comes a time when people get tired of being trampled over by the iron feet of oppression. . . . We are not here advocating violence. . . . The only weapon that we have in our hands this evening is the weapon of protest," he continued. "There will be no crosses burned at any bus stops in Montgomery. There will be no white persons pulled out of their homes and taken out on some distant road and lynched for not cooperating. There will be nobody among us who will stand up and defy the Constitution of this nation." And here, he built to a magnificent crescendo:

> And we are not wrong; we are not wrong in what we are doing. If we are wrong, the Supreme Court of this nation is wrong. If we are wrong, the Constitution of the United States is wrong. If we are wrong, God Almighty is wrong. If we are wrong, Jesus of Nazareth was merely a utopian dreamer that never came down to Earth. If we are wrong, justice is a lie; love has no meaning. And we are determined here in Montgomery to work and fight until justice runs down like water and righteousness like a mighty stream.[59]

King was part preacher, part organizer, and part philosopher—a mixture, as Branch writes, "of the exalted and the common."[60] The civil rights historian

David L. Chappell believed it "misleading to view the civil rights movement as a social and political event that had religious overtones." Rather, as its participants' own language demonstrates, it was "for them, primarily a religious event, whose social and political aspects were, in their minds, secondary or incidental." Chappell compares it to the First and Second Great Awakenings in early American history. [61]

The boycott itself proved a test of the mettle and endurance of ordinary people. Cars were few and far between, and those forced to walk to work were met with the harassment of local officials, and were often subjected to "vagrancy" arrests. (King himself was arrested when driving boycotters.) Throughout the ordeal King kept firm in his insistence on nonviolence, even when his own house was bombed, and the city's black citizens redoubled their determination. In the end, as the organization teetered and its participants struggled to hold out just a little longer, the courts intervened to allow the strikers to declare victory. On November 13, 1956, the Supreme Court upheld a decision by a three-judge panel for Alabama's Middle District Court that the city's segregated bus lines were unconstitutional. "God Almighty has spoken from Washington, D.C.!" shouted one black man in the back of the courtroom.[62] King greeted his followers with a sense of joy and jubilation as they had "awaken[ed] a sense of shame within the oppressor and challenge[d] his false sense of superiority. . . . The end is reconciliation; the end is redemption; the end is the creation of the beloved community."[63]

The success of the boycott thrust the young preacher into the national spotlight. In February of 1957 he helped to organize a civil rights organization to be called the Southern Christian Leadership Conference to try to replicate his victory across the South, and that month his image graced the cover of *Time*. His organization's purpose was opposed, however, not only by NAACP's executive secretary Roy Wilkins but also by Thurgood Marshall, both of whom viewed King as an unwelcome (and uncontrollable) rival for leadership of the rapidly growing civil rights movement. The lawyer felt he had "save[d] King's bacon" and caustically complained, "All that walking for nothing. They might as well have waited for the Court decision."[64]

King's lieutenant, Bayard Rustin, a World War II conscientious objector, had risen through the ranks of marginalized pacifist organizations, and then in 1955 visited Montgomery, where he impressed King with the relevance to his movement-building tasks of the nonviolent resistance techniques practiced so successfully in India by India's Mohandas Gandhi and his followers. Until the bus boycott, Rustin explained, "the major emphasis in our struggle to obtain civil rights has been legal and legislative." But now, "the center of gravity has shifted from the courts to community action."[65]

In 1957 the cause of racial equality also received its first twentieth-century vote of support from the United States Congress, since Reconstruction, a bastion of segregationist southern conservatives. Due largely to the tireless and often quite brilliant legislative maneuvering efforts of Majority Leader Lyndon Johnson, who needed to prove his bona fides to liberal northerners were he ever to achieve his goal of one day becoming president, Congress passed its first Civil Rights Act since 1875, giving the U.S. attorney general the power to "correct any abuses of any constitutional rights."[66] It was, in truth, a weak, almost toothless bill with extremely vague language and precious little enforcement power over local abuses of citizens' rights. Roy Wilkins decided to throw the NAACP's weight behind it on the basis of the argument "If you are digging a ditch with a teaspoon, and a man comes along and offers you a spade, there is something wrong with your head if you don't take it because he didn't offer you a bulldozer."[67]

Still, the legislation was sufficiently dangerous to segregationists' accustomed domination that South Carolina's Strom Thurmond, who had bolted the Democratic Party over its antilynching legislation in 1948 and would soon lead an exodus of ex-Confederates into the arms of the Republicans, felt compelled to launch a filibuster on the floor of the Senate that lasted a full twenty-four hours. (He was occasionally spelled by future Republican presidential nominee Barry Goldwater.[68]) But Johnson was able to get the bill passed, and when President Eisenhower was, reluctantly, forced to intervene to ensure the integration of the schools in Little Rock, Arkansas, the movement for integration could credibly claim to have all three branches of the federal government on its side.

Meanwhile, A. Philip Randolph, founder of the Brotherhood of Sleeping Car Porters, now a vice president in the merged AFL-CIO, pressed its socially conservative president, George Meany, to lend labor's support to the cause. He sought the expulsion of unions that continued to practice discrimination, including the International Longshoremen's Association, the Brotherhood of Railroad Trainmen, and the Brotherhood of Locomotive Firemen and Enginemen. Aided by Walter Reuther (and frequently with little more than the reluctant acquiescence of Meany), the labor movement invested more and more of its resources in the civil rights struggle, on more than one occasion alienating any number of the white workers who made up its majority.[69] As Congressman Richard Bolling would later observe, "We never would have passed the

Civil Rights Act without labor. They had the muscle; the other civil rights groups did not."[70]

Over time the civil rights struggle would grow to become a multifront war involving almost all institutions of American social, political, and cultural life. In Hollywood, Stanley Kramer returned to the theme of race in his 1958 film, *The Defiant Ones*. In it two men, one white and one black, escape from a chain gang, hitched together. Although they don't like each other, they are forced to cooperate to escape to freedom and eventually find themselves competing in self-sacrifice to save the other. Sidney Poitier, the only black actor in Hollywood allowed to play leading roles in A-level movies for the coming decade, brought to his role his typical mixture of smarts, sex appeal, and overall suavity.[71]

By the late 1950s, however, strictures were crumbling all around Cold War America. Communism no longer presented much of a worry for most Americans, according to late-fifties opinion polls, despite the failed Hungarian uprising against the Soviets in 1956 and the successful Cuban revolution of 1959.[72] In 1957, three years after *Brown*, as James Patterson notes, the Court "strengthened constitutional guarantees against self-incrimination, construed the anti-Communist Smith Act of 1940 narrowly so as to guard against political trials, protected individuals from having to answer questions (from HUAC) about others, and ruled that certain defendants had rights to see reports by FBI-paid informants. As a result of these decisions, the government virtually gave up all efforts to convict Communists under the Smith Act."[73]

The year 1957 would also see a significant victory in the fight against censorship when the American Civil Liberties Union (ACLU) won its case against the state of California defending the bohemian City Lights Bookstore for selling copies of Allen Ginsberg's seminal poem, "Howl"; that case inspired its lawyer, Charles Rembar, to challenge next the nearly thirty-year ban on D. H. Lawrence's *Lady Chatterley's Lover*.[74] He did not defend its graphic depictions of various forms of fornication, but asked, instead, "What if a book was considered obscene yet also presented ideas or possessed even the slightest bit of 'redeeming social importance'?"[75] Two years later he won that case as well, and with it opened the floodgates of American culture to literature that might upset the bluenoses of Boston but was nevertheless legitimately challenging to those who encountered it. Bernard DeVoto did not live to see this day, but it is no exaggeration to say that in hastening it, he helped America finally enter its long adolescence.[76]

This thawing in the overall culture had an impact on liberals as well. Ten years earlier, for instance, Arthur Schlesinger, Jr., had been praising the virtues of "hard-boiled" realism. By 1957, however, he had grown enamored of the social criticism of dissident figures such as Walt Whitman, Ralph Waldo Emerson, and Henry David Thoreau. The historian was now deriding the "phoniness" of American culture and calling for a "rebirth of satire, of dissent" rather than the ethic of responsibility that he had championed at the moment of *The Vital Center*.[77] Martin Luther King, Jr., another Thoreauvian , also spoke on behalf of "maladjustment" in an age of conformity.[78] Liberalism was opening itself up and learning to laugh a bit, even at itself, as Jewish comedians such as Mort Sahl and Lenny Bruce challenged the limits of censorship on stage. (An example of Sahlian humor: "Every time the Russians throw an American in jail, the HUAC retaliates—by throwing an American in jail."[79])

A small peace movement arose as well. In 1957 ordinary citizens and some leading cultural figures created the National Committee for a Sane Nuclear Policy (SANE), which grew into a nationwide membership organization with 130 chapters and twenty-five thousand members within a year of its founding.[80] The 1958 midterm elections brought future liberal leaders Ernest Gruening, Eugene McCarthy, and Edmund Muskie to the Senate, along with a gain of forty-eight seats for Democrats in the House. As the fifties drew to a close, so too ended the "invisibility" of America's original sin: legally sanctioned racism. Led by the men and women who risked their lives to challenge segregation, and the words and actions of the ministers, farmhands, students, and rabble-rousers who inspired them, history was again on the march. It was long past time for liberals to get on the bus and ride along with them.

9

The Liberal Hour

What do our opponents mean when they apply to us the label "Liberal"? If by "Liberal" they mean, as they want people to believe, someone who is soft in his policies abroad, who is against local government, and who is unconcerned with the taxpayer's dollar, then . . . we are not that kind of "Liberal." But if by a "Liberal" they mean someone who looks ahead and not behind, someone who welcomes new ideas without rigid reactions, someone who cares about the welfare of the people—their health, their housing, their schools, their jobs, their civil rights, and their civil liberties—someone who believes we can break through the stalemate and suspicions that grip us in our policies abroad, if that is what they mean by a "Liberal," then I'm proud to say I'm a "Liberal."

—Senator John F. Kennedy, September 14, 1960[1]

By the 1960s liberals had had enough of their beautiful loser, Adlai Stevenson. With Eisenhower constitutionally prevented from running for a third term by the passage of the Twenty-second Amendment, far fewer liberals found themselves eager for merely "moral" victories this time around. Fortunately, Richard Nixon, an unpopular vice president with a reputation as a right-wing hatchet man, was a candidate who could be beat. More important, JFK was no Adlai.

Like both Stevenson and FDR, John Fitzgerald Kennedy was, in most respects, an odd choice for a liberal icon. Raised during the Depression in what was then one of the greatest fortunes in America, he belonged to perhaps the closest thing America has ever had to a "royal family." (And in authentic American fashion, that status was bought and paid for in cash, much of it built on bootlegging, financial speculation, and no less appropriate, moviemaking.) Its patriarch, Joe Kennedy, an Irish Catholic financier, stock-market manipulator, film producer, and failed politician, consciously set out to raise (and bank-roll) America's first Catholic president. When the oldest son, Joe junior, was killed while on a bombing raid off the coast of England late in the war, it fell to Jack to assume the family mantle and realize his father's ambition. After attending Canterbury and Choate preparatory schools, JFK initially picked Princeton before settling at Harvard, which would become a kind of finishing school and private brain trust for all three remaining Kennedy sons through-out their respective political careers. His classmates found him to be a "charm-ing, irreverent young man with a fine sense of humor and a passion for sports and the good life."[2] He was a world-class playboy with a superhuman libido—one that was probably increased by the medication he was forced to take for his myriad ailments—and the many women he bedded undoubtedly provided a source of not only physical enjoyment but also psychological self-confidence. Unlike his passionate, brooding, and "ruthless" younger brother, however, JFK pursued women as he pursued politics: with a devil-may-care insouciance that both charmed and frustrated the objects of his brief affections.[3] As the journalist Richard Reeves observed, JFK "squeezed people like tubes of paint, gently or brutally, and the people around him . . . were the indentured inhab-itants serving his needs and desires. . . . He liv[ed] his life as if it were a race against boredom."[4]

Joseph Kennedy was obsessive about many things: money, power, respect, sexual conquest—he enjoyed a shamelessly unconcealed extramarital affair with the film star Gloria Swanson during his producer days in Hollywood—but these paled beside his compulsion for winning, one he instilled in his sons. "We don't want any losers around here," the old man would explain. "In this family we want winners. Don't come in second or third—that doesn't count—but win."[5] It was a ruthless demand given that of the nine children, only one could emerge the winner at any given time.

Jack had early health problems, including scarlet fever at age three (requir-ing two months in the hospital, then two weeks in a sanatorium), chicken pox, numerous ear infections, undiagnosed spells of dizziness and weakness, con-stant flu in his teen years, a dangerous weight problem, and the colitis of his early adulthood.[6] Dealing with constant pain not only toughened the young man, but engendered an attractive, easygoing disposition that allowed him to take his enormous wealth and good fortune in stride. Like his brother Joe, Jack served heroically in World War II, saving the lives of one of the men of the PT boat he captained by swimming miles with a rope between his teeth, tethered to an injured sailor. The fact that his father milked this incident for enormous local publicity, and used it to launch his second son's political career in Congress, does not diminish either the bravery it required or the physical pain it caused that almost never left him.

Though Jack's famous back troubles would be attributed to his war injuries for political reasons, they were actually already present in 1938, when he was heard to complain about occasional pain in his right sacroiliac joint. Upon returning home for back surgery, stateside doctors arrived at a new diagnosis: Addison's disease, due, most likely, to hormones he had ingested for all of his health problems since the 1930s.[7] Kennedy would continue to ignore the severity of his multiple illnesses and consumed a dizzying array of legal and illegally obtained medications, including cortisone, penicillin, procaine, and Nembutal while enduring secret hospitalizations.[8] He understood that his image of youth and vigor, together with his good looks, charm, grace, and intelligence, were his primary political selling points.

Politics, like pretty much everything in life, came remarkably easily to Jack Kennedy. His first run for Congress in 1946 began an unbroken string of victories that brought him to the White House at age forty-three. A Cold War liberal who unambiguously rejected the isolationism that had marred his father's political career, he was dubbed by the columnist Joseph Alsop "Stevenson with balls."[9] Charlie Peters, a young lawyer just entering West Virginia politics in 1960, detected in the young man the "smell of a winner."[10]

However reckless in his personal life, Kennedy was cautious to a fault in politics. From the standpoint of the liberals whose support he needed, Kennedy's record was significantly tarnished by his decision to absent himself when his fellow senators finally found the courage to censure Senator McCarthy. His reticence here points to a number of complicated characteristics about Kennedy. The first was obviously caution. The second was political self-interest, and third, toughness. Kennedy was under no illusions about the blustery buffoonery of the senator from Wisconsin. Personally, he wanted nothing to do with McCarthy or anybody like him, and publicly he did not dare defend him. Kennedy understood that Massachusetts Catholics had little to gain by attacking anti-Communist Catholic heroes, however much they may have been despised at Harvard. Kennedy already had the support of the sophisticates; he needed to solidify his appeal to average, workaday voters. (Rather typically, he mocked himself, rather ruefully, in private to Arthur Schlesinger, Jr., at a get-to-know-you dinner between the two in July 1959. Kennedy told the liberal thinker that he thought he should admit his mistake in being insufficiently "forthright" about McCarthy. When Schlesinger tried to smooth over the issue by pointing out that JFK had written *Profiles in Cour-*

age as penance—though in fact, Theodore Sorensen had almost certainly written most of the book—Kennedy replied, "Yes, but I didn't have any chapter in it about myself.") Kennedy went on to blame his unwillingness to go on record against McCarthy on the fact that brother Bobby had worked on the senator's committee and that his father and the senator had been "great friends."[11]

Kennedy's unshakable sangfroid left hard-core liberals understandably uncertain about his true motives. During the course of his brief and unremarkable—indeed, almost invisible—career in Congress, he evinced little passion for favored liberal issues and paid few if any liberal dues. Many colleagues shared the view of political journalist Theodore White that Kennedy was "a lightweight who had bought his Senate seat with his father's money."[12] Jimmy Wechsler initially labeled JFK a "charm boy," but then found himself alternately impressed and confused by what he called Kennedy's "mingled intelligence and lack of visceral reponses."[13] His ADA colleague James Loeb worried that "ice water" ran in Kennedy's veins and that there was "something very mechanical where his heart ought to be."[14] Eleanor Roosevelt, still the grand dame of American liberalism, developed a particularly intense dislike for Kennedy. She detested his father and thought his son to be a coward when it came to McCarthy.[15] Though she remained emotionally committed to her close friend Stevenson, when asked by a panel of college students who would make the best presidential candidate in 1960, she claimed that Hubert Humphrey "came closest to having 'the spark of greatness,'" indicating that JFK was not even her second choice for the job.[16] Eventually, however, the charm won out. After Kennedy did what was necessary, paying a courtesy call to her in order to, as he put it, "kiss her ass," Mrs. Roosevelt came around as well. "I liked him better than I ever had before, because he seemed so little cocksure."[17]

For the novelist Norman Mailer, who captured much of what he deemed to be the candidate's appeal to an America on the cusp of social revolution in his famous 1960 essay, "Superman Comes to the Supermarket," Kennedy was a "hipster" in "existential" revolt against mass society, a man with "a cool grace" and a "good lithe wit," a "subtle, not quite describable intensity."[18] Arbiters of style for decades to come would wax poetic about the candidate's "sunglasses and convertible cars"; his "confident, carefree style" that proved a "radical departure from the copycat boxy gray suits and felt hats that had defined men's fashion for previous generations."[19]

Whatever his ideological deficiencies, in one significant respect Kennedy's candidacy advanced an aspect of liberalism that Stevenson (or Humphrey or Johnson) could not: religious tolerance. No Catholic before JFK had ever been elected president, and none had been nominated since Al Smith ran in 1928.

Kennedy courageously faced the issue head on during the primaries, making his campaign a call for religious tolerance and a battle against one of America's longest-held prejudices. In an appearance before the Greater Houston Ministerial Association without any aides or even any notes before him, he asserted, "If this election is decided on the basis that forty million Americans lost their chance of being President on the day they were baptized, then it is the whole nation that will be the loser in the eyes of Catholics and non-Catholics around the world, in the eyes of history, and in the eyes of our own people."[20]

The old order died slowly. When Minnesota Democrat Eugene McCarthy, who believed himself to be both a better liberal and a better Catholic than Kennedy, nominated Stevenson at the 1960 convention to cheering crowds, it felt very much like a desperate last gasp of a man whose time had passed. "Do not reject this man," McCarthy bellowed. But of course a majority of Democrats were now eager to do just that.[21] Humphrey, a more likely alternative, as Eleanor Roosevelt's support implied, ran as the guardian of the New Deal tradition, offering a sixteen-point program designed to highlight his liberal bona fides and strong commitment to civil rights.[22] Kennedy figured he would beat Stevenson under any circumstances but naturally preferred to do so without earning the rancor of the diehard liberals who stuck with him. He first offered a promise of the job of secretary of state in return for the liberal standard-bearer's endorsement. But when Stevenson not only rejected the deal, but confided to reporters that Jack was "too young" to be president and "not up to the job," the Massachusetts senator threatened him, saying, "Look, I have the votes for the nomination, and if you don't give me your support, I'll have to shit all over you."[23] (And perhaps more than any other, Kennedy kept this promise.)

Meanwhile, his campaign painted the fiery, onetime ADA-wunderkind Humphrey as temperamentally unsuited to the times. ("Hubert is too hot for the present mood of the people. He gets people too excited, too worked up. What they want today is a more boring, monotonous personality, like me," Kennedy privately joked.[24]) He tacked rightward to defeat Humphrey during the primaries and then leftward to assuage the hurt feelings of his supporters once the Minnesotan had been handily dispatched. ("I want to be nominated by the liberals," he told Schlesinger. "I don't want to go screwing around with all those southern bastards."[25]) When he picked Lyndon Johnson, a real "southern bastard" whom he thought to be a "chronic liar" and who had lived up to none of the assurances he had given Kennedy during his time in the Senate, as his running mate, he again insulted the party's liberals but reassured its old pros that, despite his youth, he had the killer instinct necessary to go all the way.[26]

Meanwhile, as part of his peacemaking efforts with the party's liberal wing, Kennedy allowed the passage of the most progressive platform in the Democratic Party's history, one that tracked in many specifics of ADA's own wish list. "The time has come," it announced, "to assure equal access for all Americans to all areas of community life, including voting booths, schoolhouses, jobs, housing, and public facilities." It demanded that school districts comply with *Brown v. Board of Education* and instructed the next president to empower "the Attorney General to file civil injunction suits in federal courts to prevent the denial of any civil rights on grounds of race, creed or color," adding a call for the Fair Employment Practices Commission "to secure for everyone the right to equal opportunity for employment."[27] Significant, however, was the fact that Kennedy's people met secretly with southern white delegations at the same time to assuage their concerns, promising them that the candidate, like most candidates, did not consider platform language to be terribly important, much less legally or morally binding.[28]

The transition from Stevenson to Kennedy is nicely illustrated by the migration of liberalism's most influential political intellectuals, Arthur Schlesinger, Jr., and John Kenneth Galbraith, from one camp to the other. Schlesinger arrived in Los Angeles guilty and unhappy but felt Stevenson had no chance, which loosened for him what remained strong "ties of loyalty, of affection, of personal admiration" for the two-time loser. Personally Schlesinger felt "that as a consequence of Kennedy's victory and Stevenson's defeat something I greatly value has gone out of national politics." Yet Schlesinger perceived in Kennedy a "cool, sharp mind" and "Rooseveltian political genius" that would likely lead to his being a "the better President." "I believe him to be a liberal," he confided to his journal, "but committed by a sense of history rather than consecrated by inner conviction. I also believe him to be a devious and, if necessary, ruthless man."[29]

Kennedy had quite naturally sought Galbraith's counsel on economic matters but also on more far-reaching questions, such as the proper U.S. response to the shock of *Sputnik*. They met frequently for long discussions over lobster stew at Boston's Locke-Ober restaurant, and soon Schlesinger began to join them, the three men plotting out the likely themes of the coming presidential campaign without Kennedy's demanding, yet, that either man renounce his loyalty to Stevenson. In fact, when Galbraith's book *The Liberal Hour* was published in June of 1960, he flattered Stevenson by sending a copy with an enclosed note that read "My strategy is to keep in good with you in case you are nominated despite my support of John Fitzgerald Kennedy."[30]

In that book Galbraith drew on the arguments he and Schlesinger had made in favor of their notion of qualitative liberalism. He worried that Americans enjoyed "no enduring sense of national purpose."[31] He developed what would soon be recognized as the Kennedyesque themes of "tackling the arms race and disarmament," "forging a new development compact with the Third World," producing 'Growth with balance,'" and "rebuilding America" with emphasis on "schooling and health, medical research, housing and urban development, public transit, and the environment."[32] Kennedy could, in Galbraith's own words, make politics move beyond the satisfaction of "the comfortable and the contented."[33] These notions coalesced during the fall campaign into the rubric of Kennedy's "New Frontier": "The New Frontier of which I speak is not a set of promises—it is a set of challenges. It sums up not what I intend to *offer* the American people, but what I intend to *ask* of them," he explained. "Are we up to the task—are we equal to the challenge? That is the question of the New Frontier. That is the choice our nation must make—a choice between the public interest and private comfort, between national greatness and national decline."[34]

Standing before a frigid crowd on January 20, 1961, Kennedy delivered an inaugural address that embodied a youthful idealism that would continue to inspire millions of people for decades to come: "Let the word go forth from this time and place, to friend and foe alike that the torch has been passed to a new generation of Americans—born in this century, tempered by war, disciplined by a hard and bitter peace, proud of our ancient heritage—and unwilling to witness or permit the slow undoing of those human rights to which this nation has always been committed, and to which we are committed today at home and around the world." The words "at home" were included at the insistence of Harris Wofford, a young man who wanted the president to at least mention the issue on which he had been hired to help the president: the struggle for civil rights in America.[35] Kennedy wanted to focus his speech and presidential energy on foreign affairs, and in one particularly ill-considered moment of rhetorical hyperbole, he promised America would "pay any price, bear any burden" in order to ensure "the survival and the success of liberty," a vow that would later come back to haunt both Kennedy and his successor when the price rose above America's or any nation's means.

But braggadocio aside, the speech proved significant in many respects. Borrowing a line from John Kenneth Galbraith, he urged: "Let us never negotiate out of fear. But let us never fear to negotiate." He followed this with what would become one of the signature lines in all political oration, one that put him in a rhetorical league with Franklin Roosevelt, if not Abraham Lincoln: "And so my fellow Americans: ask not what your country can do for you—ask what you can do for your country."[36]

Following his final debate with Richard Nixon, candidate Kennedy had flown to Michigan, landing at 2 a.m. due to delays. Bleary-eyed, he rode straight to the University of Michigan, where a throng of students had stayed awake to greet him. Having no prepared remarks, he began by joking. "I come here tonight," he grinned, "to go to bed." (Lascivious laughter followed, as Kennedy's reputation had apparently preceded him.) Then the candidate got serious and challenged the assembled students: "How many of you are willing to spend ten years in Africa or Latin America or Asia working for the United States and working for freedom? On your willingness to contribute part of your life to this country will depend the answer whether we as a free country can compete." As the microphone began to shriek, Kennedy yelled over the noise, "I think it can! And I think Americans are willing to contribute, but I think the effort must be far greater than we've ever made in the past!"[37]

Earlier in the year, on a college TV show, Kennedy had been asked what he thought about Congressman Henry Reuss's bill calling for a study of a youth corps. The candidate was entirely unfamiliar with the idea but responded positively to the notion of sending young Americans to work in developing countries. Angered at what he considered to be bad staff work, he later asked Richard Goodwin to learn more about it.

The original inspiration for the Peace Corps can be traced to the settlement house movement of the Progressive Era in which Eleanor Roosevelt worked. As president, her husband had initiated the Civilian Conservation Corps (CCC), both to create jobs for the unemployed and indigent but also to nurture a sense of civic participation for all Americans. It was Hubert Humphrey who proposed, in 1957, sending young Americans abroad for peaceful purposes. He failed, however, three years later to pass a bill that would have ensured its creation.[38] Barely six weeks into his presidency, Kennedy created the Peace Corps by executive order. It was a temporary pilot program, but soon it would become Kennedy's signature congressional victory and an important symbol of his belief in the importance of inspiring a new generation of Americans to the cause of democratic idealism and personal service.[39]

Kennedy appointed his brother-in-law Sargent Shriver to head the program. Raised in Baltimore, Shriver was educated in Catholic schools, and instead of the predictable rebellion, it led to his embrace of the Social Gospel.[40]

He married Eunice Kennedy in 1953, and her father hired him to run the family's Merchandise Mart business in Chicago, where Shriver became enamored with the burgeoning civil rights movement. He joined with the Catholic Interracial Council to press for school desegregation in the city, and befriended Adlai Stevenson. Although he was asked to run for governor of Illinois in 1959, his ambitions for elective office were quickly shut down by his autocratic father-in-law: "Under no circumstances are you to run for governor next year," Joe Kennedy told him, "Jack needs your help on the campaign."[41]

Jack would tease "Sarge" by calling him his house Communist, a term that was interchangeable within the campaign with "goody-goody."[42] "Initially, the general impression I got was that Sarge was kind of a weak sister," recalled Charlie Peters, who met Shriver while working for Kennedy in West Virginia, and was later recruited to the Peace Corps. "Bobby tended to condescend to Sarge and sometimes just pissed all over him." But "within a couple of months, I knew I was in the presence of a great leader in terms of exciting people, in terms of getting an organization moving."[43]

Among Shriver's earliest recruits was Harris Wofford, who happened to be the first white man to enroll at Howard Law School (though he transferred to Yale after his first year), and was the founder of the Student Federalists, which had proposed a "'peace force' of volunteers for development projects in communities abroad."[44] Wofford's dedication to the civil rights movement—and JFK's apparent lack of it—was a key factor in his decision to join Shriver rather than fight internal battles within the White House itself.[45] Shriver also lifted the twenty-six-year-old wunderkind Bill Moyers from Lyndon Johnson's staff. An Oklahoma native raised in Marshall, Texas, Moyers was educated to be a Baptist minister before becoming a journalist, and then, by a series of unlikely incidents, LBJ's closest political adviser. Despite, or perhaps because of, his astonishing youth, Moyers proved virtually unique in his ability, and willingness, to stand up to the famously autocratic majority leader. He also played an invaluable role as a kind of ambassador between the two unfriendly camps within the White House. "I understood the Boston Mafia and I understood the Texas Cowboys," he explained many years later to Danielle Ivory.[46] When Shriver asked the White House for him, the Kennedy team tried to persuade Moyers to stay, for as Kenneth O'Donnell complained, "He's the only one on Johnson's staff we trust."[47] But Shriver would not stand down and soon Moyers became the Peace Corps deputy director (and the youngest person ever to be confirmed by the United States Senate).[48]

In many respects, sending people abroad to deploy America's financial and technological resources to find ways to improve the lives of the people of developing nations proved a hopelessly naive notion. Little thought was given, at least initially, to the complications likely to arise when young Americans, largely ignorant of local customs and mores, tried to bring ancient cultures into the secular, Western twentieth century. Overseeing both the projects and the money was also a significant problem, as local warlords, potentates, and tribal leaders were accustomed to receiving their cut of all goods and funds that flowed through the localities where their word was law.[49]

Yet the Peace Corps managed to capture some of the spirit of liberal idealism that inspired the country at the beginning of the sixties. Its "internal structure and organizational culture," Elizabeth Cobbs-Hoffman wrote, "blossomed like time-lapse photography [as] three emphases emerged immediately: democracy, individualism, and reform."[50] The program proved wildly popular, and volunteers flocked to serve.[51] Norman Cousins, the editor of *Saturday Review,* wrote, "Words like purpose and commitment are [now] used without apology" in Washington, D.C., circles. "Idealism is back in style," he announced, thanks to the Peace Corps.[52] In 1964 it was followed up with a domestic version, Volunteers in Service to America (VISTA).[53] Together, with all their shortcomings, the programs represented an almost perfect distillation of the liberal creed.

An enthusiast of Ian Fleming's James Bond novels, and eager to rid the United States of the continuing embarrassment of Fidel Castro, who taunted him from ninety miles off the coast of Florida, Kennedy proved eager to embrace a plan conceived by the Eisenhower administration for the island's liberation by a group of anti-Communist Cuban exiles, trained and equipped by the CIA.[54] Hearing of the scheme, liberals, led by Arthur Schlesinger, Jr., balked, worried that it would unleash a "wave of massive protest, agitation, and sabotage throughout Latin America, Europe, Asia, and Africa."[55] But Schlesinger knew that men of action—especially the Joint Chiefs of Staff and CIA director Allen Dulles—had gotten the ear of a president who almost always preferred deeds to words.[56]

Of course, the Bay of Pigs invasion of April 1961 proved a fiasco, as if planned and executed by the Marx Brothers or perhaps the Three Stooges. The invaders were ill equipped, ill trained, and ill prepared to fight the Cuban military. When the popular uprising that U.S. planners naively expected failed to materialize, the only chance for the survival of the counterrevolutionaries lay in their hopes for American airstrikes against their enemy. But when the moment of truth came, Kennedy refused to play along. The invasion force was cut loose; some of its members drowned, some were captured, and more than a few lost their lives, sowing bitterness among Cuban Americans toward the president and the party that had sold out their patriots and leaving Kennedy and his advisers deeply embarrassed at having been snookered by their own spies and generals. "How could I have been so stupid as to let them proceed?" he repeatedly asked himself during those fateful hours, eventually engineering the replacement of CIA director Allen Dulles.[57] *The New York Times* editors spoke for a consensus when they observed that the Bay of Pigs invasion left the United States "look[ing] like fools to our friends, rascals to our enemies, and incompetents to the rest."[58]

But credit must be given to John Kennedy. He not only resisted the urge to blame others for his mistakes, but he learned from them as well. Realizing he had made a massive error in unquestioningly trusting the judgment of those who had steered him onto this disastrous path, Kennedy renewed his commitment to the central principle that Truman had defended during the Korean War and General MacArthur's insubordination: namely, the importance of civilian control over the armed forces. "We're not going to plunge into an irresponsible action just because a fanatical fringe in this country puts so-called national pride above national reason," he promised.[59] In early May, Arthur Schlesinger, Jr., saw the president looking, "as usual, cool and composed. We talked again about Cuba," Schlesinger recorded in his journal. " 'If it hadn't been for Cuba,' " he said, " 'we might be about to intervene in Laos now.' " Kennedy had waved a sheaf of cables from Air Force general Lyman Lemnitzer apparently urging such intervention. "I might have taken this man's advice seriously."[60] The CIA and Joint Chiefs would never have the final word again.

Nearly a year after the Bay of Pigs, on March 13, 1962, JFK announced a "vast cooperative effort" to promote economic development throughout Latin America that he called the Alliance for Progress.[61] The United States "pledged $20 billion for Latin American development over ten years, keyed to proportional commitments by recipient governments and to reforms in land tenure and the tax structure."[62] This, too, did not work out as planned, falling victim in many places to both bureaucratic inertia at home and the predictable obstruction of those in power abroad.[63] But it constituted a clear example of the development of liberal thinking about foreign policy: Butter must at least accompany guns and idealism if the United States was to be able to appeal to nations looking to assert their freedom and independence in a postcolonial world.

At the same time, however, Kennedy committed himself to an almost obsessive effort to overthrow Fidel Castro, to the point where, as he himself privately admitted, America's allies "think that we're slightly demented on the subject."[64] Under his brother's orders Robert Kennedy informed CIA director John McCone that ending Castro's rule was "the top priority in the US Government—all else is secondary—no time, no money, effort or manpower is to be spared."[65] In February, Brigadier General Edward Lansdale was putting together a plan for a "revolt which can take place in Cuba by October 1962." Three weeks later General Maxwell Taylor concluded that "final success will require decisive US military intervention."[66]

But the famous missile crisis of that October intervened, and their plans were superseded by the need to solve the more pressing problem. What, exactly, Soviet Premier Nikita Khrushchev was thinking when he decided to build a nuclear weapons launching facility in Cuba will never be answered in full. But with a half century behind us, we have an increasingly detailed and nuanced understanding of the contemporaneous thoughts and actions of the American actors in the crisis, as well as some of those of the Soviets.[67]

Two aspects of the dramatic resoloution of the crisis are often misunderstood in popular discourse. First, Kennedy and company made it appear as if they were the innocent victims of a Soviet/Cuban plot, when in fact they were in the midst of a risky cat-and-mouse game with the Soviets, using the Cubans as proxies, that got completely out of hand when the Soviets raised the stakes with nuclear missiles. Second, for all of the genuine drama associated with Kennedy's decision-making process and the bipartisan group of so-called wise men he assembled, nicknamed the ExCom, the historical record reveals that no matter what his advisers suggested in pubic or in private, Kennedy was determined to resolve the crisis peacefully. He was unwilling to ignore the missiles entirely, though he might have, as they lacked any genuine strategic or military significance in an era when the Soviets could just as effectively have launched an atomic attack from their own soil as from Cuba. But Kennedy worried about both the domestic and international political implications of appearing weak in the face of so ostensibly serious a Soviet challenge. Rather than risk a nuclear exchange for the perception of victory, as many of his advisers insisted he must, Kennedy offered the Soviets what amounted to a straightforward trade: they would remove their missiles from Cuba publicly, and in exchange the United States would not long afterward remove its missiles from Turkey, in secret. Aside from his brother, who actually negotiated the deal via Soviet Ambassador Anatoly Dobrynin, and two other advisers, Secretary of State Dean Rusk and the diplomat Llewellyn E. "Tommy" Thomson, Jr., none of Kennedy's advisers, including the rest of the ExCom, were aware it was taking place. Like the American public, they believed that the United States and the Soviets had been "eyeball to eyeball and the other guy blinked."[68] Kennedy lied about the deal to the American public and sent his advisers out in the world to do the same. Had Khrushchev refused the secret offer and demanded an open trade, evidence indicates that Kennedy would likely have agreed to that as well.[69]

Some on the right did continue to complain that Kennedy had given away the store—even Dean Acheson, whom Kennedy had consulted during the crisis, "felt we were too eager to liquidate this thing. So long as we had the thumbscrew on Khrushchev, we should have given it another turn every day."[70] But for the most part, Kennedy was treated as a conquering hero, his popularity ratings rising to as high as 76 percent, just in time for midterm elections.[71] "For the first time in twenty years," wrote Walter Trohan, Washington bureau chief for the deeply conservative *Chicago Tribune,* "Americans can carry their heads high because the President of the United States has stood up to the premier of Russia and made him back down. . . . Mr. Kennedy ended a course of appeasement [that included the] shameful surrender at Yalta of the peoples of Eastern Europe and Asia. . . . Americans were proud when youthful Mr. Kennedy thrust his jaw in a fighting attitude and faced up to the bully in the Kremlin."[72] *Time* editors mused, "Generations to come may well count John Kennedy's resolve as one of the decisive moments of the twentieth century. For Kennedy was determined to move forward at whatever risk. And when faced by that determination, the bellicose Premier of the Soviet Union first wavered, then weaseled, and finally backed down."[73]

Theodore Sorensen says he believed that the effect of the crisis on the president's advisers "was to purge their minds, at least temporarily, of Cold War clichés."[74] This is a widely accepted view, bolstered by the speech Sorensen wrote and Kennedy delivered in June 1963 at American University, where he pronounced: "World peace, like community peace, does not require that each man love his neighbor—it requires only that they live together in mutual tolerance, submitting their disputes to a just and peaceful settlement."[75] This was followed, moreover, two months later by an American signature on the first significant effort to try to control the nuclear arms race: the U.S.-Soviet Limited Test Ban Treaty.[76]

But the decision to play tough had significant consequences that Kennedy and his men could not have predicted. As the Soviet missiles were being withdrawn, a Soviet negotiator warned his American counterpart, "You Americans will never be able to do this to us again."[77] Nikita Khrushchev, apparently, hoped to use the resolution of the crisis to embark on what Averell Harriman termed, in a secret memo to McGeorge Bundy, a "palpable relaxation of tensions, presumably of some duration" with the United States.[78] But Khrushchev could not even keep his job after the humiliation he suffered at Kennedy's hands. What the world got instead was a massive nuclear arms race that endangered the populations of both nations—and, indeed, those of much of the world—as it simultaneously demanded greater and greater levels of investment, starving human needs on both sides in the process.

No less significant, the crisis cemented in the minds of American policy makers the idea of force as a ladder whose rungs an American president could climb at a pace of his own choosing to communicate will and toughness to a recalcitrant adversary. This was particularly true of liberals who almost always felt themselves to be on the defensive when it came to the willingness to use force. To make matters worse, the president, with the help of some friendly journalists, decided to use the crisis to take care of some personal business and destroy the career of now UN representative Adlai Stevenson. "Adlai wanted a Munich" was the quote offered in describing the two-time presidential candidate and Kennedy rival's suggestion that the United States propose a public missile trade very much like the one the Kennedys had proposed but insisted remain secret. The opprobrium directed against Stevenson that accompanied this (false) revelation would serve as a future warning to anyone thinking along similar lines when a president was forced to choose between the relative risks of war or diplomatic compromise.[79] Examining these results, historian Barton J. Bernstein wonders, "What influence, analysts may profitably speculate, did the widespread belief in Kennedy's great victory in the missile crisis play as President Johnson struggled on, even against the counsel of advisors, for his own triumph in Southeast Asia in 1966–1968? Might he have felt psychologically, and even politically, more free to change policy if he had known, along with his fellow Americans, the truth of the October 1962 secret settlement?"[80] As Cyrus Vance, a high-ranking official in both Kennedy's and Johnson's Pentagon, later observed, "We had seen the gradual application of force applied in the Cuban Missile Crisis, and had seen a very successful result. We believed that if this same gradual and restrained application of force were applied in . . . Vietnam, that one could expect the same kind of result."[81] At a crucial meeting of President Johnson's advisers during which the decision to send massive numbers of ground troops was under consideration, Secretary of State Dean Rusk compared the plan to Kennedy's decision to face down the Russians during the Cuban missile crisis.[82]

Much the same context was adopted in the U.S. media. In late 1965, the influential pundit Joseph Alsop, a JFK intimate, attacked Johnson for being too timid in prosecuting the war. "For Lyndon B. Johnson," the hawkish Alsop taunted, "Viet-nam is what the second Cuban crisis was for John F. Kennedy.

If Mr. Johnson ducks the challenge, we shall learn by experience about what [it] would have been like if Kennedy had ducked the challenge in October, 1962."[83] In February 1966 Bobby Kennedy made particularly shameless use of this metaphor, considering that it was he who conducted the last-minute negotiations to trade missiles with the Soviets and thereby ended the crisis, by insisting Hanoi "must be given to understand as well that their present public demands are in fact for us to surrender a vital national interest—but that, as a far larger and more powerful nation learned in October of 1962, surrender of a vital interest of the United States is an objective which cannot be achieved."[84]

To be fair to all sides, while many of Kennedy's advisers pressed for a more aggressive position in Vietnam, Kennedy resisted, hoping to put off any commitment until the 1964 elections were behind him. His best advice at the time probably came from John Kenneth Galbraith, who had been appointed ambassador to India. As early as 1961 he had complained to the president that the United States was "propping up incompetent governments principally because they are anti-communist. Then we have been subject to a species of blackmail—'keep paying or we collapse.'"[85] A year later he warned, "We are increasingly replacing the French as the colonial military force and we will increasingly arouse the resentments associated therewith."[86] But he was a decidedly minority voice among the president's advisers, and Kennedy undoubtedly felt the pressure of the Republican contestants he would face in 1964, particularly the extreme hawk, Barry Goldwater, who spoke as if all that were needed to salvage the situation was a nuclear bomb or two.

Meanwhile, it has since become a kind of political parlor game to predict just how John Kennedy eventually would have handled Vietnam. David Talbot correctly terms his statements on the Southeast Asian conflict close to the time of his death as a "blur of ambiguity," though in recent years, a group of scholars practicing what they term "virtual history" have strengthened the case for a planned post-1964 withdrawal of U.S. military forces.[87] The fact remains, however, that the Kennedy administration was responsible for the massive increase in resources devoted to weapons spending, and displayed a willingness—and even an eagerness—to use those weapons.[88]

In part owing to his heroic command of Allied forces during World War II, Eisenhower was able to keep his own generals in check when it came to demands for funding new weapons as well as places to use them. (Ike did approve CIA-driven coups in Iran and Guatemala, though neither required the deployments of U.S. military forces.) But because of a policy of "massive retaliation"—that is, a willingness to threaten the use of nuclear weapons whenever any nation appeared to evince hostile intent toward a U.S. ally—Eisenhower was able to reduce military spending in the aftermath of Korea and keep foreign deployments to a minimum.[89] What's more, in his famous farewell address, the retiring president warned:

> This conjunction of an immense military establishment and a large arms industry is new in the American experience. The total influence—economic, political, even spiritual—is felt in every city, every Statehouse, every office of the Federal government. We recognize the imperative need for this development. Yet we must not fail to comprehend its grave implications. Our toil, resources and livelihood are all involved; so is the very structure of our society.
>
> In the councils of government, we must guard against the acquisition of unwarranted influence, whether sought or unsought, by the military-industrial complex. The potential for the disastrous rise of misplaced power exists and will persist.
>
> We must never let the weight of this combination endanger our liberties or democratic processes. We should take nothing for granted. Only an alert and knowledgeable citizenry can compel the proper meshing of the huge industrial and military machinery of defense with our peaceful methods and goals, so that security and liberty may prosper together.[90]

The Kennedy administration ignored these warnings and instead vastly extended the power and influence of the military-industrial complex. The president had campaigned on the existence of a "missile gap" with the Soviets, and particularly after the debacle of the Bay of Pigs, followed by a disastrous summit with Khrushchev in Vienna, he felt he had to demonstrate his strength to the premier, who had concluded that the young president "had no guts."[91]

Under former Ford Motors executive Robert S. McNamara, Kennedy's choice for secretary of defense (and among the most intellectually self-confident individuals ever to serve in any president's cabinet), the Pentagon was staffed with a new generation of "whiz kids" who, in attempting to rationalize U.S. defense strategy, called for vastly increased investments in all manner of weaponry as well as command-and-control systems to ensure their greater usefulness. Military spending began a steady, significant increase under Kennedy that continued right up through the end of the Vietnam War.[92] Kennedy's advisers, moreover—particularly McNamara, National Security Adviser McGeorge Bundy, and State Department Policy Planning chief Walter Rostow—believed that the nation needed to take a much more aggressive attitude toward containing Communist expansion in the Third World now that the contours of Europe had hardened across Cold War lines, including the ability to institute a "flexible response" to problems requiring the use of military force abroad.[93] The net result of Kennedy's presidency was the progressive militarization of U.S. foreign policy, with a vast increase of human misery among innocent populations of the nations who suffered and died at the hands of both Soviet and U.S.-armed elites, with few if any positive achievements for liberalism in the areas of increased democracy, prosperity, or respect for human freedom and dignity to show for it.[94]

Liberal concerns about the managerial/technocratic nature of President Kennedy's approach to politics proved prescient as well. Kennedy's economic advisers were roughly evenly divided between corporate conservatives and liberal academics. He picked the Republican C. Douglas Dillon to head the Treasury Department over the far more liberal Albert Gore of Tennessee, a fiery southern populist whom Kennedy feared he could not trust or control, and Galbraith was shuttled off to India. He named the liberal Keynesian economist and former Humphrey adviser Walter Heller chief of his Council of Economic Advisers. But when Kennedy laid out his administration's economic philosophy in a speech at Yale University, he borrowed from Daniel Bell's *The End of Ideology*, published two years earlier, and announced an end to the class-based fight on behalf of the "common man" that characterized Roosevelt's rhetoric. The president's job, as he described it, was merely "the practical management of a modern economy."[95] There would be no declarations of war against "economic royalty" as FDR had declared; instead Kennedy proclaimed a state of affairs that might have been fairly dubbed "peace in our time."[96]

But with growth stalled during Kennedy's first year, Walter Heller lobbied the president to cut corporate taxes to "get the country moving again." Such unapologetic Keynesianism in the service of deficit spending struck some of Kennedy's advisers as ill advised, as even FDR never fully accepted deficit spending on principle. When he first heard Heller's pitch in December 1960, the president-elect was hardly sympathetic, complaining that the notion did not "fit very well with my call for sacrifice."[97] By the autumn of 1962, however, Kennedy had come to see things Heller's way. Galbraith was also opposed, and in one of his many missives from Mumbai, he pointed out to the president that "a very large part of American conservative and business opinion" would embrace the tax cut, which would line their pockets, but then "attack you for an unbalanced budget."[98] Galbraith feared that "once we start talking about tax cuts we will take the pressure off the rest of your program. . . . We now say that housing, school building and urban renewal are needed both for themselves and for their effect on employment. Given the tax cut conservatives will not be slow to say that this will do the job."[99] But the cut went through, reducing taxes for the rich, and was widely viewed as a success by corporate America, though, as Galbraith predicted, it did next to nothing to address America's "social imbalance."[100] Kennedy even defended the move in conservative economic terms. In a speech to the Economic Club of New York, he explained, "The best means of strengthening demand among consumers and business is to reduce the burden on private income and the deterrents to private initiative which are imposed by our present tax system."[101]

Of course tax cuts were not the sum total of Kennedy's economic program, and one might argue that they were part and parcel of a new liberal economic philosophy, one that put the federal government at the center of the maintenance of the nation's economic well-being. In the long run, he promised, as much as by its military power or diplomatic influence, America's security would be determined "by the decisions of finance ministers . . . by the deployment of fiscal and monetary weapons . . . and above all by the strength of this nations' economy. . . ."[102]

Kennedy went on to unleash a dizzying array of economic initiatives. In 1961 he supported legislation to raise the minimum wage.[103] His Omnibus Housing Act attempted to address the problem of inner-city slums, though it ended up inviting private real estate developers to displace poor people's homes to put up more profitable housing for the middle class. The 1962 Manpower Development and Training Act provided vocational training for those displaced by technological innovation.[104] Kennedy was also a good friend to the labor movement. His Executive Order 10988, signed in 1962, secured the right to union membership for most federal workers, a measure AFL-CIO president George Meany termed "a Wagner Act for public employees." Numerous state legislatures followed suit. And while these measures did meet with some success, their benefits were addressed almost exclusively to the middle class and well to do.

At the beginning of 1963, however, Kennedy read a lengthy review in *The New Yorker* by the New York intellectual Dwight Macdonald focusing on a book called *The Other America* by a young writer named Michael Harrington, who called himself a democratic socialist (and was also an anti-Communist). The article inspired him to rethink the nature of the government's responsibility to America's least advantaged citizens. "Ernest Hemingway's celebrated deflation of Scott Fitzgerald's romantic notion that the rich are 'different' somehow—'Yes, they have money'—doesn't apply to the poor," Macdonald wrote.

> They are different in more important ways than their lack of money, as Mr. Harrington demonstrates: Emotional upset is one of the main forms of the vicious circle of impoverishment. The structure of the society is hostile to these people. The poor tend to become pessimistic and depressed; they seek immediate gratification instead of saving; they act out. The middle class looks upon this process and sees "lazy" people who "just don't want to get ahead." People who are much too sensitive to demand of cripples that they run races ask of the poor that they get up and act just like everyone else in the society. The poor are not like everyone else.[105]

Borrowing from anthropologist Oscar Lewis's "culture of poverty" thesis and deploying statistics drawn from reports by the U.S. Federal Reserve and the Commerce Department, Harrington focused on the shameful fact that the world's richest nation also boasted an "economic underworld" of nearly fifty million people, or roughly a quarter of the nation—"the unskilled workers, the migrant farm workers, the aged, the minorities"—who lived in poverty, creating a "subculture of misery, but not enough of them to challenge the conscience and imagination of the nation."[106] "Until these facts shame us," he concluded, "until they stir us to action, the other America will continue to exist, a monstrous example of the needless suffering in the most advanced society in the world."[107]

Against all odds Kennedy took up the challenge. The president instructed his advisers to find a way to attack not only the symptoms but also the causes of poverty: causes that were now understood to relate less to matters of psychology than of sociology. Macdonald wrote of what he termed an "obvious" solution: "to provide, out of taxes, the kind of subsidies that have always been given to the public schools (not to mention the police and fire departments and the post office)—subsidies that would raise incomes above the poverty level, so that every citizen could feel he is indeed such."[108]

But this "obvious" solution presented a no less obvious problem for liberal policy makers. Any initiatives that attacked poverty would, by their very nature, need to be *targeted*, and were therefore unlikely to enjoy the widespread political support of programs like Social Security or unemployment insurance, which were universal in their application and formed the foundation of the New Deal's appeal to working-class Americans. After all, most people prefer not to give their money to others, especially when forced to do so via the mechanism of taxation for the purpose of redistribution. It was part of the most fundamental ethos of America's self-identity that the poor were poor because of their own character flaws rather than any systemic denial of opportunity. Charity, alms, and the like were for church collection plates, not government tax forms. Meanwhile, the citizens who were likely to benefit from such redistribution—the poorest of the poor—were hardly a dependable voting bloc. When these issues were thrown into the blender with racial resentments caused by forced integration, it created an explosive cocktail indeed, and one that would over time undermine much of what liberalism had achieved in the past, to say nothing of laying a now-shaky foundation for its future.

As a senator, John F. Kennedy had a record on civil rights—like his record on all political matters—that was unexceptional. Kennedy had supported the Civil Rights Act of 1957, helping Johnson get the bill through the Senate, but he had also supported the strategic efforts of southern senators to weaken it, including, for instance, an amendment that guaranteed (likely sympathetic) jury trials for individuals accused of civil rights violations. As Nicholas Lemann observes, Kennedy's "presidential campaign in 1960 operated on the assumption that blacks in the North were machine voters who could be reached through businesslike dealings with their political bosses—not people with special problems and a unique moral claim on the government's help."[109] Consistent with this approach, the candidate, on the advice of Shriver and Wofford, placed a supportive call to Coretta Scott King when her husband was jailed, which may have resulted in significant movement of blacks from their traditional Republican voting patterns in key northeastern cities, though the riskiness of this was underlined by the fury expressed by Robert Kennedy when he found out about it. (He reportedly threatened Wofford, saying, "This is the last thing you bomb throwers are going to do in this campaign."[110]) Like so many liberals, however, Dr. King shared the view that while Kennedy "had the intelligence and the skill and the moral fervor to give the leadership we've been waiting for and do what no other President has ever done . . . the moral passion is missing."[111]

Though the civil rights movement had stalled at the end of the fifties, it exploded with new energy in 1960 when young students led sit-ins at southern lunch counters. When Kennedy assumed power, the Freedom Rides began, many of which were inspired by the Supreme Court's decision in *Boynton v. Virginia* (1960) outlawing segregated facilities in interstate travel. These symbolized an enormous transformation in strategy, for while the Montgomery bus boycott and the student sit-ins were designed to end segregation on a local level, Freedom Riders sought to prick the conscience of the entire nation. As James Farmer, the Texas-born cofounder of the Committee of Racial Equality and now the national director of its successor organization, the Congress of Racial Equality (CORE), who acted as a principal organizer of the rides, explained, "We planned the Freedom Ride with the specific intention of creating a crisis. . . . We figured that the government would have to respond if we created a situation that was headline news all over the world, and affected the nation's image abroad."[112]

Violent confrontations did erupt, especially when the Freedom Riders arrived in Alabama. As Klansmen and their supporters attacked the Riders, the Greyhound Bus Company balked at the prospect of asking drivers to face more firebombings or tire slashings. When the drivers refused to move out of Birmingham, Robert Kennedy himself got on the telephone and screamed, "I think you should—had better be getting in touch with Mr. Greyhound or whoever Greyhound is, and somebody better give us an answer . . . I am—the Government is—going to be very much upset if this group does not get to continue their trip."[113] Kennedy finally decided to send in federal marshals to enforce the Interstate Commerce Commission's ban on segregated interstate travel, putting the government on the side of the protesters, rather than their tormentors.[114]

Robert Kennedy, however, remained in a panic, no doubt not only about ongoing violence but also its political ramifications for his brother. He summoned civil rights workers to meet with him at the White House and sought to persuade them to focus not on bus rides but on voter registration drives, promising draft exemptions for young people who participated. However expedient, it was also a principled position, as he genuinely believed that registering black voters would be "the key to opening the door to all of what they wanted to accomplish in education, housing, jobs, and public accommodation."[115] But the Riders, who had risked their lives for rights guaranteed by the U.S. Constitution, did not see it that way. Charles Sherrod, one of the organizers, told Kennedy, "It's not your responsibility before God or under the law to tell us how to honor our constitutional rights. It's your job to protect us when we do."[116] Kennedy was soon enough forced to call in the federal marshals again to enable a young African American named James Meredith to enroll at "Ole Miss" (the University of Mississippi) in the face of yet another violent mob of white segregationists and little discernable local police protection.[117]

The distance between the brothers and the leaders of the movement they sought to guide can be gleaned in a May 1963 meeting in Robert Kennedy's New York apartment, organized by the film and recording star, as well as tireless behind-the-scenes movement fund-raiser, organizer, and wrangler of his fellow entertainers, Harry Belafonte. (Though often critical of liberals and liberalism, Belafonte stands virtually alone as one of the few entertainers in all American history to set aside his own spectacularly successful career to devote himself full time to serving the cause of racial and economic justice.[118]) Coming after a series of violent attacks on civil rights protesters in Birmingham, Alabama—from which came the iconic images of "lashing fire hoses that washed human beings along slippery avenues" and vicious guard dogs unleashed on proud demonstrators—the meeting took on all of the tensions of the time.[119] It was led in large measure by the writer James Baldwin, who had, of late, come to displace Ralph Ellison as the leading African American literary voice of the moment, and who had been featured on the cover of *Time* magazine just a week earlier.

Baldwin had invited a number of friends and associates, including Lena Horne, Lorraine Hansberry, and others described by *The New York Times* the following day as "angry young negroes."[120] Among them was a young Freedom Rider named Jerome Smith, who had been assaulted in Macomb, Mississippi, during a voter registration drive there. Baldwin had stoked the young man before the meeting by commenting, "This guy," RFK, "doesn't understand the seriousness of the problem."[121, 122] But when Baldwin asked Smith if he'd fight for his country, and the young man shouted, "Never! . . . These are poor people who did nothing to us. They're more my brothers than you are. Never!" Baldwin hoped to illuminate the sense of desperation among civil rights workers, but Robert Kennedy responded in shock and horror. "You will not fight for your country?" he asked, as amazed as he was angry. "How can you say that?"[123] Lorraine Hansberry, the black playwright, tried to intervene. "Look, if you can't understand what this young man is saying then we are without any hope at all because you and your brother are representatives of the best that a white America has to offer; and if *you* are insensitive to this, then there's no alternative except chaos."[124] Kennedy continued to counsel patience, pointing out that no one ever believed his brother, a Catholic, could become president, and ventured that within forty years, a black might one day do so as well. Baldwin rolled his eyes, later explaining, "That sounded like a very emancipated statement to white people . . . [but] we were here for 400 years and now he tells us that maybe in 40 years if you are good, we may let you become President."[125] The social psychologist Kenneth Clark recalled it as "the most intense, traumatic meeting in which I've ever taken part . . . the most unrestrained interchange among adults, head-to-head, no holds barred . . . the *most* dramatic experience I have ever had."[126]

After it ended, Belafonte offered sympathy to Kennedy, but the attorney general—accustomed by now to a degree of deference particularly from those whose bidding he believed himself to be doing—was not easily consoled. "The[se people]" he exploded, "they don't know anything. They don't know what the laws are—they don't know what the facts are—they don't know what we've been doing or what we're trying to do."[127] Arthur Schlesinger, Jr., worried that the meeting might drive RFK to "a sense of the futility rather than of the urgency of trying to bridge the gap."[128] Eventually, Kennedy would lay most of these and related concerns to rest, as he developed into a full-throated champion of civil rights in the years after his brother's death.

An increasingly obsessive and unbalanced J. Edgar Hoover was eager to unleash the bureau on alleged Communists advising King. Hoover had long equated civil rights with Communist subversion. ("The Negro situation," Hoover said in 1958, "is being exploited fully and continuously by Communists on a national scale."[129] He complained especially about Stanley Levison, a Jewish lawyer who helped King with speeches and strategy and had also been active in the Communist Party in the fifties, and Jack O'Dell, who had been an energetic fellow traveler in his youth, but never a party member. King was further compromised, from a political standpoint, by the presence on his staff of the gay Bayard Rustin, who had introduced Levison to King in 1956, just a year before Levison ceased his work with the party.

Aware that Hoover was gunning for Levison, the Kennedys were unnerved by the possibility that the FBI director would use his and Rustin's prominence in King's leadership circle to try to ruin the reverend and undermine the cause of civil rights. King said he understood the danger, but proved noncommittal. The attorney general procrastinated in the face of Hoover's pressure to sign off on an FBI request for an open wiretap on any address associated with King but eventually capitulated, agreeing to the wiretapping on a "trial basis," to "continue if productive results were forthcoming."[130] Hoover maintained his surveillance until King's death, using his frequent affairs with white women to try to discredit him in the press and to attempt to drive King to suicide by humiliating him both publicly before the world and privately to his wife and children.[131] Kennedy's decision always haunted him, but it remained secret until 1968, when Hoover sought to undermine RFK's credentials as a civil rights champion during his aborted presidential campaign.[132]

President Kennedy eventually grew convinced that he had no choice but to take action—indeed, he was beginning to look weak in the face of the bravery of the Freedom Riders and the violence of the segregationists. Finally, in the spring of 1963, he introduced his own civil rights bill. In doing so he articulated his own amazing self-transformation from the impatient political pragmatist who demanded that somebody solve the "god damn civil rights mess" to a moral leader who embraced the elevated rhetoric to which King and others so eloquently gave voice. "We preach freedom around the world, and we mean it," the president proclaimed. "But are we to say to the world—and much more importantly, to each other—that this is the land of the free, except for Negroes, that we have no second-class citizens, except Negroes, that we have no class or caste system, no ghettos, no master race, except with Negroes?" He made it clear that the country faced a "moral crisis as a country and a people," arguing that passing civil rights legislation would make America a "better country." Martin Luther King, Jr., wired his congratulations immediately after the speech. The president had finally spoken "passionately to the moral issues involved in the integration struggle."[133]

But of course it was not enough; no speech could be. So much remained to be done before racial equality—even mere formal political equality—might become a reality in America. The leaders of the movement decided to organize a march on Washington in August 1963 to build pressure for legislation that would ensure the enforcement of their constitutional rights everywhere in America.

The March on Washington grew into a kind of golden moment for American liberalism, the beloved community glimpsed, however briefly, across the reflection pool at the foot of the Lincoln Memorial. The Kennedys initially opposed the protest, believing it might turn violent and thus set back efforts to pass civil rights legislation in Congress. But the movement leaders were adamant this time. Belafonte recalls telling Robert Kennedy, "Bobby, I appreciate the position you're in but you're not going to stop us. So you better start getting used to the fact that it's going to happen and start trying to help us make it work."[134] Unable to dam this particular river of justice, the Kennedys threw themselves into the task of attempting to ensure its success. The president contacted Walter Reuther and pleaded with him "to arrange substantial white participation by church and labor union members" in order to prevent the opposition from writing off the protest.[135]

While George Meany's AFL-CIO kept itself safely at arm's length from the movement, Reuther and the UAW worked tirelessly with the aging but much admired A. Philip Randoph and reached out to the rest of the largely white labor brotherhood. From the beginning of his presidency of the union, Reuther had confronted racism in southern locals of the UAW, albeit with mixed results. When the Birmingham protests began, he had helped raise significant sums for bail in order to help keep them going.[136] He was particularly thrilled when King invited him to address the marchers (as he had done repeatedly for the civil rights leader at national UAW conventions) and would deliver one of the day's most salient speeches, at least from Kennedy's standpoint, when he proclaimed, "We cannot *defend* freedom in Berlin so long as we *deny* freedom in Birmingham!"[137]

By 1963, King had become in many respects larger than life. In his famous "Letter from a Birmingham Jail," published in *The Nation*, King condemned the "white moderate," whom he judged to be more "devoted to 'order' than to justice . . . [who] prefers a negative peace which is the absence of tension to a positive peace which is the presence of justice" and who "paternalistically feels that he can set the timetable for another man's freedom."[138] Still, despite his impatience with well-meaning liberals, King remained, if just barely, in the fold, unlike the increasingly popular militants Malcolm X and Elijah Muhammad, a fact recognized by the Kennedy administration.

The march was a huge success—and a peaceful one—with thousands showing up and spilling out along the reflecting pool in front of the Lincoln Memorial. Events from the podium included not only the speeches of civil rights leaders from across the spectrum but also readings by Marlon Brando and songs by Mahalia Jackson; Marian Anderson; Bob Dylan; Joan Baez; Odetta; and Peter, Paul, and Mary. At the suggestion of King, who thought it valuable to have a few famous nonliberals on the program, Belafonte recruited Charlton Heston—then famous to Americans for his role as Moses in Cecil B. DeMille's 1956 epic, *The Ten Commandments*—as cochair, with Brando, of the Hollywood delegation. The famous Second Amendment activist and soon-to-be conservative icon said he'd be "delighted."[139]

Some backstage drama ensued when young John Lewis, who had planned to speak in angrier tones than those desired by the day's organizers, was prevailed upon by Walter Reuther and Philip Randolph to keep the tone uplifting. "I've waited all my life for this opportunity," the latter pleaded with the young man. "Please don't ruin it."[140] The day's climax came with King's great "I Have a Dream" speech. He stood in front of the Lincoln Memorial before a crowd of more than a quarter million people who had sacrificed so much to be there to bear witness, and he cried out, in the intonations of the traditions of his church, "When we allow freedom to ring, when we let it ring from every village and every hamlet, from every state and every city, we will be able to speed up that day when *all* of God's children, black men and white men, Jews and Gentiles, Protestants and Catholics, will be able to join hands and sing in the words of the old Negro spiritual:

Free at last! Free at last!
Thank God Almighty, we are free at last!

As much as King spoke to American ideals, he also warned of the dangers of continuing to ignore the problem: the nation needed to live up to "the promises of democracy" lest the alternative result in a violent reaction to continued denial, repression, and injustice.[141] It was, in the end, the kind of speech that can change history, at the level of Pericles' funeral oration or Lincoln's Gettysburg Address. Jack Kennedy watched King's speech on television at the White House and told his advisers, "He's damned good. Damned good!"[142]

Indeed, the whole march was damned good, a magnificent spectacle of hope, optimism, and a belief that the promise contained in the word "America" would soon be available to all of its citizens. Rustin would later recall the "electricity in the air. Everyone who was there knew that the event was a landmark . . . one of the great days in American history."[143] Indeed, *The New York Times* called it "the greatest assembly for redress of grievances the capital has ever seen." Its influential television critic Jack Gould observed that "the gentle entrance and exit of so much petitioning humanity was an editorial in movement."[144]

The networks gave the event wall-to-wall coverage. NBC aired eleven special reports during the day, totaling more than three hours; ABC only slightly less, while CBS committed to continuous reporting throughout the afternoon. Television crews arrived from West Germany, Japan, and France. Meanwhile, Telstar, a new communications satellite launched a year earlier, enabled live coverage of the event to be broadcast to six nations, and Communist countries broadcast it on a delayed basis.[145]

Massachusetts senator Ted Kennedy, whose brother the president had barred him from attending the march owing to his fears of violence, watched it from his office. He recalled, in his posthumously published memoir, that he felt himself "fully baptized into the civil rights movement that day. The Reverend Dr. Martin Luther King Jr. has spoken of his dream that had become my own."[146]

By the time of his death, Jack Kennedy was certainly no longer the "bystander" he had been to the civil rights struggle for most of his life, but neither was he a political conjurer.[147] During his final month, the political columnists Rowland Evans and Robert Novak were warning of a "white backlash" in the coming 1964 elections, and predicting that "Mr. Kennedy would survive the white reaction, but his forces in Congress would be so badly depleted that he would enter his second term with incomparably less authority than he has today." *The New York Times*'s Anthony Lewis warned that the "race question" was now jeopardizing Democratic campaigns in the North as well as the South, and Teddy White noted, rather prophetically, that "the black revolt of 1963 is pushing the white liberal leadership in the North further away from the white working class."[148] JFK's unfinished business included not only civil rights but also his planned $11 billion tax cut, the creation of Medicare, and increasing federal aid to education. Looking back at that moment of optimism, it is easy for liberals to feel the tug of nostalgia for a time when it appeared that America might indeed "overcome" its tragic past and move toward an era not only of peace and prosperity but also of genuine racial reconciliation and global cooperation.

10

Master of Disaster

I want you to tell your friends—Arthur Schlesinger, Galbraith and other liberals—that . . . I'm no budget slasher. . . . If you looked at my record, you would know that I am a Roosevelt New Dealer. As a matter of fact, to tell the truth, John F. Kennedy was a little conservative to suit my taste.

—Lyndon Johnson to Walter Heller, 1963[1]

I am not going to have anything more to do with the liberals. They won't have anything to do with me. . . . I'm going to get rid of everybody who doesn't agree with my policies. . . . I'm not going in the liberal direction. There's no future with them. They're just out to get me, always have been.

—Lyndon Johnson to Richard Goodwin, 1965[2]

Lyndon Baines Johnson, Dean Acheson once noted, had "as many sides to him as a kaleidoscope."[3] His aide Joseph A. Califano, Jr., added that Johnson was a man who could be "altruistic and petty, caring and crude, generous and petulant, bluntly honest and calculatingly devious—all within the same few minutes."[4] "In dealing with people," Clark Clifford admitted, "I often had the feeling that he would rather go through a side door even if the front door were open."[5] This was true on matters large and small. Johnson would occasionally construct a family legacy for himself in which he descended from a grandfather who died at the Alamo, as if such a detail were unverifiable. (When one writer did go to the trouble to check, Johnson simply replaced it with a second lie, saying he meant San Jacinto.[6])

Power and self-doubt have rarely mixed so volubly in one man. "When I was young," LBJ once said, "poverty was so common that we didn't know it had a name."[7] He grew up in the Texas hill country and attended Southwest

Texas State Teachers College, which, at the time, boasted exactly one faculty member with a doctorate during the time of Johnson's attendance, and fifty-six professors with no degree whatever.[8] Deeply insecure about his meager educational background, Johnson would often prove particularly pliable in the presence of men like John Kennedy, who had enjoyed the advantages of Eastern establishment institutions, much as he hated them and hated to admit this to himself. At the same time, it is difficult to imagine a politician who could be more stubborn or wily in pursuit of whatever it was he wanted or thought he needed. "I can't stand the bastard," Robert Kennedy once admitted, "but he's the most formidable human being I've ever met."[9]

When Johnson became a congressman in 1937, his biographer Robert Caro notes, electricity had not yet reached the Texas hill country. By the time he became a senator, in 1948, he had helped bring it there. "Johnson drove advisers crazy with requests for electrification projects, despite the fact that the counties were insufficiently populated to justify them according to the regulations. He simply wore down the president and his men." "No matter what Lyndon was like," residents told Caro decades later, "we loved him because he brought us the lights."[10] "The kid," as judged by FDR adviser "Tommy the Cork" Corcoran, was "the best congressman for a district that ever was."[11] Like other New Dealers, Lloyd Gardner observes, "Johnson was enthusiastic (and probably a bit amazed) at the discovery that government really did have immense powers to change the life of the downtrodden."

As a young congressman, Lyndon Johnson made a great show of expressing exaggerated affection for FDR. One reporter encountered LBJ soon after he learned of Roosevelt's death and found the big towering Texan was crying his eyes out. "He was just like a daddy to me always," he explained to the startled reporter. "He always talked to me just that way. He was the one person I ever knew—anywhere—who was never afraid."[12] It was a typical Johnson performance, as he in fact barely knew FDR and had done nothing in particular to promote the president's programs legislatively. (Johnson did not introduce a single significant piece of legislation as a House member or for much of his career in the Senate.) Throughout his rise from an anonymous freshman congressman to the most effective Senate majority leader in its history, Johnson would constantly attach himself to lonely, older, more powerful men and accept their favors and advice as they greased the wheels of his limitless ambition.

Johnson would often purposely intimidate his opponents, towering over them, literally sweating on top of them, as he berated, cajoled, and pleaded with them until they submitted to his will. It was called the treatment, and after three hours of it, George Wallace once claimed, he was just about ready to embrace the cause of civil rights. "You really felt as if a St. Bernard had pawed you all over," *Washington Post* executive editor Ben Bradlee explained. "He never just shook hands with you. One hand was shaking your hand; the other hand was always someplace else, exploring you, examining you."[13] The romantic view of Johnson's powers of persuasion, however, is belied by the fact that, at the same time, he funneled significant amounts of Texas oil money to those politicians willing to see things his way. This constant flow of secret campaign cash helped ensure that Johnson's "treatment" would prove considerably more effective than if it had been accompanied by merely a hardy "Thank you."[14]

Johnson's insecurity increased with his influence. "I don't want loyalty," he once told an aide. "I want him to kiss my ass in Macy's window at high noon and tell me it smells like roses."[15] Johnson was constantly reminding aides that he, not they, was the boss, as if the presidential seal in his office might be considered counterfeit. "Just you remember this," he lectured one. "There's only two kinds at the White House. There's elephants and there's pissants. And I'm the only elephant."[16]

Upon finally achieving his dream of the presidency, Johnson acted immediately and decisively. In the midst of what was an almost unbearable moment of shock and horror for the nation, as well as for those close to the president, Johnson demanded to be sworn into office aboard Air Force One on the tarmac in Texas. Some family loyalists, including especially Bobby—whose hatred of the man had practically metastasized since he failed to talk his brother out of his choice for a running mate—felt that Johnson had demonstrated a lack of sensitivity toward Jackie and the family. But most Americans understood that under the circumstances, concern for the stability of the presidency and the country had to come first. The conservative *Wall Street Journal* editorial page concluded soon after the assassination that LBJ had "done much to command respect and encourage confidence."[17]

Johnson used the assassination, as he used everything, to bend men to his political purposes: in this case, toward the most far-reaching liberal agenda any post-FDR president would ever imagine. Five days after the assassination, Johnson addressed Congress: "John F. Kennedy lives on. . . . As he did not shrink from his responsibilities but welcomed them, so he would not have us shrink from carrying on his work beyond this hour of national tragedy."[18] As Johnson would charcterize it years later, "I had to take the dead man's program and turn it into a martyr's cause."[19]

The president pressed forward on two policies that JFK had proposed but had been unable to move through Congress: tax cuts and civil rights. On the latter Johnson showed much more resolve than Kennedy and, not infrequently, considerably more political skill and finesse. He achieved much that Kennedy could not, including, perhaps most significant, passage of the Civil Rights Act, which was signed into law on July 2, 1964, without amendments and with solid backing in both parties.[20] "I wanted power to give things to people—all sorts of things to all sorts of people, especially the poor and the blacks," as he put it.[21]

On January 8, 1964, LBJ appeared before Congress and the nation to deliver his State of the Union address. He boldly declared, "This Administration today, here and now, declares unconditional war on poverty in America."[22] Five months later, speaking to students at the University of Michigan, Johnson gave one of the landmark speeches in the history of American liberalism. "For in your time," he said to the young students gathered around him, "we have the opportunity to move not only towards the rich society and the powerful society, but upward to the Great Society."[23] Here LBJ articulated a fundamental faith of 1960s liberalism: America had entered a new, potentially perpetual cycle of economic abundance, and that abundance could be deployed to ensure the creation of a fairer and more equal society without any segment of society being asked to endure significant sacrifice.[24] "Will you join in the battle to give every citizen the full equality which God enjoins and the law requires?" President Johnson asked the nation. "Will you join in the battle to build the Great Society, to prove that our material progress is only the foundation on which we will build a richer life of mind and spirit?"[25] His decisiveness was the expression of a boldness rare in liberalism, but amid the soaring ideals and inspirational rhetoric, little attention would be paid to the potential unintended consequences of what Johnson and his administration believed to be noble purposes.[26]

Lyndon Johnson's liberalism was a grandiose, bastardized version of the same vision that Schlesinger, Galbraith, and Stevenson had proffered throughout the 1950s: a responsibility to use political power to correct historical injustice. This was qualitative liberalism, supported by the power of the presidency, just as they had always dreamed—or thought they had. But Johnson wanted more than "merely" to end poverty, discrimination, and social dysfunction. He also wanted to clean up the air and water, the countryside, and the nation's cities. He planned to fund the arts, explore space, protect consumers, and young children's pets.[27] Johnson believed that America's bounty, and his now nearly limitless power, gave him not just the opportunity but the responsibility to try to right almost all of society's wrongs. And he planned to do all this while fighting a land war in far-off Southeast Asia in a country whose name few Americans had ever even heard, much less could identify on a map.

As with all matters dear to his heart, LBJ demanded immediate action for his Great Society programs. He appointed Sargent Shriver to be in charge of the war on poverty. Initially Shriver balked; he enjoyed leading the Peace Corps. But LBJ insisted, and Shriver proved no match for "the treatment." His fiefdom would be the Office of Economic Opportunity (OEO), created by the Economic Opportunity Act of August 1964. He called in academics from across the country to serve on task forces and put their knowledge to use for the good of the country, and even invited Michael Harrington, the writer who had done so much to "discover" poverty, to join the agency's organizing group. When the latter objected to the notion that the problem could be abolished with what he termed "nickels and dimes," Shriver responded, only semi-ironically, "Oh really, Mr. Harington. I don't know about you, but this is the first time I've spent a billion dollars."[28]

Almost everyone involved in the effort quickly settled on a single organizing theme: "maximum feasible participation," the gist of which was that the federal government would nurture grassroots activism to involve poor people themselves in attacking the root causes of poverty. The Great Society thus sought to link social relief with participatory democracy; it was social democracy, American style, rather than the straightforward economic redistribution model popular in Europe and Great Britain. As Shriver explained it, the goal was to "mobilize public and private resources to reduce poverty; provide services to the poor; draw on the 'maximum feasible participation' of the poor themselves; and be administered by a local agency that fairly represented its surrounding community."[29] For Johnson, the idea of maximum feasible participation was rooted in the simple, commonsense notion that "local citizens best understood their own problems."[30] It promised a "hand up, not a handout."[31]

Rushing ahead at full speed in every direction at once, Johnson refused to countenance any opposition. Remaining among the wary was Michael Harrington, who warned: "When you have a governmental program to organize the poor on their own behalf . . . the first thing those people are going to do is hold a rent strike. The second thing they're going to do is send a committee to their local Congressman, and the third thing they're going to do is picket the Mayor. Can you expect, given the political structure of this country, governmental funds being used to overthrow governments?"[32]

The idea behind the Freedom Summer of 1964 was perfectly consistent with what Robert Kennedy had said he wanted from civil rights activists as well as from liberal democratic theory: voter registration. Idealistic northern college students traveled to the South to register black voters, who would then vote the segregationists out of office. It was dangerous work, particularly in light of the fact that local law offices were staffed by the people who made up the KKK and White Citizens' Councils. By the end of the summer project, workers had been arrested more than a thousand times, been shot at thirty-five times, had suffered thirty bombings and eighty beatings; at least six people were murdered.[33]

The movement generated its own leaders. Chief among these after King was Bob Moses, a young African American who had grown up in Harlem and received a BA from Hamilton College before studying philosophy at Harvard. A former New York City schoolteacher, Moses was younger than King but still more mature than most of the student protesters.[34] An admirer of the French Algerian existentialist author Albert Camus, his commitment to nonviolence derived less from the tradition of Christian martyrdom than from the existentialist imperative that individuals should refuse the destiny of becoming either history's "victim" or its "executioner."[35] Moses, in the words of King biographer Taylor Branch, was a moralist who "fought leadership's compulsion to dominate the common people even in democratic causes" and "who tumbled through doubts that his anti-leadership convictions merely shielded him from inevitable responsibility."[36] Like King, Moses also viewed the movement as a means not only to liberate blacks in the South but also to redeem the promise of America itself. "Before the Negro in the South had always looked on the defensive, cringing," he later recalled. "This time they were taking the initiative. They were kids my age, and I knew this had something to do with my own life . . . for a long time I had been troubled by the problem of being a Negro and at the same time being an American. This was the answer."[37]

Another unlikely leader whom the movement inspired to rise to the demands of the moment was Fannie Lou Hamer, the twentieth child of a Mississippi sharecropper. Untested in politics but well schooled in activism and steeped in scripture, she spoke with unyielding passion and homegrown eloquence born of personal self-sacrifice. She had experienced jail beatings and seen her house riddled with bullets, and had survived both to become a "fierce warrior."[38]

Moses, Hamer, and company had already decided to construct an alternative to the Democratic Party in Mississippi called the Mississippi Freedom Democratic Party (MFDP), which mirrored the official version with its own precinct, county, and statewide meetings.[39] Advised by ADA lawyer Joseph Rauh, they chose their own delegates and planned to travel to the 1964 Democratic Convention in Atlantic City to displace the official all-white state delegation. In the end, they did receive encouragement from King, who told them, "I say to you that any party in the world should be proud to have a delegation such as this seated in their midst. For it is in these saints in ordinary walks of life that the true spirit of democracy finds its most profound and abiding expression."

The Freedom delegation faced two significant roadblocks in its path toward official recognition: the first was the state of Mississippi, and the second was the president of the United States. Johnson had grown especially nervous about the potential disruption of his anticipated coronation and had little sympathy for troublemakers, particularly when those making the trouble were people he felt should have been grateful for all he had done for them. (Texas governor John Connally allegedly told Johnson, "If you seat those black buggers, the whole South will march out."[40]) When the network cameras turned away from the official proceedings and focused instead on Fannie Lou Hamer's describing the abuse she had endured in jail for the crime of trying to vote in an election, Johnson demanded that they cut her mike. But Hamer would not be silenced. "And if the Freedom Democratic Party is not seated now, I question America!" she cried.[41]

LBJ asked Clark Clifford to phone Walter Reuther for help, and together with Hubert Humphrey and Bill Moyers they negotiated a deal with the protesters to accept just two seats in Atlantic City along with a "formal call to future conventions" that gave "notice of disqualification for segregationist creed or practice."[42] Contrary to conventional wisdom, LBJ made it clear to all parties—civil rights reformers and regular southern delegates alike—that he did not propose this compromise merely as a short-term, stopgap measure to ensure peace at the 1964 convention. Rather he viewed the new nondiscrimination rule as a justified extension of the national party's power over state delegations that carried on discriminatory practices.[43]

Bayard Rustin, supported by Reuther, viewed this as a victory and pressed his comrades to embrace it, but Joe Rauh judged it to be a sellout. Reuther predicted that a floor fight over so racially charged an issue would cause the Democrats to lose in November. Hamer and Moses, in any event, remained unmoved. "We didn't come all this way for no two votes," Hamer explained.[44] Moses took a more philosophical tack. "We're not here to bring politics to our morality but to bring morality to our politics."[45] Perhaps the most astute observer of the situation was King. Todd Gitlin explains: "As a Negro leader, King said, he wanted the MFDP to accept the compromise: it would help the prospects for Negro voter registration throughout the South. If he were a Mississippi Negro, though, he would vote against it."[46]

As it happened, the anti–civil rights backlash so feared by Walter Reuther and Lyndon Johnson would only grow, eventually, as Johnson had predicted to Moyers upon signing the Voting Rights Act, destroying the Democratic Party in the South (and much of the North) for generations to come. Almost every side saw potential disaster in the compromise, but for the protesters it was mixed with betrayal: The "system" had failed them. Lewis and Moses left Atlantic City deeply embittered. (Moses quit the Student Nonviolent Coordinating Committee [SNCC] a year later, and soon stopped talking to white people at all.[47]) They would eventually be supplanted as the public face of the civil rights movement by Black Power activists like the anti-white rabble-rouser Stokely Carmichael. The militant Black Muslim leader Malcolm X grew stronger in the black community at King's expense, ominously preaching black liberation "by any means necessary."[48] Violence soon became inextricably linked with these new black leaders, terrifying many whites and alienating potential supporters in and out of politics. In 1966, SNCC would make its separatist stance explicit by expelling all its white members.[49]

This truly was a lost moment for liberalism, as Johnson had offered the MFDP a genuinely promising foundation for the future. Though disappointed, Joseph Rauh cautioned that "we shouldn't forget that we made great progress."[50] Indeed, the MFDP did achieve most of its aims; they were just asked to wait until 1968 for racial discrimination to be eradicated from the local party structure. But justice delayed is justice denied to the people demanding it, and despite his increasing emotional commitment to civil rights, Johnson could not deliver enough to satisfy all of the demands of either side.

The president did continue along the legislative path he had chosen, passing a strong Voting Rights Act. On March 15, 1965, he addressed the nation in language that shocked and delighted even his most liberal supporters. "Their cause must be our cause, too," he said of the marchers being beaten in Alabama, Mississippi, and elsewhere, "because it is not just Negroes, but really all of us who must overcome the crippling legacy of bigotry and injustice. And we shall overcome."[51] Just five days after the bill's August 6 signing ceremony, however, massive riots broke out in Watts, Los Angeles, when a black driver was pulled over by a policeman for drunk driving. Violence there continued for five days and was televised across the land, signaling to everyone that America was not about to "overcome" just yet.

Under less volatile circumstances, Bayard Rustin's path might have suggested a potential future for the movement. Shortly after the convention, he left his job as executive secretary of the pacifist War Resisters League to head up the A. Philip Randolph Institute, where he sought to create a coalition between labor unions and civil rights organizations to expand the fight for both causes. He argued that the time had come to move from the struggle for formal equality and toward one for substantive equality, including a "refashion[ed] political economy." This could only be done through coalition work between unions and civil rights workers and through the normal electoral channels that civil rights workers too often ignored for direct action. "The future of the Negro struggle," he wrote, "depends on whether a coalition of progressive forces becomes the effective political majority." He argued also that this new coalition would have to pay attention to the growing backlash among white Americans, citing Goldwater's rise on the right. The time was now for the movement to switch—in his evocative title—"from protest to politics."[52]

The National Organization for Women (NOW)—"for," rather than "of" because it welcomed enlightened men into its fold—came together in 1966, just one year after the Voting Rights Act.[53] This was no coincidence. Frustration had been growing among feminists about the lack of attention paid to gender in the Civil Rights Act of 1964. Organized as a kind of feminist version of the NAACP, NOW was made up of "middle-class leaders and activists in the liberal tradition." Its membership rose immediately after its formation as it agitated for the Equal Rights Amendment (ERA), legalized abortion, and other gender-based struggles.[54] It soon had chapters in every state in the union, save Hawaii, with some boasting as many as thirty or forty.[55]

NOW's story can be told through the biography of its first and most famous president, Betty Friedan. Born Bettye Naomi Goldstein in Peoria, Illinois, in 1921 to Jewish immigrant parents, she drifted from an early age toward journalism, beginning in high school a literary magazine that was too controversial and thus went unpublished. She then set out for Smith College in 1939, where she took a class with Dorothy Wolff Douglas, the wife of future senator Paul Douglas, who opened her mind to the problem of female oppression.[56]

A onetime supporter of Henry Wallace, Goldstein began gravitating toward Marxism and landed a job as a left-wing labor journalist. After marrying—and becoming Betty Friedan—she quit her job and attempted to settle down into a life of peaceful suburban domesticity. Deeply unhappy, she got back in touch with a number of her Smith classmates and discovered she was not alone in her feelings of unworthiness and lack of fulfillment. So Betty Friedan set out to name the "disease" she diagnosed for herself and her friends. The result was *The Feminine Mystique*, published in 1963, a "spirited intervention in a particular time and place," as the historian of feminism Christine Stansell aptly notes, "a flag planted by an outrider on a battlefield where armies were starting to assemble."[57]

The first paperback edition sold 1.4 million copies, and letters began arriving with messages to Friedan that read: "I feel, today, as though I had been filled with helium and turned loose!" "Like light bulbs going off again and again." "I understood what I was feeling and felt validated!!"[58] And a movement was born.

The Feminine Mystique began with Friedan's attempt to describe her "sense of dissatisfaction" that sprang from a question asked by a housewife: "Is this all?" "The Problem That Has No Name," as her first chapter was titled, described a vague sense of unhappiness that Friedan had discovered in interviewing numerous women from Smith and elsewhere. She made clear that "the problem" went beyond "material" concerns into a terrain that was more psychological and spiritual. "Our culture does not permit women to accept or gratify their basic need to grow and fulfill their potentialities as human beings," she wrote, drawing upon the teachings of the psychologist Erik Erikson, whose classes she had taken at the University of California. (She would claim in her memoirs that her then-boyfriend had talked her out of pursuing a PhD after she had won a fellowship because it made him nervous.[59]) She struck a chord with millions of women when she called for them to find "creative work of [their] own" outside the home, proposing a kind of female GI Bill that would enable them to go to college and get a degree so they could find work. Women, she quoted the president of Mills College, "should be educated so that they can argue with their husbands."[60]

If Friedan's book suggested to some that she was calling for a social revolution, her own politics were quite conventional. She was a liberal who wanted to extend the rights that men enjoyed to women just as liberal civil rights leaders wished to do for blacks (and later, gay civil rights would seek to do for homosexuals). Friedan sturdily resisted pressure to link feminism to issues of sexual freedom, particularly free love or separatist lesbianism.[61] She tried to steer NOW in a respectable reform direction, making it simply a logical extension of liberalism. And in this respect, she succeeded magnificently, achieving a degree of success in challenging the comfortable thought and life patterns of an entire country as few authors had since Thomas Paine published *Common Sense* in 1776.

Both the civil rights and feminist movements stemmed from liberalism's successful rights revolution of the late fifties and early sixties. If a single individual can be credited with being first and foremost in leading this battle, a strong contender for the title would be Supreme Court Associate Justice William O. Douglas, known to friends and adversaries alike as "Wild Bill." Douglas did more than any other individual to extend the language of rights, and with it the fact of civil liberties, into new areas of American life and law.

Douglas's most significant accomplishment lay in his assertion of a constitutional right to privacy. Developing the idea through a series of dissents during the 1950s, he made the argument public in the *The Right of the People* (1958), in which he drew upon not only the U.S. Constitution, especially the Bill of Rights, but also moral and religious writings without any particular legal authority. Douglas audaciously argued that "natural rights" existed to "protect man, his individuality, and his conscience against direct and indirect interference by the government." These rights were stipulated in the First Amendment as well as in the Fourth and Fifth. The right to privacy, while not directly enunciated anywhere in the Constitution, itself could be found, he argued, in its "penumbras"—shadows and reflections "implied from the very nature of man as a child of God."[62]

In the mid-1960s the Warren Court faced a series of cases that offered the opportunity to extend the rights of everyday Americans. *Gideon v. Wainwright* (1963) had already ensured the right to legal defense irrespective of the ability to pay for it; *Engel v. Vitale* (1962) had already outlawed mandated school prayer.[63] In *Griswold v. Connecticut* (1965) the Court not only found for the right to the purchase and "the open sale of birth control devices," but was also the philosophical foundation for extending privacy rights such as abortion as well. "It was this opinion," avers his biographer, Bruce Allen Murphy, "that simultaneously made Douglas the icon of the liberals and the devil incarnate to generations of conservatives."[64]

"Only 40 years old when President Franklin Roosevelt named him to the Supreme Court in March 1939," notes the historian David J. Garrow, "Douglas could very well have revolutionized constitutional protection for individual rights and liberties in a permanently expansive manner." He had been a "crusading liberal" as chairman of the Securities and Exchange Commission, after earning himself a reputation, in the words of University of Chicago president Robert Maynard Hutchins, as "the most outstanding law professor in the nation."[65] But Douglas ended up squandering most of his gifts and largely failed to make a meaningful difference in the thinking of his fellow justices. Garrow notes that the leadership on the Court "throughout the 1940s and '50s instead devolved into an unproductive tussle between the conservative Felix

Frankfurter and the simple-minded Hugo Black with Douglas often following in Black's footsteps."[66]

It was neither Douglas's philosophy nor his voting record that stood in the way of his becoming the influential justice so many expected him to be, but rather his character. One of his former law clerks, Lucas "Scot" Powe, told Douglas's biographer that the justice "stood for the individual as no other justice ever has. . . . The intensity of his fear of government, with its ability to oppress individuals in body and spirit, was genuine and unmatched." Yet Douglas could not be bothered to give his judicial arguments any philosophical heft or even much attention, and so, Powe lamented, "they are easy to ignore." Steven Duke, another of Douglas's former law clerks, noted that his boss's "published opinions often read like rough drafts," which is not surprising because "many were drafted in twenty minutes." The legal philosopher Ronald Dworkin credits Douglas with a "a developed and general constitutional philosophy," and adds that many of his most significant decisions were grounded in the "idea that individuals have certain moral rights against their government that are prior to all law including the Constitution." Yet Douglas "only mentioned, and never elaborated or defended, this theory of individual pre-legal rights," or what is often loosely called "natural law." Justice Brennan later admitted to his own disappointment with what he called "the slovenliness" of Douglas's writing "and the mistakes that he constantly made."[67] The most important of these, and one that applied to nearly all of Douglas's opinions, said Brennan, "was his insistence, and he repeated it time and again, [that] I have no soul to worry about but my own."[68]

One frequently offered explanation for Douglas's failure to take his responsibilities on the Court altogether seriously is his disappointment at having been rejected as FDR's running mate in 1944, followed by his own rejection of Truman's offer of same office four years later. Douglas appeared to lose interest in everything else in his life save the pursuit of extremely young women. Following a series of ruined marriages and semiscandalous affairs that forever estranged him from his children, Douglas married his fourth wife, Cathy Heffernan, a college senior barely a third his age, in 1966.[69] That same year George Andrews of Alabama called for the House Judiciary Committee to investigate Douglas's character and moral fitness for sitting on the bench.[70] While Douglas lived out his commitment to radical individual liberty, beyond *Griswold* and his reliable vote on the Court, he did not do much to advance its cause in the courts, and likely set it back, providing conservatives with evidence for their desire to equate liberalism with libertinism.

Meanwhile, in Congress, 1965 witnessed a veritable explosion of liberal legislation to accompany the Voting Rights Act, including two key programs that helped to establish and codify America's welfare state. In January, LBJ made his case for Medicare, which would provide free medical care to those over the age of sixty-five, subsidizing hospitalization and other costs. This was a classic case of Johnson's extending the shadow of Roosevelt, as the program built upon Social Security. But what made the move crafty was how he piggybacked Medicaid, directed toward the poor, on Medicare, which, owing to its universalism, was considerably more popular with taxpayers."[71] With this legislation the president took a major step toward Harry Truman's unrealized goal of national health insurance for all Americans.

Johnson also continued to push his own version of qualitative liberalism with the creation that year of the National Foundation on the Arts and Humanities (eventually the National Endowment for the Humanities [NEH] and the National Endowment for the Arts [NEA]), the Water Quality Act, and the Motor Vehicle Air Pollution Control Act. The first lady, Lady Bird Johnson, contributed to the cause by championing the Highway Beautification Act, which regulated billboards and highway junkyards—a cause inspired almost directly by Galbraith's *The Affluent Society*.[72] The Elementary and Secondary Education Act of 1965 exerted more federal oversight and gave aid to poorer students; it was capped off later in the year with the Higher Education Act, which created college and university community service programs for poorer students.[73]

As Doris Kearns Goodwin points out, the list of the Great Society's accomplishments "would offer something to almost everyone." It was good politics, at least in theory: "Medicare for the old, educational assistance for the young, tax rebates for business, a higher minimum wage for labor, subsidies for farmers, vocational training for the unskilled, food for the hungry, housing for the homeless, poverty grants for the poor, clean highways for drivers, legal protection for blacks, improved schooling for Native Americans, rehabilitation for the physically challenged, higher benefits for the unemployed, considerable changes in the methods by which immigrants were admitted, auto safety for everyone, pensions for retirees, fair labeling for consumers, conservation for hikers and campers, and more and more."[74] But theory and practice are often at odds, more so in politics perhaps than in any arena of life. Almost all of these programs ran into trouble, either from recalcitrant opponents or unforeseen consequences.

A significant proportion of the Johnson administration's problems derived from the president's inability to consider taking seriously the suggestions of anyone whose metaphoric "pecker" he did not already have in his pocket. Many of the factors that eventually undid his presidency in 1968 were already manifest in 1965. For instance, in the autumn of that year Chicago mayor and machine boss Richard J. Daley berated Vice President Humphrey over the fact that "OEO [was] building and funding in the community action committees opposition elements to the city administration," though the mayor apparently made his point in language considerably more colorful.[75] The administration's Community Action Program (CAP) became, in the words of one historian, "an ugly series of local brawls" between local politicians and those receiving federal money.[76] Michael Harrington's prediction that CAP would likely fund tenant organizing proved prophetic.[77]

In New York City, CAP money went to fund a play by Leroi Jones, later known as Amiri Baraka, which enacted Jack Benny's valet, Rochester, murdering the beloved comedian and then inciting blacks to kill whites.[78] In Oakland federal funds for CAP wound up buttressing those who were organizing the Black Panther Party, which called for blacks to arm themselves for a coming race revolution.[79] In certain respects these were unavoidable functions of timing. The Great Society came into being during the same period that Black Power militancy was displacing the platform of integration through moderation promoted by the Southern Christian Leadership Conference (SCLC). "The image of the Negro in 1966 was no longer that of the praying long-suffering nonviolent victim of southern sheriffs; it was a defiant young hoodlum shouting 'black power' and hurling 'Molotov cocktails' in an urban slum," wrote James L. Sundquist, a liberal political scientist who worked for both presidents Kennedy and Johnson.[80]

Were one to try to locate a particular moment in history to encapsulate the hubris that liberals displayed in the face of genuine democratic dissent, one could do worse than to examine the political battle that took place in New York City in 1966 over the decision of its newly elected liberal patrician Republican mayor, John V. Lindsay, to appoint actual civilians to the police department's Civilian Complaint Review Board. The board had been created in 1953 in response to community complaints about police mistreatment of blacks and Puerto Ricans. But because it was peopled and staffed exclusively by the police, it was viewed quite reasonably in these same communities as a means of diverting rather than addressing such complaints.

The idea of creating a civilian panel to oversee New York City cops had originated among more militant black leaders in the 1950s, but had been taken up by leaders like Martin Luther King, Jr. It lay fallow, however, until the summer of 1964, when Harlem broke out in riots and the police response was deemed less than polite even by the police. The official recommendation to move ahead with it had come from former federal judge Lawrence E. Walsh and was conceived of as part of an overall package of department modernization—also part of the liberal agenda—but was designed specifically to instill confidence in blacks and Puerto Ricans that City Hall was on their side.

The board was supported by all of the pillars of New York's reformist liberal establishment, including its two senators, Democrat Robert Kennedy and Republican Jacob Javits, and its governor, Republican Nelson Rockefeller, as well as *The New York Times*. *The New York Post*, the ACLU, the NAACP, the Liberal Party, the City Bar Association, the Anti-Defamation League, the American Jewish Committee, the American Jewish Congress, and the Council of Protestant Churches; even Cardinal Spellman threw in.

The police force, however, wanted no part of it. Patrolmen's Benefit Association (PBA) president John Cassese announced, "I'm sick and tired of giving in to minority groups with their whims and their gripes and shouting." He earmarked the PBA's entire $1.5 million budget for that year to fund a campaign to have the decision overturned. Joined by New York's Conservative Party, which had just benefited from an energetic mayoral campaign of the young magazine editor William F. Buckley, Jr., they collected more than ninety thousand signatures (more than three times the necessary number) to force a referendum.

The liberals made much of the presence in their opponents' camp of not only American Legion posts and small business and local neighborhood groups, but also the John Birch Society, the American Renaissance Party, and the American Nazi Party. Lindsay's reaction, like that of most of the measure's proponents, was a mixture of moralism, fear mongering, and character assassination—almost all of it aimed at the liberals' traditional base of white workers. When questioned about the issue, the mayor haughtily replied: "I have no doubt in my mind whatsoever, so convinced am I of its rightness." He said he expected the board would "receive the support of all those who care and think, who know and believe in rightness in this our city."[81]

Clearly, most of the city's white inhabitants cared and thought differently, particularly those living outside the borough of Manhattan. The mayor found himself repeatedly heckled around the city. "Why do you always kowtow to the coloreds?" yelled one woman in Flatbush. While many liberals subscribed to novelist James Baldwin's contention that urban crime and violence were actually forms of social protest, Buckley instructed his followers to resist the notion that, owing to past oppression, "Negro crime is any less criminal."[82] Robert Kennedy mused, worriedly, that the campaign was "taking on the aspect of a Jewish-negro cabal against everyone else."[83] (In fact, they didn't even have the Jews.)

As liberals grew more desperate, they resorted to increasingly histrionic scare tactics, with little or no thought of achieving compromise, much less consensus. The mayor hired the young political consultant David Garth to run the city's political campaign for the measure, which asked voters, "Do New Yorkers Want a Police State?"[84] The political scientist James Q. Wilson observed at the time that the mayor and his supporters came to symbolize to the cops "that segment of the urban middle class which has deserted the police ... [and] represents the hypocritical liberal who wants both to maintain law and order and to win the votes of the lawless."[85] And it was the police, not the liberals, who had the support on the ground. Less than a year after his own election to city hall, Lindsay's initiative was defeated by a more than two-to-one margin. Years later Lindsay would admit that "in recognizing the demands of deprived neighborhoods ... we did not realize how much the vast bulk of city people—hard-working white middle-class citizens—felt estranged, too, from the process of government."[86] At some level, that would be the liberals' problem for the coming generation.

Even Lyndon Johnson had by now begun to grow wary of many of his own initiatives. More troubling was the fact that his paranoia was getting the best of him. Nothing, one imagines, gave Lyndon Johnson more pleasure regarding his landslide 1964 victory than the fact that Robert Kennedy was forced to cling to his coattails in order to win his run for the Senate in New York.[87] But the threat that the slain president's brother—and those loyal to him—represented to his presidency began to color all of LBJ's decisions. He became fearful, even after having aggressively recruited him, that Sargent Shriver was more loyal to Robert Kennedy than himself, as Shriver started to articulate some criticisms of the president's programs as being too little and too late. (Shriver's loyalty was, in fact, the subject of considerable speculation in the Kennedy camp as well.[88]) The president watched passively as Congress began to slash funds to the OEO, cuts that continued in 1967 following Republican success at the polls.[89] Soon enough the OEO's budget fell well below what its administrators considered to be the "irreducible minimum" necessary merely to keep the agency functioning."[90] Shriver now found himself the embattled liberal, attacked from all sides, and in 1968 was grateful to accept the ambassadorship to France, abandoning the dreams he and Johnson had shared four years earlier.

The president's contrite 1967 State of the Union address offered little to please liberals. As Steven Gillon pointed out, "Only once in his 1967 State of the Union Message, a thirteen-page single-spaced text, did he refer to the Great Society."[91] *The New York Times*'s James Reston called it a speech of "guns and margarine," referring to the cost of the ever-expanding war in Vietnam and the reduced spending for domestic priorities that appeared to accompany it. (Johnson had committed nearly half a million U.S. troops to the conflict by this time.[92]) In LBJ's own language, that "bitch of a war" in Vietnam destroyed "the woman I really loved—the Great Society."[93] It was Vietnam, not his support for civil rights or the Great Society, that ultimately did in Johnson. The historian Allen Matusow writes: "Vietnam cut short the rush to the Great Society, smashed his consensus, widened the credibility gap, and made him one of the most hated chief executives in a hundred years."[94]

This is not the place to try to answer the question of what drove LBJ to pursue "Americanization" of the Vietnam War. It is enough to say that starting with a lie about an attack on American forces in the Gulf of Tonkin in 1964—a lie that would help poison both the war effort and the politics it produced—Vietnam not only ended Lyndon Johnson's presidency but destroyed the Democratic Party's dominance of presidential politics and dealt Roosevelt's liberal coalition a blow from which it has still not recovered.[95]

As one of the best recent histories of the war observes, "Liberals in America were divided on the war from an early stage, and many were among the first to challenge the need for a continued commitment to the GVN [government of South Vietnam]."[96] Certainly, liberal arguments could be made in favor of intervention in Vietnam. Yes, the Vietcong were nationalists, but they were also Communist totalitarians. And while the various regimes governing South Vietnam were almost unimaginably corrupt, they were relatively benign beyond those urban areas in and around Saigon, where they exercised control. In most instances Johnson and his advisers made the public case for war not on the merits of Vietnam itself, which was five thousand miles from the United States and enjoyed virtually no strategic value beyond the symbolic, but by appealing to the rhetoric of "freedom and democracy." In private, however, and almost without exception, the case was made in terms of the perceptions of others should the United States "lose" yet another country to communism.

LBJ relied heavily on JFK's brain trust—particularly Bundy, Rusk, and McNamara—but these men were hardly committed liberals. They remained, in the aftermath of the Cuban missile crisis, intoxicated by their belief in the ability of the United States to calibrate its response to any given threat to coerce its adversaries into capitulation, as they had, albeit mistakenly, believed President Kennedy had done with Cuba and the Soviets. George Ball would later comment that "President Johnson was overawed by these [Kennedy] people around him," and Bill Moyers later recalled that privately "Johnson would look at the Kennedy people around him" and would later muse out loud as to what they would think if he had taken a position which in their minds would have seemed softer.[97] He told the dovish Ball, "Don't worry about the hippies and the students and the Commies, they'll raise a lot of hell but can't do real damage. (Another version of this same story has Johnson saying, "Don't pay attention to what those little shits on the campuses do.") The terrible beast we have to fear is the right wing; if they ever get the idea I am selling out Vietnam, they'll do horrible things to the country, and we'll be forced to escalate the war beyond anything you've ever thought about."[98] Indeed, memories of what McCarthyism had done to Truman were never far from his mind. "I am not going to be the president who saw Southeast Asia go the way China went," he pledged early on in the decision-making process.[99]

Johnson was hardly alone in such concerns; most of the Kennedy advisers he inherited shared them, particularly the two with the greatest sway over his thinking, Bob McNamara and Mac Bundy. Bundy advised the president that "as an ex-historian," he saw that "the political damage to Truman and Acheson from the fall of China arose because most Americans came to believe that we could and should have done more than we did to prevent it. This is exactly what would happen now if we should seem to be the first to quit in Saigon."[100] He reinforced Johnson's fears with warnings of "wild men waiting in the wings," assuring Johnson that the "Goldwater crowd," was "more numerous, more powerful and more dangerous than the fleabite professors" who were likely to object.[101]

In fact, these fears of "wild men" were wildly exaggerated. In 1964 the U.S. public was deeply disengaged from the issue. At the end of that year, 25 percent of Americans surveyed by the Council on Foreign Relations were not aware of any fighting going on in Vietnam. Of those who did have knowledge of it, half favored withdrawal and just under a quarter, the use of U.S. ground forces if necessary, numbers confirmed in a University of Michigan poll conducted later in the year. According to a Gallup Organization poll in early 1965, 81 percent of those questioned answered affirmatively when asked whether the president should "arrange a conference with the leaders of Southeast Asia and China and see if a peace agreement can be worked out."[102] Senate majority leader Mike Mansfield, moreover, argued against further involvement,[103] as did Foreign Relations Committee chairman J. William Fulbright.[104] Privately, Johnson even heard the same sentiment expressed by his trusted ally, the conservative chairman of the Senate Armed Services Committee, Richard Russell, the single most important senator when it came to military issues. Russell warned him that Vietnam would likely prove "the damnedest mess on earth," with the United States ending up "in quicksands up to its neck." "It'll be the most expensive venture this country ever went into," he continued. "It'll take a half million men, [and] they'd be bogged down in there for ten years."[105]

A decision to stand down would have earned Johnson powerful support in the media, including, for starters, the editors of *The New York Times* and the nation's most influential pundit, Walter Lippmann.[106] In the academy, Hans Morgenthau, the influential father of the American "realist" school of foreign policy analysis, argued for withdrawal. In June of 1964 his name appeared atop a petition from five thousand academics calling for just such a policy, a petition that *The New York Times* editors considered to be front-page news.[107] These were not "hippies," "Commies," or "fleabite professors," but the most respected members of the political establishment. In fact, as Mac Bundy later admitted, if Johnson "had decided that the right thing to do was to cut our losses, he was quite sufficiently inventive to do that in a way that would not have destroyed the Great Society."[108] Bundy's brother, William, who was assistant secretary of state for East Asian and Pacific affairs and also, as it happens, one of the war's key architects, concurred on this point. Lyndon Johnson, he later wrote, would have carried public opinion with him, he averred, "on whatever course he chose."[109]

But the problem was that what Johnson feared even more than losing a war was debating one. He was, as he admitted to Robert Kennedy, "fearful that if we move without any authority of the Congress that the resentment would be pretty widespread and it would involve a lot of people who normally would be with us." And yet, "if we asked for the authority . . . ," he worried aloud, "I would shudder to think that if they debated it for a long period of time, and they're likely to do that. So I don't think the choice is very good."[110] Here again Johnson found his fears and insecurities reinforced by the advice of the Kennedy brain trust. McNamara advised him in the spring of 1964 that "it would be wise for you to say as little as possible."[111] Reflecting on his failures in Vietnam in their aftermath, LBJ remained adamant on this point. "I knew that if we let Communist aggression succeed in taking over South Vietnam, there would follow in this country an endless national debate—a mean and destructive debate—that would shatter my Presidency, kill my administration and damage our democracy," he would explain to Doris Kearns. "I knew that Harry Truman and Dean Acheson had lost their effectiveness from the day that Communists took over in China. I believed that the loss of China had played a large role in the rise of Joe McCarthy. And I knew that all these problems, taken together, were chickenshit compared with might happen if we lost Vietnam."[112]

Many of those close to the president urged him to go before Congress and the country and lay out the truth. Henry Cabot Lodge, Jr., whom General Maxwell Taylor replaced as ambassador to South Vietnam, asked Johnson, "How do you send young men there in great numbers without telling why?"[113] But the president explained, "I can get the Great Society through right now—this is a golden time. We've got a good Congress, and I'm the right President and I can do it. But if I talk about the cost of war, the Great Society won't go through and the tax bill won't go through. Old Wilbur Mills will sit down there and he'll thank me kindly and send me back my Great Society, and then he'll tell me that they'll be glad to spend whatever we need for the war."[114]

As the war turned sour, the Great Society stalled, and Johnson's paranoia only increased. He became convinced, with J. Edgar Hoover, that his former ally and later adversary in the Senate, J. William Fulbright, was purposely working on behalf of the Communists and pushing liberals to desert the president in droves.[115] In the fall of 1965, Richard Goodwin was one of the first to leave his staff, disagreeing about the war and concerned about the president's obsession with liberal protests against it. He was soon joined by the historian Eric Goldman, a liberal who had been playing the same role Schlesinger had had in the JFK White House and who was an accomplished historian of liberalism. When he found himself disagreeing with the Vietnam policy, Goldman had tried during the early years of 1966 to get the president to "keep at least part of" his mind "on domestic problems."[116] But as he recalled, "By the Summer and Fall of 1966 the domestic reformer of the Great Society days had become a war chief, finding more and more congeniality with conservatives."[117] When Goldman quit in September 1966, LBJ sent Bill Moyers to a press conference to condemn him. Ironically, a few months later Moyers also departed. Explaining his rationale to Arthur Schlesinger, Jr., he said, "You know, Arthur, I would not be leaving if I thought I could do any good by staying."[118] (He would go on to spend the next forty or so years working tirelessly as perhaps America's most influential liberal journalist and, almost certainly, its most accomplished television journalist.)

Public opinion polls in 1967 suggested that "the war was weakening support for Great Society programs,"[119] and Goodwin complained, "The Great Society did not fail. It was abandoned."[120] There is some merit to this argument if we focus only on Medicare, Medicaid, Head Start, Legal Services, and other programs that continued to gain respect from the American public and that could have inspired more to follow. But it's not entirely fair if we also consider the chaos generated by numerous CAP initiatives, whose failures mimicked those of the war. Whatever the case, one thing is for certain: a president who had done more for the liberal cause than any other postwar president had managed, in the course of a few years, to destroy the prospects of liberalism in this country for some time to come.

One way to measure the damage LBJ left in his wake is to examine his role in undermining the career of his would-be successor, Hubert Humphrey. The vice president ended the administration all but chewed up and spit out. His political instincts never deserted him, but the courage he had shown at the 1948 convention (and elsewhere) certainly did. Humphrey was no match whatever for LBJ's "treatment"; he recalled an early meeting with LBJ as being "an almost hypnotic experience. I came out of that session covered with blood, sweat, tears, spit—and sperm."[121] On a visit to LBJ's ranch, recounts biographer Robert Dallek, the president "made Hubert kill two deer, which repelled him" and got him to "don a cowboy outfit many sizes too big and [insisted that] he ride a large, spirited horse to which he clung 'like a tiny child on his first merry-go-round ride.'"[122]

In fact, Humphrey had initially been both brave and prescient about the war. On February 17, 1965, he sent the president a memo, drafted with Thomas Hughes, who headed the State Department's Bureau of Intelligence and Research, in which he argued that a large attack on North Vietnam would likely prove disastrous. Humphrey told LBJ that the bombing and troop increase struck him as Goldwater mimicry and that he feared China might get involved.[123] From a political standpoint, moreover, the vice president advised that 1965 would be "a year of minimum political risk for the Johnson administration," and so the president could without great difficulty become free of the trap he appeared to be setting for himself.[124] Johnson's response was to bar Humphrey from all national security meetings at which the conflict was to be discussed.

Humphrey got the message, and following a trip to Vietnam in January 1966, he reversed himself completely.[125] When Schlesinger, James Wechsler, and Joe Rauh—all opponents of the war by now, all longtime ADA allies of Humphrey—met with the vice president on April 17, 1967, he had become an apologist for a cause in which he did not believe, striking his friends as an almost pathetic caricature of his formerly vivacious self.[126] Schlesinger had already noticed the change a year earlier, confiding to his diary that he found "a new and different Hubert—hard-faced, except for some unctuous smiles, and uncharacteristically coarse in his language."[127] Joe Rauh concluded, "Most of us were struck by the sense that he was increasingly conscious of the dead-end into which his own political life might be headed as the result of the war."[128]

Appropriately, Americans for Democratic Action, or ADA, postwar liberalism's most important organization, was also torn asunder by the war. John Kenneth Galbraith, chosen to head the organization in early 1967, had been a critic of U.S. involvement when he was an ambassador to India under Kennedy.[129] After meeting with Robert McNamara in January 1966, he grew concerned about the gulf between the secretary's public optimism and his private pessimism. Afterward Galbraith sent a memo to Johnson to try to persuade him to press for negotiations and start withdrawing troops. But the memo, as to be expected, provoked no response from a president who had come to believe that any criticism of his Vietnam policy amounted to Communist treachery. Galbraith accordingly decided to go public with his protest and pushed ADA to follow.[130]

As Galbraith persuaded numerous members to support his moderate protest on Vietnam, Allard Lowenstein, who, after being elected to Congress, would eventually ascend to the organization's presidency, agitated for a more radical tack and assumed a leadership role in the burgeoning "Dump Johnson" movement.[131] As Arthur Schlesinger, Jr., described the situation in 1967: "The organization is on the verge of a split between the labor people who are irrevocably pro-Johnson, and most of the liberals who are deeply opposed to the widening of the war in Vietnam and are increasingly anti-Johnson."[132]

Lowenstein fought hard, especially with Gus Tyler, head of the Garment Workers Union and a strong supporter of LBJ. Most commentators have read this conflict as a rift between "student" protesters (even though Lowenstein was in his late thirties at the time) and labor leaders. The rift, in fact, extended far beyond the confines of ADA.[133] Even Walter Reuther, who had flirted for a moment in 1967 with pronegotiation protesters, said in 1968: "The UAW is for President Johnson all the way."[134] Tyler, like many labor leaders, worried about breaking with the president and therefore losing the influence labor had gained within the party establishment. It was hardly a winning gamble on the part of labor, but it was, by this time, an inevitable one. For in the wake of the myriad upheavals of the sixties, begun in the bosom of liberalism but having moved well beyond it in almost all cases, politics had become less about issues than about identity. And everybody knew almost automatically which side he was on.[135]

Martin Luther King, Jr., struggled long and hard before finally speaking up against the war, as Johnson had championed the cause of civil rights beyond anything King had imagined possible. Moreover King, like Johnson, had more than enough to worry about on the home front. He hoped to bring his movement to the North with his Poor People's Campaign, begun audaciously in Chicago, but it was making little progress. Radical and violence-promoting challengers were growing in power and influence, and J. Edgar Hoover's FBI was serving him a daily diet of purposeful harassment and torment. By 1966, though, he had begun to feel that he could keep silent no longer and had the SCLC draft a statement protesting that the "promises of the Great Society top the casualty list of the conflict" in Vietnam.[136] Speaking on April 4, 1967, from the pulpit of Riverside Church in New York City, exactly one year before the day of his assassination, King announced to the congregation that the war had left America's commitment to civil rights and social justice "broken and eviscerated as if it were some idle political thing of a society gone mad on war." The United States, he concluded, had become "the greatest purveyor of violence in the world today."[137]

11

Paranoia Strikes Deep in the Heartland

> The young are honorable and see the problems, but they don't know
> anything because we have not taught them anything.
> —Paul Goodman, 1968[1]

> The issue is not the issue.
> —Mark Rudd, 1968[2]

Hollywood liberalism, as with so many cultural institutions of the era, crashed and burned in 1968. Consider the fate of *Guess Who's Coming to Dinner,* a film by Stanley Kramer. The story concerned a young couple asking their parents for permission to marry; she was white, he was black. Love ultimately triumphs over prejudice, enlightenment over ignorance, hope over fear. Released in December 1967, it played in theaters until May 1968, making it, in *Variety*-speak, "one of the industry's all-time biggest grossers."[3]

The movie proved a capstone to Kramer's career (and to that of Spencer Tracy, who barely lived long enough to complete it). As we've seen, Kramer specialized in "problem pictures" or "message movies," the kind that made Hollywood liberals feel proud. He treated racism in *The Defiant Ones* (1958), nuclear holocaust in *On the Beach* (1959), Christian fundamentalism in *Inherit the Wind* (1960), fascism and the challenges of justice in the face of such extreme evil in *Judgment at Nuremberg* (1961), and the personalization of fascism in *Ship of Fools* (1965). But by 1968 his specialty had begun to seem tired to those who looked for more edginess, more irony, and less saccharine in their movie scripts. The critic Pauline Kael mocked what she described as his "irritatingly self-righteous," "messianic," and intellectually "feeble" filmmaking.[4] Ironically, it was one of the younger actors in the movie whom some found its most outdated aspect: Sidney Poitier, who played the prospective groom. His break came in 1950, when he played a young intern and future doctor caring for a racist white man in the film *No Way Out*. Both white and black audiences responded favorably, the NAACP announced its approval, and integrationist liberalism had its hero.[5]

Poitier enjoyed a second breakthrough role in *Blackboard Jungle* (1955) and teamed up with Stanley Kramer in *The Defiant Ones* (1958) (discussed in chapter eight). By this time, Poitier's biographer claims, "the black community revered [him]" and viewed him as an artist who refused to be constricted by the narrowness of most black roles at the time and instead insisted on playing a full human being, as Poitier told David Susskind in an interview in 1959.[6] And yet not all of black America was on board. James Baldwin remembered seeing *The Defiant Ones* in a white neighborhood where the audience cheered the final scene, but in Harlem audiences were aghast. When Poitier jumped off a moving train in order to help Curtis, who couldn't make the run because of the police dogs close behind, Harlem viewers leaped out of their seats and shouted: *"Get back on the train, you fool!"* Poitier's integrationist message had started to grate.[7]

Unlike Harry Belafonte, who sacrificed his acting career to devote himself full time to the movement, Poitier managed, on a far smaller scale, to combine activism with acting. He cohosted an event with Harry Belafonte in May 1960 to celebrate the anniversary of *Brown v. Board of Education* and to raise money for Martin Luther King, Jr.[8] He participated in the March on Washington and even went down to Mississippi at Belafonte's request to help him deliver badly needed cash to support the Freedom Summer volunteers. (Their car was attacked by white racists.[9]) But Poitier believed his biggest challenge was to bring the civil rights cause to Hollywood. As virtually the only black actor in America trusted with a starring role in a major motion picture—any major motion picture—he understandably felt himself to be carrying a heavy burden. "I represent ten million people in this country," he told a reporter, "and millions more in Africa.... And I'm not going to do anything they can't be proud of."[10]

Poitier's reviews also appeared to track the shifts in movement politics. In 1967, *Los Angeles Times* film critic Burt Prelutsky described Poitier as a "Negro in white face," complaining, "We have rid the screens of one stereotype only to replace it with another. Exit Stepin Fetchit, enter Sidney Poitier."[11] Around the same time, Clifford Mason, a black playwright, asked in an article for *The New York Times Magazine*, "Why Does White America Love Sidney Poitier So?" His answer: Poitier represented the "black version of the man in the gray flannel suit, taking on white problems and a white man's sense of the world."

Mason labeled Poitier "a showcase nigger."[12] His was the acting version of the civil rights movement's "gradualism"—a term, like liberalism, now considered by leftists as morally bankrupt.[13]

It was no surprise, then, that *Guess Who's Coming to Dinner,* with its sentimental script and integrationist message, provided many such critics with an occasion to vent against the vision it represented. James Baldwin, now inching toward his own version of black nationalism, thought he saw in the movie a scarcely concealed message that it was fine for a black man to marry a white woman, so long as he didn't move into the neighborhood or exhibit any sexual longing. The new leader of SNCC, firebrand H. Rap Brown, quipped, "Even George Wallace would like that nigger."[14]

Kramer was confused by the attacks, later explaining, "I agreed with the college students in some of what they were demanding from the world—a more liberated society, an end to the Vietnam War and to racism, less hypocrisy and dishonesty of their parents' generation, less corruption in the establishment—but I didn't understand why some of them were attacking me."[15] Nor could he understand why someone like James Baldwin thought it impossible for him to draw a realistic black character.[16] At the same time, Kramer admitted that Poitier's character was purposely drawn as a kind of black superman. "I wanted the prospective black bridegroom to be a person so suitable that if anyone objected to him, it could only be due to racial prejudice."[17]

Of course conditions often lag behind transformations in consciousness, and one must ask if the critics of Kramer's somewhat utopian vision might not have done well to pay closer attention to the problems America was facing in making any racial progress at all. While *Dinner* was being filmed, miscegenation remained a crime in seventeen states. On the day of Spencer Tracy's funeral, however, the U.S. Supreme Court struck down those laws in *Loving v. Virginia.* Chief Justice Earl Warren declared: "Under our Constitution the freedom to marry, or not marry, a person of another race resides with the individual and cannot be infringed by the State."[18] That same day Lyndon Johnson nominated Thurgood Marshall to be the first black man to serve on the United States Supreme Court. Change was coming, but not fast enough for some—and too fast for many others.

In the autumn of 1967, William Styron published *The Confessions of Nat Turner,* a fictionalized account of an 1831 slave revolt told from the point of view of its leader, Nat Turner, who, not incidentally, fantasizes about raping a white woman. "Bill's going to catch it from both sides," his friend and sometime housemate James Baldwin reportedly predicted to an interviewer just before publication.[19]

The grandson of slave owners, Styron was born in 1925 and grew up in Newport News, Virginia, not far from the site of the Turner uprising. After graduating from Duke University, Styron moved to New York to pursue his career as a writer. His first novel, *Lie Down in Darkness* (1951), centered on a dysfunctional family with an alcoholic father, controlling mother, and two daughters, one suffering from mental retardation, the other precocious but dissolute. It was published when he was just twenty-six and made him famous.

Following the publication of *Lie Down in Darkness,* Styron began work on his Nat Turner novel. But he came to feel overwhelmed by the project, which he felt required more research, more thinking. Returning to the novel early in the midsixties, he spent evenings conversing with two friends, the liberal historian of the South, C. Vann Woodward, and the novelist Robert Penn Warren. He wanted his book to describe the horrors of slavery, as much of the story centers on Turner's being sold from owner to owner, but he also discovered that Turner had learned to read and was prone to religious visions (often while fasting) and apocalyptic and irrational dreams. He comes to hate the "docile equanimity and good cheer with which . . . simple black people" dealt with their misery, as he has visions of blacks and whites clashing in a holy war.[20] At the end, the rebellious slave refuses to disown his cold-blooded murder of white oppressors. "No, Mr. Gray, I have no remorse for anything," Turner explains during his confession. "I would do it all again."[21]

Like *Dinner, Nat Turner* proved a commercial success and gave rise to a cultural contretemps. Initial reviews were rapturous—writing in *The New York Times,* Eliot Fremont-Smith called the book "a convincing and stirring portrait of the crippling effects of slavery on negroes and whites alike," which "illuminates slavery as a central and inescapable fact of our history."[22] But the backlash began almost immediately. Black nationalist critics accused Styron, in his own recollection of the book's aftermath, of being "psychologically sick" and "morally senile" and of having a "vile racist imagination."[23] In a book of essays, *William Styron's Nat Turner: Ten Black Writers Respond,* published in 1968 and edited by John Henrik Clarke, Vincent Harding, a professor of history at Spellman College in Atlanta, insisted that "the whitened appropriation of our history is . . . a total negation of our power and our truth. Whose mind has [Styron] entered save his own?" he asked.[24] John Oliver Killens, a black novelist, described Styron as a "darling of the liberal critics" and argued that the white writer was "still in desperate need of emancipation from his slavemaster's psychology." He was a man who "tries to sing the blues when he has not paid his dues."[25] When Styron spoke in public following its publication, the events tended to turn confrontational. "I feel like a combination of Theodore Bilbo and Lester Maddox," he recalled, by which he mean that this white liberal had somehow become the equivalent of the hate-filled racist.[26]

"By 1968," the historian Mark Kurlansky argues, "'liberal' had become almost synonymous with 'sellout.'"[27] Liberals were now facing fire from both conservatives and radicals. The whipsaw of identity politics—the idea that whites and blacks could not communicate across their barriers—was destroying the integrationist dreams of liberalism. The events of that year threw much of urban America into chaos and liberalism toward suicidal immolation. The year began with the Tet Offensive, after the Vietcong seized the U.S. embassy in Saigon.[28] Soon afterward news anchor Walter Cronkite, America's most trusted man, according to many polls, told viewers of CBS News, "To say that we are closer to victory today is to believe, in the face of the evidence, the optimists who have been wrong in the past. . . . To say that we are mired in stalemate seems the only realistic, yet unsatisfactory, conclusion."[29] The historian H. W. Brands observes, "The sky didn't fall on American liberalism until the sky fell in Vietnam."[30]

Early in 1966, Senator J. William Fulbright, an Arkansas segregationist upon whom Johnson had relied to shepherd the ill-fated Gulf of Tonkin Resolution of August 1964, had turned on the president and set out to use his position as chairman of the Foreign Relations Committee for a set of hearings that, among other things, would establish the fact that the Johnson administration had deliberately misled the Congress, the press, and the American people not only about Tonkin itself but about almost everything related to America's entry into the now-endless war. NBC and CBS covered most of the hearings live—at considerable cost to each one in lost advertising—and millions of Americans tuned in to watch administration officials being grilled by Fulbright. Most were made to look foolish, duplicitous, or both, as they repeatedly tried to put a positive spin on what was becoming an obviously calamitous situation.[31] The administration's credibility had fallen so far by this point that I. F. Stone could write in his increasingly popular weekly newsletter, "It is no longer necessary to argue the mendacity of our leaders and the incompetence of our military. Mr. Johnson has assured us that the successful surprise attack on 100 South Vietnamese cities and towns was really a Viet Cong defeat; if they suffer a few more such defeats, we'll be lucky to settle for a coalition government in Hawaii."[32]

And here we must give the antiwar movement the credit it earned before it disintegrated into something that, sadly, reflected all too much the culture of lies, contradictions, and, occasionally, mindless violence that it had been created to oppose. All wars in American history have inspired dissenters, but none, as historian of the left Michael Kazin points out, "from the New England Federalists during the War of 1812 to the pacifists and Communists during the Korean War—had begun to organize near the start of the war or had grown larger and more powerful as the battles continued."[33] The coalition of students, socialists, pacifists, (some) liberals, (some) unions, church groups, and finally ordinary people and even the supremely moving sight of the thousands of wounded and disabled members of Vietnam Veterans Against the War came together on a scale that was all but unprecedented, and although chaotically (if at all) organized and more often than not naive about the nature of the enemy, it managed to hold itself together. No previous antiwar movement endured long enough to celebrate genuine victory in what, at the time of its inception, looked to be one of the most lopsided battles, both at home and abroad, ever undertaken.

On the fifth day of the new year, America's most famous child care expert, Benjamin Spock, and the chaplain of Yale University, William Sloane Coffin, found themselves indicted with three others for aiding and abetting draft resistance. (They had signed a document titled "A Call to Resist Illegitimate Authority," and engaged in acts of civil disobedience.[34]) The indictments illustrated how the peace movement was becoming more militant, moving "from protest to resistance," as *New Left Notes* put it in 1967—that is, from writing letters to politicians and singing folk songs to active, illegal (albeit largely nonviolent) resistance.[35] Protesters were growing not only more numerous but also more theatrical and confrontational.[36]

Much of the violence that did occur involved the Democratic Party's twin constituencies of blacks and working-class whites, and to address it LBJ created a National Advisory Commission on Civil Disorders, headed by Illinois governor Otto Kerner. Its report, issued in February 1968, was shocking in its pessimism and harsh judgment of Democrats' traditional base of support. "White racism is essentially responsible for the explosive mixture which has been accumulating in our cities since the end of World War I," it concluded. The report went on to discuss "white terrorism against non-violent protest," suggesting what many thought obvious: that Black Power had erupted only after frustration that King's strategy took so long to make an impact. Even more surprising for an official document, the Kerner Commission's report complained of "white racism and white repression" among urban police forces directed against minorities: "The Negro can never forget . . . that white society is deeply implicated in the ghetto. White institutions created it, white institutions maintained it, and white society condones it." Solving this problem, the report warned, "will require unprecedented levels of funding and performance, but . . . there can be no higher priority for national action and no higher claim on the nation's conscience."[37]

April 1968 found Martin Luther King, Jr., in Memphis, Tennessee, helping striking sanitation workers mobilize. His Poor People's Campaign (PPC) was increasingly focusing on issues of black poverty in the North, rather than segregation in the South, and inching toward an endorsement of the kind of democratic socialism that characterized many European leftist parties. Together with his uncompromising rhetorical condemnation of the war in Vietnam, the effort revealed a man becoming increasingly radicalized by events. PPC's planks drew on Bayard Rustin's "freedom budget," with calls for full employment, guaranteed income, and low-cost housing.[38] Housing, in particular, would become a crucial issue for civil rights advocates and ultimately the nut they could never crack.[39]

So long as discriminatory housing patterns continued to be enforced, no sensible solution would ever be found for opening up schools or even most workplaces. King had warned as early as 1963 that he had "come to feel that our next attack will have to be more than just getting a lunch counter integrated or a department store to take down discriminatory signs." Instead, nothing less than an "assault on the whole system of segregation in a community" would suffice.[40] But the practical problems of transportation and local taxation were too easily used by resisters to quash the entire effort. No black family could move into a white ethnic neighborhood of Chicago, and perhaps most other American cities, without facing the threat of community-supported riots and organized, often semi-officially approved arson. More than a few who tried paid with life or limb.[41]

Underfunded, understaffed, and underorganized, the PPC ultimately proved to be a dispiriting affair. King himself was deeply depressed and stressed at the time by constant FBI harassment, which included sending to his wife photos and tapes of him engaged in sexual acts with white women. Meanwhile, Hoover had instructed all of his agents not to share any information with King's lieutenants regarding the frequent death threats the Bureau had uncovered, and he refused any discussion with Johnson about offering King official protection. Instead, he ordered agents "to expose, disrupt, misdirect, discredit or otherwise neutralize the activities of black nationalist hate-type organizations," in which he explicitly included King, whom he called "an instrument in the hands of subversive forces seeking to undermine our Nation."[42]

The Memphis sanitation worker campaign, meanwhile, was not going well. At one march King led, a young man was shot by police, and King left the scene as police descended on the march.[43] The next day a Memphis paper blared its denunciation that "King's pose as leader of a nonviolent movement has been shattered." It was especially critical of how the civil rights leader had allegedly "fled the melee."[44] King considered calling off the PPC altogether, but his fellow workers calmed him and he soon announced that he would hold another march in Memphis on April 8.

In the run-up to the event, King struck a tone that was less hopeful than usual, almost passive in its acceptance of the likelihood of failure. And then on April 4 he walked out onto the balcony of the Lorraine Hotel in Memphis and was shot dead by the white racist James Earl Ray.

Rioting began in as many as 125 locations almost as soon as the news became known.[45] In Washington, D.C., troops circled the White House.[46] As James Patterson observes, "The bullet, which killed him, did much to destroy chances for non-violent leadership on behalf of social justice for blacks."[47]

On April 9, 1968, Columbia University held a memorial service for the slain civil rights leader attended by over a thousand people. As Columbia's vice president, David B. Truman, moved toward the podium of St. Paul's Chapel to begin the proceedings, Mark Rudd, a leader of the local chapter of Students for a Democratic Society (SDS), stepped in front of him and shouted, "Dr. Truman and President Kirk are committing a moral outrage against the memory of Dr. King. Columbia's administration is morally corrupt, unjust, and indulges in racist policies." Forty members of SDS then followed Rudd out of the chapel in protest.[48]

SDS had been founded in a burst of left-wing hope and optimism by a group of ambitious young radicals who began as members of the Student League for Industrial Democracy (SLID), the youth arm of the musty old League for Industrial Democracy (LID), itself the stepchild of the Intercollegiate Socialist Society, which had been around since 1905. Its founding took place in 1960 on the University of Michigan campus at Ann Arbor, Michigan. Two years later it adopted the soon-to-be-famous Port Huron statement, based on a draft by young staffer Tom Hayden. A mixture of nondoctrinaire Marxism, personalistic liberalism, and unabashed utopianism—"We regard men as infinitely precious and possessed of unfulfilled capacities for reason, freedom, and love," its signatories proclaimed—the Port Huron statement formed the basis for what would become the largest radical organization in American history, and certainly the largest one to commit itself to self-governance through participatory democracy before it eventually descended into sectarian civil war.[49]

Columbia's SDS chapter had formed in 1966, led by Michael Neumann, stepson of the New Left guru Herbert Marcuse. Like most chapters, it focused mostly on the Vietnam War, objecting particularly to CIA recruitment on campus and demanding the dismantlement of its Institute for Defense Analyses (IDA), which conducted weapons evaluation and other research for the Pentagon.[50] Much enmity also focused on a gymnasium the university had proposed to build in nearby Morningside Park, which was owned by the city and jutted into Harlem. With its relationship with the community already under scrutiny—the school had a habit of evicting local residents to build new apartments for its faculty, students, and staff—the university had promised to make the gym available for local residents' use. But architectural plans revealed that the upper two floors would be for Columbia's use alone, the bottom floor for the community, which led critics to dub it "Gym Crow."[51]

The Student Afro-American Society (SAS) led the revolt against the construction of the new gymnasium by taking over Hamilton Hall, instructing the predominantly white members of SDS to have their own protest somewhere else.[52] Rudd led his own protest and directed most of his rhetorical fire against the liberals in Columbia's administration rather than at the issues of the gym or IDA. He said contemptuously of Vice President David Truman, "He gives us this alternative [to meet with him] because he is a very *li-ber-al* man."[53] Within seventy-two hours 1,100 students were occupying five campus buildings—SDS seized four, including the executive offices of President Grayson Kirk, where they helped themselves to his brandy and cigars.[54]

Rudd's words underscore the fact that the radical student revolt of the 1960s, like the Black Power movement that eventually displaced King, Rustin, Moses, and company, was in its essence *anti-liberal*, both in form and content, aimed specifically at the policies enacted by—or at least with the cooperation and assent of—America's leading liberals.

With the arrogance, ignorance, and egocentricity of youth, the Columbia students managed to presage a new kind of politics to follow the failure of liberal reform. They made impossible demands that had little to do with their actual goals but rather were intended to separate them from those unlike themselves: the ones who didn't "get it." Politics ceased to be about actually accomplishing anything and instead became a means of establishing one's identity and through it, a power base through which to game the system. Here was a genuinely "adversary culture" unlike anything Lionel Trilling had imagined decades earlier. (With particularly painful symbolism, Diana Trilling recalled that one student "zealot . . . distributed on the Columbia campus a poster of the kind which is displayed in the post offices with pictures of dangerous criminals below a photograph of Lionel with the legend WANTED, DEAD OR ALIVE FOR CRIMES AGAINST HUMANITY."[55])

No less regrettable was the fact that while the left-wing student radicals enjoyed virtually no support among the larger American public—one can even make the case that they actually increased support for the Vietnam War because so few Americans wished to be associated with their antics—the equally irrational and angry reaction on the right found itself a powerful base among disaffected ex-Democrats in the South, in the West, and in many northeastern cities who quickly tired of what they considered to be liberal "coddling" of criminals, spoiled-brat students, and minorities who, in the opinion of many, had grown addicted to government welfare as they simultaneously mocked the values of hard work, patriotism, and respect for family that had previously served as the pillars of middle-class American life.

Ironically, given the theatrics of their actions, the Columbia students' demands were relatively modest and straightforward: stop the gymnasium, sever ties to IDA, and amnesty for all the protesters. But the Columbia administration was correct to treat the demands themselves as mere excuses for a violent power grab. As Rudd explained even then, "The issue is not the issue."[56] The Columbia rebellion was actually about "racism and imperialism," not "dorm rules or democratizing university governance or any of that bullshit."[57] This young man from the well-to-do suburb of Maplewood, New Jersey, imagined himself to be leading a genuine revolution as if he were the Che Guevara of Morningside Heights. Unlike many of the early leaders of SDS, such as Tom Hayden, Carl Oglesby, and Todd Gitlin, Rudd was not much of a reader or thinker. Hayden himself remarked after meeting Rudd: "I sense in Mark an embryo of fanaticism that made me feel slightly irrelevant in his presence."[58]

The largely liberal (and increasingly Jewish) Columbia faculty found itself forced into a difficult bind by the students' actions. Many faculty members believed that the protests against the gymnasium and IDA were legitimate and sought to separate them from the ridiculous rhetoric of Rudd and some of the other self-styled revolutionaries. But most important of all, they believed, was the need to protect and defend the norms of discussion, debate, and rational discourse represented by the university—and by liberalism itself. The liberal professors formed the Ad Hoc Faculty Committee to try to mediate

between the two sides. Daniel Bell, then in the university's sociology department, proposed a resolution to his fellow faculty members that the "university
exists as a community dedicated to rational discourse and the use of communication and persuasion as the means of furthering discourse." He called for
the students to stop using coercion and the "administration to set up a tripartite body [of students, faculty, and administrators] to discuss any disciplinary
matters."[59] The administration was initially sympathetic but the students were
not; intoxicated by his own rhetoric, Rudd attacked the "basic liberal conception" of mediation and the faculty proposals were rejected.[60]

Finally, a week after the initial takeover had begun, and after the urgings
of many alumni, Columbia called in the police. Seven hundred twelve students were arrested, during which 148 people were injured, many of them
victims of police brutality. Decades later Rudd admitted that he and his fellow
"revolutionary" John "J.J." Jacobs had themselves set fire to Hamilton Hall
and blamed the police for it afterward. Associate Professor of History Orest
A. Ranum lost irreplaceable files documenting more than ten years of his research on seventeenth-century France dating back to his graduate school studies. He never published the book he had been working on and returned the
small advance he had received from its intended publisher. Ranum, a liberal,
shared the SDS's opposition to the presence of the Institute for Defense Analyses as well the new gymnasium. He left the university a year later. Rudd later
explained, "J.J. hated hypocritical liberals, and the professor, who had tried to
stop the original occupation by saying he was sympathetic to our ends but
not our means, had become an opponent of the strike."[61]

One of the Columbia faculty members most upset by the course of events
at the university was the liberal historian Richard Hofstadter, who had written
so eloquently about the threats of anti-intellectualism and McCarthyism during the 1950s. Like Daniel Bell, Hofstadter was not without sympathy for some
of the student demands and had joined the Ad Hoc Faculty Committee. He
supported "the establishment of a representative commission to be elected by
the faculties to propose necessary changes in the structure of the University,
including the participation of junior faculty and students in decision-making."[62]
"It seemed to me," Hofstadter explained shortly after the takeover, "that the
students had diagnosed very well the distinctive weakness of the academic
liberal mentality, and that they had acted with corresponding ruthlessness."[63]
He continued to work for compromise, up to and including a call for the resignation of university president Grayson Kirk.[64] He struggled to keep up the
norms of intellectual inquiry to which he had devoted his life and kept his door

open to his critics on the left who were willing to engage in civil debate, however dwindling were their numbers.

But at the same time, he professed to witness an anti-intellectualism—and therefore anti-liberalism—on the student left similar to that of the McCarthyite right

Hofstadter's historical research heightened his concerns. He had been not just a historian of ideas—McCarthyism, anti-intellectualism, and progressive reform—but the preeminent (and, sadly, one of the few) historians of academic freedom in the United States. He recognized that colleges in colonial America and the early republic were predominantly religious in nature and demanded denominational orthodoxy. Jacksonian America was no friend to academic freedom, given the era's antipathy toward "expertise of all kinds." Only with the rise of professionalization during the late nineteenth and early twentieth centuries did academic freedom come to be taken seriously in the United States.[65] Now students on the left, as the McCarthyites on the right had once done, were threatening that tradition and with it, the underlying foundation of American liberalism: the right to speak the truth as one sees it.

In the fragile peace that followed the end of the occupation, the university invited Hofstadter to deliver the 1968 commencement address. It was a gesture laden with symbolism because Columbia's president normally gave the speech, and Hoftstadter had called for his ouster. No faculty member had ever been similarly honored.

Hofstadter stated that the occasion served as an opportune moment to highlight the principles for which the modern university stood—the ideals of "freedom, rationality, inquiry, discussion"—and explained that academic freedom was the belief that "anything can be studied," including subjects that were "difficult and inflammatory." The university relied upon a "willingness of society to support and sustain institutions part of whose business is to examine, critically and without stint, the assumptions that prevail in that society." Whatever one's causes or concerns, he continued, "to imagine that the best way to change a social order is to start by assaulting its most accessible centers of thought and study and criticism is not only to show a complete disregard for the intrinsic character of the university but also to develop a curiously self-destructive strategy for social change." He counseled students and faculty to give up on any "utopian scheme" and, through gradualism, make the university more democratic, while balancing that against the need for stability and the protection of unpopular ideas.[66]

Hofstadter's address was warmly welcomed by liberals. Irving Howe, the editor of the democratic socialist (but actually liberal) magazine *Dissent*, viewed it as a rare moment of hope in a world that was collapsing. (Howe had once famously warned one radical who had been lecturing him about his insufficient commitment to "the revolution": "You know what you're going to be? You're going to be a dentist."[67]) Hofstadter had impressed him by attacking the New Left without succumbing to stridency (as Howe himself had sometimes done) and for demonstrating a "liberalism of spirit."[68]

But the time for speeches had long since passed. Though Columbia eventually did stop construction of the gymnasium and severed relations with IDA, the radicals continued to ratchet up their demands.[69] An increasingly strident Tom Hayden called for "two, three, many Columbias," echoing Che Guevara, who had used the same expression vis-à-vis Vietnam. And he got his wish. "The 1968-9 academic year," Devin Fergus points out, witnessed "292 major student protests at over 230 college campuses around the country."[70] SDS continued its radicalization process as if in a race between utopianism, militancy, and old-fashioned left-wing sectarianism. At the SDS convention held in 1968, Bernardine Dohrn, an ally of Rudd's who was running for national office, explained her politics: "I consider myself a revolutionary communist."[71] (She would soon graduate to full-fledged terrorist.)

The Columbia fracas emboldened the right wing as well. Republican presidential candidate Richard Nixon called Columbia "the first skirmish in a revolutionary struggle to seize the universities of this country and transform them into sanctuaries for radicals and vehicles for revolutionary political and social goals."[72] What was needed to control these student outbursts in the future, Ronald Reagan would suggest not long afterward, was a "bloodbath.... No more appeasement."[73]

That same spring yet another crisis for liberalism erupted within the previously peaceful confines of the New York City classroom when a group of largely Jewish public schoolteachers found themselves "transferred"—which to them meant "fired"—from their positions in the Ocean Hill-Brownsville area of Brooklyn by the newly ensconced largely black administration there. One of the aggrieved teachers was Fred Nauman, whose parents fled the Holocaust when he was a small boy. He was a strong civil rights supporter, a man who, like many Jews, saw in the struggles of King and company a shared history of oppression and resistance.[74] Nauman asked for the intervention of his union, the United Federation of Teachers (UFT), led by Albert Shanker, who agreed to take up the challenge.

Ocean Hill-Brownsville was a typical late 1960s American ghetto. One journalist described it as resembling "Berlin after the war: block after block of burned-out shells of houses, streets littered with decaying automobile husks."[75] It boasted a generous amount of drug dealers, numbers runners, and pawnshops but few doctors, lawyers, dentists, or much else in the way of evidence of middle-class life.[76] The neighborhood had tried integration and busing, but parents in white schools pushed back against these initiatives, as they had in other areas of the city. Indeed, integration in northern cities during the late 1960s looked close to impossible; New York City schools were more segregated in the spring of 1968 than they had been in 1954, when the Warren Court had issued its decision in *Brown v. Board of Education*.[77] Black parents in Ocean Hill-Brownsville continued to worry that their kids were falling behind on tests and dropping out at astounding rates; some were frustrated that predominantly white teachers didn't live in the community in which they taught, and they thought that black teachers—or at least those chosen by local black leaders—might achieve better results. Outside the neighborhood, the idea of community control sounded just fine, so long as it didn't require any more funds expended on poorer schools.

Community control was a product of LBJ's Great Society and its experimentation with Community Action Projects (CAP) as well as of New Left visions of participatory democracy.[78] But by the late 1960s the concept had become infused with the demand for "black power," based on the belief that African Americans should direct the institutions of their own neighborhoods (even if those neighborhoods were the product of segregation). This idea had drifted into the mainstream of American political life via liberal academics and foundations, particularly those funded by the Ford Foundation, who saw it as preferable to top-down, white-directed integration efforts.[79] In Ocean Hill-Brownsville, a black educator named Rhody McCoy, who had previously specialized in teaching teenagers considered too violent for regular classes, was hired to oversee the new experiment with community control, with the blessings of the city government.[80] A Washington, D.C., native, McCoy had attended Howard University and then moved to New York to teach in public schools, by which time he had become an acolyte of the separatist teachings of Malcolm X and a regular attendee at his Harlem lectures and consciousness-raising sessions.[81]

McCoy hired Herman Ferguson as one of his school principals just months after he was indicted on charges of conspiring with radical black activists to murder liberal civil rights leaders Whitney Young and Roy Wilkins. (He would later be convicted and jumped bail.) The new principal had recently authored an article calling for black students to receive instruction in martial arts as well as "gun weaponry, gun handling, and gun safety." McCoy then transferred nineteen teachers and administrators—eighteen of whom were Jewish—from Ocean Hill-Brownsville. Despite his clear violation of UFT contracts, he announced, "Not one of these teachers will be allowed to teach anywhere in this city. The black community will see to that."[82]

Albert Shanker tried to explain to liberals why McCoy's ideas were dangerous. Born a Jew in 1928 to garment worker and newspaper deliveryman parents, Shanker had developed democratic socialist ideas by reading George Orwell before becoming a labor organizer. He had also studied philosophy as a graduate student, growing particularly interested in the work of John Dewey. His passion for Dewey's faith in democratic education made Shanker sympathetic to community control on principle, but his experiences had led him to question it in practice. He noted that the first call for community control in New York City had come from a white neighborhood that sought to stymie the integration of its schools, and reasoned that they "had the right to make final decisions in much the same way that southern governors demand the right to do as they wish in the name of states' rights."[83]

Shanker asked his old friend and ally, Bayard Rustin, for help. Rustin mobilized black labor union organizers to support the union through statements published in *The New York Times*. When he spoke at rallies, Rustin repeated Shanker's critique of community control and also pointed out that it was "a hoax when it does not include real power, democracy and the funds to carry out new programs."[84] He warned that community control was a way for liberals to absolve themselves of the responsibility of taxing wealthy members to pay for the education of society's poorest members. Together with Michael Harrington, Rustin (rather ironically) helped to mobilize white liberal support for the UFT; a pro-UFT ad in *The New York Times*, for instance, included the names of Daniel Bell, Irving Howe, Reinhold Niebuhr, Dwight Macdonald, and Arthur Schlesinger, Jr.[85]

But the division, and the anger, among liberals ran deep. James Wechsler thought "it would be hard to draw a sharper contrast between the consistently maturing spirit of compromise displayed by the Ocean Hill board in the recent stages of the crisis and the UFT's distressing retreat into sullen intransigence." Murray Kempton went him one better: "I don't know anyone who has seen one of McCoy's schools and not come away impressed with the deportment of the pupils, the quiet dignity of the corridors, the engagement of the teachers," he wrote. "Yet Shanker has been able to ride on a general public impression that Ocean Hill has no curriculum beyond drills in karate and mass recitations of the speeches of Marcus Garvey."[86]

As McCoy had begun hiring replacement teachers in violation of the UFT contract, Shanker decided to strike in support of reinstating the transferred teachers, arguing, "This is a strike that will protect black teachers against white racists and white teachers against black racists."[87] Just before the beginning of the 1968–69 school year, McCoy upped the ante by announcing that he had replaced all 350 UFT members who had gone out on strike. When the teachers won in court, Shanker called for McCoy to step down and abolish the local governing board, which had the effect of mobilizing the black community to support their own, whatever reservations anyone might have had about McCoy personally.[88] Shanker ignited the fire of black-Jewish hatred when, on behalf of the union, he distributed half a million copies of a leaflet that an anonymous partisan of McCoy's cause had left in the mailboxes of teachers and staff of a local junior high school. The leaflet called Jewish teachers "middle east murderers of colored people" and "blood sucking exploiters," as it simultaneously accused them of "brainwashing" black children into "self-hatred." It concluded, "The idea behind this program is beautiful, but when the money changers heard about it, they took over."[89] Aryeh Neier, the executive director of the New York Civil Liberties Union, called Shanker's distribution of the leaflets "a smear tactic reminiscent of the McCarthy era against the governing board in an attempt to create guilt by association."[90] The novelist Cynthia Ozick gave voice to a typically nuanced neoconservative interpretation of conflicts like this when, decades later, she unambiguously asserted, "It was the rising reality of black anti-Semitism that ended the era of passionate Jewish identification with the black condition in America."[91]

When white teachers returned to Ocean Hill on September 11, 1968, black militants blocked their entry, and a crowd gathered to shout anti-Semitic epithets and chants. New York's liberal Republican mayor, John V. Lindsay, sought to mediate, and Shanker got most of what he wanted in negotiations, and the teachers were by and large returned to their original posts. But the poison remained.[92] The liberal/labor/civil rights alliance was clearly at a point of fracture.[93] Though both Bayard Rustin and Michael Harrington were privately critical of Shanker's aggressive tone, they remained with the fold in support of the UFT.[94] Dwight Macdonald had initially supported the union and had even criticized SNCC for its black nationalism and incipient anti-Semitism just a year earlier.[95] But now, as he studied the Ocean Hill situation further, he believed Harrington and Rustin had misled him, and argued that the teachers hadn't been fired but legitimately removed and placed at different schools. He saw nothing wrong with the idea of community control.[96] Numerous liberal journalists were even harsher toward Shanker. Jimmy Breslin, for instance, characterized his speeches as merely "an accent away from those of George Wallace."[97]

On the other side of the divide fell Daniel Patrick Moynihan. Regarding the anti-Semitic tones heard among Ocean Hill-Brownsville blacks, Moynihan would later explain in his 1969 book, *Maximum Feasible Misunderstanding*: "Demanding power for a black community rather quickly became a demand for black power. This may have been therapeutic for those involved, but the reaction elsewhere, as Vice President Humphrey later declared in an interview arranged by the American Jewish Community, was 'consternation and confusion.'"[98] Too often, Moynihan believed, local community programs allowed for militants and extremists to take charge. Confrontational politics—clearly on display in Ocean Hill-Brownsville's events—seemed now the inevitable outcome of the idea of "community participation." Only two years later Moynihan's critique of "maximum feasible participation," coupled with a remarkable store of personal ambition, led him to work for Richard Nixon, who if nothing else shared his hatred of left-wing elites.

Shanker would call the 1968 racial conflict "a horrible, tragic thing."[99] But he clearly enjoyed his new role as a champion of white power, as "everywhere" he went, he explained, "taxicab drivers wouldn't charge me a fare, newspaper vendors would give me a free copy of the *Times* in the morning."[100] Shanker's experience suggested the dawn of a new kind of racial politics based on identity, antagonism, and assertion of one's inherent rights rather than on the traditional liberal coalition politics of empathy and cooperation. Of course the often violently expressed racial fears of so many white working people had always stymied the progress of liberal coalitions between union and civil rights leaders, even those with the most far-sighted leadership, such as Reuther's UAW. But black demands in housing, education, and the workplace, coupled with a deep aversion to the disrespect of traditional values by antiwar demonstrators and their Black Power allies, were turning the white working class toward an identity politics of their own: one based on resentment of blacks, of government bureaucrats, and of the intellectuals and "experts" who empowered what felt very much like an attack on their schools, their neighborhoods, their values, and, indeed, on their entire way of life. For every one of these assaults, they blamed a single culprit: liberals.

The fracturing of liberalism during this period was mirrored in the fracturing of the Democratic Party. The once unthinkable fantasy of "dumping" the sitting president, Lyndon Johnson, had already become a reality by November 1967. Minnesota senator Eugene McCarthy agreed to challenge Johnson as a means of coalescing the growing antiwar feeling both in party and in the country. "There comes a time when an honorable man simply has to raise the flag," he said, articulating his peculiar brand of protest, which was both adamant and yet curiously passive.[101]

As a young man, Eugene McCarthy considered joining a monastery but instead became a political science professor at St. Thomas College (now the University of St. Thomas), a small Catholic institution in St. Paul, Minnesota. It was here that he embraced his own brand of liberalism: "peaceful change in accordance with the needs of distributive justice," as he later defined it.[102] Like his mentor, Hubert Humphrey, he was pushed to engage in politics, winning a congressional seat in November 1948, the fateful year when Democrats split over the candidacy of Henry Wallace. McCarthy proved to be a dependable liberal of the period, siding with the civil rights movement, labor unions, and the expansion of the welfare state.[103]

Understandably, given both his politics and demeanor, he gravitated toward Adlai Stevenson, to whose cause he remained committed long after it became a lost one. "Do not reject this man who made us all proud to be Democrats. . . . Do not leave this prophet without honor in his own part." McCarthy valorized Stevenson's aloofness, insisting that "power often comes to those who seek it, but history does not prove that power is always well used by those who seek it."[104]

Though he voted for the Gulf of Tonkin Resolution, McCarthy became an early though not terribly vocal critic of Johnson's Vietnam policies. During the course of 1967, J. William Fulbright's eye-opening hearings on the Tonkin Gulf incidents and the increasingly intense opposition of groups like Clergy and Laity Concerned About Vietnam helped convince McCarthy that antiwar feeling had spread from just students and professors to ordinary middle-class citizens.[105] That year he wrote *The Limits of Power* (1967), in which he reiterated some of Senator Fulbright's earlier warnings about the "arrogance of power" and explored many of the ideas developed by Reinhold Niebuhr, including the ethical foundations of realism in American foreign policy. McCarthy concluded: "Our foreign policy should be more restrained and, insofar as prudent judgment can determine, more closely in keeping with the movement of history."[106]

Much like his hero Stevenson, McCarthy found admirers who responded to his wit and poetic grace.[107] But no less than his hero, he struck many potential supporters as cold and aloof.[108] He spoke an uncomfortable, albeit unavoidable, truth when he admitted that when it came to ending the war, he was "kind of an accidental instrument."[109] He even told one TV interviewer: "I didn't say I want to be president. I'm willing to be president."[110] McCarthy's constituent attitude of noblesse oblige toward what was for many a vital crusade drove many of his supporters to distraction.[111] Indeed, McCarthy's speechwriter Jeremy Larner thought his candidate recalled "certain athletes who would rather lose than go all-out to win. If one goes all-out and loses, then one is without excuse."[112]

McCarthy's base in the electorate was decidedly limited. His wife described "his people" as "academia united with the mobile society of scientists, educators, technologists and the new post–World War II college class."[113] But young college kids going "clean for Gene" joined stay-at-home moms eager to protect their sons from the draft and swarmed New Hampshire for the late January primary there, demonstrating a degree of democratic engagement that the country had not seen since the days of the Depression. When McCarthy claimed 42 percent against a sitting president, traditional interpretations of the dynamic of the race were upended overnight.

McCarthy's showing could not but have impressed the junior senator from New York, who had repeatedly refused the same entreaties from Allard Lowenstein that McCarthy ultimately accepted. Bobby Kennedy neither liked nor respected Gene McCarthy any more than he had Adlai Stevenson.[114] He had initially decided to postpone his presidential run until 1972, believing LBJ to be unbeatable and his own reputation for "ruthless"—that was always the word—personal ambition to be an albatross he could not escape. Kennedy and his inner circle insisted that he had already decided to enter the race before New Hampshire, but the candidate clumsily seized on the event to undermine McCarthy's success, telling reporters directly after the primary, "I am actively reassessing the possibility of whether I will run against President Johnson."[115]

Robert Kennedy struck those who knew him in his final year as a man in transition to a place no one could comfortably predict. He had never been much of a student, and Arthur Schlesinger, Jr., a close friend and admirer, recounted that Kennedy's "real field of concentration at Harvard was football."[116] After graduating from law school at the University of Virginia in 1951, he joined the Justice Department, where he impressed people primarily as the "cocky" son of a megalomaniac millionaire.[117] Kennedy's stint as assistant counsel to Senator Joseph McCarthy in 1953 certainly tarnished his reputation with liberals, in some cases permanently. He never apologized or recanted his youthful support for McCarthy, and the best he could do, ten years after quitting, was to admit, "Well, at that time, I thought there was a serious internal security threat to the United States; I felt at that time that Joe McCarthy seemed to be the only one who was doing anything about it. I was wrong."[118]

But RFK also had a talent for personal growth that could be seen superficially in his adventurous spirit, including early worldwide travel with William O. Douglas as well as hobbies like downhill skiing, white-water rafting, and dangerous hiking expeditions. When he lost his older brother—the second older brother he had lost—his personality underwent a remarkable transformation. He became vulnerable, introspective, and wrapped himself in Greek tragedy and existential philosophy. He opened his eyes to the plight of America's less fortunate. He became fascinated with the debates of intellectuals regarding Vietnam, civil rights, and the urban crises, and began a series of seminars in his home for himself and his political allies.[119]

It was this openness—the drawing up of the curtain of his otherwise limited world to the voices of the poor and downcast—combined with the flashes he showed of his brother's charisma that led many liberals to believe that this man, and this man alone, had the potential to save the country. Michael Harrington thought that Kennedy had "the better possibility of uniting the white working class and the black poor and of thus bringing middle-class liberals and radicals into a genuine majority coalition."[120] Kennedy could reach poor whites who were increasingly gravitating to the protest candidacy of George Wallace (and who would eventually land in the camp of Richard Nixon). He was trusted, to the degree any white politician was trusted, by black voters as well. Even leaders of the New Left saw hope in Kennedy's candidacy to end the war and address the urban crisis.[121]

Kennedy's opposition to the war had developed gradually, and given his brother's role in initiating American involvement in Vietnam, quite reluctantly. Soon after entering the Senate in 1965, he announced, "We must understand that while bombing targets in North Viet Nam may induce more caution in Hanoi, they will not bring peace to South Viet Nam. In the last analysis, the way to defeat the terrorists is to increase our capability to fight their kind of war."[122] But as the conflict continued to grind on, these hawkish sentiments began to yield ground to a careful reconsideration, not only of Vietnam but of America's role in the world. Little by little he became perhaps the most important opponent of the war in America. Antiwar activists were desperate for Kennedy to challenge Johnson, but he dithered, concerned about his safety and certain he would be a strong candidate in 1972. The Kennedy brain trust was itself divided: Arthur Schlesinger, Jr., and Richard Goodwin were strongly in favor, but brother Teddy advised against it, sharing Bobby's reasoning.[123] RFK came forward with an alternative, or at least an excuse for delay. Early in 1968, Kennedy announced his price for his staying out of the race against the president: he wanted a committee appointed to find an honorable solution to the war; its members Kennedy himself would designate. He offered to go to Vietnam as the president's personal emissary. He also implied that it might be necessary for Lyndon Johnson to confess his sins for the whole proposal to work—a decidedly unlikely prospect, to be sure.[124] As McCarthy was making his run for president known, RFK appeared on *Face the Nation* and ramped up his antiwar rhetoric: "Do we have the right here in the United States to say that we're going to kill tens of thousands, make millions of people, as we have, refugees, kill women and children, as we have? I very seriously question whether we have the right."[125]

This period proved a kind of custom-made torture for Lyndon Johnson. He had done his utmost to live up to the promises and potential of John Kennedy's presidency, doing a better job than Kennedy himself of bringing his legislation to fruition. He had desperately courted Kennedy's advisers and bound them, he thought, to his own fortunes. He had even, as Ted Kennedy later noted, tried to play the younger surviving brother against the older one, "which was totally bizarre, since there was no way that a Kennedy would side with an outsider against another Kennedy."[126] And he had even assumed the difficult political task of securing victory in Vietnam, left to him by Jack Kennedy. And now, fewer than five years after he had begun to serve his country and the memory of the martyred leader with every weapon in his political arsenal, here was Bobby Kennedy returning not only to defeat him but to destroy him both personally and politically, and taking the president's most trusted advisers with him.

Ironically, it had been the presence of Robert Kennedy that had helped convince Johnson that he had no choice but to go full force into Vietnam. He told Doris Kearns Goodwin of his fear of what would have happened had he chosen withdrawal back in 1964: he dreamed of crowds coming at him crying, "Coward. Weakling. Traitor. . . . There would be Robert Kennedy out in front leading the fight against me, telling everyone that I had betrayed John Kennedy's commitment to South Vietnam. That I had let a democracy fall into the hands of the Communists. That I was a coward. An unmanly man. A man without a spine."[127]

Now, in his desire to reclaim the mantle of his slain brother—and in the process brand Johnson as nothing more than an incompetent usurper—Bobby heaped piles of scorn and abuse on Johnson, all to great applause. Who was responsible for not just the war, but for the riots, the dropouts, the drugs? Kennedy asked. It was not "those who were calling for change," he cried to full-throated applause, his fists in the air. "They are the ones, the President of this United States, President Johnson, they are the ones who divide us."[128] Now came Johnson's new nightmare, in which he was again being chased by "a giant stampede" led by Robert Kennedy, but this time he was "being forced over the edge by rioting blacks, demonstrating students, marching welfare mothers, squawking professors and hysterical reporters." Next came the final straw: "The thing I feared from the first day of my presidency was actually coming true. Robert Kennedy had openly announced his intention to reclaim the throne in the memory of his brother. And the American people, swayed by the magic of his name, were dancing in the streets."[129]

Johnson was clearly in an unhealthy state of both mind and body. He worried about recurring pains in his chest, his gall bladder, and his kidneys. By 1967, LBJ had had a "secret actuarial study prepared on his life expectancy."[130] Aides around the president described him as "weathered," "battered," and "drained," and Lady Bird was pressing him to consider quitting the presidency or at least not running again. Psychologically he felt betrayed by the advisers who had jumped ship. "It is hell when a President has to spend half his time keeping his own people juiced up," LBJ told a confidant in 1967.[131] And he grew increasingly convinced that his opponents—virtually all his opponents—were in league with the enemy. When the Fulbright hearings on the Gulf of Tonkin Resolution began, deeply embarrassing Johnson, he demanded an FBI investigation to determine whether Communists were behind them, instituting full surveillance on the senator. On Johnson's orders FBI agents offered the congressional leadership what he insisted was "evidence that Fulbright was either a communist agent or a dupe of the communist powers." The motivation for the chairman of the Senate Foreign Relations Committee turning traitor was allegedly Johnson's refusal to name him secretary of state.[132]

Politically Johnson had not shown much concern about McCarthy, despite New Hampshire, but Kennedy was another matter entirely. When he was shown a poll putting New York's junior senator ahead of him among Democrats 54 to 41 percent for the nomination, he apparently decided he'd had enough.[133] Fifteen days after Kennedy entered the race, the president drew up a speech to be delivered on March 31, 1968, with two possible endings, both of which he showed to Hubert Humphrey: One version ended with an announcement of his withdrawal from the race; the other did not. Once in front of television cameras, he gave what struck viewers as a fairly typical address before turning to a new page on his lectern and announcing: "There is division in the American home now. . . . I cannot disregard the peril to the prospect for peace. . . . I do not believe that I should devote an hour a day of my time to any personal partisan course. Accordingly, I shall not seek, and I will not accept, the nomination of my party for another term as your President."[134]

Kennedy was surprised but energized. Despite his loathing for Lyndon Johnson, he could not help but respect his political acumen—a respect he did not feel for Johnson's anointed successor, the much-beaten-down Hubert Humphrey. As far as his own candidacy was concerned, Humphrey was unsure of himself, however much he had been single-mindedly working toward this moment his entire adult life. "Quite frankly, I am not sure I have the stomach for it, knowing the ruthless methods that are employed by both Kennedy and Nixon," he mused at the time.[135] But the party's old guard wanted him. After getting a call from Kennedy, George Meany, the hawkish head of the AFL-CIO, called the vice president and urged him to enter the race immediately.

Kennedy's campaign, once he finally committed to it, embodied the two elements of his personality—his toughness and his growing idealism. His first primary battle took him to Indiana, and it was here that the campaign took on a whirligig, insurrectional feel. As he barnstormed the state, drawing ecstatic, rock concert-style crowds, RFK adviser Adam Walinsky explained to reporters: "Our strategy is to change the rules of nominating a president. We're going to do it a new way. In the streets."[136] At times he appeared to break every rule of established political conduct. He consistently spoke out against college deferments when at student gatherings, arguing that only this would correct a system in which blacks and poor people died disproportionately in the jungles of Vietnam.[137] At the University of Indiana, located in a conservative, prowar state, he explained to medical students that all Americans shared a responsibility to offer the poor greater health, educational, and employment opportunities. A student called out from the back of the room, "Who is going to pay for all this?" "You are," he retorted. When boos followed, he continued, indicting those whose votes he sought. "You sit here as white medical students, while black people carry the burden of fighting in Vietnam."[138] Though he did worry about white ethnic voters and the effectiveness of the Republicans' "law and order" campaign, he refused to pander to white fears of black crime and worse, but instead focused on what he understood to be the causes of urban unrest, primarily poverty and lack of economic opportunity.[139]

Nothing demonstrated the importance of Bobby Kennedy's campaign to American liberalism—and to America itself—more than his performance on the awful night of Martin Luther King's assassination, when he gave the country perhaps its most hopeful glimpse of his potential to heal the nation as its president. Speaking to a largely black audience in Indianapolis that had not yet heard the horrible news, Kennedy gave it to them straight, and then, in a voice nearly broken with emotion, he spoke extemporaneously not only from his own broken heart, but from what felt like the broken hearts of all liberals, and indeed, of much of humanity:

> For those of you who are black and are tempted to be filled with hatred and mistrust of the injustice of such an act, against all white people, I would only say that I can also feel in my own heart the same kind of feeling. I had a member of my family killed, but he was killed by a white man. But we have to make an effort in the United States, we have to make an effort to understand, to get beyond these rather difficult times. My favorite poet was Aeschylus. He once wrote: "Even in our sleep, pain which cannot forget falls drop by drop upon the heart, until, in our own despair, against our will, comes wisdom through the awful grace of God."
>
> What we need in the United States is not division; what we need in the United States is not hatred; what we need in the United States is not violence and lawlessness, but is love and wisdom, and compassion toward one another, and a feeling of justice toward those who still suffer within our country, whether they be white or whether they be black.[140]

Indianapolis was peaceful that night as few American cities were.

Campaigning eighteen hours a day, Kennedy quickly dispatched McCarthy in Indiana.[141] Rowland Evans and Robert Novak wondered if the vote meant that Kennedy could "defuse Backlash Voting."[142] But Kennedy was flying by the seat of his pants, strategically and philosophically. Sometimes he sounded like the Catholic conservative he had long been, at others, the liberal-cum-radical he appeared to be becoming. "I think there has to be a new kind of coalition to keep the Democratic party going, and to keep the country together. We have to write off the unions and the South now, and replace them with Negroes, blue-collar whites, and the kids," he explained at one point.[143]

Whether he meant it, and whether it was ever possible, will forever remain unknown. For after a bruising victory over both McCarthy and Humphrey in California, Kennedy was shot dead at age forty-two by Sirhan Sirhan, a Palestinian refugee, because of his support for the State of Israel. For his final speech, a short victory address, an exhausted Robert Kennedy, escorted to the podium by the United Farm Workers' Dolores Huerta, congratulated McCarthy and asked his supporters to join with him "not for myself, but for the cause and the ideas which moved you to begin this great popular movement," generously acknowledging his own tardiness in joining them. He then continued: "What I think is quite clear is that we can work together in the last analysis and that what has been going on within the United States over a period of the last three years—the division, the violence, the disenchantment with our society: the divisions, whether it's between blacks and white, between the poor and the more affluent or between age groups or on the war in Vietnam—is that we can start to work together. We are a great country, an unselfish country and a compassionate country." It was, thought Jeremy Larner in McCarthy headquarters, Bobby's "best speech of the campaign."[144] Then RFK left for a short cut through the hotel kitchen and within minutes, America was another country. Kennedy secretary Frank Mankiewicz visited brother Ted at 5:30 that morning and saw him "sort of leaning over the sink with the most awful expression on his face. Just more than agony, more than anguish. I don't know if there is a word for it."[145]

Kennedy's June 8 memorial service in New York's St. Patrick's Cathedral would serve as a memorial for the death not only of a much-beloved leader but also for liberal hopes and dreams, and indeed, for the possibility of idealism regarding America's future, at least in what was then the foreseeable future. Edward Kennedy took the stage, his voice choking, and said, "My brother need not be idealized, or enlarged in death beyond what he was in life; to be remembered simply as a good and decent man, who saw wrong and tried to right it, saw suffering and tried to heal it, saw war and tried to stop it." He closed with Kennedy's favorite quotation, borrowed (and adapted) from George Bernard Shaw: "Some men see things as they are and say why. I dream things that never were and say why not."[146] Journalist Jack Newfield surveyed the crowd, seeing radicals like Tom Hayden (and himself) together with Irish political bosses, Democrats, Republicans, labor leaders, Catholics, Jews, blacks, whites, Hispanics, and the like, and thought of the quotation from Pascal that Albert Camus employed at the beginning of *Resistance, Rebellion and Death*: "A man does not show his greatness by being at one extremity, but rather by touching both at once."

Newfield concluded his memoir of Kennedy as follows:

> Now I realized what makes our generation unique, what defines us apart from those who came before the hopeful winter of 1961, and those who came after the murderous spring of 1968. We are the first generation that learned from experience, in our innocent twenties, that things were not really getting better, that we shall *not* overcome. We felt, by the time we

reached thirty, that we had already glimpsed the most compassionate leaders our nation could produce, and they had been assassinated. And from this time forward, things would get worse: our best political leaders were part of memory now, not hope. The stone was at the bottom of the hill and we were alone.[147]

Following the assassination, as liberals struggled to recover from the pain, shock, and depression that followed, Eugene McCarthy found himself facing a situation where far more depended on him than he had ever anticipated. If the war was to be ended, if the country was to be saved, then McCarthy would actually have to campaign to win the presidency, something that was far from clear he had ever intended to do. What's more, he would have to challenge his former mentor, Hubert Humphrey. It was at this moment, ironically, that he grew more aloof—more Stevensonian—than ever. At the 1968 Democratic convention in Chicago, he watched the riots from his hotel room and mused that they reminded him of the Battle of Lake Trasimene, an analogy that he subsequently amended to the Battle of Cannae. Essayist Wilfrid Sheed argued, "An average citizen looking in would have said, There you are, that's an intellectual for you—making Punic War jokes while Chicago prepares to incinerate."[148] John Kenneth Galbraith concluded, "I don't believe that Eugene McCarthy's heart was ever again wholly in the battle."[149] Whether or not that was the case, McCarthy had an extremely difficult battle in front of him, given the power of the party establishment to pick its candidate irrespective of primary vote totals.[150]

Humphrey's campaign, meanwhile, evinced an air of desperation from start to finish. His "politics of joy" sounded like a cruel joke, given the joyless times. Garry Wills, covering the campaign for *Esquire,* wrote, "Poor Hubert lived in the shadow-casting ego of Johnson, a man hated by the very people who made up Humphrey's constituency, liberals (academic and semi-academic) of an ADA sort."[151] Then came the Chicago convention, which found liberals trapped between what had quickly degenerated into a nihilistic, self-destructive attack from the left, fueled by passion and self-righteous anger on the one hand, and an angry, out-of-control police force, cheered on by much of Middle America, on the other.

Most of the young people who made their way to Chicago were aware that they could expect to face the wrath of "Boss" Daley and his brutal police force. Indeed, Eugene McCarthy advised his supporters to stay home.[152] Many of the wiser heads of the antiwar movement had counseled against confrontation, and certainly many honest committed students and activists arrived hoping to do some good and give voice to their understandable disillusionment with a presidential candidate and a party. But these were not, by and large, the ones who led the protests, nor were such sympathies evident in the chaos that ensued. In fact, the protesters who did show up in Grant Park on those hot summer nights appeared hardly less eager for a confrontation than were Daley and his police; many, apparently, believed that a televised demonstration of allegedly fascistic violence against a bunch of unarmed hippies would hasten the coming revolution.[153] Those in the more mainstream organization, MOBE (short for National Mobilization Committee to End the War in Vietnam), led by Dave Dellinger, were certainly practitioners of nonviolence but were also believers in direct action, having moved from protest to resistance. The wildest of the bunch were the Yippies (the popular name for the Youth International Party), now led by street-theater provocateurs Abbie Hoffman and Jerry Rubin. Hoffman, who called himself the Lenin of the Flower Children, described his intentions in coming to Chicago: "We want to fuck up their image on TV. It's all in terms of disrupting the image, the image of a democratic society being run very peacefully and orderly and everything according to business."[154] Rubin added, "Language does not radicalize people—what changes people is the emotional involvement of action. What breaks through apathy and complacency are confrontation and actions."[155] It goes without saying that none of these groups—SDS, MOBE, or the Yippies— gave much consideration to the likelihood of a potential backlash; one activist sounded all too accurate when he called Chicago "a revolutionary wet dream come true."[156] In fact, it was even better for the proponents of a violent anti-left backlash.

The confrontations came quickly. Protesters ran from Lincoln Park into the downtown Loop area chanting, "Pigs eat shit! Pigs eat shit!" Police and national guardsmen moved in, sometimes driving jeeps with fences attached to their fronts to plow protesters out of the way. As the beatings began, bags filled with urine were tossed at the police, along with rocks and bottles.[157] The cops were, if anything, even less restrained, targeting not only protesters but also members of the media. One *Newsweek* reporter was assaulted simply for taking notes while watching protesters being beaten up. Television newsmen Dan Rather and Mike Wallace were roughed up and punched out by uniformed police inside the convention hall as they attempted to interview delegates and report on the proceedings.[158] Norman Mailer described the event as a mixture of "outrage, hysteria, panic, wild rumor, unruly outburst, fury, madness, gallows humor, and gloom."[159]

Meanwhile, as the dovish Senator Abraham Ribicoff of Connecticut condemned the "Gestapo in the streets of Chicago" from the podium, Mayor Daley was heard to call the senator either a "faker,"according to his own recollection, or to have said, "Fuck you, you Jew son of a bitch, you lousy motherfucker, go home," as was reported in the underground Washington newspaper *Mayday* at the time.[160] Outside, SDS members started to chant, "The whole world is watching," in the belief that the masses were being radicalized before their eyes. In fact, polls would later suggest that a majority of the American people who saw the violence on television actually approved of the police violence and would not have minded even more.[161]

Humphrey won the nomination, and Johnson's policies for Vietnam were voted through by a majority.[162] As the sagagious Chicago columnist Mike Royko observed in his biography of Daley, *Boss*, "In attacking the young, the liberal and the black, Daley [proved himself] in the mainstream of America's mass prejudices. The Democratic party may have suffered by his actions, but Daley came out of the convention even more popular because 'bust their heads' was the mood of the land."[163]

Ironically, the protesters could mark the convention a success as well. They had helped to inspire the chaos and violence they had predicted. Abbie Hoffman achieved his stated desire to "bring down the Democratic Party."[164] Republicans were rejoicing as they watched what transpired in Chicago, as their message was honed and ready by this point: *Return to law and order.*[165] Once again, it was Mailer who captured the chaos better than anyone:

Children, and youths, and middle-aged men and women were being pounded and gassed and beaten, hunted and driven, sent scattering in all directions by teams of policemen who had broken out of their restraints like the bursting of a boil. . . . It was as if the war had finally begun . . . , before the television cameras of the world . . . as if the military spine of a great liberal party had finally separated itself from the skin, . . . the Democratic Party had broken in two before the eyes of the nation like Melville's whale charging right out of the sea.[166]

With the disappearance of the vital center from the political spectrum, liberals sank into a deep and frequently desperate depression. Arthur Schlesinger's gloom was undoubtedly personal, for as he explained the day he learned of RFK's assassination, every political leader to whom he had grown attached was now dead.[167] But he worried professionally, as a historian, as well: "We have suddenly been reminded of the ambiguous strains in our legacy from history, of national instincts for aggression and destruction which have long warred with a national capacity for civility and idealism."[168] Much of this was due to Vietnam. "We have become a frightening people," Schlesinger concluded. "For three years we have been wrecking a small country on the other side of the world in a war which bears no proportionate relationship to our national security or national interest."[169] The historian also began to reconsider the Cold War verities that had previously sustained him, together with his conception of the vital center. For instance, he worried that the Truman Doctrine, legitimate in its original context, had become extended to a "universal maxim."[170] He was concerned that "the idea of collective security grew beyond all rational bounds and turned into a sanction for indiscriminate unilateral intervention."[171]

Late in 1967 *Commentary* magazine conducted a symposium in which it gave voice to the uncertainty about what was once a bedrock belief among America's liberal intellectuals: the sense that "the United States, the main bulwark against Stalinism, could act as a relative force for good in international affairs."[172] It was no longer 1948, with Communists and fellow travelers on one's left and Communists and conservatives on one's right, with a strong, patriotic, and self-confident liberalism in between, pushing for peace, civil rights, and economic security. This was a world defined by a backlash against liberalism coming from both sides simultaneously, one that left liberals no longer knowing what they believed or whom they represented. The vast majority of American voters had no interest in Daniel Bell's notion of a liberal "educated elite" to mediate between their passions and the democratic institutions they assumed ought to be under their control. Liberals had little to say to the Nixon and Wallace supporters who wanted law and order restored, their values upheld, and the transgressors punished, period.

Wallace's revanchist campaign had been growing ever stronger under the rubric of the American Independent Party as he laid the political and philosophical groundwork for the Nixon, Reagan, and George W. Bush presidencies, providing southerners and northern working-class whites with a way station as they moved from the Democratic into the Republican column. In doing so, note the authors Thomas and Mary Edsall, "Wallace and Nixon added a new, pejorative meaning to the word 'liberal.' Under the influence of their rhetoric, liberalism came to connote, for key voters, the favoring of blacks over whites and permissiveness toward drug abuse, illegitimacy, welfare fraud, street crime, homosexuality, anti-Americanism, as well as moral anarchy among the young."[173] Wallace's resentments—later adopted by Nixon—

were their resentments; his revenge fantasies were theirs, too. He symbolized reaction, but the sort of reaction that drew support from union members across America, and not just in the South. (Amazingly, Wallace even received a few local AFL-CIO endorsements.[174])

Humphrey, meanwhile, could not escape the vise into which history had thrust his candidacy. Facing antiwar protesters at nearly every stop, he considered criticizing the war but lacked the confidence to take on Johnson, choosing loyalty over honesty and, ultimately, victory.[175] Johnson tried to get peace talks moving again, but he was stymied by a conspiracy to ensure their failure that could be traced directly to the Nixon camp.[176] Humphrey actually made a surprising comeback in the final weeks of the campaign, but it was a hopeless battle. Eight years after he lost a squeaker to John Fitzgerald Kennedy, the country had finally come around to supporting Ike's henchman, Richard Nixon.

Politics had become less about individual interests and more about group identity. Participants eschewed compromise for what Bayard Rustin termed "existential subjectivism," or in Irving Howe's less generous view, "kamikaze radicalism."[177] Black Panther supporters and Wallace voters fed on one another's rhetoric, much as protesters shouting "Pigs eat shit" in Lincoln Park did with the police who beat their heads in. It is not too extreme to call such appeals to unreason a kind of politics of apocalypse. Sadly, almost everyone got what they wanted, save those who remained in the liberal center, no longer vital. Indeed, it scarcely showed any pulse at all.

12

In the Darkness at the Edge of Town

We are moving from Locke to Hobbes.
— Daniel Patrick Moynihan to President Richard Nixon, 1969[1]

Every now and then, it happens that these "New York Intellectuals" do turn their attention to a specific New York problem. . . . Their general purpose, in such cases, is to wreak as much mischief as possible so that American society will bore them a little less.
— Irving Kristol and Paul Weaver, 1969[2]

D espite the many entreaties he received, Ted Kennedy was in no shape, physically or psychologically, to pick up where his brother left off in the summer of 1968. In one of history's forgotten footnotes, South Dakota's soft-spoken senator, George McGovern, decided he might be the man to hold what was now a decidedly left-leaning Democratic center together. Announcing his candidacy in the Senate Caucus Room in August 1968, McGovern explained what had prompted his decision: "Vietnam—the most disastrous political and military blunder in our national experience. That war must be ended now—not next year or the year following, but right now. Beyond this, we need to harness the full spiritual and political resources of this nation to put an end to the shameful remnants of racism and poverty that still afflict our land."[3]

McGovern's goal was to try to reanimate the antiwar passion of the Kennedy campaign with his own brand of straightforward midwestern morality. "I wear no claim to the Kennedy mantle, but I believe deeply in the twin goals for which Robert Kennedy gave his life—an end to the war in Vietnam and a passionate commitment to heal the division in our own society."[4] Despite his late entry into the race, McGovern insisted that he be allowed to participate in a televised debate between the Democratic Party candidates for president. Most who watched thought that McGovern, with his calm and reasoned presentation of the antiwar cause, bested both Humphrey and McCarthy.[5]

When Arthur Schlesinger, Jr., met with McGovern to discuss writing speeches for him, he described the senator as "placid, modest and agreeable as usual," and agreed to sign on.[6] Like almost everyone who got to know McGovern, Schlesinger was attracted to his sincerity and authenticity. Even Robert Kennedy had judged him to be "the most decent man in the Senate."[7] Like Kennedy on his best days, George Stanley McGovern combined both the old and new in American liberalism. He was a Plains boy, having grown up in the six-hundred-person farming community of Avon, South Dakota, in the 1920s and 1930s. The bashful son of a Methodist minister, he grew wary of "the excessive emotionalism of some evangelists" as he came of age in an America where his father was occasionally compensated not in cash but in cabbage.[8]

McGovern enlisted in the Army Air Force at nineteen after the attack on Pearl Harbor, and would earn a Distinguished Flying Cross for the thirty-five bombing missions he flew. He returned from Europe to earn his BA from tiny Dakota Wesleyan University in 1946 and then faced a forked road: graduate studies in history or "the clerical career of my father with a Social Gospel orientation."[9] After a brief stint at Garrett Theological Seminary in Chicago, he drifted into the history department at Northwestern University, where he deepened his commitment both to liberalism and to specific strains of midwestern radicalism. McGovern maintained that "we not only overreacted" to the USSR but "indeed helped trigger" the conflict "by our own post–World War II fears."[10] He had eagerly volunteered to work for the Progressive Party in 1948, serving as an Illinois delegate to the raucous 1948 convention at which Wallace was nominated.[11]

By 1953, McGovern had completed his doctoral studies with a thesis on the striking Colorado coal workers of 1913, which would lead him to be a remarkably class-conscious politician and far more sympathetic to organized labor than almost any other farm-belt senator of his time. He taught briefly at Dakota Wesleyan College before returning home to try to build up a local Democratic Party organization. But South Dakota was hardly fertile Democratic territory, and McGovern had to struggle to stay afloat, sleeping on friendly couches or in his car as he crisscrossed the state, personally recruiting thirty-five thousand new Democrats.[12] Inspired by the lofty visions of Adlai Stevenson, he decided to run for Congress in 1957 and then for the Senate. He lost in 1960 but succeeded two years later—serving as the head of the Kennedy administration's Food for Peace program in the meantime, and making valuable friends inside the administration. Though he had voted for the Tonkin Gulf Resolution, McGovern was beset by early doubts about Vietnam, and he soon became one of the peace camp's most dogged and eloquent proponents.

Following the debacle of Chicago in 1968, disaffected members of the Mc-Carthy and Kennedy campaigns, who saw Humphrey's delegate-driven nomination as the triumph of the backroom political bosses over the democracy-driven primary system that had invited so much new participation on the part of women, youth, and minorities, demanded changes in the party's nominating structure.[13] The newly created Commission on Party Structure and Delegate Selection and the two sides agreed on McGovern to chair it. Once again McGovern's collegiality worked to his benefit. Even Hubert Humphrey liked him and supported his selection.[14] Thus began the "New Politics" takeover of the Democratic Party.

McGovern's task was hardly a simple one. The "rights" revolution was spreading, inviting activists to carve up what remained of the Democratic Party in the name of narrow, often conflicting identities, many of whose members believed they were playing a zero-sum game. Where once stood a Democrat or even a liberal now stood a black, a woman, a Hispanic, a gay, among others. Liberalism began to look less like a coherent political vision than a crazy quilt of angry constituent groups making impossible demands on the system—a system the political scientist Theodore Lowi aptly dubbed "interest-group liberalism."[15] Before issuing its report, the McGovern commission met only four times and rarely ventured beyond the coterie of disgruntled Mc-Govern and McCarthy supporters.[16] All this led, rather mechanically, to the institution of a quota system that focused primarily on ensuring representation for blacks and women.[17]

As Thomas and Mary Edsall explain, "The new rules shifted the power to nominate presidential candidates from the loose alliance of state and local party structures, which had in the past been empowered to use party control to pick delegates, to the universe of generally liberal reform activists who were not granted direct access to the machinery of delegate selection," with the result that power shifted to "reform activists aligned with the anti-war, women's, and other rights movements—as well as with procedural 'good government types,'" who felt free to ignore the interests of lower-income blue-collar workers and white-ethnic constituencies that had formed the political backbone of the party.[18] This led, quite naturally, to backlash *within* the ranks of liberalism as well as outside it as the old guard complained of the "Harvard-Berkeley-Camelots" now shutting them out of what had once been their party.[19]

When the McGovern commission released its report in April 1970, the senator had already claimed the position of the leading voice inside Congress on Vietnam. He cosponsored an amendment with liberal Republican Mark Hatfield to cut off funding for the war by the end of the year. Taking the floor of the Senate, he accused "every senator in this chamber" of being "partly responsible for sending 50,000 young Americans to an early grave. This chamber reeks of blood," he insisted, shocking and offending many present.[20]

Norman Podhoretz would define the New Politics as "the insurgency within the Democratic Party which came out of the antiwar movement and which, having lost its chance to capture the party in 1968 either through Eugene McCarthy or through Robert Kennedy, found a second chance in the reforms developed by the McGovern commission and then seized it through the candidacy of McGovern himself."[21] After failing to move his colleagues in the Senate, McGovern took his arguments to America's universities, where antiwar fervor was high among both students and faculty.[22] His traveling and his remaking of the Democratic Party went hand in hand as students and peace activists flocked to his cause. McGovern announced his presidential candidacy in January 1971 and hired young activists to run his campaign.

Among the senior members of the McGovern brigade was Gloria Steinem. She was born in Toledo, Ohio, in 1934 to a perpetually in-debt father and a stay-at-home ex-journalist mother. Following a divorce when Gloria was eleven, her mother grew increasingly unstable mentally and emotionally, and the teenage girl endured a nightmarish adolescence in a condemned dwelling the two women shared with the local rat population. By eventually selling the house, Gloria's mother enabled her daughter to escape to Betty Freidan's alma mater, Smith College. There she became engaged to a promising young man, but in an early expression of her growing feminist consciousness, she called off the wedding at the last moment. Steinem won a fellowship that allowed her to travel to India in 1958, yet another key moment in the development of her remarkable political consciousness. This was followed by a trip to the Communist-dominated Vienna World Festival of Youth and Students a year later, which she attended through the CIA-funded National Students Association. Upon returning in 1960, she moved to New York to begin a career as a journalist.[23]

Steinem was a talented writer with an enviable wit, but she displayed genuine genius when it came to publicity. In 1963 she created a media frisson by posing as a Playboy bunny for an article in *Esquire*. Throughout the 1960s she combined serious intellectual journalism with just enough fluff to engage the interest of intellectuals and celebrity watchers alike. A fixture on the Manhattan social scene, Steinem was a natural hire (together with Tom Wolfe and Jimmy Breslin) for *New York* magazine founding editor Clay Felker, who, together with *Esquire*'s Harold Hayes, was in the process of helping to create the "new" participatory journalism. Despite her obvious talent, she was neverthe-less perceived by many to be "the mini-skirted pin-up girl of the intelligent-sia," a characterization that understandably infuriated her.[24] The final straw in her flirtation with gender-neutral protest politics came after she agreed to help with novelist (and "new journalist") Norman Mailer's absurdist run for New York City mayor in 1969. She loved its raucous nature and its mockery of traditional politics, especially how it "insert[ed] ideas into the campaign."[25] But while Mailer had many wonderful qualities, a willingness to treat women as his intellectual equals was famously not one of them. Steinem resolved never to put herself in a subordinate position to male chauvinism again.

That same year Steinem appeared at an event organized by one of femi-nism's earliest radical groups, the Redstockings. Organized by two young left-wing feminists, Ellen Willis and Shulamith Firestone, they recruited Steinem for an abortion rights rally. By publicizing just how many illegal abor-tions had been carried out in the country, many of them under unsafe condi-tions, the organizers believed they could turn the personal into the political and push for reform in the nation's abortion laws.

Steinem tried to straddle the worlds of these radical organizations and Friedan's liberal, reformist feminism, and while she did a far better job than most, it was no easy task. The specter of identity politics was already begin-ning to haunt liberalism as feminists struggled to reconcile their respective racial, ethnic, class, gender, and ideological identities. Color remained an im-placable dividing line, as any feminist movement aimed exclusively at the middle class had little to offer poor women, particularly those of color. The novelist Toni Morrison noted in 1971 that black women had "no abiding ad-miration of white women as competent, complete people."[26] And most had little sympathy for the hostility that so many feminists evinced toward men. "Black women tended to want to raise their status and take the whole race with them. White women tended to go in a separatist direction and damn the men."[27] As Ellen Willis would later recount, "Gloria's was a kind of liberal adaptation or assimilation of radical feminist ideas, which traditional liber-als like Betty Friedan were just rejecting. . . . She was sort of a liberal, New Politics feminist. She's not a radical, and I deeply disagree with her about any number of things. But, in America, radical ideas tend to assimilate into liberalism. . . ."[28]

Betty Friedan decidedly did not approve either of Steinem or the direction of the movement she represented. The ex-radical socialist was not becoming a conservative in any recognizable form, but she did worry that the revolu-tionary stance of so many feminists, together with the movement's emphases on abortion and lesbianism, would alienate middle-class American wives and mothers from the cause. Her animosity became so pronounced over time that Steinem partisans, like the author Nora Ephron, would refer to Friedan as "the Wicked Witch of the West," while remaining divided over whether to accord Steinem the role of "Glinda [the Wizard of Oz's good witch] or Dorothy." In either case, concluded Ephron, "Friedan, in her thoroughly irrational hatred of Steinem, ha[d] ceased caring whether or not the effects of that hatred are good or bad for the women's movement."[29]

When in early 1970 Friedan learned that she had been deposed as NOW president by a more radical faction, she launched an immediate counterattack in the form of a press conference at which she defiantly proposed what she called a Women's Strike for Equality, a day that women across America would take off to commemorate the victory of the suffragettes in winning the vote fifty years earlier.[30] On August 26 millions of women were galvanized to hold spontaneous events all around America, and NOW's membership lists exploded afterward.[31]

The controversy about whether feminism should concern itself predominantly with civil rights or sexuality continued to grow, however. Friedan complained that feminists must "overcome the wallowing, navel-gazing rap sessions, the orgasm talk that leaves things unchanged, the rage that will produce a backlash."[32] And so it did, as a number of influential feminist works published between 1970 and 1971—including particularly radical tomes such as Germaine Greer's *The Female Eunuch,* Shulamith Firestone's *The Dialectic of Sex,* Kate Millet's *Sexual Politics,* and Robin Morgan's *Sisterhood Is Powerful*[33]— did seek to move women to places where many middle-class mothers would be unlikely to follow. But Friedan's combative personality hardly helped matters. She took to sniping at Steinem, whom she referred to as "the Hair," thereby providing the mainstream media with the catfight theme so many chauvinist reporters and editors relished.[34] For her part, Steinem famously always kept her cool, particularly in debates with conservative women and chauvinist men.

As with all controversial movements for change, it was easy for feminism's enemies to use its most extreme proponents to attack its center. Steinem appreciated the danger and did not disagree entirely with Friedan about the need to tread lightly around the sensibilities of middle-class American mothers. That recognition helped inspire what was perhaps her most significant achievement in the period: the creation, in late 1971, of *Ms.* magazine, a glossy publication that would celebrate feminism both in politics and in everyday

life for the coming decades. It was a gutsy move at the time, given the professional mores then. It branded Steinem as an actor in the political world, rather
than that of journalism, where she had made her career, and like liberalism
itself, it placed Steinem in a vulnerable position both professionally and politically. Ellen Willis, a onetime contributer, thought *Ms.*'s brand of feminism
"mushy, sentimental . . . [and] designed to obscure political conflicts between
women." Redstocking radicals accused the magazine of being part of a CIA
conspiracy to collect information on the women's movement, a paranoid
charge seized on and repeated in *The New York Times* by none other than Betty
Friedan. Meanwhile, none other than President Nixon was recorded by the
White House taping system demanding of Henry Kissinger, "For shit's sake,
how many people really have read Gloria Steinem and give one shit about
that?"[35] Like feminism, America's burgeoning environmental movement had
little to do with the traditional economic or racial justice issues that had framed
liberalism in the past. Rather, it arose from a new attempt to reintroduce the
"qualitative liberalism" for which Schlesinger and Galbraith had argued during the fifties. The text that can be said, more than any other, to have inspired
America's environmental awakening originally appeared as a three-part series
in *The New Yorker*. It was not the first nor would it be the last time the publication played this role. Never was its influence greater than in the early 1960s,
when American culture yearned for ways to shake off the somnolence of the
Eisenhower era. Jane Jacobs's influential 1961 masterpiece, *The Death and Life
of Great American Cities*, was the subject of a lengthy critical analysis by the
polymathic social critic Lewis Mumford in *The New Yorker* the following year.[36]
Similarly, Michael Harrington's *The Other America* came to the attention of
President Kennedy and much of the rest of the world through Dwight Macdonald's passionate two-part *New Yorker* review, the longest the magazine had
ever published.[37] And so, too, Rachel Carson's *Silent Spring* led the magazine's
readership to begin to think anew of their relationship to the food they ate,
the water they drank, and the planet they inhabited when it first appeared in
three June 1962 issues of *The New Yorker*.

The work arose out of discussion between the author and *New Yorker* editor
William Shawn.[38] Carson had previously published two works that popularized science and explained the human relation to the natural world: *The Sea
Around Us* (1951) and *The Edge of the Sea* (1955). She was a rarity, a woman in
a man's world of science who had been trained in biology at Johns Hopkins
University, where she studied genetics, after attending the Pennsylvania College for Women. Having worked at the Fish and Wildlife Service before becoming a popular writer, she knew how to plod through long, cumbersome

scientific reports written in bureaucratese.[39] An avid naturalist and a member of the Audubon Society, Carson lived to spend time in her cabin in Maine, wading through coastal pools and watching the aquatic life spring to life before her eyes. She remembered growing up as a "solitary child" who "spent a great deal of time in woods and beside streams, learning the birds and the insects and flowers."[40]

Carson wrote the book under extraordinary circumstances. Suffering from cancer herself, she was also taking care of her sick and elderly mother, who had recently had a stroke.[41] Having written books about the wonders of sea life, Carson now tried to strike a balance between telling a story about the "beauty of the living world" and documenting how pesticides were killing nature and even humans (especially in the form of higher levels of cancer).[42] The first title she chose for the book was *Man Against Earth*, but that felt overly combative for the middle-class readership she wanted to reach.[43] Her literary agent, Marie Rodell, suggested she instead use her love of the spring season for her title. Mark Lytle explains, "Spring had always been a special season in her life, when fields turned green with new life, flowers burst into bloom, and bird songs filled the air."[44] So Carson opened her book by asking readers to imagine a "strange stillness" in place of a budding and chirping spring season. "The birds—where had they gone?"[45] By making environmental damage palpable and imaginable, Carson had written, in the words of her most diligent biographer, "a revolutionary book in terms that were acceptable to a middle class emerging from the lethargy of postwar affluence."[46]

Carson did a diligent job of making an extremely complex problem understandable to lay readers. She moved briskly from focused case studies to building a wider picture of humans' devastation of the natural world. She had seen that pesticides "contaminate soil, water, and food, that they have the power to make our streams fishless and our gardens and woodlands silent and birdless." She played upon Americans' fears about the new world of modern science—atmospheric tests of atomic weapons had started to raise anxieties during the early 1960s—by discussing the "aerial delivery" of DDT, "showered down indiscriminately from the skies." But as much as she played upon fears of science, she also *used* science to illustrate the dangers of the chemical industry's push for uninhibited spraying. She knew her Darwin and pointed out that species would adapt to resistance to pesticides, making even more pesticides necessary, and thus creating a perpetual circle of humans battling nature. Her warning was this: the natural world could be *understood* by science but not be *controlled*. "Nature is not so easily molded," she argued, as she warned that "insects are finding ways to circumvent our chemical attacks on them."[47]

Carson ably adapted her environmental agenda to the liberalism of the moment, arguing for a new "right" of good health for all God's creatures. "If the Bill of Rights contains no guarantee that a citizen shall be secure against lethal poisons distributed either by private individuals or by public officials," she explained, "it is surely only because our forefathers, despite their considerable wisdom and foresight, could conceive of no such problem." Ultimately, however, her case was a moral one: "The question is whether any civilization can wage relentless war on life without destroying itself, and without losing the right to be called civilized."[48] Fortuitously, the book's release came on the heels of the discovery of the relationship between the popular sedative Thalidomide and severe birth defects in the children of the pregnant woman who took it.[49] "It is all of a piece," Carson told interviewers, "Thalidomide and pesticides—they represent our willingness to rush ahead and use something new without knowing what the results are going to be"[50]

Naturally, the pesticide industry, led by DuPont, attacked both the book and its author, but their criticisms only served to bring more attention to the issue. One reader of an installment in *The New Yorker* complained about Carson's "Communist sympathies," concluding, "We can live without birds and animals, but, as the current market slump shows, we cannot live without business."[51] Supreme Court Justice William O. Douglas helped promote the book, and President Kennedy cited it as well.[52] His Science Advisory Committee endorsed Carson's view "that the burden of proof properly lay with chemical companies to show that pesticides were safe."[53]

If Rachel Carson was the literary voice of the movement, then its political face could be found atop the broad shoulders of Earth Day's founder, Wisconsin senator Gaylord Nelson. Born in 1916 in the small logging village of Clear Lake in northwestern Wisconsin, Nelson was the son of a country doctor who took in vagrants and taught his son the values of midwestern progressivism.[54] Following a relatively traditional (and athletic) childhood, Nelson attended Cal State and then the University of Wisconsin Law School. There he worked on the reelection campaign of progressive champion (and family hero) Senator Robert M. La Follette, Jr., in 1940. After graduation he served in the war, during which he grew disgusted with the Army's attitude toward its black soldiers. He returned home to work again for Republican progressive LaFollette, but decided he could not abide a party that included Joe McCarthy and quit to work as a labor lawyer. By 1948, Nelson had grown tired of legal work, and like McGovern he set out to revive a moribund local Democratic Party. As McCarthy's power surged in the Senate, Nelson helped form a Democratic truth squad to follow the senator around in public, challenging his lies and signing up those similarly disgusted by their junior senator. He ran successfully for governor in 1958, inspired by Adlai Stevenson, and especially his environmentalist message.

Nelson pushed through the Outdoor Recreation Act, a $50 million initiative funded by a cigarette tax. Secretary of the Interior Stewart Udall admired it and asked for Nelson's help in creating a program of conservation for the Kennedy administration. Nelson argued that "there is no domestic issue more important to America in the long run than the conservation and proper use of our natural resources, including fresh water, clean air, tillable soil, forests, wilderness, habitat for wildlife, minerals and recreational assets." He insisted—against popular belief—that there was a constituency for conservation politics, one that was middle class and mainstream, "from ladies with a flower box in the window to the deer hunters with high powered rifles; the boaters, who range from kids with flat-bottomed scows to the wealthy yachtsmen; family campers; bird watchers; skin-divers; wilderness crusaders; farmers; soil conservationists; fishermen; insect collectors; foresters, and just plain Sunday drivers."[55] JFK took up the cause and traveled around the West to make a series of speeches on the topic. In those written by Nelson, the president quoted the western novelist Wallace Stegner: "We simply need that wild country available to us, even if we never do more than drive to the edge and look in. For it can be a means of reassuring ourselves of our sanity as creatures, a part of the geography of hope."[56]

In 1962, Nelson was elected to the Senate, where he befriended Hubert Humphrey and championed the typical northern liberal issues of the day—especially civil rights. But it was on environmental causes that he made his mark. He called for legislation that would ban phosphate detergents, the danger of which Americans had become aware through *Silent Spring*. He helped pass the Wilderness Act, which forbade construction in areas designated wild, and a whole host of bills during the Johnson and Nixon administrations.[57] Nelson's most impressive achievement may have been Earth Day, which began in 1969. He called it a "national teach-in on the crisis of the environment"[58] and "the birth date of a new American ethic that rejects the frontier philosophy that the continent was put here for our plunder, and accepts the idea that even urbanized, affluent, mobile societies are interdependent with the fragile, life-sustaining systems of the air, the water, the land."[59] Earth Day proved a huge success. Organizers sent out newsletters to schools all over America, underwritten by the UAW. In New York City, Mayor Lindsay closed Fifth Avenue to cars, and people marched for the planet, some wearing gas masks to protest air pollution. An estimated ten million schoolchildren across the country participated, together with twenty million adults.[60]

One of Earth Day's signal accomplishments was to connect with the sensible middle-class concern for "quality of life" issues drawn from the remnants of qualitative liberalism, and disentangle it from the political views of the emerging counterculture, much as Betty Friedan had sought to do with feminism. The writer Arnold Kaufman noted at the time that "the counterculture threatens the very qualities upon which our best hope for a brighter future depends—a disciplined ability to reason and a morally passionate commitment to a politics that is both rational and relatively independent of the quest for personal salvation."[61] Such arguments were lost, however, in the face of the more grandiose claims of works such as Theodore Roszak's *The Making of a Counterculture*, which argued that the young "bring with them almost nothing but healthy instincts" as they rebelled against America's "technocratic" society and celebrated "non-intellective powers of the personality," and Charles Reich's *The Greening of America*. The latter argued for a war against the "life-denying" powers of the "Corporate State" based on the counterculture's creation of a new form of consciousness that would help to restore "the non-material elements of man's existence."[62]

Gaylord Nelson, meanwhile, continued to nurture the possibility of more significant environmental legislation even with Nixon in the White House. This turned out to be smart politics. Nixon took a hard-right public line but governed, at least domestically, just left of center. In January 1970 the bipartisan National Environmental Policy Act established the Environmental Protection Agency (EPA). The same year Nixon signed the Clean Air Act, proclaiming, "It is now or never. America pays its debt to the past by reclaiming the purity of its air, its waters, and our living environment."[63] Membership in the Sierra Club and Friends of the Earth exploded. Stewart Brand's *Whole Earth Catalog* offered advice on how to live a simpler life in greater harmony with the planet and sold in the millions. And while many business organizations and conservative billionaires would continue to fight a rearguard action against all forms of regulation that cut into their profits, others saw economic opportunities in "green" technologies and seized them, trumpeting themselves as good corporate citizens and making plenty of money as they did so. Just as the Democrats' increasing embrace of qualitative liberalism began to attract upper-income suburban voters sympathetic to feminism, environmentalism, and some aspects of youthful idealism, liberals lost what had been their primary political constituency: the white working class. Political scientist Richard Scammon and former Democratic operative (and future neoconservative strategist) Ben Wattenberg identified these trends in a book called *The Real Majority* in 1970. They looked back at the New Deal/Fair Deal period as one in which Democrats had combined economic populism and cultural conservatism to create a durable political coalition. Now liberals had allowed themselves to be sidetracked by "social values issues," which they defined as "crime, race, values, busing, drugs, disruption, quotas, welfare, pornography, patriotism, draft-dodging, dependency, permissiveness, capital punishment, [and] disparagement of America." Democrats would lose the country, they warned, unless they moved toward an overall more centrist orientation.

"We've got those liberal bastards on the run," Richard Nixon boasted in November 1969, and he was right.[64] Writing in *New York* in the spring of that year, the journalist Pete Hamill described what he prophetically noted was the beginning of a "Revolt of the White Lower Middle Class." Hamill noted the effect of what he called "the information explosion" on the residents he interviewed in the working-class boroughs of Queens, Brooklyn, and Staten Island, people who complained to him, without apology, "None of them politicians gives a good goddam [about white workers]. All they worry about is the niggers. And everything is for the niggers. . . . They take the money outta my paycheck and they just turn it over to some lazy son of a bitch who won't work." Hamill listened to these complaints night after night and concluded:

> Television has made an enormous impact on them, and because of the nature of that medium—its preference for the politics of theatre, its seeming inability to ever explain what is happening behind the photographed image—much of their understanding of what happens is superficial. Most of them have only a passing acquaintance with blacks, and very few have any black friends. So they see blacks in terms of militants with Afros and shades, or crushed people on welfare. . . . And in the past five or six years, with urban rioting on everyone's minds, they have provided themselves (or been provided with) a confused, threatening stereotype of blacks that has made it almost impossible to suggest any sort of black-white working-class coalition. . . . The working-class white man is actually in revolt against taxes, joyless work, the double standards and short memories of professional politicians, hypocrisy and what he considers the debasement of the American dream. [But if] the stereotyped black man is becoming the working-class white man's enemy, the eventual enemy might be the democratic process itself.[65]

These shifting voting patterns led sociologist Jonathan Rieder to move into the white working-class community of Brooklyn's Canarsie to try to discover what lay beneath the change in residents' voting patterns between 1975 to 1977. His ability to share their kitchen table conversations and unguarded observations about their changing world yielded a wealth of insights into the decline of liberalism among those who were once its primary constituency. Though there were differences—Italians openly expressed their contempt for African Americans in racist terms, Jews were more circumspect—both evinced fury at welfare payments to minorities and particularly plans for affirmative action. Johnson's 1965 speech at Howard University had made the case in what many at the time felt were compelling terms: "You do not take a person who, for years, has been hobbled by chains and liberate him, bring him to the starting line of a race and then say, 'You are free to compete with all the others,' and still justly believe that you have been completely fair," the president thundered.[66] But the inspirational aspects of the president's message proved no match for traditional tribal and ethnic loyalties. Canarsians rejected the entire idea of special compensations for past injustices to blacks and other minorities who had suffered discrimination when, in fact, they viewed themselves in much the same terms. They were being asked to "pay the price for those years of slavery," as one resident explained. "But I ask you," Rieder's subject continued, "who will pay the Jews for two thousand years of slavery? Who will compensate the Italians for all the ditches they dug?"

Canarsians came to equate liberalism with licentiousness—political, cultural, and sexual. Liberalism, one of them told Rieder, was like the "easy" girl in the neighborhood who "gave it away" for "cheap" and expected nothing in "return." An Italian resident told Rieder: "It's like the old maid and the prostitute. Well, liberals are like the prostitute." And all liberals did in their eyes was offer excuses. Another resident complained to Rieder, "If the blacks riot, don't hurt them, they have reasons for it." By "reasons," Rieder explains, what Carnarsians meant was excuses for deviant, destructive behavior. "To accept reasons for rioting was to take cockamamie excuses and *ferkocta* double-talk at face value. Such a reading of lawlessness indicated that liberals were suckers easily gulled by the underclasses and unworthy of respect."[67]

New winds were blowing by 1970, and whether from left or right, they blew in an illiberal direction. As Garry Wills observed, "Every campaign had taught Nixon the same lesson: mobilize resentment against those in power."[68] By constantly attacking those whom Vice President Spiro Agnew mocked as the "effete corps of impudent snobs who characterized themselves as intellectuals," the president and his minions succeeded in convincing Americans that no matter who occupied the White House, it was these smart-ass liberals who somehow always remained in power.[69] When Peter Brennan and Thomas Gleason of the International Longshoremen's Association and AFL-CIO found themselves invited to the White House, they handed a delighted president a hard hat that read "Commander in Chief." Nixon was so smitten that he picked Brennan to be his new secretary of labor.[70]

Liberals, meanwhile, struggled mightily to find a formula that would allow them to somehow hold on to their working-class constituency as they simultaneously embraced the ethos of the new antiwar, civil rights, feminist (and later gay) movements. It was, in fact, an impossible task, and one made more difficult by the need of so many of the leaders of these movements to attack blue-collar values in the often deliberately incendiary language of self-styled cultural revolutionaries. The quest for a solution to this conundrum was, in certain respects, the initial impetus for the breakaway faction of liberals who became neoconservatives and succeeded in reshaping much about American politics in their own image. Liberalism had failed to solve the social problems of the 1960s. In important respects, it appeared to exacerbate them. Poverty continued to grow. Race relations worsened. The Vietnam War expanded into Cambodia with no end in sight. Many American cities were losing their middle-class white residents as busing and forced integration brought with it racial violence, increased crime, and unsafe conditions for adults and school-children alike, destroying their economic foundations with the rapid exodus to the suburbs. The crisis appeared to come to a kind of crescendo one awful night in New York City during the summer of 1977, when Con Edison accidentially cut off all power citywide, resulting in two days of almost apocalyptic levels of lawlessness, looting, and police indifference. The shock led the liberals at the *New York Times* editorial board to ponder, literally, the collapse of its own civilization: "Is New York City, after all, a failed ultra-urban experiment in which people eventually crack, social order eventually collapses, and reason ultimately yields to despair?"[71]

In his famous 1949 introduction to *The Liberal Imagination*, Lionel Trilling had warned that liberalism had a tendency to drift "toward a denial of the emotions and the imagination," adding that it "unconsciously tends to develop theories and principles . . . that justify its limitation."[72] This is precisely what liberals, both locally and nationally, had done in seeking to address any number of social problems in a manner consistent with their own limited definitions of those problems, and according to what they believed (or hoped) would be the rational reaction of all of the parties involved. By failing to match available means to their often unpredictable ends, liberals had overpromised and underdelivered and in doing so had decimated their own political base and left themselves vulnerable to newly fortified challenges from both the left and right.

The founding of the journal *Public Interest* in 1965 owed a great deal to the realization that liberals were trying to do too much too fast and with far too little attention to the potential consequences of their actions. The road to public policy hell was everywhere paved with their often arrogant, often ignorant, albeit noble intentions, followed by reckless and often thoughtless implementation. Founded by Irving Kristol and Daniel Bell, its editors and authors sought to apply social science methodology to the problems liberals tried to address, embracing the complexity of these phenomena with a degree of hard-headed lack of sentimentality they felt liberals too often eschewed. Its maiden issue proclaimed the modest goals "to help all of us, when we discuss issues of public policy, to know a little better what we are talking about—and preferably in time to make such knowledge effective."[73] As Kristol later explained, the journal's tone "from the outset, was skeptical, pragmatic, meliorist."[74] Sounding very much like Bell's End of Ideology argument published five years earlier, the editors declared that the main obstacle to effective public policy was the blindness caused by "a prior commitment to ideology, whether it be liberal, conservative or radical." "For it is the nature of ideology," the editors went on, "to preconceive reality; and it is exactly such preconceptions that are the worst hindrances to knowing-what-one-is-talking-about."[75] *The Public Interest* purposely ignored foreign policy, as its editors feared being "swallowed up by Vietnam."[76]

The decision to found the magazine was provoked, initially, by what was deemed to be the catastrophic impact of so many of the Great Society programs that Lyndon Johnson had forced through Congress without proper attention to the consequences of failure, or even to the difficulty of delivery of services—to say nothing of the unpredictable outcome of just about every major government undertaking. The administration's hasty and ultimately ill-considered embrace of the Community Action Program (CAP) as the centerpiece of its antipoverty strategy proved particularly galling to *The Public Interest* editors, who judged it to be ill considered, badly executed, and based on faddish, likely pernicious ideas. They shared the belief, with considerable justification, that liberals should pay less attention to proving their good intentions and more to ensuring that the programs produced results consistent with their aims.

They wanted more testing, more pilot programs, more rigorous research, and a bit more modesty when it came to the goal of remaking America in a manner consistent with liberal ideals.

All *The Public Interest* editors had voted for Johnson and Humphrey for president and all initially remained within the liberal fold. Irving Kristol, however, continued to move sharply rightward. Deeply influenced by Lionel Trilling's belief that contemporary intellectuals occupied "a ground and a vantage point from which to judge and condemn ... the culture that produced [them]," Kristol launched a war on what he termed the "new class" made up of "scientists, teachers, and educational administrators, journalists and others."[77] In *On the Democratic Idea in America* (1972), he made the case that the rise of "promiscuity, homosexuality, drugs, political terrorism" could be successfully resisted with the right public policies.[78] He attributed the counterculture's assault on the values of middle-class America to "the utopian idiocies of the extreme left" and termed their adoption by the nation's leading media and intellectual personalities to be "one of the most significant events in the last half-century of Western civilization," and one of the most alarming.[79] "Has there ever been" he asked "in all of recorded history, a civilization whose culture was at odds with the values and ideals of that civilization itself? It is not uncommon that a culture will be critical of the civilization that sustains it—and always critical of the failure of this civilization to realize perfectly the ideals that it claims as inspiration. Such criticism is implicit or explicit in Aristophanes or Euripides, Dante and Shakespeare. But to take an adversary posture to the ideals themselves? That is unprecedented."[80] Daniel Bell eventually became so alienated by both the tone and substance of Kristol's bellicosity toward liberals that he resigned as *The Public Interest* editor, explaining to those who asked that he placed "friendship above ideology."[81]

While Bell found Kristol's notion of a new class to be a "muddled concept," he did worry, nevertheless, about what he viewed as a "new sensibility of black-mass ritual and violence in the arena of culture" that "undermine[d] the social structure itself by striking at the motivational and psychic-reward system which has sustained it."[82] Bell believed the adversary culture fed on capitalism itself. He argued, "In culture, today, the avant-garde has triumphed, but also exhausted itself. In the economy, the old Protestant ethos has gone, and capitalism promotes a widespread hedonism."[83] Liberalism therefore was facing not merely a crisis of confidence, but also a cultural crisis that was a product of the ethos of consumer capitalism.[84] For Bell, capitalism had dug its own grave by creating its own self-contradictions, and all society could do was adapt itself to these circumstances as best as it could. "Saving" the culture was at best a rearguard action, designed to ameliorate rather than reverse the corruption that naturally accompanied capitalist consumption.

If Kristol had always trawled the rightward edges of liberalism and Bell remained at its sensible center, Norman Podhoretz had moved sharply leftward personally, politically, and culturally. Since taking over the editorial reigns of *Commentary* following Elliot Cohen's 1960 suicide, he had shorn it of its hard-line anticommunism and flirted with some of the most subversive—for better or worse—notions of the counterculture. He even went so far as to call for "an unambiguous American defeat" in Vietnam as preferable to "the indefinite and unlimited bombardment by American pilots in American planes of every country in that already devastated region."

While Podhoretz went on to write more memoirs than most people write memos, he has never satisfactorily explained his shift from such positions to the attack dog posture he soon claimed on behalf of the enemies of the left. He had long hated the Beats—the precursors to the hippies, and whose most famous member, Allen Ginsberg, had been his competition for Lionel Trilling's most talented student at Columbia—whom he dismissed as "hostile to civilization": The "Know-Nothing Bohemians," as Podhoretz dubbed them, were "spiritually underprivileged"; they were "young men who can't think straight and so hate anyone who can."[85] At the same time, he had little but contempt for the elites who indulged the senseless complaints of the Beats, and later the hippies, the students, and others who fancied themselves to be American revolutionaries. The United States had "the only ruling class in history," he complained, "that has been unable to co-opt the 'poets,' that has not come to subsidize a class of artists who are not only hostile to it but evidently hostile to the death."[86] This antipathy only expanded its targets as the middle-class children of Podhoretz's peers began to adopt cultural attitudes he equated with these thoughtless hostile hippies, leading him to complain that the sixties had spawned women who "no longer wish to be women" and "men [who] do not wish to be men." Between the cultural and political permutations of sixties revolutions, no solid citizens could count themselves safe from the "spiritual plagues" that had been unleashed, whether the menace be communism, homosexuality, or the "appeasement" of either one.[87]

Consistent with the spirit of the times, the neoconservatives were also in the process of rediscovering their tribalistic Jewish identities. In the period of his youthful leftism, Podhoretz demonstrated a rather snobbish disdain toward the Jewish state. Indeed, it was Podhoretz's hostile account of his first trip to Israel that originally attracted him to the editors of *Commentary*. Upon his first six-week visit there, in 1951, he wrote Lionel Trilling that "despite their really extraordinary accomplishments, [they are] a very unattractive people, the Israelis. They're gratuitously surly and boorish. . . . They are too arrogant and too anxious to become a real honest-to-goodness New York of the East," as if this had been—or ought to be—the Zionist ideal. Trilling passed the letter on to then-editor Elliot Cohen, and Podhoretz was invited into the inner circle.[88] In 1965, during his brief radical phase as editor, he had published George Steiner's complaint that Israel was "alien to some of the most radical, most humane elements in the Jewish spirit."[89]

Israel's victory in the Six-Day War of June 1967 played an enormous role in forging a new, Israel-centric identity for millions of American Jews, whether religious or secular. Rabbi Arthur Hertzberg, writing two months after the war, with its memories still fresh, noted that the crisis had united American Jews "with deep Jewish commitments as they have never been united before, and it has evoked such commitments in many Jews who previously seemed untouched by them. . . . There are no conventional Western theological terms with which to explain this," he said. "[M]ost contemporary Jews experience these emotions without knowing how to define them. . . . Israel may . . . now be acting as a very strong focus of worldwide Jewish emotional loyalty and thereby as a preservative of a sense of Jewish identity."[90] "The Israelis have simply showed us all that Jews need not always be powerless before the murderous intentions of their enemies," Podhoretz himself crowed in a letter to the psychologist Erich Fromm, "and it is this rather than any stirring of militarist or chauvinist fervor, that has moved so many Jews outside Israel."[91] In 1972, Podhoretz would state his new view quite plainly in an article with the deliberately provocative title—from the point of view of *Commentary*'s history of universalism and anti-Zionism—"Is It Good for the Jews?" Podhoretz explained why Jews ought to look "at proposals and policies from the point of view of the Jewish interest."[92]

Podhoretz argued for a seamless connection between anti-Semitism and anti-Americanism among leftist and liberal intellectuals who criticized what they alleged to be American imperialism and Israeli colonialism in the same breath. Jews, moreover, proved the perfect models of middle-class values that so offended their antibourgeois posturing.[93] Affirmative action, in addition, created a particularly painful form of *tsuris* with respect to black/Jewish relations. Jewish neocons, like most conservatives, professed to support diversity in hiring and education but opposed most of the means chosen to achieve it, most particularly quotas. Again, Podhoretz stated the case both plainly and tribally:

As a liberal I believed in the traditional principle of treating individuals as individuals and not as members of a group; as a Jew, I feared that a quota system designed to overcome discrimination against blacks would almost certainly result in discrimination against Jews—and I could not bring myself to believe that the only way to achieve social justice in the United States was to discriminate against my own children; and as an intellectual, I worried about the lowering and erosion of standards entailed by any system of reverse discrimination.[94]

At the same time, black anger found in Israel a convenient target, just as it had the Jewish teachers of Ocean Hill-Brownsville. The post–Martin Luther King, Jr., civil rights leadership appeared to be taking a disturbing turn toward Jew baiting, a development that tracked an increasing self-identification of the antiwar movement with the cause of Palestinian "freedom fighters" who sought to expel Jews from the Middle East and were willing to employ terroristic tactics to do so. Jew hatred became a kind of casual form of communication among many of the self-styled revolutionaries of both the New Left and Black Power movements, and the neocons drew their conclusions accordingly. An ad for the International Committee to Support Eldridge Cleaver—signed, among others, by Allen Ginsberg, along with other leftist intellectual luminaries such as Norman Mailer, Susan Sontag, and Noam Chomsky—appeared in the same issue of the *Black Panther* that praised Palestinian Fatah militants for knowing "only the gun as the sole means to achieve victory." SDS president Tom Hayden complained of "Jewish fascists" in Israel. A SNCC publication compared the Gaza Strip with Dachau, insisting "Zionists lined up Arab victims and shot them in the back in cold blood." Stokely Carmichael, the originator of the "Black Power" slogan and, beginning in June 1966, the chairman of SNCC, proved particularly promiscuous in his antiwhite rhetoric, but he appeared to reserve a special place in his pantheon of resentments for Jews, going so far as to equate the (Jewish-populated) Democratic Party with the Nazis and to deny the very existence of anti-Semitism in America.[95] In September 1967 a left-wing "New Politics" convention was held in Chicago, largely funded by then-hard-left Jewish funder and future *New Republic* owner Martin Peretz, using, as he would for the coming decades, his wealthy second ex-wife's substantial inheritance to make himself a "macher" in the world of left-wing politics. The conference collapsed amid a storm of acrimonious accusation when the black caucus rammed though a resolution condemning the "imperialistic Zionist war," and though its members later rescinded the resolution, the damage was clearly done. Peretz moved sharply rightward, particularly on racial issues and those involving Jews, and would eventually take what had been America's flagship liberal weekly with him.[96] In another famously painful incident for liberals, blacks, and Jews that grew out of the confrontation over New York City schools, a black schoolteacher named Leslie Campbell read one of her (black) students' poems on the radical radio station WBAI during a program hosted by the noted black activist Julius Lester. The verse, dedicated to the Jewish head of the New York City teacher's union, Albert Shanker, began:

> Hey Jew boy with that yamaka on your head
> You pale faced Jew boy I wish you were dead. . . . [97]

While I. F. Stone argued that "it will not hurt us Jews to swallow a few insults from overwrought blacks," this was hardly a majority view among Jews in general or neoconservatives in particular.[98] (In an ironic denouement to the cause, Lester later converted to Judaism himself.)

Irving Kristol was first to leave the liberal fold: "I no longer had to pretend to believe—what in my heart I could no longer believe—that liberals were wrong because they subscribe to this or that erroneous opinion on this or that topic." As he explained his full-fledged neoconservative penchant: "Liberals are wrong, because they are liberals."[99] Podhoretz was not far behind. As he tells it, in February 1970 he was walking in the woods of upstate New York when he experienced a mystical vision that somehow convinced him that "Judaism was true." The editor did not, in his own words, feel a need "to go to services, eat kosher, all that stuff," but he decided at that moment to "unlearn" what he had previously believed as a liberal to be true, namely "that it was more honorable and nobler to turn one's back on one's own and fight for others and for other things in which one had no personal stake or interest." Podhoretz accordingly decided to "devote his life to standing up for himself as a Jew and as an American against an ever-lengthening list of those he deemed to be mortal enemies."[100]

If Bob Dylan was the unchallenged principal poet of the sixties counterculture, inspiring and giving voice to what millions of Americans were thinking and feeling before they knew they were thinking or feeling it, then his neoconservative counterpart might fairly be said to be Saul (né Solomon) Bellow. When Bellow opened his 1953 novel *The Adventures of Augie March* with the words, "I am an American, Chicago born," he helped to reimagine and, to a considerable degree, reinvent American literature in the image of the American Jewish immigrant experience.[101]

In fact, Bellow himself had been born in a Montreal suburb in 1915 to ortho-dox Jewish parents who had fled Czarist violence just two years earlier. His family moved to Chicago when he was nine.[102] He attended the University of Chicago and Northwestern University but soon drifted into New York intel-lectual circles. He joined the Young People's Socialist League (YPSL) and em-braced Trotskyist politics more generally during the 1930s as he found employment in the New Deal Federal Writers' Project. He published much of his writing in *Partisan Review,* and like the editors there, allowed his Marxism to drift into anti-Communist liberalism during the postwar years.

Bellow's earliest novels, *Dangling Man* (1944) and *The Victim* (1947), were primarily portents of potential. As Bellow later observed to Philip Roth, he "felt that, as the child of Russian Jews, [I had to] establish my authority, my credentials, my fitness to write books in English. Somewhere in my Jewish and immigrant blood there were conspicuous traces of a doubt as to whether I had the right to practice the writer's trade."[103] Writing in *Commentary* in 1951, Bellow condemned what he deemed to be the self-imposed timidity of Jewish authors: "As long as American Jewish writers continue to write in this way we will have to go elsewhere for superior being and beauty, and will thus continue to be foreigners."[104]

He backed up his words with the miraculous *Augie March,* the book that launched what Roth would call the American Jewish "imaginative assault upon the American experience."[105] The novel was a bildungsroman of a young man who comes of age during the Depression and World War II. The novel followed Augie from adventure to adventure and embraced America as no Jewish novelist had ever done before. If Bellow saw the novel as "the natural history of the Jews in America," it in fact signaled the Jewish arrival in Amer-ica not as Jews but as Americans. "The Jews in Germany, Poland, Hungary, French Jews, Italian Jews had been deported, shot, gassed," Bellow later ex-plained, but in America, particularly after the war, they were invited to achieve whatever their talents allowed.[106]

The novel won Bellow the National Book Award and celebrity among lib-eral New York intellectuals. Irving Howe considered it "a picaresque tale about a cocky Jewish boy moving almost magically past the barriers of Amer-ican society, it is also a kind of paean to the idea of personal freedom in hostile circumstances."[107] Bellow captured, in his friend Alfred Kazin's view, "this living, acrid style—in the suddenly chastened, too glibly precise, peculiarly assertive bitterness of postwar America writing, with its hallucinated clarity about details, its oversized sense of our existence, of too many objects all around (what desolation amidst wonders!)."[108] As the literary critic Julian

Levinson would later note, "Suddenly, every reader of American fiction, Jewish or not, was expected to understand at least a smattering of Yiddish. Terms were left untranslated, lending the same authority to Yiddish that had previously been reserved for French, German or Spanish. Stories about New York Jews were offered up and read as parables for the national soul."[109]

With the bestselling *Herzog* (1964), the story of a failed professor going through a midlife crisis who tends to his troubled soul by constantly writing imagined letters to famous people, both living and dead, Bellow pursued many of the themes explored in his earlier works. Herzog "behaved like a philosophe who cared only about the very highest things—creative reason, how to render good for evil, and all the wisdom of old books." As one of Bellow's characters, a lawyer, tells his protagonist: "You're a highbrow and married a highbrow broad. Somewhere in every intellectual is a dumb prick."[110]

Throughout this period Bellow's oeuvre emerged from deep within the bosom of postwar liberalism. He was a member of SANE and a supporter of the civil rights movement. He wrote a preface to a book about the Mississippi Freedom Summer volunteers who had been killed in the name of the cause. He lived for a while in an upstate New York house with Ralph Ellison and supported the teach-in movement that was just then emerging around Vietnam.[111] Bellow's character Herzog wrote a letter to Dr. King: "Let us hope this example by Negroes will penetrate the hypnotic trance of the majority."[112]

Bellow's fiction up to and including *Herzog* dealt with themes of freedom and, to a large extent, the existential dilemma of living without an overarching meaning in life. As the cultural historian George Cotkin points out, "For all of his emphasis on alienation, death, and the absurdity of existence, Bellow remains a writer of hope, capturing the American existential demand for a dauntless attitude. This is his home-grown brand of existentialism, straight out of the immigrant streets."[113]

Like so many writers who emerged from the *Partisan Review* circle, Bellow found New Leftists to be ignorant and immature, and his next novel, *Mr. Sammler's Planet* (1970), evolved into "a dramatic essay of some sort, wrung from me by the crazy Sixties."[114] In some respects the novel could be seen as portraying the human cost—or result—of liberalism gone out of control: what Bellow would memorably term in another context, "the Good Intentions Paving Company."[115] Its central character is the seventy-year-old "child of a second marriage, born when his father was sixty."[116] A Polish Jew, Sammler survived the Holocaust but lost his wife in the process and lives within the crime-ridden and chaotic streets of late 1960s Manhattan. The doubling of welfare rolls, the increase in criminality, the flight of middle-class Jews away from the city to the suburbs—all of these things weighed heavily on Bellow's hero.[117] "New York makes one think about the collapse of civilization, about Sodom and Gomorrah, the end of the world. The end wouldn't come as surprise here. Many people already bank on it," he muses.[118]

Sammler is a novel filled with dyspeptic observations about his dying city, particularly the minorities who appear to be taking it over in the name of the sexual revolution, spouting mindless leftist slogans that mask their own voracious appetites for sex and power mixed with sloth—as if Norman Podhoretz's infamous February 1963 essay, "My Negro Problem—and Ours," had sprung to life as a kind of personal Jewish intellectual nightmare.[119] In a scene that would offer critics and champions alike ample argument for Bellow's bravery and/or sour malevolence, Arthur Sammler is followed off his Riverside Drive bus by a black pickpocket who traps the elderly, half-blind protagonist against a wall and then, as a kind of warning of unspeakable (but clearly sexualized) violence, he takes out his penis and waves it at Sammler: "a large tan-and-purple uncircumcised thing—a tube, a snake . . . suggesting the fleshly mobility of an elephant's trunk."[120] The novelist Scott Turow wrote that he admired Bellow for "his perspicacity in recognizing the lethal admixture of crime and sexuality that was already being adopted as an underground ideal of black masculinity," but it clearly bespoke a different world than the one of civil rights marches and the now-forgotten dreams of Martin Luther King, Jr.[121]

One of the novel's climactic scenes occurs when Sammler speaks at Columbia University about his lifelong interest in two progressives of yesteryear, H. G. Wells and George Orwell. Recalling an incident that had happened to Bellow at San Francisco State College not long before he published the book, a student shouts "Old Man! You quoted Orwell before. . . . You quoted him to say that British radicals were all protected by the Royal Navy? Did Orwell say that British radicals were protected by the Royal Navy?" "Yes, I believe he did say that." "That's a lot of shit," the young man yells back. "Orwell was a fink. He was a sick counterrevolutionary. It's good he died when he did. And what you are saying is shit. . . . Why do you listen to this effete old shit? What has he got to tell you? His balls are dry. He's dead. He can't come."

Using the secular democratic socialist saint George Orwell as his lodestar, Bellow identifies what he perceives as a rupture in the history of the left, with the result a generational conflict that turned into warfare and personal attack. Ironically, and undoubtedly unknowingly, he mirrors Betty Friedan's critique of the sexual revolution as replacing old-fashioned political reform, except that Bellow's Sammler has surrendered to the enemy. "All this confused sex-excrement-militancy, explosiveness, abusiveness, tooth-showing, Barbary ape howling," he complains. The bitter old man's rant is the central voice of the novel, rendered without apology. "I am getting old," Sammler observes, but "this liberation into individuality has not been a great success."[122]

The New York intellectuals who typically gushed over Bellow's creations—Irving Howe and Alfred Kazin—were taken aback by the sour taste the novel left in their mouths. Howe, who if anything liked the New Left even less than Bellow, worried over what he identified as the "line of sensibility established by T. S. Eliot in the *Waste Land*," that is, the theme of civilizational breakdown and its concomitant loss of meaning. Despite the "heavy cloud of despair" he detected hovering above Bellow's story, he clung to the belief that "we can still find some pleasure in sociability and our bodies, or, at the least, still experience that root sense of obligation which the mere fact of being human imposes on us."[123] Like Howe (and Bellow), Alfred Kazin had long since lost patience with the strident demands of youthful radicals, having witnessed them in his own son, who at the time led a particularly militant wing of SDS at Harvard before graduating to a brief career with the even more violent and nihilistic Weathermen.[124] But still he would not go so far as his old friend Bellow with his "Jewish passion for ideological moralism."[125] *Mr. Sammler's Planet* suffered from too many "dismissive jeremiads" resting on a new "moral haughtiness" in Bellow's work.[126] Kazin found "so strong a sense of physical disgust with all one's distended, mad-eyed, pushing neighbors on the West Side that there seems nothing in the book to love but certain past opinions."[127]

Bellow's journey continued with the masterful *Humboldt's Gift* (1975). The novel is the story of Charlie Citrine and Von Humboldt Fleisher, Humboldt a talented but reckless man, and Citrine a wealthy but dissatisfied intellectual who wonders: "What kind of a writer or intellectual makes that kind of dough?"[128] Indeed, the book's inspiration, the poet Delmore Schwartz, died a pauper in the "seedy Hotel Marlton on West Eighth Street, where he lived in virtual isolation" and descended into paranoia and mental illness.[129] The conversations between Humboldt and Citrine, who appears to stand in for Bellow himself, turn on the loss of youthful enthusiasm for art, literature, and the commitments of one's youth. "Those were intoxicating books," Citrine avers, with reference to Wilde and Marx—"and I was in the thick of beauty and wild about goodness and thought and poetry and love. Wasn't that merely adolescence?"[130]

It took the 1972 election to lay bare all of the divisions that had long been tearing the Democratic Party apart and leaving postwar liberalism in tatters.

Owing to the McGovern commission's new rules, primaries became the most common means by which states picked their candidates, nearly doubling the number of delegates so chosen in just four years.[131] The early frontrunner was Maine's Edmund Muskie, who had been Hubert Humphrey's vice presidential choice four years earlier and a leader in the emerging environmental movement. But Muskie faltered and was almost beaten by the much better organized McGovern campaign in that January's New Hampshire primary, where a "radical" from South Dakota had no business nearly defeating a moderate from Maine.[132]

Hubert Humphrey and Henry "Scoop" Jackson ran to Muskie's right, but the former vice president, now a senator again, suffered from being, well, Hubert Humphrey. As Pete Hamill described him, there "was a time when [he was] a reasonably brave liberal politician, but he lost that somewhere along the line. It's possible to salute the record of his youth: all whores were once virgins. In the unlikely event that there were War Crimes trials in this country, Humphrey would be in the dock."[133] "Gonzo" journalist Hunter S. Thompson, writing in the counterculture bible, *Rolling Stone,* called Humphrey "a treacherous, gutless old ward-heeler who should be put in a goddamn bottle and sent out with the Japanese Current."[134] Humphrey ran a hapless race, and Jackson, the most hawkish candidate and the neocon favorite, didn't show well anywhere. This was surprising because, as the ex-Nixon staffer Richard Whalen pointed out, Jackson stood "where the majority of the voters presumably stand, somewhat to the right on social issues, to the left on economic issues and, withal, astride the commanding center of American politics."[135] Though both Jackson and Humphrey fared poorly, they did succeed in weakening McGovern for the November election, attacking him as conservatives attacked liberals: soft on America's enemies and indulgent toward minorities, criminals, and drug dealers.

McGovern's young staff worked until exhaustion set in and pushed their candidate to frontrunner status, helped by luck and timing. But his was in many respects a pyrrhic victory, as the party over which he emerged victorious was effectively split, with its more conservative and establishment-oriented members sticking to the "Anybody but McGovern" movement that had failed to slow the juggernaut on its way to Miami.

"The streets of '68 are the aisles of '72!" was the delegates' chant that year among New Leftists.[136] New Politics and party reform had worked their wonders. While in 1968 women constituted 13 percent of delegates, in 1972 they were 40 percent.[137] Just as important was the fact that old-fashioned political bosses and their minions had been successfully kept away. The delegation from Illinois led by Mayor Daley was rejected for its dearth of women and younger members and replaced by one led by Jesse Jackson.[138] Of the New York delegation, AFL-CIO president George Meany reportedly complained, "They've got six open fags and only three AFL-CIO representatives!"[139]

Gloria Steinem fought hard to ensure that the party would adopt a proabortion plank. It didn't fly, however, as McGovern personally opposed it. Steinem was devastated, complaining, "McGovern had first inspired hope, and then waffled. . . . Not having the gut instinct on this issue that he does on the war or the economy."[140] Soon Nora Ephron found her sobbing in the lobby of McGovern's hotel. "They won't take us seriously," Steinem cried. "And I'm just tired of being screwed, and being screwed by my friends. By George McGovern, whom I raised half the money for in his first campaign, wrote his speeches. . . . He just doesn't understand."[141]

Steinem's disillusionment suggested more than just an idealistic young woman's first experience with the politics of the real world. Rather it demonstrated that the component elements of the new Democratic Party—based largely on the self-defined identities of its constituents—could not easily accept compromise. McGovern was as liberal a candidate as any major party had ever nominated, and much of the political world viewed him as overly beholden to activists and impractical idealists. When Evans and Novak quoted an anonymous Democratic Senate colleague—later revealed to be none other than Thomas Eagleton—calling McGovern the candidate of "the triple As: acid, amnesty and abortion"—the description clung to the campaign like a bloodstain on a white suit.[142]

McGovern gave a magnificent acceptance speech, but almost nobody saw it, as the chaotic convention could not be brought to order, and it was ultimately delivered at 2:45 a.m., long after its television audience had gone to bed. Almost all that was remembered of it were the words "Come home, America," which even in the age of declining support for military adventures and the Vietnam War, would prove a decidedly double-edged sword.[143] Worse still, just a few days after the convention came the "Eagleton affair." What no one was aware of at the time was that in addition to his authorship of the awful "Triple As" quote—something that was not revealed for more than thirty years—Eagleton had as a young man undergone electroshock therapy for depression.[144] McGovern's inability to make up his mind about his running mate sunk his candidacy even lower. At first he affirmed that he was "1,000 percent" behind Eagleton, but soon changed his mind and decided to dump him.[145] He finally settled on Sargent Shriver as a kind of stand-in for a real Kennedy. Teddy White declared McGovern's reputation "as a politician somehow different from the ordinary—a politician who could not, like others, do *anything* to get elected" to be lost forever.[146]

In a move that would have been unthinkable with respect to any previous Democrat, the AFL-CIO, under its hawkish president, George Meany, refused to endorse the profoundly pro-labor McGovern.[147] An internal AFL-CIO memo suggested that the leaders' primary motivation was to "regain control of the machinery after the election."[148] When Meany rather ostentatiously golfed with Richard Nixon shortly after the convention ended, he spent the entire afternoon, according to Bob Haldeman's diary, expressing "real hatred" for the Democratic nominee.[149] But Meany and the union's bigwigs did not get any protest from their membership over the snub, as cultural politics—particularly racial politics—trumped economic self-interest for the white working class. At issue, as Evans and Novak put it, was "the gap between what really bothers the working man and what the McGovern liberals think bothers him."[150]

Come Election Day, McGovern carried only Massachusetts and the District of Columbia. Nixon's 1972 victory brought to fruition the "Republican majority" forecasted by Kevin Phillips three years earlier[151] and confirmed the growing sense among white working-class ethnics, the backbone of liberalism in the New Deal and Fair Deal eras, that their movement had been captured by the longhairs, shiftless minority welfare cheats, and bra-burning feminists. By almost any standard, it was a political upheaval that shattered what remained of the foundations of American liberalism and one whose aftershocks would continue to reverberate for decades to come.

13

Maximum Feasible Misunderstanding

> The great liberal failing of this time is constantly to over-promise and
> to overstate, and thereby constantly to appear to under-perform.
> —Daniel Patrick Moynihan, 1968[1]

> I didn't think a thousand vibrators would make much difference.
> —Betty Friedan, 1976[2]

Following the debacle of the 1972 election, a group of disaffected Democratic hawks formed the Coalition for a Democratic Majority (CDM).[3]
Scoop Jackson was the titular head, but Midge Decter, wife to Norman Podhoretz, did most of the recruitment. The organization's founders—which
included labor leaders, senators and congressmen from southern and midwestern states, and a smattering of New York intellectuals, including (now
Senator) Daniel Patrick Moynihan, Irving Kristol, Nathan Glazer, and Seymour Lipset—claimed a return to "the traditions of FDR, Truman, and Kennedy" and a "strong American role in the world."[4] A commitment to Cold War
liberal internationalism ran counter to the spirit of the times, to say the least.
Liberals such as Frank Church of Idaho and Clifford Case of New Jersey were
pulling liberalism in the opposite direction, proposing in 1973 "an amendment
forbidding the use of any American forces 'in or over' Indochina, stripping
away the guarantee of American air support if South Vietnam were attacked
again."[5]

Liberalism had by now become a house of many mansions. A countercul-
ture-inflected New Politics version faced off against the working-class ethnic
coalition, both of which were increasingly identified with an uncompromising
form of identity politics that turned the entire enterprise into a never-ending
zero-sum ethnic, racial, gender, and cultural war often driven by mutual fear
and loathing. Anticommunism was no longer a vital concern. While many
ex–New Leftists gave up on revolution and sought, instead, more personal

forms of liberation, they left a void previously occupied by collective organizing, idealism, and a willingness to ask questions of conventional wisdom that had for too long gone unchallenged and become outdated. The center would not only fail to hold; it would, for most practical purposes, disappear entirely.

In many respects the distinguished historian Gertrude Himmelfarb was right when she told her husband, Irving Kristol, "Yesterday's liberalism is today's conservatism."[6] And no one's career demonstrated how distant yesterday's liberalism had become from that of the 1970s than the career of Bella Abzug. She was born Bella Savitsky in 1920 in New York City to a family of deeply politicized immigrant Russian Jews. Her father died when Abzug was still in high school, and she marched into the synagogue and said the Kaddish prayer as if she had been his son rather than his daughter.[7] Committed to politics her entire life, she was initially drawn to both socialism and Zionism as a teenager and joined the Hashomer Hatzair ("Young Watchman") youth group, which idealistically, albeit unrealistically, supported the creation of a binational state in Palestine, rather than the Jewish state that came into being following the 1948 UN partition.[8] After high school in the Bronx, Abzug entered CUNY's Hunter College and then Columbia Law School, as Harvard was still refusing to accept women. She met a young writer named Martin Abzug on a bus trip to a Yehudi Menuhin concert to raise funds for Soviet war relief. Abzug passed the bar exam in 1947 and began practicing civil liberties law, which was unusual for non-Communist lawyers at the time, as well as civil rights and labor law. While pregnant, she traveled to Mississippi to defend Willie McGee, a black man sentenced to death after being falsely accused of raping a white woman. When she was negotiating for the Mine, Mill and Smelters Workers Union, a representative saw her and screamed, "You're sending us some fucking secretary? To handle this?"[9]

Abzug entered national politics not via elected office but by helping to establish one of the most important peace organizations prior to the Vietnam War, Women Strike for Peace (WSP), founded in 1961. The group supported JFK's test ban proposals in 1963, but it called for more sweeping disarmament moves before morphing into an anti–Vietnam War organization. But Abzug's experience at WSP left her hungry for a larger stage, and she used her movement bona fides to enter electoral politics, running for Congress in 1970 on Manhattan's liberal West Side on the slogan "This woman's place is in the House, the House of Representatives."[10] Her role, she explained, "is among the people, and I am going to be *outside* organizing them at the same time that I'm *inside* fighting for them."[11] Promising to fight for "an end to militarism and domination of our society by the corporate power structure," she became the darling of the Hollywood left, particularly its most closely feminist-identified component, a group that included Barbra Streisand, Shirley MacLaine, Lily Tomlin together with the New Yorkers Mary Travers and Gloria Steinem.[12] Abzug was also among the first-ever congressional candidates to seek and receive the support of the gay community, though this was perhaps a surprise to her. A campaign worker, Doug Ireland, had her go to Fire Island and some gay bars. Abzug called him from the Continental Baths (where Bette Midler got her start) in a fury, demanding, "You cretin. What have you done to me? I'm up here in these fucking baths—filled with guys in towels held up by Bella buttons, and some are only wearing the buttons and not the towels!"[13] When accused by her opponent, the holdover Tammany Democrat Leonard Farb-stein, of opposing the sale of sophisticated fighter jets to Israel, she denied the charge, which would have been political poison among New York Jews, though until he made the charge, it had been accurate. ("Lennie, this is one Jew you're not going to out-Jew." she warned him.) She eked out a victory despite daily protests from the Jewish Defense League, whose members chanted outside her offices, "Israel, Yes. Bella, No" and "A vote for Bella is a vote for Communism."[14]

Once elected, Abzug had little concern for the politics of civility. She saw the House of Representatives as "a male, white, middle-aged, middle- and upper-class power elite that stand with their backs turned to the needs and demands of our people," and was determined, in the words of one of her early interns, "to rock the timbers of the institution."[15] Asked by a guard to remove her trademark large floppy hat upon entering the chamber for the first time, she replied, with a voice that Norman Mailer once described as able "to boil the fat off a taxi driver's neck," that she would prefer instead that the gentle-man "go fuck himself."[16] During her first term, she agitated for the Privacy Act and to strengthen the Freedom of Information Act. She fought for the Equal Credit Opportunity Act, passed in 1974, to forbid discrimination on nonfinancial grounds. A year later she tried to persuade her colleagues to ex-tend the 1964 Civil Rights Act to gays, a notion that nearly half a century later appears to have been ahead of its time. Alas, she also called on the Speaker of the House, Carl Albert, to resign, owing to his refusal to calendar a resolution against the war. Her office received a call from his chief of staff explaining that "the congresswoman has not only written her death certificate, she has signed it, too."[17] One researcher who worked for Ralph Nader calculated that Abzug's sponsorship of any piece of legislation was likely to cost it between twenty and thirty votes.[18]

Following an unfavorable redistricting in 1970—Abzug's enemies in New York politics outnumbered her friends by a considerable margin—she lost a bitter 1972 primary against the beloved liberal Democrat William Fitts Ryan. "No wonder [the radical black Oakland congressman] Ron Dellums called her a 'white elite motherfucker,'" a Ryan constituent wrote in a letter published in *The Village Voice*. "Too bad she sees Bill Ryan as the nigger of Manhattan."[19] When Ryan succumbed to cancer, however, she defeated his widow in a special election and resumed her many crusades.

Daniel Patrick Moynihan was seven years younger than Bella Abzug, but he cultivated an impression of seniority and sagacity that somehow combined the professorial style of an Oxford don with that of an Irish barroom brawler. Raised in Tulsa, Oklahoma, and then New York City, Moynihan energetically romanticized his not especially deprived upbringing. Ultimately, most journalists gave up attempting to correct the record and when it came to Moynihan, they decided, in the director John Ford's words, simply to "print the legend." Moynihan, after all, did put in some time as a stevedore.[20]

Born lower middle class, Moynihan had an alcoholic father who deserted the family and disappeared. The experience of downward social mobility turned him into an exquisitely class-conscious politician. Settled on Manhattan's Upper West Side as a teenager, he chose to attend Benjamin Franklin High School all the way across town, where he graduated first in his class. Over the years Moynihan recounted his decision to go to City College after graduation as a kind of freak accident. "I didn't know what a college was," he told one interviewer. He took the entrance test, he said, only to prove he was "as smart as I thought I was."

After Moynihan's first year of college the Navy sent him to Middlebury College and later to Tufts, in Medford, Massachusetts, where he remained a directionless and potentially explosive combination of street fighter and belletrist. After graduation Moynihan continued to drift, at one point riding boxcars home from Montana after being fired from a job clearing brush for the Hungry Horse Dam, where he had labored for exactly one day. Soon afterward, however, in 1950, he returned to academia with a Fulbright Fellowship to study government at the London School of Economics, where he fell in love with British political history, traded his bar apron for some Saville Row suits, and held famously boisterous parties at his apartment. Moynihan would eventually complete his doctoral degree in international relations at Syracuse University, but first he returned to New York to work in politics, initially for the Tilden Democratic Club and the then-governor Averell Harriman. Moynihan also began to publish his political musings in the Cold War liberal magazine *The Reporter,* and grew friendly with a number of the New York intellectuals who also contributed to it.

In 1961, Moynihan landed in the Department of Labor, where he authored the chapter on Irish Americans in Nathan Glazer's immigration study, *Beyond the Melting Pot.* But his most significant accomplishment was the Community Mental Health Centers Construction Act, which happened to be the last bill ever signed by President Kennedy. The legislation called for the deinstitution-alization of the mentally ill across America and the treatment of them instead in as-yet-unbuilt community mental health centers. Mental hospitals across the country were soon emptied, and the new, more "humane" approach was attempted. As Moynihan later noted, however, fewer than one-fifth of the promised centers actually were built before the problem was forgotten: "The Vietnam War came, the war on poverty came, and we went off." Eventually, he explained, "the problem of the homeless appeared. . . . So how does that problem get defined? A lack of affordable housing. That is my idea of a prob-lem poorly defined."[21]

It was as assistant secretary of labor in the Johnson administration that Moynihan first came to public attention in an episode that would scar him for the rest of his life. In March 1965 he authored the infamous *The Negro Family: The Case for National Action,* popularly known as "The Moynihan Report." In it he focused on the problem of exploding rates of illegitimacy in black families. Little was known by sociologists at the time about the structure of African American families, and while Moynihan was not much of a scholar, and had no background in academic sociology whatsoever, he considered himself to be a pretty quick study when it came to deploying the research of others for political purposes. But in this case, he had no choice but to rely on studies produced a generation earlier, particularly *The Negro Family in the United States* by sociologist E. Franklin Frazier, which was published in 1939 but was largely based on his doctoral dissertation, published in 1932, together with that of historian Stanley Elkins, whose work emphasized the legacy of slavery. (His classic study was *Slavery: A Problem in American Institutional and Intellectual Life* [1959].[22]) Moynihan argued that "by destroying the Negro fam-ily under slavery . . . white America broke the will of the Negro people," and so "the principal challenge of the next phase of the Negro revolution is to make certain that equality of results will now follow. If we do not, there will be no social peace in the United States for generations."[23] By focusing on the black family, Moynihan sought to address a problem he had diagnosed in a memo he sent to the secretary of labor in May 1964 in which he described the crisis befalling black America. Noting that half the recipients of Aid to Families with Dependent Children were black, and in New York City "17 percent of the city's Negroes receive public relief"—a figure that had risen 73 percent in just seven years—Moynihan worried about the creation of what he termed "an entire subculture of dependency, alienation and despair." He insisted that what was needed instead was to give "the men proper jobs and a respectable place in their community and family" before these communities disintegrated to the point where they resembled the unhappy examples of rural Appalachia or most American Indian reservations.[24] Moynihan proposed a remarkably ambitious (and expensive) program to improve "the stability and resources of the Negro American family," which included jobs programs, housing programs, birth control assistance, and what we now know as affirmative action.[25]

Moynihan's report stirred up a furious reaction from critics on the left, who proved less interested in debating the problem than in psychoanalyzing the report's author, and in doing so, missed a historic opportunity to focus the nation's attention on the needs of its most disadvantaged citizens. Writing in *The Nation* William Ryan, a white psychologist, dismissed Moynihan's analysis as a "highly sophomoric treatment of illegitimacy" and accused its author of "blaming the victim," particularly young unwed black mothers.[26] The charge was unfair, as the report clearly laid the blame on patterns of historical discrimination, but Ryan's critique proved consistent with the increasingly popular cry on the left for a separatist Black Power movement rather than one based on civil rights and integration.[27] One hundred black civil rights and religious leaders signed a resolution demanding that "the question of 'family stability' be stricken" from the agenda of the scheduled White House conference designed to deal with issues of race and poverty.[28] As the vilified Moynihan became a political poster boy for white paternalism—apparently no less an offense than outright racism in the minds of his critics—the administration quickly disowned both the report and its author, who resigned in disgrace, exiling himself back to New York. "I can never be usefully involved in those matters that I had been involved in," Moynihan said. "It won't ever be forgiven; that's all there is to it," he worried at the time, albeit as the most famous, if notorious, assistant secretary of labor in American history.[29] Eventually the issue of black illegitimacy and underachievement was appropriated by conservatives, initially for the purposes of punishment and later in the pseudoscientific work of right-wing social scientist Charles Murray, to revive the discredited arguments for the alleged intellectual inferiority of the black race.[30]

Moynihan went on to lose a race for the presidency of the New York City Council, looking very much like a cautionary tale for any liberal who might have thought to confront the complex web of political and intellectual en-tanglements eating away at America's black families and black communities. The future senator's sensitivity to insult was such that he became, for a time, one of the most effective and eloquent enemies of liberalism in America, all the while remaining a liberal himself.[31]

Moynihan attempted to find a refuge for himself in academia, first at Wes-leyan University and then as director of the Harvard/MIT Joint Center for Urban Studies, and was granted tenure at Harvard's Graduate School of Education.[32] But he lacked the patience to do meaningful academic research and yearned to return to the political arena, refusing to allow his own feelings of liberal betrayal to deter him from seeking to ameliorate the catastrophe he predicted in his ill-fated report. He correctly adduced that while "the civil rights movement has been immensely successful in creating a national con-sensus about upholding the legal rights of Negroes in the South," it had failed with regard to "the problems of class in the North. Barring massive action on these problems, it was likely that the existing civil rights consensus would begin to crumble as lower-class urban Negroes grew more restless, violent and demanding." Moynihan was deeply critical of "most liberal Democrats"—a category in which he still included himself—for enjoying "little contact and less sympathy for the intense moralisms of conservative Catholic and Protes-tant religion [that however clumsily] . . . maintain standards of family stability that most of us would regard as eminently sane."[33] A commitment to family stability, he suggested, would benefit black Americans well beyond their pro-portionate numbers while at the same time appeal to the conservative cultural values of these communities—most of whom, it should be noted, remained, quite tenuously, in the liberal Democratic coalition. Instead, the administration had chosen to adopt the language "maximum feasible participation" as a sop to academics, poverty-program bureaucrats, and editorial writers rather than the people who were themselves in need.[34]

Moynihan's language grew increasingly confrontational vis-à-vis the direc-tion taken by American liberals, and in a speech to ADA in September 1967 he attacked "ultraliberals" and urged ADA members to "seek out and make much more effective alliances with political conservatives."[35] Again, with a fair claim to the mantle of political prophecy, Moynihan warned:

> Liberals must see more clearly that their essential interest is in the sta-
>   bility of the social order; given the present threats to that stability,
>   they must seek out and make effective alliances with political con-
>   servatives who share their interests and recognize that unyielding

rigidity is just as great a threat to continuity of the social order as an anarchic desire for change.

Liberals must divest themselves of the idea that the nation—and especially its cities—can be run from agencies in Washington.

Liberals must somehow overcome the curious condescension that takes the form of defending and explaining away everything, however violent or unlawful, that Negroes, individually or collectively, might do.[36]

Such arguments could not but capture the attention of the men around Richard Nixon who were looking to recruit Democrats to their cause, the more liberal they might once have been, the better. Though he had made it clear to the president that he was still a liberal Democrat who opposed the Vietnam War, Moynihan entered the White House in 1969 as counselor to the president for urban affairs. Responding to those who viewed Nixon as the devil incarnate, Moynihan borrowed from Benjamin Disraeli's argument that "Tory men" might be the best source for "Whig measures."[37]

Initially it appeared as if his gamble might pay off. Moynihan persuaded Nixon to support his Family Assistance Plan (FAP), which would have supplied a "guaranteed income" for families living in poverty—and again, would benefit blacks disproportionately without immediately appearing to do so. With characteristic modesty Moynihan labeled it "the most startling proposal to help poor persons ever made by a modern democratic government."[38] FAP appealed to Nixon because it would gut Great Society programs and their associated bureaucracies and simply transfer funds to the poor. Though the measure managed to pass the House of Representatives in April 1970, it died in the Senate Finance Committee, owing to both the frightening costs that conservatives had predicted as well as to the decidedly lukewarm support a divided Nixon administration offered on its behalf.[39]

Fancying himself a kind of domestic analogue to Nixon's national security adviser, Henry Kissinger, Moynihan sent a steady stream of unsolicited memos to the president. In January 1970 he wrote up a report on the status of black Americans for Nixon in which he advised, "The time may have come when the issue of race could benefit from a period of 'benign neglect.' The subject has been too much talked about. The forum has been too much taken over by hysterics, paranoids and boodlers on all sides. We may need a period in which Negro progress continues and racial rhetoric fades."[40] This was not an argument for ignoring the demands of African Americans but a suggestion that progress was best made without the racially divisive discussions that inevitably accompanied the issue whenever it seized public attention. In time, it would become the position of the "New Democrats" who succeeded in capturing the party in the generation of Bill Clinton and Al Gore. But in the meantime, the phrase "benign neglect" was taken out of context and reignited the controversy that had begun with his "Negro Family" memo.

Moynihan's already precarious tenure in the Nixon administration now became even more so, and much as he hated the counterculture and the leftist intellectuals who indulged it, he was not particularly at home among Republicans. In 1971 he decided to return to Harvard, again licking his wounds as he prepared for yet another assault on the Protestant establishment he both loathed and deeply envied.

For most men, even most men of such powerful ambition, two such public failures and personal humiliations would mean the end of their political career. But Pat Moynihan's life in American politics had only just begun. Nixon rerecruited him, this time as his ambassador to India, where he thrived amid the pomp and ceremony. Gerald Ford then appointed him to be America's ambassador to the United Nations, where he found the job that providence appeared to have had in mind for him. Moynihan had turned down the job when Nixon offered it in 1970, but having since spent a number of years in the Third World and having been subjected to all manner of lectures by leaders of nondemocratic regimes who spoke scornfully of the "bourgeois" freedoms enjoyed by liberal democracies like the United States, Moynihan could not wait to return to his street-fighter self, this time with a global audience for his antileftist musings and missives.

Once ensconced at the UN, Moynihan picked fights with virtually every tin-pot dictator he could find. He called Idi Amin a "racist murderer" and announced that "the abomination of anti-Semitism has been given the appearance of international sanction" when the General Assembly passed its infamous resolution equating Zionism with racism.[41] Also—conveniently for someone considering higher elective office in New York State—Moynihan championed Scoop Jackson's favorite cause: that of persecuted Soviet Jewry. Because this cause was inconsistent with the détente-driven policies of Nixon, Ford, and Kissinger, Moynihan again found himself out of a job within eight months. But New York, the second capital of world Jewry and still first of American liberalism, was to have an election that November 1976, in which whoever won the Democratic primary was all but sure to enter "the world's greatest deliberative body."

Moynihan faced three challengers from the left in the form of the old-fashioned machine pol Paul O'Dwyer; the ex-attorney general Ramsey Clark, who was on his way to the leftward fringes of American politics; and feminist icon and avatar of New Left liberalism, Bella Abzug. The contest soon became a skirmish between two opposing styles of liberalism: his and hers. Abzug tried to paint Moynihan as a racist, a chauvinist, and a turncoat to the liberal cause, rarely failing to mention the "benign neglect" phrase that she purposely took out of context. The most significant blow to Abzug's campaign came from *The New York Times,* whose publisher, Arthur Sulzberger, insisted on overruling his Abzug-supporting editorial board to ensure an endorsement of Moynihan. The paper's rapturous vote of confidence termed him "a rambunctious child of the sidewalks of New York, profound student and teacher of social affairs, aggressive debater, outrageous flatterer, shrewd adviser—indeed manipulator—of Presidents, accomplished diplomat and heartfelt friend of the poor—poor people, poor cities, poor regions such as ours."[42] Moynihan bested Abzug by barely 10,000 votes and the incumbent, James L. Buckley, the Republican-Conservative who had squeaked in when two liberals faced off against each other six years earlier, by a landslide.

With that loss, Bella Abzug decided she would actually make a good New York City mayor. The 1977 race saw her facing off against the old-fashioned liberal Jewish incumbent Abe Beame; Harlem clubhouse politician Percy Sutton; a liberal Queens lawyer, Mario Cuomo; and Ed Koch, a staunch Greenwich Village reformist liberal who had lately been moving rightward with the times. Koch called for an end to forced busing, embraced the death penalty, tended to blame black people for the threats they faced when moving into white ethnic neighborhoods, and attacked the teachers' unions. Despite his support for abortion rights, the legalization of marijuana, and gay rights in this Democratic city, he became the de facto conservative candidate.[43] In 1976 seventy-five felonies were being committed every hour in New York, making it the worst crime year in the city's history and effectively the only issue in the contest—underscored, as always, by race.

The primary remained contested by all four candidates, but it was definitely Koch who caught the spirit of the moment. Though Abzug had entered the race as the favorite, New York City had changed faster than she could. "She thought the city was out of control," her press secretary, Harold Holzer, later recalled. "She thought it was beyond our control to remind people of what Lincoln would call 'the better angels of our nature,' to remind them of possibilities, to remind them that harmony was more important than punitiveness. God knows it was impossible to say that people who pillaged in some pathetic effort to express anger should be pitied almost as much as punished. There was no way to get through the mood, between the murders and the heat and the blackout looting."[44] Koch, meanwhile, proceeded, in the words of his biographer, Jonathan Soffer, to "convince most New Yorkers of the legitimacy of the new neoliberal order that subsidized Manhattan business development, particularly in the finance, insurance, and real estate sectors, privatized public space, and created huge income inequalities."[45]

As for Pat Moynihan, the neocons had become so heavily invested in him as their savior—and that of their country—that some among them immediately began planning for the next step: a presidential candidacy, a somewhat comical prospect given Moynihan's heterodox politics, unique speaking style, lack of a common political touch, and fondness for self-medication. Nevertheless, one night at the senator's farm upstate, in Oneonta, New York, according to a witness, Norman Podhoretz and Midge Decter could be found pinning Moynihan's wife and political manager, Liz Moynihan, to the wall, grabbing her arms and screaming, "You're standing in the way of this man becoming president! It's you, it's you, it's you!" (Podhoretz denies the incident; screaming, he explained, "is not my style," though it should be noted that both Podhoretz's mentor, Lionel Trilling, and Sidney Hook had been, apparently, on the receiving end of similarly extravagant performances around the same time.[46]) Such splits over politics and policy were frequently characteristic of the neoconservative movement from its beginnnings, as some of its members had more grandiose dreams than others, to say nothing of the political differences between the hard-liners (Podhoretz and Kristol) who were en route to becoming right-wing Republicans, and the soft-liners (Bell and Glazer) who remained, uneasily, in the liberal Democratic fold. Diana Trilling recalls the last presidential choice that her husband would make before his 1975 passing: Gertrude Himmelfarb "phoned to ask whether we would give our names to an ad in the *New York Times* for Nixon in the '72 presidential election. . . . I had much criticism of McGovern but I wouldn't dream of giving my name to Nixon, and neither would Lionel. . . ."[47] This was at a time when, as Kristol slyly noted, that voting for Nixon among this crowd was "the equivalent of a Jew ostentatiously eating pork on Yom Kippur."[48]

Trilling's refusal to follow his students' journey into neoconservatism would prove an important deterrent to many other intellectuals of the period, given the influence he retained over the New York intellectuals for decades after his passing. And Moynihan's decision to double back into the liberal fold following the election of the conservative Republican president, Ronald Reagan, would provide them with an important ballast in the storm.

If civil rights for African Americans dominated the liberal agenda during the 1960s, then the demand for gender equality would prove to be the primary focus in the following decade. Though it would appear a relatively straightforward leap of logic to ban discrimination on the basis of gender no less than race, feminist demands prompted tricky debates not just about the relations between men and women, but about socioeconomic class, the status of the family, abortion, and the entire question of "rights" themselves.

An Equal Rights Amendment (ERA) was originally proposed following the passage of the Nineteenth Amendment in 1920, which gave women the right to vote. At the time, "social feminists," such as Jane Addams, fought against this early ERA proposal as a threat to Progressive legislation that had granted women and children special status protected by certain laws and regulations. After its initial defeat the amendment was proposed again in 1943, and in 1946 it advanced to the Senate Judicial Committee, where it won approval. This time, however, Eleanor Roosevelt opposed it on grounds similar to those of Addams, and it died there.[49] By the early 1970s, however, its proponents had reason for optimism, as there was support for the legislation in Congress on both sides of the aisle, and public opinion polling showed a majority of Americans in favor.[50]

The amendment was clearly and simply written: "Equality of rights under the law shall not be denied or abridged by the United States, or by any State, on account of sex."[51] It sailed through Congress—84 to 8 in the Senate and 354 to 23 in the House[52]—and by March 1972 it was readied for state approval. The day it was sent out, the ERA was ratified by Hawaii; two days later Delaware, Nebraska, New Hampshire, Idaho, and Iowa approved it.[53]

The amendment's support, like the women's movement itself, was composed of well-educated, well-off women who were coming to dominate the Democratic grass roots. But opposition emerged within liberalism, and it echoed the objections of Addams and Roosevelt: some union women wanted to "extend protective legislation to men" rather than end it for women.[54] They were joined by culturally conservative working-class Americans who began to worry about the changes in everyday life the amendment might bring.[55] Nonratifying states were largely located in the (increasingly Republican) South or mountain states with significant Mormon populations.[56] North Dakota would be the last state to ratify the ERA in January 1975, and the amendment died with just 35 of the 38 necessary states having voted for it.

Ultimately, the amendment's political significance probably lay in the opposition it helped galvanize. The conservative activist who led the effort, Phyllis Schlafly, turned out to be a kind of Saul Alinksy of the right—she possesses a similar genius for organizating populist political campaigns. She started her effort against the ERA early, on July 7, 1972, recruiting supporters of her "STOP

ERA" organization from those who believed in "traditional religion" and the honor of homemaking.[57] Schlafly argued that the ERA threatened the traditional family and was a "big grab for vast new federal power."[58] Her tactics included arguing that the amendment's passage would lead to "unisex toilets" and would require women to provide 50 percent of the financial support of their family.[59] Most significant, she got her supporters to pound the pavement, to walk the halls of state legislatures and thereby establish the basis for a revival of morality-based right-wing activism everywhere she went. STOP ERA organizers sent out volunteers by the bus and carload every week to lobby state legislators across America to vote against the ERA. "Neatly dressed teenage daughters with scrubbed faces and frilly blouses cried, 'Please don't draft me,'" according to one newspaper report, "while their mothers carried signs reading 'Send the Libbers to Siberia. We'll Stay Home and Keep the Beds Warm.'"[60] President Carter would extend the period of time for ratification, but by 1976 the cause seemed dead, and by 1982 the battle had been lost.[61]

In many respects, however, the more significant development for feminists was 1973's *Roe v. Wade* Supreme Court decision. The case centered on Norma McCorvey, a high school dropout living in Texas who needed an abortion but could not get one legally where she lived. McCorvey was discovered by two recent University of Texas law graduates, Sarah Weddington and Linda Coffee, while they were searching for a case to challenge abortion limitations. McCorvey adopted the name Jane Roe for anonymity, and her two feminist lawyers challenged the attorney general of Texas, Henry Wade. And so, in late 1971, *Roe v. Wade* began its progression through the courts.[62]

The Supreme Court decision built upon a long line of liberal reasoning beginning with William O. Douglas's arguments for the right to privacy (which itself grew out of Isaiah Berlin's notion of "negative liberty"). Douglas's conception of "penumbras" found in the Constitution had been the basis for asserting the right to contraception in *Griswold v. Connecticut* less than ten years earlier.[63] Now the same principle would be applied to abortion. Justice Harry Blackmun, appointed by Richard Nixon in 1970, cited the work of doctors to establish the period before the end of the first trimester as safe and protected by law.[64]

Feminists like Gloria Steinem rejoiced at the news, but perhaps what the decision best illustrated was the degree to which liberals' cultural victories would be won in the courts rather than in voting booths, thereby inspiring backlashes against them and the courts that had ruled on them, wherever they took place. For many people, *Roe* implied allowing recreational/nonprocreational sex, which they linked to other changes in the culture that further fueled the antiliberal backlash. Rising divorce rates and the increased availability of pornography—especially its permeation of the larger culture through increasingly explicit movies and magazines such as *Playboy, Penthouse,* and the much raunchier *Hustler*—turned millions of economic liberals into cultural conservatives.

Undoubtedly, the loosening of sexual ethics, and simply suggesting that women experienced sexual pleasure as much as men, constituted a cultural victory for liberalism. The Germaine Greer style of feminism concerned itself less with equal access to education or professional advancement than with orgasms, while Erica Jong's 1973 *Fear of Flying* celebrated the fantasy of the "zipless fuck," one based on anonymity and lack of commitment.[65] But such sexual liberties also presented a danger in crudely equating individual pleasure with liberation. The ERA's failure provided sufficient warning about a general popular uneasiness with the side effects of the sexual revolution and the difficulty of politically legislated and/or judicially mandated cultural change. It also created a whipping boy for conservative critics who suggested that liberalism, when it moved into cultural territory, was little more than mindless tolerance and permissiveness, ready to embrace a "zipless fuck" in virtually every aspect of public life.[66]

The myriad complications and conundrums facing the man charged with simultaneously renewing the promise of JFK's Camelot and RFK's idealism—Edward Moore "Ted" Kennedy—demonstrated just how many different faces liberalism wore during the 1970s. The last surviving Kennedy brother sought to locate a liberal ethic that could unite the Boston working class with the "Harvards" like himself, as his brother Bobby had tried so mightily to do with his coalition of ethnic blue-collar workers, blacks, farmworkers, and young people in 1968. But Teddy came of age in a time when being a Kennedy, with all the privileges and burdens it implied, had become a much less enviable enterprise.

The youngest son of Rose and Joseph Kennedy was born in February 1932, his parents' ninth child. President Hoover sent his mother flowers when he was born, together with a note that was delivered with five cents postage due. He received his first communion five years later from the pope.[67] He received little attention from his parents, both of whom had become pretty much tired of raising children by that time. Teddy had trouble fitting in anywhere and passed a lonely and frequently solitary childhood, a period during which Joe Kennedy moved his family among various properties in Bronxville, Hyannis Port, Palm Beach, and the Court of St. James, where he was FDR's ambassador.

Teddy had attended ten different schools by the age of eleven, before finally finishing at Milton Academy. It was not an "education," he recalled in his memoir, "it was a battle."

To his lasting regret, Teddy, who was largely focused on football in college, made what he called in his memoir "an immature, spontaneous, extremely poor and wrong decision" in the spring of 1951, when he allowed a good friend to take a Spanish test for him during his sophomore year at Harvard.[68] (His father chided him, Evan Thomas noted, "not for moral failure, but for stupidity. 'Don't do this cheating thing; you're not clever enough.'"[69]) He was readmitted to Harvard following a brief stint in the Army, during which his father kept him out of combat in Korea, and then followed Bobby to the University of Virginia Law School. At UVA, Kennedy did not rank highly in his class, but he did win its mock court competition, though his graduation was slightly marred by an arrest for reckless driving and driving without a license.

His first job out of school was to manage—at least officially—John Kennedy's 1958 Senate reelection campaign, and his genial mien and eagerness to connect with voters helped win his brother's record margin, one that set the stage for his next campaign—for the presidency. Following the election, Ted had hoped to stay out west to do something to stand on his own, but the patriarch would have none of it. The family, Joe Kennedy decreed, was to hold on to JFK's Senate seat, and with Bobby preferring running the Justice Department to running for senator, Teddy got the nod. An obscure family retainer named Benjamin Smith was appointed placeholder until Teddy, three years out of law school and working as an assistant district attorney for Suffolk County, turned thirty and was thus legally eligible to run for senator.

The 1962 election was never much in question but yielded plenty of drama nonetheless. When the race began, Kennedy's opponent in the Democratic primary, Eddie McCormack, famously observed, "If his name was Edward Moore, with his qualifications, with your qualifications, Teddy, your candidacy would be a joke, but nobody's laughing because his name is not Edward Moore. It's Edward Moore Kennedy."[70] It was a popular view at the time; even Reinhold Niebuhr called Kennedy's candidacy "an affront to political decency."[71] Another inevitable moment of drama occurred when the story of Ted's involuntary departure from Harvard fell into the hands of the local media. The White House staff stepped into the breach to try to get the story killed, albeit without much success. "Jesus," Jack Kennedy complained, "we're having more fucking trouble with this than we did with the Bay of Pigs." National Security Adviser (and ex-Harvard dean) McGeorge Bundy ruefully added, "Yes, and with just about the same results."[72] Even so, as his longtime friend and chronicler, the late liberal journalist Jack Newfield recalled, "Most pundits saw him as a dummy who had cheated on an exam at Harvard to stay eligible for football and who was dependent on an excellent staff to compensate for his inexperience."[73] Fortunately for Ted, this was not a view that was widely held among voters. On the night after the dramatic debate when McCormack had mocked his candidacy, Kennedy was shaking hands outside a bakery in Boston's North End when a worker stopped to offer some advice. "Ted me boy," he said. "I understand you've never worked a day in your life. [Pause for effect.] You haven't missed a thing."[74]

His early years in the Senate were marked, of course, by tragedy. On November 22, 1963, while Kennedy presided over the Senate—a job usually forced on new members—he learned of his brother's murder in Dallas. With Bobby needed in Washington, Ted had the unhappy task of informing his father that he had lost yet another son. "There's been a bad accident," he explained to the old man, who had been seriously disabled by that time by a significant stroke. "The president has been hurt very badly. As a matter of fact, he died." Then the son dropped to his knees and wept.[75]

On June 19, 1964, Kennedy's private plane crashed in bad weather in an apple orchard in western Massachusetts, killing both the pilot and an aide named Edward Moss. Kennedy was pulled from the wreckage with a punctured lung, broken ribs, internal bleeding, and a severe back injury that would pain him for the rest of his life. It was at this point that the senator decided to catch up on the schooling he had failed to take seriously as a student, engaging various members of the Harvard faculty as his personal tutors. This was also the moment that led to Kennedy's passion for health care reform, one that was redoubled by his son's fight with cancer in the decade to come. Tragedy again struck in 1968 with Bobby's murder during the presidential campaign, a campaign that Teddy had opposed unsuccessfully in discussions with his brother and the family's advisers. Once again he was given the awful task of informing his father of his son's murder.

Though few people would have predicted it at the time, the youngest Kennedy was, as it happened, in the process of building a forty-seven-year career in the United States Senate that would distinguish him in the history books to a degree that few legislators in America could hope to approach and certainly none who would proudly call themselves "liberal." He learned from his first Senate tutor, Phil Hart of Michigan, that the secret to success in the Senate was to invite others to take credit for your work, and Teddy took that lesson to heart. Gregarious by nature, Kennedy also showed a great talent for crossing political and ideological lines to work with virtually anyone, regardless of political views, including irredeemable southern racists in his own party as well as some of the most conservative members of an increasingly conservative Republican Party. Kennedy would, over the course of the next half century, establish himself as among the most effective legislators in the history of the body, and as a man whose legacy would one day be ranked with those of Daniel Webster and Henry Clay. As Newfield notes, from the time he delivered his maiden speech on the floor in support of the Civil Rights Act of 1964, Kennedy could claim to have played a pivotal role in the following:

Two increases in the minimum wage

The Voting Rights Act of 1965

The Twenty-sixth Amendment, 1971, expanding the franchise to eighteen-year-olds

The $24 billion Kennedy-Hatch law of 1997, which provided health insurance to children throught a new tax on tobacco

The 1988 law that allocated $1.2 billion for AIDS testing, treatment, and research

The 1990 Americans with Disabilities Act

The 1993 Family and Medical Leave Act

The 1,200-page Education Reform Act of 2001, which he negotiated directly with President George W. Bush and his staff

Kennedy also helped abolish the poll tax, liberalize immigration laws, fund cancer research, and create the Meals on Wheels program for shut-ins and the elderly. In 1985 he and Republican senator Lowell Weicker cosponsored legislation that imposed economic sanctions on the apartheid government of South Africa, a bill that became law despite opposition from Senate Majority Leader Bob Dole, a filibuster by Senator Jesse Helms, and a veto by President Ronald Reagan. Only Kennedy could have mustered the votes to override by 78 to 21 a veto from Reagan at the height of his power.

Kennedy also organized—and then led like a commando—the successful resistance to Robert Bork's Supreme Court nomination by Reagan in 1987. Kennedy's passionate opposition to Bork helped keep abortion legal in America, for if confirmed, Bork would have provided the fifth vote necessary to repeal *Roe v. Wade*. Instead, Reagan was forced to nominate Anthony Kennedy in Bork's place, and Justice Kennedy has supported the retention of legal abortion as settled precedent.

Kennedy's final achievement—what he called the "cause of [his] life"— came after his death (after, in fact, his Senate seat had been lost to a Republican ex-*Cosmopolitan* centerfold model): the passage of Barack Obama's health care reform plan in 2010. Kennedy had first introduced legislation to achieve this goal in 1970. House Speaker Nancy Pelosi quoted Kennedy at the moment of victory in the House of Representatives, hugging his son Representative Patrick Kennedy. President Obama signed the bill wearing a bracelet in honor of Kennedy at the White House.[76]

Part of the reason Kennedy's diligence as a legislator would have been so hard to foresee in the 1960s was a side of him that would turn out to be no less significant in his public life than his work as a senator. As James Sterling Young, the director of a Kennedy Oral History Project, would observe, "Most people grow up and go into politics. The Kennedys go into politics and then they grow up."[77] A Rabelaisian figure in the Senate, Kennedy could often be found carousing with his colleagues, and females decades younger than himself. According to the journalist Evan Thomas, Kennedy's wife, Joan, was shown a film of her wedding in which his brother, Jack, "who was wearing a microphone, could be heard advising his nervous kid brother not to worry—marriage did not require fidelity."[78] Ted did not require much convincing. His frequent indulgence in his fondness for alcohol and women, with little regard to who was watching or listening, would worsen in the wake of his two brothers' murders, particularly Bobby's, after which Ted described himself to have been "shaken to my core."[79] One friend described Kennedy's life from 1968 to 1969 as a desire to evade responsibility and throw himself into a "freneticism of booze and sex."[80]

On July 18, 1969, Kennedy held a reunion party for campaign workers and volunteers from Bobby's 1968 campaign in a little cottage on an island called Chappaquiddick, just off the coast of Martha's Vineyard. Sometime after eleven, Kennedy asked his driver for the car keys, then he left, taking with him twenty-eight-year-old Mary Jo Kopechne. According to his testimony, Kennedy made a wrong turn onto a dark dirt road, and then proceeded to miss a small, railless wooden bridge, sending the car into the water. Kennedy was able to escape the vehicle and save his life. Kopechne was not so fortunate.

Many of the details of exactly what took place that night—particularly in the hours immediately after the accident—remain mysterious. The inquest concluded that Kennedy was lying about what actually took place and that his "negligent driving" helped cause her death. He pled guilty to leaving the scene of an accident and was given a two-month suspended sentence. It was a night of "horrible tragedy" that haunted Kennedy "every day of" his life, as he revealed in his memoir.[81] It also ended his chances to become president. Had Kennedy made the proper turn that night, he would likely have been the

Democratic presidential nominee in 1972. Upon his election as Senate whip in January 1969, the opening paragraph of *The New York Times* coverage termed the position a "stepping stone to the presidency," followed quickly by cover-story profiles in both *Time* and *Newsweek*. Somebody even scratched the words "Mr. President" in his new desk.[82] Richard Nixon never spoke truer words than when he told his aide John Ehrlichman that Kennedy "would never live that down. . . . [Chappaquiddick] will be around Kennedy's neck forever."[83] Kennedy was lucky just to be returned to the Senate by Massachusetts voters in 1970, with next to no questions asked.

The rest of Kennedy's career might profitably be viewed as a kind of atonement for his behavior that night on Chappaquiddick. As Newfield noted, he "converted persistence into redemption." But before he could become a *national* statesman (and eventually, a failed candidate for his party's nomination for president in 1980), Kennedy had to deal with problems at home, problems that cut to the heart of his (or anyone's) ability to unite the "Harvards" and working class under a liberal umbrella, whether in Boston, Biloxi, or anywhere else.

On April 20, 1971, the Supreme Court issued its decision in *Swann v. Charlotte-Mecklenburg Board of Education*, ending local control of neighborhood schools and inviting districts to employ complicated busing schemes, if necessary, to achieve integrated classrooms.[84] The details of implementation were left in the hands of W. Arthur Garrity, a federal judge who took up the issue in 1974. He decided that the segregation of public schools in Boston was clearly "systematic," consciously implemented, and therefore unconstitutional.[85] Certainly the typical patterns of settlement in the city of Boston—with particular neighborhoods known as more or less exclusively white or black—gave rise to segregated schools. But as with so many localities in the United States, the question was how to address segregation that was enforced by discriminatory housing as well as by educational practices. Garrity was nothing if not persistent, and he demanded an immediate commencement of busing between segregated neighborhoods such as South Boston, which was white working class and Irish and avidly racist, and Roxbury, a poor black ghetto.

George Wallace had brilliantly exploited the issue in 1972, and per usual, what Wallace had pioneered in the realm of racist backlash, Richard Nixon made respectable in the rightward-rushing epicenter of American politics: "I have consistently opposed the busing of our Nation's schoolchildren to achieve a racial balance, and I am opposed to the busing of children simply for the sake of busing."[86] His successor, Gerald Ford, followed suit.

For liberals, though, the issue was far more problematic. Boston mayor Kevin White argued that he was "for integration" but "against forced busing."[87]

The liberal Harvard professor of psychiatry Robert Coles pointed out the unfairness of the burden's being placed on working-class people, and wondered why wealthier suburbs were not being asked to share it. Poor whites and blacks "are both competing for a very limited piece of the pie, the limits of which are being set by the larger limits of class which allow them damn little, if anything."[88] Writing in *Dissent* in 1959, following the violence in Little Rock, Hannah Arendt had questioned the wisdom, and the morality, of placing the burden of ending desegregation on schoolchildren. (She suggested starting with miscegenation laws instead.[89])

Busing "fell like an axe through the Democratic Party, severing long-standing connections and creating a new set of troubled alliances: white blue-collar northerners with southerners against blacks and upper-middle class liberals," note Thomas and Mary Edsall.[90] When the plan was implemented in South Boston, as buses of black kids entered from Roxbury, protests erupted with cascades of rocks, chants of "Get those niggers out of our schools," and picket signs that read "BUS 'EM BACK TO AFRICA."[91] With painful irony, it was now "antibusing activists who employed the tactics of the civil rights movement by organizing school boycotts, holding prayer vigils, and engaging in acts of nonviolent protest that led to arrests," as historian Louis Masur observed.[92] But Judge Garrity stood firm, even increasing the numbers over time.

Mike Barnicle, a *Boston Globe* writer who fancied himself the Jimmy Breslin of Boston, urged Ted Kennedy to get involved, pleading: "You have the one voice that can help keep this city calm, leaving the clear ring of justice and common sense in homes and streets where people sit, uncertain."[93] Kennedy listened but was unsure how to proceed. He liked Judge Garrity and had defended him against critics. But he believed, quite sensibly, that parents who resisted the idea of their kids being bused great distances to inferior and frequently unsafe schools could not be talked into sacrificing their children's education for the greater good of racial equality, particularly since most of them believed that blacks and whites were better off staying "with their own kind" in the first place. As the historian Jefferson Cowie put it, "Support for [busing] was a difficult case to make to white working-class people who felt that integration was taking place on their backs. Immediate defense of white identity, home, and school readily trumped the abstract hope of a better world someday."[94] Kennedy, seeking to play the peacemaker as his brother Bobby had done during the New/Old Politics arguments of the sixties, put the best face on the forces of opposition that he could manage. Protesting parents, he later recalled, "were worried that their children would be far away from home if they fell ill at school. And they were upset because they were being denied access to the school in the neighborhood to which, in some cases, they had moved to specifically because of the school district. I understood those concerns."[95] But he could not assuage them.

Kennedy went to Boston to tour the schools in early September, and upon hearing of a protest near city hall, asked his driver to take him there so he could talk with (and listen to) some of the protesters. Kennedy arrived at the rally just after the hanging of Judge Garrity in effigy, to the screams and cheers of the crowd. As he pulled up, one protester screamed at him: "Why don't you put your one-legged son on a bus for Roxbury?" (Teddy junior had just lost a leg to cancer the year before.) Another asked, "How would you like your daughter to be raped by one of them? Why don't you let them shoot you like they shot your brothers?" As Kennedy prepared to speak, the crowd turned their backs on him and sang "God Bless America." Eggs and tomatoes rained down on his head.[96] Realizing the futility of the situation, Kennedy withdrew, but had to fend off some in the crowd who were attempting to attack him physically, punching, elbowing, and kicking him in the shins.[97]

Nothing if not indefatigable, he showed up at another antibusing protest in Quincy, organized by the grassroots organization Restore Our Alienated Rights (ROAR), which was louder and angrier even than the previous one. He "made it back to the car with people screaming and spraying spittle in our faces. The car's tires had all been punctured. Dog feces were smeared on the door handles and all over the windshields."[98]

Liberals' mishandling of this issue offered unregenerate racists a respectable route into mainstream politics through the politics of racial masquerade. In 1981 future campaign manager for George H. W. Bush's 1988 presidential campaign, and later head of the Republican National Committee, South Carolinian Lee Atwater explained the phenomenon as follows: "You start out in 1954 by saying, 'Nigger, nigger, nigger.' By 1968 you can't say 'nigger'—that hurts you. Backfires. So you say stuff like forced busing, states' rights, and all that stuff."[99]

Kennedy found solace in being voted back to the Senate in 1976, "an especially heartening outcome in light of the recent turmoil in Boston," as he remembered it.[100] While nothing could damange his reelection prospects, it appeared, the same could not be said for liberals not named Kennedy. Busing had driven an all-but-indestructible wedge between the white working class and liberals. "Limousine liberals" became a common term of derision, and what it really meant, as then-Nixon speechwriter and amateur etymologist

William Safire explained, was someone "who will talk about the public school system but sends his children to private schools."[101] Busing was "a Harvard plan for the working-class man," a statement of elitist hypocrisy as much as it was of a bleeding heart, a division in good standing of Saul Bellow's "Good Intentions Paving Company."[102]

14

"A Government as Good as Its People"

> The people out there are getting frantic, they know the great American
> ride is ending.
>
> —John Updike, *Rabbit Is Rich*

arly on the morning of August 15, 1971—before the opening of the U.S.
stock market—Richard M. Nixon effectively brought the curtain down
on the American Century with a ninety-day wage and price freeze, a 10 percent charge on imports, and most significant, a closing of the "gold window,"
thereby informing foreigners that they would no longer be able to convert their
dollar holdings into gold at a guaranteed price of $36 per ounce. Shortly there-
after, the dollar would be devalued by 10 percent. The American underwriting
of the global financial system—the backbone of the Bretton Woods regime,
credited with preventing another depression and integrating much of Europe
and parts of Asia, Africa, and Latin America into the U.S.-led liberal capitalist
economy—had fallen into the dustbin of history.

America's unchallenged supremacy in international trade had helped frame
and support postwar liberalism. The Marshall Plan, the quintessential expression of American power and beneficence, would never have been feasible had
the country not been economically strong and secure relative to the rest of the
world. With forward-looking programs like the GI Bill, which contributed to
a boom in higher education and a well-educated workforce, liberalism was
able to forge a path to the future based on optimism, investment, and the
promise of enough prosperity to move toward the goal of genuine equal opportunity for all.

By the early seventies, however, other nations—particularly the now rebuilt
Axis nations of Germany and Japan—had begun to outpace the United States
in productivity, with newer factories, more patient investment capital, and
better labor relations. Their manufacturers also enjoyed considerably lower
labor costs, as well as next to no legacy expenses such as pension payments

and medical plans for retirees that burdened so many U.S. companies. (Most would adopt national health insurance and thereby free employers from that cost as well.) Their success was, in many respects, America's success as well. Building up these nations' economies had been a central and explicit aim of U.S. postwar ambitions, in part to demonstrate the superiority of the capital-ist model to that of the Communist bloc, and in part to provide healthy mar-kets for U.S. products. Japan's per capita GDP in 1950, the historian Judith Stein notes, was roughly equal to that of America's a hundred years earlier. In 1953 "the National Security Council urged the entry of Japanese goods to the United States to halt 'economic deterioration and falling living standards' in Japan that 'create fertile ground for Communist subversion.'" Walter Heller, chair of the Council of Economic Advisers during the Kennedy and Johnson administrations, argued on behalf of the Kennedy tax cut because it would boost U.S. purchases of Japanese goods. Indeed, the respected diplomatic historian Walter LaFeber goes so far as to argue that the need to protect and defend Japanese economic expansion in Indochina was a central motivation—albeit not the only one—for America's misguided intervention in Vietnam.[1]

These nations also did not labor under the burden of U.S. defense spending, which, while on occasion it did produce useful technological spinoffs in con-sumer products such as radios and computers, nevertheless ate up an increas-ing amount of GDP and kept many of its best scientists and engineers occupied with noncommercial weapons-oriented production. U.S. industrial capacity plummeted as unemployment ratcheted up and productivity slumped.[2] These developments coincided with, and were in many respects related to, profound changes in the nature of the global economy that weakened the U.S. govern-ment's ability to intervene in its domestic economy to improve the lot of the newly vulnerable workforce. As global capital markets grew increasingly in-tegrated, individual governments found themselves with fewer Keynesian tools at their disposal. Bond markets could punish any president or prime minister who allowed current account deficits to get out of hand, just as a globalized marketplace could destroy any firm that paid workers a wage that made their products uncompetitive in the global marketplace. Corporations pronounced themselves borderless and nationless, loyal only to the bottom line as measured by quarterly profit statements. For instance, 3M distributed a pamphlet to its workers explaining that their jobs at home depended on their employer's ability "to operate in those countries as a *local* business employing *local* people and giving *local* service, not as a foreign one." By the midseventies, in economic as well as business thinking, the ability of Congress to pass laws designed to improve the condition of America's workers—rather than in support of global economic conditions—was rapidly becoming viewed as not only more difficult than ever but possibly even anachronistic. Corporations, many simply assumed, must be freed to create their own economic efficiencies across national boundaries, and the job of individual governments was now to simply get out of the way and let them do it with as little as interference as possible. Workers, as a result, would henceforth be expected to fend for themselves.

These changes in the global economy inspired any number of dramatic changes in the lives of Americans and the liberal writers and thinkers who sought to influence them. Inflation, for instance, raised the costs of desegregation: "Democrats had assumed that a pluralistic, interest group-oriented liberalism would benefit all society," writes historian Laura Kalman, but white Americans were now being asked to forfeit precious economic gains to minorities in the name of fairness while at the same time being forced to compete "for a very limited piece of pie instead of joining forces to fight for a larger slice."[3] Additionally, an increasingly globalized economy acted as a kind of straitjacket on traditional Keynesian attempts to stimulate demand through government spending or provide support for any given industry.

This period also marks the beginning of a deliberate assault on the living standards of the poor and working class by the extremely wealthy. The share of all the nation's wealth held by the richest 1 percent of Americans more than doubled beginning in the early 1970s, from 8 to 18 percent. In Fortune 500 companies, CEOs who once earned on average twenty to thirty times what their average worker made came to expect their salaries to be four hundred times that amount or more. In no other Western democracy did anything like this transformation of wealth take place. In 1971 future Supreme Court Justice Lewis Powell wrote his famous memo warning that "the American economic system is under broad attack" and "business must learn the lesson . . . that political power is necessary; that such power must be assiduously cultivated; and that when necessary, it must be used aggressively and with determination—without embarrassment and without the reluctance which has been so characteristic of American business." That is precisely what business did, through a program of legislation, reinterpretation of labor law, election spending, and media manipulation that is well beyond the scope of this book.[4]

Jerry Wurf, president of the American Federation of State, County and Municipal Employees (AFSCME), saw the implications of these measures for the labor movement, but was unable to persuade his fellow leaders to adjust course to strengthen either the movement or the workers vis-à-vis their newly weakened position. As Wurf prophetically explained in 1974, "We can stand pat as a movement that represents a declining percentage of the workforce, and watch our influence over national direction slip away, [but] if labor is weakened, society is more likely to close out the poor and the powerless whom labor seeks to represent."[5] Union concentration in the private workforce fell from an average of more than one in three workers during the 1950s to barely one in thirteen at the close of the first decade of the twenty-first century.[6]

Even leaving aside Vietnam and the civil rights, youth, feminist, gay, and various ethnic revolutions the decade inspired, the collapse of liberalism's economic foundations made all previous assumptions of political life obsolete. Presidents Kennedy and Johnson could give to the poor without stealing from the rich, eschewing redistribution for a promise of shared prosperity, but such programs were no longer viable. Rising wages were replaced by rising prices. Increased prosperity for wage workers hit a wall as family income for wage workers "topped out" in 1973.[7] By 1979 a typical American worker's take-home pay was 6 percent below its 1972 level.[8] Meanwhile, the cost of living rose between 1973 and 1983 at an average annual rate of 8.2 percent, which was more than twice what it had been a decade earlier.[9] Entry-level wages in industry after industry fell precipitously, as did attendant benefits and opportunities for advancement. The so-called misery index, a figure combining unemployment with inflation, invented by Jimmy Carter for the 1976 presidential campaign to highlight Republican economic failures, rose from an average of just 7 percent during the Kennedy/Johnson presidencies to roughly 16 percent during Carter's.[10] Due to the diabolical double helix of rising inflation and unemployment, the historic liberal argument for full employment policies became politically untenable as the "wage-price spiral" that John Kenneth Galbraith and others had diagnosed by the 1950s had come undone.

Adding insult to injury was the onset of tax revolts pursued via direct democratic tools like the initiative and the referendum. Taxes, as honest liberals understood, would have to be the linchpin of their own social policy in the future, but these were taken away as well.[11] Next came the oil crisis. Following Nixon's decision to support Israel in its 1973 war with Egypt and Syria—a war that ended in the humiliation of both attackers—the Middle East oil-producing nations, under the rubric of OPEC, retaliated by boycotting the United States for five months, beginning on October 16, 1973, and ending in March 1974. They could hardly have picked a better target: between 1967 and 1973 the U.S. appetite for oil nearly tripled in volume.[12]

While liberals were pretty much out of answers by this time, neocons felt they knew just what to do: quit whining and get tough with the Arabs, the

Russians, and anybody else who wished America (and Israel) harm. To *Commentary's* Walter Laqueur, Washington was "shilly-shallying" in the face of challenges from third-rate Marxist dictatorships.[13] Worried about a deeper crisis in the American soul, *Commentary's* editors pointed to what they saw as the "increasing disposition among the elites—political, cultural, and even commercial—to question the legitimacy of American civilization," and to "... dwell upon its failings" and even on occasion "to acquiesce in the most hostile descriptions of the country's character, its past record, and its future prospects."[14] The clarity and simplicity of these arguments no doubt appealed to millions of Americans who were frustrated by their government's apparent inability to "fix" the oil crisis, the inflation crisis, the unemployment crisis, and were eager to feel safe and secure in their homes and neighborhoods again. (This latter problem had clear racial undertones, as crime rates often rose on the heels of forced-integration schemes.)

"Watergate babies"—Democrats elected in 1974 and 1976—tried to breathe new life into liberal issues of the day, including reforming the nation's corrupt campaign finance methods, protecting the environment, and increasing opportunities for women and minorities in education and the workplace. But the optimism and faith in humankind's ability to build a better future, which are the sine qua non of liberalism's political appeal, had all but disappeared.

Watergate buoyed liberals at first, not merely because it brought down the bogeyman, Nixon, but because it brought into office legislators who were determined to fight against corruption and secrecy and for cleaner campaign finance activities. But the suspicion of government and the paranoia that Watergate engendered ultimately did long-term damage to liberalism, shaking its central principles to the core. More and more, government was viewed by citizens to be part of the problems they faced, rather than their potential solution.[15]

Anti-Communist liberalism—the sort endorsed by Arthur Schlesinger, Jr., and Reinhold Niebuhr—was no less tarred by its association with Vietnam than was conservatism. In 1975, Senator Frank Church, a stalwart liberal from the State of Idaho, a state fast growing wary of liberalism, chaired a committee investigating the misdeeds of the CIA and found that the agency had repeatedly plotted to assassinate such world leaders as Fidel Castro of Cuba, Rafael Trujillo of the Dominican Republic, and Patrice Lumumba of the Democratic Republic of the Congo. At around the same time, discoveries about the FBI's spying on the civil rights and antiwar movements, employing disruptive techniques to try to discredit their leaders, further weakened liberals' confidence in the ability of their government to act ably and honestly in pursuit of stated national values such as "liberty and justice for all."[16]

To gauge how much had changed for liberalism as a political philosophy rooted in America's past, consider the case of Arthur Schlesinger, Jr. He had long celebrated the power and unity found in the executive branch, specifically the idea that the president, who was directly elected by the people, served as the embodiment of democracy. But Johnson's and Nixon's failed presidencies revealed problems within the presidency itself rather than the (obviously flawed) men who occupied it. "As the American Presidency came to conceive itself the appointed savior of a world," what came to be viewed by U.S. leaders as "the presumed requirements of a global and messianic foreign policy" had, in Schlesinger's newly jaundiced views, "begun to swallow up the congressional power to oversee international agreements as well as the congressional power to send armed force into battle against sovereign states."[17] The system itself was the problem.

Nowhere was the new era of paranoia more clearly evident than in Hollywood. As the old studio system of Hollywood collapsed, newly empowered young directors created a noirish vision of America and the dreams it inspired at home and abroad.[18] Typical were films such as Roman Polanski's *Chinatown* (1974), the story of the sinister seizure of water rights by private interests in California and a legacy of murder and incest; Francis Ford Coppola's *The Conversation* (1974), about a man involved in secret taping for a client who picks up information he believes exposes a plotted murder; and Sydney Pollack's *Three Days of the Condor* (1975), about a man who stumbled upon a super-secret rogue agency inside the CIA.

The director Alan Pakula was born to a family of Polish Jews in 1928 and grew up on New York's Lower East Side and then Long Island. He attended the Bronx High School of Science, and then enrolled in Yale to study theater directing.[19] He got his first lucky break as a producer for Harper Lee's *To Kill a Mockingbird* (1962), which became a classic beloved by moviegoers everywhere (especially lawyer moviegoers), including those in the South. The film would prove to be a stepping-stone in Pakula's development from a hopeful sixties-style liberal to something very different. The following decade brought his so-called paranoid trilogy, starting with *Klute* (1971), the story of a prostitute, Bree Daniels (played by Jane Fonda, fast becoming the most famous figure in the Hollywood left, with her travels to North Vietnam and her romantic relationship with ex-SDS leader Tom Hayden), connected to a murder and tracked by a small-town investigator. For *The Parallax View* (1974), Pakula teamed up with another icon in left-wing Hollywood, Warren Beatty, for a film about the murder of a presidential candidate by a mysterious corporation that hires and programs assassins. It was a natural progression to Watergate, for it was Pakula's work on *The Parallax View* that convinced Robert Redford, who was planning to film Woodward and Bernstein's *All the President's Men* (1976), that he had found his man. Redford explained that he wanted Pakula because the director "was a liberal—but he was not a knee-jerk liberal. If you directed this [movie] with a knee-jerk liberal attitude you could die, because then it would have been about Nixon, which it shouldn't be. It would have been about the good guys and the bad guys instead of about investigative journalism and treating it like a detective story."[20] For his part, Pakula was happy to be brought on board because he saw an opportunity to lead American audiences toward a new European-style cultural and political maturity. "We had a disproportionate interest in diversion therapy and too little interest in discovery. What came upon us in the Watergate era after a decade of assassinations and dirty tricks was a kind of national enlightenment. Collectively we became cynical. I thought it was healthy."[21]

Pakula's film is as accurate as any historical docudrama and remains a milestone among journalism movies, despite its simplified story lines. But while its heroes' doggedness was their defining characteristic, its subtext was perhaps the primary cliché of the period: even paranoids have real enemies. Watergate criminal Charles Colson complained, "*All the President's Men* is steeped in a paranoia as deep as that which I witnessed inside the embattled White House. Woodstein's fear that they are being bugged and that their lives are threatened? Come, come now. There was not a shred of evidence that anything of the sort was going on."[22] The movie ended, as Pakula insisted, with teletypes announcing Nixon's departure instead of just the journalists working away, as Redford would have preferred. "After Nixon's departure, it was no longer un-American to question the morality of the chief executive. The moment of farewell was a big deal."[23]

Not surprisingly, conservatives accused Redford and Pakula of releasing the film in 1976 as an election ploy, and Ronald Reagan went so far as to blame it for the defeat of Gerald Ford.[24] *All the President's Men* certainly did contribute to a widespread belief that America's government needed a wholesale moral fumigation and helped pave the way for a candidate like Jimmy Carter, who promised never to lie to anyone. Together with the Democratic wave that Watergate produced, Carter's electoral victory was a moment that interrupted the general and pervasive conservative ascendancy in American political history. Voter turnout had continued to plummet along with citizens' trust in government, which may have helped Carter in the short run.[25] In the long run, however, it only hurt liberalism. Without citizens' trust that government could effectively improve their lives, liberals were without their most foundational argument: trust in the ability to improve the lives of everyday people.

Jimmy Carter arose from a spot on American soil similar to that of Lyndon Johnson, one that had little in common with the big cities that gave birth to labor unions and liberal intellectuals. Of his rural Georgia hometown, Rosalynn Carter would recall, "Plains was very small, only one square mile with a population of about 600. . . . We had no movie theater, no library, no recreation center."[26] Electricity arrived only in 1938 through the New Deal's Rural Electrification Administration.[27] Carter enjoyed an idyllic southern childhood, at least insofar as the Great Depression and a stern father could provide. Some have compared the future president's early years to that of Huckleberry Finn, but Huck never enjoyed a cook, fancy cars, a clay tennis court, or a pond house with a jukebox. Carter himself spun the myth, recalling "an active life outdoors, spending our days in the fields and woods, either at work with mules, plows, and hoes or, on off days, fishing, riding horses and bikes, hunting, climbing trees and windmills, wading or playing in creeks and muddy ditches, or fighting and wrestling with each other."[28] His father, Earl Carter, was a hardened opponent of the New Deal who oversaw as many as 260 black sharecroppers tending his cotton, corn, cane, and peanut fields. These same workers were forced to shop at the commissary Earl owned—"a license to steal," given its inflated prices, as one neighbor told Carter biographer Kenneth Morris. Earl Carter was a man who had traditional southern political sentiments and ruled his family like many patriarchs of that era.[29] Carter remembered his father's whippings, meted out with a "small, long, flexible peach tree switch."[30]

From his mother Carter absorbed an appreciation for culture and a peculiar but unmistakable lesson in southern liberalism. Miss Lillian, as she was known around Plains, nursed whites and blacks alike, and, unusual for the time, invited blacks to enter her home through the front door. Irreverent to an impressive degree, she used to drink from a bottle of Jack Daniel's on her porch on Sunday mornings as passersby walked to church.[31] (At nearly seventy, she volunteered for the Peace Corps.[32]) She also instilled in her son a love of literature that led him to a life of reading, and writing books after his presidency. Julia Coleman, a local teacher, also made a major impression on young Jimmy. She told the small classes she taught about the demands of the outside world, that world far from the Deep South that infused the young Carter with hope and wonder, and turned her most famous student into the kind of feminist who practiced his politics out of the ingrained respect for the women he had known all his life.[33]

Carter attended Georgia Tech and then the United States Naval Academy in Annapolis, Maryland, after which he expected to serve on the Asian front during World War II, but the war ended as his training did. A year later he married Rosalynn, his childhood sweetheart, who would serve as a political sounding board throughout his life. Now an engineer with a growing family, the Navy veteran looked forward to a bright future. But in 1953, Earl Carter died, and Carter's younger (and more adventurous) brother, Billy, was too young to take over the business, and no one expected that either of his two sisters would step into his father's shoes. Carter tried to resist, and Rosalynn remembers protesting any return to Plains; she cherished their lives in the Navy and the newly won independence from family ties.[34]

As "massive resistance" to all aspects of the Supreme Court's *Brown v. Board of Education* decision set in throughout the old Confederacy, the Plains area witnessed the formation in 1958 of the violently segregationist White Citizens' Council. Its leaders immediately recruited Carter and "pointed out that it would damage my reputation and my success as a businessman in the community if I proved to be the only hold-out," Carter recalled to James Wooten. "And because of their genuine concern about my welfare, they were willing to pay the dues for me."[35] Carter refused, according to Rosalynn, telling the men to "flush it right down the john."[36]

He ran for state senator in 1962, just barely winning following the discovery of illegal voting practices and a successful recount.[37] In 1966 he ran for governor and lost to the segregationist Lester Maddox, a racist fried-chicken salesman with a ninth-grade education.[38] Personally devastated, Carter found new strength in being "born again," an experience that would come to define him not only religiously but also politically. He returned to run for governor in 1970 against the progressive ex-governor Carl Sanders and, according to Bobby Rowan, a longtime family friend and Georgia state senator, purposely pandered to "the redneck vote."[39] He placated the prejudices of poor whites by railing against "Eastern elites" and promising to invite George Wallace to visit the state, thereby earning the enmity of the liberal editorial writers at *The Atlanta Journal-Constitution* but gaining the backing of the far more influential political machine of the prosegregationist senator Richard Russell. He won the primary but, tellingly, earned only 7 percent of the black vote.[40]

Once in office, however, he ruled as a progressive southern governor, reforming state government to make it less corrupt and more efficient, and to the undoubted surprise of many of his supporters, worked to end racial seg-regation.[41] At his inauguration he announced in clear, crisp terms, "I say to you quite frankly that the time for racial discrimination is over."[42] He atoned for his earlier pro-Wallace stance by hanging a portrait of Martin Luther King, Jr., in the Georgia State Capitol, a daring act even at that time, though he never tried to meet his fellow Georgian and chose not to attend his funeral.[43]

Jimmy Carter was not a traditional liberal. Presidential historian Fred Greenstein has characterized him as "a moralist and social engineer" with a "blend of domestic liberalism and economic conservatism."[44] Like the neo-cons, Carter believed that George McGovern had pulled the party too far leftward. He believed government could be competent, economic, and effi-cient so long as it stayed within its means and respected the independence of the market.[45] He might remember fondly the electrification programs of the New Deal, but he believed that any government action to dam rivers for en-ergy during the 1970s was wasteful and antienvironmental. He supported the ERA, but he was religiously opposed to abortion.[46] He would hire liberals for his staff but tried to balance them with conservative southerners, including Wallace supporters.[47]

Carter's moralism played well in post-Watergate America. "I have never claimed to be better or wiser than any other person," he explained on the campaign trail. "I think my greatest strength is that I am an ordinary man."[48] In 1975, just after declaring his candidacy, Carter argued that it was this ordi-nariness that enabled him to avoid the culture of presidential corruption prev-alent during the Watergate crisis: "There are a lot of things I would not do to be elected," he said, offering himself as an implicit contrast to the politicians of the past from both parties. Indeed, he did not like people to think of him as a politician at all.[49]

Carter's religious commitments also secured votes in the South that by this time would have been unavailable to a Kennedy or any northern liberal.[50] He claimed to pray "about twenty-five times a day, maybe more," and to read the Bible every night, sometimes in Spanish.[51] But Carter could also play the so-phisticate when the occasion called for it. When he shared a stage with Ted Kennedy for a Law Day speech at the University of Georgia in 1974, he gave off-the-cuff remarks in which he declared his two intellectual heroes to be Reinhold Niebuhr (who taught him about sin and humility) and Bob Dylan (who taught him about "the dynamism of change in modern society"). He then took off after lawyers, lobbyists, and others who enjoyed the best of what America had to offer but failed to share their good fortune or even access to equal justice with the poor.[52] Though the message was a mite moralistic, it deeply impressed those present.[53] *Rolling Stone*'s Hunter Thompson called it a "king-hell bastard of a speech" and shortly thereafter, Carter, who had already graced the cover of *Time* under the headline DIXIE WHISTLES A DIFFERENT TUNE, began receiving attention from northern political reporters and other would-be kingmakers who perceived that a credibly religious southern (sort-of) liberal might be just the ticket.[54]

Outside the context of Watergate and the Pentagon Papers, it's hard to imagine a one-term ex-governor of Georgia even being taken seriously as a presidential candidate. But the country was hungry for moral leadership and honest governance, or so many of its denizens believed. Carter successfully promoted the idea, as he promised over and over on the campaign trail, that he would "repair the damage that has been done to the relationship between our people and our government."[55]

Carter faced a wide playing field of challengers in the Democratic Party primary, but none with the appeal or charisma of Ted Kennedy, who had opted out of the race, owing to his son's cancer (and undoubtedly concerns about the continued salience of the word "Chappaquiddick"). Some liberals were clearly hoping that Carter's candidacy would demonstrate that it was possible to be a southerner and antiracist at the same time. Meanwhile, Scoop Jackson, whom Carter had supported in 1972, could not escape the consequences of his hawkishness on Vietnam. In part to pick up some of the conservative-leaning support that would have otherwise gone to Jackson, particularly among Jews concerned with a lack of freedom for their brethren in the Soviet Union, Carter made support for the human rights of citizens of totalitarian and authoritarian dictatorships a central focus of his foreign policy, which despite the neocons' agitation, remained a decidedly minority position within the party.[56] The dyed-in-the-wool liberals Representative Mo Udall of Arizona and Senator Fred Harris of Oklahoma threw their western hats into the race and gave Carter a late run for his money but ended up splitting the vote to the left of Carter, allowing him to sneak up through the middle of the pack.

Out of the blue, meanwhile, appeared Jerry Brown, the glamorous young governor of California, son of ex-governor Pat Brown and boyfriend of pop star Linda Ronstadt. Brown's run was a strange one. A fiscal conservative and onetime Jesuit who meditated in the governor's mansion and issued philosophical policy pronouncements that read like Chinese fortune cookie haikus turned out to be a bit much even for post-Nixon America.[57] Brown won in Nevada and, less surprisingly, California, but as a presidential contender he burned out before he had a chance to fade away.

With Kennedy refusing to enter the race, liberals turned to Carter like debutantes without prom dates. As Arthur Schlesinger, Jr., recounted in his journals: "We are entering another presidential year. . . . For the first time in my life I do not have a candidate."[58] Schlesinger's fears about Jimmy Carter were echoed by Bill Moyers, himself a liberal Southern Baptist, who interviewed the future president in 1976. Moyers told Schlesinger that he found Carter "cold, tough, terrifyingly self-confident."[59]

Carter ran further to the right of the political center than had any successful Democratic nominee before him, leaving him less beholden to liberals as a result. Once his victory was assured, Carter set out to woo liberals, including some who had worked with McGovern.[60] This was the opposite tack that traditional strategy would appear to have dictated: Most candidates sell themselves to the base first and then drift rightward to try to shore up centrist and conservative support. But following eight years of Nixon-Ford and the debacle of McGovern's forty-nine-state loss, liberals were ready to embrace pragmatism over principle. With the party's southern base continuing to move into the Republican column, even a putatively progressive born-and-bred Georgia peanut farmer appeared to some as a kind of gift from the Almighty. The choice of Walter Mondale, a liberal stalwart from Humphrey's home state of Minnesota, as his running mate reassured many as well. But clearly, as far as liberals' claim on the heart, much less the mind, of their party's presidential nominee, the times were clearly a-changing.

After winning the nomination, Carter stumbled on his way to the presidency with a shotgun marriage between his evangelicalism and the remnants of the counterculture. He got the Allman Brothers and the Marshall Tucker Band to play his benefit concerts, injecting a McGovernish rock 'n' roll sensibility (albeit with a southern twist) into his otherwise moralistic outreach.[61] (The joke at the time was that the recidivist stoner Gregg Allman was slotted to head up Carter's Food and Drug Administration.) A chaotic convention party thrown for him by *Rolling Stone* publisher Jann S. Wenner horrified many. In a deeply ill-advised interview with *Playboy,* Carter, while quoting scripture, somehow admitted to having looked on a lot of women with lust, an unremarkable feeling for any married man perhaps, but not one that Americans were accustomed to hearing admitted to by a presidential candidate, especially in a girly magazine.[62] Carter also made some easily exploitable pronouncements about busing by stating that there was nothing wrong with neighborhoods wishing to preserve "ethnic purity."[63] Still, he managed to retain the support of southern civil rights leaders, most particularly Martin Luther King, Sr. In the end he managed to squeak into the White House, his wide lead collapsing but holding just enough to defeat the hapless Ford and his divided, dispirited Republican Party.[64]

Inauguration Day was unquestionably one of Carter's greatest moments. His inaugural message flowed directly from the themes developed during his campaign. He urged Americans to accept that they now lived in an era of limits, one in which "we have learned that 'more' is not necessarily 'better,' that even our great nation has its recognized limits, and that we can neither answer all questions nor solve all problems."[65] Carter not only talked the talk but literally walked the walk, eschewing the presidential limousine for a frigid stroll down Constitution Avenue before an adoring crowd. He took his own rhetoric seriously, wanting, he said, "a simpler lifestyle, more frugality, less ostentation, more accessibility" in the office of the presidency.[66] He canceled the playing of "Hail to the Chief" when he entered a room, and sold off the *Sequoia,* the presidential yacht, thereby doing away with what had been two of President Nixon's primary reasons for living.[67] He promised to reduce the White House staff by nearly one-third, and he asked members of the cabinet to do the same, adding also that his cabinet officers ought to drive themselves to work.[68] He issued new guidelines for executive employees, mandating disclosure of their finances and attempted to close the revolving door for those who sought to cash in on their old jobs in government by going to work as corporate lobbyists in the same field.[69]

Jefferson Cowie observes that Carter "had always understood race much better than class, did not understand unions at all, and felt caged rather than empowered by coalitional politics that had been the backbone of the New Deal order."[70] He thought his refusal to compromise was a strength; he seemed to enjoy infuriating the very people he would eventually need to pass his legislation. In his memoirs he referred, nonchalantly, to his "one-week honeymoon with Congress."[71] Unfortunately, his honeymoon with many segments of the American public did not last much longer.

On his first full day in office, Carter made a bold move that illustrated his desire to push Americans not just into an age of limits but beyond the grip of Vietnam. On January 21 he provided amnesty for draft resisters who had fled the country during the war (though he stopped short of extending a pardon to men in the military who deserted).[72] In a 1976 speech to the American Legion—not exactly a crowd favorably disposed to such ideas—he explained his rationale for a pardon: "I think it's time for the damage and the hatred and the divisiveness of the Vietnam war to be over."[73] Carter wanted to support the veterans who had served—he pledged to provide better services to veterans grappling with residual physical and health issues in VA hospitals and would later declare a Vietnam Veterans Week to memorialize their sacrifice—but he wanted the national community to recognize also the prodigal sons whose consciences had told them that the war was damaging something deep in America's soul.[74]

In a landmark speech given at Notre Dame in May 1977, Carter stated: "For too many years, we've been willing to adopt the flawed and erroneous principles and tactics of our adversaries, sometimes abandoning our own values for theirs. We've fought fire with fire, never thinking that fire is better quenched with water. This approach failed, with Vietnam the best example of its intellectual and moral poverty."[75] Such Niebuhr-inflected humility was hardwired into Carter, who admitted on the campaign trail that America had "made a lot of . . . mistakes" in its foreign policy.[76] As president he fought to normalize relations with Vietnam (eventually accomplished under President Clinton) and argued that the country had done enough about POW/MIAs to put the issue to rest—an issue that incited conservatives and veterans who kept returning to it as a sign that the war had not ended.[77] To neoconservatives, Vietnam had not only weakened America but had given the country a weakling for a president.[78]

Like Woodrow Wilson before him, Carter sought to place moral issues at the center of U.S. international relations. Campaigning in 1976, he condemned what he called "a kind of secretive 'Lone Ranger' foreign policy" carried out under the Nixon-Ford administration.[79] He was personally "troubled by lies our people had been told," especially in "Vietnam, Cambodia, Chile," as he later recounted in his memoirs, particularly the "CIA's role in plotting murder and other crimes" that the Church Committee hearings had exposed.[80] "Carter wanted foreign policy to flow out of the best values of America, and sought to position himself in the tradition of the "idealism of Jefferson or Wilson."[81]

In his inaugural address Carter promised: "Because we are free we can never be indifferent to the fate of freedom elsewhere. . . . Our commitment to human rights must be absolute." And in the Notre Dame speech in which he recognized America's faults in Vietnam, he famously declared: "We are now free of that inordinate fear of Communism which once led us to embrace any dictator who joined us in our fear."[82] While such sentiments reflected Carter's heartfelt wish to transcend the crimes of America's Cold War past, calling America's faith in human rights "absolute" was almost entirely rhetorical because the world was not about to cooperate. How could it? A policy of protecting the rights of everyone everywhere would have been impossible to apply consistently, given the relative differences in the oppression exercised by certain governments and the degree of influence the United States enjoyed over any of them at any one time—to say nothing of the power of traditional U.S. foreign policy concerns, including most particularly anticommunism.

If judged from a less strict standpoint, though, Carter did deliver, especially as he cast his eyes south of the country's borders. U.S. foreign policy in Central America became less motivated by reflexive anticommunism than at any time since FDR's death. Carter refused to prop up Nicaragua's disgraced dictator, Anastasio Somoza—the dictator to whom FDR was referring when he spoke of "our son of a bitch" and to whom Kissinger had pledged fealty—and even exerted pressure on him to hold elections. Instead of elections, though, the Sandinista rebels rose in armed revolt and eventually seized power in July 1979. Although Carter worried about growing evidence that Cuba and the Soviet Union were infiltrating and would ultimately guide the Sandinista revolution, he declined to send in troops, as the old order would have demanded.[83]

But even in "America's backyard," Carter could hardly keep to a consistent standard. Despite the soaring rhetoric of his alleged commitment to Christian ethics, he allowed his advisers to petition Pope John Paul II to prevail upon Salvadoran archbishop Oscar Arnulfo Romero to refrain from promoting human rights in the region, a cause that eventually led to Romero's assassination (on the direct order of General [and future Salvadoran president] Roberto D'Aubuisson) by death squads that operated with impunity within that nation's U.S.-trained and -supplied military establishment.[84]

It was on the Panama Canal Treaty that Carter really moved beyond America's traditional diplomacy in Central America. This was the longest, most drawn-out battle on foreign policy during his presidency, and one that required considerable cajoling of Congress—hardly Carter's forte. The fight over the treaty stretched from 1977 to 1979, with the key votes in the Senate taking place in March and April of 1978. The central issue was whether America should cede control over the "big ditch," built by the United States under President Teddy Roosevelt, to Panama by December 31, 1999.

The Canal issue proved to be a terrific organizing tool for right-wing Republicans, because conservatives considered relinquishing it to be a retreat in America's own hemisphere, though the Nixon and Ford administrations had pursued a similar course with the Panamanians.[85] Ronald Reagan went around the country claiming, "We built it, we paid for it, it's ours!"[86] The American Conservative Union placed a newspaper ad insisting, "There is no Panama Canal. There is an American canal. Don't let President Carter give it away."[87] The debate soon centered on American "impotence" under Carter. A surprising supporter of the treaty, the conservative pundit William F. Buckley, Jr., complained that his own party had grown obsessed with "our national masculinity."[88] The newly resurgent right, however, had made up its collective mind.

For Carter, as for many Democrats and liberals, the treaty was seen as a healthy abandonment of America's outdated neocolonialist practices—the sort that Teddy Roosevelt had used to buttress his nationalistic vision of progressivism and the "big stick" he waved around in America's backyard. Carter recalled that "at the time, polls indicated that 78 percent of the American people did not want to 'give up' the Canal, and only 8 percent found the idea acceptable."[89] Nonetheless, the president stood firm, and uncharacteristically began working the legislature, sending out personal letters and speaking with legislators one on one. The historian Gaddis Smith recalls that the president "kept a loose-leaf notebook on his desk with a page for every senator, and recorded there his tireless phone calls, personal notes, and arm twisting."[90] Not until September 27, 1979, was Carter able, finally, to sign the legislation into law, and though the treaties squeaked through, Sean Wilentz recounts that "twenty of those who voted in favor were defeated for reelection either in 1978 or in 1980."[91] Pat Caddell, the president's pollster, would consistently point to the Panama Canal treaty to argue that Carter was not a poll-driven president but a leader with deep conviction.[92]

No doubt the proudest moment of Carter's presidency came on March 26, 1979, when President Anwar Sadat and Prime Minister Menachem Begin signed the first-ever peace treaty between Israel and an Arab nation. It was the product of thirteen grueling days at Camp David in September 1978, when Carter met personally with Begin and Sadat, with an emergency presidential trip to the Middle East when the deal teetered toward collapse.

James Fallows, a disillusioned speechwriter who went on to become a distinguished journalist, quit his White House job and published a tough critique of the president in *The Atlantic Monthly* shortly after the Camp David triumph. In it, Fallows complained that the president believed in "fifty things, but no one thing."[93] In the case of the endlessly complex Camp David negotiations, however, this worked to Carter's advantage. He prepared for the summit meeting by drawing up list upon list of potential concessions that might conceivably break the logjam. On his own he authored a single document that addressed "more than fifty intertwined issues."[94] Both Begin and Sadat were impressed by Carter's knowledge of the issues and his willingness to work through technical aspects of their historic dispute.

Carter also personally rose to the occasion. Though perceived to be a cold fish in Washington and a thankless boss in the White House, Carter, Fallows wrote, was able to demonstrate "remarkable charm in face-to-face encounters."[95] Because the relationship between Begin and Sadat was one of mutual antipathy, Carter was forced to shuttle between individual meetings with each of them, while lower-level advisers met in small groups in other lodges. The personal trust that inspired in Carter elicited another rare exhibition from him—his understated humor. For instance, after Sadat put forth a proposal that Carter knew would irritate Begin, the president turned to the Israeli prime minister and said, "If you would just accept and sign the Egyptian proposal as written, it would save us all a lot of time."[96] The guffaws and laughter that followed lightened the situation enough to enable a difficult discussion to follow.

The treaty that was finally agreed upon provided a timetable for Israeli withdrawal from Sinai, set out some vague arrangements for government of Gaza and the West Bank, and pledged U.S. military assistance to both countries.[97] But there was one glaring weakness that troubled Carter: nothing had been done on the Palestinian question. Secretly, Secretary of State Cyrus Vance deputized a Palestinian American professor of literature at Columbia University, Edward Said, to fly to Beirut and offer Yasser Arafat official U.S. recognition of the Palestine Liberation Organization (PLO) as the "sole, legitimate representative" of the Palestinian people in exchange for an endorsement of the Camp David accords and a willingness to enter into immediate negotiations with Israel. Arafat refused, proving once again the sad adage that the Palestinian leadership "never missed an opportunity to miss an opportunity."[98]

Not long after Camp David, Andrew Young, Carter's outspoken African American appointee as ambassador to the United Nations, was forced to resign his post after it was revealed (originally by Israeli intelligence, and under official Israeli government protest) that he, too, had met with representatives of the PLO, resulting in yet another tear in the deeply frayed relationship between blacks and Jews.[99] The fact that Jewish leaders would demand the head of Young—the highest-profile black member of the Carter administration, a civil rights hero, and a former lieutenant to Martin Luther King, Jr., who had been an unyielding friend to Israel—infuriated black leaders and caused the anger that had been building for almost a decade to spill out in public.

Yes, in the early 1960s, the American Jewish Congress had called the Freedom Rides "a historic attempt to make the constitutional guarantee of equality meaningful," and had lobbied the Defense Department and Attorney

General Robert Kennedy to intervene on their behalf.[100] The Jewish Labor Committee supplied many volunteers for the Freedom Rides as well.[101] Unlike their better known liberal intellectual counterparts, Conservative and Reform Jewish rabbis, most prominently the famous theologian Abraham Joshua Heschel, had been the most stalwart foot soldiers in the civil rights movement, marching arm in arm with King in Selma and, as Heschel famously put it, "praying" with his "feet."[102] And most famously, two of the first three martyred civil rights workers, Andrew Goodman and Mickey Schwerner, were themselves Jews.[103] But the civil rights marches were already a long time ago and black leaders were now far more concerned with the present one in which Israel was supporting South Africa abroad and Jewish leaders were fighting affirmative action at home. Jesse Jackson described Young's resignation as a White House "capitulation" to Jewish leaders.[104] The Reverend Joseph Lowery, president of the Southern Christian Leadership Conference (SCLC), announced to American Jews, "If we have to maintain your friendship by refraining from speaking to Arabs, then that friendship must be reassessed."[105] Writing in *The Nation*, James Baldwin went a step further: American Jewish liberals who supported Israel, he insisted (combining Marxist rhetoric with age-old anti-Semitic innuendo), had undertaken the "Christian's usurious dirty work" in the Middle East. "The state of Israel was not created for the salvation of the Jews; it was created for the salvation of Western interests."[106]

A week after Young's resignation, two hundred black leaders, including Bayard Rustin, Jesse Jackson, and the celebrated sociologist and television personality Kenneth Clark met in New York with representatives of the NAACP, the SCLC, and almost every significant black civil rights organization. They attacked the "double standard" that had cost Young his job. They condemned Israel's ties with South Africa and endorsed another meeting with the leaders of the PLO. "It is a fact that within the past 10 years some Jewish organizations and intellectuals who were previously identified with the aspirations of black Americans for unqualified educational, political, and economic equality with all other Americans, abruptly became apologists for the racial status quo," they announced.[107] Jews needed to "show more sensitivity and be prepared for more consultation before taking positions contrary to the best interests of the black community." What was particularly unnerving to many Jewish liberals was the "near-euphoria that engulfed the meeting as the resolutions were adopted and read in public," as the author Jonathan Kaufman notes. "This," explained Clark, when the session was over, "is our Declaration of Independence."[108]

Meanwhile, back in the Middle East, Anwar Sadat found himself returning to an Arab world increasingly incensed by his willingness to negotiate with Israel and America. His moderate version of Islam was being challenged not merely by Palestinian radicalism but also by a rising tide of Islamic fundamentalism all across the Middle East. Mohammad Reza Shah Pahlavi had been a model U.S. dictator. Placed in power by the CIA in 1953, the shah served as a beachhead against Soviet communism and appeared to be a modernizing, Westernizing force in the region, despite his liberal use of a hated secret police force (SAVAK) and his amassing of literally billions of dollars in ill-gotten gains for himself and his cronies.[109] Carter's willingness to indulge the shah was consistent with previous presidents' policies, although in glaring contradiction to his own professed devotion to human rights.[110] Whatever private communications Carter might have had with the shah regarding his treatment of his political opponents were vastly overshadowed by his toast to the shah on New Year's Eve, 1977, in Tehran, in which he proceeded to describe Iran as "an island of stability in one of the most troubled areas of the world" and Pahlavi as a great leader who had won "the respect and the admiration and love" of his people. Carter said these words in the midst of one of the shah's increasingly brutal crackdowns on his opposition, which was fueling a theocratic revolution led by the exiled Muslim cleric Ayatollah Ruhollah Khomeini, who denounced America as a satanic nation with Pahlevi as its puppet.

Carter was not much more consistent regarding America's main adversary, the USSR. The decade of the 1970s might be best known as the era of Alexander Solzhenitsyn, the great dissenter who had exposed the brutality of the gulag prison system with the 1973 publication in the West of *The Gulag Archipelago*. Soviet dissidents dominated American consciousness throughout the decade, including Andrei Sakharov, the physicist turned antiarms race and human rights activist who was later arrested for protesting the Soviet invasion of Afghanistan, and Anatoly Sharansky, a Jewish activist who helped inspire the massive Save Soviet Jewry movement that turned many Jews against Carter and his policies.[111] But despite the political gains to be found in taking on the cause of these dissidents—Democrats from the hawkish Scoop Jackson to the dovish Ted Kennedy had done so—Carter wanted an arms control treaty even more than he wanted to crusade for human rights. Given Soviet sensitivities on the issue, the two were incompatible, as Soviet premier Leonid Brezhnev had already made clear on repeated occasions.

Carter's own psyche was divided on this fundamental question, and the arguments of his advisers mirrored this division, especially two chief architects of Carter's foreign policy: the patrician establishment lawyer and secretary of state, Cyrus Vance, and the brilliant fiery academic and adviser for national security, Zbigniew Brzezinski. The former, who had been deputy secretary of defense under LBJ and had helped wind down the Vietnam War, operated from a legalistic perspective and was extremely cautious about the use of force. Brzezinski, on the other hand, a Polish-born political scientist, hated the Soviets as befitted his patrimony and saw opportunities to attack the Russians whenever they arose and sometimes when they did not. The late historian Betty Glad noted that Vance "appealed to one side of Carter's brain, Brzezinski the other. If Carter had a clear sense of his goal and how to achieve it the dovish Vance and his colleagues in the State Department would have an open field." But when it came to matters of strategic thinking, Brzezinski, who felt certain that the Soviets were "bent on world domination," tended to hold sway in Carter's convoluted decision-making process.[112] When genuinely torn, Carter, on occasion, would simply absorb their antagonistic talking points and then smilingly contradict himself as if he hadn't noticed. It is one of the great ironies in the history of foreign policy that, according to Brzezinski deputy Robert Pastor, it was Vance who recommended the volatile Pole for his job and Brzezinski who advocated on behalf of the establishment WASP lawyer for his.[113]

By the summer 1979 ceremony to sign SALT II—the second Strategic Arms Limitation Treaty between the United States and the USSR—relations had soured to the point where the agreement no longer had much support in the Senate, where it required a two-thirds majority to pass. Carter understood that the personal lobbying he'd have to do for the treaty to pass would make, in his own words, "the Panama Canal treaty's effort pale into relative insignificance."[114]

All these issues became moot once the Russians invaded Afghanistan that December and reignited the Cold War in earnest. Carter joined the hawks' team overnight, calling for a boycott of grain against the Soviet Union. He argued to reinstate the Selective Service System—essentially the first preparation for a military draft—and even insisted that U.S. athletes skip the 1980 Summer Olympics in Moscow. Carter's admission that he had "learned more about the Soviet Union" in the previous two weeks than he had in the lifetime that had preceded it infuriated his neoconservative critics, who resented how little respect their views had been accorded (and who had by now moved en masse to the Republican Party).[115] The dovish side of the foreign policy debate, which was represented by Vance and arms control negotiator Paul C. Warnke, appeared discredited by the Soviet invasion and was discarded in discussion by Carter's conversion. Such voices would never again rise to so great a degree of prominence in a Democratic administration, and following Carter, candidate after candidate would be forced to prove to the media and to the country that he or she was "no Jimmy Carter"—that is, he or she could be tough on America's adversaries and as committed to fighting evil abroad as to curing domestic problems at home.

Domestically Carter supported the Public Works Act, which helped create a general stimulus package, and the Earned Income Tax Credit, a program of tax credits for low-income working families with children that perhaps would turn out to be the most effective antipoverty program that any president would pass since the Great Society.[116] But Carter's heart was not in these efforts, and when he discovered the size of the federal deficit created under Nixon and Ford, he balked at future spending initiatives and turned into as much a fiscal hawk as a foreign policy hawk. His commitment to balancing the budget created a firestorm of liberal criticism.[117] Always happy to be a majority of one, he offered tepid support for the Humphrey-Hawkins Full Employment Bill, one of the last vestiges of New Deal/vital center liberalism. Carter likewise dropped his plans to pursue comprehensive health insurance for all Americans and adopted instead a much less ambitious (and less expensive) program. In doing so he made an enemy of the one man who, more than any other, had the power to undermine his presidency: Ted Kennedy.[118]

As the historian Peter Carroll put it, "The very traits that had made the Georgian such an attractive candidate in 1976—images of compassion, homeyness, innocence—contradicted popular expectations of presidential authority, the decisive manipulation of power."[119] The gregarious old pol Tip O'Neill, now House Speaker, was eager for Carter to succeed in Congress for reasons both personal and political. But when he attempted to advise Carter about which members of Congress might need some special pleading, or even favors with regard to certain issues, to O'Neill's amazement Carter begged to differ. "No," he replied, "I described the problem in a rational way to the American people. I'm sure they'll realize I'm right." O'Neill later said he "could have slugged" the president for this combination of arrogance and naïveté.[120]

For a politician who had traveled so far so fast, Carter proved remarkably prickly and unwilling to engage in the kind of backslapping and horse-trading that make for success in any political environment. (The priggish president even stopped serving hard liquor at White House receptions.) Carter's obsessive need to micromanage his presidency did not help matters, and while it remains a matter of historical dispute as to whether Carter himself actually scheduled the use of the White House tennis courts, the fact that almost everyone in Washington believed he did spoke volumes about the contempt with which he was viewed. Part engineer, part Sunday school preacher, he tended to forget to pay people compliments, praise a good job, or recognize numerous social niceties. He was also extremely impatient with the foibles of others, as his extremely detailed presidential diary (published in 2010) repeatedly demonstrates in its characterizations of people: Scoop Jackson ("acted like an ass"), Harrison Schmitt ("one of the biggest jerks in the Senate"), Russell Long ("a complete waste of time"), Eleanor Smeal of NOW ("crazy women's organization"), Frank Church (an "ass . . . who ought not be in the Senate"), and Helmut Schmidt ("a paranoid child")[121] The journalist Haynes Johnson, who doled out advice to the president on occasion, went so far as to call Carter "friendless."[122] Carter himself would later explain to a group of political scientists after leaving the presidency, "A lot of my advisors, including Rosalynn, used to argue with me about my decision to move ahead with a project when it was obviously not going to be politically advantageous, or to encourage me to postpone it until a possible second term and so forth. It was just contrary to my nature. . . . I just couldn't do it. Once I made a decision I was awfully stubborn about it. I think if I could have one attribute as the cause of my success to begin with, it would be tenacity. Once I set my mind on something I'm awfully hard to change. And that may also be a cause of some of my political failures."[123]

Liberals were not the first to jump ship, but they may have been the angriest. Though the president supported the Equal Rights Amendment, any enthusiasm on his part would have been difficult to discern. He appointed Bella Abzug to his National Advisory Committee for Women and fired her almost immediately, inspiring a majority of the committee to quit in protest.[124] While her departure marked the end of her official influence—Abzug would lose a series of congressional races before finally giving up and retiring—it also marked an important step in Carter's own march to defeat as well.

At the May 1977 convention of Americans for Democratic Action (ADA), George McGovern declared that liberals should not be "a cheering section for tinkering symbols signifying nothing." Joseph Rauh followed him with a condemnation of "the conservative doctrine of donothingism dressed up in five-dollar words. It's not a New Deal, or a Fair Deal, or even a Square Deal. It's a Bum Deal for the nation!"[125] Michael Harrington, leader of the Democratic Socialist Organizing Committee (DSOC), an influential group of intellectuals and labor leaders, also moved into unmistakable opposition, and Douglas Fraser, the much-respected leader of the UAW and inheritor of Walter

Reuther's mantle as the most progressive of American labor leaders, went into opposition and took his union with him.[126] Like Abzug, Fraser publicly broke with Carter over the work of a commission to which he had been appointed by the president, and which he quit in protest in 1978, charging that "leaders of the business community, with few exceptions, have chosen to wage a one-sided class war. . . . [They] have broken and discarded the fragile, unwritten compact previously existing during a past period of growth and progress." Over the course of eight years, organized labor had gone from Meany's complacency to a "realization that much of their power rested on an ephemeral deal, not a permanent realignment of class power."[127]

At the Democratic Party's midterm convention in Memphis in 1978, Kennedy laid his cards on the table and offered the delegates a rousing address in opposition to Carter's rightward drift on both foreign and domestic policy. According to one witness, he "absolutely electrified the delegates with a passionate address on the need for universal health care. The delegates stood and cheered straight through the last two minutes of Kennedy's delivery."[128] Kennedy challenged his party with the admonition that times arose when "a party must sail against the wind" on behalf of the priorities that had helped make it great in the past and would do so again in the future.[129] Carter followed up with a lackluster address that won him few friends and left many in the party clamoring for a Kennedy candidacy. By the summer of 1979 eighteen "Draft Kennedy" committees had formed in states with upcoming Democratic primaries.[130]

Jimmy Carter could not catch a break anywhere in the world. In Iran, the revolution whose warning signs so many of his advisers and he himself had missed continued to foment, and the shah was overthrown and expelled at the end of 1978. As had been the case with Somoza, Carter let the shah go down, which infuriated his allies among conservatives, pro-Israel types, and the Washington establishment. After the shah's downfall, his supporters pleaded with the president to let him into the United States to obtain the medical care he'd need if he was to survive cancer much longer. Carter knew the risk involved: Angry Iranian revolutionists had loudly denounced any support from the United States for the shah as a continuation of the unacceptable imperialism of the past. But the pressure from the establishment heavyweights, including particularly Henry Kissinger, David Rockefeller, and other beneficiaries of the shah's largesse over the years, proved too intense. On October 20, 1979, Jimmy Carter allowed the shah to enter the United States for medical treatment; on November 4 angry Iranian students, blessed and encouraged by the Ayatollah Khomeini, responded by taking over the American embassy and seizing all of its employees as hostages.

Carter focused his energy on finding an end to the hostage crisis, while each night television news counted the days of its duration for viewers, who watched in increasing despair over America's impotence. In March 1980 Carter was briefed on a helicopter reconnaissance mission that might free the hostages, to which he gave the go-ahead in April (much to the consternation of Vance, who resigned in protest when Carter approved it). The helicopters, unfortunately, ran into dust storms and malfunctioned. The mission was aborted, and eight men were left dead in the desert. It was an unmitigated failure that made Carter appear both rash and incompetent.

Iran created not only a foreign policy issue that dominated the last year of Carter's presidency but also a huge domestic problem. When oil production in Iran fell and the Saudis could not make up the deficit, OPEC shorted the United States on supplies, and Americans returned to gas lines and their ensuing chaos, with Carter, in the eyes of many Americans, to blame.[131] Picking up his failed National Energy Plan, Carter decided on a renewed energy plan that would create an Energy Mobilization Board to search for alternative energy sources as well as to coordinate efforts at conservation. To placate the business community, Carter agreed to decontrol oil prices but tried to offset these with a windfall profits tax to capture the money needed for alternative energy.

At this point, Carter retreated to Camp David and returned on July 15, 1979, to give one of the strangest orations in American presidential history: the famous "malaise" speech. As if having descended from the mountaintop, the president finally found his voice. Speaking to Americans from his heart, Carter argued that his fellow countrymen and -women had lost faith in their own civic traditions after witnessing the "murders of John Kennedy and Robert Kennedy and Martin Luther King" as well as the "agony of Vietnam" and the "shock of Watergate."[132] "Self-indulgence and consumption" were in part to blame for the oil crisis Americans now faced. Only if the nation united as if it were fighting a war could it throw off the shackles of foreign oil dependence and slavishness to the whims of OPEC. And so the Energy Mobilization Board, as well as the other policies he outlined, would undergird the civic sacrifice that Americans would have to embark upon to create energy independence and conservation.[133]

Briefly, Carter bounced back. Certainly liberals might have found much to embrace in the speech—including national unity and a coherent planning initiative to conserve resources, if not the decontrol of oil prices (which Kennedy had protested). But life for Carter went "from sugar to shit" overnight, in Walter Mondale's words, when the president followed this speech with an ill-considered decision to fire his entire cabinet, leaving him in worse shape than when he had begun and facing political crises everywhere he turned. [134]

Ted Kennedy had already had enough of Jimmy Carter by early 1978, and pretty much everything Carter did afterward only made matters worse. The so-called malaise speech—though Carter never actually used the word— infuriated Kennedy. Already angered by what he felt to be Carter's betrayal of his personal promise on health care, Kennedy felt the president was now abandoning optimism itself, a turn that not only repudiated his brother's legacies but also "violated the spirit of America." Kennedy's polling showed Carter easily defeated by Ronald Reagan in the general election but Kennedy able to beat both men. [135] After consulting with members of his informal White House-in-waiting, Kennedy decided to do what his brother Bobby had done so reluctantly (and what Teddy himself had strongly urged him not to do): challenge a sitting president for the nomination of his party.

But in an interview with broadcaster Roger Mudd on November 4, 1979, Kennedy was caught by surprise by a question about his presidential campaign—he thought he'd had a deal with Mudd not to bring the subject up, because the interview took place before he was planning to announce—and he not only failed to articulate a reason he should be the country's leader but could scarcely express a coherent thought at all. When asked about Chappaquiddick, a topic for which he should have been fully prepared, he answered, "Oh, there's, the problem is, from that night, I, I found the conduct, the behavior almost beyond belief myself. I mean that's why it's been, but I think that's the way it was. Now, I find that as I have stated that I have found the conduct that in, in that evening and in, in the, as a result of the accident of the, and the sense of loss, the sense of hope, and the, and the sense of tragedy, and the whole set of circumstances, that the behavior was inexplicable." [136] On the night the interview was broadcast, to universally negative reviews, the Iranians took American embassy workers hostage in Tehran, creating a national security crisis that appeared to undercut Kennedy's dovish critique of Carter's foreign policies.

Kennedy formally declared his candidacy before a cheering crowd in Boston's Faneuil Hall on November 7, 1979. While he began his campaign with a two-to-one advantage over Carter among self-described Democrats, it soon became clear just how ill prepared he was to run, and how unpropitious the times had grown for his full-throated liberalism. [137] The calendar did not help either, as the tenth anniversary of the Chappaquiddick tragedy rolled around in July 1979. More significant, the New Deal/Fair Deal coalition of working-class and white-collar workers with blacks, students, intellectuals, and the like was effectively dead, a fact Kennedy should have realized following his horrific experience defending busing in Boston. His personal demons also continued to dog him, including the burden of an alcoholic wife and an on-again, off-again marriage.

Moreover, Carter benefited, however ironically, from the emergencies his policies had helped create in Iran and Afghanistan, as Americans, in times of crisis, tend to rally around their president. This posed particular problems for Kennedy. When he pointed out the injustices perpetrated by the shah before the Iranian revolution, he was met with self-righteous patriotic rage.[138] Foreign policy, where Carter was becoming much more vulnerable, became off-limits to Kennedy, as only right-wing critiques of his "softness" and idealistic focus on "human rights" at the expense of U.S. national security were given any credence in the media.

Kennedy did go on to prevail in a few primaries and give Carter a scare in big cities where union voters, minorities, and committed liberals remained in the majority, but he never really looked likely to win once he became an actual candidate. The power of the presidency, combined with Carter's ability to manipulate the twin crises of Iran and Afghanistan, robbed his campaign of the oxygen it needed to survive. While still enthralling to many, and filled with sparks of eloquence and passion, Kennedy looked and felt like a throwback, running the kind of campaign that liberals imagined Bobby Kennedy might have tried to run in 1968, while the nation itself had moved well beyond the concerns that had then inspired liberalism. The "We Shall Overcome" moment in American politics was now a distant memory. Busing, riots, forced integration, and the battles over morality, sexuality, and patriotism had divided the nation, and liberals were unarguably left with the shorter end of the stick.

At the same time that social tensions between resentful working-class whites and increasingly impatient minorities were eroding the foundation of the historic liberal coalition, the global economy joined in the conspiracy by blunting the economic tools that liberal policy makers had employed in the past to provide the kind of optimism-breeding prosperity that peaceful social progress almost inevitably demands for success. Newly porous financial borders gave capital the opportunity to flee any nation whose regulations, whether regarding taxation or environmental or consumer protection, it found onerous. This meant that one nation, even the United States, could no longer stimulate its economy without risking either a capital flight or a backlash in the bond market that might cripple capital markets and begin an inflationary run on its currency, or both. Overproduction in global markets of products such as steel and automobiles put the United States at an additional disadvantage. Not only were aging U.S. industries facing more and more difficulties competing with younger, more nimble manufacturers in Germany, Japan, South Korea, Taiwan, and elsewhere, but these nations enjoyed long traditions of government subsidies and protected markets, which allowed them to dump their products in the U.S. market at a loss. American companies could not compete with their pricing, and the American economic ideology would not even entertain the notion of adopting similarly dirigiste policies. Nor were U.S. officials yet prepared to protect its markets; not only would this have conflicted with America's business-driven ideology, but it would also have run up against U.S. Cold War strategy, which sought to rebuild these foreign economies as a bulwark against Soviet advancement. Hence, it turned a blind eye to unfair trade advantages that hurt U.S. workers and saw its current accounts deficits disappear in dollar-denominated (and therefore inflatable) debt.

The foundation of the American liberal hegemonic order of the postwar world was now crumbling after a generation of perceived political and economic success: Europe and Japan (and, of course, South Korea and Taiwan) deferred to the United States in security matters in exchange for America's willingness to put its own workers at a disadvantage regarding trade and investment. As the political scientist Michael Mastanduno noted, "The United States encouraged, indeed demanded, the integration of the Western European economies and the formation of a European customs union even though the latter discriminated against US exports." As regards Japan, U.S. officials not only tolerated import barriers, both implicit and explicit, they also "accommodated the desire of the Japanese government to minimize US foreign direct investment and thereby granted a significant edge to Japan in the 'rivalry beyond trade.'"[139] The policy "worked," thanks in significant measure to the impressive capacity for consumption by American households—and the stability of postwar borders between the Soviets and the West in Europe, Japan, and eventually, the Koreas.

But with "success" came the decimation of entire Amercian manufacturing industries, with a subsequent loss of millions of well-paying jobs. These losses were particularly concentrated in the industrial Midwest and in the steel and auto industries. Meanwhile, the lethal combination of inflation plus stagnation led to a worldwide loss of confidence in progrowth Keynesian economics. In this respect—and in light of a rejuvenated, largely corporate-funded libertarian right wing—the decision of so many labor leaders, particularly in the AFL-CIO, to conspire in secret with CIA programs to meddle in the larger world on behalf of U.S. political interests turned out to be a poisoned chalice. "By working to make the world safe for US business in the 1950s, 1960s, 1970s," postulates the leftist labor scholar Gregory Mantsios, these unions laid the foundation for the labor movement's decline as "the world became all too safe for US corporations interested in cheap labor and unregulated environments."[140]

Meanwhile, Carter's economic plan, which placed much of the blame on the government's fiscal deficit, sought to fight its way out of the morass with what had previously been the typical conservative panacea: widespread spending cuts and thereby a forced recession. Without much debate or discussion, notes the historian Judith Stein, the nation's corporate managers and elites chose to replace the assumption "that capital and labor should prosper together with an ethic claiming that the promotion of capital will eventually benefit labor—trading factories for finance—a very different way of running a nation that produced very different results."[141]

Liberals had no answers to this conundrum. Indeed, they mostly failed to perceive it, much less come up with a workable political, economic, or even philosophical response. To a considerable degree they never did. But conservatives could and would solve the crisis, at least rhetorically, and their solution happened to be the same one they had been promoting for nearly every problem that had arisen since modern conservatism was born in Barry Goldwater's 1964 presidential campaign: lower taxes, less government, more military spending, and an invitation to God to return to America's classrooms. This time around, however, the formula was invested with new relevance by the media and revived energy by its followers, as the foundational pillars of economic growth appeared to be in a state of permanent collapse.

First, and perhaps most important for its novelty and potency, came the tax revolt of 1978. It started in California with Proposition 13, citizen-initiated legislation that limited property taxes and thereby placed strictures on government spending. It passed, after a grassroots campaign, by a margin of 65 to 35 percent.[142] Prop 13's antigovernment sentiment quickly spread across the West, and twelve more states passed antitax initiatives that year.[143] This all "set the stage for the Reagan era," in the words of longtime California chronicler Peter Schrag, because it built upon grassroots hostility to government and grew out of Reagan's home state.[144]

The western tax revolt was parallel to yet another in America's repeated period of localized right-wing religious revivals, further contributing to a rejuvenation of conservatism across America. It had any number of origins, including a revolt in the hill country around Charleston, West Virginia, against what they deemed to be the "secular humanism" found in children's text-books.[145] It built momentum in Anita Bryant's fight against civil rights protec-tions for gays in Florida, in what amounted to another huge victory for grassroots organizing and direct democracy.[146] Conservative Christians were particularly angered by a 1978 IRS ruling that a religious school's exemption from federal income tax would be withdrawn if those schools could be dem-onstrated to be discriminatory on grounds of race.[147] This was a galvanizing decision, as was the Supreme Court's legalization of abortion in *Roe v. Wade,* turning a formerly apolitical group of citizens into full-time activists, most of whom saw it as their godly duty to wage political war against liberalism.[148] In June 1979 the so-called Moral Majority, formed under the leadership of the Baptist and televangelist Jerry Falwell, created a network of activists ready to work against whatever issue offended fundamentalist sensibilities. Almost all were ready to desert the Democrats over issues of "faith" and "family."[149] The New Right also planned to target select politicians in the upcoming election—not just Jimmy Carter but also John Culver of Iowa, Birch Bayh of Indiana, and Frank Church of Idaho, all of whom were proud and vocal liber-als and all of whom would go down to defeat in 1980.

The 1980s conservative revival had many factions—the neoconservatives were largely Jewish and elite minded, while the conservative Christians were decidedly neither—but almost all rallied around the unifying personality of Ronald Wilson Reagan. Ironically, Carter and his aides thought Reagan emi-nently beatable and showed far more concern about the possibility that Gerald Ford might re-enter the presidential race. What Reagan offered conservatives, however, and what the Carter people failed to recognize, was his optimistic belief in the imminent return of America to national greatness. His ads beamed with national pride: "This is the greatest country in the world. We have the talent, we have the drive, we have the imagination. Now all we need is the leadership."[150] That sounded not unlike Ted Kennedy's attack on Carter's malaise speech, a speech that Reagan himself derided, and much better than Kennedy ever could. The conservative pundit Kevin Phillips remarked that the American people didn't want to be preached at by a dour Baptist about their lack of virtues but wanted "to be number one again." James Roberts, a right-wing author, stated in 1980 that what mobilized support for Reaganism was the idea that "God has bestowed upon" America "both a special grace and a special responsibility; that America has a mission in the world."[151] This language was almost perfectly interchangeable with the giddy rhetoric of the Jewish neoconservative Norman Podhoretz, who explained, "Anything within reason we wanted to do we believed we had the power to do."[152] As Garry Wills has observed, the coming contest between Jimmy Carter and Ronald Reagan was about the clash between "two theologies of America." Carter believed in "the fallibility of America," while Reagan found such an idea nearly treasonous.[153]

In this supercharged atmosphere Ted Kennedy and company were increasingly treated by many in the media and among political elites as an anachronism from another time. For many it was difficult to believe that Kennedy was preaching the same old-time religion that had sustained previous generations of liberals (and Kennedys). But still he soldiered on, and his last hurrah as a presidential candidate proved to be a stem-winder for the ages. It did the Democrats no good whatsoever in political terms, as it was understood by all to be a personal and political rebuke to the president himself, but it did warm hearts on many a cold winter night ahead when the "last brother" took the podium inside New York City's Madison Square Garden on August 12, 1980. Kennedy looked across the cheering crowds holding signs bearing his family name, shook his head and smiled, and then, after what felt like a half hour of applause, finally began to speak. The applause built to a crescendo as Kennedy gave the speech for which he would be best remembered at the end of his life, nearly thirty years later:

> Let us pledge that we will never misuse unemployment, high interest rates, and human misery as false weapons against inflation.
>
> Let us pledge that employment will be the first priority of our economic policy.
>
> Let us pledge that there will be security for all those who are now at work, and let us pledge that there will be jobs for all who are out of work; and we will not compromise on the issues of jobs.
>
> These are not simplistic pledges. Simply put, they are the heart of our tradition, and they have been the soul of our Party across the generations. It is the glory and the greatness of our tradition to speak for those who have no voice, to remember those who are forgotten, to respond to the frustrations and fulfill the aspirations of all Americans seeking a better life in a better land. We dare not forsake that tradition. We cannot let the great purposes of the Democratic Party become the bygone passages of history. . . .
>
> For me, a few hours ago, this campaign came to an end. For all those whose cares have been our concern, the work goes on, the cause endures, the hope still lives, and the dream shall never die.[154]

Reagan beat Carter so profoundly in November that the president lost pretty much every category of voter, save blacks and Jews. In a final act of contempt toward his own party, he refused Tip O'Neill's entreaties to hold off conceding until after all the polls had closed, lest Democrats decide not to bother to turn out and thereby not vote either for their senators or representatives.[155] But Carter characteristically ignored the advice, and his bitter concession speech would be the final act in what his speechwriter Hendrik Hertzberg called his "Jesus-in-the-wilderness mode of decision making."[156] The election proved a personal repudiation of him, or so he believed, by both left and right—and here he had a point. Remarkably, one postelection poll reported that fewer than a third of those who described themselves as liberal voted for Carter. Many voted for the Republican congressman John Anderson, who ran as a good government independent; many others stayed home.[157]

Among the former was Arthur Schlesinger, Jr.[158] Back in June 1979 Schlesinger had appeared at the ADA convention and promised, "We can be confident that sometime in the 1980s the dam will break, as it broke at the turn of the century, in the 1930s and in the 1960s. Our sense of adventure will revive. Our blood will start flowing again. There will be a breakthrough into a new political epoch, a new conviction of social possibility, a new demand for innovation and reform, new efforts to redeem the promise of American life."[159] Schlesinger was a fine historian, but as a political prognosticator, his predictions significantly overestimated the appeal of an exhausted liberalism and, no less important, underestimated the increasing appeal of Ronald Reagan. The dam did indeed break, but the waters it released were not mighty rivers of liberal social justice but oceans of conservative reaction in which a war on the poor, the disadvantaged, and the powerless would soon become a synonym for patriotism and optimism; it was a kind of political hijacking of the emotional symbolism that Roosevelt, Truman, and Kennedy had once claimed for liberalism.

Once the dust had settled on the 1980 election, liberals realized that they were now facing the possibility of choosing between two paths for the future—one mapped out by Jimmy Carter, the other by Ted Kennedy. Carter's legacy was more complex than Kennedy's, given his complicated relationship with liberals and liberalism. He had wanted the Democrats to reject McGovernism and position themselves toward the center, mindful of the realities of American politics, especially the backlash that George Wallace had helped create. His own victory during the primaries in 1976 suggested the wisdom of this strategy. Though he had campaigned then on the slogan "A Government as

Good as Its People," his experience of the gas crisis of 1979—when fights broke out on gas lines and the selfishness of Americans turned insolent—he came to understand that the populist pieties of his campaign had little relationship to reality. He had learned from his reading of Reinhold Niebuhr that simplistic faith in human goodness could lead only to a trail of tears. The need to find answers to America's energy crisis and the other problems Americans faced would require technical and scientific expertise, but any response to them, he recognized, had to take into account a growing populist distrust of any and all government-based solutions. Liberals would have to seize some of the issues that conservatives had made popular and find a way to claim them as their own. These included fiscal responsibility, a faith in traditional morality, and respect for religious faith.

Kennedy's legacy was simpler. He believed that liberals needed to stick to their principles—especially a faith in government's capacity to provide for greater equality and social progress among citizens, including, particularly, universal health care. Liberals must be willing to "sail against the wind," to remain liberal even if that meant becoming a party of protest rather than one of power, if only temporarily. Kennedy's decent showing during the 1980 primary demonstrated that many Americans remained attracted to principled leaders, even if those principles may have themselves been unpopular, and their champions, deeply flawed.

In the end, the coming decade would provide arguments for both paths as the correct one. Liberals would reexamine their core values and try to reposition themselves toward the center. They would also stand on principle and protest the conservative ascendancy growing at the time. The future looked no brighter as the 1980s began, merely more challenging.

15

Where's the Beef?

If we do not stand up for the hungry, if we do not speak up for those
who work with their hands, if we do not fight on for the desperate
millions of our inner cities, who will?
                            —Ted Kennedy, 1982[1]

The masquerade is over. It's time to . . . say the dreaded L-word; to say
the policies of our opposition are liberal, liberal, liberal.
                            —Ronald Reagan, 1988[2]

Jimmy Carter had picked Walter Mondale to run with him in 1976 to shore
up the Democratic Party's base, made up of liberals, labor, and what was
left of the New Deal coalition. The choice of Mondale made sense. He had
risen out of the Democratic-Farmer-Labor Party, a unique entity in Minnesota
politics. His father had taught young Fritz the principles of the Social Gospel
and Farmer-Labor populism. When he went off to Macalester College, he was
immediately recruited into SDA, the student branch of ADA, where he worked
on Humphrey's first Senate campaign. Later he was appointed attorney general before running to replace now Vice President Humphrey in the Senate.
Mondale proved a kind of fainter, second-generation carbon copy of Humphrey, minus the joie de vivre. Mondale's somber Norwegian mien made it
impossible for him to do the retail part of politics with anything like the verve
the job of vice president demanded, much less that of a presidential candidate.

Mondale's 1984 run for the White House had a zombielike quality to it,
Uninspiring in person, he was widely viewed as a prisoner of "the special
interests that support him," as Arthur Schlesinger, Jr., recorded in his journal.[3]
If Hubert Humphrey had run the same campaign, say, twenty years earlier,
before the collapse of the New Deal coalition and the internecine warfare that
ensued as a result, such a campaign might have made sense. But by 1984, it
was anomalous at best. Mondale was at pains to figure out how to appeal to

the "Reagan Democrats"—white working-class males who voted against their own economic interests out of a distaste for a Democratic Party that they believed represented only blacks, minorities, hippies, Communist college professors, and lazy welfare cheats—without at the same time alienating the liberals, minorities, and union members who had been willing to stick with him in the first place.[4] He never managed to do so, though to be fair, neither would any other Democrat—at least for another eight years. Examining the middle-class politics of Macomb County, Michigan, around this time, the pollster Stanley Greenberg would discover:

> These white Democratic defectors express a profound distaste for blacks, a sentiment that pervades almost everything they think about government and politics. . . . Blacks constitute the explanation for their vulnerability and for almost everything that has gone wrong in their lives; not being black is what constitutes being middle class; not living with blacks is what makes a neighborhood a decent place to live. These sentiments have important implications for Democrats, as virtually all progressive symbols and themes have been redefined in racial and pejorative terms.[5]

It is fair to conclude that a number of those Macomb residents had at least one image in their collective mind when responding to Greenberg's surveys: that of the Reverend Jesse Louis Jackson. Unlike Mondale (and Ted Kennedy), Jackson approved of Carter's malaise speech and had bonded with the president on matters relating to faith. The two men enjoyed a rare rapport across lines of race and class. Jackson had grown up impoverished in Greenville, South Carolina, an area with a brutal lynching history.[6] He was raised poor but proud by his single mother and grandmother, with a strong dollop of help from the local church community.[7] A star quarterback in high school, he landed a football scholarship to the University of Illinois, class of '63. He did not last long there, however—Jackson would later blame racial prejudice—and headed off for North Carolina Agricultural and Technical State University (A&T) in Greensboro, North Carolina. There Jackson found he had landed in a hotbed of activism in the early days of SNCC, but he balked at joining fellow students risking their lives to fight segregation and revealed a cautious side to his personality that became harder to discern later in his career. From A&T he headed to seminary in Chicago, in 1964, where he joined the SCLC, and soon became, at twenty-four, the youngest of King's lieutenants.[8] Moving from a purely civil rights agenda to one more focused on economic disparities, Jackson took over Operation Breadbasket, pressing local businesses to hire black employees and drawing up agreements with grocery and department stores ending discrimination policies.

Despite his youth, Jackson was frequently reluctant to defer to King. King had doubts about Jackson's narcissistic side, as did almost everyone who met him.[9] They had substantive disagreements as well, largely focused on what King biographer David Garrow termed "the implicit conflict between Breadbasket's black capitalism focus and King's increasingly socialist economic views."[10] Jackson believed that black consumers could press their demands for a bigger piece of the pie, which differed from King's belief in a multiracial movement for economic justice. These disagreements went largely unspoken, however, and the two of them worked together until the day when King died.

When King was shot, Jackson saw an opportunity and he took it, rushing to speak to the media, his shirt splashed with King's blood. It was understood by all as an attempt to claim symbolic ownership of King's mantle as the movement's leader. But that position was still technically held by the Reverend Ralph Abernathy, King's successor at the helm of SCLC, so in December 1971 Jackson left to form Operation People United to Save Humanity, or PUSH, headquartered in Chicago. The organization promoted black capitalism together with his own brand of church-based cultural conservatism. "Black Americans must begin to accept a larger share of the responsibility for their lives," he said in 1976. "There is a definite welfare mentality in many black communities that derives perhaps from slavery, but that must now be overcome."[11] His rhetorical reach, balancing rights with responsibilities, helped broaden his appeal among black conservatives as well as corporate supporters.

Jackson's talents as both a speaker and an organizer were multifaceted. His patented rhymed slogans could move crowds into enthusiastic chants:

> "Down with dope, up with hope."
> "If my mind can conceive it and my heart can believe it then I can achieve it."
> "It's not my aptitude but my altitude that determines my attitude."
> "My mind is a pearl; I can do anything in the world."[12]

But even the man's most devoted followers would be forced to admit that Jackson's ego often got the best of him, up to and apparently including having "Jesus Christ Superstar" play as he came on stage to talk at a PUSH gala event.[13] Nonetheless, his work brought him to the attention of Carter, among many other power brokers looking to make deals for black economic and political support. Jackson became the ultimate insider-outsider, bringing the voice of the streets into the suites, along with the demand—which some experienced as a shakedown—for jobs, contracts, and the like, for those who had not been invited to the party in the first place (except to change the sheets and empty the ashtrays when it was over).

Jackson worked hard for Carter-Mondale in 1980, and saw potential in the size of the largely black crowds he drew for a run of his own. Whether Jackson ever seriously entertained the possibility that he might actually be elected president is known only to him, but he undoubtedly saw an opportunity to be the de facto president of black America. In November of 1983 he announced his campaign for the presidency. He would, he promised, speak for "the desperate, the damned, the disinherited"—exactly the people Democrats were trying to convince the rest of the country they did not represent, except by default.[14] He attempted, as the sometime conservative critic Stanley Crouch observed, to demonstrate that "an Afro-American could definitely represent more than racial interests."[15] In the end, and as evidence of the problems that had been facing liberals since FDR, Jackson ended up doing far better among the best-earning blacks than he did among the lowest,[16] receiving 21 percent of the total primary and caucus votes, including 80 percent of the black vote.[17] He would have done even better, but unfortunately for all concernd, the "damned and disinherited" did not vote in sufficient numbers to sway American presidential elections.

What Jackson had named his Rainbow Coalition turned out to be genuinely multicolored and multicultural, long before the word came into common use. It included gays, Latinos, white students, and some organized labor-based leftists. Most prominent in its ranks, however, were blacks, and most of the whites who were drawn to it saw themselves as continuing the protest politics of the civil rights movement, such as it still was. When a white southern politician with a strong Texas twang named Jim Hightower threw in his lot with Jackson, it was enough of a man-bites-dog news story to merit national attention. Conspicuously absent from Jackson's rainbow were Jews, who, typically, had made up the lion's share of the white supporters of the civil rights movement and postwar liberalism in general. Part of the problem was the anti-Semitic attitude that had been prevalent among numerous African American spokespeople since the late sixties. Jackson also made no secret of whom he felt deserved the blame when former King lieutenant Andrew Young—the most prominent black member of the Carter administration—was forced to resign over his willingness to meet with PLO leader Yasser Arafat, who was still committed to a policy of terrorist resistance to the Israeli occupation of the West Bank and Gaza.[18] Jackson appeared on occasion to go out of his way to offend Jewish sensibilities. He traveled to the West Bank to hold hands with Arafat to sing "We Shall Overcome," and when speaking with the black *Washington Post* journalist Milton Coleman about New York City, Jackson, thinking he was off the record while speaking what he called "black talk," complained, "All hymie wants to talk about is Israel; every time you go to Hymietown, that's all they want to talk about."[19] Worst of all, perhaps, he allied himself with Louis Farrakhan, who had inherited the leadership of the Nation of Islam from the murdered Elijah Muhammad. Like his predecessors, Farrakhan was an unapologetic Jew-hater and Jew-baiter, referring to Judaism as a "gutter religion" and calling Hitler "a very great man." Owing in part to his refusal to accede to their repeated demand that he renounce his relationship with Farrakhan and, indeed, denounce every negative statement made by any black person about Jews or Israel anywhere in the United States (for starters), Jewish organization leaders and neoconservative writers in *The New Republic* and *Commentary* treated Jackson as if he were the single greatest threat to the safety and security of the Jews since the Third Reich. A *New Republic* cover story in 1984 featured him on the cover under the heading "I Have a Scheme," and termed him a "visceral anti-Semite."[20] *Commentary* frequently featured articles attempting to exploit Jackson's prominence in the Democratic Party to persuade Jews to abandon liberalism entirely.

Yet despite these problems, Jackson was able to cause considerable consternation in the Mondale campaign. Chaotic as it was, Jackson's traveling carnival of a campaign and inspirational call-and-response speaking style only served to highlight what a cold fish the Democrats were on their way to actually nominating.

Jesse Jackson would have been problem enough for Walter Mondale had he not also had to contend with Gary Hart, the leading "neoliberal" in the Senate. Hart had run George McGovern's campaign in 1972, the same campaign that Jimmy Carter had done everything he could to try to stop. Hart had won a seat in Colorado in the post-Watergate election of 1974 and had earned a reputation as one of the most cerebral—and least approachable—members of the Senate.[21]

The dashing young insurgent candidate had been born Gary Hartpence in the tiny town of Ottawa, Kansas, in 1936 to deeply conservative Republican parents who raised him in the Church of the Nazarene, a strict Methodist sect that aimed for "perfectionism" among its members and forbade drinking, smoking, dancing, movies, "female adornment," and most forms of popular culture as "the Devil's work."[22] He graduated from Bethany Nazarene College in Bethany, Oklahoma, before finally seeing the wider world via his enrollment in Yale Divinity School, planning to become a philosophy or religion professor. But Hart became smitten by politics in the form of John Kennedy's 1960 campaign. As the journalist Randall Rothenberg observed, "Hart came to a conclusion that would carry him through his subsequent career: that power—even power within a single ideological discipline, such as liberalism—must be wrested by each generation from its predecessors, who have grown complacent and conservative, and will fight internal change."[23] After working in the Kennedy campaign, Hart enrolled in Yale Law School. Though Kennedy's assassination profoundly disillusioned him, he returned to political work by serving as special assistant to Stewart Udall, Kennedy's appointee as secretary of interior (who continued under Johnson) before joining Bobby Kennedy's 1968 crusade. When George McGovern asked him to become campaign manager of western states for his presidential run in 1972, Hart felt drawn to the senator's opposition to the Vietnam War and his desire to continue the work of the Kennedys.[24] Hart soon advanced to campaign manager for the entire country.[25]

The McGovern campaign had a profound and transformational effect on him, as he came to see in it the final collapse of the New Deal coalition. When he ran successfully for Senate in 1974, his stump speech was titled "The End of the New Deal."[26] He went to particular lengths to disassociate himself from those candidates he termed "little Hubert Humphreys"—a not at all thinly veiled reference to Mondale, whom Hart once called "the greatest heir . . . to the classic New Deal traditions."[27] Hart worried that Democrats were too beholden to interest groups, particularly organized labor, and were losing their ability to speak to the country's shared national interest. He embraced progrowth politics over more traditionally redistributionist policies. He hoped to prepare the nation for its postindustrial future with a vigorous new program of "industrial strategy, vigorous global trade, and worker retraining."[28] The fresh nature of his ideas and the sheer youthfulness of his appearance garnered Hart support in 1984, even winning him the New Hampshire primary. Voters not only responded to the energy that seemed lacking in Mondale, but many perceived in him an updated version of JFK, with the charm, the intelligence, and the self-confidence to match.

But as with JFK's first appearance on the national scene in 1956, the novelty of Hart's appeal was both a blessing and a curse. The label "new" was as vague as it was appealing. As a politician, moreover, Hart was lacking in empathy. His speeches were awfully long on technical arguments but decidedly short on emotional appeal or inspirational vision. When, during a primary debate, Mondale responded to Hart with the commercial catchphrase "Where's the beef?" he crystallized much of the anxiety that Hart had inspired, drawing "a huge laugh" that "caught Hart completely flat-footed," as Mondale happily recalled.[29] In the end the greatest contribution of neoliberalism was not to liberal politics, but to liberal journalism. Charlie Peters's *Washington Monthly* helped to train some of the most important and influential journalists of the coming half century, including especially Michael Kinsley, James Fallows, Nicholas Lemann, and Jonathan Alter, among many others. Unfortunately for liberals, however, the most favored target for this talented group was not conservatives but liberals themselves, particularly those institutions, such as unions, upon which liberal politicians could depend to bring their message to working-class people and nonreaders of elite publications.

The trio of Mondale, Hart, and Jackson illustrated the extent to which liberalism wore different faces and galvanized different constituencies in the 1980s, echoing the split among Harry Truman, Henry Wallace, and Eleanor Roosevelt four decades earlier. But voters don't decide elections based on the impressive quality of a party's internal debates. Mondale had the strength within the Democrats' institutional elements—particularly the labor movement—which ultimately ensured him the nomination. But beyond these core party constituencies he had almost no support at all. Though a lost cause from the start, Mondale did an honorable job with what little hope he had.[30] By picking New York congresswoman Geraldine Ferraro as his running mate, he inspired feminists to get on board for the first-ever female vice presidential nominee.[31]

Even here, however, the campaign was cursed, for Ferraro turned out to be a kind of Manchurian candidate, setting back rather than advancing the feminist cause. Her husband had conducted some extremely shady real estate deals—particularly unfortunate for a candidate with an Italian American last name—and she knew nothing of foreign affairs, proving unable to hold her own with journalists such as ABC's Ted Koppel or in debate with Vice President George H. W. Bush. (The latter, however, upended his own victory by bragging unmanfully afterward that he had "kicked a little ass."[32])

Reagan-Bush ultimately trounced Mondale-Ferraro in the general election in the largest electoral-vote landslide since FDR's 1936 victory, winning forty-nine of fifty states, leaving the Democrats with only Mondale's home state of Minnesota (which he won by less than a single percentage point) and the District of Columbia.[33] What had been called Reagan Democrats were no longer Democrats at all.[34] It was the "Morning in America" message that Reagan broadcast in 1984—hope and confidence in the American nation, as contrasted to the dour pessimism that Carter and now Mondale seemed to embody—that crushed Democrats in 1984 and left liberals to worry whether their country had abandoned them forever.[35]

Now even the elite establishment media, which had tended for the previous decades to see things the way their liberal friends did, began to back away, both bemused and confused. The general aura and dimensions of Reagan's victory were far beyond what the press imagined might happen. Many felt, as the liberal journalist William Greider recalled, "My God, they've elected this guy who nine months ago we thought was a hopeless clown. . . . There's something going on here we don't understand and we don't want to get in the way."[36] Greider's boss at the *Washington Post,* the legendary Ben Bradlee, concurred, observing a "return to deference" in his own paper and those of his colleagues. Bradlee attributed the media's generosity to Reagan as "part of the subconscious feeling . . . that we were dealing with someone this time who really, really, really disapproved of us, disliked us, distrusted us, and that we ought not give him any opportunities to see he was right."[37] "Okay, guys, now that's enough, that's enough," he thought, or at least he thought he heard, coming from the public. "The criticism was that we were going on too much, and trying to make a Watergate out of everything. And I think we were sensitive to that criticism much more than we should have been, and that we did ease off."[38]

Though he enjoyed countless acolytes and political hangers-on, Ronald Reagan had no real friends, with the significant exception of his deeply devoted wife, Nancy. But not since FDR had any politician connected so deeply on an emotional level with the tens of millions of voters who decide presidential elections. His genial smile and "aw shucks" demeanor could strike fear into the hearts of many liberals, and for good reason. The man's biography embodied a great deal about the changed status of American liberalism. As Reagan thrived in the world of B movies, his politics were those, as he put it, of a "near hopeless hemophiliac liberal."[39] He was a leader of a key labor union in the entertainment world, the Screen Actors Guild (SAG); a member of ADA; and a dedicated Truman man.[40] Disillusioned by Hollywood liberals' unwillingnesss to purge Communists from their midst, he moved further and further rightward during the 1950s as the host of General Electric's weekly radio and television broadcasts—too far even for his corporate employers—before ending up near the fringe of Goldwaterism when he became the governor of California in 1967.

But while Barry Goldwater frightened voters, Ronald Reagan relaxed and inspired them.[41] The conservative pundit George F. Will accurately identified his appeal when he noted that Reagan enjoyed a "talent for happiness."[42] His unthreatening likability and his confidence in both himself and his country carried Reagan into the presidency in 1980, and his brilliant "Morning in America" campaign of 1984 returned him to office for a second term. In him the right had finally found its own Roosevelt.[43]

Reagan's polished communication skills threw off numerous liberals from his actual ambitions. Anger and frustration with Carter's performance had clouded their vision and allowed them to ignore the emboldened conservatism that stood behind Reagan's election. In 1980, Arthur Schlesinger, Jr., wrote in his journal: "We might come out a little better with Reagan surrounded and contained by a Democratic Congress than with a Carter compromising and stultifying the liberal opposition."[44] Again, good historian, lousy prognosticator.

Reagan's 1981 tax cut—the largest in American history—was heavily skewed toward the wealthy while doing nothing at all for the working poor,[45] but Democrats felt themselves all but defenseless to oppose it.[46] Reagan not only cut taxes for the rich and slashed services for the poor and middle class, but he created a deficit that would make future investments in government services far more difficult—a conscious strategy his radical Office of Management and Budget (OMB) director, David Stockman, termed "starving the beast." The former Screen Actors Guild president also dealt organized labor a near-deadly blow when, in the summer of 1981, he fired more than eleven thousand members of the nation's striking Professional Air Traffic Controllers Organization (PATCO), destroying their union and sending a burst of metaphorical grapeshot across the bow of any public union that might be considering a similar show of militancy. He launched secret wars in Central America to overthrow Marxist regimes and ensure the survival of pro-American dictatorships, unleashing the CIA abroad to do its dirty work regardless of the price in innocent lives or popular support for the United States. And he also sent the Pentagon—together with U.S. intelligence agencies—on a spending spree that rivaled those that took place during World War II and Korea. Everywhere one looked, liberals were either on the run or hiding out. If Joseph McCarthy's attacks on "eggheads" and Richard Nixon's southern strategy challenged any faith in a liberal consensus in the past, Reaganism threatened liberals from all sides simultaneously.

During Reagan's presidency, as Ted Kennedy ruefully recalled, friends and colleagues upon whom he had "counted as reliably liberal began to move rightward from the issues we had championed together over the years."[47] Kennedy himself would admit his admiration for Reagan, whom, at a March

1985 Hofstra University conference on his brother's presidency, he credited—in a dig at Carter—for having "restored the Presidency as a vigorous, purposeful instrument of national leadership." He also signaled that he understood the need for liberals to demonstrate to voters that they had embraced the lessons of the previous decades, including those involving their own mistakes: "The answer is simply not more dollars and more spending," he explained. "As we create new programs, we must regard them as replacements, not additions. . . . For who can deny that some traditional programs have failed—and that others, precisely because they have succeeded, can thankfully be set aside. The mere existence of a program is no excuse for its perpetuation—whether it is a welfare plan or a weapons system."[48] After winning reelection to the Senate in 1982 (a good midterm year for Democrats), Kennedy gave up on his hopes to be president and decided to model himself after Henry Clay or Daniel Webster and use the United States Senate as a lifelong political platform and vehicle for change. A fierce competitor, he nevertheless had a genuine gift for friendship and cooperation across party lines, a skill that enabled him to achieve significant accomplishments for many causes that appeared hopeless during the heyday of Reaganism. He was joined in his efforts by fellow Massachusetts Irish Catholic House Speaker Tip O'Neill, a man who shared Kennedy's personal animosity toward Carter as well as his fondness for Reagan, without sacrificing the principles that divided them (nor the drinking that bonded them). Raised in the blue-collar precincts of North Cambridge, Massachusetts, O'Neill was a throwback to the days of Boston mayor John F. "Honey Fitz" Fitzgerald.[49] He remained loyal to the New Deal; stuck with the people that "brung" him to Congress, the working men and women who increasingly felt themselves left behind during the go-go eighties; and worked tirelessly to bring attention to the various injustices inflicted on those least able to bear them.[50]

One of the few positive developments for liberals during this bleak decade of reactionary Reaganism was the unwillingness of so many at the grassroots level to give up hope. Historically the relation between grassroots mobilization and liberalism had been a complicated one, as liberals often found themselves in sympathy with the ideals of grassroots activists but put off by their tactics and rhetoric and, remembering the sixties, feared a general dynamic toward increased militancy.

But the signal political movement of the period turned out to be one in which liberals had every right to feel both pride and comfort. Not only did the movement aim at one of Reagan's most unpopular policies—the buildup of the country's nuclear stockpile and the apparently limitless funding of defense with little accountability—it did so with a respectable and reformist face. Mobilized by popular fears and predictions of nuclear war's devastation—the onset of a vast nuclear winter and much worse—citizens engaged in protest within the bounds of civility. They wrote letters to newspapers and contacted their representatives, attended peaceful protests, knocked on doors, and ensured that their proposals were not only moderate in tone but also approved in advance by relevant scientific and even military experts.

The movement's starting point emanated from the work of Randall Forsberg. A former English teacher and graduate of Barnard College, she had followed her husband to Stockholm, where she landed a job as a typist for the Stockholm International Peace Research Institute (SIPRI) and developed a passion for disarmament. After her divorce, Forsberg returned to the States and enrolled in a doctoral program at the Massachusetts Institute of Technology, where she drafted "Call to Halt the Nuclear Arms Race," published in 1980, and proposed a mutual freeze of nuclear weapons by both the Americans and the Soviets. The demands for unilateral U.S. disarmament that had previously characterized the peace movement never had any hope of achieving much of a following among the larger public, much less actually being enacted as government policy.[51] Now, by focusing on a legislative proposal with genuine support in Congress—one on which ex-generals, diplomats, arms negotiators, and nuclear scientists could testify in favor from both a scientific and security perspective—antinuclear and anti-Reagan activists could organize without fear that they would be labeled pro-Communist or "soft" on the Russians, except by the most recalcitrant Cold Warriors.[52]

The leading profreeze organization, Mobilization for Survival, had been founded in 1977, and was really a coalition of more than 280 affiliated groups, including 40 national organizations active in the antiwar movement.[53] The Union of Concerned Scientists, one of many organizations that reflected the middle-class and highly educated nature of the movement, carved out a day of teach-ins at 150 colleges nationwide, from which they spun off a separate organization, United Campuses Against Nuclear War.[54] As the movement started to become more popular, it began marginalizing radical activists who called for immediate disarmament and who often took up direct action and civil disobedience in opposition to the slower reform path of the freeze proponents.[55]

By June 1982, after a round of town meeting victories, the freeze counted the support of 169 U.S. representatives and 25 senators."[56] Its biggest victory occurred when supporters were able to turn out 750,000 people to fill New York's Central Park for a rally that featured politicians, activists, and rock stars, including a surprise rare appearance by Bruce Springsteen together with six-ties stalwarts Joan Baez and Pete Seeger.[57] The peaceful, largely white, largely middle-class protest was filled with church groups, theater troupes, students, and the kind of people who had proved to be the backbone of progressive movements in America for the past century. Newspaper and television reports celebrated it as part of the grand American tradition of peaceful and polite dissent.

Because the resolution could not make it through the Senate, despite the energetic promotion of Ted Kennedy and Republican Mark Hatfield of Oregon, citizens groups began to agitate for localities to pass resolutions in favor of it as a means of pressuring their senators, and ultimately the president, to embrace the cause of turning back the arms race once and for all. While their faith in the democratic process was heartening to many, the exact mechanism by which these resolutions would result in a freeze was always rather murky. After all, no localities in America controlled their own nuclear arsenals, and Ronald Reagan and company were not really interested in the foreign policy views of state legislatures and city councils. The passage of these resolutions, most often in college towns and the like, may have created political problems for the assorted candidate here or there, but if they can be said to have had any enduring effect on policy, it was probably the opposite of what was intended. Inspired to respond to the arguments coming from the proponents of the freeze, Ronald Reagan decided, almost entirely on his own, to counter with a game-changing response, one that has come to be known as the Strategic Defense Initiative (SDI), or Star Wars, and has so far cost the U.S. Treasury hundreds of billions of dollars.

Reagan's proposal that the United States embark on an immediate emergency research program to build a shield in the stars to make nuclear weapons "impotent and obsolete" enjoyed almost no support in the scientific community. It was said to require the equivalent of "eight Manhattan projects" simultaneously and would likely have proved enormously destabilizing to the nuclear balance were it to show any progress in actually working. Yet SDI captured the imagination of many Americans and, more important, the money spigot it turned on captured the affection of the entire military-industrial sector together with their lobbyists and the congressmen and senators whose campaigns they funded. Reagan's proposal, tacked on to the end of his State of the Union address without any consultation with his military or scientific advisers, successfully shifted the terms of the debate and capitalized on the fears that had been stoked by the proponents of the freeze. [58]

The origins of SDI might very well have been the book that helped inspire many to embrace the freeze initially. Jonathan Schell, author of the 1982 best-seller *The Fate of the Earth*, followed up with *The Abolition*, which called for a scientific solution to the problem of nuclear vulnerability much like the one Reagan imagined.[59] Whatever the source, the fact was that the freeze move-ment turned out to be so reasonable in its arguments and mild in its tactics that when it was co-opted to expand rather than contract the nuclear arms race, its enemies needed only to build on those arguments of its leaders that served their purposes. "What if free people could live secure in the knowledge that their security did not rest upon the threat of instant U.S. retaliation to deter a Soviet attack?" Reagan asked. Wasn't mutually assured destruction "a sad commentary on the human condition"?[60]

When Reagan won his landslide reelection in 1984, it became obvious that the freeze was effectively powerless save as a statement of values. The dem-onstrations soon abated. Reagan's Star Wars program, meanwhile, though almost unimaginably expensive and plagued by all manner of budgetary and scientific fraud, established a beachhead in the Pentagon and defense industry and was soon boasting its own command within the armed services. It remains in place today, costing tens of billions of dollars to achieve a goal that remains as chimeric as the day Reagan proposed it. Conservative historians and many journalists continue to assert that the program, however ineffective from a scientific point of view, played a key role in convincing Soviet leaders that they had no choice but to capitulate in the Cold War. But more cautious Soviet experts see internal factors as far more central to Soviet decision making and point to the increased dangers of an actual nuclear exchange.

The second domestic front in Reagan's Cold War turned on events in the jungles of Central America. Its nations had traditionally served as a kind of backyard playpen for U.S. officials and corporations, which typically bribed local strongmen to keep peasants and workers under control (and in pov-erty).[61] The presence of Fidel Castro in nearby Cuba gave Cold Warriors a reason to invest the region with strategic significance, even if its primary pur-pose from an American standpoint was to provide coffee and bananas to American consumers. When the Sandinistas came to power in Nicaragua dur-ing Jimmy Carter's presidency and proclaimed themselves to be allies of Cuba, they were met by a remarkably indulgent response by the U.S. government—at least when judged by historical standards. Conservatives, meanwhile, viewed the revolution as an insult that could not be allowed to stand. Re-versing the revolution in Nicaragua would teach the rest of the Marxist re-gimes in the world—as well as El Salvador, where a Sandinista-supported guerrilla movement sought to overthrow a murderous military junta—a lesson about the changing tides of history. Reagan believed the Nicaraguan counterrevolutionaries—called Contras—to be the "moral equivalent of the Founding Fathers" and warned of a "red tide" washing across Central America if the United States did not support their efforts.[62] Meanwhile, U.S. spending on both foreign and military aid to Central America's regimes increased twenty times over.[63]

A popular movement erupted against Reagan's policies that included leftists, union leaders, and students as well as significant numbers of clergy and laity. Many within the movement were moralistic and absolutist in their opposition, and were willing to break laws and work outside of representative institutions of government in order to express their anger at Reagan's policies.[64] Even so, their energy and anger managed to reach the top echelon of liberal power in the 1980s, those who did hold faith in representative institutions and their ability to articulate opposition. In 1982, recognizing Reagan's desire to support the Contras, Congress passed the Boland Amendment, named after an otherwise little-known Democratic congressman from Massachusetts, Edward Boland, who sponsored it. The bill prohibited the CIA and the Department of Defense from using funds to overthrow the Sandinistas and passed without any significant opposition in either house of Congress.[65]

The desire to keep the United States out of war in Central America drew support from any number of quarters. America's allies in both Nicaragua and El Salvador were not only vicious murderers of peasants and partisans but also had a particular proclivity for murdering nuns and priests, whom they accused of filling up the minds of the uneducated with dangerous ideas about Jesus' teachings. When four women, two of the them Maryknoll nuns coming from New York to do humanitarian work, were murdered in cold blood, and the Reagan administration sought to excuse the crime, the state's congressional delegation went into permanent opposition.

Ted Kennedy, Tip O'Neill, and literally hundreds of Democrats stayed focused on the issue. Haunted by his regret for having voted in favor of the Gulf of Tonkin Resolution as a young congressman, O'Neill saw Central America as a means of atonement. O'Neill's nonagenarian aunt, the Maryknoll Sister Mary Eunice Tolan, had exercised a strong influence on his thinking on moral matters and when she passed away a Maryknoll sister named Peggy Healy, who was based in Nicaragua, sent him a steady stream of reports of the brutality of the U.S.-supplied forces, not only toward the peasantry, but toward the church itself.[66] "I have a lot of friends in the Maryknoll Order, and they keep me highly informed," O'Neill explained at the time. "They look at it . . .

like Vietnam."[67] O'Neill rarely carried half of the House of Representatives with him, and almost never more than a third of the Senate, but he did ensure a pitched battle—and, hence, a fresh harvest of Reagan administration lies— every time the issue arose.

Meanwhile, the Reagan administration was ready, if necessary, to fight the war with U.S. troops. On April 17, 1985, *The New York Times* published portions of a leaked copy of a secret document in which the White House asserted that "direct application of US military force . . . must realistically be recognized as an eventual option, given our stakes in the region, if other policy alternatives fail."[68] But the campaign of the Central American peace movement, together with the still-potent effect of the "Vietnam syndrome," the memory of chaos and catastrophe both at home and abroad associated in millions of Americans' minds with all foreign military intervention, proved a sufficiently strong barrier against Reagan's hopes for military intervention in the area. Poll after poll indicated that the bumper sticker formula "El Salvador is Spanish for 'Vietnam'" continued to hold sway.[69] Mainstream churches also began a sanctuary movement to offer shelter to the thousands of Central Americans escaping political persecution in El Salvador, Guatemala, Honduras, and other close Reagan administration allies where leftists and liberals risked their lives for criticizing local oligarchies or giving voice to the values of democracy and human rights.

Liberals tried to steer clear of being painted as sympathetic to the Latin American leftists themselves, as the memory of McCarthyism remained fresh, and conservatives were not exactly shy about giving that tried and true tactic another try. *The New Republic,* though ostensibly liberal, had developed a nasty neoconservative bent when it came to foreign policy, and as such developed the frequent habit of impugning the motives of those liberals with whom it disagreed in brazenly McCarthyite terms. Those who did not see the issues the magazine's way were dismissed as "second-rate thinkers," "self-indulgent, solipsistic," and "fellow-travelers and their ilk." One editorial accused "Democrats, including some in Congress [of] positively identifying with the Sandinistas, their social designs, their political ends and even their hostility to the United States."[70] Tip O'Neill did not genuinely care about the welfare of Central America but rather wanted "so badly to wound his nemesis Ronald Reagan that the real issues at stake count for very little."[71] Human rights groups who reported on the Contras' lax standards toward the murder, rape, and torture of innocents were slandered in *The New Republic*'s pages as "Sandinista sympathizers."[72] Those in Congress who focused on such abuses, which, after all, were being conducted courtesy of U.S. taxpayer dollars, found themselves slurred as a "Sandinista Chorus" that "cares genuinely neither for liberties nor for law, but for the dictatorships and their causes."[73]

Writing in *Commentary*, Norman Podhoretz warned, "In a conflict where the only choice is between Communists and anti-Communists, anyone who refuses to help the anti-Communists is helping the Communists."[74] And UN ambassador and former Democrat Jeane Kirkpatrick, who earned her position in the administration solely on the merit of an article published in *Commentary* during the Carter administration, insisted that "there are people in the US Congress . . . who would actually like to see the Marxist forces take power" in Central America.[75]

Buoyed by such arguments, the Reagan administration did everything it could to evade the strictures that Congress had placed on it, including secretly mining Nicaragua's harbors, an obvious act of war.[76] Rumors of extraconstitutional efforts involving mercenaries and massacres led to "Boland II," passed into law in October 1984, which barred the use of any funds "available to the Central Intelligence Agency, the Department of Defense or any other agency or entity involved in intelligence activities" for the purpose of "supporting, directly or indirectly, military or paramilitary operations in Nicaragua by any nation, group, organization or individual."[77]

Reagan's response was to take his foreign policy private, outside the purview of Congress and the rest of the executive branch. The extent of the operations that were subsequently undertaken was astounding. As Reagan biographer Lou Cannon recounts, "Operating first in cooperation with the Israelis and then through a covert U.S. initiative managed by Oliver North, the Reagan administration from the late summer of 1985 to mid-autumn of 1986 supplied antitank and antiaircraft weapons to Iran in violation of its proclaimed policy of withholding weapons from nations that sponsored terrorism and of a specific embargo on arms sales to Iran." The operation became part of an impossibly complicated effort to fight two wars simultaneously without admitting to either. The profits secured by overcharging the Iranians were turned over to Americans running guns to the Contras (and occasionally carrying cocaine back into the United States). It was a dirty business, conducted by U.S. officials working with arms dealers, drug smugglers, mercenaries, and murderers. And it was all done in defiance of Congress.[78]

In October 1986, Sandinista sharpshooters brought down a U.S. plane in Nicaragua filled with U.S. arms destined for the Contras, and the entire criminal conspiracy began to unravel. Former U.S. Marine Eugene Hasenfus, who survived the crash, confessed that he was working for the CIA, much like

Francis Gary Powers had done in Moscow nearly three decades earlier.[79] Suddenly impeachment was in the air. Bob Woodward started breaking new stories. Congress assembled special investigative hearings. Reagan was forced to appoint Republican litigator Lawrence E. Walsh as independent counsel to investigate criminal wrongdoing. Democrats believed themselves to be in a strong political position, given the president's inability to defend his own behavior and the nation's resistance to war, much less aid to a terrorist-supporting regime that had taken Americans hostage. But then the handsome, charismatic Marine lieutenant colonel Oliver "Ollie" North, who somehow managed to mastermind (and finance) much of the entire effort from his tiny office within the National Security Council staff, appeared, his chest shining with military medals earned in Vietnam, questioning the patriotism of his congressional interrogators and by extension their courage. His performance recalled that of Douglas MacArthur, who had behaved with a similarly cavalier attitude toward the U.S. Constitution more than three decades earlier. But while President Truman successfully faced down MacArthur and his minions, the Democratic senators and congressmen who were subject to the attacks of North and his supporters enjoyed no such self-confidence. As Sean Wilentz recounts, "Mail supporting North and denouncing the committee poured into Washington; individual members were alarmed by how many letter writers expressed a desire to see them hanged."[80] The spectacle had become all, with little of the substance that underlay it allowed to enter public debate. The Reagan administration had made a mockery of the constitutional separation of powers doctrine; it had engaged with drug smugglers, terrorists, and mass murderers; and it had lied to the American people about its actions and been caught. From a constitutional perspective, these actions were in many respects more serious than those that had led to Richard Nixon's resignation during the Watergate scandal. The administration laid much of the blame on CIA director William Casey, who conveniently died shortly after the scandal broke. And yet Democrats lacked the wherewithal to make even the most fundamental arguments about democratic accountability. They read their mail, examined the polls, and fearing accusations of being "soft" on or "pro" Communist, they joined the praise for the juntalike actions of North and CIA Director William Casey and company. Had it not been for Lawrence Walsh's tireless (and in official Washington, much-mocked and derided) investigation, the top members of the Iran-Contra conspiracy would have gotten away without suffering any significant consequences at all. In light of "Olliemania," the frightening celebration of a man who had pursued secrecy to get around elected officials, some activists fell into what Christian Smith labeled "the sardonic and dispirited paralysis of cynicalized radicalism."[81]

With so much of Reagan's attention on foreign policy, he was distracted from mounting problems at home. Chief among these was a "gay cancer" that had struck certain neighborhoods of San Francisco, Los Angeles, and New York City as early as 1981, and first surfaced with symptoms such as purple lesions and severe flu symptoms. Four years later 5,600 Americans had died from what was now being called acquired immune deficiency syndrome (AIDS); by 1989 that number had risen to 46,344. As AIDS ravaged the gay community, Ronald Reagan remained nearly silent on the issue. Only the 1985 death of Rock Hudson, an old Hollywood friend, prompted any response from him at all, and many months passed before he asked the surgeon general, in February 1986, "to draw up a report on the problem."[82] Still, as the gay journalist Randy Shilts pointed out, not only had the Reagan administration "not increased AIDS funding but the budget called for reducing AIDS spending from the current level of $96 million to $85.5 million in the next fiscal year."[83]

The demand for action on the AIDS crisis was part of a larger struggle to bring gay rights into the larger civil rights movement, and it exploded on the national stage with the Stonewall riots of 1969. New York City police raided gay bars on a regular basis, but usually with a warning beforehand. On June 27, however, their raid on the Stonewall Inn came as a surprise. A number of patrons were arrested, but then the unexpected happened: instead of running away or complacently entering the paddy wagons, the men fought back. "Limp wrists were forgotten," as *The Village* Voice would report in the next few days, and the stunned police retreated. The following morning the words "Gay Power" were spray painted in the streets around the Stonewall Inn.[84]

Stonewall led to the formation of the Gay Liberation Front (GLF), the first of many organizations that sprang up throughout the next few years. The timing of its emergence colored the politics of GLF. After all, this was not 1963 but 1969, a year when the civil rights movement was in the process of a meltdown and Black Power, separatism, and a smorgasbord of Maoist, anarchist, and Marxist/Leninist cadres and cults were in the ascendance. John D'Emilio called it "the queer version of the National Liberation Front in Vietnam, whose flag was often brandished in demonstrations of the late 1960s."[85] GLF rejected the approach of the leading gay organization that predated it, the Mattachine Society, which had roots in progressive and Communist circles during the 1950s but was now regarded as middle class and respectable (and, many argued, ineffective).[86] The GLF's noisy meetings were notorious for participants "high on drugs, marijuana or speed usually" and for a celebration of liberated sexuality and free expression not tempered by liberal demands for rights or inclusion. [87] This was a difficult time for a new movement to take up the cause of "rights," because the country was growing weary of the demands of women, blacks, and a host of ethnic minorities. Gay activists would also consistently face the difficulty of convincing people that they had been born with ascribed identities, like African Americans or women.

Beginning in 1969 the movement began its decades-long march into the mainstream. By December 1969 the Gay Activists Alliance (GAA) had broken from the GLF. It was founded by organizers unhappy with GLF's radical agenda and often chaotic decision-making process.[88] In 1973 the National Gay and Lesbian Task Force (NGLTF) was formed to serve as a voice in Washington—another identity-oriented rights lobby accepted by fellow liberals as such.[89] Its mainstream focus yielded dividends throughout the rest of the decade. The year of its formation, the American Psychiatric Association removed homosexuality from its list of mental disorders,[90] a measure that helped change the broader American perception that homosexuality was an illness or perversion. The following year, the U.S. Civil Service Commission lifted its ban on the employment of gay men and lesbians in 1975, just a year after Bella Abzug introduced her own gay rights bill to end discrimination in public and private housing, employment, and education against individuals on the basis of sexual orientation.[91] A year later Carter's pugnacious assistant to the president for public liaison, Midge Costanza, organized the first-ever meeting between the NGLTF and a White House staff member.

In 1977, San Francisco's District 5 elected forty-seven-year-old Harvey Milk to the San Francisco Board of Supervisors—America's first openly gay public official. Milk had grown up on Long Island in a middle-class Jewish family, hiding his sexuality and playing linebacker for Bay Shore High School.[92] Following college at the State University of New York at Albany, he entered the Navy as a diving officer, serving for four years during the Korean War before earning an honorable discharge. Milk's career jumps and starts included stints as a schoolteacher, insurance company actuary, financial clerk and analyst on Wall Street, and then coproducer of *Hair* and *Jesus Christ Superstar* on Broadway.[93] He met his lover, Scott Smith, in the Christopher Street subway station on his forty-first birthday.[94] They settled in San Francisco's Castro district and opened a camera shop.

Though new to the neighborhood, Milk ran for the Board of Supervisors in 1973, reaching out to the labor movement with strong support for a boycott of the Coors Brewing Company, known for both its antigay and antilabor practices. This didn't win him political office, nor did finally cutting his long hair and shaving his beard for a second run in 1975, though Mayor George Moscone did appoint him to the city's Board of Permit Appeals. Shunned, ironically, by the city's increasingly powerful gay business establishment, two years later Milk ran a populist campaign fueled by a volunteer army and focused on the issues of public transportation, the cost of child care, and rent control—and won. He introduced a gay rights ordinance his first day in office, and the vote went 10–1 in favor. Only a newly elected supervisor named Dan White refused to support the measure, even though Milk had gone out of his way to attend the christening of White's child.

Harvey Milk's next problem was John Briggs, a conservative state legislator from Orange County. To protect the "rights of parents to determine who will be teaching their children," he introduced an amendment to ban gays from teaching in California's schools.[95] The language in his proposal would have legalized firing not only gays but also anyone who happened to support gay rights.[96] Milk's pushback against the bill—which had 61 percent favorability when originally introduced—started to win some allies, and even Ronald Reagan came out against it on libertarian grounds. An extensive grassroots campaign based on old-fashioned home visits, together with help from liberal Hollywood; public unions; and the state's governor, Jerry Brown, helped overcome the prejudice and parental fears upon which the bill played and turned the issue around.[97] When 60 percent of Californians supported the right of the state's gay teachers to keep their jobs, it provided a place for optimism in a nation where Anita Bryant and other New Right activists were turning states like Florida, Oregon, and Kansas toward antigay persecution and prejudice.[98]

Like Milk, Dan White had been elected to the board in 1977. A white, working-class Catholic, he hated gays, hippies, and everyone else he thought was undermining the values he held dear. Around the time of the Briggs Initiative, White quit his position for what he claimed was financial need but then suddenly asked for it back; Milk pleaded with Moscone to give the position to someone more progressive. On November 27, 1978, the day that Moscone planned to announce his replacement, a distraught White entered City Hall through a window, walked first to Moscone's office and then to Milk's, shooting both men at point-blank range.

The shock of the murders was bad enough, but the trial that followed proved hardly less disheartening. The jury contained no gays. The prosecutor never mentioned White's animosity toward Milk and failed to prove premeditation. A taped confession, taken by White's former softball coach, made jurors weep in sympathy for the defendant. Even prosecution witnesses, such as then-mayor Dianne Feinstein, praised the killer's moral character. The verdict was a mere seven years and eight months for manslaughter, of which White would serve little more than five years. Gays rioted in response, smashing windows and overturning cars.

Milk's martyrdom served the cause in a way no amount of activism ever could have. He had been arguing with other gay leaders about the need for a gay march on Washington modeled after the 1963 civil rights protest.[99] On October 14, 1979, even without a bill to support, an estimated one hundred thousand proud gay Americans descended on the nation's capital to announce their political coming of age and willingness to stand up and be counted. The role of the march could not be underplayed in the larger attempt to link the gay rights movement to the civil rights movement.[100]

The arrival of the AIDS epidemic in the 1980s threatened the movement's momentum. As the disease spread, an antigay backlash reemerged. Conservatives in Congress such as Jesse Helms complained on the Senate floor, "I have never heard once in this Chamber anybody say to the homosexuals and drug users. . . . 'Stop what you are doing.' . . . If they would stop what they are doing, there would not be one additional new case of AIDS in America."[101] William F. Buckley, Jr., suggested that AIDS sufferers be tattooed on the forearms and buttocks (a move the *New York Native*, a leading gay paper, termed "Buckley's Buchenwald").[102] Pat Buchanan, working in the White House communications office between pundit jobs and presidential campaigns, declared, "The poor homosexuals. They have declared war on nature and now nature is exacting an awful retribution."[103]

The crisis rallied leaders in the gay community. Larry Kramer, a New York–based writer whose rage fueled his activism, started the Gay Men's Health Crisis (GMHC), a nonprofit that worked to inform the gay community about safer sexual practices while demanding more support from the city and more money to research AIDS at the federal level.[104] Liberal leaders in Congress such as California's Henry Waxman pressed activists' demands with the vigor that a plague demanded. But in 1986 the Supreme Court dealt the movement yet another blow in *Bowers v. Hardwick*, when, in a 5–4 vote, it upheld Georgia's antisodomy law, which outlawed gay sex even in the privacy of one's own home. Justice Harry Blackmun's dissent, which argued that "the concept of privacy embodies the 'moral fact that a person belongs to himself and not others nor to society as a whole,'" offered some hope for the future.[105] So, too, did Justice John Paul Stevens's argument that the rights established in *Griswold*, a 1965 ruling that a Connecticut law prohibiting the use of contraceptives violated the right to privacy, should protect the "right to engage in nonreproductive, sexual conduct that others may consider offensive or immoral."[106]

In October of 1987 gay leaders decided to launch a second march, this time in support of full equality. In broadening their demands, march organizers also made a concerted effort to link up with previous civil rights causes, inviting leaders like Cesar Chavez, Eleanor Smeal of NOW, and most prominently (and controversially, given some of his public criticisms of the gay rights movment) in light of the upcoming election, Jesse Jackson. The march also tried to turn grief to the service of the cause, humanizing gays for people growing unnerved by AIDS. Gay activist Cleve Jones had decided to create a huge memorial quilt and began soliciting individual panels from the loved ones of victims of the disease, each of which included an emotional reminder of the person who had died. When it was unfolded onto the nation's mall, the quilt stretched out over a space larger than a football field.

The march coincided with the final year of Bayard Rustin's life. The elderly civil rights activist was asked by his young lover, Walter Naegle, and the Coalition for Lesbian and Gay Rights, to speak out about AIDS. In a series of reflective interviews, he drew connections between the past and present. "The barometer of people's thinking" in the past "was the black community. Today, the barometer of where one is on human rights questions is no longer the black, it's the gay community. . . . There are great numbers of people who will accept all kinds of people: blacks, Hispanics, and Jews, but who won't accept fags. That is what makes the homosexual central to the whole political apparatus as to how far we can go in human rights."[107]

But the gay rights movement was hardly a monolith, and not all of its elements were as committed to mainstream politicking and liberal coalition building. ACT UP, formed in 1987, was prompted in large part by the playwright and novelist Larry Kramer, who, standing before an audience of about two hundred activists gathered at the Lesbian and Gay Community Services Center in New York City on March 10, cited his own—and what he thought should be other gay activists'—"anger, fury, and rage."[108] Frustration about the inadequate reaction to the AIDS crisis and Reagan's near silence had to turn itself into confrontational, direct action, he insisted. ACT UP grew out of that electrifying speech, but it was in some respects a return to the militant spirit of the Gay Liberation Front and the Gay Activists Alliance. Kramer himself had grown frustrated with the slow bureaucratic pace of the Gay Men's Health Crisis (GMHC), the organization he had helped found in 1982 but that now disillusioned him. He thought the AIDS crisis required comparison to previous acts of genocide, including the Holocaust.

ACT UP demanded more federal dollars for medical research, easier access to AIDS drugs, and the promotion of safe-sex practices in the gay community. Mimicking some of the tactics of Yippies, the group's preferred tactic was guerrilla theater. For instance, in a "Stop the Church" protest of the Catholic Church's objection to safe-sex education, thousands of angry activists descended on St. Patrick's Cathedral in New York City, chanting and waving signs. Some entered the church and disrupted services, tossing communion wafers onto the floor (and no doubt alienating attendees of services). The language of "queer pride," a confirmation and celebration of gay sexuality and difference, and an embrace of identity politics were hallmarks of ACT UP. Anger at the failure to respond to the disease was understandable, but it was unclear what ACT UP's militancy ultimately accomplished in terms of achieving more funding for AIDS research or the drugs that might one day cure the disease. Comparisons to the Holocaust were unlikely to win much of a hearing on the part of the American public, who obviously stood guilty if the argument was accepted. Indeed, the gay journalist Randy Shilts worried that all ACT UP achieved was "expressing anger for the sake of expressing anger," something he found "infantile" and "counterproductive."[109]

When the Democratic convention was held in San Francisco (a city hit particularly hard by AIDS) in July of 1984, all of the different currents of liberal protest came together well aware that the party had little chance of regaining power against a popular president buoyed by a booming economy. Many had expected that Ted Kennedy would provide the keynote speech, but Walter Mondale, perhaps nursing grudges from 1980, insisted upon a lesser-known if no less compelling political figure: Mario Cuomo.[110]

New York's first-term governor drew upon a deeply compelling life story as he rose to the platform and introduced himself to the rest of America. He was born in 1932, the youngest son of Italian immigrants. His father, Andrea, had arrived six years earlier and cleaned storm sewers before acquiring a small grocery store in South Jamaica, Queens, the year before Mario's birth. The store was open twenty-four hours a day, and as a boy Mario worked there after school with the rest of his family. Often hiding out in the back of the store, Mario developed a quiet and thoughtful persona. He became an altar boy and, unlike many of his fellow young South Jamaica residents, actually enjoyed Sunday school and the solitary act of reading. Like so many second-generation sons and daughters of immigrants, Mario struggled with his parents' ethnic provincialism, particularly their embarrassing difficulties learning English.[111]

Cuomo attended St. John's University, where he played baseball well enough to make it to the minor leagues, and then went on to St. John's Law School, earning his degree in 1956. St. John's was hardly the Ivy League, a fact that burned inside young Mario, who never lacked confidence in his intellectual abilities or affinity for hard work. When he received no offers from elite law firms, he blamed anti-Italian prejudice, which undoubtedly played a role.[112] This early experience with exclusion, whatever its inspiration, served as a blessing in disguise because it facilitated his entry into public service and inspired the passion he brought to it. Cuomo served as a law clerk with the New York State Court of Appeals and then became an advocate for Italian residents in Queens who were fighting the development of a high school in their neighborhood that would have destroyed sixty-nine homes—the so-called Corona Fighting 69.[113] Mayor Lindsay noted his skills and hired Cuomo as a mediator in a heated dispute over a public housing development proposed for Forest Hills. He won both community and political support and impressed pretty much every political professional in the city. (Jimmy Breslin, the 1970s equivalent of Damon Runyon, went so far as to compare the young lawyer to the now-sainted Bobby Kennedy.[114])

But Cuomo's success in politics proved fitful at best. Famously, even ostentatiously cautious, he had been compared with Hamlet in the outer boroughs of New York long before he began to drive the national press corps to distraction with his inability to make up his mind about his next move. After considering and rejecting a 1973 run for New York City mayor, he ran for lieutenant governor in 1974 and was badly defeated, but Governor Hugh Carey came to his rescue by appointing him secretary of state for New York. Then, in 1977, Cuomo did decide to run for mayor and stepped into a protracted political battle. In the Democratic primary—the only one that mattered—he faced not only Bella Abzug and Abe Beame but also Ed Koch, who, like Cuomo, enjoyed considerable outer-borough appeal with the kind of people who were almost ready to give up on the national Democratic Party and become what would be called Reagan Democrats. A huge stumbling block for Cuomo was his adamant opposition to the death penalty. However symbolic his stance on it might have been—New York City mayors had no authority related to criminal penalties whatsoever—the issue resonated loudly, as did any related to race and crime, particularly after the city's horrific 1977 blackout and crime spree. Cuomo found himself spit upon at campaign events whenever he spoke against the death penalty, which, against all advice, he insisted on doing.[115] After Koch won handily in a nasty runoff between the two, Cuomo began to take on the persona of a beautiful loser—a man who stuck to his principles and picked fights that increased his unpopularity but won him the admiration of pundits and romantics.

Cuomo avenged this defeat five years later when Koch foolishly tried to make a run for the governor's mansion, a job for which he was particularly unsuited, given his open contempt for rural and suburban life outside the city. Cuomo, in contrast, shined in the governor's office, delivering beautiful speeches that somehow combined the best elements of sermons, seminars, and stem-winders, and demonstrated his thoughtfulness on issue after issue as he sought to find a middle ground between contemporary liberalism and those who felt themselves to be its victims.

Hopes were high among convention delegates as Cuomo took the stage, more than a few of them already wondering whether he might be their candidate four years hence. And he did not disappoint. The speech's opening lines became etched in the permanent memory of liberal moral stock:

> Ten days ago, President Reagan admitted that although some people in this country seemed to be doing well nowadays, others were unhappy, even worried, about themselves, their families, and their futures. The President said that he didn't understand that fear. He said, "Why, this country is a shining city on a hill." And the President is right. In many ways we are a shining city on a hill. But the hard truth is that not everyone is sharing in this city's splendor and glory. A shining city is perhaps all the President sees from the portico of the White House and the veranda of his ranch, where everyone seems to be doing well. But there's another city; there's another part to the shining city; the part where some people can't pay their mortgages, and most young people can't afford one; where students can't afford the education they need, and middle-class parents watch the dreams they hold for their children evaporate.

Continuing to deploy this "two cities" theme, he documented elderly people sleeping in basements and the rise of homeless people on city streets. Cuomo explained: "In fact, Mr. President, . . . this nation is more a 'Tale of Two Cities' than it is just a 'Shining City on a Hill.'" He then made clear that Reagan could never really understand this problem, because he believed that "what falls from the table will be enough for the middle class and those who are trying desperately to work their way into the middle class." Cuomo then reminded his listeners of the moral vision and the alternative that was at the heart of American liberalism.

Cuomo understood that he was addressing an audience of fiercely polyglot groups, and he could no longer draw upon the image of America as a melting pot, a blending together of difference into a stew of assimilation and nationalism. Cuomo recognized how their identities gave many people's lives their principal meaning, in conjunction with their families and communities. He spoke of his father as "a small man with thick calluses on both his hands" who came to America "uneducated, alone, unable to speak the language." But, Cuomo argued, his father's background hadn't locked him into his identity but pushed him to something larger. From the identity of white ethnics was carved the massive edifice of the New Deal, Cuomo reminded his listeners. His parents had "asked to be protected in those moments when they would not be able to protect themselves. This nation and this nation's government did that for them." And Cuomo wanted to do so again.

Pluralistic identities could be retained, but liberalism depended on something that transcended them as well—a sort of "transnational America" that the social critic Randolph Bourne had envisioned earlier in the century, a recognition of identity as against assimilation, an appreciation of difference, but also a pluralism that could still weave together a wider sense of a "beloved community" at the national level (what Bourne called a "cosmopolitan federation of national colonies" to replace the now obsolete "melting pot").[116] Cuomo came to this vision not from left-wing ideology or commitment to political activism but from his grounded Italian Catholicism and his love and loyalty to family and neighbors:

> We Democrats believe that we can make it all the way with the whole family intact, and we have more than once. Ever since Franklin Roosevelt lifted himself from his wheelchair to lift this nation from its knees—wagon train after wagon train—to new frontiers of education, housing, peace; the whole family aboard, constantly reaching out to extend and enlarge that family; lifting them up into the wagon on the way; blacks and Hispanics, and people of every ethnic group, and native Americans—all those struggling to build their families and claim some small share of America. For nearly fifty years we carried them all to new levels of comfort, and security, and dignity, even affluence. And remember this, some of us in this room today are here only because this nation had that kind of confidence.

The cheers resounded for what felt like hours. Delegates hugged one another and wondered, however briefly, if the Democrats might not have a shot at winning the election after all. They didn't, but Mario Cuomo did succeed in helping to forge a new liberal vision so desperately needed by all sides at once, one that honored cultural difference but embraced the ethic of teamwork and economic opportunity for all: a patchwork quilt rather than a melting pot.

Despite booming times for many, particularly on Wall Street, Cuomo struck a powerful chord with millions of Americans. In his infamous malaise speech of 1979, Jimmy Carter had worried about a nation that invited "human identity" to be defined by "what one owns" rather than "what one does." Carter had foreseen the materialistic obsession that came to define Reagan's America for better and for very much worse. Liberal critics such as John Kenneth Galbraith had likewise warned about a middle-class squeeze and growing inequality between the rich and the poor in 1980s America, the very few Donald Trumps at the top and the growing number of makeshift "tent cities" of homeless people floundering at the bottom.[117]

Sociologist Robert Bellah joined with colleagues to interview numerous Americans and in 1985 published a collective portrait of the country, the highly influential *Habits of the Heart*. A kind of analogue to David Riesman's 1950 masterwork, *The Lonely Crowd, Habits* described a nation struggling over the conflicting values projected by Reagan (individualism and wealth) and Cuomo (community and familial obligations). Bellah and his colleagues found Americans who had grown up in small towns but had moved to cities and were now struggling with anomie and the hollow rewards of a life based upon material acquisition. These were people who desired a sense of civic belongingness as well as their ability to protect their privacy and individual freedoms. What alarmed so many Americans during the 1980s seemed to be the loss of language about shared sacrifice—the sort that Cuomo sought to revive from the New Deal—and its overshadowing by the rapacious power of global capitalism. "American cultural traditions define personality, achievement, and the purpose of human life," they worried, "in ways that leave the individual suspended in glorious, but terrifying, isolation."[118] It was an observation that could be found manifest not only in politics but in the work, social, and cultural lives of millions of Americans, and one that liberals needed to overcome if they were ever to rebuild themselves into a majority movement.

The films of Oliver Stone released during the second half of the 1980s spoke powerfully to the political crosscurrents buffeting liberalism at the time.[119] The liberal messages conveyed by filmmakers like William Wyler, Elia Kazan, and Stanley Kramer were too earnest to serve as models for the 1980s, as post-Vietnam and post-Watergate American culture had become far more cynical and even paranoid, as could be seen in the work of directors like Alan Pakula,

Martin Scorsese, and the pioneering black director Spike Lee.[120] How could movies credibly return to the good-guy-slays-the-social-evils themes of the past? That was precisely Oliver Stone's dilemma. Speaking before the ACLU while working on *Wall Street* (1987), Stone spoke about balancing hope with despair. He fretted about the "military-industrial monolith dedicated to the Cold War" and his belief that "fear and conformity have triumphed." He confessed to feeling "lost" but added "somewhere on the back burner of a bewildered mind, I feel I gotta go back to those movies I believed in as a kid . . . where my hero is facing certain extinction surrounded on all sides by enemy swordsmen, but, by some shining light of inner force and greater love, turns the tables of fate and triumphs over all odds."[121]

Stone had been raised by a stern conservative father who had abandoned his youthful aspirations to the literary life to become a stockbroker with a socialite wife, a Manhattan brownstone, and private schools for his son.[122] Lou Stone shipped young Oliver off to the Hill School in Pottstown, Pennsylvania, before divorcing his wife, which shocked the young man.[123] Stone applied to and was accepted at Yale, but dropped out to travel and teach abroad, ending up at the Free Pacific Institute near Saigon. For reasons he could hardly explain at the time, but undoubtedly have a great deal to do with rejecting the privilege into which he was born as well as his father's expectations for him, Stone volunteered in 1967 for the 2nd Platoon of Bravo Company, serving near the Vietnamese-Cambodian border.

To say that Vietnam transformed Stone would be an understatement. He entered the war, in the words of his biographer James Riordan, "a rich college boy who, through his own absurd choice, had condemned himself to a hell mostly populated by poor whites and uneducated blacks."[124] The experience almost drove Stone mad, especially after he came close to killing an innocent elderly peasant out of nervousness.[125] He had once followed in his father's conservatism, supporting Goldwater in 1964, but now came to hate his country and drifted toward radical leftism. Stone later admitted that at the time, he "would have joined the Black Panthers if they'd asked me."[126]

Upon returning home he attended New York University's film school, with the ambition of making a definitive film about Vietnam. After writing a number of unfilmed screenplays, the one for 1978's *Midnight Express* won him an Oscar and paved a path for the future. Stone had a particular eye for violence. His bloody vision for Brian De Palma's *Scarface* (1983) became a classic, especially among teenage boys. Filled with gratuitous, almost sexualized violence, it told the story of a Cuban exile whose version of the Horatio Alger myth comes laced with cocaine and murder in almost orgiastic quantities. Throughout the film, the character Tony Montana praises America as a "land of opportunity," making the movie's message about the destructive nature of capitalism unmistakable.

Scarface likewise boosted Stone's professional standing as well as his ambition. The result was the first of his mid-1980s message movies, *Salvador* (1986). Set during the transition from the Carter to the Reagan administration, like many future Stone projects, it interwove genuine historical events, personal memoir, and fiction. It was the story of a rogue photojournalist who tries, unsuccessfully, to tell the story of the horrors of U.S.-supported El Salvador. The film did not do much business; it did receive a favorable critical response and raised Stone's stock in liberal, Reagan-hating Hollywood, where he was now finally able to make his autobiographical Vietnam film, *Platoon*, also released in 1986. Stone filmed in the jungles of the Philippines and subjected his actors to a grueling physical regimen that included digging foxholes and performing military exercises. "The idea," the director explained, "was to fuck with their heads so we could get that dog-tired attitude, the anger, the irritation, the casual way of brutality, the casual approach to death."[127] Within the platoon's cramped contours are two commanders, an Ahab-like figure and a sweet man who has developed doubts about the aims of the war (and who thus symbolizes American innocence). The clash between these two signified America's internal division, at least as experienced by Stone, and the platoon not only divides but descends into fragging their officers, as also happened with some frequency toward the end of the Vietnam War. "We fought ourselves."[128]

Platoon was nominated for eight Oscars, and went on to win four, including Best Picture and Best Director. Hollywood had found a "message" moviemaker who had the requisite grit to suit the post-Vietnam era. The payoff for Stone was a huge advance for his next film, *Wall Street*, which was serendipitously released just as the crash of 1987 arrived as a kind of real-life advertising campaign.

The story centered on a fictional character, Gordon Gekko, a fictionalized version of the notorious arbitrageur and inside trader Ivan Boesky, and the corruption of a young protégé, who ruins his father's company in pursuit of profits for his boss.[129] The plot was less significant than the credo of the evil genius at its center: "Greed, for lack of a better word, is good," a sentiment Gekko delivers to the shareholders' meeting of a company he is planning to take over. Moreover, the feel of the film, as James Lardner wrote in *The Nation*—its "pulsing rhythm" made up of "vistas of hotheaded young brokers working their phones and computer terminals" coupled with the "razzmatazz of skyline and traffic that is Hollywood shorthand for Manhattan"—made the whole world of money appear like a drug one could never shake.[130]

Stone closed out the decade with a return to Vietnam, or at least its aftermath, with *Born on the Fourth of July* (1989), based on the memoir of Ron Kovic, a onetime gung ho Marine who suffers extreme physical and psychological damage in Vietnam and returns home to become an antiwar activist. The movie was, in some respects, a modern version of William Wyler's post–World War II classic, *The Best Years of Our Lives* (1946), mixed with angry antiwar activism. The movie ends with Kovic's protest at the Republican Party's 1972 convention as the leader of a group of wounded vets, followed by his embrace, four years later, of the Democrats. The film, which earned Stone another Best Director Oscar, showed his control of both his emotions about America and of what Garry Wills called his "excess of rage," which often got the best of him later in his career.[131]

In 1991's *JFK*, he began to lose his bearings entirely, weaving a vast conspiratorial myth about Kennedy's assassination and America's entry into Vietnam that was difficult to imagine even he could believe. The devastated idealist was turning into a paranoid and delusional critic of American power. The misfire of *JFK* need not overshadow Stone's accomplishments during the 1980s, but it did illustrate the difficulty liberals had in explaining how, by the end of the 1980s, their hopes for America had gone so horribly wrong.

Nineteen eighty-eight proved yet another nightmare year for Democrats in general and liberals in particular, as that year's Democratic presidential primary was repopulated by many of the same candidates from 1984. Although Mondale did not run again, Gary Hart did, though he was undone by a sex scandal that sank his numbers throughout the campaign. Jesse Jackson was back as well, with exciting rallies and rhyming rhetoric, but he ran a more serious campaign this time around, inspiring any number of previously disaffected voters to enter the process and build for the future. But for all his talents and contradictions, Jesse Jackson was not the black candidate to break the barrier to the presidency or even the nomination. That man was still in his twenties at the time, working as a community organizer in Jackson's hometown of Chicago.[132]

Michael Dukakis was a "neoliberal" much like Gary Hart and, like Hart, he claimed to be inspired by JFK. But where Hart seemed to respond to Kennedy's idealism and youthful zeal, Dukakis clearly embraced his technocratic side, with an emphasis on competent governance rather than an emotional appeal to voters' values or economic self-interest. The campaign was emblematic of liberals' chronic lack of self-confidence at the time that the ostenta-tiously anti-ideological Dukakis—"the candidate of cool reason," "Governor Fix-It"—became the keeper of its barely flickering flame.[133] He lacked almost any ability to communicate personal emotion or human appeal. Greek by background, he nevertheless evinced even less charisma than the taciturn Norwegian, Walter Mondale.

Dukakis allowed himself to be defined, absurdly, by an advertisement fea-turing a frighteningly murderous felon named Willie Horton, who had been imprisoned in the early 1970s and later furloughed. In 1987, Horton took ad-vantage of his furlough and tried to kill a man and raped his fiancée.[134] Du-kakis had earlier vetoed a bill that prevented criminals from getting furloughs, based upon his own belief in rehabilitation, and Horton's crimes now proved, in the words of one Bush supporter, "a wonderful mix of liberalism and a big black rapist."[135] Ads quickly went on the air showing sinister-looking men walking through rotating doors at a prison, as if Bush were running for sher-iff of Birmingham, Alabama, circa 1948, on Strom Thurmond's ticket rather than for president of the United States after four decades of racial progress.

Dukakis failed to return fire on this and virtually every other attack on his character and the liberalism for which he allegedly stood. During the final Bush-Dukakis presidential debate, Bernard Shaw, a black reporter at CNN, asked Dukakis if he'd support the death penalty—something he opposed on principle—if his own wife had been raped and murdered. Failing to show any emotion whatever, Dukakis gave an extremely matter-of-fact response, which was understandable because it was an irresponsible question barely worthy of one.[136] But it played perfectly into the Bush strategy of portraying Dukakis as an unfeeling liberal machine, a robocandidate with a ready-made excuse for every social deviant known to mankind.

The fact that the demonization of the liberal label helped win Bush the presidency exasperated liberals, as did Dukakis's unwillingness to defend it.[137] But the moment had been a long time coming. Under challenge from neoliberal Gary Hart, who had assaulted what he called the "Eleanor Roo-sevelt wing" and insisted that "American liberalism was near bankruptcy" four years earlier, Walter Mondale had insisted that the time had come to "adjust liberal values of social justice and compassion to a new age of limited resources." In his farewell address to the Republican convention that year, Ronald Reagan brought the crowd to near ecstasy with his enthusiastic dam-nation of the now satanic creed: "The masquerade is over. It's time to . . . say the dreaded L-word; to say the policies of our opposition are liberal, liberal, liberal."[138] Heir apparent George H. W. Bush followed suit with his own sneers of "liberal, liberal, liberal" at Dukakis. "My opponent's views on defense are the standard litany of the liberal left," Bush explained to a San Diego audience. "The way he feels, I don't know if he could be comfortable in a great Navy town like this. I wouldn't be surprised if he thinks a naval exercise is something you find in the Jane Fonda Workout Book."[139] Out on the proverbial hustings Bush was far harsher: "I don't understand the type of thinking that lets first-degree murderers who haven't even served enough time to be eligible for parole so they can rape and plunder again, and then isn't willing to let the teachers lead the kids in the Pledge of Allegiance."[140] Per usual, Dukakis said nothing in his own defense, up until the campaign's final moments, when he offered up a tepid: "Yes, I'm a liberal in the tradition of Franklin Roosevelt and Harry Truman and John Kennedy." Yet what his left hand had given, his right immediately took away as Dukakis promised to terminate "the most liberal borrowing and spending spree in American history."[141] But in truth Dukakis was no liberal at all—just a sign of the desperate times into which American liberalism had fallen in its apparently endless quest for solid political ground upon which it might once again stand.

16

A Place Called "Hope"

> If we are somehow to keep our tradition alive for the next century, we
> are going to have to return to Trilling.
> —Daniel Patrick Moynihan to the legal scholar Louis Henkin, 1989[1]

In the decades since the 1960s the American university had grown deeply
politicized. Student activism and protest—even if on the margins—renewed
itself during the 1980s, focusing on opposition to Ronald Reagan's wars in
Central America, support for the antinuclear movement, and most successfully, divestiture from all investments benefiting the racist regime of South
Africa. It was a smarter and savvier form of activism than the students' older
brothers and sisters—and sometimes their parents—had engaged in and, in
the case of the divestiture movement, impressive in its success both on a local
and national level. But not all such efforts were as intelligently guided and
intellectually self-disciplined. In May 1987, for instance, students at Stanford
University chanted, "Hey, hey, ho, ho, Western culture's got to go!" as they
demanded a quota-driven diversification of the school's recently instituted
Western civilization curriculum, irrespective of the relative merit of the works
under consideration: less Shakespeare and Shaw; more Swahili and Sioux.
Jesse Jackson arrived to march with these misguided students, and the media
made much of the apparent (and actual) anti-intellectualism at one of America's most prestigious universities.[2]

These activists represented a broader development in American politics:
yet another New Left, but one that de-emphasized economics and equality of
opportunity and focused, instead, on culture, diversity, and "difference," particularly as these factors related to the life of the university. Postmodernity,
numerous critics explained, was about the triumph of the particular and the
diverse over the universal, and the particulars in this case generated an incessant set of protests on their own behalf.[3]

Identity politics was just one part of the new cultural and academic left.

Some professors in the humanities—conservatives called them "tenured radicals"—rejected not only the traditional canon but with it the entire Enlightenment.[4] Many were ex-student activists, who, disillusioned with their unsuccessful forays into genuine politics amid the simultaneous collapse of the antiwar and civil rights movements, had chosen to make the "long march" through America's institutions to battle what, in his famous "Prison Notebooks," the Marxist Italian philosopher Antonio Gramsci termed the "cultural hegemony" of the ruling elite.[5] This was actually a quite sensible reaction to the failure of "the revolution," given the power that these institutions enjoyed in shaping the boundaries of America's democratic discourse. But in practice, it frequently resulted in absurd strategies and pronouncements in which radical political analyses and postmodern theories were areas of acadmic inquiry where they struck outsiders as comically inappropriate. Andrew Ross, a professor of English who turned to "cultural and social analysis" at New York University, for instance, would profess to be "glad to be rid of English departments. I hate literature, for one thing, and English departments tend to be full of people who love literature."[6] In 1991, Ross published a book that focused much of its attention on the aesthetics and politics of the Weather Channel.[7] That same year members of the Modern Language Association (MLA) attended standing-room-only sessions on the "Sodomitical Tourist" and "Victorian Underwear and Representations of the Female Body."[8] Among the most frequently cited literary essays of the period were Eve Kosofsky Sedgwick's "Jane Austen and the Masturbating Girl" and "'Is the Rectum Straight?: Identification and Identity in 'The Wings of the Dove.'"[9]

Many of these activities would make for easy targets for both the right and the wider public, who looked upon academics as living in an imaginary universe. Beyond the ridicule of the "cult studs"—the rough equivalent to the 1950s "egghead"—came a floodtide of attacks on the phenomenon of "political correctness." Originally intended as a term of leftist self-mockery, it became an all-purpose term of abuse in the wider world used to describe the attempts of tenured radicals to indoctrinate innocent students into their anti-American, Marxist-tinged nihilistic perversity.[10] Todd Gitlin counted the term's usage in popular magazines and newspapers and found just 7 instances in 1988 and 4,643 five years later.[11] As a political matter, this attempt to police people's behavior by policing the language they used would prove to be pure poison, particularly given its emphasis on combating what it viewed to be an oppressively racist, sexist, and classist hierarchy in American society, and no sensible politician outside of Berkeley, California, or Burlington, Vermont, even thought to embrace any of it. But liberals paid the price in any case.

A new niche opened up on national bestseller lists for books that mocked the silliness and bemoaned the dangers of trendy academic posturing. The most audacious and interesting of these was undoubtedly Allan Bloom's *Closing of the American Mind* (1987), which boasted a foreword by none other than his colleague on the University of Chicago's Committee of Social Thought, Saul Bellow. An acolyte of the philosopher Leo Strauss, Bloom applied the arguments of Friedrich Nietzsche and Martin Heidegger to Rolling Stones riffs, suggesting that the Dionysian rituals of rock music, leftist politics, and postmodern academic theory represented "the same dismantling of the structure of rational inquiry as had the German university in the thirties."[12]

Bloom's apocalyptic warnings were followed by more journalistic jeremiads about the dangerous indoctrination taking place in America's elite academic institutions, including Roger Kimball's *Tenured Radicals* (1990), Richard Bernstein's *Dictatorship of Virtue* (1995), and Dinesh D'Souza's *Illiberal Education* (1991). In each case the author wove together fears about affirmative action, speech codes, and deconstruction, all of it eventually aimed at liberals who— just as had happened during the 1960s—were scorned and blamed for the excesses of the left.[13] Once again, self-styled academic revolutionaries on elite college campuses saw themselves as the vanguard of some imagined rebellion, though in this case it was to take place solely in the imagination. (As Gitlin memorably characterized the situation, while the left was marching on the English Department, the right was taking over the government.[14]) As these academic radicals manned the barricades of resistance against "phallocentrism" and the like, conservatives mounted a massive campaign against the already tattered social safety net and the poor and politically dispossessed forced to depend on it.

Though these debates may have appeared "academic" in the patronizing, politically irrelevant sense of the term frequently employed by journalists and politicians, they were actually central to the fate of American liberalism. As the sociologist James Davison Hunter pointed out, the culture wars—conflicts around abortion, federal funding of the arts, support for gay rights, and the linguistic battle inspired by calls for political correctness—all centered on "the secular Enlightenment of the eighteenth century and its philosophical aftermath."[15] Given the fact that these battles took place in the area that liberals had traditionally considered to be their home ground, they could not avoid confronting the issues they raised, however much they may have sought to avoid them. They would now need to define themselves not only against the traditional cast of conservative characters but also against a newly rejuvenated cultural left as well. It would be a two-front war for what remained of liberalism's cultural hegemony in the face of declining political power almost everywhere save urban America, the Northeast, and the assorted college and ski resort towns across America.

Arthur Schlesinger, Jr., took on the threat to liberalism from multiculturalism much as he had forty-three years earlier when combating communism in *The Vital Center,* suggesting that he saw himself in the center again, blasting away at left and right simultaneously.[16] Intellectual life during the 1990s might well open a new center—between right and academic left—that liberals could occupy just as the international force of communism waned. In *The Disuniting of America* (1991), Schlesinger reminded readers that America's democratic creed sought to create a "new man," in the words of J. Hector St. John de Crèvecoeur, author of *Letters from an American Farmer* (1782), out of divergent backgrounds, a unity amid plurality. Schlesinger was alarmed by how the new academic left treated so contemptuously the "American Creed" espoused by Gunnar Myrdal as an engine for racial and economic inclusion and, ultimately, social justice and greater equality. Schlesinger worried that activists had become transfixed with the cult of "self-esteem," employing education to help women and minorities feel better about themselves as it simultaneously encouraged their separatist claims and identities. He argued that without "a common adherence to ideals of democracy and human rights," American politics would fracture and lose sight of egalitarian ideals. He pointed out that the Western canon was full of house critics like Ralph Waldo Emerson, Herman Melville, and Walt Whitman, and could accommodate many more within the Enlightenment tradition.[17] At the same time, Schlesinger recognized that the cultural left brandished powerful weapons. Criticisms of the metanarrative of unilinear progress came easily to academics in the 1990s, given that they had experienced the flourishing of the environmental movement, nuclear meltdowns at Three Mile Island, and the catastrophe of Skylab, which understandably gave rise to doubts about the benefit of progress, scientific and otherwise.

Liberal historian John Patrick Diggins pronounced the academic left to be "the first Left in American or European history to distrust the eighteenth-century Enlightenment."[18] The cultural left had rejected "logocentrism," the elevation of rational argumentation based on universal principles, and had descended into a cynicism that viewed truth as almost entirely contingent and reliant on power relationships. They provided an intellectual rationale for dismissing reform and humanitarianism, two of the central foundations of postwar liberalism. Like Schlesinger, Diggins identified in liberalism's history a tradition of a "skeptical Enlightenment" that posited the existence of truth—

however difficult it might be to discover—but understood the challenge that humans, finite by nature, faced in attempting to recognize and locate it. Drawing upon Calvinism and Scottish skepticism, America's founders could be seen "lowering their hopes and raising their consciousness to the point where the framers were suspicious even of themselves."[19] This tradition continued in the thought of Schlesinger, Niebuhr, and Trilling, who embraced a liberalism of humility based on the recognition of man's hubristic intentions and limited capacities for self-criticism.

From the forties through the midsixties—once Marxism had lost its appeal to American intellectuals—most mainstream historians, led by Richard Hofstadter, Daniel Boorstin, and the history-minded political scienist Louis Hartz, had argued on behalf of, and later simply assumed, a liberal consensus among Americans, albeit one tinged with some deeply conservative habits. Because America had been born free of feudalism, Hartz argued in his magnum opus, *The Liberal Tradition in America* (1955), the country had also been *born liberal*.[20] Americans embraced individualism and markets; the "proletarian" believed himself to be an "incipient entrepreneur";[21] Lockean individualism and the social contract remained the pillars of American thought. Even the New Deal accepted the strictures of democratic capitalism and private property, Hartz argued, and was beholden to "experimentation" rather than radical departures from markets.[22]

By the late sixties, however, historians no longer felt secure in painting a consensual picture of America's past. In what the historian Robert Shalhope called the "republican synthesis," a new portrait of American history informed contemporary political theory in the 1980s and 1990s.[23] Colonial revolutionaries were now seen to be the true inheritors of British liberalism.[24] They spoke of "civic virtue" rather than individualism, and of active and armed citizenship, whose sacrifices benefited the common good.[25] They feared the influence of "luxury" and soft-hearted corruption of personal virtue.[26] As Gordon Wood, a highly esteemed historian of early America, explained, "Republicanism was essentially anti-capitalistic, a final attempt to come to terms with the emergent individualistic society that threatened to destroy once and for all the communion and benevolence that civilized men had always considered to be the ideal of human behavior."[27]

The potency of this tradition in the country's past supplanted what had been a belief in an almost immaculately conceived American liberal consensus and transformed the way many public intellectuals viewed not only the country's past but also the possibilities for its future. For instance, *Habits of the Heart* emphasized the "sense of public solidarity espoused by civic republicans" in explaining the authors' hope of replacing rights-based liberalism with what would become communitarianism in the 1980s.[28] With this discovery of a fractured past and a lack of consensus, liberals now had to acknowledge that their own political tradition was neither simple nor unified. In the 1990s the liberal historian James Kloppenberg tried to square this circle with the argument that American political thought since the Revolution had become an amalgam of "Christian notions of sinfulness and salvation, the public spiritedness and autonomy joined in the ideal of republican citizenship, and the concern for responsible individual freedom."[29]

The key text in this debate turned out to be a contribution by the philosopher John Rawls, who almost single-handedly revived the discipline of political theory in the English-speaking world with *A Theory of Justice* (1971). Drawing on a host of Enlightenment philosophers, most particularly Immanuel Kant, Rawls based his argument on the assumption of what he called a "veil of ignorance."[30] Through this veil—that is, without any prior knowledge regarding one's position in any social hierarchy—a liberal could imagine a community that was simultaneously "fair and egalitarian" to all its members.[31] He referred to this as the "original position." As the legal philosopher Ronald Dworkin explained it, "A political community treats people with equal concern when it respects the principles of justice that would be chosen by their representatives in the original position."[32]

Rawls so revolutionized American political theory in general and liberal political philosophy in particular that eleven years would pass before Michael Sandel offered up a fully cogent communitarian challenge. The theory of the "original position," he would argue, ignored the fact that citizens were not "unencumbered" individuals inhabiting ethereal and universal worlds. Rather, they were deeply *encumbered*—informed by their particularities, including their familial and local commitments. Sandel argues that it is these powerful bonds of community that help to define the individual. This is not merely a choice to be embraced or rejected on the basis of personal preference but it is how individuals "conceive of their identity . . . as defined to some extent by the community of which they are a part."[33] Hence the "original position" cannot hope to do justice to the reality of individual lives. Another critic of liberalism, ex-leftist historian Christopher Lasch, argued similarly in 1991: "The morally neutral state set up by liberals drew heavily on borrowed moral capital, from religion and other character-forming agencies, such as the traditional family and local community." Believing only in "the rights of the abstract individual," liberals didn't provide sufficient substance for a healthy polity.[34] As a philosophical doctrine, liberalism was premised on false assumptions about how people actually lived their lives, failing to appreciate that rights without responsibilities did not ensure the creation of healthy communities. These philosophers were identifying a central weakness of liberalism: It left people feeling all alone and lacked the mechanism to sustain solidarity over time. Community mores proved far more powerful than liberal principles, particularly when these principles appeared to be so inconsistently applied. The "veil of ignorance" existed, alas, exclusively in Rawls's imagination. In the real world, politicians, often corrupt ones, made the decisions about who got what.

The debate inspired liberal thinkers to try to present their philosophical beliefs in less dry, less rigid fashion so that they might be understood by and appeal to real people, rather than just liberal political philosophers. In so many ways they started to explain why the term "liberal" was not—pace Ronald Reagan, George Bush, and communitarian and republican political theorists— a paltry justification of public life. The political theorist and later White House adviser William Galston argued, "Liberalism contains within itself the resources it needs to declare and to defend a conception of the good and virtuous life that is in no way truncated or contemptible."[35] These values required certain virtues: reasonableness, patience, toleration, respect for opponents, mutuality, and freedom. "The liberal citizen must have the capacity to discern, and the restraint to respect, the rights of others," and must possess the patience to work within a system of laws and constraints.[36]

On this point Galston was joined by Stephen Macedo, a young political theorist at Princeton University, who argued that liberal virtues included the "public and moderate form of reflective justification" for policies and the belief in enlightened rationality and autonomous decision making. Macedo elaborated that liberal citizens needed "broad sympathies, self-critical reflectiveness, a willingness to experiment, to try and to accept new things, self-control and active, autonomous self-development, an appreciation of inherited social ideals, an attachment and even an altruistic regard for one's fellow liberal citizens."[37] The philosopher Stephen Holmes added to this the liberal belief in the constraint of political passion—a virtue in itself.[38] The more conservative liberal thinker Peter Berkowitz wrote numerous pieces throughout the 1990s that argued for the liberal virtues of "reflective judgment, sympathetic imagination, self-restraint, the ability to cooperate, and toleration."[39]

Other liberal political thinkers reminded their fellow citizens that conservative attacks and Republican criticisms inadvertently demonstrated a peculiar virtue of the liberal tradition—precisely its inability to inspire passionate or absolutist convictions. Liberals didn't need to find an alternative to the armed civic sacrifice and virtues that Republican critics of liberalism touted, because they possessed a certain sense of what the philosopher Richard Rorty called irony. [40] Liberal ironists hated cruelty and injustice but also dogmatism. Instead of constructing grandiose philosophical schemes, like those developed by Rawls, liberal citizens relied instead on stories from the past that encouraged fairness and justice.[41] Just because liberal ironists gave up "metaphysical attempts" to ground their beliefs didn't mean they couldn't "speak as the contingent historical selves we find ourselves to be."[42] Rorty famously labeled his own beliefs "postmodernist bourgeois liberalism" and insisted that despite contingency and conflict, the virtues to which liberals clung remained robust and worthy of a spirited defense.[43]

Rorty was born into the world of New York intellectuals and Cold War liberalism. His father, James Rorty, had been a Communist Party member during the twenties and thirties, and a founding editor of *New Masses*.[44] Breaking with the Communist Party in 1932, the year after his son Richard's birth, James became a Trotskyist, even hiding Trotsky's secretary, John Frank, from assassins sent by Stalin.[45] With Sidney Hook and James Burnham, he had helped to organize the American Workers Party before rejecting, along with Hook, revolutionary politics entirely.[46] James Rorty's second wife (and Richard's mother) was Winifred Raushenbush, the daughter of Walter Raushenbush, the famous Social Gospel theologian who had articulated a liberal version of Christianity that sought the "Kingdom of God" on earth and that influenced both Reinhold Niebuhr and Martin Luther King, Jr.[47] The Rortys' home in rural western New Jersey became a gathering place for New York intellectuals who shared their penchant for activism and ideas, including not just Hook but Irving Howe and Lionel Trilling. From these surroundings the young Richard Rorty learned how to "argue the world."[48]

A prodigy by any measure, at the ripe age of fifteen Rorty headed off for Hutchins College at the University of Chicago. He completed his MA in 1952 and moved away from Platonism toward what was then being called historically oriented philosophizing, a fancier term for the study of ideas in historical context.[49] Rorty then left Chicago for Yale, where he earned a PhD in philosophy in 1956. When his graduate training ended, he was drafted into the military, but because the war in Korea was over, Rorty's two years of service meant boredom more than valor while he worked for the Signal Corps. Once he returned from service, he turned to teaching philosophy, first at Wellesley College and then at Princeton University, where he arrived in 1961.

This was a boom time in American academe, a time when professorships were available in abundance and a hefty publication record wasn't a requirement. Following some difficult years in which his work foundered and his first marriage ended, Rorty began to read John Dewey much more seriously and then saw "resemblances" to other postmodern philosophers such as Ludwig Wittgenstein, Jacques Derrida, and Martin Heidegger.[50] He authored the classic *Philosophy and the Mirror of Nature* (1979), which challenged the notion that ideas and knowledge were reflections of some reality "out there" based upon permanent or objective foundations. His biographer Neil Gross recounts Rorty's transition throughout the mid-1960s to the late 1970s: "Years earlier he had been a hard-nosed analyst himself, engaged in rarefied debates in the philosophy of mind. Now he encouraged his fellow philosophers to take a 'relaxed attitude' towards the question of logical rigor, to stop drawing arbitrary boundaries between philosophy and other humanities fields, to open up more to the history of philosophy, to put the social and political concerns raised by Continental philosophers back on the table, and to cease worrying whether philosophy has a coherent paradigm."[51]

Rorty had decided, in the words of Simon Blackburn, that philosophers had to "scrap the idea that thought, and the language in which it is couched, is there to enable us to represent the world." Following Dewey and James before him, he depicted ideas and language as tools that won only partial knowledge; the search for truth was a never-ending process, rather than an objective or final state of mind. Rorty wrote, "To see the employment of words as the use of tools to deal with the environment, rather than as an attempt to represent the intrinsic nature of that environment, is to repudiate the question of whether human minds are in touch with reality. . . . No organism, human or non-human, is ever more or less in touch with reality than any other organism."[52] With the publication of these arguments, Rorty was now in new territory, one in which he was comfortable with giving up certainty—and in the process annoying his colleagues at Princeton. Rorty now inhabited the world that John Dewey had imagined in 1918 when he linked pragmatism to democracy—a world of "real uncertainty and contingency, a world which is not all in, and never will be, a world which in some respect is incomplete and in the making, and which in these respects may be made this way or that according as men judge, prize, love and labor."[53]

Personally Rorty was never really a man of his times. "I smoked a little pot and let my hair grow long," he explained, but "I soon decided that the radical students who wanted to trash the university were people with whom I would never have much sympathy."[54] He was one of those unlucky few who provided the name Hubert Humphrey to describe his own brand of politics—and without apology. Indeed, he remained his father's son, a Cold War liberal, and his anti-Communist liberalism and respect for institutional forms and norms never left him.

In 1982, Rorty accepted a position at the University of Virginia, where he had been invited, according to E. D. Hirsch, chair of the English Department, to "teach on the theoretical edges of several different fields."[55] Rorty had come to see literature as no less important than philosophy in teaching life lessons: the moral pull of narrative storytelling conveyed ideas more effectively than cold-blooded logic (an idea gleaned from the writings of Lionel Trilling and Irving Howe).[56] The intellectual freedom he had at Virginia allowed his mind to travel widely and write for a larger audience about themes of contingency, irony, and liberalism. By 1990, *The New York Times Magazine* could proclaim Rorty "the most influential contemporary American philosopher."[57]

Critics complained that Rorty's liberalism was little more than "an old-fashioned version of Cold War liberalism dressed up in fashionable 'postmodern' discourse."[58] And yet, Rorty was ultimately serious, scrappy, and willing to fight for these complicated definitions of what it meant to be a liberal at the end of the twentieth century. In *Achieving Our Country* (1998) he took aim at the academic left in whose waters he had always swum. The book surprised some readers who were expecting an author of postmodernist prose to enter into what Rorty had termed the usual "America Sucks Sweepstakes."[59] While Rorty was deeply critical of his country, he sought to find ways to hold it true to its ideas, a line of argument that positioned him not far from where Lionel Trilling had found himself in the 1940s and 1950s—a "liberal" caught between warring extremes.

The book took its title from James Baldwin's *The Fire Next Time* (1963), in which the black writer articulated a vision for the civil rights movement that was perched on the cusp of victory. It was a book filled with anger and frustration but also, in Baldwin's words, the idea that "great men have done great things here, and will again, and we can make America what America must become." Baldwin spoke of the civil rights movement as the "handful that we are" who wanted to "end the racial nightmare" and "achieve our country."[60] This was the core of Richard Rorty's liberal patriotism: the belief that the country had done regrettable things in the past but could be changed to live up to its higher ideals (what James Kloppenberg had termed "aspirational nationalism").[61] Rorty had gleaned his own variety of this not just from novelists like Baldwin but from his intellectual godfather, John Dewey. "We Deweyans are sentimentally patriotic about America—willing to grant that it could slide into fascism at any time, but proud of its past and guardedly hopeful about its future."[62] In order to renew a reformist left, intellectuals would have to renew liberal patriotism. Rorty opened his first lecture and the book with the sweeping declaration: "National pride is to countries what self-respect is to individuals: a necessary condition for self-improvement."[63]

Much of what Rorty wanted to accomplish in *Achieving Our Country* was to resuscitate the fighting liberal spirit that had vanished in the acrimony of the Vietnam War. It was the frustration with Vietnam within the New Left that stood as a turning point in Rorty's story about liberal patriotism. As he explained in a 1996 essay that articulated the themes developed in *Achieving Our Country:* "When the students began to burn flags, they did deeper and more long-lasting damage to the American left than they could ever have imagined."[64] Burned flags produced the "spectatorial, disgusted, mocking Left" that inhabited academe and that displaced the reformist left that had "struggled within the framework of constitutional democracy to protect the weak from the strong." The turning point, Rorty wrote, came between 1964 and 1966, when hope gave way to despair, a development Rorty regretted, but understood. He mused:

> There is no way to decide whether [the New Left's] patience should have run out in those years, rather than earlier or later. But if their patience had not run out at some point, if they had *never* taken to the streets, if civil disobedience had *never* replaced an insistence on working within the system, America might no longer be a constitutional democracy. Their loss of patience was the result of perfectly justified, wholly sincere moral indignation—moral indignation which, the New Left rightly sensed, we reformists were too tired and too battered to feel. . . . The New Left was right to say that America was in danger of selling its soul in order to defeat Communism.

This was precisely the aspect of Rorty's style of argument that drove his critics to distraction: his penchant for articulating distinctions that melted within historical reality.[65] The left had been justified in dividing in the past but now needed to patch itself back together. Such prescriptions often made Rorty's project sound simultaneously both too easy and too difficult. Nonetheless, Rorty's call to return to the vision of a "reformist left" flowed naturally from his thinking about the virtues of pragmatism. A reformist left would be a pragmatic left, not beholden to grandiose ideas so much as partial victories and "piecemeal reform." He distinguished between "movements" that were difficult to achieve and tended to get out of hand, and "campaigns" for particular issues and finite changes in our political and cultural lives. Rather than seeking grandiose ideas or philosophical abstractions like Marxism for inspiration, which would devolve into becoming a religion and a source of "purity," "the Left should put a moratorium on theory." A reformist left would be content finding its messages and inspiration in stories and literature rather than weighty philosophical arguments. Alas, given the state of the cause itself, not much more was available.[66]

Liberal political theorists recognized that throughout the 1980s and 1990s many citizens lacked a sense of civic belongingness—the "bowling alone" syndrome diagnosed by the political scientist Robert Putnam in 1995.[67] William Galston called for a more rigorous form of civic education, the sort already taking place in public schools, and the journalist Mickey Kaus, following John Kenneth Galbraith, called for creating public spaces that could "restrict the sphere of life in which money (and merit) matters while expanding the public sphere in which income differences are ignored."[68] Civic-minded liberals looked to venues of voluntary service that could nurture civic virtue and public-mindedness. But they recognized that they needed better answers to the conservative defense of organic communities that found themselves threatened by liberals' commitment to change regardless of the political principles that might underlay their arguments.

One group of politically minded players who tried to establish a new position for liberals were the founders of the Democratic Leadership Council, formed in 1985 in the wake of the Mondale debacle. From 1985 to 1992, the DLC helped formulate the ideas that propelled Bill Clinton into the presidency and pushed the Democratic Party to the center. The DLC's initial success proved to be largely in its ability to attract wealthy donors who liked the idea of making the Democrats a more corporate-friendly party and of meeting potential future presidents at its retreats.[69] Corporate lobbyists dominated early DLC meetings, leading Jesse Jackson to label the group "Democrats for the Leisure Class."[70] Arthur Schlesinger, Jr., went even further, terming it a "quasi-Reaganite formation," the conservative analogue to the Communist threat Robert Kennedy had once characterized as "the enemy within."[71]

This derisiveness ignored the evidence that the old-fashioned New Deal–style liberalism had become virtually unsalable outside the Northeast. Poll after DLC poll showed Democrats shedding moderate and swing voters. A survey conducted in 1987 by Stanley Greenberg revealed that 61 percent of the voters now swinging Republican believed Democrats were "too eager to satisfy special-interest groups," had "lost touch with the needs of middle-class and working people," and could not be "trusted to spend our tax dollars wisely."[72] Race undoubtedly underlay many of these complaints, but Democrats could not expect to win elections by accusing Americans of being racists, so they had to work around the problem without ever admitting it existed.

With the labor movement shrinking at an alarming pace—under pressure from both transformations in the global economy and the legal and political assault from Reagan and the Republicans—Democrats needed to find another source of funding for their campaigns if they were to compete in a political system that ran on private contributions (or less politely, "legal bribery"). As the economy transformed from one in which Americans produced things to one in which they sold or serviced them, new sectors of corporate America could be convinced that their fortunes rested with Democrats rather than with their traditional Republican allies. But the money would not be given to candidates who did not sing the tune of the men and women who signed the checks.

One important component of the DLC's critique of traditional liberalism was its argument that "rights talk" had come to dominate liberal public philosophy.[73] Liberals had grown fearful of discussing anything but what benefits government could provide citizens, forgetting that President Kennedy had challenged Americans "to ask not what your country can do for you—ask what you can do for your country." The DLC's Al From worked closely with Charles Moskos, a sociology professor at Northwestern University who was studying the ways in which voluntary public service could nurture a sense of civic equality among participants. Moskos's call for public service became the DLC's "central, defining proposal," and in May 1988 the council released "Citizenship and National Service: A Blueprint for Civic Enterprise," a document that called for a "Citizen Corps" that would require a year of voluntary service in return for pay toward college loans, job training supplements, or assistance for housing. [74] This voluntarism would revive citizenship and be "rooted in the Democratic Party's progressive tradition of equal sacrifice for the common good," the argument hinting at what many liberals thought had gone wrong during the gilded age of Reagan. Public service thus became the way to balance rights with obligations, individualism with duty and responsibility. It would also allow more of a role for local institutions to coordinate service initiatives. And perhaps most important, it would appeal to political independents and cultural conservatives such as the Reagan Democrats who had been deserting the party in droves.[75]

In 1989, Will Marshall, the head of the DLC's newly founded think tank, the Progressive Policy Institute, authored an attack on "welfare state paternalism" in which he called for the replacement of the "politics of entitlement with a new politics of reciprocal responsibility."[76] Coupled with its tough-on-crime stance, it sent an unmistakable signal that the Democrats would no longer allow themselves to be portrayed as the party of minorities, homosexuals, and welfare recipients. It was not just a matter of shifting the focus away from the civil liberties of alleged criminals but of offering an array of proposals for initiatives like community policing, designed to inspire commitment on the part of citizens as well as government to improve delivery of basic services, such as school safety and policing. In this regard, it was an attempt to move liberalism toward a vision more amenable to its communitarian critics.[77]

Two of these critics, William Galston and Elaine Kamarck—like Galston, a political scientist turned political operative—offered up a comprehensive argument of the political premises that underlay their critique of the liberalism of the late eighties in a paper titled "The Politics of Evasion" in 1989. They had seen the future, they argued, and it was not pretty. "The public has come to associate liberalism with tax and spending policies that contradict the interest of average families; with welfare policies that foster dependence rather than self-reliance; with softness towards perpetrators of crime and indifference towards its victims; with ambivalence toward American values and interests abroad; and with an adversarial stance toward mainstream moral and cultural values." Philosophically, they complained, "Democrats have become the party of individual rights but not individual responsibility; the party of self-expression but not moral accountability." They argued for Democrats to embrace "middle-class values—individual responsibility, hard work, equal opportunity—rather than the language of compensation." Galston and Kamarck believed that Democrats could use this culturally conservative language to reframe traditional Democratic and liberal policies.[78]

Echoing its corporate-friendly rhetoric, the DLC was also in the forefront of moving the Democrats toward an embrace of business-friendly ideology. As the organization's historian, Kenneth Baer, explained, "The New Democrats took a position that embraced the free market and was relatively anti-statist" and also endorsed free trade and deregulation.[79] Although President Kennedy had observed that "economic growth without social progress lets the great majority of people remain in poverty, while a privileged few reap the benefits of rising abundance," his youngest brother learned two decades later that the opposite was true as well: social progress was all but impossible without the foundation of economic growth as its engine. As early as 1985, America's most famous liberal had warned: "We cannot and should not depend on higher tax revenues to roll in and redeem every costly program," adding that "the mere existence of a program is no excuse for its perpetuation, whether it is a welfare plan or a weapons system."[80]

Despite widespread agreement on the need for a new vision for the party, the DLC approach involved significant risks and some rather obvious flaws. Its proponents—for funding purposes, no doubt—chose to ignore the fact that their relentless emphasis on mainstream values and hard work was belied by the easy money available to newly minted millionaires on Wall Street and in Silicon Valley, to say nothing of the jobs moved overseas from declining industrial areas. And by focusing so exclusively on the elusive (and frequently contradictory) demands of the swing voter on the one hand and corporate donors on the other, they risked offering confirmation to those like Jackson and Schlesinger who worried that its leaders were merely seeking to transform the party into a weak and unprincipled simulacrum, unable to stand up for itself in the political arena and therefore for America in the wider world—a liberalism, in other words, that would not take its own side in a street fight.

Born the year after World War II ended, in Hope, Arkansas, Bill Clinton was fortunate to have had both a difficult and demanding, but also loving and empowering, upbringing. His mother, Viriginia Kelly, named him William Jefferson Blythe III after his father, who died in a car accident before ever seeing his son. A vivaciously independent spirit, she smoked, drank, flirted, and gambled, without apology. She then married a man named Roger Clinton, who turned out to be an abusive alcoholic.[81] The boy took his stepfather's name, but frequently found himself forced to put himself between his stepfather and his mother or his stepfather and his younger stepbrother, Roger junior, who gave Bill the nickname Bubba.[82]

Clinton became the typical overachieving student: doing well in school while learning to play music and grooming his natural social skills. In addition, he joined Boys Nation, a civic organization that pointed young men toward careers in politics by engaging them in mock debates, public speaking, and elections.[83] In 1963, he traveled with fellow Boys Nation members to visit the White House, where he shook the hand of JFK—an event that stuck with Clinton for the rest of his life.

Embarking for Georgetown University in the fall of 1964 made perfect sense for a young man thinking of a career in public service. As a Southern Baptist amid Jesuit and Catholic teachers, Clinton was remembered for his jovial, outgoing persona and his "irrepressible glad-handing."[84] Though conservatives would later demonize Clinton as a far-left activist, he never really engaged the civil rights movement in college the way many students did during Freedom Summer (he could have simply by reaching out to Father Richard McSorley, Georgetown's activist antiwar priest). The early protests and widening debates about Vietnam that struck Georgetown and Washington, D.C., did not inspire Clinton much either. What really piqued the young man's interest was student government. There he developed a skill for listening to people's life stories and committing them to memory, as he was clearly planning for a future in politics. As president of the sophomore class, Clinton was remembered for making students feel welcome.[85] A common tendency among children of alcoholics, this personality characteristic would also prove an invaluable tool for political advancement.

Clinton would return to Arkansas at every opportunity to help out on Democratic Party political campaigns. In 1966 he worked on Frank Holt's primary campaign for governor, only to watch Jim Johnson, a racist and attack dog, walk all over his candidate. Holt refused to play ugly or fight back, and Clinton thought that a big mistake.[86] Later, perhaps recollecting Holt's loss and certainly thinking about some of his own, Clinton explained his view of political combat: "When someone is beating you over the head with a hammer, don't sit there and take it. Take out a meat cleaver and cut off their hand."[87] Clinton also did some work for Arkansas senator J. William Fulbright. He admired the firebrand's iconoclastic antiwar stance, but he worried that Fulbright's attachment to Washington might be alienating to his constituents back home (and indeed, Fulbright would subsequently lose his Senate seat to Dale Bumpers in a 1974 Democratic primary).[88]

After graduating from Georgetown in 1968, Clinton traveled to Oxford University on a Rhodes Scholarship as his uncle worked with a lawyer back home to keep him out of the draft.[89] Clinton didn't want to go to Vietnam, though he felt intense guilt about it. Plenty of boys his age from his hometown did not enjoy student deferments, much less Rhodes scholarships, and were being shipped off to Vietnam. A friend of Clinton's told him that he tried to "avoid" those "in the service" when back home in the States, a sentiment Clinton understood.[90]

At Oxford, Clinton became more politically engaged in protest movements but also continued to build his networks, making connections with people important to his future political life. He met with Strobe Talbott, who was developing an expertise on Soviet history, as well as Rick Stearns, who would head up the McGovern campaign of 1972. He also became friends with Robert Reich; one fellow student remembered Reich and Clinton as "kind of a double act . . . like Laurel and Hardy."[91] Hearing Allard Lowenstein speak at Oxford in 1969 helped to enhance the lesson he had learned from Fulbright: a young person could protest while remaining within the mainstream of the political system.[92] That same year Clinton worked for the Vietnam Moratorium Committee and pointed overseas students to venues of protest.[93] He was now a committed antiwar activist, but it bears reminding that this stance came only after a large segment of American people had expressed doubts about the war. Though he grew a shaggy beard, Clinton never really became a radical; rather, he remained a liberal, which, given his environment, was not a popular or an easy position to maintain.

From Oxford Clinton went on to Yale Law School and then the McGovern campaign of 1972. Of all places, he landed in Texas, a state that would make most McGovern campaign workers slip into Sisyphean despair. Watching the campaign, Clinton realized that McGovern had few contacts or prior groundwork in Texas. It was no surprise then that Clinton spent the last few days of the campaign at headquarters taking down people's names on note cards.[94]

After finishing at Yale Law School, Clinton married Hillary Rodham and looked to begin his political career back home. He lost his first run for Congress in 1974, but won the race for attorney general in 1976 and the governor's office in 1978. After losing his race for reelection in 1980, he decided in 1982 to apologize to voters for his decision to raise car license fees in order to increase state revenues. This worked, and taught him the importance of the "permanent campaign" and consistent polling about how his policies played with voters. Because his governorship correlated with a bleak period for Democrats nationally, Clinton, as a successful southern governor who went out of his way to pay his respects to the elders of the party, naturally won a great deal of attention. Rising in the ranks of the National Governors Association, he was known for creative thinking about public policy.[95]

Clinton's burgeoning national reputation landed him the golden opportunity of giving the keynote address at the 1988 Democratic convention. Something went horribly wrong, however, and by the time Clinton's long-winded and pedestrian address ended, the convention resembled the Apollo Theater on Amateur Night. The only real excitement came when he mentioned Dukakis's name; otherwise, he heard "Get the hook! Get the hook!"[96] Clinton recovered a few nights later by going on late-night television and making fun of himself, but he had clearly demonstrated that he was not yet ready for prime time, literally and figuratively.

Like Jimmy Carter, Clinton governed from just left of the center, making as many friends in business as he did in unions, if not more. Given his limitless ambition, he was a natural fit for the DLC and eagerly accepted Al From's invitation to chair the organization in 1990.[97] The organization would help with speeches, coaches, money, and expert advance work, and Clinton did his part, singing the DLC hymn across the nation. He told one DLC gathering: "I will let you in on a secret—governments do not raise children, people do, and it is time they were asked to assume their responsibilities and forced to do it if they refuse."[98] In another, he lifted lines from "The Politics of Evasion" by arguing on behalf of "the very burdened middle class" who no longer trusted Democrats to "take their tax money and spend it with discipline."[99] He sought to find a language to reconnect the Democratic Party to the white working class, a task he sometimes undertook one voter at a time, as if he gained energy from each such encounter. The journalist Joe Klein described the manner in which Clinton "embraced audiences and was aroused by them in turn."[100] His evident human weaknesses and lack of personal self-discipline—he was hours late for everything and could not help himself when scarfing down junk food—endeared him to voters who judged their leaders on their likability and may have helped shield him when the weight of evidence of his decades of sexual escapades threatened to overwhelm his campaign.[101]

Clinton faced a wide playing field during the 1992 primary, but his chief opponent up front was Senator Paul Tsongas. Like Hart, Tsongas was a smart neoliberal eager to challenge party orthodoxies. Unfortunately, and more to the point, he was, like Michael Dukakis, another Greek American from Massachusetts who exuded a peculiar brand of anticharisma. He left the Senate when he was diagnosed with cancer, and so was also considered a health risk. Tsongas did well with upscale and highly educated voters of the kind who had flocked to John Anderson in 1980 and to Hart in 1984, but only a party committed to its own self-destruction would have gone this route four years after the Dukakis debacle. Tsongas's combination of stiffness and stuffiness, however, invited flattering comparisons to Bill Clinton, who had had the field of working-class white populism—at least within the Democratic contest—all to himself. Clinton emphasized his cultural conservatism to the point of returning to Arkansas during the election to preside over the execution of the seriously brain-damaged Ricky Ray Rector.[102]

After he came in second in the New Hampshire primary—Jerry Brown, running at Clinton from the far left, had upended Tsongas—Clinton's star began to rise. While Brown had the best rallies, attended regularly by California's showbiz cognoscenti, no one among party professionals was particularly eager to see "Governor Moonbeam" at the top of the ticket, and soon pretty much everyone rallied around Clinton, who easily carried all of the southern states despite his dodgy draft status. Bob Kerrey, an extremely attractive war hero/ex-governor and senator from Nebraska, who was romantically attached to the actress Debra Winger, also proved a spectacular flameout—or, more accurately, a flake out. By April even liberals like Ted Kennedy, who resented and resisted the DLC's attempted party takeover, had come over to Clinton's team.[103]

With voters, however, Clinton still needed to overcome the suspicion that Democrats cared about sexual deviants and snooty professors, and the like, more than they did "real" Americans. He seized the opportunity to do precisely this when, at a meeting of Jesse Jackson's Rainbow Coalition in June 1992, he assailed the black rap star Sister Souljah for suggesting, following the Rodney King riots, "If black people kill black people every day . . . why not have a week and kill white people?" Clinton described Souljah as a kind of black David Duke, a white supremacist leader of the Klan who was now running for the Republican presidential nomination. Clinton impressed not only middle-class, middle-American white people, but many in the no longer terribly liberal media with his willingness to go into the political equivalent of the lion's den to make his case. When Jackson acted hurt, it only helped cement Clinton's bona fides with the media and white ethnic voters, with whom Jackson was deeply unpopular. Together with his enthusiastic support for the death penalty and antiunion right-to-work laws—that is, the right to bar unions from the workplace—Clinton was able to credibly sell himself to suspicious Americans as a genuinely new kind of Democrat, one who was almost as suspicious of liberals as they were.[104]

Early in the campaign, with George Bush still flush from his victory in the Gulf War, many Democrats were dubious about the possibility of victory regardless of who emerged as their nominee. But Bush was beatable, and he ran a campaign in which he helped beat himself. The candidate appeared oddly disengaged, and his campaign manager and best friend, James Baker—annoyed that he had been asked to give up his job as secretary of state—could barely deign to pay any attention to the race until it was almost too late to win it.[105] Bush alienated conservatives by breaking his "Read my lips" promise not to raise taxes. He allowed Patrick Buchanan to alienate moderate voters at the Republican convention by declaring a "culture war" on those who disagreed with his Joe McCarthy–style Catholic conservatism. The patrician president began to strike much of the public as not merely out of touch, but also entirely unaware of the human cost of the economic recession America was then undergoing. He was filmed in a supermarket looking at a price scanner as if it came from Mars. During one of the presidential debates, Bush looked profoundly befuddled when an African American woman in the audience asked how he had been personally affected by the recession. It was a pointless question—presidents don't suffer during recessions or even depressions—but it proved to be catnip for Clinton, who bit his lip, crinkled his brow, and felt the woman's pain within an inch of her life.[106]

For all of Bush's weaknesses, Clinton might never have made it in a straightforward two-person race. But the eccentric Texas billionaire Ross Perot, who had made his fortune in information-processing companies, got it into his head that he could spend enough of his own money to make a credible, possibly even victorious run at the White House. Perot did strike a populist chord, railing against politicians in general and deficits in particular. In February 1992 he announced on television that if his supporters were willing to collect the thousands of signatures necessary to get him on the ballot in all fifty states, he would finance his own campaign to the tune of well over a hundred million dollars.[107] Soon an organization calling itself THRO (for Throw the Hypocritical Rascals Out) did just that. Bizarre as he often came across—he was a small man with enormous ears and an easily mockable series of cornpone expressions—Perot stuck to his populist script, conservative on some issues (deficits) and liberal on others (trade and campaign finance). A fellow Texan, he nursed a particular animosity toward George H. W. Bush, whom he considered a spoiled Eastern elitist transplant rather than an honest born-and-bred son of Texas.[108] Perot had unmistakable authoritarian tendencies, particularly in his impatience with political give and take, as well as a paranoid streak wider than the Rio Grande. (In one case he attacked President Bush for allegedly seeking to sabotage his daughter's wedding.) But he managed to keep these under control for much of the early part of the campaign, and to the amazement of almost every political professional in America, Perot emerged in the early summer of 1992 as the campaign's front-runner.[109]

Perhaps this frightened him, because his behavior began to grow ever more bizarre. Just as the Democratic convention got under way at New York's Madison Square Garden, he quit the race, implicitly endorsing Clinton, whom he credited with adopting his issues, particularly the need to control the deficit. This gave Clinton an enormous boost at a time when he had been running third in the race, and turned the convention from a kind of wake into a rock concert. Perot, however, changed his mind again, just in time for the presidential debates, and given that his polling numbers remained quite high, the parties lacked the nerve to exclude him. By this time, however, all Perot wanted to do, it appeared, was to torture George H. W. Bush. By focusing on Bush's broken promise not to raise taxes, he undermined the president's character, and offered himself to antitax conservatives as an option for voting against Bush without having to vote for a Democrat.

For all his oddness, Perot's role in the history of the period was considerable. Pollsters and political scientists disagree on whether his voters would have chosen Bush, Clinton, or none of the above. But by amassing almost 20 percent of the vote—by far the best showing for a third-party candidate since Teddy Roosevelt's 1912 campaign—he kept Clinton's total down to 43 percent of the popular vote, and therefore gave right-wingers an opportunity to challenge his legitimacy. Second, by connecting his populist appeal to the issue of deficit reduction, he gave birth to a movement that would not only weaken Clinton's ability to use government to stimulate the economy and invest in the kinds of innovative programs laid out in his quite progressive manifesto, *Putting People First*, but help to create a political force that would one day take over much of the Republican Party.

Clinton, meanwhile, stuck to his script and let Perot do his dirty work. Stealing the language of FDR and Richard Nixon simultaneously, Clinton focused on the "forgotten middle class." "While the rich got richer, the forgotten middle class—the people who work hard and play by the rules—took it on the chin," he never tired of saying. A true Democrat, if not exactly a liberal, Clinton always insisted that government had a role to play in helping families navigate the economic and cultural minefields that faced them at the close of the twentieth century. In *Putting People First* Clinton argued: "The Republicans have lectured America on the importance of family values. But their policies have made life harder for working families: they have forced parents to choose between the jobs they need and the families they love."[110] Perhaps most important, Clinton promised, in the poll-tested words of his adviser, Stan Greenberg, to "end welfare as we know it." This promise proved absolutely necessary to get white working-class voters to consider a Democrat for the first time in nearly a generation—welfare remained a code word for "lazy black" in many parts of the country—but it created all sorts of problems for Clinton once he became president. Finally, Clinton and Al Gore, his running mate, were new and young, while Bush was tired and his vice president, Dan Quayle, remained a national joke. Clinton's postconvention campaign began with a bus tour in which he and Gore tossed a football–around during breaks. Nobody needed any reminder that another touch football–playing politician named John Kennedy had also once sought to replace a likable but out-of-touch president whose party had been in power too long.

At the same time he was running a brilliant campaign, Clinton had to deal with some unique political problems along the way, problems that threatened to undo him and would have cost a less determined candidate—indeed, almost any candidate before Clinton appeared on the scene—any chance of being president. The days when the press corps had run interference for philandering presidents had long passed, and now everything was fair game if it related to "character." Owing to the penchant of his (apparent) longtime girlfriend, nightclub singer Gennifer Flowers, to try to make as much as she could of their affair, Clinton was forced to endure a post–Super Bowl interrogation with Hillary by his side about how often he had strayed from the bonds of matrimony and with whom. He also had to explain how it was that he had managed to miss the draft without any special help, and here his answers were not much clearer. Asked if he had tried pot as a young man, he gave birth to a new adjective, "Clintonesque," by parsing his answer in the straight-faced response: "I experimented with marijuana a time or two and I didn't like it. I didn't inhale."[111] Clinton had many more personal problems than Carter, Mondale, and Dukakis put together, but he also demonstrated a willingness to do something they wouldn't or couldn't, and that was *whatever it took*. On Election Day, the final results showed Clinton with 43 percent of the popular vote against Bush's 37.5 percent and Perot's 19 percent. Bush's showing was the worst for a sitting president since Theodore Roosevelt helped Woodrow Wilson beat William Howard Taft in 1912, but only in Arkansas and Washington, D.C., could Clinton boast a majority of the vote.[112]

In February 1993, Clinton got off to a hopeful start by signing the Family and Medical Leave Act and thereby "guaranteed many workers up to twelve weeks a year in unpaid leave in case of family medical emergencies," including the birth or adoption of a new child. (Bush had vetoed the act twice.[113]) It proved a powerful signal of the new president's support for the forgotten man and demonstrated how a family-friendly Democrat could help ordinary citizens, especially when coupled with Clinton's expansion of the Earned Income Tax Credit in his first budget for 1993. (By 2005, this tax credit could "raise the annual income of a low-wage worker with children by as much as 40 percent."[114]) This measure made it possible for people to leave welfare for work without suffering in the process, and it enabled Clinton to deliver on his campaign promise to find new, innovative ways to use government effectively to help people who "worked hard and played by the rules."

But hope for a smooth-sailing start to the first Democratic presidency in twelve years proved decidedly short-lived. Almost immediately he found himself the victim of a political ambush by Republicans, conservative Democrats, and career military men on the issue of allowing gays to serve in the military. Clinton had answered a reporter's question on the topic in the affirmative, but he had hardly planned for the integration of gays into the military to be a priority of his presidency the way that Harry Truman had made racial integration one of his. Neither the military nor, likely, the country was ready for it. But Clinton could not appear to walk away from a campaign commitment as perhaps his first major act as president, which would be all too clear a signal to his enemies that he could be easily rolled.[115] So he took both sides at once, prompting cartoonist Gary Trudeau to stick him with the image of a waffle in "Doonsbury" for the duration of his presidency. Joint Chiefs head Colin Powell, a beneficiary of Truman's racial policies and the closest thing the country had to a genuine national hero following the Gulf War, eventually rode to Clinton's rescue with an intellectually incoherent but politically palatable compromise called Don't Ask, Don't Tell, which allowed gays to serve as long as they didn't make too big a deal about their sexuality.[116] This did nothing for the estimated ten thousand servicemen and servicewomen who revealed their homosexual orientation or were exposed by others and forced to leave, and it left Clinton looking amateurish as well as weak.[117] As he later recalled, "In the short run, I got the worst of both worlds—I lost the fight, and the gay community was highly critical of me for the compromise, simply refusing to acknowledge the consequences of having so little support in Congress."[118]

Clinton was more successful when he focused on his campaign promise that reinforced his focus on connecting rights to responsibilities. In September 1993 he signed a bill creating AmeriCorps, which sent volunteers throughout the country to serve fellow citizens—in many respects, a continuation of LBJ's VISTA program. Clinton recollected in his memoirs: "Over the next five years, nearly 200,000 young Americans would join the ranks of AmeriCorps, a larger number than had served in the entire forty-year history of the Peace Corps."[119]

In decided contrast to previous Democratic administrations, Clinton pressed for a crime bill featuring more police and prisons, longer sentences for repeat offenders, boot camps for young drug users, and an expansion of the federal death penalty. But the bill also included "crime-preventing social programs," such as midnight basketball and public transportation support, which led to its derision by conservatives.[120] What made the bill almost impossible to pass, however, was its inclusion—at the request of police associations across America—of a ban on armor-piercing "cop killer" bullets and assault weapons (including the semiautomatic pistol that was used to shoot Representative Gabrielle Giffords and twenty other people at an Arizona meet-and-greet in January 2011). He won that victory, but at enormous cost, energizing the NRA to devote itself to defeating every Democrat who supported it. The same was true of his economic program, which raised taxes on the wealthy and infuriated economic conservatives at *The Wall Street Journal* and the U.S. Chamber of Commerce. These same conservatives hailed his strong support and successful passage of the North America Free Trade Agreement (NAFTA)—a slap in the face to his core supporters in the labor movement—but Clinton felt as if he had no choice but to prove repeatedly his bona fides as a "New Democrat."

His biggest failure came early into his presidency when Clinton chose to revamp the nation's health care system before he had attempted to honor his far more popular promise to end welfare. His first mistake was to appoint his wife, Hillary, to lead the entire effort. As historian William Chafe observes, by putting Mrs. Clinton "in charge, he made it difficult if not impossible for supporters of the principle of health care to voice any criticism of the process being followed."[121] Hillary proceeded to gather as many as five hundred people to work on the proposal and refused to reveal their identities to the media, leading to all kinds of conspiracy charges from conservatives and bad blood among those who thought they should have been included but weren't.[122]

Hillary's health care initiative was the quintessential centrist enterprise. Rejecting the Canadian-style single-payer system, the president had argued for regulation rather than revolution. The Clintons hoped to create regional insurance-purchasing cooperatives to compete with the insurance companies and thereby lower prices and improve services through competition.[123] But the 1,342-page bill that Hillary's task force finally issued was so complicated, both in conception and execution, that it proved as impossible to explain as it was easy to mock.[124] Worse still, Clinton here, as nowhere else, refused to compromise, leading not only to the loss of half a loaf, which would have been easy to pass, but also to whispers that the president feared crossing his wife, lest she decide to take greater notice of all of his poorly hidden extramarital sexual adventures. (David Gergen, who had consulted with Nixon, Ford, and Reagan before coming to Clinton's side, said that they were "heading into the most important months of the health care fight with a president who was tiptoeing around the person in charge."[125]) Clinton probably could have passed a modified version of reform by reaching out to some of the more moderate Republicans, such as Senator Lincoln Chafee of Rhode Island, who had a plan for universal coverage that included an individual mandate, that is, a tax credit system, of the kind later embraced by President Obama.[126] Or he might, as historian David Courtwright speculated, have "invited congressional leaders to frame legislation consistent with his broad goals," as Barack Obama also did.[127] Instead, when it came to Hillary's plan, the president, like Frank Sinatra, wanted "all or nothing at all." And nothing was what he got.

Republicans had been inclined to cooperate with the president on some sort of reform—the party had not yet been taken over by its extreme right wing—until a former aide to Dan Quayle named William Kristol (the son of Irving Kristol and Gertrude Himmelfarb) challenged Republicans to refuse to cooperate with the president under any circumstances. In what would become a history-making memo to Republican leaders, he warned that the plan could "re-legitimize middle-class dependence for 'security' on government spending and regulation. It will revive the reputation of the party that spends and regulates . . . as the generous protector of middle-class interests. And it will at the same time strike a punishing blow against Republican claims to defend the middle class by restraining government."[128] In other words, passage of so generous a new benefit to so many voters credited to a Democratic president would, in Kristol's estimation, revive the reputation of American liberalism and undo much if not all the damage that he and his fellow conservative operatives had so successfully wreaked on its good name during the previous generation.

Democrats being Democrats, they lent support to Kristol's cause. The increasingly neoconservative *New Republic* ran an extremely effective, but deeply dishonest, attack on the plan that—because of the magazine's outdated reputation as America's liberal flagship publication—successfully swayed significant numbers of readers well beyond the magazine's typical audience.[129] The White House issued a nine-page rebuttal, but as the novelist Tom Wolfe pointed out, "That one article shot down the entire blimp."[130] (Andrew Sullivan, then the magazine's editor, later admitted, "I was aware of the piece's flaws but nonetheless was comfortable running it as a provocation to debate.[131]) Business lobbies that were initially favorable to health care reform due to rising costs for their own employees' plans soon swung around and began funding commercials designed to mock the plan as a government takeover of family-related health decisions. After taking up more time than any other issue of Clinton's early presidency, the plan never even came up for a vote in either the House or Senate, so hopeless were its prospects.

For these reasons among others, 1994 became what pundits came to term the year of the "angry white male." The National Rifle Association—often considered Washington's most powerful lobby—was determined to punish the president who had restricted the right to own automatic assault weapons. Seven in ten gun owners voted Republican in the midterm elections of 1994, and they voted in significantly higher numbers than their unarmed fellow citizens. Conservative Christians also turned out in massive numbers.[132] As Clinton's young aide and sometime alter ego George Stephanopoulos complained, "By the spring of 1994, even our legislative successes were working against us. The Brady Bill and the assault weapons ban had enraged and energized members of the National Rifle Association, but the general public didn't know yet that crime was down. Voters heard Republicans call our economic plan 'the largest tax increase in the history of the universe,' but they had yet to feel the benefits of lower interest rates and stronger growth. Our labor base was depressed by the president's all-out effort on the NAFTA agreement they considered a job killer, but the corporate interests profiting from the pact showed their gratitude by attacking our health care plan."[133] The Republican victory in that election, spurred on by Newt Gingrich's poll-tested "Contract for America," was the most impressive off-year comeback in modern times, and included a takeover of the Senate.[134]

Luckily for Clinton, the political architect of the Republican tsunami would also provide an almost perfect political foil for the president's Chinese menu–style politics. A onetime history professor at West Georgia College who left his cancer-ridden wife, Gingrich viewed politics as "war without blood" and spoke grandiosely, if not apocalyptically, about "a whole new debate with new terms."[135] He loved to combine out-of-context historical allusions with simplistic management theories to predict the complete transformation of humankind, led by none other than himself.[136]

Just as journalists were writing Clinton off forever and declaring Gingrich to be the de facto leader of the nation, the political dynamic was transformed on April 19, 1995, when a far-right fanatic named Timothy McVeigh, furious about the assault weapons ban, drove an explosives-laden truck into a government building in Oklahoma City, murdering 168 people and injuring hundreds more.[137] Clinton rose to the occasion magnificently, giving voice to the nation's grief and calling upon all Americans to take a healing step back from the politics of anger and animosity. "I say to you . . . there is nothing patriotic about hating your country, or pretending that you can love your country but despise your government."[138] He was rebuking not only the fringes but also the irresponsible antigovernment rhetoric of Gingrich and his minions on behalf of liberalism in its largest sense.

Gingrich continued to conspire, albeit inadvertently, in Clinton's political recovery with bizarre pronouncements, backroom deals, and petulant complaints about the lack of respect he was being accorded by Clinton and his aides. His biggest miscalculation, however, was to force a game of chicken over the size of the federal budget, which led to the shutdown of the federal government. Looking at the budget details offered by Gingrich and company, Clinton got to play Gary Cooper on behalf of America's middle class: "If you want to pass your budget, you're going to have to put somebody else in this chair. . . . I don't care if I go to five percent in the polls. I am not going to sign your budget."[139] The shutdown aggravated ordinary citizens and threw many federal employees out of work just as the holidays approached. Clinton successfully painted the Republicans as dangerous radicals until Gingrich and company realized they had no choice but to concede their loss and do their best to save face.[140]

Clinton decided to use his 1996 State of the Union address to embrace, insofar as a Democratic president could, the nation's new, more conservative mood. "The era of big government is over," announced the president to Republican cheers. "But"—and then he signaled to quiet the cheering Republicans—"but we cannot go back to the time when our citizens were left to fend for themselves. Instead, we must go forward as one America, one nation working together to meet the challenges we face together. Self-reliance and teamwork are not opposing virtues; we must have both." Here was the new center that Clinton succeeded, however briefly, in defining. But how "vital" was it?

Clinton still had to deal with his promise "to end welfare as we know it,"[141] a promise with which he had earned the votes of people who, in the recent past, would not have considered pulling the Democratic lever. But not only did welfare reform demand a great deal of support for those who needed to be trained for jobs and for whom jobs needed to be found, but it also had to be accomplished in the face of a Republican opposition that considered welfare to be a kind of addictive drug for people too lazy, too dishonest, or simply too pampered.[142] The fact that so many of them were also black or Hispanic made them seem even less attractive as victims rather than as perpetrators of a scheme to game the system. While repeatedly promising to "liberate" welfare recipients, Republicans effectively sought to destroy the system simply by turning the program into block grants for states, which, in a race with one another, would grow stingier and stingier in order to force the problem onto another state's doorstep. (In many places in the South, for instance, the "welfare" program consisted of a bus ticket to another state.[143]) Clinton vetoed two early versions of the bill and called the final version of the legislation "a decent welfare bill wrapped in a sack of shit."[144] But his conservative Svengali-like adviser, Dick Morris—upon whom Clinton had grown increasingly dependent, politically and psychologically, in the aftermath of the 1994 debacle—insisted that a third veto could cost him his reelection in 1996. Clinton accordingly decided he'd risk passing the the bill, however distasteful it might be, and then try to amend it after his reelection.

Stanley Greenberg, the president's pollster for the early days of the 1992 campaign, who had argued that Democrats had been seen by many Americans as those "for the giveaways, and we are the ones that pay all the taxes," noted that once Clinton signed welfare reform, "such frustrations nearly disappeared from the public consciousness."[145] What's more, it worked. Welfare rolls fell from 12.2 million Americans in 1996 to fewer than half that number five years later.[146] Once again, Clinton drew to an inside straight and pulled it off, no matter what the odds advised.

With welfare reform passed and with the economy riding high, his Republican opponent, longtime Kansas senator and war hero Bob Dole, had no hope of winning the 1996 election. Clinton, unlike Dole, loved campaigning, and when he took off by train through the heartland state of Ohio, he would shout to supporters from the caboose as Harry Truman had done in 1948.[147] He raised and spent a fortune and won reelection handily, becoming the first Democrat to do so since Roosevelt. He ultimately did manage to lift restrictions on immigrants in the welfare bill and raise federal funding for child care and Head Start, and while it wasn't much for liberals who cared about expanding effective programs for the most vulnerable, neither was it nothing. [148]

In winning reelection in this manner, Clinton lost the support of a great many liberals. Peter Edelman—a former close aide to Bobby Kennedy and the husband of Marian Wright Edelman, founder of the Children's Defense Fund and close friend of Hillary Clinton, who served on its board—quit his high-level position in the Department of Health and Human Services to protest his boss's willingness to sign the Republican welfare bill.[149] Edelman explained, "I have devoted the last 30-plus years to doing whatever I could to help in reducing poverty in America. I believe the recently enacted welfare bill goes in the opposite direction."[150] Edelman's remarks reflected a growing concern that Clinton's "triangulation" strategy—to take the best of liberalism, conservatism, and everything in between—was little more than cynicism, designed to cut the opposition off at the knees at the price of screwing the poor and disadvantaged.

Secretary of Labor Robert Reich was another longtime liberal friend of the president's who found himself on the outs. A close friend since their Oxford days, Reich had gone on to become an important and innovative thinker in liberal policy circles during Clinton's political rise.[151] In one of his best-known books, *The Work of Nations* (1992), he sought to address the fundamental conundrum facing the liberal political economy in the post–New Deal/Great Society era: the shocking rise in economic inequality between the rich and everyone else. Recognizing the correlation between education and income, Reich argued for a massive investment in education and infrastructure, renewing John Kenneth Galbraith's call from the 1950s to buttress public spending. Clinton had made such a program the basis of his campaign tract, *Putting People First*, upon taking office. The president's heart was with Reich on the issue of public investments, but he feared being tarred as a tax-and-spend Democrat just about as much as he feared being viewed as a liberal lover of blacks and welfare. And so Reich argued and lost, and then argued and lost some more, as the road to investing America's way out of the inequality conundrum disappeared in its rearview mirror. Like Edelman before him, Reich finally gave up and got out.[152]

The liberal departures paved the way for Clinton to rely on a new set of advisers, particularly the pollster Morris, who not only lacked liberal sympathies but had worked for the right-wing racist Republicans Trent Lott and Jesse Helms before rejoining Team Clinton. Even when Morris left the White House due to his own sex scandal, Clinton turned to the hardly less conservative Mark Penn. A believer in "micropolitics," Penn liked to divide Americans into tiny demographic groups and conquer them with small-ball policies that catered to their narrowest needs.[153] As the DLC's Will Marshall observed, "For years, the self-satisfied left has been arguing that our program was nothing more than a shallow political calculation. Dick Morris's career must give them great satisfaction."[154] The historian Gil Troy described Clinton's two terms as those of a president who "thought big and talked big, but ultimately governed small."[155]

At the same time, hopeful signs abounded. A revival of sorts appeared to be under way in the labor movement when the progressive insurgent, John Sweeney, who had risen in the ranks of the Service Employees International Union, replaced the neoconservative Lane Kirkland as the head of the AFL-CIO with a mandate to reverse labor's losses through militant action. A 1997 victory by UPS workers to protect part-time workers pointed to a new direction for a movement that badly needed it, given the changes in the way the economy operated and the massive losses suffered by private-sector unions that began in the 1970s.[156] Students were striking successfully across college campuses not only on behalf of South Africans, but also for the right to organize clerical and technical workers and teaching assistants.[157] Intellectuals rediscovered the cause of the working man and woman and sought to find ways to help the movement reinvent itself in a multicultural age with mobile capital and a globalized workforce. But the combined blows of 1970s deindustrialization, the Reagan administration's war on the movement during the 1980s, and Clinton's betrayal in pushing NAFTA through the Senate had all taken their toll.[158] Moreover, the vast service economy described by Reich and others—the temp agencies and employees of Walmart, the fast food chains and the dot-com businesses—would prove particularly difficult to organize. But despite some impressive victories with janitors in Los Angeles and hotel workers in Las Vegas, five years after Sweeney's rise and promise to embark on an aggressive organizing campaign, the percentage of unionized workers stood at 13.5 percent of the workforce, with barely 9 percent of them employed in the private sector, a fraction of the average rate across industrialized democracies in most of Western Europe.[159]

In the opening pages of *The Human Stain* (2000), Philip Roth described his moment of inspiration for the novel two years earlier as follows:

> In America [it was] the summer of an enormous piety binge, a purity binge—when terrorism—which had replaced communism as the prevailing threat to the country's security—was succeeded by cocksucking, and a virile, youthful middle-aged president and a brash, smitten twenty-one-year-old employee carrying on in the Oval Office like two teenage kids in a parking lot revived America's oldest communal passion, historically perhaps its most treacherous and subversive pleasure: the ecstasy of sanctimony. In the Congress, in the press, and on the networks, the righteous grandstanding creeps, crazy to blame, deplore, and punish, were everywhere out moralizing to beat the band: all of them in a calculated frenzy with what Hawthorne . . . identified in the incipient country of long ago as "the persecuting spirit"; all of them eager to enact the astringent rituals of purification that would excise the erection from the executive branch, thereby making things cozy and safe enough for Senator Lieberman's ten-year-old daughter to watch TV with her embarrassed daddy again. No, if you haven't lived through 1998, you don't know what sanctimony is.[160]

It was one of the many ironies of American politics that it was Bill Clinton's inability, even as president, to control his sexual appetites—or when that failed, to admit the truth about them—that ultimately drove liberals to take his side in the sex and political wars to which his behavior gave rise. Though his presidency can be viewed in some respects as one long scandal investigation, whether for prepresidential financial misdoings or postpresidential fund-raising, all accusations and inquiries paled beside those involving his affair with the young White House intern Monica Lewinsky, which began in November 1995 and continued through December 1997. A Republican fishing expedition that began in pursuit of some complicated (and money-losing) real estate deals made by Hillary and Bill with their friends from Arkansas, Jim and Susan McDougal, during the 1970s and 1980s, long before Clinton's presidency, took a twisted path and ultimately led directly to impeachment proceedings.[161]

To recount this story here would require page upon confusing page of argument, innuendo, and still-unsolved accusations. It is enough to say that Republicans and conservatives in the media, particularly *The Wall Street Journal* editorial page, used these events as a cudgel with which to undermine the Clinton presidency and frustrate virtually his entire second-term agenda. Over his wife's strong objection, Clinton conceded to demands for an independent counsel to be appointed in 1993, and Attorney General Janet Reno chose Robert Fiske to head up investigations into what was called popularly the Whitewater affair (named after an Arkansas river near one of the money-losing land deals). In 1994, just before Fiske, a moderate Republican, was about to exonerate the Clintons, a three-judge panel appointed the right-wing ideologue Kenneth Starr to replace him. Starr extended the investigation in almost every direction imaginable, bullying witnesses and even jailing those who refused to cooperate. Meanwhile, a woman named Paula Jones was pursuing a sexual harassment lawsuit against the president—announced with great fanfare at a conservative political action conference—whom she accused of exposing himself to her while he was governor and demanding sexual favors with a particularly distasteful frat-boy sense of entitlement. This investigation led Starr's staff of fanatical right-wing lawyers to a woman named Linda Tripp, who had pretended to befriend Ms. Lewinsky in order to hear her incriminating stories about Clinton, which she planned to turn into a tell-all. Tripp secretly taped the two women's extremely intimate conversations and, with the help of yet another right-wing agent provocateur, Lucianne Goldberg, set up Lewinsky to be ambushed by Starr's men. With her arrest, one of the great media circuses of the twentieth century commenced.

Once again, Bill Clinton grew fortunate in his political enemies. "A dimpled, flutily warbling Pillsbury Doughboy," Garry Wills described him. Starr's obsessive desire to destroy Clinton recalled Victor Hugo's Inspector Javert and served to alienate almost all but the most devoted of the Clinton haters.[162] Samuel Dash, who had been a former Watergate prosecutor and was now an ethics adviser to Starr, recalled, "I saw decisions made on moral grounds that had nothing to do with criminal grounds. They believed that someone was a bad person, a sinful person, who ought to be punished for it."[163] Starr would sometimes hold impromptu press conferences in his suburban driveway, at one of which he seemed to view himself as a latter-generation Old Testament prophet: "You cannot defile the temple of justice. There's no room for white lies. There's no room for shading. There's only room for truth. . . . Our job is to determine whether crimes were committed."[164] He was a man simultaneously possessed of his own power and drunk on his own sense of self-righteousness, but he had almost unlimited power and government funding to pursue his prey.

Legally speaking, the charge that always dogged Clinton was less adultery—however one defined it—than perjury. The president did not help matters by acting like a man who was probably guilty but thought he might escape on a legal technicality. Having not yet confessed to his wife, he attempted maneuver after maneuver to avoid the inevitable. He made certain to speak in the present tense—suggesting that because something wasn't happening at the moment, perhaps it hadn't happened at all—and responded angrily to any insinuation otherwise.[165] Clinton finally admitted to his dalliance with the young intern in August 1998 but continued to argue that he had done nothing illegal, much less anything warranting impeachment.

Still, on December 19, 1998, the proceedings finally commenced, and what took place proved to be a bizarre show trial on a par with the O. J. Simpson trial of three years earlier. But as Clinton's trial got under way, allegations of sexual misconduct began to spread throughout the capital. House Speaker Newt Gingrich had an affair with a congressional aide young enough to be his daughter. House Majority Leader Robert Livingston of Louisiana had one, too, and resigned his seat.[166] Henry Hyde, the gray-haired chairman of the House Judiciary Committee who presided over the impeachment inquiry, was revealed to have had an extramarital affair thirty years earlier that broke up the family of his paramour. Even the right-wing gun advocate, Helen Chenoweth, found herself forced to admit to a six-year-long affair with a married man.[167]

The Senate trial began in January 1999. Daniel Patrick Moynihan sat in the chamber on the eve of his impending retirement. Moynihan had no love for Clinton. He was furious, from the earliest days of Clinton's presidency, upon reading the words of his aide—later revealed to be Rahm Emanuel: "He's cantankerous, but he couldn't obstruct us even if he wanted to. The gridlock is broken. . . . We'll roll right over him if we have to." Moynihan wanted "the son of a bitch" fired and did his best to prove him wrong, up to and including using his high-public profile and key committee appointments to torpedo Clinton's single most important priority: his health care bill. He remained decidedly uncomfortable—personally, politically, and to a degree, culturally—with much of modern liberalism as well as countless modern liberals, whom he had come to conclude were "utterly dysfunctional. So much so of late, that one would dare to suggest that the causes liberals advocate are likely as not to fare better when they are out of office."[168]

And yet, to the shock and dismay of his neocon supporters and the some-times confused delight of liberals in New York and elsewhere, Moynihan had been nevertheless moving steadily leftward beginning with the election of Ronald Reagan in 1980. As the French historian of neoconservatism, Justin Vaisse, aptly noted, the change in Moynihan's position had been particularly noticeable in two areas: "Central America (on which he opposed the Reagan policy, which in this case was truly neoconservative) and international law, to which he attached more and more importance, while other neoconservatives turned toward unilateralism. He supported the 'nuclear freeze' movement and voted against the MX missile. In 1983 he opposed the invasion of Grenada and protested the mining of Nicaragua's ports. Speaking at New York University's commencement ceremony in 1984, he flung a challenge in the neo-conservatives' faces: 'The Soviet idea is spent. It commands some influence in the world; and fear. But it summons no loyalty. History is moving away from it at astounding speed. We must be less obsessed with the Soviets. If we must learn to live with nuclear parity, let us keep all the more in mind that we have consolidated an overwhelming economic advantage.'"[169]

While creating headache after headache for Clinton, Moynihan had clearly been taken by surprise by Newt Gingrich's ascendance in 1994 and blind-sided by the relentlessness of the radical right. Now he faced a new set of op-ponents squarely and argued—as he had earlier against Reagan—that their revolutionary brand of politics of impeachment was anathema to the health of the republic. He worried that presidential authority would be destroyed if impeachment was allowed to proceed on purely political grounds. Suffering from back pain throughout the impeachment procedures, Moynihan rose to speak and warned: "Senators, do not take the imprudent risk that removing William Jefferson Clinton for low crimes will not in the end jeopardize the Constitution itself. Censure him by all means. He will be gone in less than two years. But do not let his misdeeds put in jeopardy the Constitution we are sworn to uphold and defend."[170]

Most liberals rallied around the president about whom they had previously felt so divided.[171] Sidney Zion, a longtime New York City journalist and famous barroom raconteur, explained the phenomenon as follows: "You want to know why the left swallows hard and defends Clinton? It's because they don't want to give a victory to the racist scum, the anti-abortionists and the Christian right. That's who's trying to bring him down, and that's what's at stake here."[172] Circa 1999 liberals may no longer have been certain about their friends, but, like Pat Moynahan, they knew their enemies.

One unforeseen result of these unhappy events was the liberal rediscovery of their need for some sort of connection to real people: the so-called grass roots. But in this case, the roots turned out to be virtual. Wes Boyd and his wife, Joan Blades, lived in Silicon Valley on the fortune they had made selling the software for the flying toasters that populated screen savers on personal computers across the country during the 1990s.[173] They were dedicated liberals but disconnected from electoral politics. "We were businesspeople," Blades explained in an interview. "So we thought about the opportunity costs of our government being obsessed with the scandal when in theory they had real work to do."[174] They founded an organization they called MoveOn.org., which began with a single e-mail to friends and colleagues asking them to sign a petition to end the impeachment proceedings with a simple censure vote. By the end of a week, as friend passed the petition along to friend, and others posted it on academic and work-related bulletin boards, 100,000 signatures had been collected. By week two the number had risen to 250,000.[175] Their effort succeeded because, as Boyd explained, "[e]ssentially we stepped into a vacuum of leadership, and we said something sensible."[176] The new communications technology of the Internet had given birth to a new form of activism, one that worked particularly well for busy people who could not be bothered to drag themselves to a rally, much less a party meeting. And it would prove the beginning of a political infrastructure that would help sustain liberal activism long after Bill Clinton's sex life ceased to be a topic of polite conversation around the water coolers of the nation.

Clinton had the public on his side. Polls consistently revealed a populace that looked beyond Clinton's infidelities and believed him to be a basically good man and an excellent president who was almost undone by his singular weakness. Conservatives could not understand their forgiving nature, and "Where's the outrage?" became a mantra on the right.[177] Clinton's approval ratings, meanwhile, stayed constant at a remarkable 60 percent and rose to nearly 70 on the day of the impeachment vote.[178] Congressional Republicans—and the pundits who praised them—looked ridiculous in light of their own lapses, lapses that were as old as the human race.

Clinton's legacy is so complicated that it resists any simple summary. Speechwriter Michael Waldman accurately described him as a "one-man coalition." The former McGovern organizer certainly moved the party beyond McGovernism; no longer could Democrats be pegged as the party of "out-of-control government, welfare, crime, or stagflation."[179] He was a man of optimism, "from a town called Hope," and depending on one's viewpoint, he either reinvigorated liberalism or helped bury it. He did not, after all, re-create the "vital center" of Schlesinger's now half-century-old argument, and indeed, the septuagenarian historian condemned Clinton as representing only the "'middle of the road' preferred by cautious politicians of our own time," a "dead center."[180] But what were liberals to do now that they had lost the power to define "the center," whether in the media, in the policy arena, or in politics itself? It was a different world and one that required a new liberal synthesis for leaner times ahead. And it would be a long time in coming.

17

What's the Matter with America?

God have mercy on the man who doubts what he's sure of.
—Bruce Springsteen, "Brilliant Disguise"

A l Gore grew increasingly distant from his boss in the aftermath of the scandal. His daughters were about the same age as Monica Lewinsky, and his wife, Tipper, was roundly considered to be a famous prig when it came to matters of sex, owing to her campaign to rid the world of suggestive lyrics in rock 'n' roll.[1] Gore picked as his running mate the hawkish Connecticut senator Joseph Lieberman, the only Orthodox Jew ever to serve in the United States Congress. When it came to priggishness, however, Lieberman knew few rivals. Arthur Schlesinger, Jr., once described him to Hillary Clinton as a "sanctimonious prick," and she and her husband would have been hard pressed to disagree. During a tense moment during the Lewinsky scandal, Lieberman took to the floor of the Senate to denounce what he called the president's "disgraceful" and "immoral" behavior.[2]

Clinton, meanwhile, desperately wanted to help Gore's campaign. He naturally thought his vice president should talk up "our record of economic and social progress" and "put into sharp relief" his opponent George W. Bush's "explicit commitment to undo that progress."[3] He was privately furious at what he considered to be Gore's stubbornness in insisting on asserting his independence. Clinton had a point, though he did underestimate the animosity he had inspired among numerous voters and the phenomenon of "Clinton fatigue" that had set in among media and political elites. Gore's intractability on the matter, however, created all kinds of problems for his campaign. He could not, after all, simultaneously embrace Clinton's record and distance himself from the president himself.

Gore's independence was a powerful reed in the makeup of his character. His father, Al Gore, Sr., had been a fiercely independent senator from Tennessee whom John Kennedy decided not to make secretary of the treasury owing to his inability to accept orders from above. Young Al spent much of his life in a world of old people and bellhops, growing up mostly in the Fairfax Hotel on Washington's staid Massachusetts Avenue. He attended St. Albans, which had been established in 1909 as a "school for choirboys at the National Cathedral." Growing up in this atmosphere as the son of a senator gave Gore a kind of exaggerated seriousness at an early age that some of his peers found off-putting. Michael Kinsley famously described Gore as an "old person's idea of a young person," and he managed to live up to this assessment right through middle age.[4]

As a teenager, Al Junior had spoken of wanting to be a writer, but he continually felt the tug of the family business. At Harvard, studying first psychology and then political theory, he embraced the antiwar movement, albeit far more cautiously than most of his peers. Encouraged by the then-radical leftist instructor and funder of the McCarthy campaign Martin Peretz, Gore went "clean for Gene" (though he had not exactly proved dirty or even unbuttoned in the past). This put him on the far right-wing border of radicalized respectability at Harvard. Like Bill Clinton at Georgetown, Al Junior was a polite protester who intended to remain viable within the political system. This was essential for the son of a senator who sought to be reelected from a conservative southern state like Tennessee, where patriotism and military service were inextricably intertwined.

As his father came up for reelection in 1970, Gore worried that if he took the path of least resistance like most of his classmates and sat out the war with a student deferment, it would sink his father's hopes for reelection and end his career in ignominy. Richard Neustadt, an influential political scientist with a specialty in the American presidency and Gore's academic adviser, strongly concurred. Neustadt also suggested that the young man might wish to consider his own political future: "If you want to be part of the country twenty-five years from now, if you want any future in politics, you've got to serve."[5] And so, leaving Harvard, with a final appearance on campus in military garb—and thereby shocking pretty much everyone whose path he crossed—Al Gore left for Vietnam, where he joined an engineer brigade, though his primary duties were to serve as an in-house journalist.

Gore returned home without much direction. He attended Nashville's Vanderbilt University to study theology, which forged in him a lifelong interest in connecting spiritualism and exploration of the natural world.[6] But the years in Vietnam, his father's recent political loss, and the thinking he did at Vanderbilt also nurtured a pessimistic streak. The dean of Vanderbilt's divinity school, Walter Harrelson, recalled that Gore had developed an almost

Calvinistic theology "of how human beings, none of them, can fully be trusted, precisely because we're not God. That one of the characteristics of human life is frailty, that human beings have an enormous capacity to deceive themselves and to always put the best face on anything they see or think or do."[7] Gore's experiences and education pulled him in different directions, some optimistic and hopeful about politics, others dark and Niebuhrian, but his practical side took over when he transferred to Vanderbilt's law school. He never finished, however, so impatient was he to run for Congress when the opportunity arose in 1976.

He quickly made a name for himself with the political establishment there as a young man who was wise beyond his years. Gore was an important middleman (literally and figuratively) between Republicans and Democrats, intellectuals and politicians, and the military and Congress, going to some lengths to take on difficult issues such as the MX missile and Central America; where Democrats appeared weak, he tended to move closer to the Republican position than his own party's but garnered kudos from pundits and politicians alike for the rigorous research he undertook and the almost ostentatious pondering he displayed before arriving at his position. In 1984, the year Reagan swept his state and many Democrats went down to defeat, he moved from Congress to the Senate almost as a matter of course.

As a politically cautious young southern centrist filled with ambition, Gore was a Bill Clinton–like figure before even Clinton himself. But he never really appeared to enjoy politics and no matter how hard he tried, he was unable to communicate the warmth that Clinton could. In 1988, Gore, not yet forty, allowed himself to be talked into a premature run at the presidency. Confident that his background, coupled with his relatively conservative orientation, could carry southern states, Gore both overestimated his appeal and underestimated the potency of Jesse Jackson's insurgent campaign. Gore supported Reagan's war in Central America with reservations and, wholeheartedly, his invasion of Grenada. He opposed federal funding for abortion, supported a "moment of silence" in schools to be used for prayer, and took a weaker position than his opponents in favor of gun control. Gore did win primaries in Tennessee, Kentucky, North Carolina, Arkansas, Oklahoma, Nevada, and Wyoming, but Jackson took Alabama, Georgia, Louisiana, Mississippi, Virginia, and South Carolina, states Gore needed to win if he was to have a hope. In New York, Gore allowed the city's voluble and deeply divisive mayor, Ed Koch, to take control of his campaign and run it into the ground as he turned it into a vehicle for a kind of Jewish jihad against Jesse Jackson. The entire experience energized Jackson and his supporters and prevented most New

Yorkers from taking Gore seriously. His campaign, and his image among both voters and the press, never recovered, and soon enough he was forced to withdraw, admitting that the entire candidacy had been a kind of exercise in self-delusion. He later confessed that his decision to "ask the pollsters and professional politicians what they thought I ought to talk about" reflected doubts about his "own political judgment."[8]

In April 1989, still recovering from the humiliation of his tepid campaign, Gore took his family to the Baltimore Orioles' opening day game. His six-year-old son, Albert Gore III, ran from his father's handhold across the parking lot to see a friend and was struck by a car and thrown thirty feet into the air. Coming in midlife, the incident prompted questions about what really mattered to Gore, and he realized the answer to that—besides his son's healing—was humankind's relationship to the natural world. The first product of that realization was 1992's *Earth in the Balance,* the first book by a sitting senator to make the bestseller list since JFK's *Profiles in Courage.*

The book was both personal and profound, erudite but without Gore's famous preening. "Our dysfunctional civilization," Gore explained, "has developed a numbness that prevents us from feeling the pain of our alienation from our world." This was a problem of "addiction" and "denial," a spiritual not a material problem. "I believe deeply that true change is possible only when it begins inside the person who is advocating it." He called for a global Marshall Plan to stabilize global population growth (by promoting birth control), to develop "appropriate technologies," and to initiate global education about the environmental crisis to create policies that would encourage sustainable societies.[9]

Earth in the Balance carried with it an admission of culpability. Gore recounted how he decided to run for president in 1987 and tried to make environmentalism central to his campaign. But he remained, at heart, a politician, and his advisers thought that the environment did not poll sufficiently well to make it the centerpiece of a presidential platform. "The truth is, most voters didn't consider [the environment] an overriding issue, and I didn't do a good job of convincing them otherwise. . . . The harder truth is that I simply lacked the strength to keep on talking about the environmental crisis constantly whether it was being reported in the press or not."[10]

When he ran in 2000, he delivered a well-received speech about the dangers of global warming, the need for smart technologies to solve environmental problems, and the worrisome fact that George W. Bush's father had made his fortune in oil.[11] But that was it. Once again, he allowed himself to be talked out of focusing on the issue about which he felt most passionate. Throughout the campaign Gore could not shake the sense that he was not his own man, that he did not know—or could not bring himself to say—just what he thought, and that he was unwilling to put himself on the line for anything that had not been poll tested and focus grouped in advance.

Gore disposed of a primary challenge from neoliberal New Jersey senator (and ex–New York Knicks star) "Dollar Bill" Bradley, but the press treated him with contempt and regularly disputed his record, employing Republican press releases as fact and Gore's own statements as ipso facto self-delusion, lies, braggadocio, or a combination of all three. A study by the Project for Excellence in Journalism and Princeton Survey Research Associates examined 1,149 stories from seventeen news publications, programs, and Web sites during the election and discovered:

> The most common theme of the campaign was that Gore was scandal-tainted. This accounted for 42 percent of all the assertions about Gore's character. The second most common assertion about Gore was that he was a liar. These accounted for 34 percent of stories about him. The least common of the major themes, accounting for 14 percent of assertions, was that he was competent, experienced, and knowledgeable.[12]

Reporters found Gore's efforts to squirm away from Clinton's many White House scandals to be offensive, particularly because he frequently employed legalistic excuses rather than plainspoken explanations for his actions. His insistence that fund-raising calls he made from his office were justified by what he rather prissily termed the lack of a "controlling legal authority" was a particular bête noire for the White House press corps. *Washington Post* White House reporter Dana Milbank gave voice to a common complaint:

> Gore is sanctimonious and that's sort of the worst thing you can be in the eyes of the press. And he has been disliked all along and it was because he gives a sense that he's better than us—he's better than everybody, for that matter, but the sense that he's better than us as reporters. Whereas President Bush probably is sure that he's better than us—he's probably right, but he does not convey that sense. He does not seem to be dripping with contempt when he looks at us, and I think that has something to do with the coverage.[13]

Moreover, while running to his right against Bush, Gore was dogged by his own Henry Wallace problem: Ralph Nader coming at him from the left. Nader had run in 1996, but that race was never in doubt, and so the decision for disappointed liberals to cast a protest vote against the various sellouts they felt they had been forced to swallow during the Clinton administration was not a particularly painful one. Four years later, however, the race was up in the air. As Nader's biographer observed, his candidacy "drew its share of the pink-haired and the multipierced, who brought with them a mélange of issues: legalize drugs, illegalize sport utility vehicles, free [accused African American police murderer/life-without-parole-poet] Mumia Abu-Jamal."[14] Nader touted his previous line that there was not "a dime's worth of difference" between the two big-money, corporate-dominated parties.

The threat he posed to Gore's candidacy was well understood at the time, but neither Nader nor his fanatical backers appeared to care about the prospects of a George W. Bush administration. His celebrity-laden rallies in the very states that might hand the election to Bush forced Gore to run to his left and right simultaneously, compounding his problem of appearing inauthentic to Americans. As with Henry Wallace, Nader focused his wrath on the candidate with whom he shared more matters of agreement than the one they both opposed, chastising "frightened liberals" and "well-intentioned cowards" who lacked the courage to join his kamikaze candidacy.[15] Gore, he said, was "more reprehensible" than Bush: "He knows so much and refuses to act on his knowledge. George W. Bush can plead ignorant, but Al Gore cannot."[16] Right up until Election Day 2000, Nader and his supporters allowed themselves the luxury of believing that a presidential vote was nothing more than an expression of one's ideological identity rather than a responsible choice between however imperfect alternatives. Sadly, there were enough of those supporters in Florida and elsewhere to allow the U.S. Supreme Court to hand the presidency to George W. Bush.

The nightmare of the election of 2000 need not be relived in detail here. The days that followed Gore's concession and then his decision to retract it included a chaotic examination of ballots punched in decrepit, undermonitored voting machines that left "hanging, dimpled, and pregnant" chads.[17] Although Gore won the popular vote by about 537,000 votes—a slim margin, but far larger than that enjoyed by either John Kennedy in 1960 or Richard Nixon in 1968—and without a doubt a plurality of the intended votes of Floridians on Election Day, he did not manage to win the election.

A fair recount of the vote, however, was never undertaken. Almost without exception, it was Republicans, whether in the courts or in the streets, who sought to prevent one from taking place. As IRS documents would later show, conservative activists were flown in from out of state on private jets lent to the

Bush campaign by supportive corporations, including Enron and Haliburton; they were put up gratis in local hotels and entertained by Wayne Newton, all courtesy of Republican Party donors. Many were recruited by House Majority Whip Tom DeLay and given directions from a communications-equipped Winnebago manned by party operatives. Their value was best demonstrated when, on November 22, a Miami-Dade canvassing board attempted to undertake the hand recounts the courts had ordered. With just a few phone calls, the Republican street operation produced hundreds of "volunteers" who, according to *Time*, provoked a "'mob scene' . . . screaming . . . pounding on doors and . . . [threatening an] alleged physical assault on Democrats."[18]

Despite these actions, and many others like them, it was Gore's side that came in for most of the criticism from the allegedly liberal media. *The Washington Post*'s Michael Kelly, formerly editor of *The New Republic*, complained of Gore's "revolting" campaign filled with "hacks and political thugs":[19] "If he doesn't get his way he threatens to delegitimize democracy itself. Got to burn that village down."[20] "Even if Gore ultimately loses in Florida," Kelly wrote, "with the help of reasonably sympathetic coverage from a largely Democratic and liberal national press corps, [Gore] has managed to spin his extraordinary, radical, unprecedented behavior as reasonable—and legitimate."[21]

Democrats failed to rise to the challenge of Republican attempts to shut down a fair, court-ordered recount and allowed the election to be taken away from them by a transparently partisan U.S. Supreme Court. All five of the justices appointed by either Ronald Reagan or George H. W. Bush somehow concluded that a fair vote count in this election—and this election only— would violate the Equal Protection clause of the U.S. Constitution. It was nonsense, but the Bush campaign had so successfully created an aura of panic among the media and political establishment that Gore did not dare contest it. Minutes after the Supreme Court announced its decision, he conceded. He had been in the process of drafting an op-ed article for *The New York Times* asking for Republicans' support for his presidency.

Liberal foreign policy thinking remained deeply contested terrain during the Clinton-Gore years. Clinton had been the first Democratic president since the fall of communism in 1989 who was far enough removed from the legacy of Vietnam even to begin to articulate a new foreign policy for the post–Cold War period. Like everything else about his presidency, it was murky, but it veered toward cautious humanitarian intervention as he stumbled through some early failures on his way there. First came Somalia, where President George H. W. Bush had sent troops to stabilize a country sinking into tribal war. Clinton initially doubled down on the policy, at least until Somalian rebels shot down U.S. Black Hawk helicopters and dragged the pilots' corpses through the streets of Mogadishu in October 1993. As the mission appeared to change from peacekeeping to active engagement, Clinton precipitously withdrew U.S. troops in what looked and felt like complete humiliation. Not long afterward he did much the same when U.S. Navy ships met unexpected resistance in Haiti, where they were accompanying that tortured nation's democratically elected leader, Jean-Bertrand Aristide, on his return to power following a brutal 1991 coup. In Rwanda, where Hutus conducted a systematic genocidal murder of hundreds of thousands of Tutsis, the United States, and the rest of the world, simply stood by. As the scholar, activist, and later U.S. government official Samantha Power put it in her study *A Problem from Hell* (2002), "The real reason the United States did not do what it could and should have done to stop genocide was not a lack of knowledge or influence but a lack of will. Simply put, American leaders did not act because they did not want to. They believed that genocide was wrong, but they were not prepared to invest the military, financial, diplomatic, or domestic political capital needed to stop it."[22]

Finally, in the Balkans liberals forged a new foreign policy. But just as bad cases make bad law, so, too, do impossibly complex and intractable foreign policy problems make for flawed foreign policy doctrines. In 1991, after the Soviet empire had collapsed and a new world in East and Central Europe was born in its wake, Bosnia and Herzegovina declared independence from Yugoslavia. Immediately both descended into warfare—"ethnic cleansing" was the Orwellian term applied—between Serbs, Croats, and Muslims, much of it based on conflicts hundreds of years old that had remained simmering beneath the artificial state apparatus of Marshal Joseph Tito's Yugoslavia. Bush had all but ignored the problem, while Secretary of State James Baker had famously pronounced, "We don't have a dog in this fight."[23] Clinton, meanwhile, had flirted with the neocons and the hawkish *New York Times* columnist William Safire by implying a tougher policy. But he could not get America's European allies—where, after all, the conflict was taking place—to come around to his view. He eventually became intrigued by a "lift and strike" proposal that would lift an arms embargo on the victims—in this case the Bosnian Muslims—and punish the Bosnian Serb aggressors with NATO airstrikes.[24]

In July 1995, however, Serbs carried out a massacre in the town of Srebrenica, murdering more than seven thousand Muslims and dumping their bodies into mass graves as they also began bombing the beautiful multicultural city of Sarajevo. Finally, the Europeans paid attention, and Clinton got the policy that NATO had resisted for so long: a mixture of military force and diplomatic talks guided by a vision of humanitarian defense. Though Clinton ruled out the use of U.S. ground troops from the start, the bombing was sufficient to persuade both sides to agree to U.S.-sponsored peace talks, which were held in Dayton, Ohio, beginning in November 1995. Richard Holbrooke, the assistant secretary for European and Canadian affairs and a tireless and driven diplomat, hammered out an agreement through which Muslims and Croats would govern themselves together via the creation of a new multiethnic state. To oversee the peace, the United States sent twenty thousand troops to the region (NATO would have sixty thousand in toto), but Clinton committed the troops for only a year in order to convince a nervous public (and an increasingly isolationist Republican Party) that the U.S. "mission is clear and limited."[25]

Bosnia turned any number of formerly dovish liberals into aggressive hawks. "Multilateral solutions to the world's problems are all very well, but they have no teeth unless America bares its fangs," wrote the Canadian intellectual and future politician Michael Ignatieff, temporarily ensconced at Harvard's Carr Center for Human Rights Policy.[26] The relevant debacle analogy for the use of military force had ceased to be Vietnam and had reverted to Munich, which had served for the two decades after World War II. With no opposing great power, and the ineffectiveness of UN forces, America was all that stood between genocide and its likely victims. "If we have to use force, it is because we are America," Clinton's second secretary of state, Madeleine Albright—the first woman ever to hold the job—announced. "We are the indispensable nation. We stand tall, and we see further than other countries into the future."[27]

One person changed by Bosnia was Hillary Clinton. A tour of the country after it was safely pacified convinced her that, despite the tragedy of Vietnam, U.S. military engagement could better the world.[28] The lesson also stuck with Al Gore, who had been one of the most vocal proponents of action in Bosnia when Clinton dithered, as it was a logical extension of the hawkish tendencies he had developed during his earlier years in Congress and the Senate.

It may have come as a surprise, therefore, that when faced with the prospect of George W. Bush's push for war with Iraq in late 2002 and then the actual invasion of 2003, Senator Clinton and ex-Vice President Gore came to opposite conclusions. Clinton faced a direct vote on the matter when the Senate debated the Joint Resolution to Authorize the Use of United States Armed Forces against Iraq in 2002. On October 10 she explained her vote in favor: "Bipartisan support for this resolution makes success in the United Nations more likely and, therefore, war less likely."[29] Hillary later explained that Bush's adviser for national security, Condoleezza Rice, had promised that the real goal was to pressure the UN to send more inspectors to find out what weapons Saddam Hussein possessed, though Rice's memory of the conversation was decidedly different.[30]

On September 23, 2002, addressing the Commonwealth Club in San Francisco, Gore explained to his listeners that he supported the war Bush had waged in Afghanistan after the attacks of 9/11. But now he condemned the way Bush was rushing to war, as the president pressed Congress to "speedily affirm" his position and thus "foreshorten[ed] . . . deliberation in the Congress." Gore reminded listeners that he was "one of the few Democrats in the U.S. Senate who supported the war resolution" in Iraq in 1991 and said he felt betrayed when George H. W. Bush pulled out troops and refused to overthrow Hussein but now realized that the president had been right to pursue a policy of containment. The elder Bush had also "built a broad international coalition" and had a "strong United Nations resolution . . . in place"—measures that were absent in his son's push for war. George W. Bush was embarking on a policy that would squander "the international outpouring of sympathy, goodwill, and solidarity that followed the attacks of September 11th." Preemption, moreover, was not a doctrine that the United States could keep for itself. And so "the rule of law [would] quickly be replaced by the reign of fear—any nation that perceives circumstances that could eventually lead to an imminent threat would be justified under this approach in taking military action against another nation."[31]

The debate over war with Iraq would have been unimaginable, of course, without the Al Qaeda attack on the United States of September 11, 2001. With it, America's ability to isolate itself—to feel, in Reinhold Niebuhr's words, "the paradise of our domestic security . . . suspended in a hell of global insecurity"— had ended forever.[32] Suddenly Richard Rorty's language of liberal patriotism appeared more relevant than ever. This patriotism justified a foreign war against legitimate enemies, but almost immediately, much of the nation, egged on by many in the media, embarked on a kind of orgy of anger, jingoism, and thirst for vengeance—vengeance without much direction. Bush exploited this panic not only by purposely confusing responsibility for the attack but also by failing to ask Americans for any meaningful sacrifice. Instead, almost unbelievably, he instructed Americans to go out and consume, and to refuse to consider, even for a moment, whether the attack had any implications for America's role in the world.

History has by and large ignored the voices calling for a policy of prudence vis-à-vis Iraq, but among liberals, Gore was hardly alone. In September 2002,

Ted Kennedy delivered a prescient speech at the National Press Club, where he argued that the Bush administration had failed to make "a convincing case that we face . . . an imminent threat to our national security" that could require a "unilateral, preemptive American strike." The administration had not "acknowledged . . . the immense post-war commitment that will be required to create a stable Iraq." Taking an eye off Afghanistan could, he warned, "worsen, not lessen, the threat of terrorism."[33] At a rally organized by Chicagoans Against War in Iraq in October 2002, a young African American Illinois state senator, Barack Obama, explained his opposition to the U.S. invasion: not because it was an imperialist war for oil but a "dumb war." "I am opposed to," he added, "the cynical attempt by [neoconservative Iraq war hawks] Richard Perle and Paul Wolfowitz and other armchair, weekend warriors in this Administration" who want to "shove their own ideological agendas down our throats, irrespective of the costs in lives lost and in hardships borne." He continued: "I . . . know that Saddam poses no imminent and direct threat to the United States, or to his neighbors, that the Iraqi economy is in shambles, that the Iraqi military [has] a fraction of its former strength, and that in concert with the international community he can be contained until, in the way of all petty dictators, he falls away into the dustbin of history. I know that even a successful war against Iraq will require a US occupation of undetermined length, at undetermined cost, with undetermined consequences. I know that an invasion of Iraq without a clear rationale and without strong international support will only fan the flames of the Middle East and encourage the worst, rather than best, impulses of the Arab world, and strengthen the recruitment arm of Al Qaeda."[34] Years later, Hillary Clinton undoubtedly would have wished she had listened to these arguments. She might have been president if she had.

That the Bush administration case for war was fundamentally flawed was evident to almost anyone who examined the evidence with any care, as America's European allies, particularly France and Germany, realized, and so, finally, refused to commit to the cause. Long before the postwar postmortems demonstrated the degree to which their arguments and those of their supporters were based on a combination of wishful thinking and doctored evidence, one could discern an administration pattern of discounting evidence that interfered with their arguments and demonstrating a willingness to trump up, exaggerate, and frequently invent incidents and eyewitnesses to further its case.

While the liberals who embraced the war may not have adopted the administration's arguments as their own, they were unwilling to subject its contentions to the kind of skepticism they clearly warranted. In retrospect liberal hawks sounded less as if they were seeking to convince undecided Americans about the pragmatic case for war as they were to convince themselves of their ability to support an imperialist adventure while at the same time remaining true to their principles. These liberals were men of ideas wanting to be men of action—to embrace what the historian Christopher Lasch called "the anti-intellectualism of the intellectuals," to be bold, to reject doubt, and to fight with ideas rather than guns.[35] Once again the history train was leaving, and they aimed to book a first-class carriage.

Arguments naturally varied. Some focused on the perceived threat of terrorism; others, on the need to combat what was called Islamo-fascism. Others still grew excited about the opportunity to spread democracy where it had previously never existed and among a people routinely thought to be impervious to its benefits and incapable of assuming its responsibilities. Oddly, many thought the war was necessary to prop up America's self-regard, rather than as a response to any particular threat that Bush or anyone else professed to see. When the twin towers went down, the liberal journalist George Packer opened a collected set of essays, *The Fight Is for Democracy* (2003), with his memory of his first thoughts on 9/11: "Maybe this will make us better."[36] Packer's former friend and sometime intellectual tutor, the liberal hawk Paul Berman, argued in his influential book *Terror and Liberalism* (2003), that liberals could now fight against the writings of the Islamic prophet Sayyid Qutb, whose writings he compared to fascist theorists and their "irrationalist cult of death and murder." This too-easy equation with the threat of fascism invited Berman's comrades to imagine themselves in the historical role of these liberals—later smeared as "premature antifascists"—who had sought to convince their countrymen that the fight against Hitler could not be postponed.[37] Almost all bought into the notion that military force was the only option to deal with the problem, mocking liberals at home and abroad who thought diplomatic containment a more prudent option.

Not all of the so-called liberal hawks were actually liberals, but they happily adopted the appellation as its implied counterintuitiveness significantly increased the political caché associated with their opinions. Labels aside, almost all were, like Packer, Berman, Ignatieff, Christopher Hitchens, Andrew Sullivan, Richard Cohen, David Rieff, Bill Keller, Roger Cohen, and Jacob Weisberg, successful media personalities who, almost without exception, lacked any professional expertise regarding military strategy, Iraqi society, or even the Arab world in general. "Enamored of [their] own morality," as Andrew Sullivan later admitted of himself as well,[38] they saw their own ideas,

as the author Jacob Heilbrunn would write, "as weapons in a moral struggle."[39] While each came up with his own argument for why, in the end, war
was preferable to peace, almost all rested on the same kind of wishful thinking
that led ex-Reagan official Kenneth Adelman to promise a "cakewalk" of a
war,[40] or Dick Cheney to predict that U.S. soldiers in Iraq would "be greeted
as liberators."[41] Few if any of the group appeared willing to submit the Bush
administration's claims to the same sort of scrutiny they might have offered
even to a lengthy novel. As Christopher Hitchens, one of the most vociferous
of the not really so liberal hawks, would explain in his 2010 memoir, *Hitch 22*,
they "rather tended to assume that things of [the] more practical sort were
being taken care of."[42] What they did understand was that the United States
was facing a moment of unprecedented import, one in which it behooved the
nation to assume its role as the enforcer of global norms, even if that meant
ignoring the express will of the UN Security Council as well as the publicly
professed preferences of the entire Arab world. Strengthened through struggle
abroad, America would become invincible, all-powerful, and capable of setting aside the "irony" and contingencies of American power that Reinhold
Niebuhr had cited in his arguments against hubris.

The liberal hawks, Keller later mused, were decidedly "pleased with [them-
selves] for defying the caricature of liberals as, to borrow a phrase from those
days, brie-eating surrender monkeys."[43] And so in addition to turning a blind
eye to the myriad weaknesses of the Bush and neoconservative arguments for
war, many felt compelled to focus their energies on disciplining fellow liberals
who failed to get with the plan. "Damn the doves," wrote formerly Trotskyist,
now neoconservative Hitchens in the right-wing London *Spectator* in 2001.[44]
His compatriot, the "gay Catholic Tory" former editor of *The New Republic*,
Andrew Sullivan, warned Americans to be alert about traitors in their midst,
whom he identified not as people living in "the middle part of the country—
the great red zone that voted for Bush"—but as Gore voters, the majority, by
the way, and particularly in the city where the Twin Towers attack had taken
place.

This attitude was particularly useful to the administration, which, together
with its supporters in the media, was conducting a campaign of vilification
against any prominent figure who raised questions about the data it circulated
in support of the war. This campaign went so far as to use the right-wing columnist Robert Novak to reveal the identity of CIA agent Valerie Plame, because her husband, longtime diplomat Joseph Wilson, had returned home
from an officially sanctioned trip to Africa without the evidence of Iraq's
nuclear ambitions that Cheney and company had demanded he provide.[45]

Liberal hawks, particularly those associated with *The New Republic*, were constantly on the lookout for liberals who failed to live up to their standards of "toughness" and "militance" when it came to the battle against Islamofascism.

Another favorite tactic of liberal hawks was to equate honest dovish liberals who disagreed with their analyses, distrusted the Bush administration, or resisted U.S. unilateralism in the face of clear and concerted allied opposition with unserious or reflexively anti-American opponents of the war, such as the far-left organizers of certain protest marches along with some of the speakers they invited. As the critic Michael Bérubé explained: "The Manichean left [which included pacifist and anti-American opponents of the war] and the liberal hawks worked to produce and sustain each other."[46] Among their most vociferous critics was the late British-born historian Tony Judt, who attacked American liberals as "Bush's Useful Idiots." Writing in 2006: "In today's America, neo-conservatives generate brutish policies for which liberals provide the ethical fig-leaf. There really is no other difference between them."[47] This was unfair, as Judt's broad-brush assault did not bother to distinguish between liberals who jumped into bed with Bush and the neoconservatives and those who fought them. Judt wrote, for instance, as if the harsh criticism of Bush's plans published in *The New York Review of Books*—for which he wrote—and *The Nation*, which nearly doubled its circulation under editor Katrina vanden Heuvel during the Bush years to the point where it was triple that of *The New Republic*, did not exist.[48] (And an even more nuanced view would have forced Judt to take notice of the existence of some strong antiwar arguments in the pages of *The New Republic* itself.) Even so, the balance of the magazine's writers were so effective at pushing neocon-style arguments for war, they began cropping up in right-wing publications like *The Weekly Standard* and *Commentary*. Its chief foreign policy writer, Lawrence Kaplan, even coauthored a brief with *Weekly Standard* editor and neoconservative strategist William Kristol.[49] Whatever the motivation and whatever the result regarding Iraq, one consequence was unarguable: the purpose of these liberal hawkish attacks was to marginalize their liberal dovish opponents from mainstream political and strategic debate over the future of America's role in the world. And to an amazing degree, given what even most of them would later recognize as the disastrous effects of the invasion for which they agitated, they succeeded.

While some liberal hawks did feel compelled to reexamine the assumptions that had led them to follow so destructive a path after Iraq descended into bloody chaos, more than a few remained wedded to the view articulated by hawkish liberal pundit Richard Cohen, who, borrowing from the French ex-Stalinist Pierre Courtade, insisted, "You and your kind were wrong to be right; we were right to be wrong." George Packer went so far as to insist that those who had been prescient about the coming catastrophe, by virtue of this understanding, were in possession of "second-rate minds."[50] In June 2005, Thomas Friedman, *The New York Times*'s extraordinarily influential foreign affairs columnist, whose own analysis had proved misguided, accused liberals of "deep down" wanting America to fail in Iraq because "they thought the war was wrong."[51]

This was not only consistent with the accusations of contemporary neoconservatives, it was also oddly reminiscent of the style of Joseph McCarthy. In the case of some of those making the argument, this was clearly no accident. William Kristol demanded to know "why the Ted Kennedy wing of the Senate Democrats, the Nancy Pelosi faction of the House Democrats, a large majority of Democratic grass-roots activists, the bulk of liberal columnists, *The New York Times* editorial page, and Hollywood" were all opposed to Bush's foreign policy. His answer: "These liberals—better, leftists—hate George W. Bush so much they can barely bring themselves to hope America wins the war to which, in their view, the president has illegitimately committed the nation. They hate Don Rumsfeld so much they can't bear to see his military strategy vindicated. They hate John Ashcroft so much they can't bear to see his military strategy vindicated. They hate conservatives that seems to burn brighter than their love of America." And just as his father, Irving Kristol, had praised Senator McCarthy in order to vilify liberals back in 1952, so too William used virtually identical phraseology a half century later: "The American people, whatever their doubts about aspects of Bush's foreign policy, know that Bush is serious about fighting terrorists and terrorist states that mean America harm. About Bush's Democratic critics, they know no such thing."[52]

Despite the obvious strength of their case against Bush, the 2004 presidential election evinced extreme nervousness among liberals. They knew they had been right about both Bush and the dubiousness of his rush to war. But being right was somehow equated with being weak in the ideological twilight zone of post-Iraq America. To try to gain traction in this topsy-turvy political context, Democrats chose not Howard Dean, the leader of the McCarthy-RFK-style antiwar movement, whose own warnings had been prescient, but the far more staid Massachusetts junior senator and former Vietnam hero, John Kerry, who had voted for the Iraq war.

Indeed, Kerry's choice as the party's standard-bearer was almost entirely dependent on his status as a war hero. His service in Vietnam from 1968 to

1969 included three Purple Hearts, a Bronze Star "for heroic achievement," and a Silver Star "for conspicuous gallantry and intrepidity in action."[53] He had also been an antiwar hero, which is just the kind of war hero liberals like best when it comes to unpopular wars like Vietnam. When he stood at the lectern at the Democratic Party convention in 2004 to accept his nomination to a sea of waving American flags, Kerry gave a salute and a beaming smile and told the crowds he was "reporting for duty," as if the commander-in-chief role had become the single determinant of the qualifications for the American presidency.[54]

Kerry's paternal grandfather, Fritz Kohn, was a Czech Jew who had come to the United States in 1905. He chose the name Frederick Kerry and converted from Judaism to Catholicism; he made his fortune in footwear. On November 23, 1921, however, he committed suicide. His widow returned to Europe, but her son, Richard Kerry, returned for college at Yale and law school at Harvard before becoming a test pilot for B-29 bombers in the Army Air Corps during World War II. Richard met and fell in love with Rosemary Forbes, a wealthy descendent of Massachusetts Puritans.[55] John was born on December 11, 1943, while Richard was on a rest cure in Colorado recovering from tuberculosis. After the war Richard Kerry turned to a law career and then entered public service by joining the Bureau of United Nations Affairs housed in the State Department. Thus began John Kerry's cosmopolitan childhood, during which he traveled to Germany, France, Norway, and Switzerland, moving from one boarding school to another.[56] His rootlessness nurtured an aloofness in his relationships. His face continued to grow longer as he grew to manhood, giving the impression of a morose, beardless Abe Lincoln.

Kerry entered Yale in 1962 and gave the school's class oration on June 12, 1966, delivering a strong antiwar speech. "What was an excess of isolationism has become an excess of interventionism," Kerry said. "And this Vietnam War has found our policymakers forcing Americans into a strange corner . . . that if victory escapes us, it would not be the fault of those who led, but of the doubters who stabbed them in the back—notions all too typical of an America that had to find Americans to blame for the takeover in China by the Communists, and then for the takeover in Cuba."[57] Ironically, this prediction would be one that would have important and decidedly unhappy implications not only for Kerry's political future but for American liberalism as well.

Kerry's decision to enlist after graduation, much like Gore's three years later, was fraught with ambivalence and, ultimately, confusion and complexity. In 1966 he chose the Naval Reserve, and as Douglas Brinkley writes, "As Kerry awaited assignment, he approached the war almost contemplatively:

he liked to study what was happening around him, and why, and how he could make things better. He took a scholarly approach to the war, tape-recording the occasional worthwhile conversation and constantly scribbling impressions in his ever-present notebook like a latter-day Ernie Pyle."[58]

In the Reserve, Kerry was trained to operate swift boats, small vessels that could be driven at great speeds. In his own words, swift boats "were engaged in coastal patrolling and that's what I thought I was going to be doing."[59] Recognizing that the Mekong Delta was a stronghold of the Vietcong, however, his commanders decided that swift boats could help play a role in liberating the river valley from Communist control. What Kerry had believed to be a safe choice became a dangerous one, and he saw action on scores of hazardous raids.[60] Though he came to respect his fellow swift boaters, and earned their respect in return, he grew ashamed by the recklessness among some military men and the general callousness that war encouraged.

In December of 1968, Kerry was wounded and received a Purple Heart. In February 1969 his group was ambushed by a Vietcong patrol along the shoreline of the Duong Keo River. Beaching his boat, Kerry grabbed his weapon, jumped onto shore, and pursued the Vietcong, killing one of them and seizing his rocket launcher. Less than a month later, Kerry engaged in a firefight where he was wounded once again. During still another operation, an adviser was thrown overboard from Kerry's swift boat after it hit a mine. Kerry rescued the man from the water—the action conjures up memories of John Kennedy and the PT 109—and earned both his Bronze Star as well as his third Purple Heart. This event gave him the right to return home, which he requested in March 1969.

Kerry soon married the girlfriend he had left behind, Julia Thorne, and threw himself into antiwar activism, joining Vietnam Veterans Against the War (VVAW) and finding inspiration in his newfound heroes, Allard Lowenstein and Eugene McCarthy. On Labor Day, 1970, Kerry spoke in Valley Forge, Pennsylvania, as part of a protest organized by VVAW and Operation RAW (Rapid American Withdrawal). Although two Hollywood leftists, Donald Sutherland and Jane Fonda, and a lawyer and conspiracy theorist, Mark Lane, also spoke, Kerry took the day, moving to the microphone and saying, "We are here because we above all others have earned the right to criticize the war on Southeast Asia. We are here to say that it is not patriotism to ask Americans to die for a mistake or that it is not patriotic to allow a president to talk about not being the first president to lose a war, and using us as pawns in that game."

Kerry's celebrity grew as he became a kind of button-down spokesman in the media for respectable, well-behaved antiwar agitation. From January 31 to February 2, 1971, he helped with the Winter Soldier Investigation in Detroit against the backdrop of the war crimes trial of William Calley, Jr., for the massacres at My Lai. From there he went on to Washington to offer testimony before the Senate Foreign Relations Committee, chaired by Senator Fulbright. Kerry faced the senators, with his big mop of hair framing his long face, and asked the unforgettable questions: "How do you ask a man to be the last man to die in Vietnam? How do you ask a man to be the last man to die for a mistake?"[61] It was around this time that he started to worry that VVAW was catering to its more radical elements. Some of his fellow swift boaters who had not come to oppose the war, meanwhile, grew increasingly critical, and sometimes angry.[62] The controversy did not serve Kerry's political ambitions. In 1972 he managed to win a Massachusetts Democratic primary for Congress but lost in the general election to a centrist Republican businessman, Paul Cronin, who sent hecklers to Kerry rallies chanting "Traitor" and "Loser."[63]

Kerry did not run again for another decade, allowing his anger to recede and tensions to simmer. But he won the lieutenant governorship in 1982 and the non-Kennedy family Senate seat in 1984. In the Senate he retained his reputation as a hard worker and a profoundly aloof colleague who was difficult to get to know and deeply impressed with the sound of his own voice. Divorced from Julia Thorne, he married the Mozambique-born Portuguese billionairess, Maria Teresa Thierstein Simões-Ferreira Heinz, and became, overnight, one of the wealthiest men in America. In the Senate, Kerry made his name as a stern critic of the Reagan administration's lawless behavior in Iran-Contra and joined his friend and fellow veteran John McCain in working to normalize relations with Vietnam.

When he declared his presidential campaign for 2004, any number of Democrats made unflattering analogies to both Adlai Stevenson and Michael Dukakis. But the Democratic establishment grew frightened when it appeared that the frenetic antiwar campaign of ex-Vermont governor Dr. Howard Dean appeared to catch fire with the grass roots. Dean proudly claimed to speak for the "*Democratic* wing of the Democratic Party," one animated by fury for George W. Bush.[64] Its members rallied around Kerry as a man who, despite his stiffness, could be presented as a war hero who might highlight Bush's curious and never fully explained credentials when it came to military service—and dispatch the McGovern-like threat represented by Dean and his furious following. The tactic worked, and Dean self-destructed à la Eugene McCarthy. He had, apparently, never really planned on being president and was as surprised as anyone when his Internet fund-raising took off and made him appear, however briefly, to be a potential political juggernaut. The only other serious candidate in the race, the inexperienced North Carolina senator John Edwards, looked attractive on many levels, but was understood by all to be running for the vice presidential nomination, which he won.

Beyond the foreign policy–focused war hero aspect of his résumé, however, Kerry remained undefined in voters' minds. He was wealthy beyond measure, with residences galore, and a wife with a heavy foreign accent who had a penchant for screaming at him in front of journalists and staff. His record as a politician was one of extreme caution, and like Dukakis before him, he was proved a study in the absence of charisma. Much of what was known about Kerry derived from what the journalist Harold Meyerson called, "triumphs of opposition, of liberalism out of power thwarting abuses of power. Kerry never settled into a stump speech in which he said what he most wanted to do if voters handed him power. . . . Voters got a sense of what he wanted to stop, but not . . . what he wanted to start."[65] An extremely cautious liberal, particularly given the fact that he hailed from Massachusetts, Kerry opposed the death penalty and supported the right to abortion, but this profile was leavened by his strong support for free trade, welfare reform, tax cuts for the middle class, and a modest incremental health care plan.[66]

Kerry's vote for Bush's war was also a problem. When pressed, he insisted that he had trusted the president to tell the country (and the Senate) the truth and refused to admit that he had erred in doing so. It was the same "I was right to be wrong" position adopted by the liberal hawks who would sink Hillary Clinton's campaign in 2008. In 2004, with no available electable alternative, however, it merely backed Kerry into an impossible corner, from which he tried to appeal to Dean's antiwar crowd as he simultaneously sought to build up his hawkish credentials against Bush. In the Senate he voted against an $87 billion spending measure to support military operations in Iraq but insisted he would have supported it if the Bush administration had been willing to finance it by rescinding some of its tax cuts for the wealthy.[67] This vote against funding a war—which looked like a vote against the troops in the field, an issue even Dean was careful about when addressing—led Kerry to utter an excuse that turned out to be an act of political hari-kari: "I actually did vote for the eighty-seven billion dollars before I voted against it."[68]

Karl Rove, Bush's political adviser and alter ego, knew better than to look this gift horse in the mouth. On the campaign trail, the president would repeat that line and then add: "Now I've spent some time in"—here he would mention whatever place he happened to be in and then continue—"and people out here don't talk like that."[69] But Kerry often talked in a way that Bush did not, and his "elitism" rather than any particular issue lay at the center of Bush's campaign. Unlike Bush, Kerry was a "flip-flopper," an indecisive aloof elitist who ordered Grey Poupon mustard on his hot dogs and green tea in coffee shops. He "looked French" and engaged in strange, unfamiliar sporting contests. Moreover, he was not really a war hero at all. Funded by wealthy conservatives, an "independent" organization calling itself Swift Boat Veterans for Truth released advertisements accusing Kerry of lying about his record in the war and of generally being an untrustworthy coward of questionable loyalties. Like Michael Dukakis, whose campaign should have provided a sufficient cautionary tale, the candidate did not deign to respond to these vulgar attacks until most of the country had come to believe them. They were relentlessly repeated, first in the newly resurgent right-wing media of Fox News and talk radio, and then they bled into the mainstream media regardless of the lack of evidence or credibility. George Bush, on the other hand, could tell an audience, "You may not always agree with me, but you'll always know where I stand." It wasn't always true but it sounded true. When a Bush ad warned:

> *After September 11th, our world changed.*
> *Either we fight terrorists abroad or face them here.*
> *John Kerry and liberals in Congress have a different view.*
> *They opposed Reagan as he won the Cold War.*
> *Voted against the first Gulf War.*
> *Voted to slash intelligence after the first Trade Center attack.*
> *Repeatedly opposed weapons vital to winning the War on Terror.*
> *John Kerry and his liberal allies . . . Are they a risk we can afford to take*
>   *today?*[70]

Kerry—again like Dukakis—was all but silent in response.

Liberals were shocked by Kerry's loss in 2004. The economy was suffering, and the war a catastrophe. One could find bright spots—the victory of Brian Schweitzer, the populist Democrat who won the governorship of Montana, a rural state, and the victory of Barack Obama, who had opposed the Iraq war and won a seat in the U.S. Senate after delivering a powerful and moving speech at the 2004 Democratic convention. But in general, the news was bad, and the now requisite (and chronic) liberal moping soon got under way. As Harold Ickes, a former Clinton adviser who had helped run one of the independent efforts against Bush, admitted, "We had the money, we had a ground operation the likes of which has never been seen, and we had a good candidate who stood toe to toe with the President and bested him in three debates. We had all that, and we still lost."[71] *Democracy* editor Andrei Cherny added: "On Wednesday morning, Democrats across the country awoke to a situation they have not experienced since before the New Deal: We are now, without a doubt, America's minority party. We do not have the presidency. We are outnumbered in the Senate, the House, governorships and legislatures. And the conservative majority on the Supreme Court seems likely to be locked in place for a generation. It is clearly a moment that calls for serious reflection."[72]

Suddenly there appeared two worlds at loggerheads in America—"red" versus "blue" states, or better yet, states of mind. In the words of Thomas Frank, author of *What's the Matter with Kansas?* (2004), "People getting their fundamental interests wrong is what American political life is all about."[73] Frank didn't intend it this way, but his argument caught on with liberals and fed a growing paranoia on the part of some of them about the white working class as victims of a "false consciousness." (Frank himself blamed Democrats' feebleness as much as crediting Republicans with craftiness.) An e-mail that circulated among many depressed Democrats after the 2004 election showed a map with East Coast blue states labeled "America" and then the sea of red in the South and the middle labeled "Dumbfuckistan."[74] The logical conclusion for some liberals was to secede, forget about national politics, and turn to a progressive "state strategy," passing gay marriage and liberal abortion laws, for instance, in the blue states, and leaving the red ones to fester in their own prejudices. [75] As one liberal journalist explained, "It's much easier nowadays to fancy yourself a member of a persecuted minority, bravely shielding the flickering flame of enlightenment from the increasing Christo-Republican darkness, than it is to figure out how you're actually going to win an election."[76]

Another explanation that found favor with many liberals originated with a Berkeley professor of cognitive science, George Lakoff, who insisted that liberals' problem was one of "framing." He argued that "frames" weren't *heard* but rooted in our "cognitive unconscious."[77] Chief was the way people analogized politics to parenting—a strict father model symbolizing conservatism versus a caring, nurturing, egalitarian family symbolizing liberalism. Sometimes this approach, ironically, made the situation sound hopeless, with politics rooted in people's unconscious psyches. As was always the case, no simple solution was going to fix America's historically rooted divide, which had been evident as early as the 1920s and had exploded during the 1960s backlash against liberalism.

What would enliven liberalism's prospects during the second Bush term was a principle taught by Reinhold Niebuhr: the virtue and necessity of patience.

Consolation could be found in a poll taken just after George W. Bush was re-elected that found that "Americans are at best ambivalent about Mr. Bush's plans to reshape Social Security, rewrite the tax code, cut taxes, and appoint conservative judges to the bench. There is continuing disapproval of Mr. Bush's handling of the war in Iraq, with a plurality now saying it was a mistake to invade in the first place."[78] Of course, the newly reelected president ignored such warnings. The situation in Iraq continued to worsen, and from 2004 to the middle of 2006 "the United States lost almost 1,400 soldiers in Iraq, an average of more than two a day."[79] The economy continued to falter. Gasoline prices rose. Then came Hurricane Katrina and laid bare the arrogance, incompetence, and sheer lack of seriousness of the Bush administration when it came to governance. Katrina provided Americans with an example of what happens when conservative rhetoric collides with messy reality: a teachable moment if ever there was one.

Close to two thousand people died in the course of events, and the director of FEMA (the Federal Emergency Management Agency), Michael Brown, had little to no background in emergency relief, having served two years earlier as commissioner of the International Arabian Horse Association. Brown appeared on national television admitting that he didn't know the extent of Katrina's damage or what relief was getting to people, and then he blamed state and city government for what was clearly FEMA's responsibility. In the midst of it all, Bush assured the man he called Brownie, who was increasingly being viewed as a presidential crony, that he was doing a "heck of a job."[80] Bush had in fact slashed funds to FEMA over the course of his presidency, gutting what was one of the federal government's most respected agencies. Brown ultimately had to resign, leaving Bush to look more and more like a leader who sat back and passively let disaster take hold—first in Iraq, then in New Orleans.

The Katrina disaster also illustrated what the political scientist Alan Wolfe called the why-conservatives-cannot-govern problem, meaning that the ideological fervor to shrink and delegitimize the federal government had come home to roost in the disabling of FEMA. (Joe Allbaugh, whom Bush had appointed the head of FEMA before Brown, had testified in 2001 that "many are concerned that federal disaster assistance may have evolved into both an oversized entitlement program and a disincentive to effective state and local risk management."[81]) Though average citizens might not have made the direct connections between George W. Bush's governing philosophy—death of government through a thousand cuts—and the problems faced during Katrina, enough of them were appalled at Bush's staggering lack of even basic competence, to say nothing of compassion.

In 2006, Al Gore, now a private citizen, released the film *An Inconvenient Truth,* and it soon became a runaway hit, winning Gore an Oscar in the process. The film was little more than a filmed PowerPoint presentation about the threat of environmental catastrophe in which Gore walked his audiences through science and evidence to explain the issue of global warming. In doing so, he managed to raise the same kind of educational alarm that Rachel Carson had done with pesticides in *Silent Spring* more than four decades earlier.

The Al Gore who starred in the film was a much changed character from the one who had run for president in 2000. As he came out onto the stage to begin his presentation, he announced: "I used to be the next president of the United States of America," giving the audience a glimpse of the sense of humor those closest to him always claimed for him, but had managed to keep hidden from voters for the previous thirty years. Gore's good humor and calm demeanor conveyed the serious themes of the film with the import they deserved. He explained how warmer oceans made storms like Katrina worse than usual, how the Arctic ice cap was melting and raising sea levels (showing an image of the island of Manhattan being submerged), and how species loss and the prevalence of mosquitoes at higher levels of elevation could be explained through an understanding of global warming. He recounted the story of his father's decision to stop growing tobacco on his Carthage, Tennessee, farm when his sister developed lung cancer and the connections to smoking became irrefutable.

In 2007 the Nobel Peace Prize was awarded jointly to Gore and to the Intergovernmental Panel on Climate Change. He became a hero to the very liberals who had mocked and derided him as a presidential candidate—he was like the girl they all wished they had married back when they were too young and callow to see her inner beauty. But it was too late. Gore was not running for office; he was playing the role of a kind of national conscience or secular prophet, modeled perhaps on Martin Luther King, Jr., or Dorothy Day. His next book, *The Assault on Reason* (2007), relied heavily on the work of the great liberal Frankfurt school philosopher Jürgen Habermas. Bush, Gore wrote, was not merely a rival politician with a differing political philosophy but a revolutionary who threatened America's "public sphere" and the principles of debate and dialogue. "After initially responding in an entirely appropriate way" to 9/11, Gore recalled, "the administration began to heighten and distort public fear of terrorism to create a political case for attacking Iraq." He not only squandered the moment after 9/11 that could have created a new era of international improvement, he also "resorted to the language and politics of fear in order to short-circuit debate and drive the public agenda without regard to the evidence." Bush allowed his own reactionary ideology to deny the complex realities of the world when he spoke of an "an epic struggle between good and evil" and packaged his "policy of unprovoked war in the garb of religious faith." Gore pulled no punches when it came to the delicate topic of torture. George W. Bush had "dismantled the constraints of law and the Geneva Conventions" and so "the abuse of the prisoners at Abu Ghraib flowed directly from the abuse of the truth that characterized the administration's march to war."[82]

With this brave, tough indictment not only of the president but of the political culture that had spawned and then celebrated him, Gore successfully located the rarely mentioned failure of America's political system to remain relevant in the face of the changing nature of threats to the nation's well-being. Yet Gore remained attached to his faith in the importance of deliberation and the country's need to nurture a "well-connected citizenry," putting his hopes in the possibilities awakened by the Internet. "Broadband interconnection is supporting decentralized processes that reinvigorate democracy. We can see it happening before our eyes."[83]

Al Gore set out a difficult charge: a rational, deliberative, and normatively grounded liberal opposition to an irrational and fear-based conservatism. This became what the journalist E. J. Dionne labeled "the liberal moment" of 2007. As Alan Wolfe added, "After watching a petulant, self-indulgent man occupy the White House, voters may be ready for a politics of responsibility and caution."[84] It would not be Al Gore, who claimed that he had lost the ability to speak in sound bites and, in any case, was undergoing troubles that would soon lead to the end of his thirty-year marriage. But waiting in the wings was destiny's man of the moment sent by way of Hawaii, Indonesia, and the south side of Chicago.

Culturally speaking, during the Bush years another man functioned symbolically at home and abroad as president of an alternative America: one in which working men and women were imbued with dignity, even heroism, where gays were embraced as brothers and sisters, where blacks and whites worked and played together, and where "nobody wins unless everybody wins." In this America, Woody Guthrie's "This Land Is Your Land" was the country's national anthem, and working-class hero Bruce Springsteen was its president. He made his own way in the world, relying on his own talent, dedication to his craft, and faith in his own destiny and his ability to connect that destiny to the promise of the American Dream.

Bruce Springsteen was born and raised in Freehold, New Jersey, the first-born child of Irish and Italian parents. His father, Douglas, was an embittered man who struggled to find a place for himself in the local economy. He worked, for brief periods, in the local rug mill, as a jail guard, and as a cab and bus driver. Adele Springsteen, who worked as a legal secretary, took pride in her professional identity and remained in the same job for Bruce's entire childhood. To Bruce, she "was just like superwoman. She did everything, everywhere, all the time."[85]

The Springsteens lived in a lower-middle-class section of Freehold called Texas, where a group of Appalachian refugees had come together with a smattering of white ethnics in one of America's less publicized migrations. The 1939 Federal Writers' Project's *New Jersey: A Guide to Its Present and Past* observed that "in an unobtrusive way it seems to embody America's growth from farm to factory."[86] Deeply segregated, Freehold's whites and blacks lived, respectively, on opposite sides of an actual railroad track.

A loner par excellence, in high school Bruce participated in no activities, sports, or even much in the way of academics. One of his teachers even suggested to his classmates that, for the sake of their own "self-respect," Bruce not be allowed to graduate, given the indecency of his hair. As a fledgling performer, he practiced his craft obsessively but partook in few of the late sixties rituals that characterized the life of the rock musician of the time. His early lyrics were rarely political, save the occasional mocking of the pretensions of the Woodstock generation with lyrics like "Take LSD and off the pigs." Springsteen was interested in personal freedom—the right to be who he wanted to be, even if he didn't know precisely who that was at the time—and creating his own community of like-minded folk with whom to share his life. This was the political content of his songs and would remain the fulcrum of his career as an artist for the next forty years, though he would consistently redefine what that freedom meant and what his responsibilities to his various communities would demand of him. Rock 'n' roll was the train that would "deliver" him "from nowhere."

A complete naïf when it came to business matters, Springsteen signed a usurious contract from his first manager without reading it, which not only kept him and his band in perpetual poverty but also robbed him of the artistic independence that lay at the center of all of his ambitions. Discovered by John Hammond, the legendary talent scout who also signed Bob Dylan, among countless others, Springsteen released his first two records in 1973, which received rapturous reviews but earned paltry sales. Columbia wanted to drop him, but when the son of one its top executives saw him in concert and told his father that Springsteen was the greatest performer he'd ever seen, the company gave the twenty-four-year-old Springsteen and his band all of the freedom they needed to produce a masterpiece.

On October 27, 1975, with the release of the now classic *Born to Run* album, the hitherto relatively unknown Bruce Springsteen became the first entertainer ever to grace the covers of *Time* and *Newsweek* on the same day, and became an overnight American icon in the process. *Born to Run* may be seen as a counternarrative to the culture of midseventies America, offering hope in hard times. The poetry and power of the album lay in its unwillingness to compromise, in the refusal of its protagonists to accept passively the hand that circumstances, economic and otherwise, had dealt them.[87]

Despite this taste of megastardom, Springsteen was forced to stay out of the spotlight in the years immediately following, as he fought his manager for creative control of his career. Springsteen repeatedly refused, against the advice of his lawyers, to give in on even the most minor points, despite his clear contractual obligation to do so and his inability to record while the case remained undecided. Springsteen explained to a judge that "my interest is in my career, which up until now holds the promise of my being able to significantly contribute to, and possibly influence, a generation of music. No amount of money could compensate me if I were to lose this opportunity."[88]

Freed at a cost of millions of dollars to record as he wished, Springsteen took his music gradually from the personal to the political. *Born to Run* led to the grim but powerful *Darkness at the Edge of Town*, which led to the raucous *The River*, which led to *Nebraska*, a stark, Woody Guthrie–like album. Released in 1982 as national unemployment reached 11 percent (and while President Reagan complained that he was tired of hearing about it every time someone lost a job in "South Succotash"), the album offered an internal portrait of the people victimized by America's winner-take-all economy. Springsteen sought to tell the story of people who were "isolated from their jobs, from their friends, from their family, from their fathers, mothers, not being connected to anything that's going on. . . . When you lose that sense of community, there's some spiritual sense of breakdown that occurs. You just get shot off somewhere where nothing really matters."[89]

The literary historian Bryan Garman finds in *Nebraska* what he calls "working-class geographies," through which Springsteen mapped out the class stratifications that entrapped his protagonists. While the action takes place in factories, mines, and mills, "these places no longer amount to much when the inevitable crisis arises." Decay, in the form of crime, drugs, and danger, has taken over. For Springsteen, Garman writes, "These markers—the industrial town, the factory, and the neighborhood bar—have become so marginalized that it is impossible to forge a collective working-class identity which provides people with a sense of self-worth." Garman tied the album to the history of the "hurt song." Written in working-class language, hurt songs express the collective pain, suffering, and injustice working people have historically suffered, and articulate their collective hopes and dreams for a less oppressive future. By resurrecting the tradition of the hurt song, Springsteen employed what the philosopher Raymond Williams calls a residual form, one that has been forged in the past, but is still active in present political and cultural processes. In doing so, he gave voice not only to his own battered psyche, but also connected to a thread of personal, economic, and social dislocation he sensed around him.[90]

Even so, Springsteen remained extremely cautious when it came to traditional politics. During the first decade or so of his career as a rock star, Springsteen forcefully resisted the myriad pleadings he received to lend his reputation for unshakable integrity to one political cause or another. Like many self-educated people, he was less comfortable discussing ideas and ideologies than speaking in purely "human" terms. He spent much of his adolescence and early adulthood, as he put it, "tryin' to figure out now where do the aesthetic issues that you write about intersect with some sort of concrete action, some direct involvement, in the communities that your audience comes from."[91] At his first-ever political concert appearance for a 1979 antinuclear power spectacular, he left his part of the printed concert program wordless. Three years later, when he made a surprise appearance with a single song alongside Jackson Browne at a 750,000-person rally for the nuclear freeze resolution in New York's Central Park, he again let the music do the talking.

Springsteen made his first stab into direct political involvement after reading Ron Kovic's harrowing Vietnam memoir, *Born on the Fourth of July,* which would later inspire the Oliver Stone film discussed in chapter fifteen. Springsteen asked to meet the author and then volunteered to perform with his band to raise funds for a mental health clinic for vets and awareness for his organization, Vietnam Veterans of America. Speaking from the stage, surrounded by handicapped veterans, Springsteen compared his learning process to "walking down a dark street at night and you see somebody getting a beating in an alley. You want to keep walking because you don't want to feel involved, but you feel guilty."

Springsteen's political views, formed by watching the forces that had shaped his depressed hometown and by a passion for reading history developed in his twenties—often under the tutelage of his intellectually sophisticated new manager, former rock critic Jon Landau, along with those of more politically attuned friends in the music world, including particularly Jackson Browne and Bonnie Raitt—were those of an old-fashioned New Deal social democrat in an era when that category was all but disappearing from America's political discourse. He would later liken these first small steps into political waters to a simple recognition of his responsibilities as a citizen. Decades later he would explain the connection between his music and his politics thus: "A lot of the core of our songs is the American idea: What is it? What does it mean? 'Promised Land,' 'Badlands,' I've seen people singing those songs back to me all over the world. I'd seen that country on a grass-roots level through the '80s, since I was a teenager. And I met people who were always working toward the country being that kind of place. But on a national level it always seemed very far away."[92]

If *Nebraska* had been Springsteen's quietest album, both literally and metaphorically, then the one that followed, *Born in the USA*, would be his loudest. Released in 1984, as the nation was undergoing a celebration of right-wing patriotism during Ronald Reagan's "Morning in America" reelection campaign, Springsteen suddenly found himself at the center of America's political debate. *New York Times* critic Stephen Holden cheered the artist for "us[ing] rock to express an ongoing epic vision of this country, individual social roots and the possibility of heroic self-creation." With *Born in the USA*, he argued, Springsteen had "transfused rock and roll and social realism into one another," and turned his "despairing vision of American life into a kind of celebration."[93] It soon became Columbia's bestselling album to that point in its history. And Springsteen became perhaps the most popular performer in the history of musical performance with marathon shows that somehow combined the energy of James Brown, the pathos of Hank Williams, the intellectual introspection of Bob Dylan with a healthy dose of the electrified sex appeal of Elvis Presley. Soon enough, he became a global phenomenon, drawing hundreds of thousands of people to shows all over Europe, Japan, and Australia, offering a different form of American patriotism from the one that was (no less noisily) emanating from the Reagan White House.

Embedded in the frenzy surrounding *Born in the USA* was an argument. In the album's title song a young man gets into trouble with the law and is given the choice of jail or Vietnam. His brother is killed in battle, and he returns home to an industrial dead zone with no jobs and no future. Heard properly, the rock critic Greil Marcus wrote, the song "carries the tension of a clandestine communication in a Stalinist country, the power of the argument paradoxically multiplying in a country where no censorship is necessary."[94] But this was not how the song was heard in Ronald Reagan's Washington. Attending a Springsteen concert in September 1984, the conservative pundit George F. Will somehow heard in "Born in the USA" "a grand, cheerful affirmation" of American life. Will admitted to putting cotton in his ears, and he left after the first set, but his strange misreading of the song created a minicrisis in that year's presidential campaign, particularly as the bow-tied, bespectacled pundit went on to employ this workingman hero's song to bash American workers. "If all Americans made their products with as much energy and confidence as Springsteen and his merry band make music," he insisted, our economy would not suffer from so many "slipshod products."[95]

President Reagan's political advisers read Will's column in *The Washington Post* and were inspired. Five days later, as Reagan announced his candidacy for a second term in the battleground state of New Jersey with the Statue of Liberty as a backdrop, he mentioned Springsteen's name as if the president's hopes and dreams for America's future and those expressed "in the message of hope in songs of a man so many young Americans admire: New Jersey's own Bruce Springsteen" were one and the same. Walter Mondale countered with his own Springsteen reference: "Bruce may not have been born to run, but he wasn't born yesterday." Springsteen responded to this as he responded to everything: cautiously. He began performing Woody Guthrie's "This Land Is Your Land" in his live shows, explaining that he sang it "to let people know that America belongs to everybody who lives there; the blacks, Chicanos, Indians, Chinese and the whites."[96] He began to warn the young people who came to his shows not to trust their leaders when it came to questions of war and peace. In Washington, D.C., he suggested they stroll over to the Vietnam Veterans Memorial and imagine just what politicians were thinking regarding Central America. Next he added Edwin Starr's angry antiwar classic "War. What Is It Good For?" to his concerts, with the unmistakable introduction: "Blind faith in your leaders can get you killed."

This shock of such success led Springsteen to pull back again and inspired a long period of fitful personal growth and therapy, marriage, divorce and a second marriage, breaking up his band and then reconstituting it, moving to Los Angeles and then back again to New Jersey. During this period he would occasionally emerge with musical statements that sometimes spoke to the country's cultural/political moment and sometimes stood outside of them. He took part in a worldwide tour for Amnesty International. When Springsteen wrote and sang "Streets of Philadelphia"—the title song for the film *Philadelphia,* starring Tom Hanks as an AIDS victim—he became the first prominent male singer to explicitly adopt the voice of a gay man and won an Academy Award for his efforts. His largely acoustic 1995 album, *The Ghost of Tom Joad,* was a self-conscious re-creation and updating of John Steinbeck's (and John Ford's) proletarian masterpiece *The Grapes of Wrath,* with songs literally pulled from stories in the newspapers. The lyrics are filled with railroad transients, people around a fire under a bridge, homeless people waiting in line for shelter, and families sleeping in their cars—an implicit rebuke to the corporate-friendly politics of "triangulation" practiced by Bill Clinton at the time. Springsteen chose as his next cause that of legalizing (and honoring) Latino immigration, fighting against a proposed extremely punitive California law—Proposition 187—that united him with farmworkers, home workers, and others who had hitherto been merely the subject of his songs.

After a nearly fourteen-year break, Springsteen reconstituted the E Street Band in 1999 for a reunion tour and premiered the song, "American Skin (Forty One Shots)," a pointed racial commentary in the aftermath of the shooting of an unarmed Haitian immigrant and the acquittal of four police officers who had fired at him forty-one times. The song angered some fans, particularly policemen, and once again he was roundly misinterpreted. The lyrics were actually quite sympathetic to the police officers, but their representatives roundly denounced Springsteen, and the beat cops booed the song when he performed it in concert.

September 11, 2001, returned Springsteen to the spotlit crossroads of American culture. As the story goes, he was pulling out of a New Jersey parking lot when a man rolled down his window and shouted, "We need you!" before disappearing down the road. "That's part of my job," Springsteen told *The New York Times.* "It's an honor to find that place in the audience's life. . . . I didn't set out to write a 9/11 album," he explained. "I didn't want to write literally about what happened, but the emotions in the air. In the purest sense, that's what a songwriter does."97 *The Rising* was a major cultural event of 2002, the first album with the full E Street Band that Springsteen had released since 1984's *Born in the USA,* and it was treated by the media as the equivalent of a presidential address. The album did many things, but most of all it united much of America in an entirely different spirit than the one George W. Bush and Dick Cheney attempted to exploit. Employing explicitly religious imagery, Springsteen called upon people to "rise up" to their better angels—not out of vengeance but out of mutual understanding, rising above even reality. In the Muslim/Christian love story "Worlds Apart," he sang, "Sometimes the truth just ain't enough / Or is it too much in times like this / Let's throw the truth away, we'll find it in this kiss." Springsteen closed out his world tour with a ten-night stand at the sixty-thousand-seat Giants

Stadium in his home state of New Jersey, selling more tickets in any one place at any one time than any other single act in musical history.

It was at this point, moved by his fury at Bush's agenda, particularly his manipulation of 9/11, that for the first time ever he threw himself into electoral politics, agreeing to do a minitour with a group of other artists of battleground states in support of Kerry's candidacy. His song "No Surrender" became Kerry's campaign theme. He gave speeches at these events about the darkness that had descended on the country under Bush, and then agreed to travel the country by Kerry's side, guitar in hand, singing before his speeches, the rock star giving the politician/war hero credibility with segments of the citizenry he would otherwise likely fail to connect.

Following Kerry's defeat, Springsteen toured with a makeshift folk troop he assembled in the spirit of Pete Seeger's hootenanny shows. A highlight of the show was the band's version of Blind Alfred Reed's 1929 protest song, "How Can a Poor Man Stand Such Times and Live?" adapted for the Katrina catastrophe and with added verses, including:

> *There's bodies floatin' on Canal and the levees gone to Hell*
> *Martha, get me my sixteen gauge and some dry shells*
> *Them who's got got out of town and them who ain't got left to drown*
> *Tell me how can a poor man stand such times and live*

Together with the band, he toured the country in 2006 preaching against "rendition, illegal wiretapping, voter suppression, no habeas corpus, the neglect of that great city New Orleans and its people, an attack on the Constitution. And the loss of our best men and women in a tragic war." Challenged in an interview about his patriotism by CBS News's Scott Pelley, Springsteen gave no quarter: "Well, that's just the language of the day, you know? The modus operandi for anybody who doesn't like somebody. . . . There's a part of the singer going way back in American history that is of course the canary in the coal mine. When it gets dark, you're supposed to be singing. It's dark right now. . . . The American idea is a beautiful idea. It needs to be preserved, served, protected and sung out."[98]

Springsteen kept singing all through the 2008 election, endorsing Barack Obama over Hillary Clinton for the Democratic nomination and touring the country on behalf of his candidacy in the general election against John McCain. Three months later, on the eve of Obama's inauguration, standing before the Lincoln Memorial, he sang "The Rising" for the president, the vice president, their families, and a group of American dignitaries together with a crowd estimated at four hundred thousand, while backed by a multiracial chorus of young people. He then joined onetime Communist, now liberal folk icon Pete Seeger for a rousing version of "This Land Is Your Land" that included, rather surprisingly, those rarely sung verses that question the moral basis of capitalism. The entire crowd sang boisterously along.

It was a rare and beautiful moment for American liberals but one whose ultimate meaning would remain fuzzy as it passed into history. Yes, liberals had won some decisive battles to arrive at this place; Springsteen's pride of place on stage with the president and vice president was evidence of that. But what did this victory mean for liberal hopes and dreams in the realm of actual politics? The answer, alas, was not to be found in a folk song, even one in which President-elect Barack Hussein Obama could be seen tapping his feet and singing along.

18

Hope and Change?

I don't identify myself as a Democrat so much as someone for whom it is torturing to hear George Bush speak.

—Jonathan Franzen, 2009[1]

What I am constantly trying to do is balance a hard head with a big heart.

—Barack Obama[2]

The Bush years were defined by more than a "transformational" presidency's bold policies—a war of choice in Iraq, tax cuts for the wealthy, and the disavowal of science in the rejection of stem cell research and proactive measures against global warming. They nurtured a cultural worldview rooted in the persona of the forty-third president. Bush described himself as a "gut player" and resolved complex policy arguments by declaring himself "the decider,"[3] a role that was on display with preening belligerence when he urged terrorists to "Bring it on" or declared "Mission accomplished" long before the difficult part of the Iraq war had even begun. Bush claimed not to read newspaper articles while president because they reflected mere "opinions," and such intellectual laziness and unreflective prejudice somehow came to be interpreted by conservatives as "good old-fashioned American common sense."[4]

The Weekly Standard's Fred Barnes labeled Bush "rebel in chief," praising him as "defiant of the press, scornful of the conventional wisdom, and keen to reverse or at least substantially reform long-standing policies."[5] Norman Podhoretz's son, John, who wrote mostly about popular culture (and later inherited the editorship of *Commentary* as if it were a family-run dry cleaners), penned an entire book about what made Bush's presidency so excellent, singling out his pugnacious attitude and belligerence, which were able to build popular support and "drive liberals insane."[6] Even the more thoughtful con-

servative pundit David Frum, once a speechwriter for the president, acknowledged that though Bush was "uncurious and as a result ill-informed," but
argued anyway that he was still the "right man."7 That these assessments came
from aspiring intellectuals may seem stunning in retrospect, but they barely
raised an eyebrow in the cable news/tabloid television-driven media culture
in the first decade of the twenty-first century.

A strange sort of postmodernism could be heard in the president's gut-
rendered conservatism. Not that its denizens shared Richard Rorty's commitment to "antifoundationalism," but many believed that the powerful could
construct their own "truth." As the longtime Bush adviser Mark McKinnon
told journalist Ron Suskind, "You think he's an idiot, don't you?," all those
"up and down the West Coast, the East Coast, a few blocks in southern Manhattan called Wall Street. Let me clue you in. We don't care. You see, you're
outnumbered 2 to 1 by folks in the big, wide middle of America, busy working
people who don't read *The New York Times* or *Washington Post* or the *L.A.
Times.*"8 Bush's team evinced nothing but contempt for what another (un-
named) adviser called the "reality-based community," those who "believe that
solutions emerge from your judicious study of discernible reality." In fact, he
explained: "We're an empire now, and when we act, we create our own reality.
And while you're studying that reality—judiciously, as you will—we'll act
again, creating other new realities, which you can study, too, and that's how
things will sort out."9 Such was the essence of postmodern conservatism,
wrung out of the "decider" who could rely upon those Americans whose will
to believe allowed them to remain convinced that—against all evidence—
Saddam Hussein was behind 9/11, that the U.S. military had discovered Saddam's weapons of mass destruction cache, and that anyone who thought
differently "hated America." The country's most anti-intellectual president was
sailing along blissfully on the country's historical undercurrents. Fully a quarter
of all Americans questioned during those years said they believed that "Christianity was established by the Constitution as the official government religion."10

For many Americans, this unhappy era in the nation's history was brought
to a close on January 20, 2009, when Barack Hussein Obama looked out at a
crowd of as many as a million cheering (and freezing) citizens and spoke to
"the spirit of service" that he hoped his future presidency could resurrect and
identified the present moment as one that "will define a generation."11 No
more striking contrast could be imagined than that between Obama and the
man who watched him take the pledge of office, George W. Bush. Where Bush
worked from his "gut," Obama projected a respect for knowledge and complexity. Where Bush appeared impatient with detail, Obama radiated a calm

intelligence. While Bush pronounced his commitment to evangelical religious teachings and could name only Jesus when asked what philosopher he most admired, Obama, when similarly questioned, was eager to discuss Reinhold Niebuhr's theological writings.

Obama's inaugural conjured up memories of JFK's when the forty-three-year-old senator from Massachusetts spoke of "the torch" being passed to "a new generation of Americans."[12] Comparisons between Obama and Kennedy had become commonplace. When Obama was running in the Democratic primary and heading into the Iowa caucus, Ted Sorensen, JFK's speechwriter, often introduced the candidate by musing on the similarities of the barriers faced by the country's first Catholic president and, potentially, its first black one.[13] JFK's daughter, Caroline Kennedy, was the first family member to make the connection explicit: "I have never had a president who inspired me the way people tell me that my father inspired them. But for the first time, I believe I have found the man who could be that president—not just for me, but for a new generation of Americans."[14] Soon afterward Ted Kennedy endorsed Obama: "There was another time, when another young candidate was running for president and challenging America to cross a new frontier. He faced criticism from the preceding Democratic president, who was widely respected in the party." Kennedy went on: "And John Kennedy replied, 'The world is changing. The old ways will not do. . . . It is time for a new generation of leadership.' So it is with Barack Obama."[15]

Such comparisons were in many respects misleading. John Kennedy had been blessed by millions of dollars' worth of purchased political favors by their father, one of the wealthiest men in America. Obama's father raised goats in Alego, Kenya, where there were no universities as late as 1959. Thanks to the efforts and inspiration of a Kenyan nationalist leader named Tom Mboya, Obama senior became one of eighty-one young potential leaders chosen for the opportunity to come to the United States to study.

Obama's mother, Stanley Ann Dunham—her parents had hoped for a boy—hailed from Wichita, Kansas. She met Barack Obama, Sr., as a student at the University of Hawaii, and as a deeply committed liberal had no problem considering marriage to a black man—which, fortunately for the couple, happened to be legal in Hawaii at the time. Barack Hussein Obama—the first name was a Swahili word derived from the Arabic, meaning "blessing," and the middle name is that of the grandson of the of the Prophet Muhammad—was born on August 4, 1961, in Honolulu.[16] Obama senior soon left his wife and new son in Hawaii, in 1962, to attend Harvard University, later to return to Kenya, where he led a life of bitter and angry disappointment, checkered by alcohol abuse and frequent trouble with local authorities, before being killed in a 1982 auto accident at age forty-six. Dunham filed for divorce shortly after her husband departed and in 1965 married Lolo Soetoro, an Indonesian she met at the University of Hawaii. Obama wound up spending ages four to ten in Indonesia with his new stepfather, attending "majority-Muslim" schools before returning to Honolulu in 1971, where he lived with his white grandparents and attended the Punahou School, a prep school that prepared him for departure to Los Angeles's Occidental College in 1979.[17]

Occidental was a small, highly competitive liberal arts college. Obama studied political thought and literature, tried his hand at writing free-verse poetry, and drew close to the ragtag and academic left of the time. He remembered his friends as the "more politically active black students. The foreign students. The Chicanos. The Marxist professors and structural feminists and punk-rock performance poets" who liked to smoke cigarettes, drink coffee, and discuss Eurocentrism and neocolonialism.[18] As he read the likes of Tocqueville, Marx, Weber, and Habermas, Obama sought, as he put it in *The Audacity of Hope*, "a language and systems of action that could help build community and make justice real."[19] But Obama found himself tiring of Occidental, especially its insularity; a friend and roommate of his, Phil Boerner, claimed they both disliked its "country-club atmosphere" and wanted something grittier.[20] Obama decided on Columbia University, less for its Ivy League pedigree than its proximity to Harlem. There he attended speeches by various political figures from Jesse Jackson to Kwame Ture—aka Stokely Carmichael—and wrote passionate articles for a student weekly publication in which he bemoaned the "narrow focus" of the freeze movement, for instance, and its disavowal of issues of political and economic equality.[21]

Following graduation, Obama drifted, picking up a research job for Business International Corporation in New York City, where he was known as Mr. Cool for his aloofness around the rest of the staff. During a stint with Ralph Nader's Public Interest Research Group, he organized students at the City College of New York for recycling projects and voter registration drives.[22] Around this time he noticed an advertisement in *Community Jobs*, placed by Jerry Kellman of the Calumet Community Religious Conference and the Developing Communities Project, seeking community organizers to move to Chicago and engage in grassroots campaigns aimed at improving civic life, a program modeled on the work of Saul Alinsky and the Industrial Areas Foundation. Kellman believed his whiteness was getting in the way of organizing blacks on the South Side of Chicago and was looking for a young black organizer with charisma. "Mentors very quickly ceased to be mentors with

Barack," Kellman rcalled later, "they became collaborators."[23] Obama came to the job with images of "SNCC workers standing on a porch in some Mississippi backwater trying to convince a family of sharecroppers to register to vote." These "became a form of prayer for me, bolstering my spirits, channeling my emotions in a way that words never could."[24] Those heady expectations would quickly dissolve in the face of the realities of Chicago's South Side in 1985.

It was in Chicago during the 1930s and 1940s that Saul Alinsky built his first community organization. Alinsky practiced a hard-boiled vision of political change, believing citizens needed to discover their own self-interests—identified from the bottom up but with assistance from an organizer—and then use collective forms of confrontation to win concessions from the ruling powers.[25] As Alinsky put it: "No one can negotiate without the power to compel negotiation. This is the function of the community organizer. Anything otherwise is wishful non-thinking."[26]

Young Barack Obama himself struggled with that legacy. He understood the importance of appealing to individuals' self-interest, but he could not abandon the idealism he so admired in the history of the civil rights struggle. "It's true that the notion of self-interest was critical. But Alinsky understated the degree to which people's hopes and dreams and their ideals and their values were just as important in organizing as people's self-interest." he observed.[27] Jerry Kellman believed Obama wanted to synthesize "the Alinsky teaching on self-interest" with "Dr. King's appeals to our mutuality."[28]

Obama would later reflect that he was never "wildly successful" as a community organizer, but he did learn some crucial lessons in democratic politics on the job. First and foremost, he honed his skills at listening, for taking people's concerns seriously was the founding principle of being a community organizer.[29] He learned how to translate a personal story into a larger narrative about power dynamics, telling stories about individual struggles to make a living and lead a decent life that related to public policies—job training, better public schools, more access to child care. Obama's political style embodied Richard Rorty's insight that storytelling was a more effective way to teach political philosophy than speeches, and he worked hard to help people he met see the politics embedded in their individual stories.

Jerry Kellman bemoaned the fact that his protégé "wasn't good at trading on his race to advance himself. He was an awful ethnic politician."[30] Obama found himself struggling in his conversations with black nationalists, particularly the Nation of Islam, which had its national headquarters in Chicago and played an outsized role in the life of the black community there. He became deeply alienated from their vision of "a Hobbesian world where distrust was a given and loyalties extended from family to mosque to the black race—whereupon notions of loyalty ceased to apply."[31] Obama distrusted all identity politics, as they "contradicted the morality my mother had taught me, a morality of subtle distinctions—between individuals of goodwill and those who wished me ill."[32] But he also took time to read Malcolm X's autobiography, which espoused black nationalism's "ability to instill . . . racial dignity" and "confidence that the black race needs today to get up off its knees."[33] For Obama, such language offered only "an attitude rather than any concrete program, a collection of grievances and not an organized force."[34]

Three years as a community organizer proved more than enough, however, and in 1988 Obama embarked for Harvard Law School, intent on learning about "things that would help me bring about real change" such as "interest rates, corporate mergers, the legislative process . . . the way businesses and banks were put together" with the hope of returning to Chicago to apply those lessons.[35] What he didn't recognize was that he had enrolled in what had become known as"the Beirut of legal education," with a faculty that was divided between "critical legal studies" scholars, such as Roberto Mangabeira Unger, a self-described "revolutionary," and an increasing number of combative conservatives.[36] Obama leaned toward the center, choosing to work with the respected liberal constitutional scholar Laurence Tribe. Obama navigated his way toward becoming the first-ever black president of the *Harvard Law Review*, winning the election, it was widely recognized, by capturing both the centrist and conservative voters. One of the latter, Brad Berenson, said that many "young people" at places like Harvard "often demonize folks who have differing political views," but not Obama, who "earned the affection and trust of almost everyone." Indeed, Obama didn't think the conservative students "were evil people, only misguided," so Berenson and his fellow conservatives gave him their support.[37] Obama's victory received some press attention, including a story in *The New York Times*, where Obama played up his sense of humility by arguing that his election was "encouraging" for race relations but shouldn't be interpreted as "everything is O.K. for blacks" because there were "hundreds or thousands of black students with at least equal talent who don't get a chance."[38]

Though Obama would support the cause of black scholar Derrick Bell, who had earlier staged a hunger strike in the name of diversity and affirmative action on campus, his studies and presidency of the *Harvard Law Review* pointed to a desire to build bridges to all factions. Unger, however, interpreted his behavior less charitably but perhaps more presciently. He would later explain to Obama biographer David Remnick that like other gifted students, Obama enjoyed "a very strong sense of the limits that American politics and political culture impose on what can be said and done, and ultimately what can be felt and thought." He saw in the future president

> the style of sociability that is most prized in the American professional and business class and serves as the supreme object of education in the top prep schools: how to cooperate with your peers by casting on them a spell of charismatic seduction, which you nevertheless disguise under a veneer of self-deprecation and informality. Obama did not master this style in prep school, but became a virtuoso at it nevertheless, as the condition of preferment in American society that it is. As often happens, the outsider turned out to be better at it than the vast majority of the insiders.[39]

After Harvard, Obama returned to Chicago to accept a position with the leading civil rights law firm, and agreed to teach part time at the University of Chicago Law School. He also had wedding plans to make, having become engaged to Michelle Robinson, who, as one of the few African Americans around, had been assigned to mentor him at a summer law job with the Chicago firm of Sidley Austin. In 1992 he also chose to lead a Chicago-based voter registration drive.[40] Project Vote! grew out of recognition on the part of the city's Democrats that ever since the death of Harold Washington in 1987, black voting rates had plummeted. Project Vote! registered nearly 150,000 new voters,[41] and not only would Illinois' Carol Moseley Braun become the first female black senator, but Bill Clinton became the first Democratic presidential candidate to sweep the state since Lyndon Johnson had done so twenty-eight years earlier.

Obama's idealism survived the famously cynical world of Chicago politics. Before entering the Republican-dominated Illinois statehouse, winning his first race in 1996, Obama was interviewed by the *Chicago Reader* and discussed his joining the vision of community organizing to his newfound role as political representative: "What if a politician were to see his job as that of an organizer, as part teacher and part advocate, one who does not sell voters short but who educates them about the real choices before them?"[42] In office he fought to improve the state's democratic practices, pressing for "contribution limits and public financing of campaigns." He battled against Illinois' flat tax and tried to increase its earned income tax credit as well as child support for welfare recipients.[43] In other words, he began his elective career as a fairly typical big-city liberal, but one who knew better than to stand on principle when there was a deal to be done.

Still learning his way, Obama made a major misstep four years into his career as a state legislator when he recklessly chose to challenge the former Black Panther Bobby Rush, now a representative from the First District of Chicago, for his congressional seat. Obama saw in Rush a rigid sixties ideologue, fighting yesterday's battles, representative of "a politics that is rooted in the past, a reactive politics that isn't very good at coming up with concrete solutions";[44] Rush in turn called Obama "an educated fool" with "Eastern elite degrees."[45] He mocked his youth, adding that "Barack is a person who read about the civil-rights protests and thinks he knows all about it."[46] One of Obama's advisers, Ron Davis, warned his candidate, "Motherfucker, you ain't goin' anywhere. You ain't gonna get elected dogcatcher. You're full of yourself. You have to let the air out."[47] The voters concurred, and Obama received only 30 percent of the district's vote.

Offered a seven-figure foundation job that his wife desperately wanted him to accept, Obama, financially strapped and uncertain about how to make his mortgage payments, nevertheless decided to double down on politics. He continued to make contacts that could help him run for national office and threw himself into a flurry of activity in the statehouse, working on policies that would resonate on the national level. He advocated for legislation regarding "racial profiling, death-penalty reform, and expanded health insurance for children."[48] He gave a speech at an AFL-CIO event in 2003 where he endorsed a single-payer health care system—long a dream for liberals—and continued to press flesh and make new friends.

The big leap came in 2004, when Obama, who wasn't the Democratic Party leadership's choice, won against a huge eight-candidate playing field in the 2004 Senate primary and went on to victory in the general election, as one better financed and more experienced candidate after another seemed to self-destruct in his path. The Democratic convention that year proved another enormous break for the lucky young man. Picked by Kerry from relative oblivion to deliver the keynote address, based on his obvious charisma and growing reputation as an orator, he nevertheless had to fight to be allowed to show his stuff. When Kerry and his nervous advisers read over Obama's draft speech about "red states" versus "blue states" when what really mattered was the "United States," Kerry decided he wanted the idea for himself. Informed of the decision, Obama blew up: "That fucker is trying to steal a line from my speech."[49] The "fucker" lost.

On July 27, 2004, Obama delivered a speech that excited the faithful as no speech had done at least since Mario Cuomo's keynote twenty years earlier. He opened, naturally, by introducing his amazing life story: the goat-herding father from Kenya and his mother from Wichita and their "improbable love" that could only have grown in a "tolerant" America. "Tonight, we gather to affirm the greatness of our Nation—not because of the height of our skyscrapers, or the power of our military, or the size of our economy. Our pride is based on a very simple premise, summed up in a declaration made over two hundred years ago: We hold these truths to be self-evident, that all men are created equal, that they are endowed by their Creator with certain inalienable rights, that among these are Life, Liberty and the pursuit of Happiness."[50] Then came the plain-spoken fellow: "Alongside our famous individualism, there's another ingredient in the American saga, a belief that we're all connected as one people. If there is a child on the south side of Chicago who can't read, that matters to me, even if it's not my child. If there is a senior citizen somewhere who can't pay for their prescription drugs, and having to choose between medicine and the rent, that makes my life poorer, even if it's not my grandparent. If there's an Arab American family being rounded up without benefit of an attorney or due process, that threatens my civil liberties. . . . Now even as we speak, there are those who are preparing to divide us—the spin masters, the negative ad peddlers who embrace the politics of 'anything goes.' Well, I say to them tonight, there is not a liberal America and a conservative America—there is the United States of America. There is not a Black America and a White America and Latino America and Asian America—there's the United States of America."

He finished by wrapping around to the theme of "hope," a word he distinguished from optimism (having read his Reinhold Niebuhr): "I'm not talking about blind optimism here—the almost willful ignorance that thinks unemployment will go away if we just don't think about it, or the health care crisis will solve itself if we just ignore it. That's not what I'm talking about. I'm talking about something more substantial. It's the hope of slaves sitting around a fire singing freedom songs; the hope of immigrants setting out for distant shores; the hope of a young naval lieutenant bravely patrolling the Mekong Delta; the hope of a millworker's son who dares to defy the odds; the hope of a skinny kid with a funny name who believes that America has a place for him, too." The crowds roared. They had just heard, as journalist Michael Tomasky later observed, quite "possibly the greatest convention speech by a relatively unknown politician since Hubert Humphrey's rousing plea for civil rights at the 1948 Democratic convention."[51]

The speech displayed Obama's gift both for telling a story and for articulating a public philosophy. He was a man of ideas entering the political sphere who offered, first and foremost, a language of the common good. Obama had, in the words of historian Thomas Sugrue, appropriated "for liberals a unifying language of Americanism."[52] Much of Obama's thinking about politics drew on his reading of Niebuhr. The conservative journalist David Brooks remembered a particularly bad interview he had had with the future president, enlivened only when Brooks asked about Reinhold Niebuhr. Obama's face lit up as he launched into a spirited twenty-minute discussion that turned on the liberal theologian's thinking. The future president seemed especially interested in "the idea that you have to use power while it corrupts you."[53] Obama's own religious faith, developed while attending services at Trinity United Church of Christ in Chicago, seemed peculiarly Niebuhrian, prompting less certitude and more ambivalence and humility. He described his faith as a "journey" and explained: "Faith doesn't mean that you don't have doubts."[54]

Obama developed his own conception of democratic leadership, one framed by humility and self-scrutiny, seeing a model in Abraham Lincoln, a president whom Niebuhr once described as the country's greatest. Niebuhr loved Lincoln's "brooding sense of charity" that was "derived from a religious awareness of another dimension of meaning than that of the immediate political conflict." Lincoln had a "moral resoluteness about the immediate issues with a religious awareness of another dimension of understanding of meaning and judgment," Niebuhr explained.[55] The same tones could be heard in Obama's own reflections about Lincoln: the president who led America through the Civil War "understood both the deliberative function of our democracy and the limits of such deliberation. We remember him for the firmness and depth of his convictions—his unyielding opposition to slavery and his determination that a house divided could not stand. But his presidency was guided by a practicality that would distress us today, a practicality that led him to test various bargains with the South." In doing so, Lincoln showed that "we must talk and reach for common understandings, precisely because all of us are imperfect and can never act with the certainty that God is on our side; and yet at times we must act nonetheless, as if we are certain, protected from error only by providence." From Lincoln—filtered through the reflections of Niebuhr—Obama embraced the central liberal democratic principle of "humility."[56]

This view of politics drove Obama into debates with the absolutists populating progressive circles. For instance, after voting against Bush's appointment of conservative John Roberts to be chief justice of the U.S. Supreme

Court, Obama watched as progressive bloggers—especially those on the Web site Daily Kos—attacked those who voted in Roberts's favor, including Patrick Leahy, Christopher Dodd, and Russ Feingold. The debate that Obama prompted went to the heart of his own view on politics, and he titled his letter in protest to Daily Kos "Tone, Truth, and the Democratic Party."[57] Obama had a view that held on to its own ambivalence even while engaging the opposition. He entered the fray on the Kos Web site itself: "To the degree that we brook no dissent within the Democratic Party, and demand fealty to the one, 'true' progressive vision for the country, we risk the very thoughtfulness and openness to new ideas that are required to move this country forward. When we lash out at those who share our fundamental values because they have not met the criteria of every single item on our progressive 'checklist,' then we are essentially preventing them from thinking in new ways about problems. We are tying them up in a straightjacket and forcing them into a conversation only with the converted. Beyond that, by applying such tests, we are hamstringing our ability to build a majority. We won't be able to transform the country with such a polarized electorate."[58] Heeding the procedures of deliberation—precisely because our own reason might be fallible—Obama held out a difficult and challenging vision for progressives.

Like many potential presidential candidates given the "liberal" label by the national media, Obama positioned himself for a move to the center. The difference was that he wanted to be admired for doing so as if doing so were somehow a matter of high philosophical principle. Obama had always spoken highly of President Bill Clinton's "third way," or centrist approach to politics, even though he worried about Clinton's rearguard defensive posturing. "It was Bill Clinton's singular contribution that he tried to transcend [the] ideological deadlock" that plagued American politics. He "saw that government and spending and regulation could, if properly designed, serve as vital ingredients and not inhibitors to economic growth, and how markets and fiscal discipline could help promote social justice."[59] Obama also stood by Clinton's controversial compromise on welfare reform, believing that "the old AFDC program sapped people of their initiative and eroded their self-respect," an opinion that was a major turnaround for someone who as state senator had opposed the plan.[60] The young senator described himself in 2006 to *The American Prospect* as follows:

> Sometimes the DLC camp seems to want to run to the center no matter how far right the Republican Party has moved the debate—that sense of "let's cut a deal no matter what the deal is." The old-time religion school some-

times seems unreflective and is unwilling to experiment or update old programs to meet new challenges. And the way I would describe myself is I think that my values are deeply rooted in the progressive tradition, the values of equal opportunity, civil rights, fighting for working families, a foreign policy that is mindful of human rights, a strong belief in civil liberties, wanting to be a good steward for the environment, a sense that the government has an important role to play, that opportunity is open to all people and that the powerful don't trample on the less powerful. . . . I share all the aims of a Paul Wellstone or a Ted Kennedy when it comes to the end result. But I'm much more agnostic, much more flexible on how we achieve those ends.[61]

While his heart may have beat on the left, his eyes looked toward wherever voters could be found.

Standing between Barack Hussein Obama and destiny was the now-junior senator from the great state of New York, Hillary Clinton. Having stood by her man through almost unimaginable public humiliation as first lady, she had, as senator, proved herself dutiful and hardworking. Mrs. Clinton was now, in the eyes of many of her husband's supporters and not a few women, the rightful heir to the throne.

Hillary was raised in Park Ridge, Illinois, a suburb of Chicago, in a strictly conservative family. Her father, Hugh Rodham, was a small businessman who chewed tobacco, voted Republican, and spouted conservative conventional wisdom to anyone willing to listen. Hillary's mother, Dorothy Howell Rodham, called her husband Mr. Difficult, and hid her own liberal leanings from him. She did her best to buffer the children from his rages and instill in them a sense of personal autonomy and intellectual independence.[62]

Hillary Rodham was also mentored by her Methodist minister, the Reverend Don Jones. The two engaged in theological discussions and even went to see Martin Luther King, Jr., speak in Park Ridge in 1961. That experience didn't dislodge Hillary's own conservatism, however, and when she left for Wellesley College in 1965, she carried with her a well-worn copy of Barry Goldwater's *The Conscience of a Conservative*.[63] Wellesley was still a place where girls from good homes met nice boys from nearby Ivy League colleges, studying, as the joke went, for their Mrs. degrees. But it was also a school that put a premium on inculcating a sense of confidence in its students. Don Jones suggested she try reading Paul Tillich, the theologian whom Reinhold Niebuhr had helped escape from Germany just as the Nazis seized power and who wrote about the relationship between "despair" and "courage" in choosing faith. Having gained strength through this faith, Hillary became more outgoing and self-confident.[64]

Like Al Gore a few miles north in Cambridge, Hillary showed some excitement over the civil rights and antiwar movements on campus but remained detached from their radical tendencies. She had begun to ease away from her father's politics first by moving toward Rockefeller Republicanism and then toward liberalism—still the most conservative philosophy available to a graduate of an elite American university in 1969 (where genuine conservatives were for most practical purposes entirely invisible). She read an essay in a Methodist magazine by Carl Oglesby, one of the gentlest and most eloquent voices of the SDS, whom she later misidentified as a "theologian." "It was the first thing I had ever read that challenged the Vietnam War," she explained decades later.[65] Jones wrote Hillary a soul-searching letter in which he asked "whether someone can be a Burkean realist about history and human nature and at the same time have liberal sentiments and visions."[66] Jones recognized a young woman struggling with an ageless question, one that would be at the heart of the political sensibilities she carried with her from college onward.

Hillary attended the 1968 Republican convention hoping Rockefeller would be nominated over Nixon, but she ended up supporting Eugene McCarthy. Both were lost causes, of course, and as neither satisfied her nascent political hunger, she began to look for alternatives to representative politics.[67] Like Barack Obama, she found some answers in the work of Saul Alinsky. For her senior thesis, Hillary wrote Alinksy inquisitive letters and visited organizations in Chicago that modeled themselves on his vision of grassroots organizing changing power dynamics in local neighborhoods. A consistent theme in her analysis was the relationship between Alinsky's model of community organizing and the growing interest in the Johnson administration's belief in "maximum feasible participation." Intrigued by the idea that the federal government could work in consort with grassroots power, Hillary also recognized that Alinsky's model had severe limitations (something young Barack Obama would later learn the hard way). She pointed out that many neighborhoods, in a day and age of mobility and breakdown, lacked sufficient cohesion to organize. She admired those who respected local organizing but wanted to complement it with other mechanisms of power and influence.[68]

Hillary's seriousness as a student and her political engagement made her a natural for Wellesley's commencement student speaker, and it turned into a gratifying moment of self-definition. She followed Senator Edward Brooke, the first African American senator elected from Massachusetts—a candidate for whom Hillary had campaigned for three years, and a Republican. Attacking the self-indulgence of a student "Lumpenbourgeoisie," Brooke had quoted Al Capp, ridiculing feminists with his character "Joaney Phoney." It was, noted Garry Wills, "a long and pompous and self-satisfied speech."[69] Rising to the occasion, Clinton dropped her own text and spoke up in defense of herself and her classmates: "For too long our leaders have used politics as the art of the possible. And the challenge now is to practice politics as the art of making what appears to be impossible, possible," she said. She was tough-minded but intriguingly mystical: "We're searching for more immediate, ecstatic and penetrating modes of living," hinting at her Tillich-infused idea of growth. Vague as it was, the speech showed how far Hillary Clinton had traveled from the Goldwater girl Wellesley had admitted four years earlier.[70]

She next went on to Yale Law School to study family law and children's rights, where she also met her future husband, who recognized in her a toughness he felt he lacked. The story of Hillary Clinton's role as America's first lady during her husband's presidency requires its own book at a minimum. But its tenor can be summed up in a joke frequently told among politicos during those years, in which Hillary and Bill drive up to a gas station in her hometown of Park Ridge:

Hillary: "Why my goodness, that's my old boyfriend [insert name here] pumping gas."

Bill (chuckling): "Just think what your life would have been like if you had married him instead of me."

Hillary: "That's easy. He'd be president and you'd be back in Little Rock, pumping gas.

For much if not all of Bill Clinton's political career, Hillary was, to coin a phrase, "the decider." Bill Clinton's mind was so flexible and his talent for empathy so profound that he could not help but see the merit in almost any point of view. Throughout his political career, difficult decisions would be relitigated and frequently reversed back and forth until everyone involved—save perhaps Clinton himself—grew bitter and exhausted by the process. It was not until Hillary Clinton, acting as Bill's full political partner, weighed in on a given decision that the various claimants on Bill's attention knew that whatever matter was on the table was now closed. She could be stubborn. She could certainly be wrong. But she could make a decision and make it stick. And to those who knew him well, it was hard to imagine that he could have been president without her. At the same time, some of the worst decisions of his presidency, including his refusal to compromise on health care, to put off welfare reform, and to refuse any and all cooperation in the Whitewater matter with Congress, could be traced to the president's inability to challenge her judgment.[71]

In her memoir Hillary Clinton recounted: "The most difficult decisions I have made in my life were to stay married to Bill and to run for the Senate from New York."[72] Those choices, however, were inevitably intertwined. Her fortunes in seeking political office drew upon an array of factors, including the sympathy she garnered for sticking with her philandering husband. She was recruited by Democratic Party officials who were in the market for someone who might beat the popular liberal Republican New York mayor, Rudy Giuliani. Here again the hinge of history appeared to turn on the uncontrollability of the male libido, as Giuliani's bizarre treatment of the women in his life, including an ex-wife, a current wife, and a future wife, was something of a national joke. A bout of treatable prostate cancer gave him an excuse to quit the race with the illusion of some dignity, and Hillary handily defeated his replacement, Long Island Congressman Rick Lazio.[73]

To make herself more acceptable during the campaign to New Yorkers—she was, after all, by any known definition, a carpetbagger, though one in the tradition of Robert Kennedy—she embarked on what she called a listening tour throughout the state. Observing her, *The Observer's* Tish Durkin found her so bland in her responses to constituent questions, she wondered if the aspiring senator had undergone a "controversectomy." As stiff and formal as her husband was warm and jovial, the candidate, in journalist Elizabeth Kolbert's view, sought "to elevate nodding into a kind of political philosophy."[74] While Al Gore was touting a fight for the "people against the powerful," Clinton now professed a more chastened, less populist politics, distancing herself from her original plan for health care overhaul (which would have cut funds for the teaching hospitals that New York had in large numbers), and championing incremental reform for children only.

Once in office, Clinton hewed close to the political middle, successfully transcending what Bill Galston and Elaine Kamarck called the "politics of polarization"[75] and cautiously projecting what the blogger Greg Sargent termed, "pragmatism on economic issues" with "ideological flexibility on social issues"—a strategy befitting a politician who wanted to be president rather than a senator from one of America's bluest of states.[76] She was almost ostentatiously deferential to her ideological opponents, for instance, announcing in 2005, "I, for one, respect those who believe with all their hearts and conscience that there are no circumstances under which any abortion should ever be available." She could foresee a future where "the choice guaranteed under our Constitution either does not ever have to be exercised or only in very rare circumstances."[77] Turning her back on both her husband's hard-fought compromise and the views of most New York liberals—even Robert Rubin had opposed the initial welfare compromise—she embraced a much harsher welfare reform bill proposed by George W. Bush.[78] But the controversy these conservative pivots entailed paled in comparison to the vote she cast for Bush's war. Though she steadfastly refused to admit it, that vote would soon become one of the great frustrations—and occasions for regret—of her entire life in politics.[79]

Love her or hate her, Hillary Clinton was "the dominant brand name of the Democratic Party," as Obama put it, and she began her presidential campaign with the support of the Democratic establishment; at least a third of primary voters; a big advantage with women, who made up the majority of these voters; and by far the most experienced campaign organization.[80] A late 2007 poll gave her a 53-to-20 advantage over Obama.[81] She even did extremely well with blacks, due in large measure to her husband's special rapport. (The African American novelist Toni Morrison provocatively described him as America's first black President.[82]) Hillary's campaign resembled a military operation whose generals did not worry themselves about collateral damage as their columns moved inexorably forward, crushing their enemies without breaking formation. Her primary political adviser, aside from her husband, was his pollster, Mark Penn, a public relations executive who tended mostly to corporate clients. His early campaign memo was penned soon before she declared her candidacy in January 2007. Penn argued that Hillary should model herself after the conservative British prime minister Margaret Thatcher, the "Iron Lady." She should take comfort in being the "establishment, experienced leader candidate." The only problem he foresaw was her "likability"; her steely reserve made her appear a cold and distant figure, according to Penn's polls. Penn did not worry too much about this, however. As he claimed to have told Bill Gates upon being asked to make the Microsoft chairman "more human," "Being human is overrated."[83]

In January 2006 Barack Obama appeared on *Meet the Press,* and the show's host, veteran Tim Russert, questioned the young senator about a potential presidential run. "I will not," he replied firmly, and appeared to mean it.[84] Still he was restless. "Barack hated being a Senator," his top political aide, David Axelrod, admitted.[85] He had no seniority and next to no patience. Some talked of the Illinois governorship or the presidency of the University of Chicago; others whispered about the possibility of a spot on the ticket as vice president.

In July, Obama's office received a call from that of Senate Majority Leader

Harry Reid, who wanted to see him immediately. "I wonder what we screwed up," Obama told an aide on his way out the door. Reid quickly got to the point—"You're not going to go anyplace here"—and suggested he make a run at the presidency.[86] Reid turned out to be far from alone in his thinking, as Tom Daschle, Byron Dorgan, Ben Nelson, Bill Nelson, Barbara Boxer, and Ted Kennedy all communicated to the young man that they would welcome his entry into the race as well. They had to be careful in saying so, however, for the Clintons were famous for their hardball tactics and took loyalty no less seriously than your average Mafia chieftain. A great many Democrats were worried, however, about "Clinton fatigue" among voters, and more than a few of the party's most powerful voices—including Daschle's—were suffering from it themselves. Daschle assured Obama that his time was now: he would be the "un-Washington" candidate in a year when that label was a winner. And if Obama had the nerve, he was ready to endorse.[87]

Dick Durbin, the senior senator from Illinois, offered two words of warning should Obama fail to step up: "John Kerry." Kerry's presidential campaign had been undone by decades of Senate votes easy to decontextualize as "flip-flops," a charge to which virtually any senator with a lengthy record of service was vulnerable. Legislative experience had now become a net negative for a candidate. "Do you really think sticking around the Senate for four more years and casting a thousand more votes will make you more qualified for President?" Durbin asked.[88] David Axelrod seconded the motion, warning Obama that in contemporary political campaigns, one's voting record "hangs from your neck like the anchor from the Lusitania." He added, "You will never be hotter than you are right now."[89]

Obama returned to *Meet the Press* in November, immediately after the Democrats' sweep of the midterm elections. This time Russert received a decidedly different response to his "Will you or won't you" cross-examination. Listening to a tape of his earlier appearance, Obama allowed, "Well, the—that was how I was thinking at that time. . . . I have thought about the possibility." "So, it sounds as if the door has opened a bit," Russert suggested.[90]

Coincidentally, Obama had planned a book tour in support of *The Audacity of Hope*, his second and more policy-oriented book, and crowds turned out by the thousands. In Manchester, New Hampshire, speaking to 1,500 people, Obama sounded as if he had already made up his mind. "America is ready to turn the page," he shouted. "This is our time. A new generation is prepared to lead."[91] He made it official on February 10, 2007, speaking from the Old State Capitol in Springfield, Illinois, where, coincidentally, Abe Lincoln had announced his presidential campaign. It was a blustery winter day, even by

February-in-Illinois standards, but 17,000 people turned out. Obama set the theme of his campaign to come: "I recognize there is a certain presumptuousness in this, a certain audacity to this announcement." But Obama claimed his inexperience as an asset, explaining that he "hadn't spent a lot of time learning the ways of Washington." And "ways of Washington" in the age of Bush were no longer something to brag about. He returned to his language of community organizing. "This campaign can't only be about me. It must be about us. It must be about what we can do together."[92]

The most liberal major candidate in the race was John Kerry's 2004 running mate, John Edwards. The onetime senator from North Carolina distinguished himself from the pack by arguing for universal health insurance—his wife, Elizabeth, who had been recently diagnosed with breast cancer, openly touted a single-payer health care system—and an energetic new war on poverty.[93] He had announced his campaign from "the front yard of a mangled brick house in New Orleans's Upper Ninth Ward," an area devastated by Hurricane Katrina, and not since LBJ had fighting poverty been so central to a politician's self-professed identity.[94] Edwards declared poverty "morally wrong" and a "national shame,"[95] and in addition to the typical post-Clinton policies for attacking the problem (which included "creating publicly subsidized temporary jobs, expanding the earned-income tax credit and easing college affordability"[96]), he daringly called for vouchers that would allow poor people to buy their way into middle-class neighborhoods, breaking down socioeconomic and racial segregation.[97] For a while, it appeared as if Edwards had found a way, in David Axelrod's words, to connect "viscerally" with "working-class and rural voters, which is reflected in his impressive early lead in Iowa."[98] And the unions liked him, too. Unlike his rivals, Edwards had run four years earlier. He had done well in Iowa during the 2004 Democratic presidential primary, and had preserved those connections to the state in hopes of returning in 2008. Like Hillary, he had voted in favor of the war, but unlike Hillary, he said the three words liberals needed to hear: "I was wrong."[99]

Edwards had problems, though. While he had been born to a textile millworker and was the first person in his family to go to college, he had grown accustomed to an extremely expensive lifestyle, including, as it happened, a single haircut for which he paid $1,250. Just before the campaign began, he and his wife built "a two-building complex totaling 28,200 square feet, with an indoor basketball court, swimming pool, and squash court, two theatrical stages, and a room designated 'John's Lounge.'"[100] Worst of all were the mounting rumors—fortunately for him they were playing out in *The National Enquirer* rather than the mainstream media—that he had had an affair with a

New Age rhetoric-spouting videographer on his staff with whom he was alleged to have had a child and whom he paid out of campaign funds. (That these rumors later proved to be true leaves one to wonder just what Edwards could have been thinking during the entire period of his candidacy.[101])

Despite Edwards's apparent strength in the early primaries, Mark Penn's Republican-style plan for Hillary focused on Obama. As overconfident as he was incorrect, Penn believed that Obama's "lack of American roots" would eventually sink him with the electorate: "All of these articles about his boyhood in Indonesia and his life in Hawaii are geared towards showing his background is diverse, multicultural and putting that in a new light. Save it for 2050. It also exposes a very strong weakness for him—his roots to basic American values and culture are at best limited. I cannot imagine America electing a president during a time of war who is not at his center fundamentally American in his thinking and in his values."[102]

David Axelrod had other ideas, His twelve-page strategy memo, drafted in October 2007, argued, "The fundamental idea behind this race from the start has been that this is a 'change' election."[103] Americans were tired of the Bushes and the Clintons and all the internecine battles they recalled. Obama was untouched by the culture wars those decades inspired, to say nothing of the special, never-ending dramas Hillary's husband carried with him everywhere he went.[104]

Ironically, Obama initially enjoyed little support among black civil rights leaders.[105] Andrew Young endorsed Clinton with the curious contention that Bill Clinton was "every bit as black as Barack Obama."[106] The Reverend Calvin Butts, pastor of Harlem's Abyssinian Baptist Church (which Obama had sometimes attended while an undergraduate at Columbia), invited Hillary to come to his church to give a political stump speech.[107] John Lewis, now a respected congressman and superdelegate, also threw his initial support to Clinton.[108] And Jesse Jackson, the unofficial president of black America and a Chicagoan to boot, offered Obama an extremely pro forma, arm's-length endorsement.[109]

Obama's problem with the now-graying civil rights leadership was partially generational and partially intellectual. His generation viewed these men and women as deserving of *historical* respect rather than present-day genuflection. When Obama went to Selma, Alabama, on March 4, 2007, to speak at the Brown Chapel A.M.E. Church, he paid eloquent tribute to "'the Moses generation'—to Martin Luther King and John Lewis . . .—the men and women of the movement, who marched and suffered." But he also spoke of his own "Joshua generation," who never faced a police dog or water cannon, legal segregation, or purposeful voter disenfranchisement, but were faced with more complex and, apparently, more intractable issues such as underfunded schools, a dearth of well-paying jobs, and a general lack of "political will" to undertake the hard work to address their causes in America's political structure.[110] The black leadership's tune changed, however, when it saw the power of Obama's candidacy in its communities. He may have begun with barely 50 percent of black America's leaders, on board, but he was running away with the enthusiastic support of 90 percent of its citizens.

These strengths went unrecognized by Clinton's advisers, so supremely confident were they. As a result, her entire campaign nearly collapsed when Obama soundly defeated her in the Iowa Caucuses. But she bounced back in New Hampshire—it actually helped her with voters when she choked up while discussing some of the attacks to which she had been subjected—and the two engaged in a long slog of primaries and caucuses in which Obama was almost always ahead, but never sufficiently so to clinch the race. When he trounced Hillary in South Carolina, Bill Clinton tried to explain away the victory's significance by pointing out that "Jesse Jackson won South Carolina twice, in '84 and '88." This appeared to many as an awfully clumsy attempt to denigrate Obama as the purely "black candidate" with no real hope of winning—an attitude that could reasonably be expected to offend blacks, liberals, and plenty of others.[111] At that point, with John Edwards suspending his campaign in late January, the race turned into straightforward identity politics: Obama had blacks and upscale wine drinkers; Hillary had the beer vote. Desperate, Hillary lurched rightward, calling into question Obama's likely fortitude in a national security crisis. *National Review*'s Rich Lowry complimented her for demonstrating "a Nixonian resilience," as she apparently "morph[ed] into Scoop Jackson."[112]

But as the candidates faced a lull before heading into a series of brutal primaries in Pennsylvania, Indiana, and North Carolina, all hell broke loose for the Obama campaign. Obama's personal pastor, the Reverend Jeremiah Wright, was suddenly everywhere in the media, thanks to videotapes acquired by Fox and ABC. Sounding like Louis Farrakhan, he had taken to giving speeches complaining of the "US of KKK-A" and retailed conspiracy theories popular among some Black Muslims: "The government gives them [blacks] the drugs, builds bigger prisons, passes a three-strike law and then wants us to sing 'God bless America.' No, no, no. . . . God damn America for treating her citizens as less than human."[113] Obama's campaign advisers knew he had to confront the matter, but had no idea how. When the issue continued to metastasize, Obama himself made the decision to face up to it with a speech about race and American politics. Here, he thought, was the perfect teaching moment, both in terms of confronting America's troubled past and present, but also in demonstrating what kind of president he hoped to be.[114] On March 18, 2008, he delivered his "More Perfect Union" speech at the National Constitution Center in Philadelphia, Pennsylvania, just before that state's crucial presidential primary.

Citing the location of his speech, Obama praised the Constitution but averred that it was "stained by the nation's original sin of slavery."[115] He set out his own Joshua-generation view of race. Wright was wrong, he explained, because the minister viewed "white racism as endemic" and elevated "what is wrong with America above all that we know is right with America." Wright's vision of America was "static," ignoring the fluidity that Obama had experienced in his own life. And yet wrong though Wright was, "I can no more disown him," Obama explained, "than I can disown the black community. I can no more disown him than I can my white grandmother—a woman who helped raise me, a woman who sacrificed again and again for me, a woman who loves me as much as she loves anything in this world, but a woman who once confessed her fear of black men who passed her by on the street, and who on more than one occasion has uttered racial or ethnic stereotypes that made me cringe. These people are a part of me. And they are a part of America, this country that I love." Obama counseled his audience to accept people with all their imperfections. Wright's frustration was "powerful; and to simply wish it away, to condemn it without understanding its roots, only serves to widen the chasm of misunderstanding that exists between the races." He sought to put these fears in the context of similarly angry resentments on the part of white Americans who were forced to "bus their children to a school across town" or who felt embittered by what they viewed to be the reverse discrimination of affirmative action.

After testifying to the frustrations and conflicts that crossed the color line, Obama called his fellow citizens to unify, as he had at his 2004 convention speech. He spoke here the language of the community organizer—weaving disparate stories of anger into a narrative of shared, collective purpose. "We can come together," he argued, "to talk about the crumbling schools that are stealing the future of black children and white children and Asian children and Hispanic and Native American children." He ended with a story about Ashley, a young white woman who had joined his campaign because she wanted to help do something about health care, and how she was joined by an elderly black man who saw in her an ally.

Axelrod later mused, "Barack turned a moment of great vulnerability into a moment of triumph. He said, 'I may lose, but I will have done something valuable.' He was utterly calm while everyone was freaking out. He said, 'Either they will accept it or they won't and I won't be President.' It was probably the most important moment of the whole campaign." The speech was labeled a "Profile in Courage" by *The New York Times* and a "bold gamble" not expected from a "politician" in *Time*.

More bumps inevitably came along, including a callous set of comments Obama made in San Francisco when he thought he was speaking off the record but was being recorded by a *Huffington Post* blogger. As if playing perfectly to type as an effete, wine-drinking, brie-eating liberal elitist (and sounding as if he were channeling Thomas Frank's *What's the Matter with Kansas?*), Obama worried aloud about "these small towns in Pennsylvania, and like a lot of small towns in the Midwest, the jobs have been gone now for twenty years. . . . And it's not surprising then they get bitter, they cling to guns or religion, or antipathy to people who aren't like them or anti-immigrant sentiment or anti-trade sentiment as a way to explain their frustrations."[116] Earlier on, such remarks could have sunk him, as they resonated perfectly into Hillary's attacks. But they came too late in the campaign for Clinton to do anything more than complain about them.

Oddly—indeed, inexplicably—the Clinton contingent seemed to be paying little heed to the all but insurmountable lead in pledged delegates Obama had succeeded in building. Nobody knew exactly why, but rumors abounded that Hillary was waiting for some catastrophe to strike—for instance, when someone claimed he had seen a tape of Michelle Obama talking trash about "whitey."[117] Mark Penn said he wanted to see Obama "grovel."[118] On Tuesday, June 3, Obama clinched the nomination mathematically, but Clinton remained defiant. On that very day her campaign chief, Terry McAuliffe, introduced her to a cheering New York City crowd as "the next president of the United States."[119] To much of the country, they all appeared to be out of their minds.

Clinton eventually withdrew, claiming credit for putting "eighteen million cracks" in the "hardest, highest glass ceiling," and reserved the right to cause trouble at the convention.[120] But that didn't happen, either. The Denver Democratic convention proceeded like a dream as Obama threaded the needle between liberal and centrist, pragmatist and idealist, the past and the future, and united the party for a presidential campaign that—amazingly—was the African American Barack Hussein Obama's to lose. He was the change.

Arizona Republican and onetime Vietnam POW, Senator John McCain, had quite possibly become the national press corps' favorite politician. During his unsuccessful 2000 presidential campaign, he so famously captured their hearts by playing a "maverick" on a few issues and, briefly, challenging the power of the Republican Christian conservatives and bonding with reporters long into the night. The John McCain of so many journalists' dreams had always been something of a fantasy, however, and that image faded further and further into the mists of the mythological as the real McCain decided the only hope for him to win the nomination was to hug and kiss George W. Bush both literally and metaphorically. Over and over again McCain fled from his signature issues—campaign finance reform, immigration reform, even opposition to torture, though he himself had been tortured in North Vietnam—in pursuit of his life's dream.

The McCain myth finally crumbled to dust when he chose Sarah Palin as his running mate. (He had originally wanted Joseph Lieberman, the conservative Democratic senator from Connecticut and onetime vice presidential candidate to Al Gore, but this choice was vetoed by Karl Rove and other party conservatives over Lieberman's pro-choice voting record.) McCain's opting for the obscure Alaska governor—whom he barely knew and who was clearly unprepared to assume the presidency—was a desperate move, particularly given the fact that McCain's advanced age made it possible that his choice might be called upon to do so. Palin had charisma in abundance, but her head was filled with more nutty notions than could be comfortably counted and her extensive family was ready-made for reality TV.

The McCain-Palin ticket got a bounce in the polls after the convention, as many Republicans seemed more excited by Palin and her red-meat rhetoric than by anything McCain could bring himself to say.[121] Her rallies resembled evangelical tent meetings, gathering the anti-intellectual passions of the right. When she said that Obama was "pallin' around with terrorists" and had "launched his political career in the living room of a domestic terrorist," though, the atmosphere grew worrisome. "This is not a man who sees America the way you and I see America," she warned in Clearwater, Florida. Often times, members of the audience would shout "Kill him!" and "He's a nigger!" and "Treason!" and "Go back to Kenya!" at her appearances.[122]

Democrats went into a bit of a panic over Palin's initial appeal, as many in the media were apparently losing their heads over her, but her popularity turned out to be fleeting. Her ignorance of the most basic aspects of governance coupled with the myriad scandals that arose from her brief term as governor of Alaska all served to undermine the logic of McCain's choice and confirm the general impression of both his desperation and impulsiveness.

Moreover, just two weeks after the Republican convention bounce, the U.S. economy appeared on the verge of calamity, owing to the collapse of Lehman

Brothers and the revelation that much of the rest of Wall Street was teetering on the brink of bankruptcy as well. The Dow Jones Industrial Average fell more than 500 points in a single day. That same day, in what might have been one of the worst-timed political pronouncements in recent political history, McCain assured a town hall meeting in Florida: "The fundamentals of our economy are strong."[123] A usually calm and methodical David Plouffe, who held the title of campaign manager (just below Axelrod), shouted: "No fucking way!" in much the same way Karl Rove had celebrated John Kerry's self-defeating statements about Iraq.[124] McCain quickly tried to backpedal, but it was too late. He had put the handcuffs on himself and thrown away the key. Obama could now campaign on his calm plan to be "Not George Bush." The ensuing economic collapse became "the final verdict" on a "failed economic philosophy" shared by both George W. Bush and John McCain.[125]

McCain's behavior grew ever more bizarre as the campaign drew to a close. His impulsive decisions—first to suspend his campaign to deal with the economic emergency personally, and then to refuse to cooperate with the delicate deal that Bush, Federal Reserve chairman Ben Bernanke, and congressional leaders were desperately trying to piece together—left reporters and eventually the public bewildered. Republicans were the ones who had led the country down this disastrous path, and McCain could find no compelling argument why his leadership would produce better results. Obama, meanwhile, remained calm, parrying McCain's attacks with eloquence and equanimity.[126]

Election Day saw Obama win the popular vote by 52.9 to 45.7, a better showing than Clinton had ever achieved. The victory speech of the nation's first African American president, in Chicago's Grant Park, gave liberals a moment of hope and joyful tears that few had ever expected to experience. And the sight of Jesse Jackson, once Martin Luther King's lieutenant, openly crying in the crowd as Obama spoke provided not only a vivid representation of the passing of the guard but also, and more important, a symbolic reminder of just how far America had come.[127]

To many liberals Obama's victory felt like a kind of miracle. That the very same country that had reelected George W. Bush would now turn to Barack Obama as his replacement would have appeared inconceivable little more than two years earlier. And given how progressive a campaign the candidate had run—promising universal health care, a commitment to ending global warming, getting tough on the banks along with a quick withdrawal from Iraq, and the closing of Guantánamo—a few million liberals could be forgiven for fearing they might awaken from an impossible dream if pinched too hard.

After clinching the Democratic nomination in June 2008, Barack Obama had stood before an excited group of supporters in St. Paul, Minnesota, and declared: "We will be able to look back and tell our children that this was the moment when we began to provide care for the sick and good jobs to the jobless; this was the moment when the rise of the oceans began to slow and our planet began to heal; this was the moment when we ended a war and secured our nation and restored our image as the last, best hope on earth."[128]

But if ever a president was to prove Mario Cuomo's adage that candidates "campaign in poetry" but "govern in prose," it was Barack Obama.[129] As Marshall Ganz, a community organizer and academic who helped play a large role in the campaign, explains, "'Transformational' leadership engages followers in the risky and often exhilarating work of changing the world, work that often changes the activists themselves. Its sources are shared values that become wellsprings of the courage, creativity and hope needed to open new pathways to success. 'Transactional' leadership, on the other hand, is about horse-trading, operating within the routine, and it is practiced to maintain, rather than change, the status quo." Obama, Gans conceded, "entered office wrapped in a mantle of moral leadership" but ceded it without a struggle. He never recovered from abandoning the bully pulpit of moral argument and public education and embracing the politics of compromise over those of advocacy.[130]

Barack Obama, as Jesse Jackson might have put it, was a deal maker, not a world shaker. His rhetoric, together with his legislative strategy, was always oriented toward inclusiveness, consensus building, and preemptive offers of compromise.

Whatever political calculation may have lain behind it—and countless supporters found it baffling—Obama's approach failed to take into account some fundamental changes that American politics had undergone during the Bush years, most particularly the radicalization of the Republican Party. Republicans circa 2009 were no longer interested in bipartisan solutions to America's problems. Then-Senate minority leader Mitch McConnell told *The National Journal*, "The single most important thing we want to achieve is for President Obama to be a one-term president."[131] Senator Jim DeMint famously promised health care reform could be used to "break" Obama from day one. "We're the party of 'Hell, no!'" cried Sarah Palin to a crowd of cheering southern Republicans in April 2010.[132]

By the time of Obama's election, the moderate wing in the Republican Party had been purged virtually out of existence, and in its place was a faction dominated, according to the moderately conservative commentator, Fareed Zakaria, by "Conservatives [who] now espouse ideas drawn from abstract principles with little regard to the realities of America's present or past."[133] The result, as *New Republic* editor John Judis described it, was a party that had "transformed [itself] from a loyal opposition into an insurrectionary party that flouts the law when it is in the majority and threatens disorder when it is the minority. . . . If there is an earlier American precedent for today's Republican Party, it is the antebellum Southern Democrats of John Calhoun who threatened to nullify, or disregard, federal legislation they objected to, and who later led the fight to secede from the union over slavery."[134] In the fall of 2011, Mike Lofgren, recently retired after twenty-eight years as a congressional staffer, serving sixteen of these as a professional staff member on the Republican side of both the House and Senate Budget Committees, went so far as to describe the party for which he had labored so long as "becoming less and less like a traditional political party in a representative democracy than an apocalyptic cult, or one of the intensely ideological authoritarian parties of twentieth-century Europe."[135] Democrats, meanwhile, were divided between what one pundit called their "sitting pretty faction" and "the more fragile 'scaredy cat' faction that could be carried off by even the gentlest of anti-incumbent breezes."[136] The latter voted more often like Republicans than with their president.

Asked what he wished for in 2011 during the 2010 holiday season, Obama reportedly replied, "All I want for Christmas is an opposition I can negotiate with."[137] He never got one. As a longtime student and frequent defender of Congress—the American Enterprise Institute's Norman Ornstein—observed in an article he titled "Worst. Congress. Ever.":

Republicans, having been thrashed at all levels in 2008, did not respond to the voters' rebuke by cooperating with the majority or trying to find common ground. Instead, repeating a tactic employed with great political success by Republicans in 1993 and 1994 against a newly elected President Bill Clinton, they immediately united fiercely and unremittingly against all the Obama and Democratic congressional initiatives. In the Senate they used delay tactics—the filibuster and the hold—in an unprecedented fashion, to block a large number of Obama administration nominees for executive branch positions and draw out debate to clog the legislative process and make an already messy business even messier.[138]

Republicans refused to agree to approve appointments to the federal bench, even to crucial government posts, many of which remained vacant for Obama's entire term.[139] Following the passage of the financial reform bill creating the Consumer Financial Protection Bureau, they intimidated the president into not even nominating the Democrats' most popular choice, Harvard Law School professor Elizabeth Warren, and then proceeded to refuse to schedule hearings on Obama's alternative choice, former Ohio attorney general Richard Cordray, after Obama caved in.[140] Republican willingness to threaten to filibuster just about every Democratic initiative successfully frustrated liberal priority after liberal priority. The labor movement's key issue, passage of the Employee Free Choice Act, received only tepid administration or congressional support. Nothing was done to reform America's broken (and deeply exploitative) immigration policies. (The pace of deportations actually increased during Obama's presidency by roughly 20 percent above that of an equivalent period during the Bush administration's tenure.[141]) Reproductive rights for women were actually narrowed. Money grew more powerful both in politics and in society, as campaign finance laws were weakened and the Bush-era tax cuts extended, worsening the previous era's explosion in inequality, despite the unpopularity with the public of both of these policies. These were all clear breaks from past practices. Journalist Michael Tomasky compared eight key priorities of presidents Bush and Obama in the autumn of 2011 and found, on average, 41.1 percent of Democrats tended to support Bush's legislation, while the corresponding number for Republicans under Obama was just 5.75 percent.[142]

What Richard Hofstadter had written of the extremely business-friendly Democrat Grover Cleveland turned out to be eerily true of Obama as well: "With his stern ideas of purity, efficiency, and service, he was a taxpayer's dream, the ideal bourgeois statesman for his time: out of heartfelt conviction he gave to the interests what many a lesser politician would have sold for a price."[143] The president showed little willingness to use the powers of his office to counter the hardball tactics that were strangling his agenda, such as making recess appointments when Congress was out of session or issuing executive orders to ensure that his will was done regardless of Republican filibusters or delaying efforts.[144, 145] Instead he simply curtailed his appointments and left many key positions unfilled.[146] The old joke about the liberal who showed up for a gunfight with a library book was no longer so funny.

The political circumstances Obama faced were, it must be admitted, remarkable. Barely a month into his presidency, a cable news reporter named Rick Santelli stood on the floor of the Chicago Board of Trade and, in the famous words of the character Howard Beale in the film *Network* (1976), started shouting: "I'm as mad as hell, and I'm not going to take it anymore!"[147] Santelli's hysterics were directed at the small amounts of taxpayer funds that had been allocated by the government to enable people to continue to pay their mortgages rather than lose their homes. This was a surprising choice of targets, given the billions that were being handed out to Wall Street bankers at the time, but Santelli's rant helped spark what became known as the Tea Party movement, which rapidly gelled into a free-floating protest of rage directed toward virtually any government program that sought to ameliorate inequality or offer a hand up to the poor or middle class. By April 2009 these protests—some organized and all advertised by the hosts and guests on Rupert Murdoch's Fox News—drew hundreds of thousands of supporters across America.[148] Racist signs depicting Obama as a pickaninny or even a gorilla were common at such demonstrations until the movement developed the self-discipline to ensure that such images were kept off camera. Meanwhile, a motley assortment of what *The New Yorker*'s Ben McGrath described as "gold-bugs, evangelicals, Atlas Shruggers, militia-men, strict Constitutionalists, swine-flu skeptics, scattered 9/11 'truthers,' neo-'Birchers,' and, of course, 'birthers'—those who remained convinced that the President was a Muslim double agent born in Kenya" intent on turning the United States into an Islamic Republic could be depended upon to turn up anywhere Fox News promised to send cameras for much of Obama's presidency.[149]

A study of the views and attitudes of two thousand voters sympathetic to the Tea Party presented to the 2011 annual meeting of the American Sociological Association by four academics added that their attitudes could be characterized as reflective of "four primary cultural and political beliefs" in greater measure than in other Americans: "authoritarianism, libertarianism, fear of change, and negative attitudes toward immigrants and immigration."[150] So committed were these protesters to their own paranoid view of politics that they felt free to ignore reality at every turn. A May 2011 poll found that only 48 percent of those questioned believed that Barack Obama was born in the United States. While that figure was almost double the 28 percent who believed it in February of that year, it was still remarkably low, given that Hawaii had recently released the president's long-form birth certificate.[151] Unfair levels of taxation paid by Americans was allegedly the single issue that united the Tea Party, but, apparently, this, too, was a product of either misinformation or mass hysteria. According to the 2009 figures from the Organization for Economic Cooperation and Development (OECD), Americans enjoyed some of the lowest taxation rates in the developed world.[152] And yet this group of angry ignorant agitators continued to hold remarkable sway over Republicans, terrorizing the nonbelievers into toeing their line. Despite repeated polls demonstrating that their views were never shared by much more than 20 percent of Americans, mainstream media reporters treated the Tea Party as the authentic voice of the average American.

Liberals had nothing to remotely match conservatives' Tea Party troops. David Plouffe, the 2008 campaign's top organizer, had created an e-mail list of more than thirteen million names for the future use of the president. Many organizers salivated at the prospect of using that list to build up organizations in support of environmental, economic, and various social causes on the progressive agenda. But it all ended on Election Day. Organizing for America, the successor organization to Obama for America, was allowed to atrophy into little more than a cheering section for whatever direction the administration decided to follow. Apparently, the last thing the Obama administration wanted to see develop was a large populist organization whose priorities might differ from its own and thereby interfere with his deal-making agenda. Indeed, when liberals sought to challenge Democratic incumbents who refused to support the administration's priorities, particularly regarding health care, the administration intervened to crush the dissidents and ensure smooth sailing for the disloyal Democratic senators and representatives.

At the outset of the Obama administration, many liberals mistook the 2008 near collapse of the U.S. economy for an opportunity to return to a kind of Keynesian activism associated with the early days of the New Deal.[153] This hope, too, was dashed before it had a chance, once Obama announced his team of economic advisers. Most prominent among them was Larry Summers, a brilliant if acerbic economic thinker who had once been Harvard's youngest tenured professor, and eventually the school's president, and who had held a series of important official appointments along the way, including a stint as Bill Clinton's treasury secretary.[154] Summers had long championed deregulation, and together with Obama's treasury secretary, Tim Geithner, the former president and chief executive officer of the Federal Reserve Bank of New York, he dismissed the arguments of those such as Nobel laureates Paul Krugman and Joseph Stiglitz who believed that the big banks should be held accountable for the damage their recklessness had wrought.

The battles began with the stimulus plan. Few economists doubted its necessity; the question was its scale. The country was stuck in its worst economic downturn since the Great Depression. More than 8.4 million jobs had disappeared from the economy, taking with them three million homes by foreclosure, with more to come as Obama took office. In just one year U.S. households lost $11 trillion, or nearly a fifth of all of their wealth.[155] Christina Romer, chairwoman of Obama's Council of Economic Advisers, calculated the need for an injection of $1.2 trillion into an economy she termed "grim and deteriorating."[156] Krugman's advice to the president was to "figure out how much help they think the economy needs, then add 50 percent."[157]

During the negotiations over the size and shape of the stimulus package, the president felt it necessary to grant Congress the lion's share of influence over the spending process, ensuring wasteful pork-barrel projects that would be easily open to attack, and threw in hundreds of billions in tax cuts to appeal to right-wing Republicans. The result was a package that, while costly, would be clearly insufficient to address a crisis whose size and scope, it turned out, Obama and his advisers had vastly underestimated. Chief of Staff Rahm Emanuel angrily defended it as the best that could be done "in the art of the possible, of the deal."[158] Absent in such thinking was the Reagan-like option of trying to move the country toward a more ambitious program that might have better chance at success.[159]

The end product of these negotiations—the American Recovery and Reinvestment Act—injected $814 billion into the economy,[160] which, as Obama described it, was "the largest investment in research and development in our history, the largest investment in infrastructure since Dwight Eisenhower, the largest investment in education . . . in this country in 30 years" and "the largest investment in clean energy in our history."[161] Even though Obama had compromised and turned about a third of it into tax cuts rather than public works programs, it nevertheless made many conservatives apoplectic. The columnist George Will blamed Obama for a bill that "allowed, even encouraged, self-indulgent liberal majorities in Congress to create a stimulus that confirmed conservatism's portrayal of liberalism as an undisciplined agglomeration of parochial appetites."[162]

Few Americans, it turned out, were able to distinguish between the stimulus program and the TARP (Troubled Asset Relief Program) program to bail out the banks, begun under Bush's administration. Dollars were flowing out of federal coffers, and yet unemployment could not be brought below 9 percent before it began to creep upward again.[163] Here again Obama and company painted a target on their backs. In his 2010 State of the Union address, the president admitted that bailing out the banks had been "about as popular as a root canal."[164] But he took no steps to assuage the populist anger that the measure had naturally engendered. During the fight over the financial reform legislation, he resisted congressional efforts to place any limits on executive pay as European nations had done, even for companies in which U.S. taxpayers were now the principal stockholders. This came at a time when executive compensation at America's biggest companies had quadrupled in real terms since the 1970s, even as pay for 90 percent of America had remained flat or even declined. Meanwhile, the percentage of Americans living in poverty was on its way to its highest rate in the fifty-two years since the U.S. Census Bureau had begun collecting the relevant data.[165]

As fearful of being labeled "antibusiness" as Democrats had traditionally been seen as "soft" on communism, the administration, apparently, had decided as a matter of policy to "protect the interests of creditors, no matter the cost," in Paul Krugman's words. During the fight over the financial reform bill, it consistently took the positions for which the banks were lobbying. Obama and his team were eager to weaken the "Volcker rule," which sought to prevent "large, systemically important banking institutions [from] undertaking proprietary activities that represent particularly high risks and serious conflicts of interest," as, for instance, Goldman Sachs had done by betting against the collateralized debt obligations it sold its customers.[166] At the same time that banks were being given massive loans at or near 0 percent from the Federal Reserve, they could lend back at a 100 percent profit. The administration sided with the banks in keeping the Consumer Financial Protection Bureau within the Fed, where its independence would likely be compromised, and then refused to fight for its own agency director. Finally, nothing at all was done to address the central problem that had caused the crisis in the first place: allowing banking institutions to become "too big to fail." The banks that caused the 2008 crisis had since then significantly increased their share of global assets, ensuring that the next time around, whatever crisis took place would be even worse.[167]

Obama's generosity won him no kudos from owners of the posteriors he rescued. According to one reporter's account, Obama had "enraged many financial industry executives" by "labeling them 'fat cats' and criticizing their bonuses"; hence, they were pouring money into Republican coffers in response. On Main Street, meanwhile, most public opinion polling found not only that the stimulus plan was "widely considered to have failed," but that the vast majority of Americans wrongly believed their taxes to have gone up.[168] In fact, according to the nonpartisan Congressional Budget Office, the president's emergency stimulus bill helped to create or preserve 3.7 million jobs,[169] while the tax cuts contained in the bill saved an average of nearly $1,200 for 97 percent of U.S. households.[170] Obama had, in fact, cut taxes for most Americans by a greater percentage than had George W. Bush. But nobody seemed to know it. No less significant—owing in part to the fact that they really did underestimate the weakness of the economy—Obama and his aides fell into the age-old liberal trap of overpromising and underperforming.[171] Administration figures confidently predicted that because of their economic program, unemployment would peak at 8 percent before returning to more manageable levels. But figures would later reveal that instead of a 0.5 percent contraction in the third quarter of 2008 and a 3.8 percent drop in its final quarter, the economy had actually contracted by 2.7 percent with an 8.9 percent fall in that period.[172] And so when unemployment remained sky-high by historical standards, Obama's policies received a far larger share of the blame than they would have had their initial descriptions of the extent of the crisis been more accurate.

Obama also failed in one of his most important early goals: to pass legislation to control climate-changing carbon emissions. Republican rejection of reality had progressed so far by this point that a global scientific consensus on man-made climate change was routinely dubbed a "liberal conspiracy" to increase funding and regulate industry, and the Republicans in Congress actually forbade the U.S. Environmental Protection Agency from taking any preventative measures to deal with its consequences.[173] Here again Obama came in for strong criticism from his onetime liberal supporters, most vocal among these, in many respects, being former Vice President Gore, who charged that the president had simply not made the case for action. "President Obama has never presented to the American people the magnitude of the climate crisis. . . . He has not defended the science against the ongoing withering and dishonest attacks. Nor has he provided a presidential venue for the scientific community . . . to bring the reality of the science before the public."[174]

Obama's signal accomplishment as president was undoubtedly his passage of the Affordable Care Act (ACA), the landmark reform of America's health care system. Here was a problem absolutely central to U.S. society and its economy, as well as a cause that had set liberal hearts aflutter for more than sixty years. But Obama and his advisers had overlearned the lesson of Clinton's health care failure. The last Democratic president had lost his chance to pass his legislation because he tried, and failed, to steamroll Congress. Obama tried the opposite, and invited Congress to write its own bill with merely some broad guidelines and requests from the administration. But because the rules of the Senate invited all manner of obstruction, the process of delay and the threat of a minority filibuster continually watered down the legislation. The clock ticked as Obama offered one concession after another, his most important "compromise" coming with his willingness to relinquish the promised "Public Option"—the alternative to a single-payer system in which a government-run program would compete with private insurance companies—while he stuck to his demands for mandatory insurance for everyone, including those with "prior conditions."

Overall, it was a quite conservative plan when compared with the one Richard Nixon had proposed, to say nothing of what all other modern liberal democracies offered their citizens. Indeed, its shape was actually inspired by the plan that the Republican then-governor of Massachusetts Mitt Romney had passed into law in 2006.[175] Republicans still denounced it as "socialism" and a "government takeover" of a fifth of the economy, while insisting that the inclusion of "death panels" would result in the forced euthanasia of America's grandparents.[176] But in March 2010 it finally became law. Ninety-two-year-old Robert Byrd, who was not long for this world, called out "I cast my vote for my friend Ted Kennedy" as the roll was called. It was one of the most moving moments any liberal had had the opportunity to witness from the Capitol visitors' gallery in decades, and among the last they were likely to see for an awfully long time.

Admittedly, Obama was playing a game where the rules kept changing in the other side's favor. Special interests had strengthened their vicelike grip on the process, allowing senators whose campaigns they funded to obstruct the legislation at every turn. At one point, Pharmaceutical Research and Manufacturers of America (PhRMA), the industrywide trade association of the pharmaceutical industry, employed 48 different lobbying firms, in addition to its in-house lobbyists, for a total of 165 people overall to work on Congress. This was in addition to the nearly $500 million that the oil, coal, and utility businesses collectively had spent since the beginning of 2009 to lobby against legislation to address climate change and to defeat candidates who supported it.[177] This avalanche of cash was just the tip of the new corporate spending iceberg emerging from a series of Supreme Court decisions. In the most important of these, 2009's *Citizens United v. Federal Election Commission,* the one-vote conservative majority somehow forbade Congress from limiting independent corporate expenditures to support or defeat a given candidate, and significantly weakened the disclosure rules that had previously been in place. This unleashed a virtual avalanche of conservative campaign cash designed to undermine any candidate, whether challenger or incumbent, who tried to put public interests ahead of private ones.

Added to the above was the fact that the number one cable news network in America dedicated itself to a program of purposeful misinformation about Obama. The comedian/commentator Jon Stewart aptly termed Rupert Murdoch's Fox News Channel—the most conspicuous American arm of a massive global network of media properties that occasionally delved into criminal activity on behalf of its ideological and business interests—to be "a cyclonic, perpetual emotion machine that gins up legitimate political disagreements into a full-fledged panic attack about the next coming of Chairman Mao."[178] While they may not have employed the criminal tactics that were apparently common in other parts of Rupert Murdoch's global media empire, Fox News represented a relentless assault on political truth in America carried out on multiple fronts simultaneously. Its on-air personalities often mangled the president's words on purpose and frequently cut away before letting him finish. They invited Republican politicians and conservative propagandists to come on and spout falsehoods without challenge. They invited pretend "liberals" to come on the air to attack real ones. And Fox was only a small part of the story when it came to purposeful conservative disinformation. According to a study by the Pew Research Center's Project on Excellence in Journalism (PEJ), right-wing talk radio enjoyed 48 million regular listeners, which was not only many times Fox's audience but also more than twice the collective audience for the three TV network evening news shows combined.[179] Liberals had their own voices as well, but they were no match at all, whether measured by size, scope, or vociferousness, to those of the far right; nor could they honestly be portrayed as even remotely as extreme as their conservative counterparts. The net result, both because of the reach of these outlets and also because of their gravitational pull on other, less conventionally defined media, resulted in coverage largely dictated by the priorities and assumptions of Obama's conservative opponents. To take just one illustration, in another study by the PEJ, released in October 2011 and focusing on the content of 11,500 media outlets during the previous six months, researchers found stories reflecting badly on Barack Obama exceeded favorable ones by a factor of four to one. (The negativity appeared impervious to actual events as not even the capturing and killing of Osama bin Laden could put the president in positive territory for an entire week.) Meanwhile, despite incessant complaints of an alleged liberal bias in what they had taken to calling the "lamestream media," right-wing Republicans with downright bizarre views about not only political issues but reality itself, including, especially, Rick Perry, Sarah Palin, Michele Bachmann, and Herman Cain, all enjoyed largely positive coverage.[180]

As a *New York Times* editorial aptly observed, Barack Obama "took office under an extraordinary burden of problems created by President George W. Bush's ineptness and blind ideology."[181] This was nowhere truer than in the area of U.S. foreign policy. The United States was fighting two wars, hamstrung by the hatred of many of the world's citizens, and operating secret prisons in various locations across the globe. In many respects, it was in the international arena where Obama had the clearest field in which to institute his agenda for change. His onetime opponent and now secretary of state, Hillary Clinton, stated that Obama's election allowed the world a "great exhalation of breath." At the same time, however, she warned that the new administration still had "a lot of damage to repair."[182] And yet it was in foreign policy that Obama's supporters may have felt the most profound sense of buyer's remorse.

Liberals had long argued that domestic practices of justice needed to be cleaned up if America could lay claim to the right of moral leadership abroad. As political scientist Alan Wolfe has rightly argued, "As political systems, liberal democracies are aspirational. They come into being to make the world a better place, and they fail to serve their history and ideals if they give up on that objective."[183] Liberals therefore argued that the secret prosecution of those captured in the war on terror needed to be halted in order to live up to American ideals of justice for all. Obama supported this idea when he signed executive orders that closed Guantánamo Bay's secret prison and instructed "all interrogations to follow the noncoercive methods of the Army Field Manual."[184] Just four months, later, however, he found himself blocked by the Senate when it voted to prohibit the transfer of these prisoners anywhere on American soil. Following that defeat, Obama appeared to give up entirely on this part of his agenda and in many respects decided to remain on the Bush-Cheney path on all matters relating to civil liberties and national security—a shocking reversal not only for a candidate who criticized these policies as unworthy of America as a great nation, but also for a onetime professor of constitutional law who surely knew better.

As president, and consistent, this time, with his campaign promises, Obama doubled down on the war in Afghanistan, now America's longest ever, despite its day-to-day deterioration to the point where it increasingly resembled Vietnam. As with that catastrophe, U.S. forces arrived with inappropriate training for a "nation-building" mission and even less rapport with and understanding of Afghanistan's traditional Islamic culture and politics. Once again U.S. troops were fighting in the service of a corrupt regime that rigged elections to remain in power and whose citizens appeared more interested in getting rich off heroin sales and distribution, and playing America against its enemies, than in winning a war. President Hamid Karzai regularly referred to the U.S. troops as occupying forces, acting in Afghanistan "for their own purposes, for their own goals, and . . . using our soil."[185] And as was the case with Vietnam, urgent domestic priorities went begging and created additional pressure to rethink what looked more and more like a failed policy.[186]

Obama bought himself some time with the public by accomplishing what George W. Bush had sought to do: killing Osama Bin Laden, accomplished in the spring of 2011 by a daring raid by U.S. Navy Seals. Yet even this moment of grim but undeniable glory was shadowed by the disturbing recognition that Osama had been being kept safe and sound in Pakistan, the very country that was supposed to be allied with the United States in combating him. With Pakistan on the wrong side, the Afghan war made little sense at all because it not only presented the enemy with a safe haven—just as Cambodia had done for North Vietnam—but it turned out that the war was destabilizing the very nation it had been intended to support. (And this one had nuclear weapons.) Finally, in late June 2011, Obama began the process of drawing down troops even against Pentagon objections, admitting that the United States had "lost [the] balance" between protecting the nation's national security and investing in its economy. It was long past time, he stated, to "begin nation building at home."[187]

Obama's reaction to the 2011 events that came to be known as the Arab Spring proved a riddle as well. Scenes of protesters' taking to the streets demanding democratic reform in Egypt, being shot by their own army in Syria, and arming themselves for rebellion in Libya were not easy for Obama to ignore. While his heart undoubtedly warmed to protest against these repressive dictatorships, his head prompted memories of Iraq and Afghanistan, to say nothing of Indochina. Obama had defined his own foreign policy, after the Bush disaster in Iraq, in largely realist and pragmatic terms, much like that of the first President Bush. His strategy was, in his own 2006 words, "no longer driven by ideology and politics but . . . based on a realistic assessment of the sobering facts on the ground and our interests in" the Middle East.[188]

Adapting to each crisis on a case-by-case basis, the administration wound up selectively and cautiously supporting some of those who wanted democratic reform while ignoring others.[189] He stood on the sidelines during the Tunisian people's successful uprising that began the process, and when the Egyptians rose up next, he eventually abandoned Egypt's corrupt dictator, Hosni Mubarak, long an American ally whose willingness to observe the cool peace with Israel entitled him to billions in U.S. aid—but only when the dictator's position became untenable. He stuck by the repressive conservative leaders of Saudi Arabia, Bahrain, and Dubai when they faced uprisings and did nothing to help the Syrian people when they rebelled against the dictatorial regime of Bashar al-Assad and were met with a brutal crackdown reportedly resulting in over three thousand deaths and counting during just its first six months.[190] In Libya, however, Obama made the opposite decision and committed U.S. forces to a UN- and NATO-backed mission against the dictator in order to prevent what he saw as a likely massacre.[191] But in the imperial tradition of previous postwar presidents, Obama refused to seek congressional approval for his Libyan intervention. Rejecting the opinions of top lawyers at the Pentagon and the Justice Department, he argued that U.S. involvement did not constitute the kind of hostilities designed to trigger the 1973 War Powers Act.[192] Constitutionally speaking, he had the power to do this, but it was one of many decisions that led supporters to wonder whether John McCain had actually defeated the constitutional law professor Barack Obama in the 2008 election.

Fortunately, the Libyan intervention turned out to be a remarkably successful one as the rebels managed to oust—and eventually capture and kill—the hated dictator. Reporters returned with stories of the gratitude of the Libyan people. Predictably, however, even this episode proved a political negative for Obama after a senior administration official described the president's actions to *The New Yorker*'s Ryan Lizza as "leading from behind."[193] As the magazine's editor (and Obama biographer), David Remnick, observed in the aftermath of the rebel victory, "You could almost hear the speed-dials revving at the headquarters of the Republican National Committee. The phrase ricocheted from one Murdoch-owned editorial page and television studio to the next. Obama was mocked as a "timorous pretender who, out of a misbegotten sense of liberal guilt" coupled with arrogant (and undeserved) self-regard, embraced America's decline on the world stage rather than try to shape in our own image as past presidents had done.[194]

Meanwhile, owing to its powerful focus on all of its military adventures, the crucial foreign policy issues facing the country often received short shrift. The United States made no progress with China in currency negotiations, where the undervalued yuan artificially kept the prices of dollar-denominated goods high and Chinese-manufactured goods low. This strategy helped to further weaken an increasingly decimated U.S. manufacturing base and with it, the Democrats' dwindling base in industrial unions, reflecting a Cold War–era priority that no longer made any sense in a world where American workers had trouble competing with Chinese (and Indian, South Korean, Indonesian, et cetera) workers whether measured by price or quality.[195] It achieved no agreements on global environmental issues, which grew more dangerous with each passing day. It actually achieved a kind of negative progress regarding both the Israeli-Palestinian peace process and in quieting regional fears about Iran's nuclear program.[196]

The overall problem was that it was becoming easier for other nations to ignore U.S. wishes (or pressure). So much blood and treasure had been squandered in counterproductive wars and regressive tax cuts during the Bush years that the United States lacked the mechanisms necessary to enforce its will. As representatives of a debtor nation addicted to living vastly beyond its means, President Obama and Secretary of State Clinton needed first and foremost to ensure that nothing upset the flow of funds from China and elsewhere that enabled the nation to maintain low interest rates and prevent a run of inflation.[197] Despite the giddy neoconservative crowing about America's "unipolar" moment, the United States was actually a more dependent nation than it had been in nearly a century. But such an admission would have meant political suicide for any president, much less a Democrat with Obama's particular problems.

In August 2010 Barack Obama took his family to Martha's Vineyard, where at a local bookstore he was given a galley of the not-yet-released novel *Freedom*, by Jonathan Franzen. Obama read it and called it "terrific" and later invited Franzen to the White House.[198] But if he was looking for a book to take his mind of his political troubles, he could hardly have made a worse choice.

Within days of its publication *Freedom* would be touted as "the novel of the century" in *The Guardian* and as a "masterpiece" on the front page of *The New York Times Book Review*. Franzen appeared on the cover of *Time* above the caption "Great American Novelist"[199] and was soon being compared with Norman Mailer, John Updike, and even Henry James and Charles Dickens; Franzen himself compared his ambition to that of Tolstoy. Naturally, all this soon led to a backlash. The book, naysayers were quick to observe, focused on the problems of privileged, relatively well-to-do white men and women, was written by a white man, and was celebrated by a media dominated by the same.

Born in Chicago in 1959, Franzen grew up in a suburb of St. Louis, "in the middle of the country in the middle of the golden age of the American middle class," as he recalled.[200] Neither parent encouraged literary ambitions in their son, who described himself at the time as "a nerd," with a "large vocabulary, a giddily squeaking voice, horn-rimmed glasses, poor arm strength," and "irresistible urges to shout unfunny puns."[201] Franzen attended Swarthmore, where he became editor of the college's literary magazine, and following his 1981 graduation, he married a fellow aspiring novelist with whom he shared not-so-genteel poverty. Franzen published two well-reviewed but poorly selling novels, divorced, and grew increasingly angry and isolated.[202] At the same time, he burned with a "rage against literary theory and the politicization of academic English departments," which treated the literary realism to which he was so partial as a kind of fossil from a prehistoric age.[203]

Franzen believed that novelists had a democratic responsibility to make their work accessible, but at the same time, he believed that fiction had to "raise more questions than it answer[ed]."[204] Sounding Niebuhresque, Franzen argued in an April 1996 essay in *Harper's*, "Tragic realism preserves access to the dirt behind the dream of Chosenness—to the human difficulty beneath the technological ease, to the sorrow behind the pop-cultural narcosis: to all those portents on the margins of our existence."[205] In doing so, Franzen also echoed Lionel Trilling's celebration of "possibility, complexity, and difficulty," shadowed by the need for "moral imagination" and "tragic choice" as a guide to living with the contradictions of democratic capitalism.[206] The novel, Franzen later observed, "is well suited to expanding sympathy. . . . Good novels have a lot of the same attributes as good liberal politics."[207, 208] It could, moreover, nurture moral imagination by placing readers into a "place of stillness" where they could "make responsible decisions" and "engage productively with an otherwise scary and unmanageable world."[209]

It took Franzen three books to fully develop his voice. *The Corrections* (2001), his breakthrough novel and winner of the National Book Award, was a story of entangled family members during the bubble "years in America when it was nearly impossible not to make money," along with the corruptions that arose from that temptation. Franzen's hero, Chip Lambert, had been trying to teach his students "the critical tools of resistance and analysis" to confront an insidious consumer culture, but he was at a loss to explain exactly what was so objectionable about it.[210] Throughout this section of the novel, Franzen brought to life the liberal argument that the linguistic turn that leftist academic politics had taken during the 1990s had not only eviscerated liberalism's ability to respond to the corporate and conservative assault on the living standards of the poor and the middle class, but had also created an analytical paradigm through which it became impossible to determine the morality of any given action.

When Oprah Winfrey gave *The Corrections* her blessing by selecting it as the main choice for her wildly successful televised book club,[211] Franzen, who liked to think of himself as an "egalitarian Midwesterner," recoiled from the endorsement, finding Oprah's taste to be too often "schmaltzy [and] one-dimensional" and generally beneath the standards of his literary ambitions.[212] Immediately he became American political culture's Public Enemy Number

One and was unceremoniously disinvited from appearing on Oprah's television program, though the stickers advertising its selection by her remained on the books, and its author was left to ponder how wealthy and celebrated he might have been if only he hadn't felt it necessary to sneer at the opinion of the masses for whom she so unassailably spoke. Here again was liberalism's unsolved tension regarding its love/hate relationship with consumerism and mass opinion rising up to bite Franzen from behind.

Chastened by his experience, Franzen retreated from the public eye to ruminate on the literary and political culture that found his confusion (and or pretention) to be so offensive. The decade he spent writing his next novel, *Freedom* (2010), coincided with the Bush years—a time, when, as Franzen noted, "Language was under as concerted an assault as we've seen in my lifetime."[213] "It seemed to me," he told *Time*, "that if we were going to be elevating freedom to the defining principle of what we're about as a culture and a nation, we ought to take a careful look at what freedom in practice brings."[214]

Freedom focused on a middle-class family, the Berglunds, composed of Walter, "the nicest man in Minnesota," and Patty, an ex-jock and now supermom, and their two children, a son, "effortlessly cool, ruggedly confident, totally focused on getting what he want[s], impervious to moralizing, unafraid of girls," and a daughter, who constantly tries to please her parents. A neighbor describes them as "super-guilty liberals who needed to forgive everybody so their own good fortune could be forgiven."[215]

Patty attends colleage via a basketball scholarship at the University of Minnesota, where she meets, Richard Katz, a "self-absorbed, addiction-prone, unreliable, street-smart" rock star in the making, and Richard's roommate, Walter, who is as sober and responsible as Richard is wild. Patty is torn between attraction for Richard and appreciation for Walter, who played the liberal to Richard's radical. When Walter explains, "We disagree about the likelihood of a Marxist Revolution," Richard retorts, "Walter thinks the liberal state can self-correct. He thinks the American bourgeoisie will voluntarily accept increasing restrictions on its personal freedoms."[216] In the part of the novel titled "2004," the lives of the Berglunds take on the characteristics of representative figures from George W. Bush's America. Walter and Patty move to Washington, D.C., so Walter can take a job with a conservative billionaire industrialist, acquiring land for a preservation project. The acquisition of the land comes easily enough, because residents are mired in generational poverty, looking for any way out, and Walter's good intentions end up literally paving their roads, if not to hell, then to the despoilation of the environment he was trying, so desperately and yet so naïvely, to protect. Walter and Patty's ne'er-do-well son, meanwhile, has fallen into the orbit of the head of a neo-conservative think tank "devoted to advocating the unilateral exercise of American military supremacy to make the world freer and safer," But his greed and lust get the best of him and he ends up becoming a kind of minor-league arms dealer, getting rich by selling junked and useless weaponry to the U.S. military and its Iraqi allies.[217]

Franzen's plot has too many twists and turns to be justly described here, but as the novelist Charles Baxter ruefully observed, "*Freedom* attempts to come to terms with the Bush years and is finally defeated by them"—much like liberalism itself. The public sphere is deemed to be the exclusive purview of those Walter Lippmann termed "the charlatan, the jingo and the terror-ist."[218] Americans are so busy pursuing their deeply individualized notions of personal liberty and advancement—"Freedom," in other words—they are incapable even of imagining the kind of communal cooperation that since Roosevelt's New Deal had defined the liberal sense of mission.

With polls indicating disaster in the offing for the 2010 midterm elections, Obama and company allowed their frustration to spill into the public via a series of extremely ill-advised attacks on liberals for their alleged failure to appreciate the administration's achievements. Then-chief of staff Rahm Eman-uel called liberals "fucking retarded" when a small number threatened to withdraw their support over Obama's capitulation on the public option dur-ing the health care fight. (He eventually apologized to retarded people but not, alas, to liberals.) Press Secretary Robert Gibbs, deriding what he termed "the professional left," whined, saying "They will be satisfied when we have Canadian healthcare and we've eliminated the Pentagon." And Obama him-self mocked liberal disappointment at a $30,000-per-person fund-raiser: "Gosh, we haven't yet brought about world peace and I thought that was going to happen quicker."[219]

Not surprisingly, Democrats suffered the defeat that polls had been prom-ising. They gave up 60 seats in the House, saw their Senate majority re-duced, and lost 10 governorships. At the local level, where state and federal redistricting maps were soon to be redrawn and would therefore shape future national elections for the coming decade, Republicans picked up 680 state legislative seats, smashing the previous record of 628 by the Democrats in the post-Watergate election of 1974. It was, overall, the worst performance in the party's history. The scope of defeat far exceeded what might have been expected based on a purely statistical analysis, indicating that voters appeared extraeager to punish Democrats for the previous two years. Moreover, the margin would have been even worse had Republicans not chosen unqualified Tea Party–supported candidates who held what most voters considered to be bizarre political views and thereby enabled vulnerable Senate Democrats to retain their seats.With the understatement that had become a familiar presidential trademark, Obama admitted after the election that he "had spoken of a need for unity" and a "period of postpartisanship" that "didn't work out so well."

The new breed of House Republicans consisted of a much more ideologically obsessed group of hard-liners than even the previous obstructionist one, and they set about frustrating literally every one of Obama's priorities they could, demanding massive budget cuts in exchange for simply agreeing to do business, and going so far as to threaten the good faith and credit of the U.S. government by holding hostage a routine debt-raising limit to demand massive cuts in social programs.[220] Like the Republican governors in Wisconsin, Ohio, Michigan, New Jersey, and elsewhere, they were determined not only to protect the gains of the wealthy during the past four decades from calls for common sacrifice but also to roll back whatever gains working people had been able to achieve dating as far back as the New Deal. Because public unions were seen as liberalism's last bastion of political and economic power (outside of the occasional left-wing billionaire), schoolteachers, emergency workers, and other state employees became the target of a vicious campaign to both defund their treasuries and destroy their power to act in concert. The pitched battle over teachers' right to organize in Wisconsin during the winter months of 2010 and 2011 captured the attention of the nation and, though unsuccessful in the short term from a liberal standpoint, helped to revive some of liberalism's lost fighting spirit.

Meanwhile, the new Republican majority in the House of Representatives was now faced with the task of articulating a positive program of its own, rather than simply rejecting every one of the president's. This gave Obama the opportunity he had needed to—finally—define himself and his principles following two and half bruising years as president.

Tasked with drafting the Republican budget, Representative Paul Ryan of Wisconsin presented one that, if enacted, would destroy Medicare by turning it into a voucher system, end Medicaid, cut a whole host of programs aimed at shoring up the middle class, even as it offered yet another massive cut in taxes for American multimillionaires and billionaires. Obama now had the foil with which to finally offer Americans a positive vision of the version of liberalism he was willing to embrace. Speaking to students at George Washington University, he articulated not merely the policy particulars that undergirded the programs of the New Deal, Fair Deal, and Great Society, but their philosophical foundations as well:

> Part of this American belief that we are all connected also expresses itself in a conviction that each one of us deserves some basic measure of security. We recognize that no matter how responsibly we live our lives, hard times or bad luck, a crippling illness or a layoff, may strike any one of us. "There but for the grace of God go I," we say to ourselves, and so we contribute to programs like Medicare and Social Security, which guarantee us health care and a measure of basic income after a lifetime of hard work; unemployment insurance, which protects us against unexpected job loss; and Medicaid, which provides care for millions of seniors in nursing homes, poor children, and those with disabilities. We are a better country because of these commitments. I'll go further—we would not be a great country without those commitments.

Hearkening to the formula of rights and responsibilities championed by Bill Clinton, Obama went on: "We take responsibility for ourselves and each other; for the country we want and the future we share." From there he reviewed the accomplishments of FDR and LBJ—once again under assault by the Republicans: "We sent a generation to college on the GI bill and saved millions of seniors from poverty with Social Security and Medicare." Americans believed "that in order to preserve our own freedoms and pursue our own happiness, we can't just think about ourselves. We have to think about the country that made those liberties possible. We have to think about our fellow citizens with whom we share a community." Here Obama returned to the theme of communal and aspirational nationalism at the heart of the liberal tradition in the language of the "great society" of JFK's "Ask Not What Your Country" and Martin Luther King's "I Have a Dream" speeches: "This sense of responsibility—to each other and to our country—this isn't a partisan feeling. It isn't a Democratic or Republican idea. It's patriotism."

Despite this fine, albeit long-overdue, speech, as well as the overwhelming popularity of the Democrats' defense of Medicare and Medicaid, even among self-identified Republican voters, when it came to actual policy proposals, Obama continued to play only defense, and to play it badly. When it came to actual negotiations, under Republican threat of allowing the government to default, rather than risk the results of a showdown on behalf of the policies and values he had campaigned on, Obama caved in to virtually every demand his newly empowered opposition could put forward.

The deficit deal contained an alleged, albeit decidedly ill-defined, $2.4 trillion in future cuts in government programs but made no provisions whatsoever for revenue-raising measures. Typical of such last-minute patched-together deals, it did not even address the most significant problem that had given rise to the crisis in the first place: the ballooning cost of Medicare and Medicaid. But from a political standpoint, it offered the now Tea Party–dominated Republicans, as House Speaker John Boehner bragged, "98 percent" of what he had demanded on their behalf.[221] One liberal representative termed the deal "a sugar-coated Satan sandwich."[222] As a result, *The New Republic's* Jonathan Cohn observed that America would suffer "more people eating tainted food, more people breathing polluted air, more people pulling their kids out of college, and more people losing their homes—in other words, the hardships people suffer when government can't do an adequate job of looking out for their interests."[223] Obama's former senior Senate colleague, Illinois Democrat Richard Durbin, surveyed the situation and found himself forced to pronounce "the final interment of John Maynard Keynes": "He normally died in 1946," Durbin explained, "but it appears we are going to put him to his final rest with this agreement."[224] And Obama proved him correct when he proudly proclaimed that the deal would put us on track to reduce nondefense discretionary spending to its lowest level [as a share of GDP] since Dwight Eisenhower was president."[225] This was the same president who, barely two years earlier, had bragged about the level of investment in the economy in exactly the same terms—referencing the Eisenhower presidency—to make exactly the opposite case.

Shortly afterward the author Drew Westen called attention to Obama's primary political weakness, particularly in a moment of intense Republican partisanship: his unwillingness to ascribe any motive to his opponents—or even to admit that he had opponents:

> When he wants to be, the president is a brilliant and moving speaker, but his stories virtually always lack one element: the villain who caused the problem, who is always left out, described in impersonal terms, or described in passive voice, as if the cause of others' misery has no agency and hence no culpability. Whether that reflects his aversion to conflict, an aversion to conflict with potential campaign donors that today cripples both parties' ability to govern and threatens our democracy, or both, is unclear.[226]

As with both Jimmy Carter and Bill Clinton—the only other Democrats to accede to the presidency in the past half century of American politics—Barack

Obama had found it necessary to become a far more conservative president, both in foreign and domestic policy, than the candidate who had actually won the race. Whatever commitment to liberalism Obama had carried with him to White House appeared by now to be a distant memory: American liberalism and those who still felt compelled to fight for it had proved, in three Democratic presidencies in a row, to be no match for the political pressures faced by the man once in office.

Conclusion:
"The Only Honest Place to Be"

Sapere aude! [Dare to know!]
—Immannel Kant

"Historical movements," the historian Mary Jo Buhle rightly notes, "are rarely judged solely in the light they cast themselves."[1] In that light it is a decidedly risky business to draw hard and fast conclusions about the present moment in the history of liberalism from events contemporaneous to the publication of this book. And yet one could not help but be struck by the dramatic turns in the summer months of 2011. As President Barack Obama found himself forced to begin the dismantlement of some of the most significant accomplishments of the New Deal and Great Society merely to entice his political opposition to agree to allow the U.S. government to pay its debts, the New York governor, Democrat Andrew Cuomo—son of former governor Mario Cuomo—was simultaneously concluding a remarkable run of legislative victories in what had famously been one of America's most dysfunctional state legislatures.[2]

The most significant of these was New York's new law legalizing gay marriage. To win the necessary votes, Cuomo turned to top-dollar Republican donors who, according to a *New York Times* report, "had the influence and the money to insulate nervous senators from conservative backlash if they supported the marriage measure."[3] It was a thrilling moment, not only for gays, but for liberals looking for a leader who refused to be cowed by the scare tactics of conservative Christians.[4]

Andrew Cuomo was no radical, however—the law was, in fact, popular with more than 60 percent of New Yorkers polled—and the respective roles he undertook as governor provided a picture-perfect incarnation of the transformation of American liberalism from its New Deal origins. Under Roosevelt's presidency, liberalism became a political movement focused on improving the lives of working people and those who needed a helping hand from government. In Obama's America (and Cuomo's New York), however, liberalism was primarily a movement designed to increase social and cultural freedoms for those who could afford to enjoy them. Cultural liberalism, while not without political risk, did not cost the wealthy anything or restrict their ability to become even wealthier. As such, it proved a far easier sell in a political system like that in the United States in the twenty-first century, dominated, as it was, by the power of money.

The difference between the Cuomos, father and son, offers a telling illustration of this transformation. Recall the role that Mario Cuomo had played in rejuvenating both the language and the spirit of the New Deal with the series of mid-1980s addresses he gave in opposition to Ronald Reagan's Social Darwinist reading of the American creed, culminating with his 1984 Democratic convention speech. As one journalist observed, "Mario was an FDR liberal (and child of immigrants) with an unyielding faith in the government's power to improve people's lives."[5] Andrew, in turn, was the product of a political era described by Nobel laureate economist Joseph Stiglitz as "of the one percent, by the one percent, for the one percent."[6] Despite being elected to run the bluest of blue states in 2010, Andrew Cuomo governed, in the words of the local news columnist Michael Powell, like "a bulldog for the rich." In the same legislative session that legalized gay marriage Cuomo engineered a cap on annual increases in the amount of property taxes collected by local school districts. He presided over a budget that forced the firing of twenty-six hundred New York City teachers and laid off one thousand city workers, many of whom were involved in health care for the poor, at a time when the need for both could hardly be greater.[7] And finally, and most energetically, Cuomo fought to ensure the demise of New York State's millionaire tax at the moment when its proceeds might have been able to prevent the kinds of cuts being enforced.[8] These were the priorities of a man who occupied the office once held not only by his father but also by Franklin D. Roosevelt before him.

Cuomo's commitment to the abolition of the millionaire tax was particularly illuminating and for economic liberals deeply depressing. The surcharge, which affected only citizens earning $1 million or more per year, garnered the support of 72 percent of state residents polled in October 2011. It would have generated an estimated $2.8 billion, or more than a quarter of the state's projected budget deficit. What's more, it had become a focal point of the first genuinely populist progressive movement to arise in decades. The so-called 99 Percent took to occupying public spaces—like New York's Zucotti Park near Wall Street—to demand an end to taxation and fiscal policies that served the interests of only the country's wealthiest

1 percent. The millionaire's tax enjoyed the energetic support of almost all traditional liberal constituencies in the New York legislature, including its labor union–supported representatives, as well as its black, Puerto Rican, Hispanic, and Asian caucuses. But acting in concert with the body's Republicans, Cuomo scuttled the tax and then went on to compare his lone wolf position with that of his father's unstinting opposition to the death penalty. "The fact that everybody wants it, that doesn't mean all that much," he explained, apparently without noticing that his father's lonely stand had been taken on behalf of prisoners on death row, rather than multimillionaires on Wall Street.[9]

Andrew Cuomo's agenda, like the nascent 99 Percent movement, was less a cause of the transformation of American liberalism than its product. In the years since his father had begun seeking public office, economic inequality in the United States surged into territory unseen in more than a century. In 1974 the top 0.1 percent of American families earned 2.7 percent of all income in the country. By 2007 this same tiny slice of the population had increased its holdings to fully 12.3 percent, roughly five times as great a piece of the pie as it had enjoyed just three decades earlier.[10] Half the U.S. population owned barely 2 percent of its wealth, putting the United States near Rwanda and Uganda and below such nations as pre–Arab Spring Tunisia and Egypt when measured by degrees of income inequality.[11] By the end of 2010, as corporate profits rose to 14 percent of national income—their biggest share of the economy since such statistics became available nearly seventy years earlier—the share going to workers' wages fell to its lowest level in the same period.[12] However much the election of an African American president was a point of pride for liberals, the fact remained that at two years into his historic presidency, white Americans enjoyed, on average, median wealth of twenty times that of black households and eighteen times that of Hispanic households.[13]

Months before the passage of New York's gay marriage legislation, President Obama caved into Republican demands to slash the budget for spending for the poor and middle class and extended the Bush-era tax cuts for Americans lucky enough to earn more than $250,000 annually. Shortly thereafter, during the debt limit debacle, he conceded even more on the economic front, agreeing to additional budget reductions without winning any new tax revenues from the wealthy, whose tax breaks were now secure. As a result, liberals found themselves faced with two vexing questions raised by Robert Kuttner, cofounder of the liberal public policy magazine *The American Prospect*: "First, how did we make such stunning progress in three decades on issues involving tolerance and inclusiveness? And how is it that, during the same period, we have gone steadily backwards on a whole set of economic issues?"[14]

The short answer lies in the power and influence Americans have allowed money to assume in their politics. "We can have democracy in this country, or we can have great wealth concentrated in the hands of a few," the great liberal jurist Louis Brandeis prophesied in the second decade of the twentieth century. "But we can't have both."[15] Once again, this problem has a multiplicity of tangled causes. According to the political scientists Jacob Hacker and Paul Pierson, for instance, the number of political action committees (PACs) grew from under three hundred in 1976 to nearly five thousand by 2010.[16] The amount of money these PACs control and direct toward politicians of both parties on issues of concern has the power to overcome almost any group of voters who attempt to organize themselves in opposition. One can observe this power at work on almost any issue of concern to any industry in both local and national political contests, and it has the effect not only of getting the wealthy what they want from politicians but also of destroying the faith of citizens in their democracy. When, for instance, Senator Richard Durbin (D-Ill.), speaking of the banking industry's relationship to Congress, tells the journalist Bill Moyers "They frankly own the place," he is saying something not only about the power of money to get what it wants but also about the failure of democracy.[17]

Financial power is not measured merely on the basis of the votes it controls. It can also define potential alternatives, discredit opposing arguments, inundate with propaganda, and threaten with merely hypothetical opposition, most of which is aimed at frustrating reform and maintaining the status quo. As Antonio Gramsci explained in his famous prison notebooks in the 1930s— as paraphrased by the British labor historian Gwyn Williams—such power can create "an order in which a certain way of life and thought is dominant, in which one concept of reality is infused throughout society in all its institutional and private manifestations, informing with its spirit all taste, morality, customs, religious and political principles, and all social relations, particularly in their intellectual and moral connotation."[18]

The lobbyists' power in Congress rests on the massive investment that corporations and wealthy individuals had been making since the mid-1960s to remake American political and economic thought in their own image. Their well-funded think tanks, public policy journals, and editorial writers championed the arguments of Austrian economist Friedrich von Hayek and his American counterpart, monetarist Milton Friedman, to replace what had previously been a global Keynesian consensus with their preferred model, one based on lower taxes, weaker regulation, and less government. It was in this period, as intellectual historian Daniel T. Rodgers observes, that the "near-global dominance of the new political economy" became evident. "Faith in the wisdom and the efficiency of markets, disdain for big government taxation, spending and regulation, reverence for a globalized world of flexible labor pools, free trade and free-floating capital" became the dominant ideology of American politics.[19]

Undoubtedly Americans' historic distrust of government offered fertile ground for such arguments. It was the liberal hero Thomas Paine, who, after all, first called government "a necessary evil" and Henry David Thoreau, who, writing in support of civil disobedience, observed that "the government is best which governs least." An autumn 2011 CNN/ORC international poll found that fewer than one in seven Americans trusted the government "to do what's right almost always or most of the time," an all-time low since University of Michigan pollsters began asking the question in 1958.[20] This was approximately the same anemic percentage of those questioned who, in a previous poll, expressed confidence in the government's "ability to stand up to vested interests." A related problem is a lack of trust in elites: citizens do not believe that the programs politicians propose will last or make any difference if they do, and they do not vote their own interests because all they see are the likely costs.[21]

The governing style of the Obama administration only reinforced these beliefs. As the Democratic pollster and political scientist Stanley Greenberg wrote in July 2011, "The government saved irresponsible executives who bankrupted their own companies, hurt many people and threatened the welfare of the country. When Mr. Obama championed the bailout of the auto companies and allowed senior executives at bailed-out companies to take bonuses, voters concluded that he was part of the operating elite consensus."[22]

As we have seen, liberals' inability to unite the poor and the middle classes in America is profoundly complicated by historical circumstances—specifically the divisions of race and (to a lesser extent) ethnicity—that continue to define so many citizens' identities. If the great welfare states of Northern Europe have had, at least until recently, one characteristic in common, it has been racial and ethnic homogeneity: People, it turns out, do not generally appreciate subsidizing, through tax and transfer policies, the lifestyles of those they deem to be different from themselves. The history of American liberalism through the New Deal and Fair Deal periods was one of steady progress so long as it excluded the demand for full political and social equality for minorities, particularly blacks.

As the political scientist Ira Katznelson has demonstrated, this exclusion was intentional, and from the standpoint of the success of its white beneficiaries, largely successful.[23] In areas where this de facto apartheid was not observed—for instance, the U.S. labor movement—the reaction from southerners in particular, but also many others, was to abandon the liberal alliance in favor of racist reaction. This split helped ensure that U.S. labor unions never achieved the power and influence of their European counterparts and have since dwindled to barely 8 percent of the private workforce.

When combined with the relative loss of economic autonomy experienced by all capitalist countries as a result of the transformations wrought by a technology-driven communications revolution coupled with an increasingly borderless, frictionless environment for global trade, corporations now enjoy the option of moving production to any nation that offers the "friendliest" environment for its profits. This "race to the bottom" profoundly constrains liberals' ability, when in power, to deliver on their promises to offer workers minimal meaningful protection for their right to organize and thereby defend their wages or work conditions, or their communities' ability to protect their natural resources and environments.

Today, with the never-ending spigot of corporate funding for antiunion legislation both at a local and national level, unions had to muster all of their strength merely to defend their right to exist while lacking the resources and, in many cases, the self-confidence to take the offensive. With Democratic politicians increasingly dependent on the funding by a cadre of socially liberal multimillionaires who believe not only in individual Franzen-style "freedom," but also in unfettered global trade and generally low corporate taxation policies, unions discovered that they had to fight inside as well as outside of their own troubled houses.

As a result of these and other trends, organized labor in the United States was literally fighting to survive in the private economy as the decimation of the U.S. manufacturing base not only cut into the numbers of those who joined unions but also, consequentially, undermined the ability of those unions to protect and defend their workers. The entry into the global work force of as many as two billion workers from developing nations eager to work for a fraction of what American workers had come to expect further undercut the government's power to improve their ability to compete in a global economy. Technological trends, which encouraged the outsourcing not only of manufacturing jobs, as had been happening for decades, but also of service jobs and particularly information-industry jobs that were once the purview of the educated upper-middle class but could now be done either by machines or by undercompensated workers abroad, threatened to cut out an entire swath of the economy: the middle management and semisuccessful professional class in such places as law firms and accounting firms.

Many political reversals may have been unavoidable, but liberals exacerbated them by failing to place these constituents' interests at the center of their political narrative and formulating a politics designed to address their plight. Daniel Patrick Moynihan's formulation, of "overpromising and underforming," was surely a part of the problem. But the syndrome from which liberals suffered went deeper than mere bravado. As Lionel Trilling so presciently observed, the liberal certainty of being on the side of angels can easily blind one to "all the ways good can produce bad, through unintended consequences, or unacknowledged motives, or fanatical zeal."[24] When the results of any given program fail to live up to one's hopes for it—as is almost always the case—instead of examining their assumptions or rethinking their ambitions, liberals too often blame the objects of their alleged affections: the people themselves. But the liberal failure to master the politics of class cannot be allowed to obscure the even more serious (and complicated) problems that face liberals regarding race. While the achievement of full political equality for all Americans was undoubtedly the right and proper goal in the 1960s, the word "liberal" would cease to have any meaning if those associated with it had failed to heed the call of Martin Luther King, Jr., and the nonviolent revolution he preached, no matter the political cost. Even so, the price need not have been quite as high as it turned out to be. The call for racial equality inevitably upset and angered many white Americans whose views had been formed by a time and place in which equality between the races was literally unthinkable. Even so, the callousness with which liberal politicians treated the genuine concerns of so many white working men and woman as they sought to address, and when possible, reverse the consequences of racial discrimination was truly politically perverse and morally difficult to justify. The simultaneous postsixties liberal embrace both of the politics of "victimhood" and "identity" splintered their movement as it simultaneously alienated the only people who could ensure its enactment.

When liberals began lecturing voters about whose grievances might be considered legitimate and whose might not, they granted themselves a degree of moral authority that few of their fellow citizens believed that they had earned. A degree from Harvard's Kennedy School of Government or an appointment as a Ford Foundation program officer was not viewed in middle-class America as a license to remake an entire neighborhood or rewrite a social contract that had evolved over a period of decades or even centuries. Add to this their suspicions that their taxes were being raised for the sole purpose of subsidizing those whose lifestyles and values they not only found offensive but whom they also believed to be the cause of skyrocketing crime rates and property destruction they experienced and you had all the ingredients for a genuine populist revolt—if not against liberalism itself, then certainly against liberals. In spite of resentment that programs designed to "right" the historical wrongs of officially sanctioned racial exclusion, gender and sexual discrimination, and so on, liberals added gasoline to the fire that threatened to consume them by embracing a politics that emphasized these differences rather than one that sought to forge commonality and cooperation among their various constituencies. Too often in postwar history liberal activists appeared more concerned with claiming moral victories that allowed them to remain comfortable in their small enclaves of the like-minded while conservatives concentrated on winning the votes and the allegiance of the middle classes with values and solidarity-based appeals that exploited their growing alienation from liberals as they simultaneously stoked their resentments. While idealism is a necessity to any form of liberalism, it must be grounded in the self-interest of the majority. As Barack Obama learned on the job on the South Side of Chicago, "The key to creating successful organizations was making sure people's self-interest was met and not just basing it on pie-in-the-sky idealism."[25]

At the same time that liberals were alienating their own constituents, they failed to show sufficient mettle when facing their enemies. The shock of McCarthyism drained them of much of their self-confidence, as did the debacle in Vietnam. Attacks from the right during the former period and from the left, and later the right, in the latter, led liberals to feel compelled to demonstrate their manhood in virtually every potential conflict with another nation, no matter how self-destructive this impulse might have been. Vietnam is the most obvious example of liberalism's inability to allocate resources effectively between guns and butter, but one can find any number of similar calculations regarding the liberal position vis-à-vis America's conflicts in Central America, the Middle East, Southern Asia, and the Persian Gulf. Following 1967, the need to defend Israel in whatever circumstances that might arise as a result of its conflict either with the Palestinians or the larger Arab world further restricted maneuvering room in liberal foreign policy. The powerful pro-Israel lobby American Israel Public Affairs Committee (AIPAC) would often demand of liberals that they support higher U.S. defense budgets and additional U.S. military aid not only to Israel, but also to nations friendly to Israel, regardless of how regressive their policies. Those who disagreed offered little or no political counterweight in response. As a result of the need to prove that they could be just as tough, just as reckless, just as willing to squander the blood and treasure of the United States for frivolous reasons as trigger-happy hawks, liberals never really had the opportunity to develop a foreign policy consistent with their own values as well as with the national interests of the United States. Their disinclination to challenge out-of-control expenditures on guns only complicated their attempts to persuade Americans to open their wallets to pay for butter. Americans' infamous taxophobia—particularly when compared with European nations' (and Canada's) willingness to fund far more generous welfare states—has many sources, but a key one is the fact that because so much of the discretionary budget is devoted to defense, they have not been given the opportunity to experience the benefits of social spending in the same way other nations' citizens do.

Meanwhile, liberals found themselves under relentless assault from a re-markably well-funded, well-organized—and, as political movements go—well-disciplined revanchist political right wing. Thanks to the massive ongoing investment of billions of dollars by corporations and wealthy individuals, the media, for instance, which had been generally friendly territory for liberal causes throughout the midseventies, gradually turned into hostile ground. The new American conservatives were remarkably Manichaean—if you were not conservative as they defined the term, you were de facto biased against them—and did an impressive job of persuading the men and women of the main-stream media to adopt their ideologically driven political taxonomy.

To take just one example of cable television, in prime time Rupert Murdoch's Fox News Channel regularly attracts more viewers than both competitors combined. This is a matter of considerable political significance for any ambitious liberal because the number one cable news network in America just happens to be dedicated to a program of purposeful misinformation rather than any honest accounting of the news. Fox News Channel is often described as a cable news station. On occasion, the word "conservative" or "biased" is attached to that description. But few dispute the journalistic orientation of the overall enterprise. This is a mistake. Fox is something new—something for which we do not yet have a word. It provides little if any actual journalism. Instead, it gives ideological guidance to the Republican Party and millions of its supporters, attacking its opponents and keeping its supporters in line.

But even to focus on so significant a force as Fox is to miss an entire forest for a few trees. Its parent company, NewsCorp, enjoys a media empire that is vast and wide, and it deliberately slants the news while shamelessly promoting blatant disinformation platforms all over the world. Together with the countless other right-wing political organizations funded by conservative billionaires and large global corporations, these campaigns raise the cost of liberalism to individuals and organizations to include a guarantee of a campaign of slander and purposeful disinformation should one rise to prominence in contemporary American political culture.

One result of this constant barrage of deliberately disseminated conservative disinformation—much of it thoughtlessly repeated elsewhere in the media—could be seen in poll results relating both to liberals in general and Democratic politicians in particular. In four straight polls published in the fall of 2011, for instance, voters were shown "to strongly disapprove of Obama on the economy, and are deeply pessimistic that it will get any better—even as they solidly approve[d] of the actual fiscal policies the President is championing."[26]

While the president and his team were far from blameless for their own failure to communicate their political and economic arguments more effectively, it is necessary to note as well that the problem was in part a reflection of the disjunction in the use of political labels that became the norm within the U.S. media. Consistently, polls demonstrated that while most Americans remained unwilling to answer to the "liberal" label—liberals made up roughly 37 percent of self-described Democrats and about 20 percent of voters generally—when "moderates" were questioned by pollsters, they turned out to share almost exactly the same beliefs that "liberals" did. A significant number of Americans undoubtedly shared the views of liberals, but resisted the appellation as a result, no doubt, of the avalanche of opprobrium and distortion that had been heaped on liberals—and indeed the word itself—in so much of the media and the political world at large.[27]

Due to the strength of its conservative adversaries and the structural difficulties of governing, the Obama presidency only grew more tentative, less confident, and more aware of its limitations. While the notion of a "liberal consensus" had always proved more of a hope than reality, it had now come to be regarded as a kind of impossible dream. A glib *New York Times* writer joked in May 2011 that he would not be surprised if readers "thought that liberals had been eradicated through some kind of spraying program or inoculation. No elected official has admitted to being one since the Carter administration, and the very word 'liberal' ranks right up there with 'care to respond to the rumors about your love child?' as guaranteed to make Sunday morning talk-show guests change the subject."[28]

America has undoubtedly become a fairer, more open, and less oppressive society thanks largely to the political and cultural struggles waged by the liberals described in this book. The progress in securing basic human decency for the old, the infirm, women, African Americans, and other ethnic and racial minorities, gays and lesbians, immigrants and their children, Americans with disabilities, and so many others is a testament to their courage in the face of adversity and oppression. This was the work of "those who marched and those who sang, those who sat in and those who stood firm, those who organized and those who mobilized," as Barack Obama recalled on the October 2011 occasion of the unveiling of the Martin Luther King, Jr., memorial statue on the National Mall in Washington, D.C., and "all those men and women who through countless acts of quiet heroism helped bring about changes few thought were even possible."[29] As Robert Kuttner rightly observes, "They changed norms, then laws, which reinforced the shift in norms."[30]

But the fact remains that on the economic front, contemporary liberals find themselves on the defensive in virtually every respect. Liberalism, much like Obama at the outset of his presidency, was torn between commitments to preserve the necessary civility in political life and a desire to pursue substantive values of justice and equity. Lionel Trilling had given voice to this frustration when he told Richard Sennett, "Between [was] the only honest place to be."[31] Daniel Bell and Walter Lippmann had likewise insisted on the importance of "educated elites" to "mediate between the passions of the people and the realistic needs of a modern democracy."[32] Today liberalism has pledged itself to rationality in a political culture in which anti-intellectualism runs rampant.

The practice of liberal politics, the philosopher Michael Walzer observes, is difficult "because it offers so few emotional rewards; the liberal state is not a home for its citizens; it lacks warmth and intimacy."[33] Lacking universal foundations—recall that Trilling termed it "a large tendency rather than a concise body of doctrine"—liberalism can offer only narratives of sacrifice and common purpose, ones that can easily be trumped by the tales of the right, which frequently combine libertarianism with jingoism, fear mongering, and other easily pushed emotional buttons that tend to drown out the more idealistic homilies that liberals put forth.[34] As Richard Hofstadter feared nearly sixty years ago, "in a populistic culture like ours, which seems to lack a responsible elite with political and moral autonomy, and in which it is possible to exploit the wildest currents of public sentiment for private purposes," it would be "at least conceivable that a highly organized, vocal, active, and well-financed minority could create a political climate in which the rational pursuit of our well-being and safety would become impossible."[35] By the summer of

2011 this "pseudoconservative revolt" was in the driver's seat of American politics. And all liberals could do was hold on for dear life.

Ironically, it is at moments in a nation's history when liberalism is most difficult to practice that its defense is most desperately needed. This task need not be as difficult as recent history has made it appear. While the policies that liberals support may have changed—indeed, sometimes even reversed themselves—over the past three centuries, the inspiration for them has not. To be a liberal, now, as then, means, fundamentally, to be a child of the Enlightenment. It means standing firm on behalf of the foundational freedoms of thought, expression, and the necessity of individuals to take hold of their collective fates and shape them according to the values of liberty and equality, while being fully aware that the two must always coexist in tension with each other. While the word "liberal" has come to imply many ideas and commitments over the past two centuries, only those that honor what John Kenneth Galbraith called "the emancipation of belief" are worthy of it.[36] Liberalism's guiding spirit can be found in the words of Immanuel Kant, who in 1784 proclaimed: "*Sapere aude!* [Dare to know!] 'Have courage to use your own understanding!'—that is the motto of enlightenment."[37]

The liberals who founded America believed themselves to be inventing a new form of government based on these Enlightenment precepts. They aspired to create a nation of what Thomas Jefferson termed a nation of "natural aristocrats," a term they associated not with family lineage but rather with what they deemed to be enlightened values. Gordon Wood defines these as the qualities of "being reasonable, tolerant, honest, virtuous, and candid." Further, they implied "standing on elevated ground in order to have a large view of human affairs, and being free of the prejudices, parochialism and religious enthusiasm of the vulgar and barbaric."[38] Inspired by the misery caused by the failure of private enterprise to lift the country out of the Great Depression, Franklin Roosevelt expanded this definition. Unlike what he called "the conservative party," which—then as today—"honestly and conscientiously believes" that "in the long run, individual initiative and private philanthropy can take care of all situations," the "militant liberalism" of the New Deal promised to employ the resources of government to "protect its people against disasters once considered inevitable, to solve problems once considered unsolvable."[39]

Under FDR's leadership Democrats doubled their percentage of the popular vote in presidential elections. By 1934 they held more than 70 percent of the House and Senate.[40] They won five consecutive presidential elections—a feat no party had ever or has ever matched—and nine of the next ten congressional elections, as well.[41] Roosevelt achieved these victories, it must be added, with a record of decidedly mixed success in grappling with the catastrophic economic situation he and his fellow liberals had inherited. But as the historian Lizabeth Cohen suggests, its success "should be measured less by the lasting accomplishments of its reforms and more by the attitudinal changes it produced in a generation of working-class Americans who now looked to Washington to deliver the American dream."[42]

Ronald Reagan's subsequent success in transforming the political discourse in the opposite direction was in many respects the mirror image of Roosevelt's own accomplishment. If both presidents met with decidedly mixed success in policy terms, each succeeded in reshaping American political culture because the optimism and self-confidence of the respective visions they offered captured the imagination of a majority of Americans, most particularly young Americans.

If liberal fortunes are ever to revive, liberals must find a way to recapture this simultaneously militant and optimistic spirit. The "larger message" for what Roosevelt called "the liberal party" was a clear and simple one: "As new conditions and problems arise beyond the power of men and women to meet as individuals, it becomes the duty of the Government itself to find new remedies with which to meet them."[43] Add to this John Dewey's precept "that government should regularly intervene to help equalize conditions between the wealthy and the poor, between the overprivileged and the underprivileged," while acknowledging Reinhold Niebuhr's prescient warnings about the need for "humility" in all such undertakings, and you have a concise, compelling statement of what it means—then as now—to call oneself an "American liberal."[44]

When liberals lose confidence in their ability to lead Americans toward some version of this vision, they lose their reason for being liberals. The previous pages have tried telling the story of how the men and women who spoke for and acted in this tradition have sought to turn this vision into a reality, and thereby help make American society a more free and equal place for all of its members. What they demonstrate, whether in success, failure, or more frequently, something in-between is the necessity of self-confidence. If the postwar history of liberalism has a single lesson to teach us, it is that what liberals have to fear—far more than conservatives—is fear itself.

Notes

Introduction: Nothing to Fear

1. Arthur M. Schlesinger, Jr., "Two Years Later—the Roosevelt Family," *Life* (April 7, 1947), 113.
2. Jon Meacham, *Franklin and Winston: An Intimate Portrait of an Epic Friendship* (New York: Random House, 2003), 343.
3. Diane Shaver Clemens, *Yalta* (New York: Oxford University Press, 1970), 103–4.
4. *New York Times*, April 13, 1945, 10; *Washington Post*, April 14, 1945, 1.
5. Quoted in Doris Kearns Goodwin, "Person of the Century Runner-Up: Franklin Delano Roosevelt," *Time* (January 3, 2000).
6. Bill Moyers, "Moyers & FDR," *The Nation* (December 10, 2007), 13.
7. Alan Brinkley, *Liberalism and Its Discontents* (Cambridge, MA: Harvard University Press, 1998), 17.
8. Sidney Hertzberg, "Politics after Roosevelt," *Common Sense* (May 1945), 3.
9. Brinkley, *Liberalism and Its Discontents*, 2.
10. William E. Leuchtenburg, *Franklin D. Roosevelt and the New Deal, 1932–1940* (New York: Harper & Row, 1963), 165. See also H. W. Brands, *Traitor to His Class: The Privileged Life and Radical Presidency of Franklin Delano Roosevelt* (New York: Doubleday, 2008).
11. David E. Lilienthal, *TVA: Democracy on the March* (1944; repr., Chicago: Quadrangle, 1966), 225; Roosevelt quoted in Arthur M. Schlesinger, Jr., *The Politics of Upheaval* (Boston: Houghton Mifflin, 1988), 375.
12. Harry C. Boyte and Nancy N. Kari, *Building America: The Democratic Promise of Public Work* (Philadelphia: Temple University Press, 1996).
13. Franklin D. Roosevelt, "Roosevelt's 1932 Nomination Speech," reprinted in *The Public Papers and Addresses of Franklin D. Roosevelt*, Vol. 1, 1928–32, (New York: Random House, 1938), 647.
14. FDR quoted in Frances Perkins, *The Roosevelt I Knew* (New York: Harper & Row, 1964), 330.
15. Jane Addams, *Twenty Years at Hull-House* (1910; repr., New York: Macmillan, 1960), 97; see also Louise W. Knight, *Citizen: Jane Addams and the Struggle for Democracy* (Chicago: University of Chicago Press, 2005), 173–74; Arthur M. Schlesinger, Jr., *The Crisis of the Old Order, 1919–1933* (Boston: Houghton Mifflin, 1957), 22–23.
16. Arthur M. Schlesinger, Jr., *The Age of Jackson* (Boston: Little Brown, 1945), 505, 312. See also Marvin Meyers, *The Jacksonian Persuasion* (Stanford, CA: Stanford University Press, 1957), 19–21.
17. The producerist ideology of southern farmers is discussed in Steven Hahn, *The Roots of Southern Populism* (New York: Oxford University Press, 1983), 282.
18. See for instance Richard Hofstadter, *The Age of Reform* (New York: Knopf, 1955), Chapter 7; see also Gary Gerstle, "The Protean Character of American Liberalism," *American Historical Review* 99 (1994), 1043–44. Some historians have argued that populists themselves were modern in their approach to reform. See Charles Postel, *The Populist Vision* (New York: Oxford University Press, 2007).
19. For a learned and useful discussion of the ideas and influence of many of these thinkers, see Jonathan I. Israel, *Enlightenment Contested: Philosophy, Modernity and the Emancipation of Man, 1670–1752* (New York: Oxford University Press, 2006).
20. Reinhold Niebuhr, "Liberalism: Illusions and Realities," *The New Republic* (July 4, 1955), http://www.tnr.com/article/politics/liberalism-illusions-and-realities.
21. Jo Ann Boydston, ed., *John Dewey: The Later Works 1925–1953* (Carbondale, IL: Southern Illinois University Press, 1991), 364–65.
22. "Commonwealth Club Speech," in Hofstadter, ed., *Great Issues*, 347.
23. Herbert Croly, *The Promise of American Life* (1909; repr., New York: Capricorn, 1964), 23.
24. Ibid., 284.

25. Ibid., 169.
26. On the relations between the growth in executive power and the Progressive Era, see Maureen Flanagan, *America Reformed*, 283.
27. Quoted in McGerr, *A Fierce Discontent*, 162.
28. Quoted in ibid., 317.
29. John Milton Cooper, *The Warrior and the Priest: Woodrow Wilson and Theodore Roosevelt* (Cambridge, MA: Belknap Press, 1983), 259.
30. Franklin D. Roosevelt, excerpted from the "Annual Message to the Congress, January 6, 1941," http://www.americanrhetoric.com/speeches/fdrthefourfreedoms.htm.
31. Franklin D. Roosevelt, in Hofstadter, ed., *Great Issues*, 350.
32. John Patrick Diggins, *The Proud Decades: America in War and Peace, 1941–1960* (New York: Norton, 1988), 21–22.
33. Franklin D. Roosevelt, "State of the Union Message to Congress, January 11, 1944," http://docs.fdrlibrary.marist.edu/011144.html.
34. For a useful discussion of the ideas underlying Roosevelt's foreign policy, see Warren F. Kimball, "The Sheriffs: FDR's Postwar World" in David B. Woolner, Warren F. Kimball, and David Reynolds, eds., *FDR's World: War, Peace, and Legacies* (New York: Palgrave Macmillan, 2008), 92. See also Kimball, *The Juggler: Franklin Roosevelt as Wartime Statesman* (Princeton: Princeton University Press, 1991); Richard J. Barnet, *The Rockets' Red Glare: When America Goes to War: The Presidents and the People* (New York: Simon & Schuster, 1990), 214; Robert Dallek, *Franklin D. Roosevelt and American Foreign Policy: 1932–1945* (New York: Oxford University Press, 1979). For a discussion of FDR's concept of "Americanism," specifically, see Kimball, "The Sheriffs" in *FDR's World*.
35. Jefferson to Joseph Priestley, March 21, 1801, Paul L. Ford, ed., *The Works of Thomas Jefferson*, vol. 9 (New York: Putnam, 1905), 218.
36. Leo Strauss, *Thoughts on Machiavelli* (Glencoe, IL: The Free Press, 1958), 13.
37. Thomas M. Campbell and George C. Herring, eds., *The Diaries of Edward R. Stettinius, Jr., 1943–1946* (New York: New Viewpoints, 1975), 214.
38. Warren Kimball, "The Sheriffs," 100–101.
39. Brinkley, *Liberalism and Its Discontents*, 65.
40. David M. Kennedy, *Freedom from Fear: The American People in Depression and War, 1929–1945* (New York: Oxford University Press, 1999), 767.
41. Gunnar Myrdal, *An American Dilemma: The Negro Problem and Modern Democracy* (New York: Harper & Bros., 1944), lxi; Walter Jackson, *Gunnar Myrdal and America's Conscience: Social Engineering and Racial Liberalism, 1938–1987* (Chapel Hill: University of North Carolina Press, 1990), 161–73, 197–201.
42. Quoted in Kennedy, *Freedom from Fear*, 808.
43. Richard H. Pells, *The Liberal Mind in a Conservative Age: American Intellectuals in the 1940s and 1950s* (Middletown, CT: Wesleyan University Press, 1989), 12–13; Thomas G. Paterson, *On Every Front: The Making of the Cold War* (New York: Norton, 1979), 31.
44. Alan Brinkley, "The Idea of the State," in Steve Fraser and Gary Gerstle, eds., *The Rise and Fall of the New Deal Order, 1930–1980* (Princeton: Princeton University Press, 1989). Brinkley argues that liberalism always suffered from the weak state tradition inherent in America's past. See also his *The End of Reform: New Deal Liberalism in Recession and War* (New York: Vintage, 1996).
45. On the cutting of New Deal programs, see Brinkley, *Liberalism and Its Discontents*, 97.
46. Schlesinger, Jr., *The Politics of Upheaval*, 648.
47. Ibid., 423.
48. Mary Sperling McAuliffe, *Crisis on the Left: Cold War Politics and American Liberals, 1947–1954* (Amherst, MA: University of Massachusetts Press, 1978), 10.
49. Nelson Lichtenstein, *State of the Union: A Century of American Labor* (Princeton: Princeton University Press, 2002), 72.
50. See Clark Clifford's remarks in Arthur M. Schlesinger, Jr., *A Life in the 20th Century: Innocent Beginnings, 1917–1950* (Boston: Houghton Mifflin, 2000), 487; Kenneth S. Davis, *FDR: The New Deal Years, 1933–1937* (New York: Random House, 1979), 20.
51. Pells, *The Liberal Mind in a Conservative Age*, 9.
52. Schlesinger, Jr., *The Politics of Upheaval*, 563; see for instance Howard Brick, *Daniel Bell and the Decline of Intellectual Radicalism: Social Theory and Political Reconciliation in the 1940s* (Madison, WI: University of Wisconsin Press, 1986); and Pells, *The Liberal Mind in a Conservative Age*.

53. Reinhold Niebuhr to Arthur M. Schlesinger, Jr., April 15, 1954, letter in Niebuhr Papers, Library of Congress, Washington, DC. See also Schlesinger, Jr., "Reinhold Niebuhr's Role in Political Thought," in Charles W. Kegley and Robert W. Bretall, eds., *Reinhold Niebuhr: His Religious, Social, and Political Thought* (New York: Macmillan, 1961), 143.

1 | Henry, Harry, and Eleanor: Three Faces of Liberalism

1. Alonzo L. Hamby, *Man of the People: A Life of Harry S. Truman*, 313.
2. I. F. Stone, "Farewell to F.D.R." (April 21, 1945), in Peter Osnos and Karl Weber, eds., *The Best of I. F. Stone,* (New York: Public Affairs, 2006), 311–12.
3. David McCullough, *Truman* (New York: Simon & Schuster, 1992), 459–63.
4. Robert Dallek, *Harry S. Truman* (New York: Times Books, 2008), 5.
5. Ibid., 10.
6. Ibid., 11.
7. See Jonathan Daniels, *The Man of Independence* (Philadelphia: Lippincott, 1950), 285.
8. Ibid., 278.
9. See John Lewis Gaddis, "The Insecurities of Victory," in *The Long Peace: Inquiring into the History of the Cold War* (New York: Oxford University Press, 1987).
10. See Peter Grosse, *Operation Rollback: America's Secret War behind the Iron Curtain* (Boston: Houghton Mifflin, 2000), 70; and William Taubman, *Stalin's American Policy: From Entente to Détente to Cold War* (New York: Norton, 1982), 259.
11. Quoted in Robert H. Ferrell, *Harry S. Truman: A Life* (Columbia, MO: University of Missouri Press, 1996), 265.
12. Alonzo L. Hamby, *Beyond the New Deal: Harry S. Truman and American Liberalism* (New York: Columbia University Press, 1973), 48.
13. Quoted in Arthur M. Schlesinger, Jr., *A Life in the 20th Century: Innocent Beginnings, 1917–1950* (Boston: Houghton Mifflin, 2000), 406.
14. Gardner Jackson, "Henry Wallace: A Divided Mind," *The Atlantic Monthly* (August 1948), http://www.theatlantic.com/magazine/archive/1969/12/henry-wallace-a-divided-mind/6029/.
15. Hamby, *Beyond the New Deal*, 22–23.
16. See Norman D. Markowitz, *The Rise and Fall of the People's Century: Henry A. Wallace and American Liberalism, 1941–1948* (New York: Free Press, 1973), 89–90.
17. Quoted in ibid., 16.
18. Quoted in James A. Farley, *Jim Farley's Story—The Roosevelt Years* (New York: Whittlesey House, 1948), 293–94.
19. Quoted in John C. Culver and John Hyde, *American Dreamer: The Life and Times of Henry A. Wallace* (New York: Norton, 2000), 328; Ronald Steel, *Walter Lippmann and the American Century* (New York: Vintage, 1980), 435.
20. Thorstein Veblen, *The Engineers and the Price System* (New York: Viking, 1921), esp. 30, 44. For Veblen's influence on Wallace, see Markowitz, *The Rise and Fall of the People's Century,* 12–14. For more on Veblen and liberal thinking about the economy, see Kevin Mattson, "John Kenneth Galbraith: Liberalism and the Politics of Cultural Critique," in Nelson Lichtenstein, ed., *American Capitalism* (Philadelphia: University of Pennsylvania Press, 2006), 91–95.
21. Markowitz, *The Rise and Fall of the People's Century,* 14.
22. Henry A. Wallace, *New Frontiers* (New York: Reynal & Hitchcock, 1934), 12.
23. Robert Westbrook, "Tribune of the Technostructure: The Popular Economics of Stuart Chase," *American Quarterly* 32 (1980), 388. See also Donald L. Miller, *The New American Radicalism: Alfred M. Bingham and Non-Marxian Insurgency in the New Deal Era* (Port Washington, NY: Kennikat Press, 1979).
24. Richard H. Pells, *Radical Visions and American Dreams: Culture and Social Thought in the Depression Years* (New York: Harper, 1973), 79–80; see also Markowitz, *The Rise and Fall of the People's Century,* 41.
25. John Dewey quoted in David M. Kennedy, *Over Here: The First World War and American Society* (New York: Oxford, 1980), 50.
26. Henry R. Luce, "The American Century," *Life* (February 17, 1941), reprinted in John K. Jessup, ed., *The Ideas of Henry Luce* (New York: Atheneum, 1969), 105–20.
27. Henry R. Luce, *The American Century* (New York: Farrar & Rinehart, 1941), 32–34, 38–39. See also Alan Brinkley, "The Concept of an American Century," in R. Laurence Moore and

Maurizio Vaudagna, eds., *The American Century in Europe* (Ithaca, NY: Cornell University Press, 2002), 7–10, 19.

28. Luce, *The American Century*, 27.
29. Alan Brinkley, "The Concept of an American Century," 12.
30. Blanche Wiesen Cook, "'Turn toward Peace': ER and Foreign Affairs," in Joan Hoff-Wilson and Marjorie Lightman, eds., *Without Precedent: The Life and Career of Eleanor Roosevelt* (Bloomington, IN: Indiana University Press, 1984), 117–18.
31. Philip A. Klinkner, Rogers M. Smith, *The Unsteady March: The Rise and Decline of Racial Equality in America* (Chicago: University of Chicago Press, 1999), 129.
32. Richard S. Kirkendall, "ER and the Issue of FDR's Successor," in Hoff-Wilson and Lightman, *Without Precedent*, 177.
33. Ibid., 189.
34. Quoted in Roger Daniels, "Lash's Eleanor," *Reviews in American History* 1 (1973), 136.
35. Eleanor Roosevelt quoted in John Morton Blum, *V Was for Victory: Politics and American Culture during World War II*, 292.
36. Henry A. Wallace, *The Price of Vision: The Diary of Henry A. Wallace, 1942–1946* (New York: Houghton Mifflin, 1973), 475.
37. Hamby, *Beyond the New Deal*, 83.
38. Culver and Hyde, *American Dreamer*, 389.
39. Henry A. Wallace, *Sixty Million Jobs* (New York: Reynal & Hitchcock, 1945), 15, 86.
40. Markowitz, *The Rise and Fall of the People's Century*, 142.
41. David Brinkley, *Washington Goes to War* (New York: Knopf, 1988), 116.
42. Chester Bowles, *Tomorrow Without Fear* (New York: Simon & Schuster, 1946), 37, 44, 49.
43. David M. Oshinsky, *A Conspiracy So Immense: The World of Joe McCarthy* (New York: Free Press, 1983), 64–65.
44. Meg Jacobs, "'How About Some Meat?': The Office of Price Administration, Consumption Politics, and State Building from the Bottom Up, 1941–1946," *Journal of American History* 84 (1997), 910.
45. Richard Parker, *John Kenneth Galbraith: His Life, His Politics, His Economics* (New York: Farrar, Straus and Giroux, 2005), 152.
46. Lizabeth Cohen, *A Consumers' Republic: The Politics of Mass Consumption in Postwar America* (New York: Knopf, 2003), 102.
47. Jacobs, "'How About Some Meat?'," 937.
48. Cohen, *A Consumers' Republic*, 105.
49. Blum, *V Was for Victory*, 326.
50. Ibid., 329.
51. Ibid., 330.
52. Parker, *John Kenneth Galbraith*, 218.
53. Arthur M. Schlesinger, Jr., quoted in Victor S. Navasky, *Naming Names* (New York: Viking, 1980), 53–54.
54. Kenneth S. Davis, *FDR: The New Deal Years, 1933–1937* (New York: Random House, 1979), 171, 175.
55. James T. Patterson, *Grand Expectations: The United States, 1945–1974* (New York: Oxford University Press, 1996), 43.
56. Harry S. Truman Papers, 1945, 282, 283.
57. Steven Fraser, *Labor Will Rule: Sidney Hillman and the Rise of American Labor* (Ithaca, NY: Cornell University Press, 1991), 559.
58. James A. Wechsler, *Labor Baron: A Portrait of John L. Lewis* (New York: William Morrow, 1944), 266.
59. McCullough, *Truman*, 503.
60. Quoted in James T. Patterson, *Grand Expectations*, 48.

2 | "Scare Hell"

1. Michael Kimmage, *The Conservative Turn: Lionel Trilling, Whittaker Chambers, and the Lessons of Anti-Communism* (Cambridge, MA: Harvard University Press, 2009), 186.
2. See *Life*, November 17, 1947, and March 29, 1943, quoted in Ronald Steel, *Walter Lippmann and the American Century* (New York: Vintage, 1980), 410, 447.
3. Quoted in Walter LaFeber, *The American Age: A History of the United States Since the 1890s* (New York: Norton, 1989), 461.

4. Quoted in Walter Isaacson and Evan Thomas, *The Wise Men: Six Friends and the World They Made* (New York: Simon & Schuster, 1986), 440.

5. Joseph E. Davies Journal, April 23, 1945, box 16, Joseph E. Davies Papers, Manuscript Division, Library of Congress, Washington, DC; and Joseph E. Davies Diary, April 23, 1945, box 16, Davies Papers.

6. See Warren F. Kimball, *Forged in War: Roosevelt, Churchill, and the Second World War* (New York: William Morrow, 1997), 242. For Eleanor Roosevelt's comment, see "Unfinished Notes" (August 1941), Belle Willard Roosevelt Papers, Manuscript Division, Library of Congress, Washington, DC.

7. Harry S. Truman Papers, Post-Presidential Files, box 643, Memoirs files, "Discussion, January 23, 1954," Harry S. Truman Library and Museum.

8. David McCullough, *Truman* (New York: Simon & Schuster, 1992), 338–39.

9. Ibid., 382.

10. Martin J. Sherwin suggests that while Truman wished to dramatize this meeting in his memoirs, others present at the meeting believed that the president "was already convinced of the need for 'rather brutal frankness,'" particularly on Poland, before the meeting began. See Sherwin, *A World Destroyed: The Atomic Bomb and the Grand Alliance* (New York: Knopf, 1975), 157. This interpretation is augmented by entries in the Stimson Diary, April 23, 1945; Leahy Diary, April 23, 1945; Bohlen Memo, April 23, 1945; William Leahy, *I Was There: The Personal Story of the Chief of Staff to Presidents Roosevelt and Truman* (New York: Whittlesey House, 1950), 352; and James Forrestal, The Forrestal Diaries (New York: Viking, 1951), 48–51.

11. For other memoirs and critical accounts of this meeting, see Charles Bohlen, *Witness to History: 1929–1969* (New York: Norton, 1973), 213; Robert J. Donovan, *Conflict and Crisis: The Presidency of Harry S. Truman, 1945–49* (New York: Norton, 1977), 37–39; William E. Pemberton, *Harry S. Truman: Fair Dealer and Cold Warrior* (Boston: Twayne, 1989), 47; and Andrei Gromyko, *Memoirs,* trans. Harold Shukman (London: Hutchinson, 1989), 96.

12. The latter called only for a "reorganized" version of the Polish Provisional Government; see Harry S. Truman, *Memoirs, Volume 1: Year of Decisions* (Garden City, NY: Doubleday, 1955–1956), 80–81.

13. Ibid., 82.

14. Memorandum by Mr. Charles E. Bohlen, Assistant to the Secretary of State, of a Meeting at the White House, April 23, 1945, 2:00 pm, *Foreign Relations of the United States, 1945, vol. 5: Europe,* 252–59.

15. John C. Culver and John Hyde, *American Dreamer: The Life and Times of Henry A. Wallace* (New York: Norton, 2000), 422–23; Alonzo Hamby, *Man of the People: A Life of Harry S. Truman* (New York: Oxford University Press, 1995), 357–59.

16. Culver and Hyde, *American Dreamer,* 441.

17. Ibid., 423.

18. Ibid., 424–25.

19. Ibid., 426.

20. Ibid., 429.

21. Mark Kleinman L., *A World of Hope, A World of Fear: Henry A. Wallace, Reinhold Niebuhr, and American Liberalism* (Columbus: Ohio State University Press, 2000), 275.

22. Walter LaFeber, *America, Russia and the Cold War, 1945–2002* (New York: McGraw-Hill, 2002), 56.

23. Melvyn P. Leffler, "The Emergence of an American Grand Strategy, 1945–1952," in Melvyn P. Leffler and Odd Arne Westad, eds., *The Cambridge History of the Cold War, Volume I: Origins* (Cambridge: Cambridge University Press, 2010), 87.

24. George Kennan, telegram dated March 20, 1946, Harry S. Truman administration. "Newsclippings" file, box 64, George Elsey Papers, Truman Library.

25. For more on the *Times,* see Fraser J. Harbutt, *The Iron Curtain: Churchill, America, and the Origins of the Cold War* (New York: Oxford University Press, 1986), 172. For Vandenberg, see John Lewis Gaddis, *The United States and the Origins of the Cold War: 1941–1947* (New York: Columbia University Press, 1972). For the long telegram, see George Kennan, *Memoirs: 1925–1950* (New York: Pantheon, 1967), 271–97. See also his elaboration of its central points in "The Sources of Soviet Conduct," *Foreign Affairs* (July 1946), reprinted in Hamilton Fish Armstrong, ed., *The Foreign Affairs Reader* (New York: Harper & Bros, 1947), 464–83. See also Michael J. Hogan, *A Cross of Iron: Harry S. Truman and the Origins of the National Security State, 1945–1954* (Cambridge: Cambridge University Press, 1998), 10.

26. See Peter Grosse, *Operation Rollback: America's Secret War behind the Iron Curtain* (Boston: Houghton Mifflin, 2000), 89.

27. Drafts of this letter, done for Clifford by Elsey, Harry S. Truman administration, box 63, folder 2, George Elsey Papers, Truman Library.

28. The report, titled "American Relations with the Soviet Union: A Report to the President by the Special Council to the President, September—, 1946," can be found in Arthur Krock, *Sixty Years on the Firing Line* (New York: Funk & Wagnalls, 1968), Appendix A, 421–82. The original draft, titled "Comments on Soviet Compliance with International Agreements Undertaken Since January 1941," "Russia," file 4 of 8, box 15, Clark Clifford Papers, Truman Library.

29. Richard H. Pells, *The Liberal Mind in a Conservative Age: American Intellectuals in the 1940s and 1950s* (Middletown, CT: Wesleyan University Press, 1989), 65.

30. Alonzo L. Hamby, *Beyond the New Deal: Harry S. Truman and American Liberalism* (New York: Columbia University Press, 1973), 195, 196.

31. Quoted in John Patrick Diggins, "*The New Republic* and Its Times," *The New Republic* (December 10, 1984), 54.

32. Culver and Hyde, *American Dreamer*, 433–37.

33. "The Quarter's Poll," *Public Opinion Quarterly* (Winter 1947–48), 639–84.

34. "TRB: Washington Wire," *The New Republic* (September 30, 1946), 399, 396; Freda Kirchwey, "The Challenge of Henry Wallace," *The Nation* (September 28, 1946), 339.

35. Arnold A. Offner, *Another Such Victory: President Truman and the Cold War,1945–1953* (Stanford, CA: Stanford University Press, 2002), 197–99.

36. George McKee Elsey, *An Unplanned Life: A Memoir* (Columbia, MO: University of Missouri Press, 2005), 149.

37. Senator J. William Fulbright, *The Crippled Giant: American Foreign Policy and Its Domestic Consequences* (New York: Random House, 1972), 6–24.

38. LaFeber, *America, Russia, and the Cold War*, 65.

39. Clark Clifford with Richard Holbrooke, *Counsel to the President: A Memoir* (New York: Random House, 1991), 145.

40. Nicolaus Mills, *Winning the Peace: The Marshall Plan and America's Coming of Age as a Superpower* (Hoboken, NJ: Wiley, 2008).

41. Cifford, *Counsel*, 144.

42. Culver and Hyde, *American Dreamer*, 452.

43. Robert Dallek, *Harry S. Truman* (New York: Times Books, 2008), 55.

44. Hamby, *Man of the People*, 428.

45. David K. Johnson, *The Lavender Scare: The Cold War Persecution of Gays and Lesbians in the Federal Government* (Chicago: University of Chicago Press, 2004).

46. Hamby, *Beyond the New Deal*, 190.

47. Dallek, *Harry S. Truman*, 55.

48. Nelson Lichtenstein, *State of the Union: A Century of American Labor* (Princeton: Princeton University Press, 2002), 118.

49. Ibid., 120.

50. Hamby, *Man of the People*, 424.

51. See Clayton Sinyai, *Schools of Democracy: A Political History of the American Labor Movement* (Ithaca, NY: Cornell University Press, 2006), 172; and James T. Patterson, *Grand Expectations: The United States, 1945–1974* (New York : Oxford University Press, 1996), 142. See also Robert J. Donovan, *Conflict and Crisis: The Presidency of Harry S. Truman, 1945–49* (New York, 1977), 299–304; Hamby, *Beyond the New Deal*, 180–87.

52. See Richard Lentz and Karla K. Gower, *The Opinions of Mankind: Racial Issues, Press and Propaganda in the Cold War* (Columbia, MO: University of Missouri Press, 2011), 62.

53. Eleanor Roosevelt, "Making Human Rights Come Alive" (March 30, 1949), available at http://gos.sbc.edu/r/eleanor1.html; see also Joanna Schneider Zangrando and Robert L. Zangrando, "ER and Black Civil Rights," in Joan Hoff-Wilson and Marjorie Lightman, eds., *Without Precedent: The Life and Career of Eleanor Roosevelt* (Bloomington, IN: Indiana University Press, 1984).

54. Allida M. Black, *Casting Her Own Shadow: Eleanor Roosevelt and the Shaping of Postwar Liberalism* (New York: Columbia University Press, 1996), 80–81.

55. Clifford, *Counsel*, 188.

56. *New York Times*, June 17, 1947, 1; Hamby, *Beyond the New Deal*, 206.

57. Quoted in Steven M. Gillon, *Politics and Vision: The ADA and American Liberalism, 1947–1985* (New York: Oxford University Press, 1987), 33.

58. *New York Times*, July 11, 1948, 2; *Time* (July 19, 1948), 21.
59. Quoted in Zachary Karabell, *The Last Campaign: How Harry Truman Won the 1948 Election* (New York: Knopf, 2000), 151.
60. Ibid., 158.
61. "Essie Mae on Strom Thurmond," *60 Minutes*, CBS News, Dec. 17, 2003, transcript available at http://www.cbsnews.com/stories/2003/12/17/60II/main589107.shtml.
62. Culver and Hyde, *American Dreamer*, 485–89.
63. Quoted in Arthur M. Schlesinger, Jr., *A Life in the 20th Century: Innocent Beginnings, 1917–1950* (Boston: Houghton Mifflin, 2000), 456. Stone is quoted in D. D. Guttenplan, *American Radical: The Life and Times of I. F. Stone* (New York: Farrar, Straus and Giroux, 2009), 231.
64. Culver and Hyde, *American Dreamer*, 493–95.
65. Quoted in Joshua M. Zeitz, "Saving Grace: Henry Wallace Was Right about Race," *The New Republic* Online, post date 12.30.04, accessed on that date but no longer available.
66. Pells, *The Liberal Mind in a Conservative Age*, 260–61.
67. Clifford, *Counsel*, 225.
68. Morris Dickstein, *Leopards in the Temple: The Transformation of American Fiction, 1945–1970* (Cambridge, MA: Harvard University Press, 2002), 28.
69. McCullough, *Truman*, 586.
70. Hamby, *Beyond the New Deal*, 252.
71. "TRB: Washington Wire," *The New Republic* (October 4, 1948), 4. See also "TRB: Washington Wire," *The New Republic* (July 26, 1948), 3.
72. Allida M. Black, ed., *Courage in a Dangerous World: The Political Writings of Eleanor Roosevelt* (New York: Columbia University Press, 1999), 249.
73. Amanda Ripley, "The Relentless Mrs. Roosevelt," *Time* (July 6, 2009), http://www.time.com/time/specials/packages/article/0,28804,1906802_1906838_1906798,00.html.
74. Quoted in Mary Ann Glendon, *A World Made New: Eleanor Roosevelt and the Universal Declaration of Human Rights* (New York: Random House, 2001), 39.
75. Black, ed., *Courage in a Dangerous World*, 193.
76. See David Levering Lewis, *W. E. B. Du Bois: The Fight for Equality and the American Century, 1919–1963* (New York: Holt, 2000).
77. Schlesinger, Jr., *A Life in the 20th Century*, 456.
78. Pells, *The Liberal Mind in a Conservative Age*, 113
79. 1948 Presidential General Election Results, http://uselectionatlas.org/RESULTS/national.php?year=1948.
80. Henry A. Wallace, "Where I Was Wrong," *This Week Magazine, New York Herald Tribune*, September 7, 1952, 7, 39, 46.
81. Eliot Cohen, "Citizen's Victory: Defeat of the 'Common Man,'" *Commentary* (December 1948), 511–13.
82. "TRB: Washington Wire," *The New Republic* (November 15, 1948), 3.
83. Hamby, *Beyond the New Deal*, 264.
84. Hamby, *Man of the People*, 488.

3 | "The Self-Righteous Delusions of Innocence"

1. Reinhold Niebuhr, "American Liberals and British Labor," *The Nation* (June 8, 1946), 683.
2. Dialogue from *The Maltese Falcon* is quoted from James Harvey, *Movie Love in the Fifties* (New York: Da Capo, 2001), 224.
3. Biographical details are largely drawn from Richard Wightman Fox, *Reinhold Niebuhr: A Biography* (New York: Pantheon, 1985).
4. For more on this, see Walter Rauschenbusch, *A Theology for the Social Gospel* (New York: Macmillan, 1917) and Heather A. Warren, *Theologians for a New World Order: Reinhold Niebuhr and the Christian Realists, 1920–1948* (New York: Oxford University Press, 1997).
5. Niebuhr, Reinhold, *Moral Man and Immoral Society: A Study of Ethics and Politics* (New York: Scribner, 1932), 172, 197.
6. Archibald MacLeish, "The Irresponsibles" (1940), reprinted in *A Time to Speak* (Boston: Houghton Mifflin, 1940), 109.
7. Henry Beckett, "Niebuhr," *New York Post*, April 20, 1943, 39.
8. Reinhold Niebuhr Papers, Library of Congress, UDA Folder: Niebuhr to Roy Jacobson, January 11, 1943.
9. Fox, *Reinhold Niebuhr*, 200.

10. Reinhold Niebuhr in *Christianity and Crisis* (April 3, 1944), 1.
11. Reinhold Niebuhr, *The Children of Light and the Children of Darkness* (New York: Scribner, 1944), xii, 21, 105.
12. See Arthur Schlesinger, Jr., *A Life in the 20th Century: Innocent Beginnings, 1917–1950* (Boston: Houghton Mifflin, 2000), 78.
13. Arthur M. Schlesinger, Jr., "Orestes Brownson: An American Marxist Before Marx," *Sewanee Review*, 47 (1939), 317–23; Orestes A. Brownson, *A Pilgrim's Progress* (Boston: Little Brown, 1939), 61.
14. Martin E. Marty, "Reinhold Niebuhr and *The Irony of American History*: A Retrospective," *The History Teacher* 26 (1993), 161–74.
15. See Arthur M. Schlesinger, Jr., *A Life in the 20th Century*, 293.
16. Arthur M. Schlesinger, Jr., *The Age of Jackson* (Boston: Little Brown, 1945), 366, 505.
17. See Sam Tanenhaus, *Whittaker Chambers: A Biography* (New York: Random House, 1997), 172.
18. Reinhold Niebuhr in *Christianity and Society* (Spring 1946), 38–39.
19. Arthur M. Schlesinger, Jr., "The U.S. Communist Party," *Life* (July 29, 1946), 85, 87.
20. Arthur M. Schlesinger, Jr., "The Future of Socialism III: The Perspective Now," *Partisan Review* 14 (1947), 235.
21. Arthur M. Schlesinger, Jr., "Liberal Faith Needs Guts," *Labor and Nation* (November–December 1948), 13.
22. Arthur M. Schlesinger, Jr., "Forgetting Reinhold Niebuhr," *New York Times Book Review*, September 18, 2005, G12.
23. Quoted in Richard Cook, *Alfred Kazin: A Biography* (New Haven, CT: Yale University Press, 2007), 44–45.
24. James A. Wechsler, *The Age of Suspicion* (New York: Donald I. Fine, 1953), 67.
25. Ibid., 157.
26. Paul Milkman, *PM: A New Deal in Journalism, 1940–1948* (New Brunswick, NJ: Rutgers University Press, 1997).
27. Kevin Mattson, *When America Was Great: The Fighting Faith of Postwar Liberalism* (New York: Routledge, 2004), 31.
28. Wechsler, *The Age of Suspicion*, 210–11.
29. James A. Wechsler, "Labor's Bright Young Man," *Harper's* (March 1948), 264–271.
30. Clayton Sinyai, *Schools of Democracy: A Political History of the American Labor Movement* (Ithaca, NY: Cornell University Press, 2006), 176.
31. Steven M. Gillon, *Politics and Vision: The ADA and American Liberalism, 1947–1985* (New York: Oxford University Press, 1987), 13. See also John Barnard, *Walter Reuther and the Rise of the Auto Workers* (Boston: Little Brown, 1983); Frank Cormier and William J. Eaton, *Reuther* (Englewood Cliffs, NJ: Prentice-Hall, 1970); Jean Gould, *Walter Reuther: Labor's Rugged Individualist* (New York: Dodd, Mead, 1972); Irving Howe and B. J. Widick, *The UAW and Walter Reuther* (New York: Random House, 1949); Roger Keeran, *The Communist Party and the Auto Workers Unions* (Bloomington, IN: Indiana University Press, 1977).
32. *Harper's* (May 1942), quoted in Philip Dray, *There Is Power in a Union: The Epic Story of Labor in America* (New York: Doubleday, 2010), 509.
33. Quoted in John Barnard, *American Vanguard: The United Auto Workers During the Reuther Years, 1935–1970* (Detroit: Wayne State University Press, 2004), 213.
34. Ibid., 214.
35. Ibid., 219.
36. Ibid.
37. C. Wright Mills, quoted in Nelson Lichtenstein, *State of the Union: A Century of American Labor* (Princeton: Princeton University Press, 2002), 157–58.
38. Clifton Brock, *Americans for Democratic Action: Its Role in National Politics* (Washington, DC: Public Affairs, 1962), 51.
39. Wechsler, *The Age of Suspicion*, 216–17.
40. *New York Times*, January 4 1947, 1, cited in Gillon, *Politics and Vision*, 21–24.
41. "A World to Live In," *New York Post*, January 3, 1947, 48.
42. Americans for Democratic Action, *Toward Total Peace: A Liberal Foreign Policy for the United States* (Washington, DC: ADA, nd), 9. Found in ADA Papers, Wisconsin Historical Society.
43. ADA, *Toward Total Peace*, 26.
44. Niebuhr, *The Children of Light*, 186.
45. Arthur M. Schlesinger, Jr., "What Is Loyalty?" *New York Times Magazine*, November 2, 1947, 50.

46. Arthur M. Schlesinger, Jr., "Ideas to Watch in Politics," *Vogue* (January 1949), 174.
47. Carl Solberg, *Hubert Humphrey: A Biography* (New York: Norton, 1984), 136.
48. Ibid., 51–52.
49. Ibid., 76.
50. Ibid., 78.
51. Robert A. Caro, *Master of the Senate: The Years of Lyndon Johnson* (New York: Random House, 2002), 440.
52. Hubert H. Humphrey, *The Education of a Public Man: My Life and Politics* (Garden City, NY: Doubleday, 1976), 111.
53. Gillon, *Politics and Vision*, 48–52.
54. Schlesinger, Jr. *A Life in the 20th Century*, 463.
55. Caro, *Master of the Senate*, 441.
56. Gillon, *Politics and Vision*, 48–52.
57. See Michael E. Parrish, *Citizen Rauh: An American Liberal's Life in Law and Politics* (Ann Arbor, MI: University of Michigan Press, 2010), 89.
58. Caro, *Master of the Senate*, 443.
59. Brock, *The Americans for Democratic Action*, 98.
60. Caro, *Master of the Senate*, 445.
61. Solberg, *Hubert Humphrey*, 133.
62. Caro, *Master of the Senate*, 444.
63. Gillon, *Politics and Vision*, 48–52.
64. Reinhold Niebuhr, "Hazards and Resources," *Virginia Quarterly Review* 25 (1949), 196–97.
65. Mark L. Kleinman, *A World of Hope, A World of Fear: Henry A. Wallace, Reinhold Niebuhr, and American Liberalism* (Columbus: Ohio State University Press, 2000), 257.
66. Clark Clifford with Richard Holbrooke, *Counsel to the President: A Memoir* (New York: Random House, 1991), 225.
67. This section is based on Barbara Griffith, *The Crisis of American Labor: Operation Dixie and the Defeat of the CIO* (Philadelphia: Temple University Press, 1988); Michael Goldfield, "The Failure of Operation Dixie," in Gary M. Fink and Merl E. Read, eds., *Race, Class, and Community in Southern Labor History* (Tuscaloosa, AL: University of Alabama Press, 1994), 166–89; Michael Honey, "Operation Dixie, the Red Scare, and the Defeat of Southern Labor Organizing," in Robert W. Cherny, William Issel, and Kieran Walsh Taylor, eds., *American Labor and the Cold War: Grassroots Politics and Postwar Political Culture* (New Brunswick, NJ: Rutgers University Press, 2004), 216–44; F. Ray Marshall, *Labor in the South* (Cambridge, MA: Harvard University Press, 1967); William Regensburger, "'Ground Into Our Blood': The Origins of Working Class Consciousness and Organization in Durably Unionized Southern Industries, 1930–1946," (Ph.D. diss., University of California, Los Angeles, 1987); William Jones, "Black Workers and the CIO's Turn Toward Racial Liberalism: Operation Dixie and the North Carolina Lumber Industry, 1946–1953," *Labor History* 41 (2000), 279–306.
68. Douglas S. Massey, "Original Sin: Race and the Stunted Growth and Rapid Decline of American Liberalism," Logosjournal.com, May 2011, http://logosjournal.com/2011/race-and-the-stunted-growth-and-rapid-decline-of-american-liberalism/.
69. Sartre quoted in Carol Brightman, *Writing Dangerously: Mary McCarthy and Her World* (New York: Clarkson Potter, 1992), 332.
70. George Cotkin, *Existential America* (Baltimore: Johns Hopkins, 2003), 117–18.
71. Arthur M. Schlesinger, Jr., *The Vital Center: The Politics of Freedom* (1949; repr., New York: DaCapo, 1988), xvii.
72. Ibid., 2, 7.
73. Ibid., 115, 38, 43, 40, 159.
74. Ibid., 169.
75. Schlesinger, Jr., *The Vital Center*, 160, 163.
76. Ibid., 245, 196.
77. Richard H. Pells, *The Liberal Mind in a Conservative Age: American Intellectuals in the 1940s and 1950s* (Middletown, CT: Wesleyan University Press, 1989), 82–83.

4 | Patient, Firm, and Vigilant

1. Quoted in Ronald Steel, *Walter Lippmann and the American Century* (New York: Vintage, 1980), 425.
2. "Rear Platform and Other Informal Remarks in Ohio," October 11, 1948, Harry S. Truman

Papers, 1945–1953, Harry S. Truman Library and Museum, http://www.trumanlibrary.org/publicpapers/index.php?pid=1981.

3. Philip Roth, *American Pastoral* (New York: Houghton Mifflin, 1997), 40–41.
4. Eric Hobsbawm, *Interesting Times: A Twentieth-Century Life* (New York: Pantheon, 2002), 404.
5. Alonzo L. Hamby, *Beyond the New Deal: Harry S. Truman and American Liberalism* (New York: Columbia University Press, 1973), 4.
6. Mary Ann Glendon, *A World Made New: Eleanor Roosevelt and the Universal Declaration of Human Rights* (New York: Random House, 2001), 18–19.
7. Townsend Hoopes and Douglas Brinkley, *FDR and the Creation of the U.N.* (New Haven, CT: Yale University Press, 1997), 179.
8. Tony Judt, *Postwar: A History of Europe Since 1945* (New York: Penguin, 2005), 23.
9. Lois Scharf, *Eleanor Roosevelt: First Lady of American Liberalism* (Boston: Twayne, 1987), 147.
10. Mary Ann Glendon, *A World Made New*, 34.
11. Quoted in ibid., 148.
12. See Lloyd C. Gardner, *Architects of Illusion: Men and Ideas in American Foreign Policy: 1941–1949* (Chicago: Quadrangle Books, 1970), 61–62.
13. I. F. Stone, "Trieste and San Francisco," *The Nation* (May 26, 1945).
14. Robert L. Beisner, *Dean Acheson: A Life in the Cold War* (New York: Oxford University Press, 2006), 211.
15. G. John Ikenberry, *Liberal Leviathan: The Origins, Crisis and Transformation of the American World Order* (Princeton: Princeton University Press, 2011), 159–60.
16. H. W. Brands, *The Strange Death of American Liberalism* (New Haven, CT: Yale University Press, 2001).
17. John A. Davis, "Negro Employment: A Progress Report," *Fortune* (July 1952), 102–103.
18. Dean Acheson, *Present at the Creation: My Years in the State Department* (New York: Norton, 1969), xvi.
19. Martin Weil, *A Pretty Good Club: The Founding Fathers of the U.S. Foreign Service* (New York: Norton, 1978), 258.
20. Dean Acheson, *Power and Diplomacy* (Cambridge, MA: Harvard University Press, 1958), 29.
21. John Lewis Gaddis, "The Gardener," *The New Republic* (October 16, 2006), http://www.tnr.com/article/the-gardener.
22. See David F. Schmitz. *Henry L. Stimson: The First Wise Man* (Wilmington, DE: SR Books, 2001).
23. Henry L. Stimson, "Memorandum for the President," September 11, 1945, http://nuclear files.org/menu/library/correspondence/stimson-henry/corr_stimson_1945-09-11.htm.
24. Beisner, *Dean Acheson*, 12.
25. Alonzo L. Hamby, *Man of the People: A Life of Harry S. Truman* (New York: Oxford University Press, 1995), 340.
26. Scharf, *Eleanor Roosevelt*, 145.
27. Quoted in John Lewis Gaddis, *The United States and the Origins of the Cold War: 1941–1947* (New York: Columbia, 1972), 251, 252.
28. Beisner, *Dean Acheson*, 12.
29. John Patrick Diggins, *The Proud Decades: America in War and Peace, 1941–1960* (New York: Norton, 1988), 51.
30. Quoted in Michael Wreszin, *A Rebel in Defense of Tradition: The Life and Politics of Dwight Macdonald* (New York: Basic Books, 1994), 154.
31. Ibid., 164, 166.
32. David E. Lilienthal, *TVA: Democracy on the March* (1944; repr., Chicago: Quadrangle Books, 1944), 219.
33. Steven M. Neuse, *David E. Lilienthal: The Journey of an American Liberal* (Knoxville: University of Tennessee Press, 1996), 167.
34. Kai Bird and Martin J. Sherwin, *American Prometheus: The Triumph and Tragedy of J. Robert Oppenheimer* (New York: Knopf, 2005), 340.
35. Neuse, *David E. Lilienthal*, 169.
36. Ibid., 172.
37. Diggins, *The Proud Decades*, 62.
38. Beisner, *Dean Acheson*, 34. See also Jordan A. Schwarz, *The Speculator: Bernard M. Baruch in Washington, 1917–1965* (Chapel Hill: University of North Carolina Press, 1981), 464.
39. Schwarz, *The Speculator*, 492.
40. Ibid., 495–505; Walter LaFeber, *The American Age: A History of the United States Since the 1890s* (New York: W.W. Norton, 1989), 447–48; Beisner, *Dean Acheson*, 35.

41. Beisner, *Dean Acheson*, 44.
42. Quoted in Lloyd C. Gardner, *Architects of Illusion: Men and Ideas in American Foreign Policy, 1941–1949*, 219.
43. Beisner, *Dean Acheson*, 52.
44. Ibid., 46.
45. Ibid., 142.
46. Ibid., 47.
47. Anders Stephanson, "George F. Kennan, 1904–2005," *Dizionario del comunismo nel XX Secolo*, ed. Silvio Pons and Robert Service (Turin: Einaudi, 2006).
48. George F. Kennan, *The Cloud of Danger: Current Realities of American Foreign Policy* (Boston: Little Brown, 1977), 6.
49. U.S. Department of State, *Foreign Relations of the United States: Eastern Europe; the Soviet Union*, vol. VI, 1946 (Washington, DC: Government Printing Office, 1969), 696–709. See also George F. Kennan, *American Diplomacy, 1900–1950* (New York: Mentor, 1951), 91–104.
50. Richard Wightman Fox, *Reinhold Niebuhr: A Biography* (New York: Pantheon, 1985), 238.
51. George F. Kennan, *Memoirs, 1925–1950* (New York: Pantheon, 1967), 310.
52. John Lewis Gaddis, *Strategies of Containment: A Critical Appraisal of Postwar American National Security Policy during the Cold War* (New York: Oxford University Press, 1982), 40.
53. Quoted in John Lewis Gaddis, *George F. Kennan: An American Life* (New York: Penguin Press, 2011), 693.
54. Quoted in Andrew J. Bacevich, *The Nation*, October 25, 2011. See also Louis Menand, "Getting Real: George F. Kennan's Cold War." *The New Yorker*, November 14, 2011, http://www.new yorker.com/arts/critics/atlarge/2011/11/14/111114crat_atlarge_menand?currentPage=all.
55. Daniel Kelly, *James Burnham and the Struggle for the World* (Wilmington, DE: ISI, 2002), 125.
56. Quoted in Richard Gid Powers, *Not Without Honor: The History of American Anticommunism* (New York: Free Press, 1995), 206.
57. James Burnham, *The Coming Defeat of Communism* (New York: John Day, 1950), 12, 24, 61, 254.
58. In Richard Hofstadter, ed., *Great Issues in American History: From Reconstruction to the Present Day, 1864–1969* (New York: Vintage, 1969), 413, 414.
59. Kennan, *Memoirs*, 320, 356.
60. See Walter Lippmann, *The Phantom Public* (New York: Macmillan, 1924), 13–14.
61. Steel, *Walter Lippmann*, 437, 438.
62. Walter Lippmann, *The Cold War* (New York: Harper, 1947), 26.
63. Lippmann, *The Cold War*, 54.
64. See Max Hastings, "A Very Chilly Victory," *The New York Review of Books*, August 13, 2009, http://www.nybooks.com/articles/article-preview?article_id=22975.
65. Ed Cray, *General of the Army: George C. Marshall, Soldier and Statesman* (New York: Norton, 1990), 584.
66. Ibid., 590.
67. George Kennan quoted in Walter Isaacson and Evan Thomas, *The Wise Men: Six Friends and the World They Made* (New York: Simon & Schuster, 1986), 422.
68. Greg Behrman, *The Most Noble Adventure: The Marshall Plan and the Time When America Helped Save Europe* (New York: Free Press, 2007), 55.
69. Kennan, *Memoirs*, 335, 343.
70. In Hofstadter, ed., *Great Issues*, 416–19.
71. Diggins, *The Proud Decades*, 78.
72. Greg Behrman, *The Most Noble Adventure*, 149.
73. Ibid., 91–92.
74. Quoted ibid., 58.
75. Ibid., 123, 124, 153.
76. Steven M. Gillon, *Politics and Vision: The ADA and American Liberalism, 1947–1985* (New York: Oxford University Press, 1987), 31.
77. Michael Hogan, "American Marshall Planners and the Search for a European Neocapitalism," *American Historical Review* 90 (1985), 45.
78. Giles Scott-Smith, *The Politics of Apolitical Culture: The Congress for Cultural Freedom, the CIA, and Postwar American Hegemony* (New York: Routledge, 2002), 86.
79. See Peter Coleman, "Arthur Koestler and the Congress for Cultural Freedom," *Polanyiana* 2005 no. 1–2, http://www.polanyi.bme.hu/folyoirat/2005/2005_21_ARTHUR%20KOETLER %20AND%20THE.pdf.

80. See Sidney Hook, *Out of Step: An Unquiet Life in the 20th Century* (New York: Harper & Row, 1987), 263–65.

81. C. Wright Mills, *The Power Elite* (1956; repr., New York: Oxford University Press, 2000).

82. This draws from Frances Stonor Saunders, *The Cultural Cold War: The CIA and the World of Arts and Letters* (New York: Free Press, 1999). See also Peter Coleman, *The Liberal Conspiracy: The Congress for Cultural Freedom and the Struggle for the Mind of Postwar Europe* (New York: Free Press, 1989).

83. Quoted in Saunders, *The Cultural Cold War*, 74.

84. Ibid.

85. Ibid.

86. Richard H. Pells, *Not Like Us: How Europeans Have Loved, Hated, and Transformed American Culture Since World War II* (New York: Basic Books, 1997), 50.

87. Pells, *Not Like Us*, 50, 107–10.

88. Louis Menand, "Unpopular Front," *The New Yorker* (October 17, 2005), 174, 175. See also David Caute, *The Dancer Defects: The Struggle for Cultural Supremacy during the Cold War* (New York: Oxford, 2003), 544.

89. *Partisan Review* 19 (September–October 1952) 593, quoted in Gerald Sorin, *Irving Howe: A Life of Passionate Dissent* (New York: New York University Press, 2002), 114.

90. Hugh Wilford, *The Mighty Wurlitzer: How the CIA Played America* (Cambridge, MA: Harvard University Press, 2008), 113–16.

91. Quoted in John Summers, "Daniel Bell and *The End of Ideology*," *Dissent* (February 1, 2011), http://www.dissentmagazine.org/online.php?id=441.

92. See Stanislao G. Pugliese, *Bitter Spring: A Life of Ignazio Silone* (New York: Farrar, Straus and Giroux, 2009), 247–48.

93. Wreszin, *A Rebel in Defense of Tradition*, 428.

94. Letter from Irving Kristol to Dwight Macdonald, April 11, 1967, Dwight Macdonald Papers, box 26, folder 291, Yale University. On Kristol's denial, see also Joseph Dorman, *Arguing the World: The New York Intellectuals in Their Own Words* (New York: Free Press, 2000), 114–15.

95. Quoted in James T. Patterson, *Grand Expectations: The United States, 1945–1974* (New York: Oxford University Press, 1996), 171; Beisner, *Dean Acheson*, 187, 283.

96. Reinhold Niebuhr, "The Plight of China," *Christianity and Society* (Winter 1949), 6.

97. Nicolaus Mills, *Winning the Peace: The Marshall Plan and America's Coming of Age as a Superpower* (Hoboken, NJ: Wiley, 2008), 193.

98. See "United States Objectives and Programs for National Security," April 14, 1950, *Foreign Relations of the United States, 1950*, vol. I (Washington, DC: GPO, 1977), 244, 234–92. See also Ernest R. May, ed., *American Cold War Strategy: Interpreting NSC 68* (Boston: Bedford/St. Martin's Press, 1993).

5 | The Best Years of Our Lives

1. Lionel Trilling, "Preface" (dated December 1949), in *The Liberal Imagination: Essays on Literature and Society* (1950; repr., Garden City, NY: Anchor, 1953), xiii.

2. Irving Howe, *Decline of the New* (New York: Harcourt, Brace, and World, 1970), 249.

3. Trilling, *The Liberal Imagination*, x.

4. Lionel Trilling to the editors of *The New Republic* (April 4, 1937), Trilling MSS, box 7, Columbia University Library.

5. Irving Kristol, "Arnold and Trilling," *New Leader*, July 2, 1949, Trilling MSS, box 59, Columbia University Library.

6. Mark Royden Winchell, *Too Good to Be True: The Life and Work of Leslie Fiedler* (Columbia, MO: University of Missouri Press, 2002), 69; William Graebner, *The Age of Doubt: American Thought and Culture in the 1940s* (Prospect Heights, IL: Waveland, 1991), 48–49.

7. Dizzy Gillespie quoted in Lewis Erenberg, "Things to Come: Swing Bands, Bebop, and the Rise of a Postwar Jazz Scene," in Lary May, ed., *Recasting America: Culture and Politics in the Age of Cold War* (Chicago: University of Chicago, 1989), 221.

8. David Lehman, *The Last Avant-Garde: The Making of the New York School of Poets* (New York: Doubleday, 1998), 305.

9. Quotes from Erika Doss, "The Art of Cultural Politics: From Regionalism to Abstract Expressionism," in May, *Recasting America*, 215, 214.

10. Jed Perl, *New Art City: Manhattan at Mid-Century* (New York: Knopf, 2005).

11. Quoted in John Patrick Diggins, *The Proud Decades: America in War and Peace, 1941–1960* (New York: Norton, 1988), 238–39.
12. Ibid.
13. Richard Cook, *Alfred Kazin: A Biography* (New Haven, CT: Yale University Press, 2007), 71.
14. Bellow is quoted in Cynthia Ozick, "Lasting Man," *The New Republic* (February 10, 2011), www.tnr.com/article/books-and-arts/.../saul-bellows-letters-review.
15. See Norman Mailer, *The Naked and the Dead* (1948; repr., New York: Picador, 1998) (the term "fug" can be found on page 7 and then throughout); Saul Bellow, *The Dangling Man* (New York: Vanguard, 1944) and *The Victim* (New York: Signet, 1947); Richard Wright, *Native Son* (Stockholm: Jan Förlag, 1943).
16. Alfred Kazin, *On Native Grounds* (1942; New York: Doubleday, 1956), ix.
17. John Egerton, *Speak Now Against the Day: The Generation Before the Civil Rights Movement in the South* (New York: Knopf, 1994), 265.
18. David Margolick, *Strange Fruit: Billie Holiday, Café Society, and an Early Cry for Civil Rights* (Philadelphia: Running Press, 2000), 37. On Popular Front culture in general, see Michael Denning, *The Cultural Front: The Laboring of American Culture in the Twentieth Century* (New York: Verso, 1996).
19. Trilling, *The Liberal Imagination*, 19.
20. Malcolm Cowley quoted in Richard H. Pells, *Radical Visions and American Dreams* (New York: Harper & Row, 1973), 174. See also Alan M. Wald, *Exiles from a Future Time* (Chapel Hill: University of North Carolina, 2002)
21. Quoted in Anne C. Loveland, *Lillian Smith* (Baton Rouge: Louisiana State University Press, 1986), 63.
22. Lillian Smith, *Strange Fruit* (New York: Reynal & Hitchcock, 1944), 65.
23. Lillian Smith, "Personal History of 'Strange Fruit,'" *Saturday Review of Literature* (February 17, 1945), 10.
24. Lillian Smith, "Addressed to White Liberals," *New Republic* (September 18, 1944), 331.
25. Ibid., 332.
26. Lillian Smith, *How Am I to Be Heard? Letters of Lillian Smith*, ed. Margaret Rose Gladney, (Chapel Hill: University of North Carolina Press, 1993), 109.
27. Arthur M. Schlesinger, Jr., to Joe Rauh and James Loeb, January 25, 1950, found in ADA Papers, reel 103, Microfilm Records.
28. Smith, *How Am I to Be Heard?* (letter dated May 2, 1944), 83.
29. Wallace Stegner, *The Uneasy Chair: A Biography of Bernard DeVoto* (New York: Doubleday, 1974), 7.
30. Arthur M. Schlesinger, Jr., *The Politics of Hope* and *the Bitter Heritage* (Princeton: Princeton University Press, 2008), 196.
31. DeVoto to Mat (Garrett Mattingly), March 2, 1942, DeVoto Papers, box 2, folder 15, Stanford University Library.
32. Bernard DeVoto, "The Home Town Front," in DeVoto Papers, box 52, folder 3.
33. See Judy Kutulas, *The American Civil Liberties Union and the Making of Modern Liberalism, 1930–1960* (Chapel Hill: University of North Carolina Press, 2006).
34. Wallace Stegner, ed., *The Letters of Bernard DeVoto* (New York: Doubleday, 1975), 172.
35. *Harper's* (July 1944), 148.
36. Bernard DeVoto, "The Decision in the Strange Fruit Case," *The New England Quarterly* (June 1946), 153. DeVoto is quoting the court here.
37. Ibid., 157.
38. *Harper's* (July, 1944), 150.
39. *Harper's* (May 1944), 526.
40. Stegner, *The Uneasy Chair*, 263.
41. Ibid., 252.
42. Kazin, *On Native Grounds*, 175, 165.
43. Quoted in Louis Menand, "Browbeaten: Dwight Macdonald's War on Midcult," *The New Yorker* (September 5, 2011), 72–78.
44. Nicholas Lemann, "The Outcast," *Washington Monthly* (January/February, 1999), http://www.washingtonmonthly.com/books/1999/9901.lemann.outcast.html.
45. Lionel Trilling, "Preface to *Beyond Culture*," in Leon Wieseltier, ed., *The Moral Obligation to Be Intelligent: Selected Essays* (New York: Farrar, Straus and Giroux, 2000), 552.
46. Alfred Kazin, *Starting Out in the Thirties* (Boston: Little Brown and Co., 1965), 3–4.
47. Nicholas Butler's decision is described in Wieseltier, *The Moral Obligation to Be Intelligent*, ix.

Barzun is quoted in Ann Hulbert, "'It's Complicated. . . . It's Very Complicated,'" *New York Times Book Review*, October 24, 1993, http://www.nytimes.com/1993/10/24/books/it-s-complicated-it-s-very-complicated.html?pagewanted=all.

48. Howe, *Decline of the New*, 241.

49. "Under Forty: A Symposium on American Literature and the Younger Generation of American Jews," *Contemporary Jewish Record* (February 1944).

50. Quoted in Edward Mendelson, "The Hidden Life of Alfred Kazin,"*The New York Review of Books*, August 18, 2011, http://www.nybooks.com/articles/archives/2011/aug/18/hidden-life-alfred-kazin/.

51. Shapiro is cited in Stephen J. Whitfield, "Why America Has Not Seemed Like Exile," *Michigan Quarterly Review* 41 (2002), 668–93.

52. We are speaking of the word "fug" in Norman Mailer's case, and obviously "Catch-22" in Joseph Heller's novel by that title.

53. Stephen L. Tanner, *Lionel Trilling* (Boston: Twayne, 1988), 13–15.

54. Lionel Trilling, "Under Forty," 17.

55. Quoted in Terry A. Cooney: *The Rise of the New York Intellectuals: Partisan Review and Its Circle* (Madison, WI: University of Wisconsin Press, 1986), 5.

56. Emily Miller Budick, *Blacks and Jews in Literary Conversation* (Cambridge: Cambridge University Press, 1998), 96.

57. Sidney Hook, *Out of Step: An Unquiet Life in the 20th Century* (New York: Harper & Row, 1987), 33.

58. Trilling, "Under Forty."

59. See Isaac Deutscher, *The Non-Jewish Jew and Other Essays* (New York: Oxford University Press, 1968), 33.

60. Leslie Fiedler quoted in Cooney, *The Rise of the New York Intellectuals*, 244.

61. Edward S. Shapiro, *A Time for Healing; American Jewry Since World War II* (Baltimore: Johns Hopkins University Press, 1992), 25.

62. Susanne Klingenstein, *Jews in the American Academy, 1900–1940: The Dynamics of Intellectual Assimilation* (New Haven, CT: Yale University Press, 1991), 141.

63. "From the Notebooks of Lionel Trilling," *Partisan Review* 51–2 (1984–85), 508.

64. Lionel Trilling, "A Rejoinder to Mr. Barrett," *Partisan Review* 16 (1949), 655.

65. "The Other Margaret," reprinted in Lionel Trilling, *Of This Time, Of That Place, and Other Stories* (New York: Harcourt, Brace, Jovanovich, 1979).

66. Lionel Trilling, *The Middle of the Journey* (1947; repr., New York: Avon, 1966), 111–12, 137, 119, 166, 153, 194; George Cotkin, *Existential America* (Baltimore: Johns Hopkins University Press, 2003), 126.

67. Arthur Schlesinger, Jr., to Lionel Trilling, August 26, 1947, found in the Lionel Trilling Papers, Correspondence: box 5.

68. Quoted in Adam Kirsch, *Why Trilling Matters* (New Haven, CT: Yale University Press, 2011), 72.

69. Quoted in Cynthia Ozick, "Novel or Nothing," *The New Republic,* May 28, 2008, http://www.tnr.com/story_print.html?id=b12db0e0-c81d-417d-b138-c7c633dbbbc1.

70. Quoted in Cynthia Ozick, "Novel or Nothing."

71. Quoted in Richard H. Pells, *The Liberal Mind in a Conservative Age: American Intellectual Life in the 1940s and 1950s* (Middletown, CT: Wesleyan University Press, 1989), 138.

72. Trilling, *The Liberal Imagination*, ix.

73. Ibid., 215.

74. Edward Rothstein, "Dated? Perhaps, But His Insights Remain Powerful," *New York Times*, July 29, 2000, http://www.nytimes.com/2000/07/29/books/dated-perhaps-but-his-insights-remain-powerful.html.

75. Ibid.

76. Trilling, *The Liberal Imagination*, xi.

77. Gertrude Himmelfarb, "The Trilling Imagination," *The Weekly Standard* (February 14 –21, 2005), http://www.weeklystandard.com/Content/Public/Articles/000/000/005/213jfgtq.asp.

78. Trilling, *The Liberal Imagination*, xiii.

79. Richard Sennett quoted in Introduction to John Rodden, ed., *Lionel Trilling and the Critics* (Lincoln, NE: University of Nebraska Press, 1999), 19.

80. Quoted in Hulbert, "'It's Complicated.'"

81. Robert Sklar, *Movie-Made America: A Cultural History of American Movies* (New York: Random House, 1975), 269.
82. See John Mason Brown, *The Worlds of Robert E. Sherwood* (New York: Harper & Row, 1965).
83. Harriet Hyman Alonso, *Robert E. Sherwood* (Amherst, MA: University of Massachusetts Press, 2007), 280.
84. *New York Post*, May 26, 1947, 4; James T. Patterson, *Grand Expectations: The United States, 1945–1974* (New York: Oxford University Press, 1996), 14–15; on Goldwyn, see Nora Sayre, *Running Time: Films of the Cold War* (New York: Dial Press, 1982), 51–54.
85. Edward Dmytryk would later become an "unfriendly" to HUAC, go to jail, and then later name names in order to obtain his release.
86. John Huston had made a documentary, *Let There Be Light,* in 1946 that tried to grapple honestly with the psychological damage the war did to returning vets, only to find the movie too upsetting to the government and Hollywood alike. It didn't reach audiences until much later.
87. Quoted in Pells, *Radical Visions,* 257.
88. Margaret Brenman-Gibson, *Clifford Odets: American Playwright* (New York: Atheneum, 1981), 259.
89. "Waiting for Lefty," in *Six Plays of Clifford Odets* (New York: Grove Press, 1979), 28.
90. Elia Kazan, *A Life* (New York: Knopf, 1988), 129.
91. Ibid., 63.
92. Ibid., 242.
93. Ibid., 245.
94. J. Hoberman and Jeffrey Shandler, "Hollywood's Jewish Question," in J. Hoberman and Jeffrey Shandler, eds., *Entertaining America: Jews, Movies and Broadcasting.* (Princeton: Princeton University Press, 1994), 68.
95. Quoted in Gary Fishgall, *Gregory Peck: A Biography* (New York: Scribners, 2002), 124.
96. Kazan, *A Life,* 333.
97. Richard Schickel, *Elia Kazan: A Biography* (New York: HarperCollins, 2005), 163.
98. Shapiro, *A Time for Healing,* 20.
99. Elia Kazan, *Kazan: The Master Director Discusses His Films,* ed. Jeff Young (New York: Newmarket Press, 1999) 59.
100. Sayre, *Running Time,* 18; and Nancy Lynn Schwartz, *The Hollywood Writers' War* (New York: McGraw-Hill, 1982), 268.
101. Schwartz, *The Hollywood Writers' War,* 254.
102. See Steven J. Ross, *Hollywood Left and Right: How Movie Stars Shaped American Politics* (New York: Oxford University Press, 2011) 108–109.
103. Ibid., 142.
104. Gary Cooper quoted in Patterson, *Grand Expectations,* 189.
105. See Robert D. McFadden, "J.Parnell Thomas, Anti-Red Crusader, Is Dead," *New York Times,* November 20, 1970, 44.
106. Ross, *Hollywood Left and Right,* 149.
107. Ibid., 144
108. A. M. Sperber and Eric Lax, *Bogart* (New York: William Morrow, 1997), 368.
109. Quoted in Patterson, *Grand Expectations,* 189.
110. Sperber and Lax, *Bogart,* 379.
111. Quoted in Schwartz, *The Hollywood Writers's Wars,* 281.
112. Sperber and Lax, *Bogart,* 397.
113. Quoted in Schwartz, *The Hollywood Writers' Wars,* 281.
114. Quoted in Larry Ceplair and Steven Englund, *The Inquisition in Hollywood: Politics in the Film Community, 1930–1960* (New York: Anchor, 1980), 329.
115. Schwartz, *The Hollywood Writers' Wars,* 266.
116. Michael Wilson quoted in Joseph McBride, *Frank Capra: The Catastrophe of Success* (New York: Touchstone, 1992), 543.
117. Waldorf Statement reprinted in Ceplair and Englund, *The Inquisition in Hollywood,* 445.
118. Ibid., 340; for how Wyler continued to make movies on his own ground, at least for the most part, see Sarah Kozloff, "Wyler's Wars," *Film History* 20 (2008).
119. Deborah Peterson, *Fredric March: Craftsman First, Star Second* (Westport, CT: Greenwood Publishing Group, 1996), 161.

120. Ronald Radosh and Allis Radosh, *Red Star over Hollywood: The Film Colony's Long Romance with the Left* (San Francisco: Encounter, 2005), 186.

121. Robert Nott, *He Ran All the Way: The Life of John Garfield* (New York: Limelight Editions, 2003), 289–90, 308.

122. See Jennifer Delton, "Rethinking Post–World War II Anticommunism," *The Journal of the Historical Society* 10 (2010). 1–41.

123. Philip Dunne, *Take Two: A Life in Movies and Politics* (New York: Limelight Editions, 1992), 217.

6 | The Two Joes

1. Quoted in Lois Scharf, *Eleanor Roosevelt: First Lady of American Liberalism* (Boston: Twayne, 1987), 154.

2. David Caute, *The Great Fear: The Anti-Communist Purge Under Truman and Eisenhower* (New York: Simon & Schuster, 1978), 52.

3. Richard H. Pells, *The Liberal Mind in a Conservative Age: American Intellectuals in the 1940s and 1950s* (Middletown, CT: Wesleyan University Press, 1989), 264, 265.

4. Steven M. Gillon, *Politics and Vision: The ADA and American Liberalism, 1947–1985* (New York: Oxford University Press, 1987), 108.

5. Quoted in Richard Cook, *Alfred Kazin: A Biography* (New Haven, CT: Yale University Press, 2007), 131.

6. Quoted in Caute, *The Great Fear*, 46.

7. Benjamin Balint, *Running* Commentary: *The Contentious Magazine That Transformed the Jewish Left into the Neoconservative Right* (New York: Public Affairs, 2010), 71.

8. Richard Gid Powers, *Not Without Honor: The History of American Anticommunism* (New York; Free Press, 1995), 237.

9. David A. Horowitz, *Beyond Left and Right: Insurgency and the Establishment* (Urbana, IL: University of Illinois Press, 1997), 219–20.

10. William Martin, *A Prophet with Honor: The Billy Graham Story* (New York: Morrow, 1991), 125, 165–66. See also Angela Lahr, *Millenial Dreams and Apocalyptic Nightmares: The Cold War Origins of Political Evangelicalism* (New York: Oxford University Press, 2007).

11. Richard Hofstadter, *Anti-Intellectualism in American Life* (New York: Vintage, 1963), 13.

12. Horowitz, *Beyond Left and Right*, 269.

13. Quoted in Jefferson Cowie, "From Hard Hats to the NASCAR Dads," *New Labor Forum* 13 (2004), 1.

14. Dean Rusk, as told to Richard Rusk, *As I Saw It* (New York: Norton, 1990), 158.

15. Ellen W. Schrecker, *Many Are the Crimes: McCarthyism in America* (Boston: Little Brown, 1998), 298.

16. Allan J. Lichtman, *White Protestant Nation: The Rise of the American Conservative Movement* (New York: Atlantic Monthly Press, 2008), 157.

17. Alistair Cooke, *A Generation on Trial: U.S.A. v. Alger Hiss* (New York: Knopf, 1950), 121; Richard Nixon, *The Memoirs of Richard Nixon* (New York: Grosset & Dunlap, 1978), 52–53.

18. Cooke, *A Generation on Trial*, 92.

19. See Sam Tanenhaus, *Whitaker Chambers* (New York: Random House, 1997), 226.

20. Whittaker Chambers, *Witness* (New York: Random House, 1952), 195.

21. "Testimony of David Whittaker Chambers," August 3, 1948, open session before the U.S. House Committee on Internal Security, See U.S. Congressional Record, 81st Congress, 1st session, 1949, XCV, Part 3, 3767–71.

22. Ibid. See also Chambers, *Witness*, 689; and Alger Hiss, *In the Court of Public Opinion* (New York: Knopf, 1957), 147.

23. W. H. Lawrence, "Communists Solid for Dewey to Win, Truman Declares," *New York Times*, September 29, 1948, 1.

24. Cooke, *A Generation on Trial*.

25. Quoted in Susan Jacoby, *Alger Hiss and the Battle for History* (New Haven, CT: Yale University Press, 2009), 113–14.

26. *New York Herald Tribune*, July 10, 1949. See also Sam Tanenhaus, *Whittaker Chambers: A Biography* (New York: Random House, 1997), 412.

27. See U.S. Congressional Record, 81st Congress, 2nd session, 1950, XCV, Part 3, 900–904. See also Allen Weinstein, *Perjury: The Hiss–Chambers Case* (New York: Vintage, 1978), 453.

28. See U.S. Congressional Record, 81st Congress, 2nd session, 1950, XCV, Part 3, 756.
29. See U.S. Congressional Record, 81st Congress, 1st session, 1949, XCV, Part 1, A1047–48.
30. *Witness* was the ninth bestselling book of 1952, *New York Times Book Review,* June 8, 1952; and *Time* (May 26, 1952). See Tanenhaus, *Whittaker Chambers,* 463; and Stephen J. Whitfield, *The Culture of the Cold War* (Baltimore: Johns Hopkins University Press, 1991), 18.
31. Sidney Hook, "The Faiths of Whittaker Chambers," *New York Times Book Review,* May 25, 1952, 1; Philip Rahv, "The Sense and Nonsense of Whittaker Chambers," in Arabel J. Porter and Andrew J. Dvosin, eds., *Essays on Literature and Politics, 1932–1972* (Boston: Houghton Mifflin, 1978), 322–23.
32. Richard M. Fried, *Nightmare in Red: The McCarthy Era in Perspective* (New York: Oxford University Press, 1990), 62.
33. Arthur M. Schlesinger, Jr., to Adlai Stevenson, August 5, 1953, Arthur M. Schlesinger Papers, Series 1, John F. Kennedy Presidential Library and Museum.
34. Fried, *Nightmare in Red,* 77.
35. Hofstadter, *Anti-Intellectualism in American Life,* 13.
36. Weinstein, *Perjury,* 451.
37. Fried, *Nightmare in Red,* 124.
38. Quoted in Richard H. Rovere, *Senator Joe McCarthy* (New York: Meridian, 1959), 30.
39. David M. Oshinsky, *A Conspiracy So Immense: The World of Joe McCarthy* (New York: Free Press, 1983), 430–32.
40. James T. Patterson, *Grand Expectations: The United States, 1945–1974* (New York: Oxford University Press, 1996), 269.
41. Allida M. Black, *Casting Her Own Shadow: Eleanor Roosevelt and the Shaping of Postwar Liberalism* (New York: Columbia University Press, 1996), 133–36, 148.
42. Murray Kempton himself and quoting Truman, quoted in John Patrick Diggins, *The Proud Decades: America in War and Peace, 1941–1960* (New York: Norton, 1988), 118.
43. Powers, *Not Without Honor,* 255.
44. James F. Simon, *Independent Journey: The Life of William O. Douglas* (New York: Penguin, 1980), 293, 298.
45. Leslie A. Fiedler, *An End to Innocence: Essays on Culture and Politics* (Boston: Beacon Press, 1955), 57.
46. Quoted in Eric Foner, "The Education of Richard Hofstadter" in *Who Owns History? Rethinking the Past in a Changing World* (New York: Hill & Wang, 2002), 25–46.
47. For Hofstadter's biography, in addition to Foner, see David Brown, *Richard Hofstadter: An Intellectual Biography* (Chicago: University of Chicago Press, 2006); Susan Stout Baker, *Radical Beginnings: Richard Hofstadter and the 1930s* (Westport, CT: Greenwood Press, 1985); Alfred Kazin, "Richard Hofstadter, 1916–1970," *American Scholar* 40 (1971); and Michael Kazin, "Hofstadter Lives: Political Culture and Temperament in the Work of an American Historian, *Reviews in American History* 27.2 (1999) 334–48.
48. Alfred Kazin, "Richard Hofstadter, 1916–1970," *American Scholar* 40 (1971), 399.
49. Brown, *Richard Hofstadter,* 79.
50. Richard Hofstadter, "Democracy and Anti-Intellectualism in America," *Michigan Alumnus Quarterly* (August 8, 1953), 282, 286.
51. Richard Hofstadter, "The Pseudo-Conservative Revolt," in Daniel Bell, ed., *The Radical Right (The New American Right Expanded and Updated)* (Garden City, NY: Anchor Books, 1964), 77, 84, 78.
52. See Richard Hofstadter, "The Paranoid Style in American Politics" (1964), in Hofstadter, *The Paranoid Style in American Politics and Other Essays* (Chicago: University of Chicago Press, 1965) and *Anti-Intellectualism in American Life,* 433.
53. Hofstadter, "The Pseudo-Conservative Revolt," 95.
54. Ibid., 77, 78. See also Michael Paul Rogin, *The Intellectuals and McCarthy: The Radical Specter* (Cambridge, MA: MIT, 1967), 93–94, 247. On the Frankfurt School and the "authoritarian personality," see Martin Jay, *The Dialectical Imagination: A History of the Frankfurt School and the Institute of Social Research, 1923–1950* (Boston: Little Brown, 1973).
55. Daniel Bell, "Interpretations of American Politics," in Bell, *The Radical Right,* 71.
56. David Riesman and Nathan Glazer, "Intellectuals and the Discontented Classes" (1955), in Bell, *The Radical Right,* 108, 119, 133.
57. Daniel Bell and Reinhold Neibuhr are quoted and elaborated upon by Alan Brinkley, "Liberalism and Belief," in Neil Jumonville and Kevin Mattson, eds., *Liberalism for a New Century* (Berkeley: University of California Press, 2007), 82.

58. Elia Kazan, *A Life* (New York: Knopf, 1988), 449, 464.
59. Quoted in Caute, *The Great Fear*, 508.
60. Quoted in Victor Navasky, *Naming Names* (New York: Viking, 1980), 242.
61. Ronald Radosh and Allis Radosh, *Red Star over Hollywood: The Film Colony's Long Romance with the Left* (San Francisco: Encounter, 2005), 189.
62. See Navasky, *Naming Names*, 200.
63. Quoted in ibid., 205.
64. See Christoper Bigsby, *Arthur Miller: 1962–2005* (Cambridge, MA: Harvard University Press, 2009), 549–65.
65. Quoted in Navasky, *Naming Names*, 199.
66. Quoted in Kazan, *A Life*, 470.
67. Kevin Mattson, *When America Was Great: The Fighting Faith of Postwar Liberalism* (New York: Routledge, 2004), 72.
68. Ibid., 68–69.
69. Joseph Dorman, *Arguing the World: The New York Intellectuals in Their Own Words* (New York: The Free Press, 2000), 118.
70. Ibid.
71. Diggins, *The Proud Decades*, 166
72. Arthur M. Schlesinger, Jr., to Sidney Hook, March 11, 1953, American Committee for Cultural Freedom Records, box 8; the letter to the *New York Times* dated July 13, 1953, is found in the same box.
73. *ADA World* (April 1953), 2 . This publication can be found in the Americans for Democratic Action Records at the Wisconsin Historical Society or in the microfilm copy of the ADA Records.
74. Gillon, *Politics and Vision*, 79.
75. Whitfield, *The Culture of the Cold War*, 163; Oshinksy, *A Conspiracy So Immense*, 187; Edwin R. Bayley, *Joe McCarthy and the Press* (Madison, WI: University of Wisconsin Press, 1981), 216.
76. Thomas Doherty, *Cold War, Cool Medium: Television, McCarthyism, and American Culture* (New York: Columbia University Press, 2003), 161.
77. Powers, *Not Without Honor*, 268.
78. Steven Stark quoted in Doherty, *Cold War, Cool Medium*, 162; for a critique of the rehabilitation of Murrow, see Jack Shafer, "Edward R. Movie," Slate.com, October 5, 2005, http://www.slate.com/id/2127595/.
79. *New York Post*, March 14, 1950, 33.
80. Marilyn Nissenson, *The Lady Upstairs: Dorothy Schiff and the* New York Post (New York: St. Martin's Press, 2007), 135, 155.
81. *New York Post*, September 4, 1951, 3, 32.
82. Max Lerner, *The Unfinished Country* (New York: Simon & Schuster, 1959), 184.
83. Mattson, *When America Was Great*, 55.
84. James A. Wechsler, *The Age of Suspicion* (New York: Donald I. Fine, 1953), 279.
85. "Excerpts from Testimony of Wechsler before McCarthy Inquiry," *New York Times*, May 8, 1953, C14; *Stenographic Transcript of Hearings before the Senate Permanent Subcommittee on Investigations, U.S. Senate*, May 5, 1953, vol. 83, 6145–46.
86. Mattson, *When America Was Great*, 56.
87. Arthur M. Schlesinger, Jr., to Adlai Stevenson, May 11, 1953, Schlesinger Papers, Series 1, Kennedy Library.
88. Quoted in Gillon, *Politics and Vision*, 69.
89. Ibid., 69.
90. Patterson, *Grand Expectations*, 221.
91. Alonzo L. Hamby, *Man of the People: A Life of Harry S. Truman* (New York: Oxford University Press, 1995), 555.
92. J. Ronald Oakley, *God's Country: America in the Fifties* (New York: Dembner, 1990), 87.
93. Patterson, *Grand Expectations*, 230.
94. Hamby, *Man of the People*, 564.
95. Ibid., 534.
96. Gillon, *Politics and Vision*, 91.
97. Irving Kristol, "'Civil Liberties,' 1952—A Study in Confusion," *Commentary* (March 1952), 299; also quoted in Pells, *The Liberal Mind in a Conservative Age*, 296.
98. Nathan Glazer quoted in Dorman, *Arguing the World*, 124.

7 | Eggheads in the Wilderness

1. Jeff Broadwater, *Adlai Stevenson and American Politics: The Odyssey of a Cold War Liberal* (New York: Twayne, 1994), 156.
2. Eric Goldman, *The Crucial Decade—And After: America, 1945–1960* (New York: Vintage, 1956), 223.
3. There was supposedly a slogan among women during his presidential campaigns: "Idlai Adlai Gladlai."
4. Richard Parker, *John Kenneth Galbraith: His Life, His Politics, His Economics* (New York: Farrar, Straus and Giroux, 2005), 263.
5. James T. Patterson, *Grand Expectations: The United States, 1945–1974* (New York: Oxford University Press, 1996), 252–53.
6. Broadwater, *Adlai Stevenson and American Politics*, 6.
7. Kevin Mattson, *When America Was Great: The Fighting Faith of Postwar Liberalism* (New York: Routledge, 2004), 23–24.
8. Porter McKeever, *Adlai Stevenson: His Life and Legacy: A Biography* (New York: Morrow, 1989), 373.
9. Arthur M. Schlesinger, Jr., "Stevenson and the American Liberal Dilemma," *Twentieth Century* 153 (1953), 25.
10. Broadwater, *Adlai Stevenson and American Politics*, 71.
11. Steven M. Gillon, *Politics and Vision: The ADA and American Liberalism, 1947–1985* (New York: Oxford University Press, 1987), 84.
12. Richard H. Pells, *The Liberal Mind in a Conservative Age: American Intellectuals in the 1940s and 1950s* (Middletown, CT: Wesleyan University Press, 1989), 397; Patterson, *Grand Expectations*, 252–53.
13. Broadwater, *Adlai Stevenson and American Politics*, 156.
14. John Kenneth Galbraith, "Three Generations of Democrats," 3, found in John Kenneth Galbraith Personal Papers, John F. Kennedy Presidential Library and Museum.
15. Arthur M. Schlesinger, Jr., *Journals: 1952–2000* (New York: Penguin, 2007), 12, 22.
16. Bernard DeVoto, "Stevenson and the Independent Voter," *Harper's* (April 1952), 64. As a civil libertarian, DeVoto was quick to endorse Stevenson.
17. Adlai Stevenson's speech found in *The Papers of Adlai E. Stevenson, vol. III* (Boston: Little Brown, 1973), 413–18.
18. Schlesinger, Jr., *Journals*, 6.
19. Broadwater, *Adlai Stevenson and American Politics*, 115.
20. David Halberstam, *The Fifties* (New York: Fawcett, 1993), 232.
21. David McCullough, *Truman* (New York: Simon & Schuster 1992) 907.
22. Schlesinger, Jr., *Journals*, 12–13.
23. Broadwater, *Adlai Stevenson and American Politics*, 116.
24. Schlesinger, Jr., *Journals*, 12–13.
25. McKeever, *Adlai Stevenson*, 215–16.
26. Alonzo L. Hamby, *Beyond the New Deal: Harry S. Truman and American Liberalism* (New York: Columbia University Press, 1973), 496–97.
27. John Patrick Diggins, "*The New Republic* and Its Times," *The New Republic* (December 10, 1984), 58.
28. William E. Leuchtenburg, *A Troubled Feast: American Society Since 1945* (Boston: Little, Brown, 1973), 34; J. Ronald Oakley, *God's Country: America in the Fifties* (New York: Dembner, 1986), 135.
29. Patterson, *Grand Expectations*, 255.
30. Halberstam, *The Fifties*, 236
31. Schlesinger, Jr., *Journals*, 12–13.
32. See Barton Bernstein's contribution to *History of American Presidential Elections*, vol. VIII (New York: Chelsea House, 1985), 3254.
33. Leuchtenburg, *A Troubled Feast*, 34; Oakley, *God's Country*, 135.
34. Arthur M. Schlesinger, Jr., "Stevenson and the American Liberal Dilemma," *Twentieth Century* 153 (1953), 26.
35. Benjamin Balint, *Running* Commentary, *The Contentious Magazine That Transformed the Jewish Left into the Neoconservative Right* (New York: Public Affairs, 2010), 45–46.
36. Quoted in Jackson Lears, "A Matter of Taste: Corporate Cultural Hegemony in a Mass Consumption Society," in Lary May, ed., *Recasting America: Culture and Politics in the Age of the Cold War* (Chicago: University of Chicago Press, 1989), 40.

37. John Patrick Diggins, *The Proud Decades: America in War and Peace, 1941–1960* (New York: Norton, 1988), 266.

38. "America and the Intellectual: The Reconciliation," *Time* (June 11, 1956), quoted in Balint, *Running* Commentary, 227.

39. "Our Country and Our Culture," *Partisan Review* 19 (1952), 284. Citations here and following are the page numbers from the symposium; this ran in a series throughout 1952).

40. Ibid., 574.

41. Ibid., 450.

42. Ibid., 577.

43. Ibid., 302.

44. Ibid., 592–93.

45. Patterson, *Grand Expectations*, 312.

46. Ibid., 348.

47. David Riesman, "A Personal Memoir," in Walter W. Powell and Richard Robbins, eds., *Conflict and Consensus: A Festschrift in Honor of Lewis A. Coser* (New York: Free Press, 1984).

48. David Riesman, *Individualism Reconsidered and Other Essays* (New York: Free Press, 1954), 106.

49. David Riesman et al., *The Lonely Crowd* (1950; repr., New York: Doubleday, 1955), 106.

50. Ibid., 63.

51. David Riesman, *Individualism Reconsidered*, 100. See also James P. Young, *Reconsidering American Liberalism: The Troubled Odyssey of the Liberal Idea* (New York: Westview, 1996), 184.

52. Quoted in Michael Wreszin, *A Rebel in Defense of Tradition: The Life and Politics of Dwight Macdonald* (New York: Basic Books, 1994), 262.

53. Daniel Bell and Irving Howe quoted in Pells, *The Liberal Mind in a Conservative Age*, 218.

54. Irving Howe, "This Age of Conformity," in *Selected Writings, 1950–1990* (New York: Harcourt Brace Jovanovich, 1990), 26–49.

55. Sloan Wilson, *The Man in the Gray Flannel Suit* (1955; repr., New York: Four Walls Eight Windows, 2002), 61.

56. John Cheever, "The Country Husband," in *The Stories of John Cheever* (New York: Ballantine, 1978); Scott Donaldson, *John Cheever: A Biography* (New York: Random House, 1988), 143. See also Blake Bailey, *Cheever: A Life* (New York: Knopf, 2009), esp. 208–11.

57. Lionel Trilling, *Matthew Arnold* (New York: Norton, 1939). This discussion of Trilling and Arnold is also indebted to the arguments made by Michael Kimmage, *The Conservative Turn: Lionel Trilling, Whittaker Chambers, and the Lessons of Anti-Communism*, especially Chapter 3, 78–109.

58. Ibid., 188, 254.

59. Ibid., 384.

60. Parker, *John Kenneth Galbraith*, 30.

61. John Kenneth Galbraith, *A Life in Our Times: Memoirs* (Boston: Houghton Mifflin, 1981), 81.

62. Parker, *John Kenneth Galbraith*, 149.

63. Ibid., 151–52.

64. Ibid., 234.

65. John Kenneth Galbraith, *Ambassador's Journal: A Personal Account of the Kennedy Years* (Boston: Houghton Mifflin Co, 1969), 45.

66. Jordan A. Schwarz, *Liberal: Adolf A. Berle and the Vision of an American Era* (New York: Free Press, 1987), 61; on advising Stevenson, see 296–97.

67. John Kenneth Galbraith, *American Capitalism* (1952; repr., New York: Houghton Mifflin, 1962), 119, 120.

68. Parker, *John Kenneth Galbraith*, 237.

69. Max Lerner, *America as a Civilization* (New York: Simon & Schuster, 1957), 350.

70. Galbraith, *American Capitalism*, 95. See also Galbraith, "The Unseemly Economics of Opulence," *Harper's* (January 1952), 58–63.

71. John Kenneth Galbraith to Jonathan Bingham, May 12, 1954, Galbraith Papers, Kennedy Library.

72. Parker, *John Kenneth Galbraith*, 267; Galbraith, *A Life in Our Times*, 307–308.

73. John Kenneth Galbraith, *The Affluent Society* (1958; repr., Boston: Houghton Mifflin, 1976), 195.

74. Parker, *John Kenneth Galbraith*, 294.

75. See Wreszin, *A Rebel in Defense of Tradition*, 278; and Carol Brightman, *Writing Dangerously: Mary McCarthy and Her World* (New York: Clarkson Potter, 1992), 358–61.

76. Arthur M. Schlesinger, Jr., to Adlai Stevenson, September 22, 1955, Schlesinger Papers, Kennedy Library.
77. See James T. Kloppenberg, "Aspirational Nationalism in America," *Intellectual History Newsletter* 24 (2002), 60–71.
78. For Galbraith's views on conservation, see his "How Much Should a Country Consume?" in Henry Jarrett, ed., *Perspectives on Conservation* (Baltimore: Johns Hopkins University Press, 1958).
79. Bernard DeVoto to Schlesinger, January 18, 1955, found in Schlesinger Papers, Kennedy Library. For more on the environmental activism of the 1940s and 1950s that informed DeVoto's work, see David Backes, *A Wilderness Within: The Life of Sigurd F. Olson* (Minneapolis: University of Minnesota Press, 1997), especially Chapter 10; Mary Street Alinder, *Ansel Adams: A Biography* (New York: Holt, 1996), 215–17; Mark Harvey, *Wilderness Forever: Howard Zahniser and the Path to the Wilderness Act* (Seattle: University of Washington Press, 2005), 132; Paul Sutter, *Driven Wild: How the Fight Against Automobiles Launched the Modern Wilderness Movement* (Seattle: University of Washington Press, 2002).
80. John Bartlow Martin, *Adlai Stevenson and the World: The Life of Adlai Stevenson* (Garden City, NY: Anchor Books, 1978), 255.
81. Letter quoted in Martin, *Adlai Stevenson and the World,* 256.
82. Quoted ibid., 234–35.
83. Broadwater, *Adlai Stevenson and American Politics,* 171.
84. Jean H. Baker, *The Stevensons: A Biography of an American Family* (New York: Norton, 1996), 363.
85. Quoted in Martin, *Adlai Stevenson and the World,* 122.
86. Quoted ibid., 258–59.
87. Quoted in Fred Kaplan, *1959: The Year Everything Changed* (Hoboken, NJ: Wiley, 2009), 59.
88. Schlesinger, Jr., *Journals,* 41–43.
89. Marilyn Nissenson, *The Lady Upstairs: Dorothy Schiff and the* New York Post (New York: St Martin's Press, 2007), 193.
90. Allen J. Matusow, *The Unraveling of America: A History of Liberalism in the 1960s* (New York: Harper & Row, 1984), 8.

8 | We Shall Overcome

1. Ralph Ellison, "An American Dilemma: A Review," *The Collected Essays of Ralph Ellison,* ed. John Callahan (New York: Modern Library, 1995), 339.
2. Max Lerner, *The Unfinished Century* (New York: Simon & Schuster, 1959), 541.
3. Arnold Rampersad, *Ralph Ellison: A Biography* (New York: Knopf, 2007), 30.
4. Booker T. Washington in Francis L. Broderick and August Meier, eds., *Negro Protest Thought in the Twentieth Century* (Indianapolis: Bobbs-Merrill, 1966), 6.
5. Arnold Rampersad, *Ralph Ellison,* 67.
6. Ibid.
7. W.E.B. Du Bois in Broderick and Meier, *Negro Protest Thought,* 35.
8. Charles Flint Kellogg, *NAACP: A History of the National Association for the Advancement of Colored People, 1909–1920* (Baltimore: Johns Hopkins University Press, 1967); John Hope Franklin, *From Slavery to Freedom: A History of Negro Americans* (New York: Knopf, 1988), 287–88.
9. W.E.B. Du Bois, *The Souls of Black Folk* (1903; repr., New York: Bedford/St. Martin's Press, 1997), 37.
10. David Levering Lewis, *W. E .B. Du Bois: The Fight For Equality and the American Century, 1919–1963* (New York: Holt, 2000), 535–38.
11. Rampersad, *Ralph Ellison,* 90, 92.
12. Richard Wright, *Native Son* (Stockholm: Jan Förlag, 1943), 48.
13. Richard Wright in Richard H. Crossman, ed., *The God That Failed* (New York: Harper and Brothers, 1949), 127.
14. The quote is from Rampersad, *Ralph Ellison,* 162; see also Lawrence Jackson, *Ralph Ellison: Emergence of Genius* (Hoboken, NJ: Wiley, 2002), 403.
15. Ralph Ellison, *The Collected Essays of Ralph Ellison,* ed. John Callahan (New York: Modern Library, 1995), 339.
16. Ibid., 306, 308.
17. Ralph Ellison, *Shadow and Act* (New York: Random House, 1964), 103, 104, 169.

18. James Baldwin, "Everybody's Protest Novel," *Partisan Review* 16 (1949), 584.
19. Morris Dickstein, *Leopards in the Temple: The Transformation of American Fiction, 1945–1970* (Cambridge, MA: Harvard University Press, 2002), 209.
20. John S. Wright, "To the Battle Royal," in Lary May, ed., *Recasting America: Culture and Politics in the Age of Cold War* (Chicago: University of Chicago Press, 1989), 247.
21. Juan Williams, *Thurgood Marshall: American Revolutionary* (New York: Times Books, 1998), 17, 22, 27–28.
22. Howard Ball, *A Defiant Life: Thurgood Marshall and the Persistence of Racism in America* (New York: Crown, 1998), 17.
23. Michael D. Davis and Hunter R. Clark, *Thurgood Marshall: Warrior at the Bar, Rebel on the Bench* (Secaucus, NJ: Carol Publishing, 1992), 4.
24. Ball, *A Defiant Life*, 43.
25. Davis and Clark, *Thurgood Marshall*, 44–45.
26. Ibid., 56.
27. Williams, *Thurgood Marshall*, 169.
28. Risa L. Goluboff, *The Lost Promise of Civil Rights* (Cambridge, MA: Harvard University Press, 2007), 228.
29. Williams, *Thurgood Marshall*, 174.
30. See on this point Randall Kennedy, "Schoolings in Equality," *The New Republic* (June 24, 2004), 29–39.
31. Richard D. Kluger, *Simple Justice: The History of Brown v. Board of Education and Black America's Struggle for Equality* (New York: Vintage, 1975), 635.
32. Ibid., 355–56; John P. Jackson, Jr., *Social Scientists for Social Justice: Making the Case against Segregation* (New York: New York University Press, 2001), 145, 176.
33. See Kevin Mattson, *Rebels All!: A Short History of the Conservative Mind in Postwar America* (New Brunswick, NJ: Rutgers University Press, 2008), 52–54.
34. Davis and Clark, *Thurgood Marshall*, 171.
35. James F. Simon, *Independent Journey: The Life of William O. Douglas* (New York: Penguin, 1980), 242; Bruce Allen Murphy, *Wild Bill: The Legend and Life of William O. Douglas* (New York: Random House, 2003), 233–34.
36. Jim Newton, *Justice for All: Earl Warren and the Nation He Made* (New York: Riverhead, 2006), 318.
37. Eric Alterman's interview, April 1977, U.S. Supreme Court, Washington, DC.
38. See Richard Hofstadter, ed., *Great Issues in American History: From Reconstruction to the Present Day, 1864–1969* (New York: Vintage, 1969), 60, 62, 63.
39. Quoted in Gene Roberts and Hank Klibanoff, *The Race Beat: The Press, the Civil Rights Movement, and the Awakening of the Nation* (New York: Knopf, 2006), 72.
40. Quoted in John D'Emilio, *Lost Prophet: The Life and Times of Bayard Rustin* (New York: Free Press, 2003), 224.
41. "Declaration of Ninety-Six Southern Congressmen on Integration," in Hofstadter, *Great Issues*, 64.
42. Michael O'Donnell, "Without Artifice: On William Brennan," *The Nation* (November 17, 2010), http://www.thenation.com/article/156517/without-artifice-william-brennan.
43. Taylor Branch, *Parting the Waters: America in the King Years, 1954–63* (New York: Simon & Schuster, 1988), 114.
44. David J. Garrow, *Bearing the Cross: Martin Luther King, Jr., and the Southern Christian Leadership Conference* (New York: Vintage, 1986), 15.
45. Branch, *Parting the Waters*, 41.
46. Garrow, *Bearing the Cross*, 34.
47. Branch, *Parting the Waters*, 63.
48. Ibid., 68.
49. King, Jr., in Washington, *A Testament of Hope*, 35–36.
50. Branch, *Parting the Waters*, 86.
51. Quoted in Gary Dorrien, *Economy, Difference, Empire: Social Ethics for Social Justice* (New York: Columbia University Press, 2010), 81.
52. Branch, *Parting the Waters*, 92.
53. See David J. Garrow, "King's Plagiarism," *Journal of American History* 78 (1991), 90.
54. Garrow, *Bearing the Cross*, 48.
55. Branch, *Parting the Waters*, 114.

56. Stephen B. Oates, *Let the Trumpet Sound: The Life of Martin Luther King, Jr.* (New York: Harper & Row, 1982), 68.

57. Branch, *Parting the Waters*, 138.

58. Quoted in Branch, *Parting the Waters*, 139–40.

59. Branch, *Parting the Waters*, 161.

60. David L. Chappell, *A Stone of Hope: Prophetic Religion and the Death of Jim Crow* (Chapel Hill: University of North Carolina Press, 2004), 87.

61. Branch, *Parting the Waters*, 159–60.

62. Ibid., 193.

63. Quoted in Garrow, *Bearing the Cross*, 81.

64. Quoted in James T. Patterson, *Grand Expectations: The United States, 1945–1974* (New York: Oxford University Press, 1996), 405.

65. D'Emilio, *Lost Prophet*, 246, 247–48.

66. Gilbert Jonas, *Freedom's Sword: The NAACP and the Struggle Against Racism in America, 1909–1969* (New York: Routledge, 2005), 164.

67. Quoted in Harvard Sitkoff, *The Struggle for Black Equality, 1954–1980* (New York: Hill and Wang, 1981), 35.

68. Nadine Cohodas, *Strom Thurmond and the Politics of Southern Change* (New York: Simon & Schuster, 1993), 294–96.

69. Paula F. Pfeffer, *A. Philip Randolph, Pioneer of the Civil Rights Movement* (Baton Rouge: Louisiana University Press, 1990), 206–13.

70. Clayton Sinyai, *Schools of Democracy: A Political History of the American Labor Movement* (Ithaca, NY: Cornell University Press, 2006), 202.

71. Stanley Kramer, with Thomas M. Coffey, *A Mad, Mad, Mad, Mad World: A Life in Hollywood* (New York: Harcourt Brace, 1997), 147–48.

72. Susan Jacoby, *Alger Hiss and the Battle for History* (New Haven, CT: Yale University Press, 2009), 132.

73. Patterson, *Grand Expectations*, 416.

74. See Bill Morgan and Nancy J. Peters, eds., *Howl on Trial: The Battle for Free Expression* (San Francisco: City Light Books, 2006).

75. Fred Kaplan, *1959: The Year Everything Changed* (Hoboken, NJ: Wiley, 2009), 51.

76. Elisabeth Ladenson, *Dirt for Art's Sake: Books on Trial from* Madame Bovary *to* Lolita (Ithaca, NY: Cornell University Press, 2007), 221.

77. Arthur M. Schlesinger, Jr., "Where Does the Liberal Go from Here?" *New York Times Magazine*, August 4, 1957, 38.

78. King, Jr., in Washington, *A Testament of Hope*, 14.

79. LeRoy Ashby, *With Amusement for All: A History of American Popular Culture Since 1830* (Louisville: University Press of Kentucky, 2006), 315.

80. Maurice Isserman, *If I Had a Hammer: The Death of the Old Left and the Birth of the New Left* (New York: Basic Books, 1987), 149; Lawrence S. Wittner, *Rebels Against War: The American Peace Movement, 1933–1983* (Philadelphia: Temple University Press, 1984), 228.

9 | The Liberal Hour

1. John F. Kennedy, "Acceptance of the New York Liberal Party Nomination," New York City, September 14, 1960, http://www.pbs.org/wgbh/amex/presidents/35_kennedy/psources/ps_nyliberal.html.

2. Robert Dallek, *An Unfinished Life: John F. Kennedy, 1917–1963* (Boston: Little Brown and Company, 2003), 43.

3. Lance Morrow, *The Best Year of Their Lives: Kennedy, Johnson, and Nixon in 1948* (New York: Basic Books, 2004), 8.

4. Richard Reeves, *President Kennedy: Profile of Power* (New York: Simon & Schuster, 1993), 18, 19.

5. Quoted in Arthur M. Schlesinger, Jr., *Robert Kennedy and His Times* (New York: Ballantine, 1978), 14.

6. Dallek, *An Unfinished Life*, 33–35, 75.

7. Ibid., 81, 101, 105.

8. Ibid., 212.

9. Ibid., 259.

10. Charles Peters, *Tilting at Windmills: An Autobiography* (Reading, MA: Addison-Wesley, 1988), 100.

11. Arthur M. Schlesinger, Jr., *Journals, 1952–2000* (New York: Penguin, 2007), 17.

12. Theodore H. White, *In Search of History: A Personal Adventure* (New York: Warner, 1978), 594.

13. James A. Wechsler, *Reflections of an Angry Middle-Aged Editor* (New York: Random House, 1960), 38. See also *ADA World* (February 1960), 3. This publication can be found in the Americans for Democratic Action Records at the Wisconsin Historical Society or in the microfilm copy of the ADA Records.

14. Quoted in Steven M. Gillon, *Politics and Vision: The ADA and American Liberalism, 1947–1985* (New York: Oxford University Press, 1987), 132.

15. Quoted in Dallek, *An Unfinished Life*, 233.

16. Carl Solberg, *Hubert Humphrey: A Biography* (New York: Norton, 1984), 193.

17. Lois Scharf, *Eleanor Roosevelt: First Lady of American Liberalism* (Boston: Twayne, 1987), 171.

18. Norman Mailer, *The Presidential Papers* (New York: Bantam, 1964), 45, 47; see also George Cotkin, *Existential America* (Baltimore: Johns Hopkins University Press, 2003), 208.

19. Kate Betts, "The Cool Factor," *Time* (June 21, 2007), 62–63.

20. Quoted in White, *In Search of History*, 629–30.

21. Dominic Sandbrook, *Eugene McCarthy: The Rise and Fall of Postwar American Liberalism* (New York: Knopf, 2004), 104.

22. Solberg, *Hubert Humphrey*, 199–200.

23. Quoted in James A. Bill, *George Ball: Behind the Scenes in U.S. Foreign Policy* (New Haven, CT: Yale University Press, 1997), 56. See also Mark J. White, *The Cuban Missile Crisis.* (Basingstoke, UK: Macmillan, 1996), 177; and Michael R. Beschloss, *The Crisis Years* (New York: Harper-Collins, 1991), 467.

24. Schlesinger, Jr., *Journals*, 63.

25. Ibid., 67.

26. Ibid., 68.

27. Quoted in Gillon, *Politics and Vision*, 132.

28. See Nick Bryant, *The Bystander: John F. Kennedy and the Struggle for Black Equality* (New York: Basic Books, 2006), 145.

29. Schlesinger, Jr., *Journals*, 77–79.

30. John Kenneth Galbraith to Adlai Stevenson, June 30, 1969, John Kenneth Galbraith Personal Papers, box 40, John F. Kennedy Presidential Library and Museum.

31. John Kenneth Galbraith, *The Liberal Hour* (New York: Houghton Mifflin, 1960), 11.

32. Quoted in Richard Parker, *John Kenneth Galbraith: His Life, His Politics, His Economics* (New York: Farrar, Straus and Giroux, 2005), 333.

33. Speech to the Economic Policy Committee, Democratic Advisory Council, found in Galbraith Papers, box 75, Kennedy Library.

34. Dallek, *An Unfinished Life*, 276.

35. Reeves, *President Kennedy*, 39.

36. John F. Kennedy in Richard Hofstadter, ed., *Great Issues in American History: From Reconstruction to the Present Day, 1864–1969* (New York: Vintage, 1969), 453, 454, 456. See also Thurston Clarke, *Ask Not: The Inauguration of John F. Kennedy and the Speech That Changed America* (New York: Holt, 2004).

37. Elizabeth Cobbs Hoffman, *All You Need Is Love: The Peace Corps and the Spirit of the 1960s* (Cambridge, MA: Harvard University Press, 1998), 11–12; Scott Stossel, *Sarge: The Life and Times of Sargent Shriver* (Washington, DC: Smithsonian, 2004), 169–70.

38. Solberg, *Hubert Humphrey*, 216, G. Calvin Mackenzie and Robert Weisbrot, *The Liberal Hour: Washington and the Politics of Change in the 1960s* (New York: Penguin, 2008), 261.

39. Hoffman, *All You Need Is Love*, 53.

40. Sandbrook, *Eugene McCarthy*, 40.

41. Stossel, *Sarge*, 139, 141.

42. Nicholas Lemann, *The Promised Land: The Great Black Migration and How It Changed America* (New York: Vintage, 1991), 114.

43. Charles Peters, quoted in in Danelle Ivory, "Rebels with a Cause: American Journalism and the Independent Peace Corps," Undergraduate Thesis, Princeton University, Princeton, NJ, 2005.

44. Stossel, *Sarge*, 196. On Wofford, see David J. Garrow, *Bearing the Cross: Martin Luther King, Jr., and the Southern Christian Leadership Conference* (New York: Vintage, 1986), 83–84.

45. Bryant, *The Bystander*, 313–14.

46. Bill Moyers is quoted in Ivory, "Rebels with a Cause."
47. Elizabeth Cobbs Hoffman, *All You Need Is Love*, 47.
48. Stossel, *Sarge*, 214–15.
49. Peters, *Tilting at Windmills*, 117.
50. Hoffman, *All You Need Is Love*, 54.
51. Ibid., 41.
52. Ibid., 33.
53. Schlesinger, Jr., *Robert Kennedy and His Times*, 444–45.
54. Dallek, *An Unfinished Life*, 362.
55. Ibid., 358.
56. Parker, *John Kenneth Galbraith*, 353.
57. New details about the operations became public owing to the CIA's declassification of its own history of the operation. For a discussion of these, see Robert Dallek, "Untold Story of the Bay of Pigs," *Newsweek* (August 14, 2011), http://www.thedailybeast.com/newsweek/2011/08/14/bay-of-pigs-newly-revealed-cia-documents-expose-blunders.html.
58. George Tindall, *America: A Narrative History*, vol. 2 (New York: Norton, 1988), 1356.
59. Quoted in David Talbot, "Warrior for Peace," *Time* (June 21, 2007), http://www.time.com/time/specials/2007/article/0,28804,1635958_1635999,00.html.
60. Schlesinger, Jr., *Journals*, 120.
61. Lawrence Freedman, *Kennedy's Wars: Berlin, Cuba, Laos, and Vietnam* (New York: Oxford University Press, 2000), 124.
62. Mackenzie and Weisbrot, *The Liberal Hour*, 255.
63. Freedman, *Kennedy's Wars*, 229.
64. Quoted in Sheldon M. Stern, *Averting "The Final Failure": John F. Kennedy and the Secret Cuban Missile Crisis Meetings* (Stanford, CA: Stanford University Press, 2003), 100.
65. Donald F. Chamberlain, CIA Inspector General, to Walt Elder, June 5, 1975, Rockefeller Commission Papers, Gerald R. Ford Presidential Library Materials, JFK Assassination Materials Project, National Archives, College Park, MD. Chamberlain's letter quotes from Operation Mongoose documents including Robert Kennedy's January 19, 1962, memo to McCone. See also Alexandr Fursenko and Timothy Naftali, *One Hell of a Gamble: Khrushchev, Castro, and Kennedy, 1958–1964* (New York: Norton, 1997), 150.
66. Barton J. Bernstein, "Commentary: Reconsidering Khrushchev's Gambit—Defending the Soviet Union and Cuba," *Diplomatic History* 14 (1990), 234.
67. For a detailed account of what was known about the crisis circa 2004, see Eric Alterman, *When Presidents Lie: A History of Official Deception and Its Consequences* (New York: Viking, 2004), 90–160.
68. Alterman, *When Presidents Lie*, 104.
69. If the initial offer had been rejected, Kennedy had deputized Secretary of State Dean Rusk to arrange with Columbia University president Andrew Cordier to have Cordier telephone his close friend, UN Secretary-General U Thant. Cordier would then instruct him as to the exact language through which the United States would be willing to accept a missile trade if publicly requested by the UN chief. Kennedy would likely have acceded to a public deal with the previously authorized language that he, together with Rusk and Bobby Kennedy, had themselves scripted. For more on "the Cordier Ploy," see James G. Blight and David A. Welch, *On the Brink: Americans and Soviets Reexamine the Cuban Missile Crisis*, 2nd ed. (New York: Noonday, 1990), 82–83; and Dean Rusk, as told to Richard Rusk, *As I Saw It* (New York: Norton, 1990), 240–41.
70. See Ronald Steel, "Endgame," *The New York Review of Books* (March 13, 1969), 15–22.
71. Freedman, *Kennedy's Wars*, 249.
72. Walter Trohan in the *Chicago Tribune*, October 27, 1962, 4.
73. *Time* (November 2, 1962), 15.
74. Raymond L. Garthoff, *Reflections on the Cuban Missile Crisis* (Washington, DC: Brookings Institution Press, 1989), 87; and Theodore C. Sorensen, *The Kennedy Legacy* (New York: Macmillan, 1969), 192.
75. Freedman, *Kennedy's Wars*, 267.
76. Reeves, *President Kennedy*, 552.
77. Charles E. Bohlen, *Witness to History, 1929–1969* (New York: Norton, 1973), 495–96.
78. See Kai Bird, *The Color of Truth: McGeorge and William Bundy: Brothers in Arms: A Biography* (New York: Simon & Schuster, 1998), 249.

79. Kennedy did this in the first and best read of the allegedly comprehensive treatments of the crisis, Stewart Alsop and Joseph Alsop, "In a Time of Crisis," *Saturday Evening Post* ccxxxv (December 8, 1962), 15–21. The authors allowed Kennedy to read, edit, and amend the article before it was published. See Alterman, *When Presidents Lie*, 356

80. See also Barton J. Bernstein, "Reconsidering the Missile Crisis: Dealing with the Problems of the American Jupiters in Turkey," James A. Nathan, ed., *The Cuban Missile Crisis Revisited* (New York: St. Martin's Press, 1992), 106.

81. Cyrus Vance Oral History Interview, March 9, 1970, Interview no. 3, 11, Lyndon Baines Johnson Library and Museum.

82. David Kaiser, *American Tragedy: Kennedy, Johnson, and the Origins of the Vietnam War* (Cambridge, MA: Harvard University Press, 2000), 370.

83. Brian VanDeMark, *Into the Quagmire: Lyndon Johnson and the Escalation of the Vietnam War* (New York: Oxford, 1991), 50.

84. Robert A. Divine, ed., *The Cuban Missile Crisis*, 2nd ed. (New York: M. Weiner, 1988), 160.

85. John Kenneth Galbraith to JFK, February 28, 1961, John Kenneth Galbraith Papers, box 77.

86. Galbraith, *Letters to Kennedy* (Cambridge, MA: Harvard University Press, 1998), 98.

87. See Talbot, "Warrior for Peace." See also James G. Blight, Janet M. Lang, and David A. Welch, *Vietnam If Kennedy Had Lived: Virtual JFK* (New York: Rowan and Littlefield, 2009) and James K. Galbraith, "Exit Strategy," *Boston Review*, October/November, 2003, www.bostonreview .net/BR28.5/galbraith.html.

88. See Julian E. Zelizer, *Arsenal of Democracy: The Politics of National Security—From World War II to the War on Terrorism* (New York: Basic Books, 2009), 125–27.

89. Available online at http://mcadams.posc.mu.edu/ike.htm.

90. Zelizer, *Arsenal of Democracy*, 152.

91. Available online at http://www.infoplease.com/ipa/A0904490.html.

92. See William K. Domke, "Do Leaders Make a Difference? Posture and Politics in the Defense Budget," in Alex Mintz, ed., *The Political Economy of Military Spending in the United States* (New York: Routledge, 1992), 41.

93. For discussions of the costs of these foreign military interventions, see for instance, Ronald Steel, *Pax Americana* (New York: Viking, 1967); Robert H. Johnson, *Improbable Dangers: U.S. Conceptions of Threat in the Cold War and After* (New York: St. Martin's Press, 1994); Stephen Kinzer, *Overthrow: America's Century of Regime Change from Hawaii to Iraq* (New York: Times Books, 2006), 148–259; and Charles S. Maier, *Among Empires: American Ascendancy and Its Predecessors* (Cambridge, MA: Harvard University Press, 2006), 151–91.

94. John F. Kennedy's Commencement Address at Yale University, in Hofstadter, *Great Issues*, 459.

95. For more on how the history of Keynesian thought put strong limitations on liberal economic policy, see Alan Brinkley, "The New Deal and the Idea of the State," in Steve Fraser and Gary Gerstle, eds., *The Rise and Fall of the New Deal Order, 1930–1980* (Princeton: Princeton University Press, 1989).

96. Quoted in Parker, *John Kenneth Galbraith*, 392.

97. Dallek, *An Unfinished Life*, 507.

98. Quoted in Parker, *John Kenneth Galbraith*, 360.

99. See White, *In Search of History*, 653; and Allen J. Matusow, *The Unraveling of America: A History of Liberalism in the 1960s* (New York: Harper & Row, 1984), 55.

100. Quoted in H. W. Brands, *The Strange Death of American Liberalism* (New Haven, CT: Yale University Press, 2001), 86.

101. Ibid., 87–88.

102. Matusow, *The Unraveling of America*, 99.

103. Ibid., 105.

104. Dwight Macdonald, "Books: Our Invisible Poor," *The New Yorker* (January 19, 1963), http://www.newyorker.com/archive/1963/01/19/1963_01_19_082_TNY_CARDS_000075671?printable=true.

105. Michael Harrington, *The Other America: Poverty in the United States* (Baltimore: Penguin, 1963), 2, 12.

106. Ibid., 191.

107. Dwight Macdonald, "Books: Our Invisible Poor."

108. Lemann, *The Promised Land*, 112.

109. Stossel, *Sarge*, 165; and Lemann, *The Promised Land*, 115.

110. Garrow, *Bearing the Cross*, 170.

111. Ibid.,156.
112. Taylor Branch, *Parting the Waters: America in the King Years, 1954–63* (New York: Simon & Schuster, 1988), 443.
113. Garrow, *Bearing the Cross*, 161.
114. Quoted in Schlesinger, Jr., *Robert Kennedy and His Times*, 312.
115. Branch, *Parting the Waters*, 480.
116. Arthur M. Schlesinger, Jr., *A Thousand Days: John F. Kennedy in the White House* (Boston: Houghton Mifflin, 1965), 941; William Doyle, *An American Insurrection: The Battle of Oxford, Mississippi, 1962* (New York: Doubleday, 2001). In one conversation with Governor Barnett of Mississippi, Kennedy asked, "Are you getting out of the Union?" Schlesinger, Jr., *Robert Kennedy and His Times*, 342. The conflicts in Oxford had resulted in a foreign journalist killed and "160 marshals . . . injured, including 27 with gunshot wounds." See also Dallek, *An Unfinished Life*, 517.
117. See Harry Belafonte with Michael Shnayerson, *My Song: A Memoir* (New York: Knopf, 2011).
118. "Man of the Year: Martin Luther King, Jr., Never Again Where He Was," *Time* (January 3, 1964), http://www.time.com/time/magazine/article/0,9171,940759,00.html.
119. See Layhmond Robinson, "Robert Kennedy Consults Negroes Here About North," *New York Times*, May 25, 1963, 1.
120. Carol Polsgrove, *Divided Minds: Intellectuals and the Civil Rights Movement* (New York: Norton, 2001), 178.
121. Branch, *Parting the Waters*, 810.
122. Harry Belafonte, *My Song*, 267–69.
123. Polsgrove, *Divided Minds*, 179.
124. James Baldwin, "The American Dream and The American Negro," *New York Times Magazine*, March 17, 1965, http://select.nytimes.com/mem/archive/pdf?res=F70D12FC3E5812738D DDAE0894DB405B858AF1D3.
125. Schlesinger, Jr., *Robert Kennedy and His Times*, 360.
126. Quoted in Polsgrove, *Divided Minds*, 177.
127. Schlesinger, Jr., *Journals: 1952–2000*, 193.
128. Quoted in John D'Emilio, *Lost Prophet: The Life and Times of Bayard Rustin* (New York: Free Press, 2003), 345.
129. Schlesinger, Jr., *Robert Kennedy and His Times*, 387.
130. Ibid., 386; Taylor Branch, *Pillar of Fire: America in the King Years, 1963–1965* (New York: Simon & Schuster, 1998), 153–54, and Branch, *Parting the Waters*, 903.
131. Branch, *Parting the Waters*, 909.
132. Ibid., 824
133. Harry Belafonte, *My Song*, 272.
134. Dallek, *An Unfinished Life*, 643.
135. Garrow, *Bearing the Cross*, 273.
136. Nelson Lichtenstein, *The Most Dangerous Man in Detroit: Walter Reuther and the Fate of American Labor* (New York: Basic Books, 1995), 371, 370; and Branch, *Parting the Waters*, 881–85. For more on how the UAW helped the civil rights movement and even the burgeoning New Left, see Peter B. Levy, *The New Left and Labor in the 1960s* (Urbana, IL: University of Illinois Press, 1994).
137. Martin Luther King, Jr., in James M. Washington, ed., *A Testament of Hope: The Essential Writings of Martin Luther King, Jr.* (New York: HarperCollins, 1991), 295.
138. Harry Belafonte, *My Song*, 272.
139. John D'Emilio, *Lost Prophet*, 353, 354.
140. Available online at http://www.americanrhetoric.com/speeches/mlkihaveadream.htm.
141. Martin Luther King, Jr., in Washington, *A Testament of Hope*, 219, 218.
142. Reeves, *President Kennedy*, 584.
143. D'Emilio, *Lost Prophet*, 357.
144. Gene Roberts and Hank Klibanoff, *The Race Beat: The Press, the Civil Rights Struggle, and the Awakening of a Nation* (New York: Knopf, 2006), 348.
145. Ibid., 348.
146. Edward M. Kennedy, *True Compass* (New York: Twelve, 2009), 201.
147. This is the evocative image used by Nick Bryant in his extremely thorough study, *The Bystander*.
148. Evans and Novak, Lewis and White are quoted in ibid., 452.

10 | Master of Disaster

1. Quoted in William E. Leuchtenburg, *In the Shadow of FDR: From Harry Truman to Barack Obama* (Ithaca, NY: Cornell University Press, 2001), 137.

2. Richard N. Goodwin, *Remembering America: A Voice from the Sixties* (Boston: Little Brown, 1988), 392.

3. Dean Acheson cited in George C. Herring, *LBJ and Vietnam: A Different Kind of War* (Austin: University of Texas Press, 1994), 16.

4. Joseph A. Califano, Jr., *The Triumph and Tragedy of Lyndon Johnson: The White House Years* (New York: Simon & Schuster, 1991), 10.

5. Clark Clifford, with Richard Holbrooke, *Counsel to the President: A Memoir* (New York: Random House, 1991), 386.

6. Fredrik Logevall, *Choosing War: The Lost Chance for Peace and the Escalation of War in Vietnam* (Berkeley: University of California Press, 2001), 145.

7. Quoted in Frederick E. Siegel, *Troubled Journey: From Pearl Harbor to Ronald Reagan* (New York: Hill and Wang, 1984), 152.

8. Robert A. Caro, *The Path to Power: The Years of Lyndon Johnson* (New York: Vintage, 1990), 141–42.

9. Quoted in H. W. Brands, *American Dreams: The United States Since 1945* (New York: Penguin, 2010), 119.

10. See Robert A. Caro, "Lyndon B. Johnson" in Robert A. Wilson, ed., *Power and the Presidency* (New York: Public Affairs, 1999), 80; and Caro, *The Path to Power*, xviii.

11. Caro, "Lyndon B. Johnson," 81.

12. Quoted in Leuchtenburg, *In the Shadow of FDR*, 121.

13. Robert Dallek, *Flawed Giant: Lyndon Johnson and His Times, 1961–1973* (New York: Oxford University Press, 1998), 5.

14. Robert A. Caro, *Master of the Senate: The Years of Lyndon Johnson* (New York: Knopf, 2002), 406–409.

15. Quoted in David Halberstam, *The Best and the Brightest* (New York: Fawcett, 1972), 434.

16. Quoted in James T. Patterson, *Grand Expectations: The United States, 1945–1974* (New York: Oxford University Press, 1996), 528.

17. Steven M. Gillon, *The Kennedy Assassination* (New York: Basic Books, 2009), 227.

18. Dallek, *Flawed Giant*, 56.

19. Ibid., 63.

20. Taylor Branch, *Pillar of Fire: America in the King Years, 1963–1965* (New York: Simon & Schuster, 1998), 233.

21. Dallek, *Flawed Giant*, 6.

22. Nicholas Lemann, *The Promised Land: The Great Black Migration and How It Changed America* (New York: Vintage, 1991), 144.

23. Dallek, *Flawed Giant*, 82.

24. Ira Katznelson, "Was the Great Society a Lost Opportunity?," in Steve Fraser and Gary Gerstle, eds., *The Rise and Fall of the New Deal Order, 1930–1980* (Princeton: Princeton University Press, 1989), 199–200; Robert M. Collins, *More: The Politics of Economic Growth in Postwar America* (New York: Oxford University Press, 2000).

25. Goodwin, *Remembering America*, 280.

26. Doris Kearns Goodwin, *Lyndon Johnson and the American Dream* (New York: Harper & Row, 1976), 218.

27. G. Calvin Mackenzie and Robert Weisbrot, *The Liberal Hour: Washington and the Politics of Change in the 1960s* (New York: Penguin, 2008), 100.

28. Quoted in Gary Dorrien, *Economy, Difference, Empire: Social Ethics for Social Justice* (New York: Columbia University Press, 2010), 119.

29. Scott Stossell, *Sarge: The Life and Times of Sargent Shriver* (Washington, DC: Smithsonian, 2004), 370.

30. Goodwin, *Remembering America*, 286.

31. Maurice Isserman and Michael Kazin, *America Divided: The Civil War of the 1960s* (New York: Oxford University Press, 2000), 110.

32. Maurice Isserman, *The Other American: The Life of Michael Harrington* (New York: Public Affairs, 2000), 214.

33. David Farber, *The Age of Great Dreams: America in the 1960s* (New York: Hill and Wang, 1994), 94.

34. Clayborne Carson, *In Struggle: SNCC and the Black Awakening of the 1960s* (Cambridge, MA: Harvard University Press, 1981), 26.

35. Todd Gitlin, *The Sixties: Years of Hope, Days of Rage* (New York; Bantam, 1987), 148; George Cotkin, *Existential America* (Baltimore: Johns Hopkins University Press, 2003), 234.

36. Branch, *Pillar of Fire*, 55.

37. Quoted in Carson, *In Struggle*, 17.

38. Kay Mills, *This Little Light of Mine: The Life of Fannie Lou Hamer* (New York: Plume, 1994), 116.

39. John D'Emilio, *Lost Prophet: The Life and Times of Bayard Rustin* (New York: Free Press, 2003), 384–85.

40. Branch, *Pillar of Fire*, 460.

41. Quoted in Nelson Lichtenstein, *The Most Dangerous Man in Detroit: Walter Reuther and the Fate of American Labor* (New York: Basic Books, 1995), 393.

42. Mills, *This Little Light of Mine*, 121.

43. Branch, *Pillar of Fire*, 465.

44. Sidney Milkis, "The Modern Presidency, Social Movements, and the Administrative State: Lyndon Johnson and the Civil Rights Movement," Paper for Conference on Race and American Political Development, University of Oregon, May 11–12, 2006, 29.

45. William H. Chafe, *Never Stop Running: Allard Lowenstein and the Struggle to Save American Liberalism* (New York: Basic Books, 1993), 198.

46. Branch, *Pillar of Fire*, 474.

47. Gitlin, *The Sixties*, 160.

48. Branch, *Pillar of Fire*, 590.

49. Isserman and Kazin, *America Divided*, 174.

50. Carson, *In Struggle*, 233–43.

51. Gitlin, *The Sixties*, 159.

52. Quoted in Patterson, *Grand Expectations*, 582.

53. D'Emilio, *Lost Prophet*, 396–403.

54. Judith Hennessee, *Betty Friedan: Her Life* (New York: Penguin, 1999), 98.

55. Ibid., 103–4.

56. Christine Stansell, *The Feminist Promise: 1792 to the Present* (New York: Modern Library, 2010), 276.

57. Daniel Horowitz, *Betty Friedan and the Making of* The Feminine Mystique: *The American Left, the Cold War, and Modern Feminism* (Amherst, MA: University of Massachusetts Press, 2000), 50–52.

58. Stansell, *The Feminist Promise*, 206.

59. See Louis Menand, "Books as Bombs: Why the Women's Movement Needed 'The Feminine Mystique,'" *The New Yorker* (January 24, 2011), http://www.newyorker.com/arts/critics/books/2011/01/24/110124crbo_books_menand.

60. Patricia Sullivan, obituary, *Washington Post*, February 5, 2006, A01.

61. Betty Friedan, *The Feminine Mystique* (New York: Dell, 1963), 11, 17, 21, 69, 294, 332, 356; Menand, "Books as Bombs."

62. Ruth Rosen, *The World Split Open: How the Modern Women's Movement Changed America* (New York: Viking, 2000), 83.

63. Quoted in James F. Simon, *Independent Journey: The Life of William O. Douglas* (New York: Penguin, 1980), 347.

64. Patterson, *Grand Expectations*, 565.

65. Bruce Allen Murphy, *Wild Bill: The Legend and Life of William O. Douglas* (New York: Random House, 2003), 388. See also in this context David J. Garrow, *Liberty and Sexuality: The Right to Privacy and the Making of* Roe v. Wade (New York: Macmillan, 1994).

66. David J. Garrow, "The Tragedy of William O. Douglas," *The Nation* (April 14, 2003), http://www.thenation.com/article/tragedy-william-o-douglas.

67. Garrow, "Doing Justice," *The Nation* (February 27, 1995), http://www.davidgarrow-com.hb2hosting.net/File/DJG%201995%20HLBHandNationReviewEssay.pdf.

68. Garrow, "The Tragedy of William O. Douglas."

69. See Seth Stern and Stephen Wermiel, *Justice Brennan: Liberal Champion* (New York: Houghton Mifflin, 2010), 219. See also Justin Driver, "Robust and Wide-Open," *The New Republic* (February 17, 2011), 38–39.

70. John W. Johnson, *Griswold v. Connecticut: Birth Control and the Constitutional Right to Privacy* (Lawrence, KS: University Press of Kansas, 2005), 130.

71. Simon, *Independent Journey*, 391.

72. Farber, *The Age of Great Dreams*, 108.

73. Mackenzie and Weisbrot, *The Liberal Hour*, 208–209.
74. Dallek, *Flawed Giant*, 202.
75. Goodwin, *Lyndon Johnson and the American Dream*, 216.
76. Lemann, *The Promised Land*, 165.
77. Jeff Shesol, *Mutual Contempt: Lyndon Johnson, Robert Kennedy, and the Feud That Defined a Decade* (New York : Norton, 1997), 241.
78. Allen J. Matusow, *The Unraveling of America: A History of Liberalism in the 1960s* (New York: Harper & Row, 1984), 248.
79. David Osborne, "The Great Society Revisited," *Mother Jones* (June 1986), 16, 17.
80. Lemann, *The Promised Land*,180.
81. Thomas Byrne Edsall with Mary D. Edsall, *Chain Reaction: The Impact of Race, Rights, and Taxes on American Politics* (New York: Norton, 1992), 52.
82. Quoted in Vincent J. Cannato, *The Ungovernable City: John Lindsay and His Struggle to Save New York* (New York: Basic Books, 2001), 177.
83. Tamar Jacoby, "The Uncivil History of the Civilian Review Board: How the Issue Divided the City Three Decades Ago," *City Journal* (Winter 1993), http://www.city-journal.org/article01.php?aid=1151.
84. Cannato, *The Ungovernable City*, 182.
85. Ibid., 179.
86. Ibid., 183.
87. Sam Roberts, "The Legacy," in Sam Roberts, ed., *America's Mayor: John V. Lindsay and the Reinvention of New York* (New York: Columbia University Press, 2010), 238.
88. Shesol, *Mutual Contempt*, 223.
89. Stossell, *Sarge*, 413.
90. Edsall, *Chain Reaction*, 59.
91. Stossell, *Sarge*, 459.
92. Gillon, *Politics and Vision*, 190.
93. Martin Binkin, William W. Kaufmann, *U.S. Army Guard and Reserve: Rhetoric, Realities, Risks* (Studies in Defense Policy) (Washington, D.C.: Brookings Institution Press, 1989) 52.
94. Quoted in Herring, *America's Longest War*, 133.
95. Matusow, *The Unraveling of America*, 155.
96. For a detailed study of the lies regarding the Gulf of Tonkin incidents and their impact on America's politics and culture, see Eric Alterman, *When Presidents Lie: A History of Official Deception and Its Consequences* (New York: Viking Books, 2004), 160–238.
97. Logevall, *Choosing War*, 57.
98. Robert Scheer, "The Hoax of Tonkin," in Scheer, *Thinking Tuna Fish, Talking Death: Essays on the Pornography of Power* (New York: Hill and Wang, 1988), 157.
99. Quoted in Mackenzie and Weisbrot, *The Liberal Hour*, 308.
100. Patterson, *Grand Expectations*, 593.
101. Kai Bird, *The Color of Truth: McGeorge and William Bundy: Brothers in Arms: A Biography* (New York: Simon & Schuster, 1998), 272.
102. Ibid., 20; Jack Snyder, *Myths of Empire: Domestic Politics and International Ambition* (Ithaca, NY: Cornell University Press, 1991), 300.
103. Logevall, *Choosing War*, 282.
104. Michael R. Beschloss, *Taking Charge: The Johnson White House Tapes, 1963–1964* (New York: Simon & Schuster, 1997), 398. See also "Mansfield memo to the President, 7 December, 1963," Files of McGeorge Bundy, NSF, Country File, Vietnam, box 1, Lyndon Baines Johnson Library and Museum, and his memo to the president of February 1, 1964, Files of McGeorge Bundy, NSF, Memos to President, box 1, Johnson Library.
105. See, for instance, telephone conversation between the President and Senator Fulbright (to Senator Fulbright), December 2, 1963, JFK Assas. Related Conversations, Johnson Library.
106. Beschloss, *Taking Charge*, 370.
107. Ronald Steel, *Walter Lippmann and the American Century* (Boston: Little Brown, 1980), 550. See also Logevall, *Choosing War*, 143.
108. Logevall, *Choosing War*, 168.
109. Ibid., 391.
110. Michael Barone, *Our Country: The Shaping of America from Roosevelt to Reagan* (New York: Free Press, 1990), 399. See also Logevall, *Choosing War*, 288.
111. Beschloss, *Taking Charge*, 390.

112. Ibid., 258.
113. See Valenti notes, "July 21–27, 1965, Meetings on Vietnam," MNF, box 1, Johnson Library. See also Brian VanDeMark, *Into the Quagmire: Lyndon Johnson and the Escalation of the Vietnam War* (New York: Oxford University Press, 1991), 207.
114. Ibid., 207
115. William Manchester, *The Glory and the Dream: A Narrative History of America, 1932–1972* (New York: Bantam, 1975), 1053.
116. Randall Bennett Woods, *Fulbright: A Biography* (Cambridge: Cambridge University Press, 1995), 407–408; see also William C. Berman, *William Fulbright and the Vietnam War: The Dissent of a Political Realist* (Kent, OH: Kent State University Press, 1988), 68.
117. Eric Goldman, *The Tragedy of Lyndon Johnson* (New York: Dell, 1969), 488.
118. Ibid., 499.
119. Arthur M. Schlesinger, Jr., *Journals: 1952–2000* (New York: Penguin, 2007), 257.
120. Dallek, *Flawed Giant*, 461.
121. Goodwin, *Remembering America*, 424.
122. Quoted in Gillon, *The Kennedy Assassination*, 7.
123. Dallek, *Flawed Giant*, 186.
124. Carl Solberg, *Hubert Humphrey: A Biography* (New York: Norton, 1984), 272.
125. Hubert H. Humphrey, *The Education of a Public Man: My Life and Politics* (Garden City, NY: Doubleday, 1976), 320–24; see also Logevall, *Choosing War*, 347.
126. Gillon, *Politics and Vision*, 195.
127. Schlesinger, Jr., *Journals*, 258–59.
128. Ibid., 246.
129. Gillon, *Politics and Vision*, 196.
130. Gene Rising, *Clean for Gene: Eugene McCarthy's 1968 Presidential Campaign* (Westport, CT: Greenwood Press, 1997) 54.
131. Richard Parker, *John Kenneth Galbraith: His Life, His Politics, His Economics* (New York: Farrar, Straus and Giroux, 2005), 430–31.
132. Rising, *Clean for Gene*, 54.
133. Schlesinger, Jr., *Journals*, 263.
134. Gillon, *Politics and Vision*, 192.
135. Lichtenstein, *The Most Dangerous Man*, 422.
136. Peter B. Levy, *The New Left and Labor in the 1960s* (Urbana, IL: University of Illinois Press, 1994), 46–47.
137. Garrow, *Bearing the Cross*, 470.

11 | Paranoia Strikes Deep in the Heartland

1. Quoted in Casey Nelson Blake, "Disappointed but Not Resigned," *Dissent* (Fall, 2010), 21.
2. Quoted in Maurice Isserman and Michael Kazin, *America Divided: The Civil War of the 1960s* (New York: Oxford University Press, 2000), 229.
3. Aram Goudsouzian, *Sidney Poitier: Man, Actor, Icon* (Chapel Hill: University of North Carolina Press, 2004), 284.
4. Mark Harris, *Pictures at a Revolution: Five Movies and the Birth of the New Hollywood* (New York: Penguin, 2008), 113.
5. Details of Poitier's life are taken from Goudsouzian, *Sidney Poitier*.
6. Goudsouzian, *Sidney Poitier*, 179.
7. James Baldwin, *The Devil Finds Work* (New York: Dell, 1976), 62.
8. Goudsouzian, *Sidney Poitier*, 195.
9. Ibid., 224.
10. Quoted in Harris, *Pictures at a Revolution*, 350.
11. Goudsouzian, *Sidney Poitier*, 254.
12. Ibid., 275.
13. Harris, *Pictures at a Revolution*, 348.
14. Ibid., 425.
15. Stanley Kramer, with Thomas M. Coffey, *A Mad, Mad, Mad, Mad World: A Life in Hollywood* (New York: Harcourt Brace, 1997), 216.
16. Kramer, *A Mad, Mad, Mad, Mad World*, 228.
17. Harris, *Pictures at a Revolution*, 188.

18. Jim Newton, *Justice for All: Earl Warren and the Nation He Made* (New York: Riverhead, 2006), 477.

19. William Styron, "Nat Turner Revisited," in *The Confessions of Nat Turner* (1967; repr., New York: Vintage, 1992), 454.

20. Ibid., 223.

21. Ibid., 403.

22. Eliot Fremont-Smith, "Books of the Times: *The Confessions of Nat Turner,*" *New York Times*, October 4, 1967, http://select.nytimes.com/mem/archive/pdf?res=FB0B13F6395C107B93 C6A9178BD95F438685F9.

23. Styron, "Nat Turner Revisited," *The Confessions of Nat Turner*, 448.

24. Quoted in James L. W. West, III, *William Styron, A Life* (New York: Random House, 1998), 386; see also John Henrik Clarke, ed., *William Styron's Nat Turner: Ten Black Writers Respond* (Boston: Beacon Press, 1968), 26.

25. Quoted in West, *William Styron*, 386; see also Clarke, *William Styron's Nat Turner*, 35 (for "darling of liberal critics" remark) and 43.

26. West, *William Styron*, 392.

27. Mark Kurlansky, *1968: The Year That Rocked the World* (New York: Ballantine, 2004), 166.

28. George C. Herring, *America's Longest War: The United States and Vietnam, 1950–1975* (New York: Knopf, 1986), 186.

29. Quoted in G. Calvin Mackenzie and Robert Weisbrot, *The Liberal Hour: Washington and the Politics of Change in the 1960s* (New York: Penguin, 2008), 334.

30. Brands is quoted in Bernard von Bothmer, *Framing the Sixties: The Use and Abuse of a Decade from Ronald Reagan to George W. Bush* (Amherst, MA: University of Massachusetts Press, 2010), 25.

31. See Daniel Hallin, *The "Uncensored War:" The Media and Vietnam* (New York: Oxford University Press, 1986), 142–47.

32. D. D. Guttenplan, *American Radical: The Life and Times of I. F. Stone* (New York: Farrar, Straus and Giroux, 2009), 419.

33. Michael Kazin, *American Dreamers: How the Left Changed A Nation* (New York: Knopf, 2011), 237.

34. Thomas Maier, *Dr. Spock: An American Life* (New York: Harcourt, 1998), 290.

35. Allen J. Matusow, *The Unraveling of America: A History of Liberalism in the 1960s* (New York: Harper & Row, 1984), 325.

36. Quoted in Maier, *Dr. Spock*, 304.

37. Report of the National Advisory Commission on Civil Disorders (Washington, DC: U.S. Government Printing Office, 1968), http://www.eisenhowerfoundation.org/docs/kerner.pdf.

38. David J. Garrow, *Bearing the Cross: Martin Luther King, Jr., and the Southern Christian Leadership Conference* (New York: Vintage, 1986), 595–96.

39. "Man of the Year: Martin Luther King, Jr., Never Again Where He Was," *Time* (January 3, 1964), http://www.time.com/time/magazine/article/0,9171,940759,00.html.

40. Ibid.

41. For detailed examination of this issue, see Beryl Satter, *Family Properties: Race, Real Estate, and the Exploitation of Black Urban America* (New York: Metropolitan Books, 2009). For details on particular episodes of violence in Chicago, see Mike Royko, *Boss: Richard J. Daley of Chicago* (New York: New American Library, 1971), 134–40.

42. Quoted in Anthony Lewis, "The Whirlwinds of Revolt," *New York Times Book Review*, February 5, 2001, 1.

43. Garrow, *Bearing the Cross*, 611.

44. Ibid., 615.

45. Rick Perlstein, *Nixonland: The Rise of a President and the Fracturing of America* (New York: Scribner, 2008), 256.

46. Clay Risen, *A Nation on Fire: America in the Wake of the King Assassination* (Hoboken, NJ: Wiley, 2009), 55.

47. James T. Patterson, *Grand Expectations: The United States, 1945–1974* (New York: Oxford University Press, 1996), 685. See also Robert Weisbrot, *Freedom Bound: A History of America's Civil Rights Movement* (New York: Norton, 1990), 266–70.

48. Vincent J. Cannato, *The Ungovernable City: John Lindsay and His Struggle to Save New York* (New York: Basic Books, 2001), 238.

49. The Port Huron Statement can be found in many sources, including "Students for a Democratic Society Port Huron Statement (June 15, 1962)," http://history.hanover.edu/courses/

excerpts/111hur3.html. For a detailed history of SDS, see James Miller, *Democracy Is in the Streets: From Port Huron to the Siege of Chicago* (New York: Simon & Schuster, 1987).

50. Jerry Avorn, *Up Against the Ivy Wall: A History of the Columbia Crisis* (New York: Atheneum Press, 1969), 9, 15.
51. Cannato, *The Ungovernable City*, 233.
52. Matusow, *The Unraveling of America*, 333.
53. Mark Rudd, *Underground: My Life with SDS and the Weathermen* (New York: William Morrow, 2009), 59.
54. Isserman and Kazin, *America Divided*, 229.
55. Quoted in Adam Kirsch, *Why Trilling Matters* (New Haven, CT: Yale University Press, 2011), 154.
56. Ibid.
57. Matusow, *The Unraveling of America*, 334.
58. Quoted in Kurlansky, 178.
59. Avorn, *Up Against the Ivy Wall*, 76–77; see also Daniel Bell's comments in Joseph Dorman, *Arguing the World: The New York Intellectuals in Their Own Words* (New York: Free Press, 2000), 154.
60. Cannato, *The Ungovernable City*, 247.
61. John Castellucci, "The Night They Burned Ranum's Papers," *Chronicle Review* (February 14, 2010), http://chronicle.com/article/The-Night-They-Burned-Ranums/64115/.
62. Quoted David S. Brown, *Richard Hofstadter: An Intellectual Biography* (Chicago: University of Chicago Press, 2006), 179.
63. Quoted Brown, *Richard Hofstadter*, 180; see also Daniel Bell's account in "Columbia and the New Left," in Daniel Bell and Irving Kristol , eds., *Confrontation: The Student Rebellion and the Universities* (New York: Basic Books, 1969), 93–99.
64. Brown, *Richard Hofstadter*, 186.
65. Richard Hofstadter, *Academic Freedom in the Age of the College* (1955; repr., New York: Columbia University Press, 1964), 245, 261–62.
66. Richard Hofstadter, "The 214th Columbia University Commencement," *American Scholar* (Autumn 1968), 583–88; see also Hofstadter, "Uncle Sam Has Cried 'Uncle!' Before," *New York Times Magazine*, May 19, 1968, 125, and Daniel Bell's comments in Dorman, *Arguing the World*, 152.
67. See Richard Bernstein, "Irving Howe, 72, Critic, Editor and Socialist, Dies," *New York Times*, May 6, 1993, http://www.nytimes.com/1993/05/06/obituaries/irving-howe-72-critic-editor-and-socialist-dies.html?pagewanted=1.
68. Irving Howe, *A Margin of Hope: An Intellectual Autobiography* (New York: Harcourt Brace Jovanovich, 1982), 323.
69. Rudd, *Underground*, 115.
70. Isserman and Kazin, *America Divided*, 230; Devin Fergus, *Liberalism, Black Power, and the Making of American Politics, 1965–1980* (Athens, GA: University of Georgia Press, 2009), 37.
71. Tom Wells, *The War Within: America's Battle Over Vietnam* (Berkeley: University of California Press, 1994), 273.
72. Mark Hamilton Lytle, *America's Uncivil Wars: The Sixties Era from Elvis to the Fall of Richard Nixon* (New York: Oxford University Press, 2006), 254.
73. Wallace Turner, "Reagan Remark a Campaign Issue: 'Bloodbath' Comment Fuels Oratory in California," *New York Times*, April 19, 1970, 43; see also Lou Cannon, *Governor Reagan: His Rise to Power* (New York: Public Affairs, 2003), 335–47.
74. Jerald E. Podair, *The Strike That Changed New York: Blacks, Whites, and the Ocean Hill–Brownsville Crisis* (New Haven, CT: Yale University Press, 2002), 95–96.
75. Richard D. Kahlenberg, *Tough Liberal: Albert Shanker and the Battles over Schools, Unions, Race, and Democracy* (New York: Columbia University Press, 2007), 73.
76. Ibid.
77. Podair, *The Strike That Changed New York*, 22.
78. See ibid., 33–34; Wini Breines, *Community and Organization in the New Left, 1962–1968: The Great Refusal* (New York: Praeger, 1982), 126.
79. Podair, *The Strike That Changed New York*, 80.
80. Cannato, *The Ungovernable City*, 305.
81. Podair, *The Strike That Changed New York*, 80.
82. Joshua M. Zeitz, *White Ethnic New York; Jews, Catholics, and the Shaping of Postwar Politics* (Chapel Hill: University of North Carolina Press, 2007), 162–63.

83. Kahlenberg, *Tough Liberal*, 86.
84. John D'Emilio, *Lost Prophet: The Life and Times of Bayard Rustin* (New York: Free Press, 2003), 470.
85. Kahlenberg, *Tough Liberal*, 102–103.
86. Marilyn Nissenson, *The Lady Upstairs: Dorothy Schiff and the* New York Post. (New York: St. Martin's Press 2007), 332.
87. Kahlenberg, *Tough Liberal*, 97.
88. Podair, *The Strike That Changed New York*, 123.
89. Zeitz, *White Ethnic New York*,163–64.
90. Quoted in *The American Jewish Yearbook 1969* (New York: The American Jewish Committee and the Jewish Publication Society of America, 1969), 81.
91. Cynthia Ozick, "Literary Blacks and Jews," in Paul Berman, ed., *Blacks and Jews: Alliances and Arguments* (New York: Delacorte Press, 1994), 67–68.
92. Kahlenberg, *Tough Liberal*, 111.
93. Peter B. Levy, *The New Left and Labor in the 1960s* (Urbana, IL: University of Illinois Press, 1994), Chapter, 4.
94. Maurice Isserman, *The Other American: The Life of Michael Harrington* (New York: Public Affairs, 2000), 282.
95. Michael Wreszin, *A Rebel in Defense of Tradition: The Life and Politics of Dwight Macdonald* (New York: Basic Books, 1994), 440.
96. Ibid., 462.
97. Kahlenberg, *Tough Liberal*, 104.
98. Daniel P. Moyhinan, *Maximum Feasible Misunderstanding: Community Action in the War on Poverty* (New York: Free Press, 1969), 117.
99. Kahlenberg, *Tough Liberal*, 109.
100. Ibid., 119.
101. William H. Chafe, *Private Lives/ Public Consequences: Personality and Politics in Modern America* (Cambridge, MA: Harvard University Press), 168.
102. Dominic Sandbrook, *Eugene McCarthy: The Rise and Fall of Postwar American Liberalism* (New York: Knopf, 2004), 81.
103. See in general ibid.
104. Eugene McCarthy, *Parting Shots from My Brittle Bow: Reflections on American Politics and Life* (Golden, CO: Fulcrum, 2004), 13.
105. Sandbrook, *Eugene McCarthy*, 147–49.
106. Ibid., 153.
107. William L. O'Neill, *Coming Apart: An Informal History of America in the 1960's* (New York: Times Books, 1971), 377.
108. Patterson, *Grand Expectations*, 690.
109. Francis Clines, "Eugene McCarthy, Senate Dove Who Jolted '68 Race, Dies at 89," *New York Times*, December 10, 2006, http://www.nytimes.com/2005/12/10/obituaries/10cnd-mccarthy .html.
110. Quoted in Richard N. Goodwin, *Remembering America: A Voice from the Sixties* (New York: Harper & Row, 1988), 491.
111. Wells, *The War Within*, 225.
112. Matusow, *The Unraveling of America*, 407.
113. Quoted in Arthur M. Schlesinger, Jr., *Robert Kennedy and His Times* (New York: Ballantine, 1978), 959.
114. Thurston Clarke, *The Last Campaign: Robert F. Kennedy and 82 Days That Inspired America* (New York: Holt, 2008), 35–36.
115. Schlesinger, Jr., *Robert Kennedy and His Times*, 912.
116. Ibid., 72.
117. Ibid., 102.
118. Ibid., 113.
119. Ibid., 638–39.
120. Quoted in Isserman, *The Other American*, 284.
121. Goodwin, *Remembering America*, 443.
122. Jeff Shesol, *Mutual Contempt: Lyndon Johnson, Robert Kennedy, and the Feud That Defined a Decade* (New York, Norton, 1997), 251–52.
123. Edward M. Kennedy, *True Compass: A Memoir* (New York: Twelve, 2009), 253.

124. See Randall Bennett Woods, *Fulbright: A Biography* (Cambridge: Cambridge University Press, 1995), 482.
125. Thurston Clarke, "The Last Good Campaign," *Vanity Fair* (June 2008), http://www.vanityfair .com/politics/features/2008/06/rfk_excerpt200806.
126. Kennedy, *True Compass*, 228.
127. See Lloyd C. Gardner, *Pay Any Price: Lyndon Johnson and the Wars for Vietnam* (Chicago: Ivan R. Dee, 1995), 442.
128. Shesol, *Mutual Contempt*, 425.
129. Doris Kearns Goodwin, *Lyndon Johnson and the American Dream* (New York: Harper & Row), 342–43.
130. Robert Dallek, *Flawed Giant: Lyndon Johnson and His Times, 1961–1973* (New York: Oxford University Press, 1998), 522.
131. Ibid., 523.
132. See William C. Berman, *William Fulbright and the Vietnam War: The Dissent of a Political Realist* (Kent, OH: Kent State University Press, 1988), 68.
133. Dallek, *Flawed Giant*, 528.
134. Patterson, *Grand Expectations*, 685.
135. Adam Clymer, *Edward M. Kennedy: A Biography* (New York: William Morrow, 1999), 107.
136. Evan Thomas, *Robert Kennedy: His Life* (New York: Simon & Schuster, 2000), 363.
137. Clarke, *The Last Campaign*, 189–90.
138. Evan Thomas, *Robert Kennedy*, 371.
139. Clarke, *The Last Campaign*, 139–40, 177.
140. "Robert Kennedy on the Death of Martin Luther King," April 4, 1968, http://www.historyplace .com/speeches/rfk.htm.
141. Goodwin, *Remembering America*, 532.
142. Thomas, *Robert Kennedy*, 375.
143. Quoted in Shesol, *Mutual Contempt*, 473.
144. Schlesinger, Jr., *Robert Kennedy and His Times*, 914.
145. Clymer, *Edward M. Kennedy*, 110.
146. Edward M. Kennedy, "Address at the Public Memorial Service for Robert F. Kennedy," http://www.americanrhetoric.com/speeches/ekennedytributetorfk.html.
147. Jack Newfield, *RFK: A Memoir* (1969; repr., New York: Thunder Mouth Press, 2003), 304.
148. Sandbrook, *Eugene McCarthy*, 211.
149. Richard Parker, *John Kenneth Galbraith: His Life, His Politics, His Economics* (New York: Farrar, Straus and Giroux, 2005), 470.
150. Sandbrook, *Eugene McCarthy*, 201.
151. Garry Wills, *Nixon Agonistes: The Crisis of the Self-Made Man* (New York: Mentor, 1979), 115.
152. Lytle, *America's Uncivil Wars*, 261.
153. For this point, see Susan Braudy, *Family Circle: The Boudins and the Aristocracy of the Left* (New York: Knopf, 2003), 161.
154. Quoted in Jonah Raskin, *For the Hell of It: The Life and Times of Abbie Hoffman* (Berkeley: University of California Press, 1996), 147, 143.
155. David Farber, *Chicago '68* (Chicago: University of Chicago Press, 1988), 20.
156. David Farber, *The Age of Great Dreams: America in the 1960s* (New York: Hill and Wang, 1994), 224.
157. See Farber, *Chicago '68*, Chapter 7.
158. A video of the Rather incident can be seen at http://www.youtube.com/watch?v=TrlYRWD _tnA.
159. Norman Mailer, "Miami and the Siege of Chicago," in Mailer, *The Time of Our Time* (New York: Modern Library, 1998), 696.
160. Patterson, *Grand Expectations*, 696; Royko, *Boss*, 188–89.
161. Patterson, *Grand Expectations*, 697.
162. Matusow, *The Unraveling of America*, 419.
163. Royko, *Boss*, 193–94.
164. Raskin, *For the Hell of It*, 148, 149.
165. For a broader and more in-depth treatment of law and order arguments in the 1960s and how they played against liberalism, see Michael W. Flamm, *Law and Order: Street Crime, Civil Unrest, and the Crisis of Liberalism in the 1960s* (New York: Columbia University Press, 2005).

166. Quoted in Braudy, *Family Circle*, 166.
167. Arthur M. Schlesinger, Jr., *Journals: 1952–2000* (New York: Penguin, 2007), 294.
168. Arthur M. Schlesinger, Jr., *The Crisis of Confidence: Ideas, Power, and Violence in America* (New York: Bantam, 1969), xi; these words were written in February 1969.
169. Ibid., 5.
170. Ibid., 116.
171. Ibid., 117.
172. Norman Podhoretz, syposium introduction, *Commentary* (September, 1967), 31.
173. See Thomas Byrne Edsall with Mary D. Edsall, *Chain Reaction: The Impact of Race, Rights, and Taxes on American Politics* (New York: Norton, 1992), 9.
174. Arthur M. Schlesinger, Jr., *The Imperial Presidency* (Boston: Houghton, Mifflin, 1973), 206.
175. Carl Solberg, *Hubert Humphrey: A Biography* (New York: Norton, 1984), 385.
176. For details, see Dallek, *Flawed Giant*, 588; Perlstein, *Nixonland*, 350.
177. Ronald Berman, *America in the Sixties: An Intellectual History* (New York: Harper & Row, 1970), 128.

12 | In the Darkness at the Edge of Town

1. Daniel Patrick Moynihan to Richard Nixon, January 9, 1969, in Daniel P. Moynihan, *A Portrait in Letters of An American Visionary*, ed. Steven R. Weisman (New York: Public Affairs, 2010), 172.
2. Irving Kristol and Paul Weaver, "Who Knows New York?—Notes on a Mixed-Up City," *Public Interest* (Summer 1969), 55–56; also quoted in Peter Steinfels, *The Neoconservatives: The Men Who Are Changing America's Politics* (New York: Simon & Schuster, 1979), 195.
3. Quoted in Gloria Steinem, *Outrageous Acts and Everyday Rebellions* (New York: Holt, Rinehart, and Winston, 1983), 87–88.
4. George McGovern, *Grassroots: The Autobiography of George McGovern* (New York: Random House, 1977), 121.
5. Bruce Miroff, *The Liberals' Moment: The McGovern Insurgency and the Identity Crisis of the Democratic Party* (Lawrence, KS: University Press of Kansas, 2007), 17.
6. Arthur M. Schlesinger, Jr., *Journals: 1952–2000* (New York: Penguin, 2007), 297.
7. Quoted in Hunter S. Thompson, *Fear and Loathing: On the Campaign Trail '72* (New York: Warner, 1973), 127.
8. McGovern, *Grassroots*, 5.
9. Ibid., 36.
10. Ibid., 41.
11. Ibid., 43.
12. Miroff, *The Liberals' Moment*, 23.
13. Byron E. Shafer, *Quiet Revolution: The Struggle for the Democratic Party and the Shaping of Post-Reform Politics* (New York: Russell Sage, 1983), 14–16.
14. Carl Solberg, *Hubert Humphrey: A Biography* (New York: Norton, 1984), 422.
15. Theodore Lowi, *The End of Liberalism* (New York: Norton, 1969).
16. Rick Perlstein, *Nixonland: The Rise of a President and the Fracturing of America* (New York: Scribner, 2008), 512.
17. See McGovern, *Grassroots*, 148.
18. Thomas Byrne Edsall with Mary D. Edsall, *Chain Reaction: The Impact of Race, Rights, and Taxes on American Politics* (New York: Norton, 1992), 92.
19. Perlstein, *Nixonland*, 514.
20. Miroff, *The Liberals' Moment*, 38.
21. Norman Podhoretz, "Between Nixon and the New Politics," in *The New York Intellectuals Reader*, ed. Neil Jumonville (New York: Routledge, 2007), 408.
22. Ibid.
23. For more details, see Carolyn G. Heilbrun, *The Education of a Woman*, and Sydney Ladensohn Stern, *Gloria Steinem: Her Passion, Politics, and Mystique* (Secaucus, NJ: Carol Publishing, 1997).
24. Heilbrun, *The Education of a Woman*, 144.
25. Gloria Steinem, interview compiled in Peter Manso, *Mailer: His Life and Times* (New York: Simon & Schuster, 1985), 501, 502.
26. Toni Morrison, "What the Black Woman Thinks About Women's Lib," Dawn Keetley and John Pettegrew, eds., *Public Women, Public Words: A Documentary History of American Feminism,* (Madison, WI: Madison House, 1997), 71–77.

27. Frances Beal, "Speaking Up When Others Can't," *Crossroads* (March 1993).
28. Stern, *Gloria Steinem*, 275.
29. Nora Ephron from *Crazy Salad* (1975) quoted in Abigail Pogrebin, "How Do You Spell Ms." *New York*, October 30, 2011, http://nymag.com/news/features/ms-magazine-2011-11/.
30. Judith Hennessee, *Betty Friedan: Her Life* (New York: Penguin, 1999), 135.
31. Ruth Rosen, *The World Split Open: How the Modern Women's Movement Changed America* (New York: Viking, 2000), 92–93.
32. Quoted in Bruce J. Schulman, *The Seventies: The Great Shift in American Culture, Society, and Politics* (New York: DaCapo, 2001), 165.
33. Rosen, *The World Split Open*, xxi–xxii.
34. Hennessee, *Betty Friedan*, 152.
35. Quoted in Abigail Pogrebin, "How Do You Spell Ms."
36. Lewis Mumford, "'THE SKY LINE' Mother Jacobs Home Remedies," *The New Yorker*, December 1, 1942, 148.
37. Dwight Madconald, "Books: Our Invisible Poor," *The New Yorker* (January 19, 1963), http://www.newyorker.com/archive/1963/01/19/1963_01_19_082_TNY_CARDS_000075671?printable=true.
38. Mark Hamilton Lytle, *The Gentle Subversive: Rachel Carson, Silent Spring, and the Rise of the Environmental Movement* (New York: Oxford University Press, 2007), 1.
39. Ibid., 19.
40. Quoted in G. Calvin Mackenzie and Robert Weisbrot, *The Liberal Hour: Washington and the Politics of Change in the 1960s* (New York: Penguin, 2008), 198.
41. Lytle, *The Gentle Subversive*, 146–47.
42. Linda Lear, *Rachel Carson: Witness for Nature* (New York: Holt, 1997), 397.
43. Lytle, *The Gentle Subversive*, 2.
44. Ibid., 7.
45. Rachel Carson, *Silent Spring* (Boston: Houghton Mifflin , 1962), 2.
46. Lear, *Rachel Carson*, 4–5.
47. Carson, *Silent Spring*, 59, 188, 156, 245.
48. Ibid., 12–13, 99.
49. Lytle, *The Gentle Subversive*, 145.
50. Quoted in Lear, *Rachel Carson*, 412.
51. Quoted in ibid., 409.
52. Ibid., 419.
53. Mackenzie and Weisbrot, *The Liberal Hour*, 199.
54. The information in this paragraph and those following comes from Bill Christofferson, *The Man from Clear Lake: Earth Day Founder Senator Gaylord Nelson* (Madison, WI: University of Wisconsin Press, 2004).
55. Ibid., 177–78.
56. Quoted in ibid., 178.
57. Mackenzie and Weisbrot, *The Liberal Hour*, 207, 206.
58. Schulman, *The Seventies*, 90.
59. Quoted in Christofferson, *The Man from Clear Lake*, 7.
60. James T. Patterson, *Grand Expectations: The United States, 1945–1974* (New York: Oxford University Press, 1996), 727; Mackenzie and Weisbrot, *The Liberal Hour*, 225.
61. Arnold Kaufman, "Beyond Alienation," *The Progressive* (February 1970), 45.
62. Charles Reich, *The Greening of America* (1970; repr., New York: Bantam, 1971), 236, 255, 382.
63. Peter N. Carroll, *It Seemed Like Nothing Happened: America in the 1970s* (New Brunswick, NJ: Rutgers University Press, 1990), 125.
64. H. W. Brands, *American Dreams: The United States Since 1945* (New York: The Penguin Press, 2010), 171.
65. Pete Hamill, "The Revolt of the White Lower Middle Class," *New York Magazine* (April 14, 1969), http://nymag.com/news/features/46801/; this essay is also reprinted in Pete Hamill, *Irrational Ravings* (New York: Putnam, 1971), 384–95.
66. Lyndon B. Johnson's Commencement Address at Howard University: "To Fulfill These Rights," June 4, 1965, Lyndon Baines Johnson Library and Museum, http://www.lbjlib.utexas.edu/johnson/archives.hom/speeches.hom/650604.asp.
67. Jonathan Rieder, *Canarsie: The Jews and Italians of Brooklyn against Liberalism* (Cambridge, MA: Harvard University Press, 1985), 108.
68. Garry Wills, *Nixon Agonistes: The Crisis of the Self-Made Man* (New York: Mentor, 1979), 89.

69. See "The Vice Presidency: Agnew Unleashed," *Time* (October 31, 1969), http://www.time.com/time/magazine/article/0,9171,839090,00.html.
70. Perlstein, *Nixonland*, 499.
71. See Jonathan Mahler, *Ladies and Gentlemen, The Bronx Is Burning: 1977, Baseball, Politics, and the Battle for the Soul of a City* (New York: Farrar, Straus and Giroux, 2005), 256.
72. Lionel Trilling, *The Liberal Imagination: Essays on Literature and Society* (Garden City, NY: Anchor Books, 1953), xi.
73. Edward Rothstein, "Mission Accomplished, a Journal Folds," *New York Times*, May 9, 2005, http://www.nytimes.com/2005/05/09/arts/09conn.html?_r=1.
74. Irving Kristol, "American Conservatism 1945–1995," *Public Interest* (Fall 1995), http://delong.typepad.com/pdf/20061226_Kristol_American_Conservatism.pdf.
75. Rothstein, "Mission Accomplished."
76. Irving Kristol, "Looking Back: Forty Good Years," *Public Interest* (Spring 2005), 7.
77. Irving Kristol, "The Adversary Culture of Intellectuals," in Neil Jumonville, ed., *The New York Intellectuals Reader* (New York: Routledge, 2007), 411–426; this essay originally appeared in *Encounter* (October 1979).
78. Irving Kristol, *On the Democratic Idea in America* (New York: Harper & Row, 1972), 29.
79. Kristol, "American Conservatism."
80. Lionel Trilling, *Beyond Culture: Essays on Literature and Learning* (New York: Viking, 1965), 3.
81. Eric Alterman's interview with Daniel Bell, Cambridge, 1994.
82. Daniel Bell, "The Cultural Contradictions of Capitalism," *Public Interest* (November 1970), 36; and "The New Class: A Muddled Concept" in B. Bruce-Biggs, ed. *The New Class?* (New Brunswick, NJ: Transaction Books, 1970), 169.
83. Daniel Bell, *The Winding Passage: Sociological Essays and Journeys* (New York: Basic Books, 1980), 232.
84. See Peter Steinfels, *The Neoconservatives: The Men Who Are Changing America's Politics* (New York: Simon & Schuster, 1979), 55.
85. Norman Podhoretz, "The Know-Nothing Bohemians" (1958), in Jumonville, *The New York Intellectuals Reader*, 315.
86. Benjamin Balint, *Running Commentary, The Contentious Magazine That Transformed the Jewish Left into the Neoconservative Right* (New York: Public Affairs, 2010), 146.
87. Norman Podhoretz, *Breaking Ranks: A Political Memoir* (New York: Harper & Row, 1979), 363.
88. Balint, *Running* Commentary.
89. Ibid.,111.
90. Edward S. Shapiro, *A Time for Healing; American Jewry Since World War II* (Baltimore: Johns Hopkins University Press, 1992), 207–208.
91. Balint, *Running* Commentary, 110.
92. Ibid., 114.
93. Justin Vaïsse, *Neoconservatism: The Biography of a Movement* (Cambridge, MA: Harvard University Press, 2010), 69.
94. Ibid., 69.
95. See Balint, *Running* Commentary, 110–11 and Clayborne Carson, "Black-Jewish Universalism in the Era of Identity Politics" in Jack Salzman and Cornel West, eds., *Struggles in the Promised Land: Toward a History of Black-Jewish Relations in the United States* (New York: Oxford University Press, 1997), 187.
96. See Eric Alterman, "My Marty Peretz Problem—And Ours," *American Prospect* (June 18, 2007), http://www.prospect.org/cs/articles?article=my_marty_peretz_problem_and_ours.
97. See Carol R. Sternhell, "WBAI's Problems," *The Harvard Crimson*, February 27, 1969, http://www.thecrimson.com/article/1969/2/27/wbais-problems-pwbai-fm-new-york-citys/.
98. Balint, *Running* Commentary,109.
99. Irving Kristol, "My Cold War," *National Interest* (Spring, 1993), http://delong.typepad.com/egregious_moderation/2009/10/irving-kristol-my-cold-war-april-1-1993.html.
100. See the discussion of this incident in Damon Linker, "Turning Right," *New York Times Book Review*, July 30, 2010, http://www.nytimes.com/2010/08/01/books/review/Linker-t.html?_r=2&ref=books.
101. Saul Bellow, *The Adventures of Augie March* (New York: Viking, 1953), 1.
102. Edward Mendelson, "The Obedient Bellow," *The New York Review of Books* (April 28, 2011), http://www.nybooks.com/articles/archives/2011/apr/28/obedient-bellow/.
103. Philip Roth, "'I GOT A SCHEME!' The Words of Saul Bellow," *The New Yorker* (April 25, 2008), www.newyorker.com/archive/2005/04/25/050425fa_fact_roth.

104. Balint, *Running* Commentary, 57.
105. Ibid., 55.
106. Roth, "'I GOT A SCHEME!' The Words of Saul Bellow."
107. Irving Howe, *Decline of the New* (New York: Harcourt, Brace, and World, 1970), 203.
108. Alfred Kazin, "The Earthly City of the Jews: Bellow, Malamud, and Roth," in Ted Solotaroff, ed., *Alfred Kazin's America: Critical and Personal Writings* (New York: Perennial, 2003), 257.
109. Julian Levinson, *Exiles on Main Street: Jewish American Writers and American Literary Culture* (Bloomington, IN: Indiana University Press, 2008), 144.
110. Saul Bellow, *Herzog* (New York: Viking, 1964), 229, 103, 374.
111. James Atlas, *Bellow: A Biography* (New York: Random House, 2000), 344.
112. Bellow, *Herzog*, 87.
113. George Cotkin, *Existential America* (Baltimore: Johns Hopkins University Press, 2003), 125.
114. Quoted in Atlas, *Bellow*, 392.
115. This quote can be found, among other places, in Christopher Hitchens, "The Great Assimilator," *The Atlantic Monthly* (November, 2007), http://www.powells.com/review/2007_11_06.html.
116. Saul Bellow, *Mr. Sammler's Planet* (New York: Viking, 1970), 72.
117. See Schulman, *The Seventies*, 32–33; Vincent J. Cannato, *The Ungovernable City: John Lindsay and His Struggle to Save New York* (New York: Basic Books, 2001), 127.
118. Bellow, *Mr. Sammler's Planet*, 277.
119. Norman Podhoretz, "My Negro Problem—And Ours," *Commentary* (February, 1963), http://www.time.com/time/magazine/article/0,9171,909452,00.html#ixzzotO5Wq1V6.
120. Bellow, *Mr. Sammler's Planet*, 48.
121. Scott Turow, "Missing Bellow: A Family Story," *Atlantic Monthly* (December 2005), http://www.theatlantic.com/magazine/archive/2005/12/missing-bellow/4421.
122. Bellow, *Mr. Sammler's Planet*, 42, 43, 208.
123. Irving Howe, "Fiction: Bellow, O'Hara, Litwack," *Harper's* (February 1970), 106, 108, 112.
124. Richard Cook, *Alfred Kazin: A Biography* (New Haven, CT: Yale University Press, 2007), 258. Michael Kazin is now co-editor of *Dissent* and a much admired liberal historian and public intellectual.
125. Alfred Kazin, "Though He Slay Me," *The New York Review of Books*, December 3, 1970, 3.
126. Ibid., 4.
127. Kazin, "The Earthly City of the Jews," in Solotaroff, *Alfred Kazin's America*, 262.
128. Saul Bellow, *Humboldt's Gift* (New York: Viking, 1975), 2.
129. James Atlas, *Delmore Schwartz: The Life of an American Poet* (New York: Avon, 1977), 308.
130. Bellow, *Humboldt's Gift*, 298.
131. Vaïsse, *Neoconservatism*, 84.
132. Thompson, *Fear and Loathing*, 117.
133. Quoted in Solberg, *Hubert Humphrey*, 426.
134. Thompson, *Fear and Loathing*, 135.
135. Perlstein, *Nixonland*, 610.
136. Ibid., 694.
137. Schulman, *The Seventies*, 166.
138. Vaïsse, *Neoconservatism*, 84.
139. Meany is quoted in Philip A. Klinkner, *The Losing Parties: Out-Party National Committees, 1956–1993* (New Haven, CT: Yale University Press, 1994), 106.
140. Steinem, *Outrageous Acts and Everyday Rebellions*, 106.
141. Stern, *Gloria Steinem*, 249.
142. Upon Eagleton's death, Novak revealed his source on *Meet the Press*, July 15, 2007, http://www.msnbc.msn.com/id/19694666/page/7/.
143. Theodore H. White, *The Making of the President 1972* (New York: Atheneum, 1973), 196–97.
144. Perlstein, *Nixonland*, 700.
145. Norman Mailer, *St. George and the Godfather* (New York: Signet, 1972), 96.
146. White, *The Making of the President 1972*, 207.
147. Patterson, *Grand Expectations*, 761.
148. Jefferson Cowie, *Stayin' Alive: The 1970s and the Last Days of the Working Class* (New York: New Press, 2010), 113.
149. Ibid.
150. Ibid., 99.
151. Edsall, *Chain Reaction*, 76.

13 | Maximum Feasible Misunderstanding

1. Quoted in Peter Steinfels, *The Neoconservatives: The Men Who Are Changing America's Politics* (New York: Simon & Schuster, 1979), 128.
2. Betty Friedan quoted in Godfrey Hodgson, *More Equal Than Others: America from Nixon to the New Century* (Princeton: Princeton University Press, 2004), 155.
3. Robert G. Kaufman, *Henry M. Jackson: A Life in Politics* (Seattle: University of Washington Press, 2000), 241.
4. Richard D. Kahlenberg, *Tough Liberal: Albert Shanker and the Battles over Schools, Unions, Race, and Democracy* (New York: Columbia University Press, 2007), 193.
5. David Frum, *How We Got Here: The 70's: The Decade That Brought You Modern Life—For Better or Worse* (New York: Basic Books, 2000), 305.
6. Benjamin Balint, *Running Commentary: The Contentious Magazine That Transformed the Jewish Left into the Neoconservative Right* (New York: Public Affairs, 2010), 117.
7. See Jonathan Soffer, *Ed Koch and the Rebuilding of New York City* (New York: Columbia University Press, 2010), 97.
8. Suzanne Braun Levine and Mary Thom, *Bella Abzug* (New York: Farrar, Straus and Giroux, 2007), 6.
9. Ibid., 28.
10. Ibid., 85.
11. Bella Abzug, *Bella!: Ms. Abzug Goes to Washington* (New York: Saturday Review Press, 1972), 5.
12. Levine and Thom, *Bella Abzug*, 85.
13. Ibid., 99.
14. See Soffer, *Ed Koch and the Rebuilding of New York City*, 99.
15. Jonathan Mahler, *Ladies and Gentlemen, The Bronx Is Burning: 1977, Baseball, Politics, and the Battle for the Soul of a City* (New York: Farrar, Straus and Giroux, 2005), 68; and Soffer, *Ed Koch and the Rebuilding of New York City*, 99.
16. Mahler, *Ladies and Gentlemen, The Bronx Is Burning*, 67.
17. See Soffer, *Ed Koch and the Rebuilding of New York City*, 101.
18. Mahler, *Ladies and Gentlemen, The Bronx Is Burning*, 68.
19. Soffer, *Ed Koch and the Rebuilding of New York City*, 103.
20. Godfrey Hodgson, *The Gentleman from New York: Daniel Patrick Moynihan: A Biography* (Boston: Houghton Mifflin, 2000), 25.
21. These quotes are taken from Eric Alterman, "The Power and the Glory," *New York Magazine* (May 2, 1994). Alterman conducted the interviews, http://books.google.com/books?id=Oe QCAAAAMBAJ&pg=PA3&dq="Eric+Alterman"&hl=en&ei=Ro4fTLXFB4S8lQfHhJyZDg& sa=X&oi=book_result&ct=result&resnum=9&ved=0CEkQ6AEwCDiWAQ#v=onepage&q= %22Eric%20Alterman%22&f=false,
22. See E. Franklin Frazier, *The Negro Family in the United States* (Chicago: University of Chicago Press, 1939); and Stanley Elkins, *Slavery: A Problem in American Institutional and Intellectual Life* (Chicago: University of Chicago Press, 1959).
23. U.S. Department of Labor, "The Negro Family: The Case for National Action Office of Policy Planning and Research," March 1965, http://www.blackpast.org/?q=primary/moynihan -report-1965.
24. Daniel P. Moynihan, *A Portrait in Letters of an American Visionary*, ed. Steven R. Weisman (New York: Public Affairs, 2010), 80.
25. Nicholas Lemann, *The Promised Land: The Great Black Migration and How It Changed America* (New York: Vintage, 1991), 181.
26. Thomas Byrne Edsall with Mary D. Edsall, *Chain Reaction: The Impact of Race, Rights, and Taxes on American Politics* (New York: Norton, 1992), 54.
27. Lemann, *The Promised Land*, 174–76.
28. Sam Tanenhaus, *The Death of Conservatism* (New York: Random House, 2009), 72.
29. Eric Alterman, "Moynihan Rules," *New York* (May 2, 1994), http://books.google.com/books ?id=OeQCAAAAMBAJ&pg=PA42&lpg=PA42&dq=eric+alterman,+new+york,+"Moynihan +Rules"&source=bl&ots=9P7nFGLXKV&sig=GlynEEoqeLH40Y2_a10Pk9qaqEc&hl=en&ei =DY8fTIyoJIO88gaaosiiDA&sa=X&oi=book_result&ct=result&resnum=1&ved=0CBIQ6A EwAA#v=onepage&q&f=false.
30. See for instance the discussion and sources cited in Eric Alterman, *What Liberal Media?: The Truth About Bias and the News* (New York: Basic Books, 20013), 89–103.
31. Daniel P. Moynihan, "The President & the Negro: The Moment Lost," *Commentary* (February,

1967), http://www.commentarymagazine.com/viewarticle.cfm/the-president---the-negro-the-moment-lost-4304.

32. See here especially Robert A. Katzmann, ed., *Daniel Patrick Moynihan: The Intellectual in Public Life* (Baltimore: Johns Hopkins University Press, 1998); and Steinfels, *The Neoconservatives*, 109.

33. Moynihan, *A Portrait in Letters*, 126–28.

34. Hodgson, *The Gentleman*, 122.

35. Ibid.,139.

36. Steinfels, *The Neoconservatives*, 125; Gareth Davies, *From Opportunity to Entitlement: The Transformation and Decline of Great Society Liberalism* (Lawrence, KS: University Press of Kansas, 1996), 169; see also Justin Vaïsse, *Neoconservatism: The Biography of a Movement* (Cambridge, MA: Harvard University Press, 2010), 55–57.

37. Hodgson, *The Gentleman*, 149.

38. Ibid., 173.

39. Katzmann, *Daniel Patrick Moynihan*, 116.

40. Hodgson, *The Gentleman*,158.

41. Ibid., 244.

42. Ibid., 267.

43. Jonathan Mahler, *Ladies and Gentlemen, The Bronx Is Burning*, 270, 272, 274.

44. See ibid., 281.

45. Ibid., 231; and Soffer, *Ed Koch and the Rebuilding of New York City*, 6.

46. See Sidney Blumenthal, *The Rise of the Counter-Establishment: The Conservative Ascent to Political Power* (New York: Union Square Press, 2008), 124.

47. Joseph Dorman, *Arguing the World: The New York Intellectuals in Their Own Words* (New York: Free Press, 2000), 166.

48. Irving Kristol, "Looking Back: Forty Good Years," *Public Interest* (Spring 2005), 8.

49. Cynthia Harrison, *On Account of Sex: The Politics of Women's Issues, 1945–1968* (Berkeley: University of California, 1988).

50. Jane J. Mansbridge, *Why We Lost the ERA* (Chicago: University of Chicago Press, 1986), 14.

51. James T. Patterson, *Restless Giant: The United States from Watergate to Bush v. Gore* (New York: Oxford University Press, 2005), 52.

52. Alan Wolfe, "Mrs. America," *The New Republic* (October 3, 2005), http://www.tnr.com/article/politics/mrs-america.

53. Bruce J. Schulman, *The Seventies: The Great Shift in American Culture, Society, and Politics* (New York: DaCapo, 2001), 169.

54. Ruth Rosen, *The World Split Open: How the Modern Women's Movement Changed America* (New York: Viking, 2000), 82.

55. Mansbridge, *Why We Lost the ERA*, 15–16.

56. Schulman, *The Seventies*, 170.

57. Frum, *How We Got Here*, 247–48.

58. Schulman, *The Seventies*, 169; William A. Link, *Righteous Warrior: Jesse Helms and the Rise of Modern Conservatism* (New York: St. Martin's Press,), 182–83, 176.

59. Judith Hennessee, *Betty Friedan: Her Life* (New York: Penguin, 1999), 233.

60. Donald T. Critchlow, *Phyllis Schlafly and Grassroots Conservatism: A Woman's Crusade* (Princeton: Princeton University Press, 2005), 236.

61. Ashley Kahn, Holly George-Warren, and Shawn Dahl, eds. *Rolling Stone: The '70s* (Boston: Little Brown, 1998), 204.

62. Hodgson, *More Equal Than Others*, 147.

63. David J. Garrow, *Liberty and Sexuality: The Right to Privacy and the Making of* Roe v. Wade (New York: Macmillan, 1994), 264.

64. Jeffrey Toobin, "Still Standing: The Resilience of *Roe v. Wade*," *The New Yorker* (November 18, 2005), 74.

65. Erica Jong, *Fear of Flying* (New York: Holt, Rinehart, and Winston, 1973), 12.

66. For more on this theme, see Tom Waldman, *Not Much Left: The Fate of Liberalism in America* (Berkeley: University of California Press, 2008); on criticisms of liberalism as mindless tolerance, see also Lisa McGirr, *Suburban Warriors: The Origins of the New American Right* (Princeton: Princeton University Press, 2001), 159.

67. See Michael Crowley, "Teddy Bear," *The New Republic* (August 8, 2001), 9.

68. Edward M. Kennedy, *True Compass: A Memoir* (New York: Twelve, 2009), 95–97.

69. Evan Thomas, "His Dream Shall Never Die," *Newsweek* (August 26, 2009), http://www.newsweek.com/2009/08/25/his-dream-shall-never-die.html.

70. Adam Clymer, *Edward M. Kennedy: A Biography* (New York: William Morrow, 1999), 40.

71. Joe McGinniss, *The Last Brother: The Rise and Fall of Teddy Kennedy* (New York: Simon & Schuster, 1993), 283, 299.

72. Thomas, "His Dream Shall Never Die."

73. Jack Newfield, "The Senate's Fighting Liberal," *The Nation* (March 25, 2002), 11.

74. Clymer, *Edward M. Kennedy*, 41.

75. Thomas, "His Dream Shall Never Die."

76. See Niall O'Dowd, "Ted Kennedy's Gamble on Obama Pays Off as Health Care Passes," "Periscope," Irish Central, March 21, 2010, http://www.irishcentral.com/story/news/peri scope/ted-kennedys-gamble-on-obama-pays-off--as-health-care-passes-88788517.html; and Mimi Hall, "Health care bill supporters jubilant at signing," *USA Today*, March 24, 2010, A1.

77. John M. Broder, "Edward M. Kennedy, Senate Stalwart, Is Dead at 77," *New York Times*, August 26, 2009, A1.

78. Thomas, "His Dream Shall Never Die."

79. Kennedy, *True Compass*, 272.

80. McGinniss, *The Last Brother*, 481.

81. Kennedy, *True Compass*, 288.

82. Clymer, *Edward M. Kennedy*, 129.

83. Ibid., 173.

84. Frum, *How We Got Here*, 253; see also Schulman, *The Seventies*, 57.

85. Louis P. Masur, *The Soiling of Old Glory: The Story of a Photograph That Shocked America* (New York: Bloomsbury, 2008), 40.

86. Ibid., 38.

87. Ibid., 42.

88. J. Anthony Lukas, *Common Ground: A Turbulent Decade in the Lives of Three American Families* (New York: Knopf, 1985), 506.

89. Hannah Arendt, "Reflections on Little Rock", *Dissent* (Winter 1959), 47–58.

90. Edsall, *Chain Reaction*, 89.

91. Masur, *The Soiling of Old Glory*, 45.

92. Ibid., 46.

93. Clymer, *Edward M. Kennedy*, 222.

94. Jefferson Cowie, *Stayin' Alive: The 1970s and the Last Decade of the Working Class* (New York: New Press, 2010), 99.

95. Kennedy, *True Compass*, 348.

96. Clymer, *Edward M. Kennedy*, 224.

97. Lukas, *Common Ground*, 262.

98. Kennedy, *True Compass*, 350.

99. Atwater is quoted in Bob Herbert, "The Ugly Side of the GOP," *New York Times*, September 25, 2007, http://www.nytimes.com/2007/09/25/opinion/25herbert.html.

100. Kennedy, *True Compass*, 352.

101. Vincent J. Cannato, *The Ungovernable City: John Lindsay and His Struggle to Save New York* (New York: Basic Books, 2001), 428.

102. Frum, *How We Got Here*, 263.

14 | "A Government as Good as Its People"

1. See Judith Stein, *Pivotal Decade: How The United States Traded Factories for Finance in the Seventies* (New Haven, CT: Yale University Press, 2010), 7, 118; See also Walter LaFeber, *America, Russia, and the Cold War, 1945–2006*, 10th ed. (New York: McGraw-Hill, 2006).

2. Beth Bailey and David Farber, eds., *America in the Seventies* (Lawrence, KS: University of Kansas Press, 2004), 84; "Economy and Politics Since 1970," in Michael Kazin, ed., *The Princeton Encyclopedia of American Political History*, vol. 1 (Princeton: Princeton University Press, 2010), 274–77.

3. Laura Kalman, *Right Star Rising: A New Politics, 1974–1980* (New York: Norton, 2010), 39–46.

4. For the Powell Memo, see "The Powell Memo," http://www.Reclaimdemocracy.Org/Corporate_Accountability/Powell_Memo_Lewis.Html.

5. Quoted in Jefferson Cowie, "Red, White, and Blue Collar," *Democracy* (Spring 2011), http://www.Democracyjournal.Org/20/Red-White-And-Blue-Collar.Php?Page=2. For more detail, see Eric Alterman, *What Liberal Media? The Truth About Bias and the News* (New York: Basic

Books, 2003) and Alterman, *Why We're Liberals: A Handbook for Restoring America's Most Important Ideals* (New York: Viking, 2009) for specifics on tax policy and inequality.

6. Steven Greenhouse, "Union Membership in U.S. Fell to a 70-Year Low Last Year," *New York Times*, January 21, 2011: http://www.nytimes.com/2011/01/22/business/22union.html?_R=1&pagewanted=print.

7. Thomas Byrne Edsall, "The Changing Shape of Power," in Steve Fraser and Gary Gerstle, eds., *The Rise and Fall of the New Deal Order, 1930–1980*, (Princeton: Princeton University Press, 1989), 278.

8. Edward D. Berkowitz, *Something Happened: A Political and Cultural Overview of the Seventies* (New York: Columbia University Press, 2006), 55.

9. Godfrey Hodgson, *More Equal Than Others: America from Nixon to the New Century* (Princeton: Princeton University Press 2004), 16.

10. See Daniel T. Rodgers, *The Age of Fracture* (Cambridge, MA: Harvard University Press, 2010), 43.

11. Robert M. Collins, *More: The Politics of Economic Growth in Postwar America* (New York: Oxford University Press, 2000), 160.

12. Berkowitz, *Something Happened*, 2.

13. Walter Laqueur, "Why the Shah Fell," *Commentary* (March 1979), 55.

14. Midge Decter, "America Now: A Failure of Nerve?," *Commentary* (July 1975), http://www.commentarymagazine.com/article/america-now-a-failure-of-nerve/

15. See H. W. Brands, *The Strange Death of American Liberalism* (New Haven, CT: Yale University Press, 2001).

16. David Frum, *How We Got Here: The 70's: The Decade That Brought You Modern Life—For Better or Worse* (New York: Basic Books, 2000), 50.

17. Arthur M. Schlesinger, Jr., *The Imperial Presidency* (Boston: Houghton Mifflin, 1973), 213.

18. On "New Hollywood," see Peter Biskind, *Easy Riders, Raging Bulls: How the Sex-Drugs-and-Rock 'n' Roll Generation Saved Hollywood* (New York: Simon & Schuster, 1998).

19. Jared Brown, *Alan J. Pakula: His Films and His Life* (New York: Back Stage Books, 2005), 24. Biographical details come from this book.

20. Quoted in Brown, *Alan J. Pakula*, 154.

21. Quoted in Michael Feeney Callan, "Washington Monument," *Vanity Fair* (April, 2011), 125.

22. Quoted in William E. Leuchtenburg, "All the President's Men," in Mark C. Carnes, ed., *Past Imperfect: History According to the Movies* (New York: Holt, 1995), 288.

23. See Callan, "Washington Monument," 132.

24. Brown, *Alan J. Pakula*, 201.

25. Frum, *How We Got Here*, 284.

26. Rosalynn Carter, *First Lady from Plains* (New York: Fawcett, 1984), 9.

27. Jimmy Carter, *An Hour Before Daylight: Memories of a Rural Boyhood* (New York: Simon & Schuster, 2001), 70; Dan Ariail and Cherly Heckler-Feltz, *The Carpenter's Apprentice: The Spiritual Biography of Jimmy Carter* (Grand Rapids, MI: Zondervan, 1996), 28.

28. Carter, *An Hour Before Daylight*, 78.

29. Quoted in Nicholas Dawidoff, "The Riddle of Jimmy Carter," *Rolling Stone* (February 3, 2011), 74.

30. Jimmy Carter, *Why Not the Best?* (New York: Bantam, 1976), 12.

31. Quoted in Dawidoff, "The Riddle of Jimmy Carter," 74.

32. Bruce Mazlish and Edwin Diamond, *Jimmy Carter: A Character Portrait* (New York: Simon & Schuster, 1980), 45–48.

33. Peter G. Bourne, *Jimmy Carter: A Comprehensive Biography from Plains to Post-Presidency* (New York: Scribner, 1997), 25, 39–40.

34. Carter, *First Lady from Plains*, 33.

35. James Wooten, *Dasher: The Roots and the Rising of Jimmy Carter* (New York: Summit, 1978), 236.

36. Quoted in Dawidoff, "The Riddle of Jimmy Carter," 74.

37. Betty Glad, *Jimmy Carter: In Search of the Great White House* (New York: Norton, 1980), 89–93.

38. Laura Kalman, *Right Star Rising: A New Politics, 1974–1980* (New York: Norton, 2010), 149.

39. Quoted in Dawidoff, "The Riddle of Jimmy Carter," 74.

40. Glad, *Jimmy Carter*, 130.

41. William Lee Miller, *Yankee from Georgia: The Emergence of Jimmy Carter* (New York: Times Books, 1978), 28–9.

42. Kalman, *Right Star Rising*, 149.

43. Glad, *Jimmy Carter*, 152.
44. Fred I. Greenstein, *The Presidential Difference: Leadership Style from FDR to George W. Bush* (Princeton: Princeton University Press, 2004), 132.
45. Kalman, *Right Star Rising*, 149.
46. John Dumbrell, *The Carter Presidency: A Re-Evaluation* (Manchester, UK: Manchester University Press, 1995), 71–72.
47. Burton Hersh, *The Shadow President: Ted Kennedy in Opposition* (South Royalton, VT: Steerforth Press, 1997), 25; Glad, *Jimmy Carter*, 206.
48. Jimmy Carter, *A Government as Good as Its People* (New York: Pocket Books, 1977), 106.
49. Ibid., 55.
50. See Maurice Isserman and Michael Kazin, *America Divided: The Civil War of the 1960s* (New York: Oxford University Press, 2000), 245.
51. Kalman, *Right Star Rising*, 149.
52. Jimmy Carter quoted in Glad, *Jimmy Carter*, 220.
53. Hunter S. Thompson, *The Great Shark Hunt: Strange Tales from a Strange Time* (New York: Fawcett, 1979), 527–579.
54. Quoted in Dawidoff, "The Riddle of Jimmy Carter," 74.
55. Carter, *A Government as Good as Its People*, 71.
56. Jeffrey Bloodworth, "Senator Henry Jackson, The Solzhenitsyn Affair, and American Liberalism," *Pacific Northwest Quarterly* (Spring 2006), 75.
57. Garry Wills, *Lead Time: A Journalist's Education* (Garden City, NY: Doubleday, 1983), 175.
58. Arthur M. Schlesinger, Jr., *Journals: 1952–2000* (New York: Penguin, 2007), 405.
59. Ibid., 409.
60. Glad, *Jimmy Carter*, 268.
61. Ibid., 234.
62. Haynes Johnson, *In the Absence of Power: Governing America* (New York: Viking Press, 1980), 175–76.
63. Glad, *Jimmy Carter*, 291–96.
64. Ibid., 253.
65. Jimmy Carter, *Keeping Faith: Memoirs of a President* (Fayetteville, AR: University of Arkansas Press, 1995), 23.
66. Ibid., 28.
67. Timothy Stanley, *Kennedy vs. Carter: The 1980 Battle for the Democratic Party's Soul* (Lawrence, KS: University Press of Kansas, 2010), 43; Hendrik Hertzberg, "Jimmy Carter," in Robert A. Wilson, ed., *Character Above All*, ed. (New York: Simon & Schuster, 1995), 183.
68. Glad, *Jimmy Carter*, 412.
69. Peter N. Carroll, *It Seemed Like Nothing Happened: America in the 1970s* (New Brunswick, NJ: Rutgers University Press, 1990), 208.
70. Cowie is quoted in Mark Schmitt, "When It All Went Wrong," *The American Prospect* Online (September 2, 2010), http://www.prospect.org/cs/articles?article=when_it_all_went_wrong.
71. Carter, *Keeping Faith*, 69.
72. John Dumbrell, *American Foreign Policy: Carter to Clinton* (New York: St. Martin's Press, 1997), 11.
73. Carter, *A Government as Good as Its People*, 149.
74. For more, see Bernard Weinraub, "Now, Vietnam Vets Demand Their Rights," *New York Times Magazine*, May 27, 1979, 30–33, 66–67.
75. The speech in both video and text is available at http://millercenter.org/scripps/archive/speeches/detail/3399.
76. Carter, *A Government as Good as Its People*, 67.
77. On the POW/MIA issue and its relation to conservative politics, see Tom Engelhardt, *The End of Victory Culture: Cold War America and the Disillusioning of a Generation* (Amherst, MA: University of Massachusetts, 1995), 275.
78. See Gary Dorrien, *The Neoconservative Mind: Politics, Culture, and the War of Ideology* (Philadelphia: Temple University Press, 1993), 169–70.
79. Carter, *A Government as Good as Its People*, 115.
80. Carter, *Keeping Faith*, 147.
81. Ibid., 146.
82. Frum, *How We Got Here*, 309.
83. For discussions of Carter's foreign policy, see Gaddis Smith, *Morality, Reason, and Power: American Diplomacy in the Carter Years* (New York: Hill and Wang, 1986); Alexander Moens,

Foreign Policy Under Carter: Testing Multiple Advocacy Decision Making (Boulder: Westview, 1990); Burton Kaufman, *The Presidency of James Earl Carter, Jr.* (Lawrence, KS: University Press of Kansas, 1993); Timothy P. Maga, *The World of Jimmy Carter: U.S. Foreign Policy, 1977–1981* (West Haven, CT.: University of New Haven Press, 1994); Richard C. Thornton, *The Carter Years: Toward a New Global Order* (New York: Paragon House, 1991); Joshua Muravchik, *The Uncertain Crusade: Jimmy Carter and the Dilemmas of Human Rights Policy* (Lanham, MD: Hamilton Press, 1986); Erwin C. Hargrove, *Jimmy Carter as President: Leadership and the Politics of the Public Good* (Baton Rouge: Louisiana State University Press, 1988); Steven Hurst, *The Carter Administration and Vietnam* (New York: Macmillan, 1996); Robert A. Strong, *Working in the World: Jimmy Carter and the Making of American Foreign Policy* (Baton Rouge: Louisiana State University Press, 2000); Dumbrell, *The Carter Presidency*; Mary E. Stuckey, *Jimmy Carter, Human Rights, and the National Agenda* (College Station, TX: Texas A&M University Press, 2008); Burton I. Kaufman and Scott Kaufman, *The Presidency of James Earl Carter, Jr.*, 2nd ed. (Lawrence, KS: University Press of Kansas, 2006); Scott Kaufman, *Plans Unraveled: The Foreign Policy of the Carter Administration* (Dekalb, IL: Northern Illinois University Press, 2008).

84. "Betty Glad, *An Outsider in the White House: Jimmy Carter, His Advisors, and the Making of American Foreign Policy*," H-Diplo Roundtable Review, www.h-net.org/~diplo/roundtables, March 1, 2011, cited by Kaufman, *Plans Unraveled*, 9.

85. Walter LaFeber, *The Panama Canal: The Crisis in Historical Perspective* (New York: Oxford University Press, 1978), 205.

86. Quoted in Carter, *Keeping Faith*, 158.

87. Quoted in William A. Link, *Righteous Warrior: Jesse Helms and the Rise of Modern Conservatism* (New York: St. Martin's Press, 2008), 190.

88. Kalman, *Right Star Rising*, 270.

89. Carter, *Keeping Faith*, 163.

90. Smith, *Morality, Reason, and Power*, 115.

91. Sean Wilentz, *The Age of Reagan: A History, 1974–2008* (New York: HarperCollins, 2008), 102.

92. "Playboy Interview: Pat Caddell," *Playboy* (February 1980), 73.

93. James Fallows, "The Passionless Presidency," *Atlantic Monthly* (May 1979), 38.

94. Bourne, *Jimmy Carter*, 408.

95. Fallows, "The Passionless Presidency," 35.

96. Quoted in Bourne, *Jimmy Carter*, 406.

97. Dumbrell, *American Foreign Policy*, 30.

98. Author's interview with Edward Said, 1993 (Stanford, California). The coining of the sad saying is usually credited to the late Israeli scholar and diplomat, Abba Eban.

99. See Bernard Gwertzman, "Vance Chides Young for Holding Talks with P.L.O. Official," *New York Times*, August 15, 1979, A1; "Ambassador Young's Offense," *New York Times*, August 15, 1979, A22; "Carter Summons Young to White House," *Los Angeles Times*, August 15, 1979, A1; Don Oberdorfer, "Young Admits PLO Talks, Draws Rebuke from Vance," *Washingon Post*, August 15, 1979, A1.

100. Naomi Levine, American Jewish Congress director of programming, to Jewish Community Relations Councils, "The Freedom Riders," June 8, 1961, Vertical Files, Folder "Negroes: Civil Rights Movement," The American Jewish Committee Archives, New York, NY.

101. See "Monthly Activities Review: Jewish Labor Committee," April 7, 1961, July 6, 1961, September 6, 1961, Student Nonviolent Coordinating Committee Papers, Subgroup A, reel 5.

102. Marc H. Ellis, *Encountering The Jewish Future: With Wiesel, Buber, Heschel, Arendt, Levinas* (Minneapolis, MN: Augsburg Fortress Publishers, 2010), 135.

103. Steven F. Lawson and Charles M. Payne, *Debating the Civil Rights Movement, 1945–1968* (Lanham, MD: Rowman and Littlefield, 1998), 30–31.

104. Paul Delaney, "Leaders Try to Halt a Black-Jewish Rift," *New York Times*, August 19, 1979, 12.

105. Laurie Johnson, "Black Leaders Back Young; Jews Still Fearful on P.L.O.," *New York Times*, August 16, 1979, A16.

106. James Baldwin, "Open Letter to the Born Again," *The Nation* (September 29, 1979), 263–64.

107. "Statement from the National Urban League," box 9, folder 5, Robert S. Browne Papers, Schomburg Center for Research in Black Culture, New York, NY.

108. See Jonathan Kaufman, *Broken Alliance: The Turbulent Times Between Blacks and Jews in America* (New York: Scribner, 1988), 245.

109. See Rashid Khalidi, *Sowing Crisis: The Cold War and American Dominance in the Middle East* (Boston: Beacon Press, 2009), 172–75.

110. Smith, *Morality, Reason, And Power*, 184–85

111. For a history of this movement, see Gal Beckerman, *When They Come for Us, We'll Be Gone: The Epic Struggle to Save Soviet Jewry* (New York: Houghton Mifflin Co, 2010).
112. Glad, *An Outsider in the White House: Jimmy Carter, His Advisors, and the Making of American Foreign Policy* (Ithaca, NY: Cornell University Press, 2009), 39, 25.
113. "Glad, *An Outsider in the White House*," H-Diplo Roundtable Review.
114. Carter, *Keeping Faith*, 267.
115. See for instance, the disdain that drips from the pens of William Kristol and Robert Kagan, in "Toward A Neo-Reaganite Foreign Policy," *Foreign Affairs* (July/August, 1996), http://carnegie-mec.org/publications/?fa=276.
116. James T. Patterson, *Restless Giant: The United States from Watergate to* Bush v. Gore (New York: Oxford University Press, 2005), 113.
117. Johnson, *In the Absence of Power*, 164.
118. Garland A. Haas, *Jimmy Carter and the Politics of Frustration* (Jefferson, NC: McFarland, 1992), 74.
119. Carroll, *It Seemed Like Nothing Happened*, 212.
120. Kalman, *Right Star Rising*, 210.
121. Quoted in Garry Wills, "The Strange Success of Jimmy Carter," *The New York Review of Books*, October 28, 2010, 23–24.
122. Haynes Johnson, *Sleepwalking Through History: America in the Reagan Years* (New York: Doubleday, 1992), 35; see also his interesting account in *The Absence of Power*.
123. Jimmy Carter interview, available online at http://www.hnet.org/~diplo/roundtables/pdf/roundtable-XII-6.pdf.
124. Glad, *Jimmy Carter*, 438.
125. Both quoted in Steven M. Gillon, *Politics And Vision: The ADA And American Liberalism, 1947–1985* (New York: Oxford University Press, 1987), 234.
126. Stanley, *Kennedy vs. Carter*, 66.
127. Mark Schmitt, "When It All Went Wrong."
128. Harold Meyerson, "Keeper of the Liberal Flame," *American Prospect* (August 29, 2009), http://www.prospect.org/cs/articles?article=ted_kennedy_keeper_of_the_liberal_flame.
129. Edward M. Kennedy, *True Compass: A Memoir* (New York: Twelve, 2009), 363.
130. Jeanie Kasindorf, "Waiting for Kennedy," *New West* (August 13, 1979), 71.
131. Dankwart A. Rustow, *Oil and Turmoil: America Faces OPEC and the Middle East* (New York: Norton, 1982), 183.
132. See Kevin Mattson, *"What The Heck Are You Up To, Mr. President?": Jimmy Carter, America's "Malaise," and the Speech That Should Have Changed the Country* (New York: Bloomsbury, 2009), 156–59.
133. Ibid.; and Adam Clymer, *Edward M. Kennedy: A Biography* (New York: William Morrow, 1999), 275.
134. Kalman, *Right Star Rising*, 331.
135. Kennedy, *True Compass*, 367.
136. Clymer, *Edward M. Kennedy*, 286–87.
137. Carroll, *It Seemed Like Nothing Happened*, 340.
138. Clymer, *Edward M. Kennedy*, 295.
139. Michael Mastanduno, "Economics and Security in Statecraft and Scholarship," *International Security* 52 (1998), 192.
140. Gregory Mantsios, "What Does Labor Stand For?" in Mantsios, ed., *A New Labor Movement for the New Century* (New York: Monthly Review Press, 1998), quoted in Philip Dray, *There Is Power in a Union: The Epic Story of Labor in America* (New York: Doubleday, 2010), 670.
141. Stein is quoted in Jennifer Klein, "Apocalypse Then and Now," *Democracy* (Winter 2011), 101.
142. Thomas Byrne Edsall with Mary D. Edsall, *Chain Reaction: The Impact of Race, Rights, and Taxes on American Politics* (New York: Norton, 1992), 130.
143. Andrew E. Busch, *Reagan's Victory: The Presidential Election of 1980 and the Rise of the Right* (Lawrence, KS: University Press of Kansas, 2005), 25.
144. Quoted in Hodgson, *More Equal Than Others*, 43.
145. William Martin, *With God on Our Side: The Rise of the Religious Right in America* (New York: Broadway, 2005).
146. Perry Deane Young, *God's Bullies: Native Reflections on Preachers and Politics* (New York: Holt, Rinehart, and Winston, 1982), 36.

147. James C. Roberts, *The Conservative Decade: Emerging Leaders of the 1980s* (Westport, CT: Arlington House, 1980), 91; see also Lee Edwards, *The Conservative Revolution: The Movement That Remade America* (New York: Free Press, 1999), 197.
148. Godfrey Hodgson, *The World Turned Right Side Up* (Boston: Houghton Mifflin, 1996), 178.
149. Richard Viguerie quoted in *U.S. News & World Report* (September 24, 1979), 38.
150. Carroll, *It Seemed Like Nothing Happened*, 344.
151. Quoted in Roberts, *The Conservative Decade*, 308, 329.
152. Norman Podhoretz, *The Present Danger* (New York: Simon & Schuster, 1980), 30.
153. Wills, *Lead Time*, 261.
154. Ted Kennedy, "1980 Democratic National Convention Address," delivered August 12, 1980, New York, NY, available online at "American Rhetoric, Top 100 Speeches", http://www.americanrhetoric.com/speeches/tedkennedy1980dnc.htm.
155. Stein, *Pivotal Decade*, 260.
156. Quoted in ibid., 179.
157. Douglas Brinkley, *The Unfinished Presidency: Jimmy Carter's Journey Beyond* Viking, 1998), 6.
158. Schlesinger, Jr., *Journals*, 503–505.
159. Speech reprinted in *The New Republic* (July 7 and 14, 1979), 16.

15 | "Where's the Beef?"

1. Quoted in Adam Clymer, *Edward M. Kennedy: A Biography* (New York: William Morrow, 1999), 339.
2. Quoted in William E. Leuchtenburg, *In the Shadow of FDR: From Harry Truman to Barack Obama* (Ithaca, NY: Cornell University Press, 2001), 257.
3. Arthur M. Schlesinger, Jr., *Journals: 1952–2000* (New York: Penguin, 2007), 574.
4. Walter Mondale, *The Good Fight: A Life in Liberal Politics* (New York: Scribner, 2010), 303, and Steven M. Gillon, *The Democrats' Dilemma: Walter F. Mondale and the Liberal Legacy* (New York: Columbia University Press, 1992), 308–309.
5. Quoted in Thomas Byrne Edsall with Mary D. Edsall, *Chain Reaction: The Impact of Race, Rights, and Taxes on American Politics* (New York: Norton, 1991), 182.
6. Marshall Frady, *Jesse: The Life and Pilgrimage of Jesse Jackson* (New York: Random House, 1996), 5.
7. Ibid., 86.
8. Ibid.,199.
9. Ibid., 217.
10. David J. Garrow, *Bearing the Cross: Martin Luther King, Jr., and the Southern Christian Leadership Conference* (New York: Vintage, 1986), 585.
11. Frady, *Jesse*, 293.
12. Richard L. Berke, "Jackson's Rhymes: Lilting to a Different Cadence," *New York Times*, April 16, 1988, http://www.nytimes.com/1988/04/16/us/jackson-s-rhymes-lilting-to-a-different-cadence.html.
13. Frady, *Jesse*, 23.
14. Stanley Crouch, *Notes of a Hanging Judge: Essays and Reviews, 1979–1989* (New York: Oxford University Press, 1990), 5.
15. Ibid., 18.
16. Adolph L. Reed, *The Jesse Jackson Phenomenon: The Crisis of Purpose in Afro-American Politics* (New Haven, CT: Yale University Press, 1986), 13.
17. Frady, *Jesse*, 14.
18. Reed, *The Jesse Jackson Phenomenon*, 94.
19. Jonathan Kaufman, *Broken Alliance: The Turbulent Times Between Blacks and Jews in America* (New York: Scribner, 1988), 256.
20. Quoted in Edward Alexander, "Multiculturalists and Anti-Semitism," *Society* 31 (1994), 58–64.
21. See for instance Gary Hart, *A New Democracy* (New York: Quill, 1983), 141–156.
22. Gary Hart, "When the Personal Shouldn't Be Political," *New York Times*, November 8, 2004, http://www.nytimes.com/2004/11/08/opinion/08hart.html?ex=1257656400&en=45d84e c7d6fb1fad&ei=5090; see also Garry Wills, "Holiness and Gary Hart," in *Under God: Religion and American Politics* (New York: Simon & Schuster, 1990).
23. Randall Rothenberg, *The Neoliberals: Creating the New American Politics* (New York: Simon & Schuster, 1984), 129.

24. Quoted in Bruce Miroff, *The Liberals' Moment: The McGovern Insurgency and the Identity Crisis of the Democratic Party* (Lawrence, KS: University Press of Kansas, 2007), 19.
25. See Rothenberg, *The Neoliberals*, 129.
26. Miroff, *The Liberals' Moment*, 286.
27. Gary Hart, *The Good Fight: The Education of an American Reformer* (New York: Random House, 1993), 212.
28. Miroff, *The Liberals' Moment*, 286; see also Hart, *A New Democracy*, 88–89.
29. Mondale, *The Good Fight*, 292.
30. Quoted in Gillon, *The Democrats' Dilemma*, 319.
31. Ibid., 354.
32. John A. Farrell, *Tip O'Neill and the Democratic Century* (Boston: Little Brown, 2001), 646.
33. Lou Cannon, *President Reagan: The Role of a Lifetime* (New York: Public Affairs, 2000), 434.
34. Edsall, *Chain Reaction*, 173.
35. SeanWilentz, *The Age of Reagan: A History, 1974–2008* (New York: HarperCollins, 2008), 174.
36. Mark Hertsgaard, *On Bended Knee: The Press and the Reagan Presidency* (New York: Farrar, Straus and Giroux, 1988), 99–100.
37. Ibid., 101.
38. Ibid.
39. William Kleinknecht, *The Man Who Sold the World: Ronald Reagan and the Betrayal of Main Street America* (New York: Nation Books, 2009), 41.
40. Garry Wills, *Reagan's America: Innocents at Home* (Garden City, NY: Doubleday, 1987), 215.
41. John Patrick Diggins, *Ronald Reagan: Fate, Freedom, and the Making of History* (New York: Norton, 2007), 30, 46; John Ehrman, *The Eighties: America in the Age of Reagan* (New Haven, CT: Yale University Press, 2005), 11.
42. Quoted in Robert M. Collins, *More: The Politics of Economic Growth in Postwar America* (New York: Oxford University Press, 2000), 192.
43. Alonzo L. Hamby, *Liberalism and its Challengers: From F.D.R. to Bush* (New York: Oxford University Press, 1992), 342, 384.
44. Schlesinger, Jr., *Journals*, 491.
45. Edsall, *Chain Reaction*, 159.
46. Kleinknecht, *The Man Who Sold the World*, 34.
47. Edward M. Kennedy, *True Compass: A Memoir* (New York: Twelve, 2009), 384.
48. Clymer, *Edward M. Kennedy*, 362.
49. Kleinknecht, *The Man Who Sold the World*, 24.
50. Quoted in Farrell, *Tip O'Neill*, 658.
51. Lawrence S. Wittner, *Toward Nuclear Abolition: A History of the World Nuclear Disarmament Movement, 1971–Present* (Stanford, CA: Stanford University Press, 2003), 75; background on Forsberg also from her obituary, *New York Times*, October 26, 2007, http://www.nytimes.com/2007/10/26/us/26forsberg.html?ref=us.
52. Thomas R. Rochon and David S. Meyer, eds., *Coalitions and Political Movements: The Lessons of the Nuclear Freeze* (Boulder, CO: Lynne Rienner, 1997), 2.
53. David S. Meyer, *A Winter of Discontent: The Nuclear Freeze and American Politics* (New York: Praeger, 1990), 147.
54. Paul Rogat Loeb, *Hope in Hard Times: America's Peace Movement and the Reagan Era* (Lexington, MA: Lexington, 1987), 148.
55. For more on the radical, direct-action element in the peace movement of the 1980s, see Barbara Epstein, *Political Protest and Cultural Revolution: Nonviolent Direct Action in the 1970s and 1980s* (Berkeley: University of California Press, 1991), 30.
56. Meyer, *A Winter of Discontent*, 183.
57. Rochon and Meyer, *Coalitions and Political Movements*, 1.
58. Ibid., 13.
59. See Jonathan Schell, *The Fate of the Earth* and *The Abolition* (Stanford, CA: Stanford University Press, 2000).
60. Quoted in Bradford Martin, *The Other Eighties: A Secret History of America in the Age of Reagan* (New York: Hill and Wang, 2011), 28.
61. See for instance Walter LaFeber, *Inevitable Revolutions: The United States in Central America*, 2nd ed. (New York: Norton, 1993).
62. Quoted in James T. Patterson, *Restless Giant: The United States from Watergate to Bush v. Gore* (New York: Oxford University Press, 2005), 208.

63. Christian Smith, *Resisting Reagan: The U.S. Central America Peace Movement* (Chicago: University of Chicago Press, 1996), 38.
64. Ibid., xvi, xvii.
65. Patterson, *Restless Giant*, 208
66. See Bob Woodward, *Veil: The Secret Wars of the CIA, 1981–1987* (New York: Simon & Schuster, 1987), 208.
67. Tip O'Neill press conference, February 23, 1982; see Farrell, *Tip O'Neill*, 612.
68. Hedrick Smith, "A Larger Force of Latin Rebels Sought by U.S.," *New York Times*, April 17, 1985; see also Arnson, *Crossroads: Congress, the Reagan Administration, and Central America* (New York: Pantheon Books, 1989), 181.
69. Smith, *Resisting Reagan*, 95.
70. The phrase "Sandinista sympathizer" appeared in Fred Barnes, "The Sandinista Lobby," *The New Republic* (January 20, 1986); "Democrats and Commandantes," *The New Republic* (July 28, 1986), 197–210.
71. "Democrats and Commandantes," 7.
72. Barnes, "The Sandinista Lobby," 11.
73. "The Sandinista Chorus," *The New Republic* (August 25, 1986), 9.
74. Eric Alterman, *Sound and Fury: The Washington Punditocracy and the Collapse of American Politics* (New York: HarperCollins, 1992), 194.
75. Quoted in Arnson, *Crossroads*, 117.
76. Haynes Johnson, *Sleepwalking Through History: America in the Reagan Years* (New York: Norton, 1991), 275–76; Patterson, *Restless Giant*, 208.
77. Cannon, *President Reagan*, 337.
78. Ibid., 521.
79. Smith, *Resisting Reagan*, 349; Wilentz, *The Age of Reagan*, 225.
80. Wilentz, *The Age of Reagan*, 238.
81. Smith, *Resisting Reagan*, 351.
82. Patterson, *Restless Giant*, 179.
83. Randy Shilts, *And the Band Played On: Politics, People, and the AIDS Epidemic* (New York: St. Martin's Press, 1987), 525.
84. Bruce J. Schulman, *The Seventies: The Great Shift in American Culture, Society, and Politics* (New York: DaCapo, 2001), 180.
85. John D'Emilio, *Making Trouble: Essays on Gay History, Politics, and the University* (New York: Routledge, 1992), 242.
86. The term "mattachine" referred to "mysterious mediaeval figures in masks" who the founders believed to be homosexuals; see John D'Emilio, *Sexual Politics, Sexual Communities: The Making of a Homosexual Minority in the United States, 1940–1970* (Chicago: University of Chicago Press, 1983), 67.
87. Dudley Clendinen and Adam Nagourney, *Out for Good: The Struggle to Build a Gay Rights Movement in America* (New York: Simon & Schuster, 1999), 46.
88. Chai Feldblum, "The Federal Gay Rights Bill: From Bella to ENDA," in John D'Emilio, William B. Turner, and Urvashi Vaid, eds., *Creating Change: Sexuality, Public Policy, and Civil Rights* (New York: St. Martin's Press, 2000), 151.
89. William B. Turner, "Mirror Images: Lesbian/Gay Civil Rights in the Carter and Reagan Administrations," in D'Emilio et al., *Creating Change*, 10.
90. John D'Emilio and Estelle B. Freedman, *Intimate Matters: A History of Sexuality in America* (Chicago: University of Chicago Press, 1997), 324.
91. Chai R. Feldblum, "The Federal Gay Rights Bill: From Bella to ENDA," in D'Emilio et al., *Creating Change*, 152–53; Suzanne Braun Levine and Mary Thom, *Bella Abzug* (New York: Farrar, Straus and Giroux, 2007), 150.
92. Randy Shilts, *The Mayor of Castro Street: The Life and Times of Harvey Milk* (New York: St. Martin's Press, 1982), 7, 10.
93. Clendinen and Nagourney, *Out for Good*, 338.
94. Shilts, *The Mayor of Castro Street*, 44.
95. *The Times of Harvey Milk*, 1984; New Yorker Video, 2004.
96. Clendinen and Nagourney, *Out for Good*, 377–79.
97. Shilts, *The Mayor of Castro Street*, 242.
98. D'Emilio, *Making Trouble*, 90.
99. Quoted in Amin Ghaziani, *The Dividends of Dissent: How Conflict and Culture Work in Lesbian and Gay Marches on Washington* (Chicago: University of Chicago, 2008), 45.

100. Quoted in Jean O'Leary, "From Agitator to Insider: Fighting for Inclusion in the Democratic Party," in D'Emilio, Turner, and Vaid, *Creating Change*, 95.
101. Clymer, *Edward M. Kennedy*, 433.
102. John B. Judis, *William F. Buckley, Jr.: Patron Saint of the Conservatives* (New York: Simon & Schuster, 1988), 455.
103. Quoted in Patterson, *Restless Giant*, 180.
104. David Roman, *Acts of Intervention: Performance, Gay Culture, and AIDS* (Bloomington, IN: Indiana University Press, 1998), 10–12.
105. Ghaziani, *The Dividends of Dissent*, 89.
106. Quoted in David J. Garrow, *Liberty and Sexuality: The Right to Privacy and the Making of* Roe v. Wade (New York: Macmillan, 1994), 665.
107. The speech is reprinted in Larry Kramer, *Reports from the Holocaust: the Making of an AIDS Activist* (New York: St. Martin's Press, 1989), 128.
108. Ibid.
109. Quoted in Deborah B. Gould, *Moving Politics: Emotion and ACT UP's Fight Against AIDS* (Chicago: University of Chicago Press, 2009), 290.
110. Robert S. McElvaine, *Mario Cuomo: A Biography* (New York: Scribner, 1988), 342–44.
111. See Jonathan Mahler, *The Bronx Is Burning: 1977, Baseball, Politics, and the Battle for the Soul of a City* (New York: Farrar, Straus and Giroux, 2005), 104.
112. See Steve Fishman, "The Cuomo Family Business," in *New York Magazine*, August 1, 2010, http://nymag.com/news/politics/67397/.
113. Mahler, *Ladies and Gentlemen, The Bronx Is Burning*, 105.
114. All the events in Cuomo's life come from McElvaine, *Mario Cuomo*.
115. See in general Mahler, *Ladies and Gentlemen, The Bronx Is Burning*.
116. Randolph Bourne, "Transnational America," in *The Radical Will: Selected Writings, 1911–1918*, Olaf Hansen, ed. (New York: Urizen Books, 1977), 258.
117. Gil Troy, *Morning in America: How Ronald Reagan Invented the 1980s* (Princeton: Princeton University Press, 2005), 224; Richard Parker, *John Kenneth Galbraith: His Life, His Politics, His Economics* (New York: Farrar, Straus and Giroux, 2005), 592.
118. Robert N. Bellah et al., *Habits of the Heart: Individualism and Commitment in American Life* (New York: Perennial, 1985), 6.
119. Garry Wills uses the term "message" moviemaker in his assessment of Stone's career; "Dostoyevsky Behind a Camera," *Atlantic Monthly* (July 1997), 100.
120. See Peter Biskind, *Easy Riders, Raging Bulls: How the Sex-Drugs-and-Rock 'n' Roll Generation Saved Hollywood* (New York: Simon & Schuster, 1998).
121. Quoted in James Riordan, *Stone: The Controversies, Excesses, and Exploits of a Radical Filmmaker: A Biography of Oliver Stone* (New York: Hyperion, 1995), 246–47.
122. Ibid., 15–16.
123. Ibid., 24–25.
124. Ibid., 43, 42.
125. Ibid., 59.
126. Ibid., 63.
127. Ibid., 196.
128. *Platoon*, MGM, 2000.
129. Quoted in Patterson, *Restless Giant*, 186.
130. James Lardner, "Films: *Broadcast News/Wall Street*," *The Nation* (January 23, 1988), 97.
131. Wills, "Dostoyevsky Behind a Camera," 98.
132. Wilentz, *The Age of Reagan*, 267.
133. Ibid., 268; and David Courtwright, *No Right Turn: Conservative Politics in a Liberal America* (Cambridge, MA: Harvard University Press, 2010), 202.
134. Edsall, *Chain Reaction*, 222.
135. Quoted in Troy, *Morning in America*, 305.
136. Courtwright, *No Right Turn*, 158.
137. See Gerald M. Pomper, "The Presidential Nominations," in Pomper et al., eds., *The Election of 1988: Reports and Interpretations* (Chatham, NY: Chatham House, 1989), 65.
138. Geoffrey Nunberg, *Talking Right* (New York: Public Affairs, 2006), 43.
139. Ann Coulter, *Treason: Liberal Treachery from the Cold War to the War on Terrorism* (New York: Three Rivers Press, 2005).
140. E. J. Dionne, Jr., *Why Americans Hate Politics* (New York: Simon & Schuster, 1991), 301.
141. Nunberg, *Talking Right*, 43.

16 | A Place Called "Hope"

1. Daniel P. Moynihan, *A Portrait in Letters of an American Visionary*, ed. Steven R. Weisman (New York: Public Affairs, 2010), 511–13.
2. Gil Troy, *Morning in America: How Ronald Reagan Invented the 1980s* (Princeton: Princeton University Press, 2005), 265–66; Robert Hughes, *The Culture of Complaint: The Fraying of America* (New York: Oxford University Press, 1993), 81.
3. Andreas Huyssen, *After the Great Divide: Modernism, Mass Culture, Postmodernism* (Bloomington, IN: Indiana University Press, 1986), 183–66.
4. Roger Kimball, *Tenured Radicals: How Politics Has Corrupted Our Higher Education* (New York: Harper & Row, 1990).
5. Antonio Gramsci, *Prison Notebooks*, ed. Joseph A. Buttigieg (New York: Columbia University Press, 1992), 233–38.
6. Rebecca Mead, "Yo, Professor," *New York Magazine* (November 14, 1994), 51.
7. Andrew Ross, *Strange Weather: Culture, Science and Technology in the Age of Limits* (New York: Verso, 1991).
8. Anne Mathews, "Deciphering Victorian Underwear, and Other Seminars," *New York Times Magazine*, February 10, 1991, 43.
9. See Dinitia Smith, "'Queer Theory' Is Entering the Literary Mainstream," *New York Times*, January 17, 1998, http://www.nytimes.com/1998/01/17/books/queer-theory-is-entering -the-literary-mainstream.html?pagewanted=all&src=pm.
10. See Geoffrey Hughes, *Political Correctness: A History of Semantics and Culture* (New York: John Wiley, 2010), 60.
11. Todd Gitlin, *The Twilight of Common Dreams: Why America Is Wracked by Culture Wars* (New York: Metropolitan, 1995), 168.
12. Allan Bloom, *The Closing of the American Mind* (New York: Simon & Schuster, 1987), 313, 314.
13. See Dinesh D'Souza, *Illiberal Education: The Politics of Race and Sex on Campus* (New York: Free Press, 1991); on the right-wing infrastructure behind his work, see John Micklethwait and Adrian Wooldridge, *The Right Nation: Why America Is Different* (Harmondsworth, UK: Penguin, 2005), 169.
14. See Gitlin, *The Twilight of Common Dreams*. See also Jonathan Alter's review in *Washington Monthly* (January/Feburary, 1996), http://findarticles.com/p/articles/mi_m1316/is_n1-2 _v28/ai_17761527/.
15. James Davison Hunter, "The Culture Wars," in Gilbert Sewall, ed., *The Eighties: A Reader* (Reading, MA: Perseus, 1998), 365.
16. Arthur M. Schlesinger, Jr., *Journals: 1952–2000* (New York: Penguin, 2007), 705.
17. Arthur M. Schlesinger, Jr., *The Disuniting of America* (Knoxville: Whittle Direct Books, 1991), 30, 67, 73.
18. John Patrick Diggins, *The Rise and Fall of the American Left* (New York: Norton, 1992), 347.
19. Ibid., 382.
20. Louis Hartz, *The Liberal Tradition in America* (1955; repr., New York: Harvest, 1991), 60–61.
21. Quoted in Richard H. Pells, *The Liberal Mind in a Conservative Age: American Intellectuals in the 1940s and 1950s* (Middletown, CT: Wesleyan University Press, 1989), 158.
22. Hartz, *The Liberal Tradition in America*, 263.
23. See Robert Shalhope, "Toward a Republican Synthesis," *William and Mary Quarterly* 29 (1972), 49–80.
24. J. G. A. Pocock, *The Machiavellian Moment: Florentine Political Thought and the Atlantic Republican Tradition* (Princeton: Princeton University Press, 1975), 506.
25. Ibid., 41.
26. Gordon S. Wood, *The Creation of the American Republic, 1776–1787* (New York: 1969), 418.
27. Ibid., 418–19.
28. Robert N. Bellah et al., *Habits of the Heart: Individualism and Commitment in American Life* (New York: Perennial, 1985), 256; for more on the connections between communitarianism and republicanism, see Ian Shapiro, *Political Criticism* (Berkeley: University of California Press, 1990), 167.
29. James T. Kloppenberg, *The Virtues of Liberalism* (New York: Oxford University Press, 1998), 125.
30. John Rawls, *A Theory of Justice* (Cambridge, MA: Harvard University Press, 1971), 12.
31. Ibid., 13.
32. Ronald Dworkin, *Sovereign Virtue: The Theory and Practice of Equality* (Cambridge, MA: Harvard University Press, 2000), 136.

33. See Michael Sandel, *Liberalism and the Limits of Justice* (New York: Cambridge University Press, 1982), 147. See also Michael Sandel, *Democracy's Discontent*, 6, 322 on this point.

34. Christopher Lasch, "Why Liberalism Lacks Virtue," *New Perspectives Quarterly* 8 (1991), 31, 33.

35. William A. Galston, *Liberal Purposes: Goods, Virtues, and Diversity in the Liberal State* (Cambridge: Cambridge University Press, 1991), 304.

36. Ibid., 211, 224, 225–26.

37. Stephen Macedo, *Liberal Virtues: Citizenship, Virtue, and Community in Liberal Constitutionalism* (Oxford: Clarendon Press, 1990), 37, 272.

38. Stephen Holmes, *The Anatomy of Antiliberalism* (Cambridge, MA: Harvard University Press, 1993).

39. Peter Berkowitz, *Virtue and the Making of Modern Liberalism* (Princeton: Princeton University Press, 1999), xi. Berkowitz made the point that Rawls himself had this set of principles behind his own political theory.

40. Diggins, *The Rise and Fall of the American Left*, 370.

41. Richard Rorty, *Contingency, Irony, and Solidarity* (Cambridge: Cambridge University Press, 1989).

42. Richard Rorty, *Objectivity, Relativism, and Truth: Philosophical Papers* (Cambridge: Cambridge University Press, 1991), 214.

43. See, in particular, Richard Rorty, *Achieving Our Country: Leftist Thought in Twentieth-Century America* (Cambridge, MA: Harvard University Press, 1999).

44. Jeffrey J. Williams, "How to Be an Intellectual: The Cases of Richard Rorty and Andrew Ross," *Dissent* (Winter 2011), 74.

45. Neil Gross, *Richard Rorty: The Making of an American Philosopher* (Chicago: University of Chicago Press, 2008), 91.

46. James Ryerson, "The Quest for Uncertainty," *Lingua Franca* (December 2000/January 2001), http://linguafranca.mirror.theinfo.org/print/0012/feature_quest.html.

47. For more on the Rauschenbusch legacy, see Casey Nelson Blake, "Private Life and Public Commitment: From Walter Rauschenbusch to Richard Rorty," in John Pettigrew, ed., *A Pragmatist's Progress?: Richard Rorty and American Intellectual History* (Lanham, MD: Rowman and Littlefield, 2000). See also Walter Rauschenbusch, *A Theology for the Social Gospel* (New York: Macmillan, 1917).

48. See Joseph Dorman, *Arguing the World: The New York Intellectuals in Their Own Words* (New York: Free Press, 2000).

49. Gross, *Richard Rorty*, 112.

50. Richard Rorty, *Philosophy and Social Hope* (New York: Penguin, 1999), 12.

51. Gross, *Richard Rorty*, 4.

52. Simon Blackburn, "Richard Rorty," *Prospect* (April 20 2003), http://www.prospectmagazine.co.uk/2003/04/blackburn-richard-rorty-profile/. John Dewey, "Philosophy and Democracy" (1918), in David A. Hollinger and Charles Capper, eds., *The American Intellectual Tradition, vol. II: 1865 to the Present*, 4th ed. (New York: Oxford University Press, 2000), 168.

53. John Dewey, "Philosophy and Democracy" (1918) in *The American Intellectual Tradition*, 4th ed., eds. David Hollinger and Charles Capper (New York: Oxford University Press, 2000), 168.

54. Patricia Cohen, "Richard Rorty," *New York Times*, June 11, 2007, http://www.nytimes.com/2007/06/11/obituaries/11rorty.html.

55. Quoted in Gross, *Richard Rorty*, 232.

56. Williams, "How to Be An Intellectual," 73.

57. Gross, *Richard Rorty*, 5.

58. Damon Linker, posting to *The New Republic* (June 12, 2007), http://www.tnr.com/doc.mhtml?i=w070611&s=linker061207; Robert Westbrook, quoted in Casey Nelson Blake, "Pragmatist Hope," *Dissent* (Spring 2007), http://www.dissentmagazine.org/article/?article=787; Richard Bernstein, quoted in Ryerson, "The Quest for Uncertainty."

59. Rorty, *Philosophy and Social Hope*, 4.

60. James Baldwin, *The Fire Next Time* (1963; repr., New York: Vintage, 1993), 10, 105.

61. James T. Kloppenberg, "Aspirational Nationalism in America," *Intellectual History Newsletter* 24 (2002), 60–71; see also Jonathan M. Hansen, *The Lost Promise of Patriotism: Debating American Identity, 1890–1920* (Chicago: University of Chicago Press, 2003).

62. Rorty, *Philosophy and Social Hope*, 17.

63. Rorty, *Achieving Our Country*, 3.

64. Rorty, *Philosophy and Social Hope*, 260.

65. Rorty, *Achieving Our Country*, 58, 35, 43, 69.
66. Ibid., 105, 46, 91.
67. James T. Patterson, *Restless Giant: The United States from Watergate to Bush v. Gore* (New York: Oxford University Press, 2005), 258.
68. Mickey Kaus, *The End of Equality* (New York: Basic Books, 1995), xiii.
69. Kenneth S. Baer, *Reinventing Democrats: The Politics of Liberalism from Reagan to Clinton* (Lawrence, KS: University Press of Kansas, 2000), 74.
70. Joe Klein, *The Natural: The Misunderstood Presidency of Bill Clinton* (New York: Broadway, 2002), 29.
71. Ibid., 29; Baer, *Reinventing Democrats*, 82, 81.
72. Baer, *Reinventing Democrats*, 95.
73. See Mary Ann Glendon, *Rights Talk: The Impoverishment of Political Discourse* (New York: Free Press, 1993).
74. Steven Waldman, *The Bill: How the Adventures of Clinton's National Service Bill Reveal What Is Corrupt, Comic, Cynical—and Noble—About Washington* (New York: Viking, 1995), 4.
75. Baer, *Reinventing Democrats*, 112.
76. Ibid., 169.
77. Ibid., 171.
78. William Galston and Elaine Ciulla Kamarck, *The Politics of Evasion: Democrats and the Presidency* (Washington, DC: Progressive Policy Institute, 1989), 3–4, 16, 18–19. See also Baer, *Reinventing Democrats*, 170.
79. Baer, *Reinventing Democrats*, 168.
80. Kennedy quoted in Dan Balz, "Always the Party of What-Went-Wrong," *Washington Post*, June 11, 2006, http://www.washingtonpost.com/wp-dyn/content/article/2006/06/09/AR2006060902001.html.
81. David Maraniss, *First in His Class: The Biography of Bill Clinton* (New York: Touchstone, 1995), 13.
82. Ibid., 13, 40.
83. Ibid., 11.
84. Ibid., 61.
85. Ibid., 69.
86. Bill Clinton, *My Life* (New York: Knopf, 2004), 87.
87. Quoted in Maraniss, *First in His Class*, 396.
88. Ibid., 115.
89. Ibid., 119.
90. Ibid., 184.
91. Ibid., 142.
92. Ibid., 158.
93. Ibid., 186.
94. Ibid., 284.
95. Klein, *The Natural*, 34–35.
96. Maraniss, *First in His Class*, 446.
97. Baer, *Reinventing Democrats*, 8.
98. Quoted in ibid., 181.
99. Clinton, *My Life*, 365.
100. Klein, *The Natural*, 40.
101. John F. Harris, *The Survivor: Bill Clinton in the White House* (New York: Random House, 2005), 147.
102. Laura Mansnerus, "Damaged Brains and the Death Penalty," *New York Times*, July 21, 2001, http://www.deathpenaltyinfo.org/node/652.
103. Adam Clymer, *Edward M. Kennedy: A Biography* (New York: William Morrow, 1999), 513–14.
104. William L. O'Neill, *A Bubble in Time: America During the Interwar Years, 1989–2001* (Chicago: Ivan R. Dee, 2009), 113; Clinton, *My Life*, 411.
105. Patterson, *Restless Giant*, 251.
106. Klein, *The Natural*, 43.
107. See Ronald B. Rapoport and Walter Stone, *Three's a Crowd: The Dynamic of Third Parties, Ross Perot, and Republican Resurgence* (Ann Arbor, MI: University of Michigan Press, 2005), 55.
108. Sean Wilentz, *The Age of Reagan: A History, 1974–2008* (New York: HarperCollins, 2008), 316.

109. Gerald Posner, *Citizen Perot: His Life and Times* (New York: Random House, 1996), 257–59.
110. Governor Bill Clinton and Senator Al Gore, *Putting People First: How We Can All Change America* (New York: Times Books, 1992), 100.
111. Clinton, *My Life*, 404.
112. "1992 Election," the Roper Center for Public Opinion Research archives, http://www .ropercenter.uconn.edu/elections/presidential/presidential_election_1992.html.
113. Wilentz, *The Age of Reagan*, 326; see also O'Neill, *A Bubble in Time*, 166.
114. Christopher Jencks, "What Happened to Welfare?," *The New York Review of Books*, December 15, 2005, http://www.nybooks.com/articles/archives/2005/dec/15/what-happened-to -welfare/.
115. Harris, *The Survivor*, 16.
116. Ibid.
117. Wilentz, *The Age of Reagan*, 329.
118. Clinton, *My Life*, 486.
119. Ibid., 547; for more in general on this, see Waldman, *The Bill*.
120. David Courtwright, *No Right Turn: Conservative Politics in a Liberal America* (Cambridge, MA: Harvard University Press, 2010), 225.
121. William H. Chafe, *Private Lives/Public Consequences: Personality and Politics in Modern America* (Cambridge, MA: Harvard University Press, 2005), 369.
122. Courtwright, *No Right Turn*, 223.
123. William C. Berman, *From the Center to the Edge: The Policies and Politics of the Clinton Presidency* (Lanham, MD: Rowman and Littlefield, 2001), 27–28.
124. Patterson, *Restless Giant*, 329.
125. Chafe, *Private Lives/Public Consequences*, 370.
126. Klein, *The Natural*, 122.
127. Courtwright, *No Right Turn*, 223.
128. "Bill Kristol's 1993 Memo Calling for GOP to Block Health Care Reform," http://theplum line.whorunsgov.com/bill-kristols-1993-memo-calling-for-gop-to-block-health-care-reform/.
129. See Betsy McCaughey, "No Exit," *The New Republic* (February 7, 1994), 21–25.
130. Tom Wolfe, "Revolutionaries: Tom Wolfe on how the Manhattan Institute changed New York City and America," *New York Post*, January 30, 2003, http://www.freerepublic.com/focus/ news/833131/posts.
131. Andrew Sullivan, "Answering Ezra," "The Daily Dish," October 11, 2007, http://andrew sullivan.theatlantic.com/the_daily_dish/2007/10/answering-ezra.html.
132. Micklethwait and Wooldridge, *The Right Nation*, 110–12.
133. George Stephanopolous, *All Too Human (A Political Education)* (Boston: Little Brown, 1999), 276.
134. Patterson, *Restless Giant*, 344.
135. Elizabeth Drew, *Showdown: The Struggle Between the Gingrich Congress and the Clinton White House* (New York: Simon & Schuster, 1996), 14.
136. David Maraniss and Michael Weisskopf, *"Tell Newt to Shut Up!"* (New York: Simon & Schuster, 1996), 193.
137. Lou Michel and Dan Herbeck, *American Terrorist: Timothy McVeigh and the Oklahoma City Bombing* (New York: Regan Books, 2001), 234.
138. Quoted in Klein, *The Natural*, 143.
139. Quoted in Harris, *The Survivor*, 216.
140. Patterson, *Restless Giant*, 372.
141. Harris, *The Survivor*, 231.
142. Quoted in Jacob Hacker, "After Welfare," *The New Republic* (October 11, 2004), http://gap .newamerica.net/publications/articles/2004/after_welfare.
143. David Glenn, "After Welfare," *Dissent* (Fall 2004), http://www.dissentmagazine.org/ article/?article=325.
144. Courtwright, *No Right Turn*, 238.
145. Stanley B. Greenberg, *The Two Americas: Our Current Political Deadlock and How to Break It* (New York: St. Martin's Press, 2004), 79.
146. Patterson, *Restless Giant*, 376.
147. Harris, *The Survivor*, 246.
148. Wilentz, *The Age of Reagan*, 367.
149. Ibid.
150. *New York Times*, September 12, 1996.

151. John Ehrman, *The Eighties: America in the Age of Reagan* (New Haven, CT: Yale University Press, 2005), 80.

152. Robert B. Reich, *Locked in the Cabinet* (New York: Knopf, 1997); Klein, *The Natural*, 196.

153. Michael Waldman, *POTUS Speaks: Finding the Words That Defined the Clinton Presidency* (New York: Simon & Schuster, 2000), 99; John Harris, "Policy and Politics by the Numbers," *Washington Post*, December 31, 2000, A01.

154. Quoted in Klein, *The Natural*, 140.

155. Gil Troy, *Leading from the Center: Why Moderates Make the Best Presidents* (New York: Basic Books, 2008), 224.

156. Nelson Lichtenstein, *State of the Union: A Century of American Labor* (Princeton: Princeton University Press, 2002), 255; see also Steven Fraser and Joshua B. Freeman, eds., *Audacious Democracy: Labor, Intellectuals, and the Social Reconstruction of America* (New York: Mariner, 1997).

157. Davidson Goldin, "Yale Teaching Assistants Vote for a Grade Strike," *New York Times*, December 13, 1995, http://www.nytimes.com/1995/12/13/nyregion/yale-teaching-assistants-vote-for-a-grade-strike.html.

158. See Thomas Geoghegan, *Which Side Are You On?: Trying to Be for Labor When It's Flat on Its Back* (New York: Plume, 1992).

159. Lichtenstein, *State of the Union*, 16.

160. Philip Roth, *The Human Stain* (New York: Houghton Mifflin, 2000), 2.

161. Richard Nixon resigned before being impeached. Andrew Johnson was impeached but never elected to the office of president.

162. Garry Wills, "The Tragedy of Bill Clinton," *The New York Review of Books*, August 12, 2004, http://www.nybooks.com/articles/archives/2004/aug/12/the-tragedy-of-bill-clinton/.

163. Chafe, *Private Lives/Public Consequences*, 378.

164. Joan Didion, *Political Fictions* (New York: Vintage, 2001), 241.

165. Harris, *The Survivor*, 306–307.

166. Patterson, *Restless Giant*, 396.

167. Haynes Johnson, *The Best of Times: The Boom and Bust Years of America Before and After Everything Changed* (New York: Harcourt, 2002), 379–80.

168. Moynihan, *A Portrait in Letters*, 513.

169. Justin Vaïsse, *Neoconservatism: The Biography of a Movement* (Cambridge, MA: Harvard University Press, 2010), 211.

170. Godfrey Hodgson, *The Gentleman from New York: Daniel Patrick Moynihan: A Biography* (Boston: Houghton Mifflin, 2000), 399.

171. John Micklethwait and Adrian Wooldridge, "It Depends on What the Meaning of 'Liberal' Is," *New York Times*, June 27, 2004, http://www.nytimes.com/2004/06/27/weekinreview/the-nation-it-depends-what-the-meaning-of-liberal-is.html.

172. Quoted in Courtwright, *No Right Turn*, 244.

173. Michelle Goldberg, "MoveOn Moves Up," Salon.com, December 1, 2003, http://dir.salon.com/news/feature/2003/12/01/moveon/index.html.

174. Christopher Hayes, "MoveOn.Org Is Not as Radical as Conservatives Think," *The Nation* (July 16, 2008), http://www.thenation.com/article/moveonorg-not-radical-conservatives-think.

175. Matt Bai, *The Argument: Inside the Battle to Remake Democratic Politics* (New York: Penguin, 2007), 77.

176. Hayes, "MoveOn.Org Is Not as Radical as Conservatives Think."

177. Harris, *The Survivor*, 241.

178. Courtwright, *No Right Turn*, 247; Johnson, *The Best of Times*, 390.

179. Waldman, *POTUS Speaks*, 269.

180. Arthur M. Schlesinger, Jr., "The Vital Center: 50 Years Later," *Society* (May/June 1998), 53.

17 | What's the Matter with America?

1. Joe Klein, *Politics Lost: How American Democracy Was Trivialized by People Who Think You're Stupid* (New York: Doubleday, 2006), 140.

2. Arthur Schlesinger, Jr., *Journals: 1952–2000* (New York: Penguin, 2007), 837; James T. Patterson, *Restless Giant: The United States from Watergate to Bush v. Gore* (New York: Oxford University Press, 2005), 408.

3. Bill Clinton, *My Life* (New York: Knopf, 2004), 927.

4. This quote can be found in many places, including Jason Zengerle, "Geek Pop Star," *New York Magazine* (November 9, 2008), http://nymag.com/print/?/arts/books/features/52014/index1.html2008.

5. David Maraniss and Ellen Nakashima, *The Prince of Tennessee: The Rise of Al Gore* (New York: Simon & Schuster, 2000), 106.

6. Ibid., 155.

7. Ibid., 157.

8. Al Gore, *Earth in the Balance: Ecology and the Human Spirit* (Boston: Houghton Mifflin, 1992), 8.

9. Ibid., 236, 223–24, 12, 14, 306–307.

10. Ibid., 8, 9.

11. Background and story on the speech are available online at, http://transcripts.cnn.com/2000/ALLPOLITICS/stories/06/27/campaign.wrap/index.html.

12. Bill Kovach and Tom Rosenstiel, "Campaign Lite: Why Reporters Won't Tell Us What We Need to Know," *Washington Monthly* (January/February, 2001), http://www.journalism.org/node/348.

13. CNN's "Reliable Sources," August 10, 2002, http://www.cnn.com/TRANSCRIPTS/0208/10/rs.00.html.

14. Justin Martin, *Nader: Crusader, Spoiler, Icon* (Cambridge, MA: Perseus, 2002), 230.

15. Ibid., 262.

16. Quoted in ibid., 254.

17. Patterson, *Restless Giant*, 413.

18. Tim Padgett, "Mob Scene in Miami," *Time* (November 26, 2000), http://www.time.com/time/nation/article/0,8599,89450,00.html.

19. Michael Kelly, "Burn that Village," *Washington Post,* November 29, 2000, A39.

20. Ibid.

21. Michael Kelly, "Send in the Thugs," *Washington Post,* November 22, 2000, A27 (also in *Jewish World Review*, same date).

22. Jacob Heilbrunn, "Samantha and Her Subjects," *The National Interest*, April 19, 2011, http://nationalinterest.org/article/samantha-her-subjects-5161.

23. Ibid.

24. John F. Harris, *The Survivor: Bill Clinton in the White House* (New York: Random House, 2005), 45.

25. Bill Clinton, "The Dayton Accords," in Alvin Z. Rubinstein, Albina Shayevich, and Boris Zlotnikow, eds., *The Clinton Foreign Policy Reader* (Armonk, NY: M. E. Sharpe, 2000), 178.

26. Michael Ignatieff, "The American Empire; The Burden," *New York Times,* January 5, 2003, http://query.nytimes.com/gst/fullpage.html?res=9B03E6DA143FF936A35752C0A9659C8B63.

27. Heilbrunn, "Samantha and Her Subjects."

28. Carl Bernstein, *A Woman in Charge: The Life of Hillary Rodham Clinton* (New York: Knopf, 2007), 461.

29. Greg Sargent, "Brand Hillary," *The Nation* (June 6, 2005), http://www.thenation.com/article/brand-hillary?page=0,4.

30. Bernstein, *A Woman in Charge,* 550.

31. Gore's speech is available online at, http://www.gwu.edu/~action/2004/gore/gore092302sp.html.

32. Reinhold Niebuhr, *The Irony of American History* (1952; repr., Chicago: University of Chicago Press, 2008), 7.

33. Eric Boehlert, "Why did the press ignore Ted Kennedy in 2002?," Media Matters, http://mediamatters.org/columns/200805280002; see also E. J. Dionne, Jr., *Stand Up, Fight Back: Republican Toughs, Democratic Wimps, and the Politics of Revenge* (New York: Simon & Schuster, 2004), 82.

34. Speech reprinted in David Remnick, *The Bridge: The Life and Rise of Barack Obama* (New York: Knopf, 2010), 346–47.

35. See Christopher Lasch, *The New Radicalism in America, 1889–1963: The Intellectual as a Social Type* (New York: Knopf, 1965); see also Joshua Micah Marshall, "The Orwell Temptation: Are Intellectuals Overthinking the Middle East?," *Washington Monthly*, May 2003, http://www.washingtonmonthly.com/features/2003/0305.marshall.html.

36. George Packer's introduction to Packer, ed., *The Fight Is for Democracy: Winning the War of Ideas in America and the World* (New York: HarperCollins, 2003), 1.
37. Paul Berman, *Terrorism and Liberalism* (New York: Norton, 2003), 40.
38. Andrew Sullivan, "How Did I Get Iraq Wrong?" Slate.com, March 21, 2008, http://www.slate.com/id/2187098/.
39. Jacob Heilbrunn, *They Knew They Were Right: The Rise of the Neocons* (New York: Doubleday, 2008), 13.
40. Quoted in George Packer, *The Assassins' Gate: America in Iraq* (New York: Farrar, Straus and Giroux, 2005), 136.
41. Quoted Dionne, Jr., *Stand Up, Fight Back,* 79–80.
42. Quoted in Eric Alterman, "Something about Christopher," *Dissent* (Fall, 2010), http://www.dissentmagazine.org/article/?article=3685.
43. Bill Keller, "My Unfinished 9/11 Business," *New York Times Magazine,* September 6, 2011, http://www.nytimes.com/2011/09/06/us/sept-11-reckoning/keller.html?_r=2&ref=global-home&pagewanted=print.
44. Heilbrunn, "Samantha and Her Subjects."
45. See Valerie Plame, *Fair Game: My Life as a Spy, My Betrayal by the White House* (New York: Simon & Schuster, 2007).
46. Michael Bérubé, *The Left at War* (New York: New York University Press, 2009), 103.
47. Tony Judt, "Bush's Useful Idiots," *London Review of Books,* September 21, 2006. http://www.lrb.co.uk/v28/n18/tony-judt/bushs-useful-idiots.
48. Based on Audit Bureau of Circulation figures, 2001–2009. See Pew Project for Journalistic Excellence, "The State of the News Media, 2010: Opinion Magazines," http://stateofthemedia.org/2010/magazines-summary-essay/opinion-magazines/.
49. See Lawrence F. Kaplan and William Kristol, *The War over Iraq: Saddam's Tyranny and America's Mission* (San Francisco: Encounter Books, 2003).
50. See Eric Alterman, "Never Mind the Truth . . . ," *The Nation* (February 6, 2006), http://www.thenation.com/doc/20060206/alterman.
51. Thomas L. Friedman, "Let's Talk About Iraq," *New York Times,* June 15, 2005, http://www.nytimes.com/2005/06/15/opinion/15friedman.html.
52. William Kristol, "The War for Liberalism," *Weekly Standard* (April 7, 2003), http://www.weeklystandard.com/Content/Public/Articles/000/000/002/452kblzf.asp.
53. Philip Gourevitch, "Damage Control," *The New Yorker* (July 26, 2004), http://www.newyorker.com/archive/2004/07/26/040726fa_fact.
54. Adam Nagourney, "The 2004 Campaign: The Massachusetts Senator; Kerry Sees Hope of Gaining Edge on Terror Issue," *New York Times,* July 25, 2004, http://www.nytimes.com/2004/07/25/us/2004-campaign-massachusetts-senator-kerry-sees-hope-gaining-edge-terror-issue.html.
55. Douglas Brinkley, *Tour of Duty: John Kerry and the Vietnam War* (New York: William Morrow, 2004), 21.
56. Ibid., 31.
57. Ibid., 61.
58. Ibid., 141.
59. Ibid., 254.
60. Ibid., 2.
61. Ibid., 11.
62. Ibid., 372.
63. Ibid., 421.
64. Ari Berman, *Herding Donkeys: The Fight to Rebuild the Democratic Party and Reshape American Politics* (New York: Farrar, Straus and Giroux, 2010), 16.
65. Harold Meyerson, "What Are Democrats About?" *Washington Post,* November 17, 2004, http://www.washingtonpost.com/wp-dyn/articles/A55689-2004Nov16.html.
66. Janet Hook, "Making 'Liberal' a Fighting Word Again," *Los Angeles Times,* October 15, 2004, http://articles.latimes.com/2004/oct/15/nation/na-liberal15; John Harris, "Truth, Consequences of Kerry's 'Liberal' Label," *Washington Post,* July 19, 2004, http://www.washingtonpost.com/wp-dyn/articles/A60419-2004Jul18.html.
67. Harris, "Truth, Consequences of Kerry's 'Liberal' Label."
68. Ryan Lizza, "Flip Side," *New Republic* (September 27, 2004), 10.
69. Ibid., 10.

70. "'Risk,' New Bush-Cheney '04 TV Ad," available online at http://blog.4president.us/2004/george_w_bush/index.html.

71. Quoted in James Carney, "What Happens to the Losing Team," *Time* (November 3, 2004): http://www.time.com/time/magazine/article/0,9171,750765,00.html.

72. Andrei Cherny, "Why We Lost," *New York Times,* November 5, 2004, http://www.nytimes.com/2004/11/05/opinion/05cherny.html/.

73. Thomas Frank, *What's the Matter with Kansas?: How Conservatives Won the Heart of America* (New York: Metropolitan Books, 2004), 114–15, 1.

74. Matt Bai, *The Argument: Inside the Battle to Remake Democratic Politics* (New York: Penguin, 2007), 52.

75. Indeed, a whole "states' rights" language started to creep into some liberal talk after the election; see Jim Holt, "A States' Rights Left," *New York Times,* November 21, 2004, http://www.nytimes.com/2004/11/21/magazine/21WWLN.html.

76. Marc Cooper, "Thinking of Jackassses," *Atlantic Monthly* (April 2005), 100.

77. See George Lakoff, *Don't Think of an Elephant!: Know Your Values and Frame the Debate* (White River Junction, VT: Chelsea Green, 2004).

78. Adam Nagourney and Janet Elder, "Americans Show Clear Concerns on Bush Agenda," *New York Times,* November 23, 2004, http://www.nytimes.com/2004/11/23/national/23poll.html.

79. Bai, *The Argument,* 156.

80. Quoted in Sean Wilentz, *The Age of Reagan: A History, 1974–2008* (New York: HarperCollins, 2008), 447.

81. Alan Wolfe, "Why Conservatives Can't Govern," *Washington Monthly* (July/August 2006), 36.

82. Al Gore, *The Assault on Reason* (New York: Penguin, 2007), 38, 175, 41, 62, 60.

83. Ibid., 270.

84. The original piece was E. J. Dionne, Jr., "The Liberal Moment," *The Chronicle of Higher Education,* September 7, 2007, B7–B8; commentary, including Alan Wolfe's, is available online at http://chronicle.com/article/The-Liberal-Moment/18579.

85. "The Backstreet Phantom of Rock," *Time* (October 27, 1975), http://www.time.com/time/magazine/article/0,9171,913583-4,00.html.

86. Federal Writers' Project, *New Jersey: A Guide to Its Present and Past* (New York: Viking, 1939), 250.

87. Louis P. Masur, *Runaway Dream: Born to Run and Bruce Springsteen's American Vision* (New York: Bloomsbury, 2009).

88. Dave Marsh, *Bruce Springsteen: Two Hearts, The Definitive Biography, 1972–2003* (New York: Routledge, 2004), 183.

89. Eric Alterman, *It Ain't No Sin to Be Glad You're Alive: The Promise of Bruce Springsteen* (Boston: Little Brown, 1999), 130–31.

90. Bryan K. Garman, *A Race of Singers: Whitman's Working-Class Hero from Guthrie to Springsteen* (Chapel Hill: University of North Carolina Press, 2000).

91. Marsh, *Bruce Springsteen,* 489.

92. Jon Pareles, "The Rock Laureate," *New York Times,* January 29, 2009, http://www.nytimes.com/2009/02/01/arts/music/01pare.html.

93. Stephen Holden, "Springsteen Scans the American Dream," *New York Times,* May 27, 1984, Section 2, 19.

94. Greil Marcus, *In the Fascist Bathroom* (Cambridge, MA: Harvard University Press, 1999), 271.

95. George F. Will, "Bruce Springsteen's USA," *Washington Post,* September 13, 1984, A19.

96. Garman, *A Race of Singers,* 72.

97. Jon Pareles, "His Kind of Heroes, His Kinds of Songs," *New York Times,* July 14, 2002, http://www.nytimes.com/2002/07/14/arts/music-his-kind-of-heroes-his-kind-of-songs.html?src=pm.

98. "Springsteen: Silence Is Unpatriotic," CBS News, July 27, 2008, http://www.cbsnews.com/stories/2007/10/04/60minutes/main3330463_page3.shtml.

18 | Hope and Change?

1. "The Liberal Form: An Interview with Jonathan Franzen," *boundary* 2, issue 36 (2009), 52.

2. Quoted in James T. Kloppenberg, *Reading Obama: Dreams, Hope, and the American Political Tradition* (Princeton University Press, 2011), 95.

3. See especially Susan Jacoby, *The Age of American Unreason* (New York: Pantheon, 2008), 281.

4. Ibid., 10.

5. Fred Barnes, *Rebel in Chief : Inside the Bold and Controversial Presidency of George W. Bush* (New York: Crown, 2006), 13.

6. John Podhoretz, *Bush Country: How Dubya Became a Great President While Driving Liberals Insane* (New York: St. Martin's Press, 2004).

7. David Frum, *The Right Man The Surprise Presidency of George W. Bush* (New York: Random House, 2003), 272.

8. Ron Suskind, "Faith, Certainty and the Presidency of George W. Bush," *New York Times Magazine*, October 17, 2004, http://www.nytimes.com/2004/10/17/magazine/17BUSH .html.

9. Ibid.

10. Jacoby, *The Age of American Unreason*, 299.

11. Obama's inaugural address is available onlnie at http://www.nytimes.com/2009/01/20/ us/politics/20text-obama.html?pagewanted=3&_r=1&adxnnl=1&adxnnlx=1302274844-ajJ Gp8FQ59cTDcuTMEPEHQ.

12. Kennedy's inaugural address is available online at http://www.americanrhetoric.com/ speeches/jfkinaugural.htm.

13. Richard Wolffe, *Renegade: The Making of a President* (New York: Crown, 2009), 84–85.

14. Quoted in David Plouffe, *The Audacity to Win: How Obama Won and How We Can Beat the Party of Limbaugh, Beck and Palin* (New York: Penguin, 2010), 165.

15. "Senator Kennedy Endorses Barack Obama," the Associated Press, January 28, 2008, http:// www.msnbc.msn.com/id/22873162/ns/politics-decision_08/.

16. Hendrik Hertzberg, "Obama Wins," *The New Yorker* (November 17, 2008), http://www .newyorker.com/talk/comment/2008/11/17/081117taco_talk_hertzberg.

17. Andrew Sullivan, "Goodbye to All That," *Atlantic Monthly* (December 2007), 46; Wolffe, *Renegade*, 236; on his childhood in Indonesia, see Jonathan Alter, *The Promise: President Obama, Year One* (New York: Simon & Schuster, 2010), 143–44.

18. Barack Obama, *Dreams from My Father: A Story of Race and Inheritance* (New York; Three Rivers Press, 1995), 100.

19. Quoted in Kloppenberg, *Reading Obama*, 17.

20. David Remnick, *The Bridge: the Life and Rise of Barack Obama* (New York: Knopf, 2010), 111; see also Phil Boerner, "Barack Obama '83, My Columbia College Roommate," available online at http://www.college.columbia.edu/cct/jan_feb09/alumni_corner.

21. Remnick, *The Bridge*, 116.

22. Ibid., 119–20.

23. Kevin Merida, "The Ghost of a Father," *Washington Post*, December 14, 2007, A12.

24. Obama, *Dreams from My Father*, 134–35; see also Ryan Lizza, "The Agitator," *The New Republic* (March 19, 2007), 24.

25. For his view of "power," see Saul Alinsky, *Reveille for Radicals* (Chicago: University of Chicago Press, 1946), 77–79; and Doug Rossinow, *Visions of Progress: The Left-Liberal Tradition in America* (Philadelphia: University of Pennsylvania Press, 2008), Chapter 5.

26. Quoted in Edward McClelland, *Young Mr. Obama: Chicago and the Making of a Black President* (New York: Bloomsbury, 2010), 43.

27. Lizza, "The Agitator," 26.

28. Quoted in Remnick, *The Bridge*, 164.

29. Quoted in Ryan Lizza, "Making It: How Chicago Shaped Obama," *The New Yorker* (July 21, 2008), 52.

30. Quoted in Wolffe, *Renegade*, 154.

31. Obama, *Dreams from My Father*, 196–97.

32. Ibid., 199.

33. *The Autobiography of Malcolm X* (New York: Grove Press, 1965), 374.

34. Obama, *Dreams from My Father*, 200.

35. Ibid., 276.

36. Remnick, *The Bridge*, 185–86.

37. Ibid., 207; see also Thomas J. Sugrue, *Not Even Past: Barack Obama and the Burden of Race* (Princeton: Princeton University Press, 2010), 38–39.

38. Fox Butterfield, "First Black Elected to Head Harvard's Law Review," *New York Times*, February 6, 1990, http://query.nytimes.com/gst/fullpage.html?res=9C0CE2DC1631F935A35 751C0A966958260.

39. Remnick, *The Bridge*.

40. McClelland, *Young Mr. Obama*, 66.
41. Remnick, *The Bridge*, 223.
42. McClelland, *Young Mr. Obama*, 111.
43. Ibid., 135, 142–43.
44. Ibid., 147.
45. Ibid., 150.
46. David Remnick, "The Joshua Generation: Race and the Campaign of Barack Obama," *The New Yorker*, November 17, 2008, http://www.newyorker.com/reporting/2008/11/17/081117fa_fact_remnick.
47. McClelland, *Young Mr. Obama*, 155.
48. Lizza, "Making It," 65.
49. Remnick, *The Bridge*, 396.
50. Barack Obama's 2004 convention speech is available online at http://www.americanrhetoric.com/speeches/convention2004/barackobama2004dnc.htm.
51. Michael Tomasky, "The Phenomenon," *The New York Review of Books*, November 30, 2006, http://www.nybooks.com/articles/archives/2006/nov/30/the-phenomenon/.
52. Sugrue, *Not Even Past*, 55.
53. David Brooks quoted at http://www.huffingtonpost.com/2008/10/08/david-brooks-sarahpalin_n_133001.html.
54. Quoted in Sullivan, "Goodbye to All That," 49.
55. Reinhold Niebuhr, *The Irony of American History* (1952; repr., Chicago: University of Chicago Press, 2008), 171, 172.
56. Barack Obama, *The Audacity of Hope: Thoughts on Reclaiming the American Dream* (New York: Three Rivers Press, 2006), 97–98.
57. Remnick, *The Bridge*, 435.
58. Jodi Enda, "Great Expectations," *The American Prospect*, January 16, 2006, http://prospect.org/cs/articles?articleId=10828
59. Obama, *The Audacity of Hope*, 34.
60. Ibid., 256.
61. Jodi Enda, "Great Expectations," *The American Prospect* (January 16, 2006).
62. Carl Bernstein, *A Woman in Charge: The Life of Hillary Rodham Clinton* (New York: Knopf, 2007), 15.
63. Ibid., 38.
64. Ibid., 44
65. Quoted in Todd Gitlin, "A Eulogy for Carl Oglesby, the Man Who Inspired the New Left and Was Then Tossed Overboard," *The New Republic*, September 17, 2011, http://www.tnr.com/article/politics/95047/carl-oglesby-new-left-sds.
66. Quoted in ibid., 50.
67. For more on the term "new sensibility" and the 1960s, see Morris Dickstein, *Gates of Eden: American Culture in the Sixties* (Cambridge, MA: Harvard University Press, 1997).
68. Clinton's thesis (parts of which are unpaginated, unfortunately) is available online at, http://www.hillaryclintonquarterly.com/documents/HillaryClintonThesis.pdf.
69. Garry Wills, "Lightning Rod," *The New York Review of Books*, August 14, 2003, http://www.nybooks.com/articles/archives/2003/aug/14/lightning-rod/.
70. Bernstein, *A Woman in Charge*, 58–59.
71. This assessment is based on multiple real-time conversations with top Clinton officials undertaken by Eric Alterman from 1992 to 2001. It is also consistent with myriad accounts of the Clinton presidency, the best of which, at this writing, probably remains John F. Harris, *The Survivor: Bill Clinton in The White House* (New York: Random House, 2005).
72. Quoted in Bernstein, *A Woman in Charge*, 537.
73. Michael Tomasky, *Hillary's Turn: Inside Her Improbable, Victorious Senate Campaign* (New York: Free Press, 2001), 185.
74. Elizabeth Kolbert, *The Prophet of Love and Other Tales of Power and Deceit* (New York: Bloomsbury, 2004), 27, 150.
75. See William Galston and Elaine Kamarck, *The Politics of Polarization* (Washington, DC: Third Way, 2005); Ezra Klein, "Sophomore Slump," *The American Prospect* (October 27, 2005), http://prospect.org/cs/articles?articleId=10522.
76. Greg Sargent, "Brand Hillary," *The Nation* (June 6, 2005), http://www.thenation.com/article/brand-hillary?page=0,2.
77. Raymond Hernandez and Patrick D. Healy, "The Evolution of Hillary Clinton; From Seeking

Major Change at Once to Taking Small Steps," *New York Times*, July 13, 2005, http://query.nytimes.com/gst/fullpage.html?res=9903E4DD103DF930A25754C0A9639C8B63.

78. Raymond Hernandez, "Hillary Clinton Taking Fire From Left as Well as Right," *New York Times*, May 30, 2003, http://www.nytimes.com/2003/05/30/nyregion/hillary-clinton-taking-fire-from-left-as-well-as-right.html.

79. See Jeff Gerth and Don Van Natta, Jr., "Hillary's War," *New York Times*, June 3, 2007, http://www.nytimes.com/2007/05/29/magazine/03Hillary-t.html.

80. Quoted in Dan Balz and Haynes Johnson, *The Battle for America 2008: The Story of an Extraordinary Election* (New York: Viking, 2009), 119.

81. John Heilemann and Mark Halperin, *Game Change: Obama and the Clintons, McCain and Palin, and the Race of a Lifetime* (New York: Harper, 2010), 99.

82. Toni Morrison, "Comment," *The New Yorker*, October 5, 1998, http://www.newyorker.com/archive/1998/10/05/1998_10_05_031_TNY_LIBRY_000016504?currentPage=all.

83. Quoted in Balz and Johnson, *The Battle for America 2008*, 51–52.

84. Ibid., 17.

85. Remnick, *The Bridge*, 444.

86. Heilemann and Halperin, *Game Change*, 33–34.

87. Ibid., 70.

88. Quoted in Remnick, *The Bridge*, 461.

89. Balz and Johnson, *The Battle for America 2008*, 30.

90. Ibid., 18.

91. Ibid., 31.

92. Heilemann and Halperin, *Game Change*, 74–75.

93. Ibid., 111.

94. Matt Bai, "The Poverty Platform," *New York Times*, June 10, 2007, http://www.nytimes.com/2007/06/10/magazine/10edwards-t.html.

95. Alec MacGillis, "On Poverty, Edwards Faces Old Hurdles," *Washington Post*, May 7, 2007, http://www.washingtonpost.com/wp-dyn/content/article/2007/05/06/AR2007050601322.html.

96. Ibid.

97. Ibid.

98. Quoted in Balz and Johnson, *The Battle for America 2008*, 30.

99. Heilemann and Halperin, *Game Change*, 39.

100. Ibid., 138–39.

101. See David Margolick, "John Edwards's Trial Will Showcase a Novel Defense," *The Daily Beast*, October 30, 2011, http://www.thedailybeast.com/newsweek/2011/10/30/john-edwards-s-trial-will-showcase-a-novel-defense.html.

102. Quoted in Wolffe, *Renegade*, 143–44.

103. Ryan Lizza, "Battle Plans: How Obama Won," *The New Yorker* (November 17, 2008), http://www.newyorker.com/reporting/2008/11/17/081117fa_fact_lizza.

104. Elizabeth Drew, "The Truth About the Election," *The New York Review of Books*, December 18, 2008, http://www.nybooks.com/articles/archives/2008/dec/18/the-truth-about-the-election/.

105. Remnick, *The Bridge*, 13.

106. William Jelani Cobb, *The Substance of Hope: Barack Obama and the Paradox of Progress* (New York: Walker, 2010), 66.

107. Ibid., 96.

108. Ibid., 101.

109. Ibid., 36.

110. Remnick, "The Joshua Generation."

111. Plouffe, *The Audacity to Win*, 161.

112. Rich Lowry, "Hillary, the New Scoop Jackson?," *National Review* (April 29, 2008), http://www.nationalreview.com/corner/162325/hillary-new-scoop-jackson/rich-lowry.

113. Quoted in Derrick Jackson, "Wright Stuff, Wrong Time," in T. Denean Sharpley-Whiting, ed., *The Speech: Race and Barack Obama's "A More Perfection Union,"* (New York: Bloomsbury, 2009), 23.

114. Heilemann and Halperin, *Game Change*, 236.

115. The speech is reprinted in Sharpley-Whiting, *The Speech*, 237–51.

116. David Plouffe, *The Audacity to Win*, 215–16

117. Heilemann and Halperin, *Game Change*, 255.

118. Ibid., 259.

119. Ibid., 258.
120. Ibid., 262.
121. Plouffe, *The Audacity to Win*, 314.
122. Max Blumenthal, *Republican Gomorrah: Inside the Movement That Shattered the Party* (New York: Nation Books, 2009), 300.
123. Andrew Leonard, "John McCain: 'The Fundamentals of Our Economy Are Strong,'" Salon .com, September 15, 2008, http://www.salon.com/technology/how_the_world_works/2008/ 09/15/mccain_fundamentals.
124. Alter, *The Promise*, 4.
125. Quoted in George Packer, "The New Liberalism," *The New Yorker* (November 17, 2008), http://www.newyorker.com/reporting/2008/11/17/081117fa_fact_packer.
126. See Rebecca Truister, "America Has Cracked Open," *Salon.com*, November 5, 2008.
127. Jeff Zeleny, "Obama Clinches Nomination; First Black Candidate to Lead a Major Party Ticket," *New York Times*, June 4, 2008, http://www.nytimes.com/2008/06/04/us/politics/ 04elect.html.
128. Kevin Sack, "Cuomo the Orator Now Soliloquizes in Book Form; Disclaiming Greatness, He Labors On: An Embryonic Idea Here, an Honorarium There," *New York Times*, September 27, 1993; see also Mario Cuomo, *More than Words: The Speeches of Mario Cuomo* (New York: St Martin's Press, 1993).
129. Marshall Ganz, "How Obama Lost His Voice, and How He Can Get It Back," *Los Angeles Times*, November 3, 2010, http://articles.latimes.com/2010/nov/03/opinion/la-oe-1103- ganz-obama-20101103.
130. Michael A. Memoli, "Mitch McConnell's Remarks on 2012 Draw White House Ire," *Los Angeles Times*, October 27, 2010, http://articles.latimes.com/2010/oct/27/news/la-pn-obama -mcconnell-20101027.
131. Jeff Zeleny, "Republicans Weighing Party's Message," *New York Times*, April 29, 2005, http:// www.nytimes.com/2010/04/10/us/politics/10memo.html.
132. Fareed Zakaria, "How Today's Conservatism Lost Touch with Reality," *Time* (June 16, 2011), http://www.time.com/time/nation/article/0,8599,2077943,00.html#ixzz1PjOJ9od6.
133. John B. Judis, "If Obama Likes Lincoln So Much, He Should Start Acting Like Him," *New Republic* (July 30, 2011), http://www.tnr.com/article/john-judis/92958/obama-lincoln-debt- ceiling.
134. Mike Lofgren, "Goodbye to All That: Reflections of a GOP Operative Who Left the Cult," TruthOut.org, September 3, 2011, http://www.truth-out.org/goodbye-all-reflections-gop -operative-who-left-cult/1314907779.
135. Ron Elving, "Beneath NPR's Poll, The 'Tyranny of Constituency,'" NPR, June 18, 2010, www .npr.org/blogs/watchingwashington/2010/06/18/127926122/watching-washington.
136. Marcus Baram, "Alter's 'The Promise' Epilogue: Obama Team's Dysfunction Prompted Lack of Focus on Jobs; Bill Clinton Annoyed at White House," Huffington Post, December 30, 2010, http://www.huffingtonpost.com/2010/12/30/alters-the-promise-epilog_n_802866 .html.
137. Norman Ornstein, "Worst. Congress. Ever." *Foreign Policy* (July 19, 2011), http://www .foreignpolicy.com/articles/2011/07/19/worst_congress_ever?page=full.
138. Statistics, which originally appeared in the *New York Times*, cited by Tom Hayden in "In Decrying Obama's Centrism, Drew Westen Ignores Role of Race," *Nation* (August 9, 2010), http://www.thenation.com/article/162642/decrying-obamas-centrism-drew-westen- ignores-role-race.
139. Binyamin Appelbaum, "Nominees at Standstill as G.O.P. Flexes Its Muscle," *New York Times*, June 19, 2011, http://www.nytimes.com/2011/06/20/us/politics/20nominate.html?ref =us&pagewanted=print.
140. See Adam Serwer, "Obama Getting Close to One Million Deportations," *Mother Jones* (September 9, 2011), http://motherjones.com/mojo/2011/09/obama-getting-close-one-million -deportations.
141. See Michael Tomasky, "The GOP's One-Sided War on Dems," The Daily Beast, September 9, 2011, http://www.thedailybeast.com/articles/2011/09/09/michael-tomasky-data-show -the-gop-s-one-sided-war-on-democrats.html.
142. Richard Hofstadter, *The American Political Tradition and the Men Who Made It*, ninth ed., (New York: Vintage, 1974), 239.
143. Scott Lemieux, "Let My Judges Go!," *American Prospect* (May 27, 2011), http://prospect.org/ cs/articles?article=let_my_judges_go.

144. Dominick Sundbrook, *Mad as Hell: The Crisis of the 1970s and the Rise of the Populist Right* (New York: Knopf, 2011), x.

145. John Amato and Dave Neiwart, *Over the Cliff: How Obama's Election Drove the American Right Insane* (Sausalito, CA: Polipoint Press, 2010), 118, 128.

146. Ben McGrath, "The Movement: The Rise of Tea Party Activism," *The New Yorker* (February 1, 2010), 43.

147. Andrew J. Perrin, Steven J. Tepper, Neal Caren, Sally Morris, "Cultures of the Tea Party," presented to the American Sociological Association, Las Vegas, Nevada, August 22, 2011.

148. See Eric Alterman, "The Problem of Republican Idiots," *Nation* (June 19, 2011); see also, http://video.foxnews.com/v/1006873447001/exclusive-jon-stewart-on-fox-news-sunday/#/v/1007046245001/exclusive-jon-stewart-on-fox-news-sunday/?playlist_id=87485.

149. "Tax Revenue as a Percentage of GDP in the Developed World," *Toronto Globe and Mail,* July 29, 2011, http://www.theglobeandmail.com/report-on-business/international-news/us/tax-revenue-as-a-percentage-of-gdp-in-the-developed-world/article2114914.

150. Packer, "The New Liberalism," *The New Yorker* (November 17, 2008).

151. David E. Sanger, "A New Economic Team: The Nominee; The Administration's Fiscal Closer," *New York Times*, May 13, 1999, www.nytimes.com/1999/05/13/business/a-new-economic-team-the-nominee-the-administration-s-fiscal-closer.html.

152. S. Mitra Kalita, "Americans See 18% of Wealth Vanish," *Wall Street Journal*, March 13, 2009, http://online.wsj.com/article/SB123687371369308675.html.

153. Wolffe, *Revival*, 176–77.

154. Paul Krugman, "Franklin Delano Obama?," *New York Times*, November 10, 2008, http://www.nytimes.com/2008/11/10/opinion/10krugman.html.

155. Ryan Lizza, "The Gatekeeper: Rahm Emanuel on the Job," *The New Yorker* (March 2, 2009), http://www.newyorker.com/reporting/2009/03/02/090302fa_fact_lizza?currentPage=all.

156. Alter, *The Promise*, 116.

157. Ibid, 153.

158. Quoted in Jann S. Wenner, "Obama in Command: The Rolling Stone Interview"; *Rolling Stone* (September 28, 2010), http://www.rollingstone.com/politics/news/obama-in-command-br-the-rolling-stone-interview-20100928; and Wolffe, *Revival*, 256.

159. George F. Will, "The Debt Deal and Obama's 2012 Problem," *Washington Post*, August 2, 2011, http://www.washingtonpost.com/opinions/the-debt-deal-and-obamas-2012-problem/2011/08/02/gIQAblZepI_story.html.

160. Motoko Rich, "Many Cities Face a Long Wait for Jobs to Return" *New York Times*, June 19, 2011, http://www.nytimes.com/2011/06/20/business/economy/20cities.html?_r=1&ref=us; and Stephanie Clifford, "Even Marked Up, Luxury Goods Fly Off Shelves," *New York Times*, August 4, 2011, A1.

161. Sheryl Gay Stolberg, "Obama Reaches Out to Doubters in State of the Union Address," *Denver Post*, January 28, 2010, http://www.denverpost.com/frontpage/ci_14283021#ixzz1QaIqG905.

162. Sabrina Tavernise, "Poverty Rate Soars to Highest Level Since 1993," *New York Times*, September 14, 2011, A1.

163. John Cassidy, "The Volker Rule," *The New Yorker* (July 26, 2010), http://www.newyorker.com/reporting/2010/07/26/100726fa_fact_cassidy.

164. Wendell Cochran, "Banks Emerging from Three-Year Financial Crisis," Bank Tracker, March 17, 2011, http://banktracker.investigativereportingworkshop.org/stories/2011/mar/17/nations-banks-emerging-three-year-financial-crisis/.

165. Guy Molyneux, "Can Obama Make the Pivot?" *The American Prospect* (June 2011), 17.

166. "New CBO Report Finds Recovery Act Has Preserved or Created up to 2.8 Million Jobs," May 26, 2010, http://www.cbpp.org/cms/index.cfm?fa=view&id=3196.

167. Jeanne Sahadi, "Your Share of Stimulus Tax Breaks," CNNMoney.com, February 21, 2009, http://money.cnn.com/2009/02/21/news/economy/tax_savings_stimulus/index.htm.

168. "Flying Blind," *The Economist* (August 3, 2011), http://www.economist.com/blogs/freeexchange/2011/08/fiscal-policy.

169. Noah Matson, "As Crops Are Killed, House Forbids USDA from Preparing for Climate Disasters," Thinkprogress.org, June 18, 2011, http://thinkprogress.org/green/2011/06/18/247507/as-crops-are-killed-house-forbids-usda-from-preparing-for-climate-disasters/; and Lisa Hymas, "Now all GOP Senate candidates deny global warming," Grist.org, September 18, 2011, www.grist.org/article/2010-09-14-now-all-republican-senate-candidates-deny-global-warming.

170. Al Gore, "Climate of Denial," *Rolling Stone* (June 22, 2011), http://www.rollingstone.com/politics/news/climate-of-denial-20110622.

171. Ezra Klein, "Obama Revealed: A Moderate Republican," *Washington Post*, April 25, 2011, and Ryan Lizza, "Romney's Dilemma," *The New Yorker*, June 6, 2011, 38–43.

172. John Heileman, "The West Wing, Season II," *New York*, January 23, 2011, nymag.com/news/politics/70829.

173. See Eric Alterman, *Kabuki Democracy: The System vs. Barack Obama* (New York: Nation Books, 2011), 32–44, 64.

174. Stewart is quoted in Chris Smith, "America Is a Joke," *New York Magazine*, September 12, 2010, http://nymag.com/arts/tv/profiles/68086/.

175. Ibid.

176. Ibid.

177. See Pew Research Center Project on Excellence in Journalism, "State of the News Media 2010," http://stateofthemedia.org/.

178. Project for Excellence in Journalism, "The Media Primary: How News Media and Blogs Have Eyed the Presidential Contenders During the First Phase of the 2012 Race," October 17, 2011, http://www.journalism.org/print/26958.

179. "The President's Moment," *New York Times*, June 12, 2010, http://www.nytimes.com/2010/06/13/opinion/13sun1.html.

180. Quoted in Paul Richter, "World Breathes Sigh of Relief, Hillary Clinton Says," *Los Angeles Times*, January 28, 2009. http://articles.latimes.com/2009/jan/28/world/fg-clinton28.

181. Alan Wolfe, *Political Evil: What It Is and How to Combat It* (New York: Knopf, 2011) 62–64.

182. Scott Shane, Mark Mazzetti, and Helene Cooper, "Obama Reverses Key Bush Security Policies," *New York Times*, January 23, 1009, http://www.nytimes.com/2009/01/23/us/politics/23obama.html.

183. Ray Rivera and Ginger Thompson, "U.S. Ambassador Responds to Karzai's Criticisms," *New York Times*, June 19, 2011, http://www.nytimes.com/2011/06/20/world/asia/20afghanistan.html?scp=2&sq=karzai&st=cse.

184. Helene Cooper, "Cost of Wars a Rising Issue as Obama Weighs Troop Levels," *New York Times*, June 21, 2011, A1.

185. Margaret Talev and Julie Hirschfeld Davis, "Obama Says Afghan Pullout Will Aid 'Nation-Building at Home,'" Businessweek.com, http://www.businessweek.com/news/2011-06-23/obama-says-afghan-pullout-will-aid-nation-building-at-home-.html.

186. Ryan Lizza, "The Consequentialist: How the Arab Spring Remade Obama's Foreign Policy," *The New Yorker* (May 2, 2011), 46.

187. BBC News, "Syria Uprising: UN Says Protest Death Toll Hits 3,000," October 4, 2011, http://www.bbc.co.uk/news/world-middle-east-15304741?utm_medium=email&utm_source=newsletter&utm_campaign=cheatsheet_morning&cid=newsletter%3Bemail%3Bcheatsheet_morning&utm_term=CheatSheet%20-%20VIP%20Email%20First.

188. Charles Savage, "2 Top Lawyers Lost to Obama in Libya War Policy Debate, "*New York Times*, June 17, 2011, A1.

189. Ibid.

190. Ryan Lizza, "The Consequentialist," 52.

191. David Remnick, "Behind the Curtain," *The New Yorker*, September 5, 2011, http://www.newyorker.com/talk/comment/2011/09/05/110905taco_talk_remnick.

192. See the arguments made by John B. Judis in "Stop Blaming Wall Street," *The New Republic* (August 4, 2011), 8–11.

193. See, for instance, Hussein Agha and Robert Malley, "Who's Afraid of the Palestinians?" *The New York Review of Books*, February 10, 2011, http://www.nybooks.com/articles/archives/2011/feb/10/whos-afraid-palestinians/?pagination.

194. See Lori Montgomery, "Running in the Red: How the U.S., on the Road to Surplus, Detoured to Massive Debt," *Washington Post*, April 30, 2011, A1.

195. Julie Bosman, "Obama Gets Franzen Novel Early, and Publishing Panic Ensues," *New York Times*, Arts Beat Blog, August 23, 2010, http://artsbeat.blogs.nytimes.com/2010/08/23/obama-gets-franzen-novel-early-and-publishing-panic-ensues/.

196. Paul Charles Griffin, "Sound and Fury, Signifying . . . What, Exactly?: Notes on the Franzen Wars," *Common Review* (Fall/Winter, 2010), 14; Sam Tanenhaus, "Peace and War," *New York Times Book Review*, August 19, 2010, http://www.nytimes.com/2010/08/29/books/review/Tanenhaus-t.html; Lev Grossman, "Jonathan Franzen: Great American Novelist," *Time*, August 12, 2010, http://www.time.com/time/arts/article/0,8599,2010000,00.html.

197. Jonathan Franzen, *The Discomfort Zone: A Personal History* (New York: Farrar, Straus and Giroux, 2006), 13.
198. Ibid., 69, 93, 96.
199. Jonathan Franzen, *How to Be Alone: Essays* (New York: Farrar, Straus and Giroux, 2002), 4–5.
200. Stephen J. Burn, "Jonathan Franzen" (an interview), *Paris Review* (Winter 2010). 59.
201. Franzen, *How to Be Alone*, 91.
202. Ibid., 92.
203. Lionel Trilling, *The Liberal Imagination: Essays on Literature and Society* (Garden City, NY: Anchor, 1950), xii; "From the Notebooks of Lionel Trilling," *Partisan Review* 51–52 (1984–85), 509.
204. "The Liberal Form: An Interview with Jonathan Franzen," *boundary 2*, issue 36 (2009), 46–47.
205. Grossman, "Jonathan Franzen: Great American Novelist."
206. Jonathan Franzen, *The Corrections* (New York: Farrar, Straus and Giroux, 2001), 103.
207. Jonathan Franzen, *How to Be Alone*, 261.
208. Quoted in Chris Lehmann, *Revolt of the Masscult* (Chicago: Prickly Paradigm Press, 2003), 9–10.
209. Burn, "Jonathan Franzen," 71.
210. Grossman, "Jonathan Franzen: Great American Novelist."
211. Jonathan Franzen, *Freedom* (New York: Farrar, Straus and Giroux, 2010), 119, 3–4, 7.
212. Ibid., 109, 102.
213. Ibid., 261, 267.
214. Charles Baxter, "'His Glory and His Curse,'" *The New York Review of Books*, September 30, 2010, http://www.nybooks.com/articles/archives/2010/sep/30/his-glory-and-his-curse/.
215. See Eric Alterman, "How Obama Screws His Base," *The Daily Beast*, September 19, 2010, http://www.thedailybeast.com/articles/2010/09/19/how-obama-screws-his-liberal-base.html.
216. Linda Feldman, "Obama Calls Midterm Elections 'Humbling,' Promises to Do Better," *Christian Science Monitor*, November 3, 2010, http://www.csmonitor.com/USA/2010/1103/Obama-calls-midterm-elections-humbling-promises-to-do-better.
217. See for instance the methodology discussed in Andrew Gelman, "Doug Hibbs on the Fundamentals in 2010," The Monkey Cage, September 23, 2010, http://themonkeycage.org/blog/2010/09/23/doug_hibbs_on_the_fundamentals/.
218. Quoted in Wolffe, *Revival*, 32.
219. Michael Tomasky, "Obama at the Edge," *The New York Review of Books*, February 10, 2011, http://www.nybooks.com/articles/archives/2011/feb/10/obama-edge/.
220. Barack Obama, "Remarks by the President on Fiscal Policy," George Washington University, Washington, DC, April 13, 2011, http://www.whitehouse.gov/the-press-office/2011/04/13/remarks-president-fiscal-policy.
221. Scott Pelley, "Boehner: I Got 98 Percent of What I Wanted," CBS News, August 1, 2011, http://www.cbsnews.com/stories/2011/08/01/eveningnews/main20086598.shtml.
222. Rebecca Stewart, "A Lucifer Panini?," CNN.com Politicker, August 1, 2011, http://politicalticker.blogs.cnn.com/2011/08/01/a-lucifer-panini/.
223. Jonathan Cohn, "This Is Not Leadership," *The New Republic*, August 1, 2011, http://www.tnr.com/blog/jonathan-cohn/92989/failure-leadership-obama-debt-deal-cuts-medicare-discretionary.
224. Matthew Yglesias, "When Did Keynesian Economics Live?" Think Progress, August 1, 2011, http://www.thinkprogress.org/yglesias/2011/08/01/283990/when-did-keynesian-economics-live/.
225. Quoted in Jared Bernstein, "A Few More Comments on the Pending Deal," *On the Economy*, August 1, 2011, jaredbernsteinblog.com/a-few-more-comments-on-the-pending-deal/.
226. Drew Westen, "Whatever Happened to Obama?," *New York Times*, August 7, 2011, http://www.nytimes.com/2011/08/07/opinion/sunday/what-happened-to-obamas-passion.html?_r=1&ref=opinion.

Conclusion: "The Only Honest Place to Be"

1. Mari Jo Buhle, *Women and American Socialism, 1870–1920* (Urbana, IL: University of Illinois, 1981), 323.
2. On the state of the New York State legislature, see Clyde Haberman, "The Stalemate in Albany: 5 Years On," *New York Times*, June 8, 2009, quoted in Alan Ackerman, *Just Words: Lillian*

Hellman, Mary McCarthy, and the Failure of Public Conversation in America (New Haven, CT: Yale University Press, 2011) 23.

3. Michael Barbaro, "Behind N.Y. Gay Marriage, an Unlikely Mix of Forces," *The New York Times*, June 25, 2011, http://www.nytimes.com/2011/06/26/nyregion/the-road-to-gay-marriage-in-new-york.html.

4. Associated Press, "Excerpt from Santorum Interview, *USA Today*, April 23, 2003, http://www.usatoday.com/news/washington/2003-04-23-santorum-excerpt_x.htm.

5. Jonathan Mahler, "The Making of Andrew Cuomo," *New York Times Magazine*, August 11, 2011, http://www.nytimes.com/2010/08/15/magazine/15Cuomo-t.html.

6. "Joseph Stiglitz, "Of the One, by the One for the One Percent," Democracy Now, April 7, 2011, http://www.youtube.com/watch?v=4CqnrEIQk0s.

7. See Eric Alterman, "Andrew Cuomo's Flawed Liberalism," The Daily Beast, June 26, 2011, http://www.thedailybeast.com/articles/2011/06/26/andrew-cuomo-s-flawed-liberalism .html.

8. Thomas Kaplan and Michael Barbaro, "Cuomo Says Curbing Public Pension Benefits Will Be His Top Goal in '12," *New York Times*, July 13, 2011, http://www.nytimes.com/2011/07/14/nyregion/cuomo-says-he-wants-to-tackle-pension-changes-in-2012.html?_r=1&sq=cuomo,%20pensions&st=cse&scp=1&pagewanted=print.

9. See Thomas Kaplan, "Despite Protests, Cuomo Says He Will Not Extend a Tax Surcharge on Top Earners," *New York Times*, October 17, 2011, http://www.nytimes.com/2011/10/18/nyregion/cuomo-says-he-will-not-renew-millionaires-tax.html?_r=1&ref=nyregion&pagewanted=print; and Mathew Cooper, "Occupy D.C.? Most Back Protests, Surtax," *National Journal*, October 19, 2011, http://nationaljournal.com/daily/occupy-d-c-most-back-protests-surtax-20111018.

10. See Seth Hanlon, "Making More, Contributing Less: Millionaires' Tax Rates Have Declined While Everyone Else Contributes to Deficit Reduction," Center for American Progress, August 4, 2011, http://www.americanprogress.org/issues/2011/08/millionaire_tax_rates .html; and Archon Fung, "Winning the Future: Should Political Scientists Care More About Politics?" *Boston Review* (May 12, 2011), http://bostonreview.net/BR36.3/archon_fung _winner_take_all_politics.php.

11. See Charles M. Blow, "The Kindling of Change," *New York Times*, February 4, 2011, http://www.nytimes.com/2011/02/05/opinion/05blow.html?_r=2&ref=opinion.

12. Floyd Norris, "As Corporate Profits Rise, Workers' Income Declines," *New York Times*, August 6, 2011, B3.

13. Rakesh Kochhar, Richard Fry, and Paul Taylor, Pew Research Center, Social & Demographic Trends, "Wealth Gaps Rise to Record Highs Between Whites, Blacks and Hispanics," July 26, 2011, http://pewresearch.org/pubs/2069/housing-bubble-subprime-mortgages -hispanics-blacks-household-wealth-disparity.

14. Robert Kuttner, "The Paradox of Social Progress and Economic Reaction," Huffington Post, June 19, 2011, http://www.huffingtonpost.com/robert-kuttner/economic-gap_b_880091 .html.

15. This quote can be found in many places, including William H. Gates, Sr., and Chuck Collins, *Wealth and Our Commonwealth: Why America Should Tax Accumulated Fortunes* (Boston: Beacon Press, 2004) 17.

16. Jacob S. Hacker and Paul Pierson, *Winner-Take-All Politics: How Washington Made the Rich Richer—and Turned Its Back on the Middle Class* (New York: Simon & Schuster, 2010), 12.

17. Richard Durban to Bill Moyers, "Bill Moyers Journal, Transcript," May 8, 2009, http://www .pbs.org/moyers/journal/05082009/transcript1.html.

18. See Daniel T. Rogers, *Age of Fracture*, Cambridge, MA: Harvard University Press, 2011), 96.

19. Ibid., 75.

20. "CNN Poll: Trust in Government at All-Time Low," CNN.com Politics Political Ticker, September 28, 2011, http://politicalticker.blogs.cnn.com/2011/09/28/cnn-poll-trust-in -government-at-all-time-low/#comments.

21. See Richard Sennett, "A Credible Left," *The Nation*, August 1–8, 2011, www. thenation.com/article/162011/credible-left.

22. Stanley B. Greenberg, "Why Voters Tune Out Democrats," *New York Times*, July 30, 2011, http://www.nytimes.com/2011/07/31/opinion/sunday/tuning-out-the-democrats.html ?scp=1&sq=stanley%20greenberg&st=cse.

23. Ira Katznelson, *When Affirmative Action Was White: An Untold History of Racial Inequality in Twentieth-Century America* (New York: Norton, 2005).

24. Trilling is quoted in Adam Kirsch, *Why Trilling Matters* (New Haven, CT: Yale University Press, 2011), 58–60.
25. Ryan Lizza, "The Agitator," *The New Republic* (March 19, 2007), 25.
26. See Greg Sargent, "The Big Disconnect: Strong Disapproval of Obama on Economy, Solid Support for His Actual Policies," *Washington Post,* September 17, 2011, http://www.washingtonpost.com/blogs/plum-line/post/the-big-disconnect-strong-disapproval-of-obama-on-economy-strong-support-for-his-actual-policies/2011/03/03/gIQAFhHiZK_blog.html?hpid=z2; see also Steve Benen, "When the Parts Are More Popular Than the Whole," *Washington Monthly,* Political Animal, September 17, 2011, http://www.washingtonmonthly.com/political-animal/2011_09/when_the_parts_are_more_popula032267.php.
27. See the discussion of this issue as well as of the overall consistency of these numbers of a period of decades in Eric Alterman, *Why We're Liberals: A Handbook for Restoring America's Most Important Ideals* (New York: Viking, 2009), 5–15. The 37 percent of Democrat figure, a slight rise over previous years, was true at the end of August 2011 and can be found in Frank Newport, Jeffrey M. Jones, and Lydia Saad, "Democrats More Liberal, Less White Than in 2008," *Gallup,* November 7, 2011, http://www.gallup.com/poll/150611/Democrats-Liberal-Less-White-2008.aspx.
28. Neil Genzlinger, "Enter Laughing, From the Liberal Wing," *New York Times,* May 20, 2011, http://www.nytimes.com/2011/05/22/nyregion/can-liberal-comics-tickle-the-right-funny-bone.html.
29. The White House, Office of the Press Secretary, "Remarks by the President at the Martin Luther King, Jr., Memorial Dedication," The National Mall, Washington, D.C., October 16, 2011.
30. Robert Kuttner, "The Paradox of Social Progress and Economic Reaction," Huffington Post, June 19, 2011, http://www.huffingtonpost.com/robert-kuttner/economic-gap_b_880091.html.
31. Richard Sennett quoted in Introduction in John Rodden, ed., *Lionel Trilling and the Critics: Opposing Selves* (Lincoln: University of Nebraska Press, 1999), 19.
32. Daniel Bell quoted in Alan Brinkley, "Liberalism and Belief," in Neil Jumonville and Kevin Mattson, eds., *Liberalism for a New Century* (Berkeley: University of California Press, 2007), 82.
33. Michael Walzer, *What It Means to Be an American* (New York: Marsilio Publishers, 1993) 96.
34. Lionel Trilling, *The Liberal Imagination: Essays on Literature and Society* (Garden City, NY: Anchor, 1950), xi.
35. Richard Hofstadter, "The Pseudo-Conservative Revolt," in Daniel Bell, ed., *The Radical Right (The New American Right Expanded and Updated)* (Garden City: Anchor Books, 1964), 95.
36. See for instance Stephen P. Dunne, *The Economics of John Kenneth Galbraith: Introduction, Persuasion and Rehabilitation* (Cambridge: Cambridge University Press, 2010), 89.
37. Immanuel Kant, "An Answer to the Question: What Is Enlightenment?" (1784), http://www.english.upenn.edu/~mgamer/Etexts/kant.html.
38. Gordon S. Wood, *The Idea of America: Reflections on the Birth of the United States* (New York: Penguin, 2011), 277–78.
39. John B. Judis, "Structural Flaw: How Liberalism Came to the U.S.," *The New Republic* (February 28, 2005), 20.
40. James L. Sundquist, *Dynamics of the Party System: Alignment and Realignment of Political Parties in the United States,* rev. ed. (Washington, DC: Brookings Institution Press, 1983), 210; Edgar Eugene Robinson, *They Voted for Roosevelt: The Presidential Vote, 1932–1944* (New York: Octagon, 1970), 4, 33.
41. Earl Black and Merle Black, *Divided America: The Ferocious Power Struggle in American Politics* (New York: Simon & Schuster, 2007), 5.
42. Cohen is quoted in Nelson Lichtenstein, *State of the Union: A Century of American Labor* (Princeton, N.J.: Princeton University Press, 2002), 27; see also Lizabeth Cohen, *Making a New Deal: Industrial Workers in Chicago, 1919–1939* (Cambridge, Cambridge University Press, 1990) and *A Consumers' Republic: The Politics of Mass Consumption in Postwar America.* (New York: Knopf, 2003).
43. James P. Young, *Reconsidering American Liberalism: The Troubled Odyssey of the Liberal Idea* (New York: Westview Press, 1996), 171.
44. Jo Ann Boydston, ed., *John Dewey: The Later Works, 1925–1953* (Carbondale, IL: Southern Illinois University Press, 1991), 284–85.

Index

About the Authors

Eric Alterman is Distinguished Professor of English and Journalism, Brooklyn College, City University of New York, and Professor of Journalism, CUNY Graduate School of Journalism. He is also "The Liberal Media" columnist for *The Nation*, a columnist on Jewish issues for *The Forward* and on politics for *The Daily Beast*. He is a senior fellow of the Center for American Progress in Washington, D.C., and of the Nation Institute, and the World Policy Institute in New York City. In the past he has been a history consultant to HBO films, a columnist for *Rolling Stone, Mother Jones, Worth, World Policy Journal*, and the *Sunday Express* (London), as well as an occasional contributor to *The New Yorker, The Atlantic Monthly*, and *Le Monde Diplomatique*. Alterman is the author of eight previous books, including the national bestseller *What Liberal Media? The Truth About Bias and the News*. His first book, *Sound & Fury: The Making of the Punditocracy* (1992), won the George Orwell Award and his *It Ain't No Sin to Be Glad You're Alive: The Promise of Bruce Springsteen* (1999) won the Jack London Literary Prize. Alterman has been called "the most honest and incisive media critic writing today" in the *National Catholic Reporter* and author of "the smartest and funniest political journal out there" in the *San Francisco Chronicle*. In 2011, he was given the Mirror Award for media criticism. Alterman received his Ph.D. in American history from Stanford, his M.A. in international relations from Yale, and his B.A. in history and government from Cornell. He lives with his family in New York City.

Kevin Mattson is the Connor Study Professor of Contemporary History at Ohio University (Athens), where he also lives, and is the author of six previous books and editor of three. He received his Ph.D. from the University of Rochester and his B.A. from The New School.